Mathematical and Computational Approaches in Applied Mechanics: A Themed Issue Dedicated to Professor J.N. Reddy

Mathematical and Computational Approaches in Applied Mechanics: A Themed Issue Dedicated to Professor J.N. Reddy

Guest Editors

Nicholas Fantuzzi
Michele Bacciocchi
Eugenio Ruocco
Maria Amélia Ramos Loja
Jose Antonio Loya

MDPI

Basel • Beijing • Wuhan • Barcelona • Belgrade • Novi Sad • Cluj • Manchester

Guest Editors

Nicholas Fantuzzi
Department of Civil, Chemical, Environmental, and Materials Engineering
University of Bologna
Bologna
Italy

Michele Bacciocchi
Department of Economics, Science, Engineering and Design
University of San Marino
Dogana
Repubblica Di San Marino

Eugenio Ruocco
Dipartimento di Ingegneria
University of Campania "L. Vanvitelli"
Caserta
Italy

Maria Amélia Ramos Loja
Instituto Superior Técnico
Universidade de Lisboa
Lisboa
Portugal

Jose Antonio Loya
Department of Continuum Mechanics and Structural Analysis
University Carlos III of Madrid
Madrid
Spain

Editorial Office
MDPI AG
Grosspeteranlage 5
4052 Basel, Switzerland

This is a reprint of the Special Issue, published open access by the journal *Mathematical and Computational Applications* (ISSN 2297-8747), freely accessible at: https://www.mdpi.com/journal/mca/special_issues/JN_Reddy.

For citation purposes, cite each article independently as indicated on the article page online and as indicated below:

Lastname, A.A.; Lastname, B.B. Article Title. *Journal Name* **Year**, *Volume Number*, Page Range.

ISBN 978-3-7258-5851-4 (Hbk)
ISBN 978-3-7258-5852-1 (PDF)
https://doi.org/10.3390/books978-3-7258-5852-1

Contents

Mathematical and Computational Applications

MDPI

Editorial

Editorial for the Special Issue Dedicated to Professor J.N. Reddy

Nicholas Fantuzzi [1,*], Michele Bacciocchi [2], Eugenio Ruocco [3], Maria Amélia Ramos Loja [4,5] and Jose Antonio Loya [6]

1 Department of Civil, Chemical, Environmental, and Materials Engineering, University of Bologna, Viale del Risorgimento 2, 40136 Bologna, Italy
2 DESID Department, University of San Marino, Via Consiglio dei Sessanta, 99, 47891 Dogana, San Marino; m.bacciocchi1@unirsm.sm
3 Engineering Department, University of Campania "L. Vanvitelli", Via Roma 28, 81100 Caserta, Italy; eugenio.ruocco@unicampania.it
4 CIMOSM—Centro de Investigação em Modelação e Otimização de Sistemas Multifuncionais, ISEL, IPL—Instituto Politécnico de Lisboa, Av. Conselheiro Emídio Navarro 1, 1959-007 Lisboa, Portugal; amelia.loja@isel.pt
5 IDMEC, Instituto Superior Técnico, Universidade de Lisboa, Avenue Rovisco Pais, 1, 1049-001 Lisboa, Portugal
6 Department of Continuum Mechanics and Structural Analysis, University Carlos III of Madrid, Avda. de la Universidad, 30, Leganés, 28911 Madrid, Spain; jloya@ing.uc3m.es
* Correspondence: nicholas.fantuzzi@unibo.it

This Special Issue of *Mathematical and Computational Applications* is devoted to innovative mathematical and computational approaches in applied mechanics and is dedicated to Professor J.N. Reddy (Texas A&M University). Professor Reddy has been a towering figure in theoretical and computational mechanics, especially through his development of the third-order shear deformation theory for beams, plates, and shells (often known as "Reddy's theory"), as well as his work on layer-wise models, nonlinear finite element formulations, and key textbooks. His vision has continuously bridged rigorous mathematics and engineering applications, and his legacy provides motivation for much of the current research in this domain.

We prepared this Editorial both to acknowledge Professor Reddy's enduring influence and to offer readers a synopsis of the articles collected in this issue. Saber et al. [1] analyze the dynamic behavior of light bridges under moving loads within the context of vibration control and structural integrity. The Authors introduce the effectiveness of nonlinear semi-active absorbers in mitigating bridge vibrations. Saadatmorad et al. [2] introduce a mode shape projection method to improve damage detection in laminated composite plates, overcoming some of the edge effects inherent in wavelet methods.

Nava and Kim [3] developed a nonlinear finite element model for circular and annular micro-plates under thermal and mechanical loading considering a third-order shear deformation theory, where the effects of material and porosity distributions were analyzed.

Fahmy and Toujani [4] present a fractional boundary element formulation for 3D thermal stress wave propagation in anisotropic materials, employing Caputo derivatives and efficient solvers. Karami and Ghayesh [5] investigate the forced vibration behavior of graphene origami–enabled auxetic metamaterial beams with elastic constraints, showing how folding geometry and foundation stiffness influence dynamic response. Sofiyev et al. [6] address the buckling of axially loaded laminated nanocomposite cylindrical shells under thermal and mechanical loading, using an extended shear deformation theory framework. Mahtabi et al. [7] propose a polynomial approximation method over arbitrary shaped domains using SVD-based Vandermonde manipulations to determine interpolation or modal points. Carvalho et al. [8] quantify how uncertainty in carbon nanotube geometry and material parameters propagates into deflection predictions for functionally graded plates. Kurpa et al. [9] apply R-function theory within a Ritz framework to handle the free vibration of porous functionally graded plates of variable thickness on elastic foundations. Loya et al. [10] examine the buckling of cracked Euler—Bernoulli columns embedded in a Winkler medium, analyzing the influence of crack location and stiffness. Murillo et al. [11] present a finite element implementation of Reddy's third-order beam theory for the thermal—structural analysis of functionally graded beams. Finally, Apalak and Reddy [12] analyze thermal stress formation in a functionally graded Al_2O_3–adhesive single lap joint under uniform temperature, showing how the gradient index moderates interface stresses.

We believe that this Special Issue showcases the potential of the interplay between mathematical finesse and computational implementation in modern applied mechanics. It honours Professor Reddy's enduring inspiration and highlights promising future directions inspired by his legacy.

Conflicts of Interest: The authors declare no conflicts of interest.

References

1. Saber, H.; Samani, F.S.; Pellicano, F.; Molaie, M.; Zippo, A. Vibration Control of Light Bridges Under Moving Loads Using Nonlinear Semi-Active Absorbers. *Math. Comput. Appl.* **2025**, *30*, 19. [CrossRef]
2. Saadatmorad, M.; Pashaei, M.-H.; Jafari-Talookolaei, R.-A.; Khatir, S. Mode Shape Projection for Damage Detection of Laminated Composite Plates. *Math. Comput. Appl.* **2025**, *30*, 18. [CrossRef]
3. Nava, E.; Kim, J. Nonlinear Finite Element Model for FGM Porous Circular and Annular Micro-Plates Under Thermal and Mechanical Loads Using Modified Couple Stress-Based Third-Order Plate Theory. *Math. Comput. Appl.* **2025**, *30*, 35. [CrossRef]
4. Fahmy, M.A.; Toujani, M. A New Fractional Boundary Element Model for the 3D Thermal Stress Wave Propagation Problems in Anisotropic Materials. *Math. Comput. Appl.* **2025**, *30*, 6. [CrossRef]
5. Karami, B.; Ghayesh, M.H. Forced Vibration Behaviour of Elastically Constrained Graphene Origami-Enabled Auxetic Metamaterial Beams. *Math. Comput. Appl.* **2025**, *30*, 5. [CrossRef]
6. Sofiyev, A.H.; Avey, M.; Aslanova, N.M. A Mathematical Approach to the Buckling Problem of Axially Loaded Laminated Nanocomposite Cylindrical Shells in Various Environments. *Math. Comput. Appl.* **2025**, *30*, 10. [CrossRef]
7. Mahtabi, M.J.; Ghasemi, A.; Ghasemi, A.; Newman, J.C., III. Polynomial Approximation Over Arbitrary Shape Domains. *Math. Comput. Appl.* **2024**, *29*, 110. [CrossRef]
8. Carvalho, A.; Martins, A.; Mota, A.F.; Loja, M.A.R. Variability on Functionally Graded Plates' Deflection Due to Uncertainty on Carbon Nanotubes' Properties. *Math. Comput. Appl.* **2024**, *29*, 22. [CrossRef]
9. Kurpa, L.; Pellicano, F.; Shmatko, T.; Zippo, A. Free Vibration Analysis of Porous Functionally Graded Material Plates With Variable Thickness on an Elastic Foundation Using the R-Functions Method. *Math. Comput. Appl.* **2024**, *29*, 10. [CrossRef]
10. Loya, J.A.; Santiuste, C.; Aranda-Ruiz, J.; Zaera, R. Buckling of Cracked Euler–Bernoulli Columns Embedded in a Winkler Elastic Medium. *Math. Comput. Appl.* **2023**, *28*, 87. [CrossRef]
11. Valencia Murillo, C.E.; Gutierrez Rivera, M.E.; Celaya Garcia, L.D. Thermal–Structural Linear Static Analysis of Functionally Graded Beams Using Reddy Beam Theory. *Math. Comput. Appl.* **2023**, *28*, 84. [CrossRef]
12. Apalak, M.K.; Reddy, J.N. Thermal Stress Formation in a Functionally Graded Al_2O_3-Adhesive Single Lap Joint Subjected to a Uniform Temperature Field. *Math. Comput. Appl.* **2023**, *28*, 82. [CrossRef]

Mathematical and Computational Applications

MDPI

Article

Vibration Control of Light Bridges Under Moving Loads Using Nonlinear Semi-Active Absorbers

Hamed Saber [1], Farhad S. Samani [1], Francesco Pellicano [2], Moslem Molaie [2] and Antonio Zippo [2,*]

[1] Department of Mechanical Engineering, Shahid Bahonar University of Kerman, Kerman 76169-14111, Iran; hamed3071@yahoo.com (H.S.)
[2] Department of Engineering "Enzo Ferrari", University of Modena and Reggio Emilia, 41121 Modena, Italy; francesco.pellicano@unimore.it (F.P.); moslem_molaie@unimore.it (M.M.)
* Correspondence: antonio.zippo@unimore.it

Abstract: The dynamic response of light bridges to moving loads presents significant challenges in controlling vibrations that can impact on the structural integrity and the user comfort. This study investigates the effectiveness of nonlinear semi-active absorbers in mitigating these vibrations on light bridges that are particularly susceptible to human-induced vibrations, due to their inherent low damping and flexibility, especially under near-resonance conditions. Traditional passive vibration control methods, such as dynamic vibration absorbers (DVAs), may not be entirely adequate for mitigating vibrations, as they require adjustments in damping and stiffness when operating conditions change over time. Therefore, suitable strategies are needed to dynamically adapt DVA parameters and ensure optimal performance. This paper explores the effectiveness of linear and nonlinear DVAs in reducing vertical vibrations of lightweight beams subjected to moving loads. Using the Bubnov-Galerkin method, the governing partial differential equations are reduced to a set of ordinary differential equations and a novel nonlinear DVA with a variable damping dashpot is investigated, showing better performances compared to traditional constant-parameter DVAs. The nonlinear viscous damping device enables real-time adjustments, making the DVA semi-active and more effective. A footbridge case study demonstrates significant vibration reductions using optimized nonlinear DVAs for lightweight bridges, showing broader frequency effectiveness than linear ones. The quadratic nonlinear DVA is the most efficient, achieving a 92% deflection reduction in the 1.5–2.5 Hz range, and under running and jumping reduces deflection by 42%.

Keywords: bridge vibrations; semi-active DVA; adjustable vibration absorber; viscous variable damping dashpot; moving load; vibration reduction

1. Introduction

Reducing vibrations is important for the serviceability and safety of light structures like bridges. The bridge structure may experience significant deflections when subjected to a moving load in near resonance conditions. There are multiple methods to reduce beam vibrations, including selecting the appropriate structural material, control of the bridge's overall condition and support strengthening, and utilizing the dynamic vibration absorber (DVA) as the most efficient technique. Samani and Pellicano [1] studied the efficacy of linear and nonlinear dampers installed on simply-supported beams subjected to moving loads. The performance of the suggested vibration absorber was evaluated based on the maximum vibration amplitude and the energy dissipation by the damper. Additionally, Samani et al. [2] conducted a study comparing the effectiveness of linear and nonlinear DVAs under dynamic loads from moving vehicles. Their findings indicated that cubic stiffness is more effective than linear stiffness. They suggested that enhancing the nonlinearity of stiffness leads to a more efficient reduction in beam deflection.

Recently, many researchers investigated the impact of the vertical component of moving loads on lightweight bridges and evaluating the efficiency of linear DVAs in mitigating induced vibrations [3–8]. Saber et al. examined how different types of DVAs can reduce vibrations in footbridges. The DVAs were fine-tuned through two methods: minimizing beam deflection and maximizing the absorbed energy by the vibration absorber [9]. Caprani and Ahmadi [10] investigated human-structure interaction models for vertical vibration induced by pedestrian excitation; in their study, the beam equation is analyzed using modal coordinates and the finite element method in the referenced study. Kei Ao and Reynolds [11] investigated an Eddy Current Damper as an alternative to the traditional viscous dampers in civil engineering structures; the damper was based on electromagnetic induction and minimal friction, it showed promising damping properties when applied to a footbridge. Finite element and analytical models confirmed its effectiveness in enhancing damping under various loading conditions. In another study, the same authors investigated the design and effectiveness of an electromagnetic shunt damper using an electrodynamic actuator to improve vibration control in civil engineering structures, specifically footbridges, by comparing its performance to a tuned mass damper. H_∞ and H_2 optimization techniques were applied to enhanced the dissipation across multiple vibration modes [12]. Pedersen and Frier [13] researched how footbridge vibrations are influenced by walking parameters by analyzing the response of a footbridge to pedestrian load models. Lievens et al. [14] demonstrated that forecasting the dominant characteristics of the finite element (FE) models of the bridges is challenging. Furthermore, the modal parameters will change over time due to variations in environmental conditions. Nimmen et al. [15] proposed that significant changes in the natural frequencies between the finite element analysis outcomes and the experimental data may arise from the assumptions incorporated in the FE model, including boundary conditions, material properties, and the impact of non-structural components.

Ding and Chen [16] carried out an extensive analysis of studies regarding nonlinear vibration absorbers. Their work focuses on the design, analysis, conclusions, and uses of nonlinear vibration absorber tools to enhance vibration mitigation in engineering contexts. Gourdon et al. [17] investigated the robustness of a new cubic nonlinear energy sink; they experimentally validated the theoretical findings through tests on a reduced-scale building model. Their findings suggest that nonlinear attachments can outperform linear ones. Ferreira et al. [18] studied semi-active dampers to mitigate synchronous lateral vibrations in pedestrian bridges. Their numerical analysis showed that the new semi-active vibration absorber could achieve similar performance of a passive absorber but requires a small mass. The DVA's self-tuning capability makes it more effective in addressing multimode control compared to a traditional passive linear Tuned Mass Damper (TMD). Maslanka [19] introduced a semi-active vibration absorber that incorporates acceleration and relative motion feedbacks optimized using frequency domain analysis. This particular variation of semi-active DVA includes a controllable viscous damper with magnetorheological properties. Saber et al. [20], presented an innovative nonlinear viscous dashpot with tunable damping for DVAs. In another study, Saber et al. [6] investigated how vibration absorbers can reduce vertical deflections of footbridges caused by various types of human activities. Chen et al. [21], investigated the influence of human-induced load models on the effectiveness of a tuned mass damper in dampening vibrations in a floor. They analyzed the floor's reactions to different types of excitations and showed that employing distinct load models, like those for walking or jumping, can greatly alter the performance of the TMD. Recently,

Nguyen et al. [22] investigated the use of semi-active tuned mass dampers (STMD) to mitigate resonant vibrations in railway bridges subjected to high-speed trains. Unlike passive controllers, which have a narrow operational bandwidth and are vulnerable to detuning, the STMD enhances the vibration suppression across a broader frequency range, demonstrating improved robustness and effectiveness in real-world conditions. Kumar and Bhushan [23], developed an innovative semi-active absorber that utilizes Magnetorheological fluids and elastomers to achieve variable damping and stiffness. Their mathematical model demonstrated significant improvements versus the passive technologies. Barrera-Vargas et al. [24], investigated semiactive tuned mass dampers for lightweight pedestrian structures. The study presented a design methodology that reduces structural acceleration and inertial forces. Simulations showed that STMDs effectively mitigate vibrations while reducing inertial mass compared to passive systems. Wang et al. [25], introduced a novel magnetorheological damper featuring an elastic ring to enhance the damper performance by optimizing the oil-film thickness distribution. Such device can be categorized as semi-active; through dynamic modeling and experimental validation, the study highlighted the improved damping characteristics compared to conventional systems. For more information on the effectiveness of nonlinearity on vibration mitigation of various test cases, the reader is suggested to analyze Refs. [26–30].

The major contribution of the present paper is the introduction of a nonlinear DVA having a viscous variable damping dashpot; more specifically, this study introduces a quadratic nonlinearity to the damping element, allowing variable damping constants based on flow rates. This newly proposed dashpot enhances the performance of the dynamic system, i.e., a footbridge subjected to moving pedestrians. The classical linear DVA typically reduces vibrations within a narrow frequency band, whereas a nonlinear DVA can operate effectively across a wider spectrum. This study investigates various types of nonlinear DVAs applied to footbridges, comparing their performance with the standard linear DVAs (Tigli and Den Hartog formulation), thereby illustrating the advantages of nonlinearity. The test case for the application of linear and nonlinear DVAs is an Euler-Bernoulli beam, simulating a pedestrian bridge, the partial differential equations (PDEs) are reduced to ordinary differential equations (ODEs) by means of the Bubnov-Galerkin and numerically integrated using the Gauss-Kronrod method. This innovative design allows for real-time adjustments of damping parameters, which is crucial for effectively mitigating vibrations caused by moving loads on light bridges. This adaptability represents a substantial improvement over traditional passive systems that operate with fixed parameters, thereby enhancing performance under varying load conditions.

Furthermore, this paper considers a nonlinear semi-active absorber as a semi-active device capable of adapting its properties in real-time using adjustable elements. Specifically, two types of nonlinearities are proposed: geometric cubic nonlinearity and quadratic nonlinear damping. However, this work does not focus on control algorithms or the engineering implementation of the application.

2. Moving Load Bridge Interaction Model

The governing equations of the beam with DVA, subjected to a moving load, are derived by projecting the PDE of the domain, obtaining the mass, damping, and stiffness matrices of the system. This involves considering the contributions from both the beam and the absorber, where the inertia effect of the spring mass is accounted for to ensure accurate modeling of the dynamic responses. The effective overall matrices are obtained by applying the appropriate boundary conditions, leading to a comprehensive representation of the beam's dynamics under the moving load [31].

A DVA is connected to the bridge to dampen the vibrations, as shown in Figure 1. As mentioned above, the PDE, which governs the bridge's dynamics, including the associated boundary and initial conditions, is the follow:

$$EIw_{,xxxx}(x,t) + \rho A w_{,tt}(x,t) + [f(u) + g(u_{,t})]\delta(x-d) = F(x,t) \\ x \in (0,L), \quad t > 0 \tag{1}$$

$$w(0,t) = 0, \quad w(L,t) = 0, \quad w_{,xx}(0,t) = 0, \quad w_{,xx}(L,t) = 0 \tag{2}$$

$$w(x,0) = 0, \quad w_{,t}(x,0) = 0, \quad u(t) = w(d,t) - z(t) \tag{3}$$

$$w_{,t} = \frac{\partial w}{\partial t}, \ w_{,tt} = \frac{\partial^2 w}{\partial t^2}, \ w_{,xxxx} = \frac{\partial^4 w}{\partial x^4} \tag{4}$$

The moment of inertia of the beam's cross-sectional area is denoted by I, while ρ represents the material density, and A represents the beam's cross-section area. The functions $g(u_{,t})$, and $f(u)$ represent the restoring forces of the dashpot, and spring of the DVA, respectively. The term $[f(u) + g(u_{,t})]\delta(x-d)$ denotes the force applied by the DVA to the bridge; The damper location on the bridge is in the midspan $d = L/2$. The vertical position of the DVA's mass (m_0) is denoted by $z(t)$, while the vertical displacement of the bridge is denoted by $w(x,t)$. The relative displacement of the DVA's mass and the beam mid-span is denoted by $u(t)$, as shown in Equation (3).

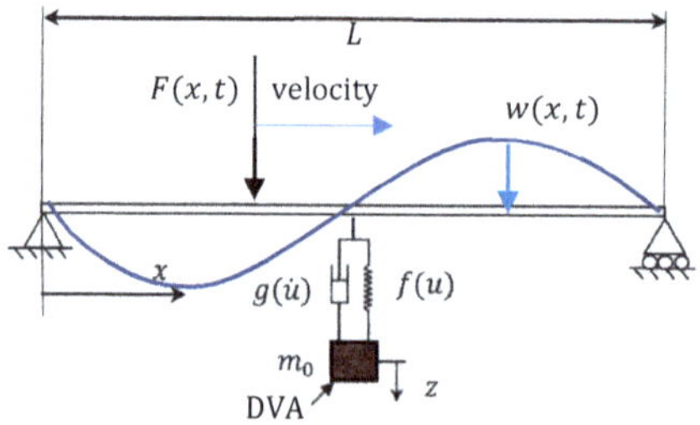

Figure 1. A bridge structure featuring a vibration absorber connected to it, exposed to a dynamic force.

The equation for the moving force can be expressed as follows:

$$F(x,t) = G(t)\ \delta(x - vt)\left[H\left(\frac{L}{v} - t\right)\right] \tag{5}$$

The Dirac delta, and Heaviside functions are denoted by δ and $H(t)$, respectively. The amplitude of the total force exerted by the moving force is denoted as *G*(*t*). The governing equations of the DVA reads:

$$m_0 z_{,tt} - ku - \lambda u_{,t}(t) = 0, \qquad t > 0 \tag{6}$$

$$z(0) = 0, \qquad z_{,t}(0) = 0, \qquad t > 0 \tag{7}$$

The position of the mass (m_0) of the DVA, $z(t)$, is represented in Equation (7).

The displacement field of the beam is expanded using the eigenfunctions of a free homogeneous beam, see Equation (8):

$$w(x,t) = \sum_{r=1}^{N} q_r(t)\varphi_r(x) \tag{8}$$

The modal coordinates are denoted by $q_r(t)$, the normalized eigenfunctions are represented by $\varphi_r(x)$, and the number of modes in the system is indicated by N. The definition of the eigenfunctions is as follows:

$$\varphi_r(x) = \left(\frac{2}{mL}\right)^{\frac{1}{2}} \sin\left(\frac{r\pi x}{L}\right), \quad \omega_r = (r\pi)^2 \left(\frac{EI}{mL^4}\right)^{\frac{1}{2}}, \quad r = 1, 2, 3, \ldots \tag{9}$$

The beam's mass per unit length is represented as $m = \rho A$, and the natural circular frequency of the rth mode is denoted as ω_r. Notably the eigenfunctions must satisfy the boundary conditions of the problem. The Bubnov-Galerkin method is used to project the PDE into the eigenfunction basis and the resulting ODEs are numerically integrated with the Gauss-Kronrod method, which employs adaptive Gaussian quadrature with error estimation evaluated at Kronrod points.

The optimization strategy used for determining the optimal parameters is a brute force approach, that involves exploring the full parameter space, the method that is computationally intensive but effective (see Refs. [2,32–35]).

The jth modal equation can be expressed as follows:

$$\ddot{q}_r + 2\xi_r\omega_r\dot{q}_r + \omega_r^2 q_r + \{f(u) + g(u_{,t})\}\varphi_r(d) = \varphi_r(vt)G(t) \tag{10}$$

$f(u)$, and $g(u_{,t})$ are expressed as the equations below:

$$f(u(t)) = k\left[\sum_{r=1}^{N} q_r(t)\varphi_r(d) - z(t)\right]^{\alpha} \left|\sum_{r=1}^{N} q_r(t)\varphi_r(d) - z(t)\right|^{\beta} \tag{11}$$

$$g(u_{,t}(t)) = \lambda\left[\sum_{r=1}^{N} \dot{q}_r(t)\varphi_r(d) - \dot{z}(t)\right]^{\gamma} \left|\sum_{r=1}^{N} \dot{q}_r(t)\varphi_r(d) - \dot{z}(t)\right|^{\delta} \tag{12}$$

The DVA's stiffness is denoted by k, while its damping is represented by λ. These values will be calculated using both numerical and analytical methods in the upcoming sections. The symbol ξ_r represents the damping ratio of the bridge.

3. Improving the DVA Parameters to Enhance Performance

This paper examines two objective functions for the optimization procedure. The primary aim of the optimization is to reduce the highest beam deflection, and the secondary goal is to increase the energy dissipated by the DVA (η), which is computed using Equation (13), as follows:

$$\eta = E_{DVA}/E_{in} = \frac{\int_0^{t_1} \lambda\left[\dot{z}(t) - \sum_{r=1}^{N} \dot{q}_r(t)\varphi_r(d)\right]^m \left|\dot{z}(t) - \sum_{r=1}^{N} \dot{q}_r(t)\varphi_r(d)\right|^n dt}{\int_0^{t_0} F_i\left[\dot{q}_r(t)\varphi_r(x_F)\right] dt} \tag{13}$$

The energy dissipated by the viscous damper of the DVA (E_{DVA}) is referred to as a nonlinear energy sink, see Refs. [1,27,36]. F_i symbolizes the force applied by the pedestrian, as defined in Equation (9). The pedestrian's position on the footbridge is denoted by x_F, which is equal to vt. The energy absorbed by the DVA is denoted as E_{DVA}, and E_{in} is the energy input from the pedestrian's feet on the bridge. The values of the integer powers m and n depend on whether a linear or nonlinear damper is utilized in diverse DVAs. The time t_1 is chosen to be long enough to ensure damping of the transient response, while t_0 corresponds to the period for which the load acts on the beam. The objective of this approach is to enhance the dissipation of energy by the DVA [1].

Figure 2 presents a flowchart outlining the steps of the computer algorithm used to solve the equations of the human-structure interaction system.

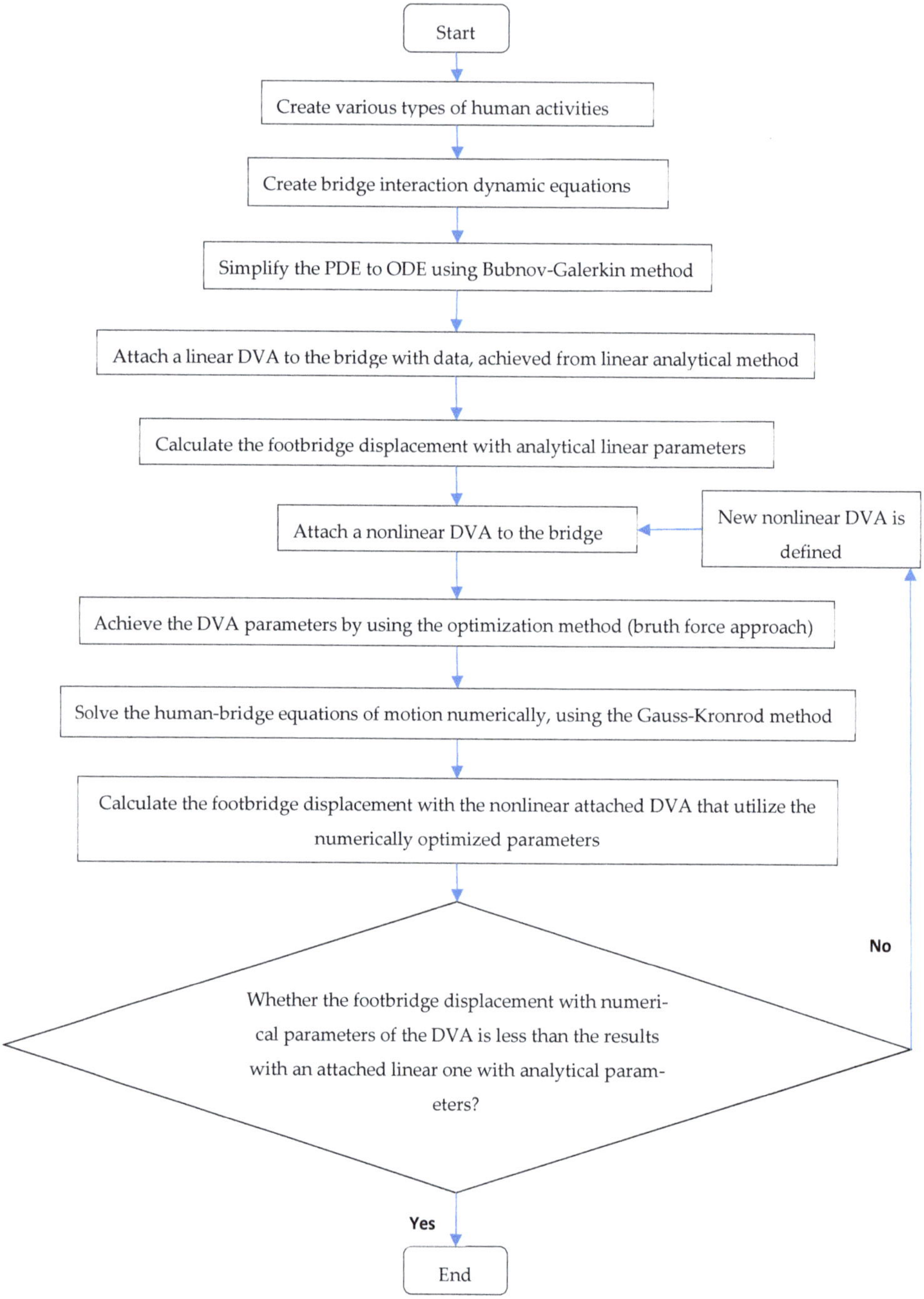

Figure 2. Flowchart outlining the steps of the computer algorithm used to solve the equations of the human-structure interaction system with attached DVA.

4. Effect of Force Amplitude and Velocity on the Optimal Values of the DVA

This section explores how force parameters like amplitude and velocity affect the optimized characteristics of the DVA, including damping and stiffness. Chen et al. studied how the load models affect the performance of a tuned mass damper in reducing vibrations in a floor [21]. They compared the floor's responses to various types of excitations and demonstrated that different load models, significantly impact the effectiveness of the tuned mass damper. Sayyad and Gadhave [37] researched a variable stiffness magnetic vibration absorber to reduce vibration in a beam structure when exposed to varying frequency harmonic excitation, aiming to decrease vibration in the main system. The present study investigates the effectiveness of various linear and nonlinear DVAs in reducing vibrations on a lightweight bridge. It considers pedestrian movement as a moving load on the bridge and explores how variations in force amplitude and velocity affect the reduction of vibrations.

4.1. Performance Analysis of Different Types of Vibration Absorbers Under Pedestrian Excitation

The vertical force generated by the pedestrian's feet is typically similar in magnitude and can be estimated by using a sine function, as illustrated in Equation (14); see [38,39].

$$G(t) = W + \sum_{k=1}^{h} W\eta_k \sin\left(2\pi k f_p\, t + \varphi_k\right) \tag{14}$$

In Equation (14), the weight of the pedestrian is represented by W, calculated as $W = m_p g$. The variable f_p represents the pedestrian's pacing rate, which is determined by the pedestrian's velocity (v) and stride length (l_p), expressed as $f_p = v/l_p$ [11]. As mentioned in Ref. [40], the coefficient in the Fourier series denoted by η_k is known as the "dynamic load factor (DLF)", while the harmonic phase angle, represented by φ_k, can be selected randomly and uniformly within the range of $[-\pi, \pi]$. Ref. [41] suggested DLF values for the first four harmonics, computed based on an assumed walking frequency between 1 and 2.8 Hz, as described in Equation (15).

$$\begin{aligned} &\eta_{1W} = 0.37\left(f_p - 0.95\right) \leq 0.5 && 1 \leq f_p \leq 2.8\,\text{Hz} \\ &\eta_{2W} = 0.054 + 0.0044 f_p && 2 \leq f_p \leq 5.6\,\text{Hz} \\ &\eta_{3W} = 0.026 + 0.0050 f_p && 3 \leq f_p \leq 8.4\,\text{Hz} \\ &\eta_{4W} = 0.010 + 0.0051 f_p && 4 \leq f_p \leq 11.2\,\text{Hz} \end{aligned} \tag{15}$$

To evaluate the accuracy of the aforementioned models, the force exerted on the footbridge by a walking pedestrian over time is analyzed and compared with the results from Kim et al. [42], which originally based their findings on the experimental investigation conducted by Wu et al. [43]. In the present study, the first four dynamic load factors for running and jumping pedestrians are derived from Rainer et al. [44]. Notably, the typical frequency of walking excitation ranges from 1.6 to 2.4 Hz [45], while the frequencies for running and jumping are between 2 and 3 Hz [44]. The system of Equation (15) is considered at a frequency of 2 Hz, and the first four DLFs are specified in Table 1. The footbridge characteristics is described in Table 2. The pedestrian weighs 724 Newtons.

Table 1. DLFs are used for regular walking at a rate of 2 Hz [9].

Reference	η_{1W}	η_{2W}	η_{3W}	η_{4W}
[25]	0.40	0.10	0.10	0

Table 2. Footbridge characteristics.

Unit Mass	Length	Cross-Section Area	Area Moment of Inertia	Fundamental Frequency	Damping Ratio	Modulus of Elasticity
500 $\frac{kg}{m}$	50 m	1.07 m^2	0.0255 m^4	2 Hz	0.004	200 GPa

In this study, the initial four phase angles of a walking pedestrian involved in any task are $\varphi_1 = 0$, $\varphi_2 = -\pi/2$, $\varphi_3 = -\pi/2$, $\varphi_4 = 0$ radians, as stated in [25]. The study's formulation accuracy for a walking pedestrian is assessed in Figure 3 using the research findings of [25].

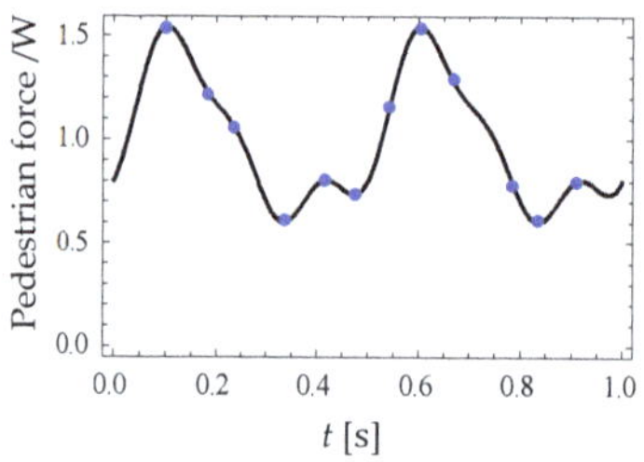

Figure 3. The force-time response produced by a walking person with a frequency of 2 Hz; —: the model presented in Equation (14); filled circles •: extracted data from [25].

Different nonlinear DVAs incorporating quadratic and cubic nonlinearity are utilized on the footbridges in the subsequent sections.

To verify the effectiveness of nonlinear DVAs under moving loads, we used data from Samani and Pellicano [1]; their study involved a nonlinear DVA with cubic stiffness and linear damping attached to a bridge; they presented the maximum mid-span deflection of the beam versus the stiffness of the nonlinear absorber. Notably, to check the accuracy of our formula in this paper we considered a constant amplitude moving force as stated in Ref. [1]. In Figure 4, one-mode and five-mode expansions are shown as dashed and solid green lines, respectively, with the five-mode expansion aligning well with the data marked by red points in Ref. [1]. The results demonstrate a strong agreement between the five-mode expansion model used in this study and the data obtained from Ref. [1].

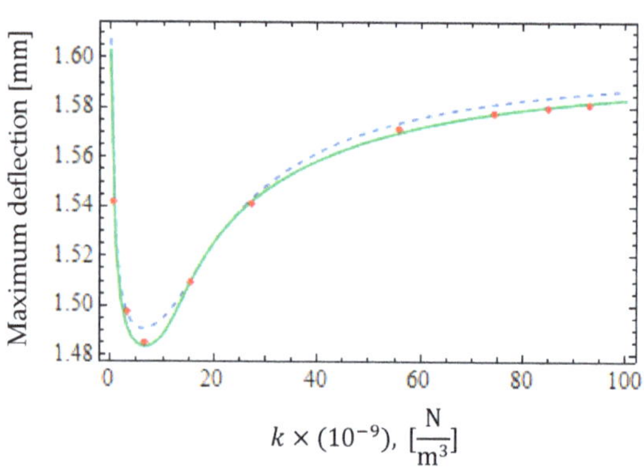

Figure 4. Verification of the bridges subjected to moving load with constant amplitude an attached DVA (cubic stiffness and linear damping) with the data extracted from Ref. [1].

4.1.1. The Optimal Configuration for a Linear DVA

To minimize the resonance effects of a beam subjected to a periodic load, it is essential to calculate the beam's equivalent mass, which is affected by the positioning of the vibration absorber. According to Den Hartog's method, the ideal stiffness and damping settings for the linear DVA attached to a simply supported beam are recommended as follows:

$$k = m_0\left(\frac{\omega_1}{1+\mu}\right)^2 \tag{16}$$

$$\lambda = 2m_0\omega_1\sqrt{\frac{3\mu}{8(1+\mu)^3}} \tag{17}$$

where ω_1 represents the primary natural frequency of the beam, μ is the ratio of m_0/m_e, where $m_e = mL/2\left(sin\,\frac{\pi d}{L}\right)^2$ represents the equivalent mass of the beam. Den Hartog's method determines the optimal values of λ and k as 5293 Ns/m and 164 kN/m, respectively, as per Equations (16) and (17). The optimal solutions for both objective functions will be achieved using the numerical approach detailed in Section 2. The main focus will be on the region where the highest efficiency (η) and lowest deflection is observed. The ranges for the parameters λ and k are from 0 to 10 kNs/m and from 50 kN/m to 300, respectively. By systematically varying the viscous damping and stiffness across a 50 × 50 grid with damping and stiffness increments of 0.2 kNs/m and 5 kN/m, respectively, the minimum deflection can be ascertained. The optimized values of λ and k for the energy-related objective function represent the points at which the DVA dissipates the maximum energy. Figure 5A,B illustrate the energy and deflection optimization approaches, respectively. The optimal parameters for λ and k, using a linear DVA for each approach, are also presented. In Figure 6A, Peaks A, B, and C depict the minimum values of the optimized DVA when utilizing the energy method. These peaks signify the least favorable situations for the optimized DVA across the anticipated frequency range of excitation. By substituting $m = 2$ and $n = 0$ into Equation (13), an efficiency of 92.80% (at point C) is attained, as illustrated in Figure 6A, for $\lambda = 6.4$ kNs/m and $k = 145$ kN/m, obtained from Figure 5A. The optimum λ and k values for the deflection method are determined by finding the combination that minimizes the maximum deflection for each frequency. The optimal parameters of $\lambda = 6$ kNs/m and $k = 180$ kN/m lead to a minimum deflection of 0.96 mm, identified through a thorough search utilizing the deflection function shown in Figure 5B. It is important to highlight that the integer powers for a linear DVA in Equations (11) and (12) are: $\alpha = 1$, $\beta = 0$, $\gamma = 1$ and $\delta = 0$. It should be noted that, in a linear DVA, the integer powers differ between the two optimization methods. The crucial difference lies in the fact that in the energy optimization approach, the footbridge's time response would exhibit quicker damping, while in the deflection optimization approach, the goal is to minimize the maximum deflection of the footbridge. The typical range of pedestrian walking frequencies falls between 1.6–2.4 Hz, see Ref. [45]. Hence, it is essential to calculate the maximum deflection of the footbridge and the energy absorbed by the DVA across a wide range of low frequencies. Utilizing a frequency domain representation is vital due to the random nature of walking parameters, including pedestrian frequencies, see Ref. [38]. Figure 6 provides a comparison between DVAs optimized according to energy and deflection criteria and DVA values from Den Hartog in the frequency domain.

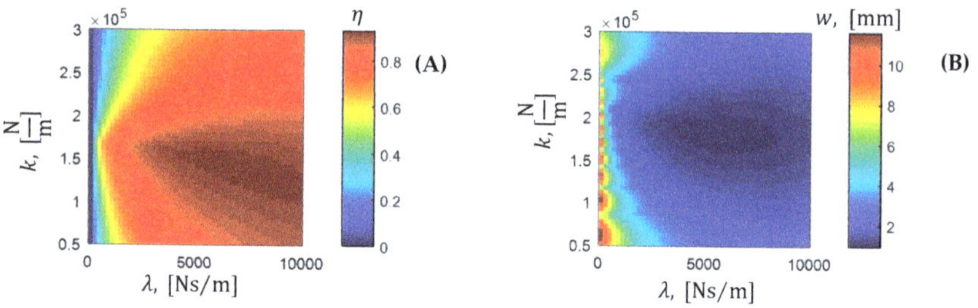

Figure 5. Parameters optimized for DVA. (**A**) Optimization method based on energy approach; (**B**) Optimization method based on deflection approach.

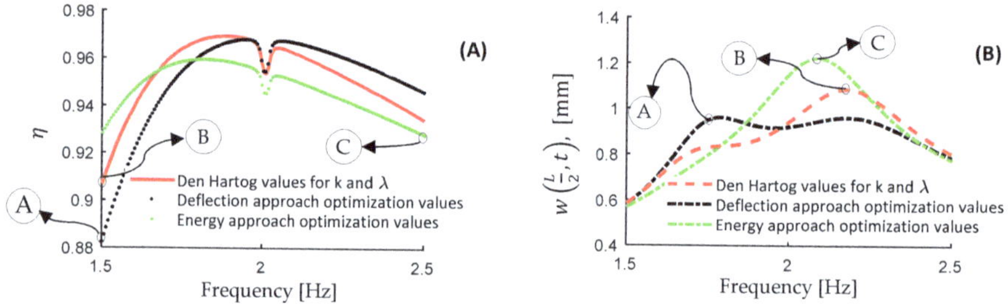

Figure 6. (**A**) The quantity of energy dissipated by linear DVAs; (**B**) Largest amount of displacement experienced by footbridges when subjected to linear DVAs in the frequency domain.

Peak points A, B, and C depicted in Figure 6 correspond to the optimized deflection approach DVA, linear DVA with Den Hartog values, and energy approach optimized DVA, respectively. These pivotal points signify the crucial frequencies that impact the determination of optimized parameters for both linear and nonlinear DVA methodologies. It should be emphasized that on the dissipated energy (η) graphs in Figure 6A, these points are associated with frequencies denoting the lowest dissipated energy, whereas on the deflection (w) graphs in Figure 6B, they indicate frequencies reflecting the highest deflections. Peak C in Figure 6A exhibits an energy dissipation of η = 92.822% in connection with energy approach optimization, surpassing peaks A and B associated with the deflection approach and Den Hartog method. The frequency dip observed at 2 Hz in Figure 6A is indicative of a resonance phenomenon. Within Figure 6B, Peak A illustrates the smallest deflection of 0.96 mm in the deflection approach method, which is lesser compared to peaks B and C. Additionally, in Figure 6B, the goal is to minimize the maximum deflection of the footbridge using different optimization methods across all frequencies related to a walking pedestrian.

4.1.2. The Optimal Configuration for Nonlinear DVAs

This section will investigate various forms of nonlinear DVAs based on the approaches outlined earlier. It is advisable to employ nonlinear DVAs when the excitation frequency varies. For instance, Starovetsky investigated a system with a nonlinear energy sink that exhibited quadratic damping characteristics [46]. In a separate study, Minaei and Ghorbani [47] introduced a novel variable stiffness mechanism that can be further developed as a practical nonlinear tool in engineering.

To investigate the effect of nonlinearity, the mathematical details of a DVA with quadratic stiffness and linear damping are checked with the parameters of elastic and damping forces defined as $\alpha = 1$, $\beta = 1$, $\gamma = 1$, and $\delta = 0$ (see Equations (11) and (12)). To optimize the nonlinear DVA parameters, the energy approach is utilized, yielding optimal values of $\lambda = 9900\ \frac{\text{Ns}}{\text{m}}$ and $k = 2.4 \times 10^8\ \frac{\text{N}}{\text{m}^2}$ when $m = 2$ and $n = 0$ in Equation (13). Additionally, using the deflection approach, the following values are obtained: $\lambda = 4750\ \frac{\text{Ns}}{\text{m}}$, and $k = 1.55 \times 10^8\ \frac{\text{N}}{\text{m}^2}$. The maximum beam deflection and energy absorbed by the DVA are illustrated in Figure 7. Peak A in Figure 7B indicates a minimum deflection of 0.97 mm, which is lower than peaks B and C, suggesting that the DVA with quadratic stiffness and linear damping outperforms the linear DVA. As shown in Figure 7B, the optimized nonlinear DVA (dashed black line) consistently exhibits enhanced performance across the frequency range of 1.5 Hz to 2.5 Hz compared to the linear DVA using Den Hartog values. In Figure 7A, peak B (Den Hartog values) reflects an efficiency η = 90.68%, exceeding that of peaks C and A, which correspond to the energy and deflection approaches. The anti-peaks at 2 Hz are associated with a resonance phenomenon, indicating that, from an energy approach standpoint, this specific nonlinear DVA is less efficient than the linear DVA.

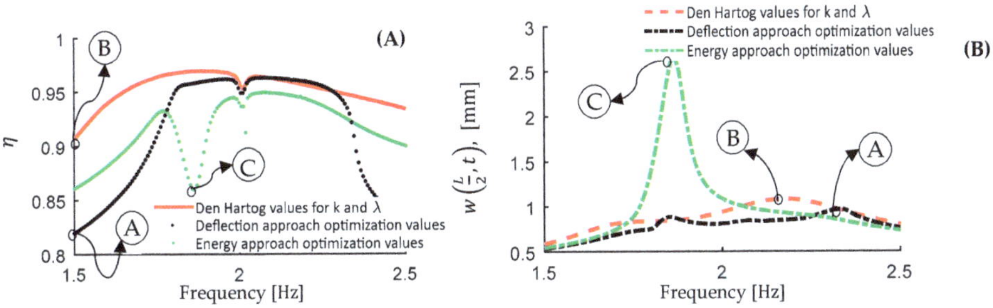

Figure 7. A footbridge connected to a Dynamic Vibration Absorber characterized by quadratic stiffness and linear damping in the frequency domain; (**A**) The quantity of energy dissipated by DVA (**B**) Maximum deflection of footbridge.

Now, the performance of a nonlinear DVA with quadratic stiffness and quadratic damping characteristics is investigated, see Figure 8. The maximum beam deflection and absorbed energy are presented in Figure 8. Notably, Figure 8A reveals a minor anti-peak at 1.88 Hz using the energy-optimized DVA, while a corresponding peak is evident in Figure 8B at point C. The integer powers for the elastic and damping forces in Equations (11) and (12) are set to $\alpha = 1$, $\beta = 1$, $\gamma = 1$, and $\delta = 1$, while in Equation (13), the values are $m = 2$ and $n = 1$. The peak A in Figure 8B indicates a minimum deflection of 0.97 mm, lower than the peaks B and C, suggesting better performance of the nonlinear DVA compared to the linear version. Optimal values obtained from the deflection approach optimization are $\lambda = 230\ \frac{\text{kNs}^2}{\text{m}^2}$ and $k = 150 \times 10^6\ \frac{\text{N}}{\text{m}^2}$, while those from the energy approach are $\lambda = 1350\ \frac{\text{kNs}^2}{\text{m}^2}$ and $k = 265 \times 10^6\ \frac{\text{N}}{\text{m}^2}$. As shown in Figure 8B, the nonlinear DVA consistently outperforms the linear model across most frequencies except within the ranges of 1.78 Hz to 1.83 Hz and 2.3 Hz to 2.4 Hz. Figure 8A indicates efficiency values of η = 90.68% for both Den Hartog and energy optimization methods, which exceed peak A from the deflection approach. The anti-peaks at 2 Hz result from resonance, indicating that this nonlinear DVA does not perform more efficiently than the linear one from an energy perspective.

Furthermore, Table 3 presents a detailed comparison of linear and nonlinear DVAs, demonstrating that the optimal parameters for minimizing deflection and maximizing energy absorption differ. This underscores the importance of defining the goals of the DVA before selecting its parameters. When the frequency of the applied excitation is variable, utilizing nonlinear DVAs is recommended [2]. Furthermore, although higher-order stiffness and damping nonlinearities (beyond cubic nonlinearity) were analyzed in this study, no significant improvements were identified, leading to their exclusion for the sake of brevity. In addition to the aforementioned nonlinearity, various types of nonlinearities, including piecewise, polynomial, monomial, magnetorheological, and others, can be used as nonlinear elements for vibration reduction in bridges. For more information, please refer to Refs. [48–50].

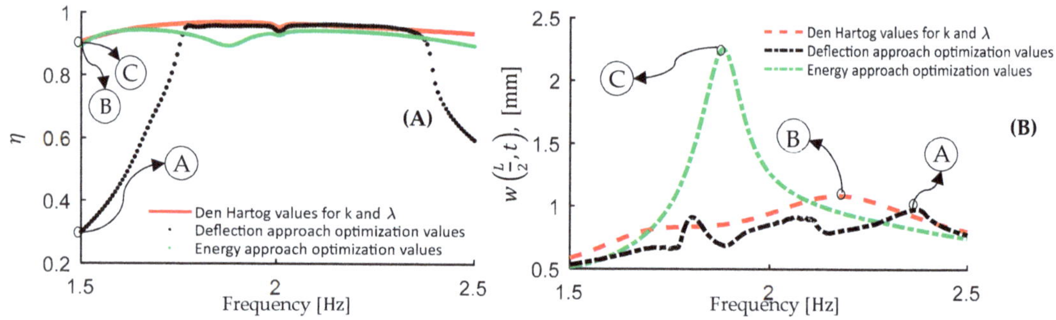

Figure 8. A footbridge equipped with a Dynamic Vibration Absorber exhibiting quadratic stiffness and quadratic damping characteristics in the frequency domain; (**A**) The energy dissipated by DVA, (**B**) Maximum deflection.

Table 3. Comparison between various optimization results under a walking pedestrian-induced excitation.

Footbridge and Type of DVA	Optimization Approach	Maximum Deflection [mm]	Minimum Value of Dissipated Energy [%]	Optimized k	Optimized λ	The Integers of Equations (11)–(13)
Bare footbridge	—	11.41	—	—	—	—
Linear DVA	Den Hartog values	1.1	90	$164 \times 10^3\ \frac{\text{N}}{\text{m}}$	$5293\ \frac{\text{Ns}}{\text{m}}$	—
Linear DVA	Energy	1.2	92.82	$145 \times 10^3\ \frac{\text{N}}{\text{m}}$	$6400\ \frac{\text{Ns}}{\text{m}}$	$m = 2$ and $n = 0$
Linear DVA	Deflection	0.96	88	$180 \times 10^3\ \frac{\text{N}}{\text{m}}$	$6000\ \frac{\text{Ns}}{\text{m}}$	$\alpha = 1,\ \beta = 0,$ $\gamma = 1,$ and $\delta = 0$
Quadratic damping and linear stiffness	Energy	1.6	92.77	$146 \times 10^3\ \frac{\text{N}}{\text{m}}$	$1.0 \times 10^6\ \frac{\text{Ns}^2}{\text{m}^2}$	$m = 2$ and $n = 1$
Quadratic damping and linear stiffness	Deflection	0.96	66	$183 \times 10^3\ \frac{\text{N}}{\text{m}}$	$0.42 \times 10^6\ \frac{\text{Ns}^2}{\text{m}^2}$	$\alpha = 1,\ \beta = 0,$ $\gamma = 1,$ and $\delta = 1$
Quadratic stiffness and linear damping	Energy	2.6	86	$240 \times 10^6\ \frac{\text{N}}{\text{m}^2}$	$9900\ \frac{\text{Ns}}{\text{m}}$	$m = 2$ and $n = 0$
Quadratic stiffness and linear damping	Deflection	0.97	82	$155 \times 10^6\ \frac{\text{N}}{\text{m}^2}$	$4750\ \frac{\text{Ns}}{\text{m}}$	$\alpha = 1,\ \beta = 1,$ $\gamma = 1,$ and $\delta = 0$
Quadratic stiffness and damping	Energy	2.2	89	$265 \times 10^6\ \frac{\text{N}}{\text{m}^2}$	$1.35 \times 10^6\ \frac{\text{Ns}^2}{\text{m}^2}$	$m = 2$ and $n = 1$
Quadratic stiffness and damping	Deflection	0.97	30	$150 \times 10^6\ \frac{\text{N}}{\text{m}^2}$	$0.23 \times 10^6\ \frac{\text{Ns}^2}{\text{m}^2}$	$\alpha = 1,\ \beta = 1,$ $\gamma = 1,$ and $\delta = 1$
Cubic damping and linear stiffness	Energy	1.8	92	$148 \times 10^3\ \frac{\text{N}}{\text{m}}$	$95 \times 10^6\ \frac{\text{Ns}^3}{\text{m}^3}$	$m = 4$ and $n = 0$
Cubic damping and linear stiffness	Deflection	0.96	27	$185 \times 10^3\ \frac{\text{N}}{\text{m}}$	$27.5 \times 10^6\ \frac{\text{Ns}^3}{\text{m}^3}$	$\alpha = 1,\ \beta = 0,$ $\gamma = 3,$ and $\delta = 0$
Cubic stiffness and Linear damping	Energy	3.5	79	$257 \times 10^9\ \frac{\text{N}}{\text{m}^3}$	$11700\ \frac{\text{Ns}}{\text{m}}$	$m = 2$ and $n = 0$
Cubic stiffness and Linear damping	Deflection	1.1	81	$129 \times 10^9\ \frac{\text{N}}{\text{m}^3}$	$7750\ \frac{\text{Ns}}{\text{m}}$	$\alpha = 3,\ \beta = 0,$ $\gamma = 1,$ and $\delta = 0$
Cubic damping and Cubic stiffness	Energy	4.7	71	$770 \times 10^9\ \frac{\text{N}}{\text{m}^3}$	$1.2 \times 10^9\ \frac{\text{Ns}^3}{\text{m}^3}$	$m = 4$ and $n = 0$
Cubic damping and Cubic stiffness	Deflection	1.1	4	$137 \times 10^9\ \frac{\text{N}}{\text{m}^3}$	$32 \times 10^6\ \frac{\text{Ns}^3}{\text{m}^3}$	$\alpha = 3,\ \beta = 0,$ $\gamma = 3,$ and $\delta = 0$

4.2. The Impact of the Force Frequencies on the Optimization of the DVA Parameters

Equation (15) includes η_{1W}, η_{2W}, η_{3W}, and η_{4W} which are the initial four DLFs utilized in simulating a pedestrian walking behavior. Furthermore, DLFs for the first four harmonics are introduced to simulate a pedestrian engaged in running and jumping activities. The dataset derived from a previous study, [44], is subjected to cubic polynomial regression for analysis, and the findings are depicted in Figure 9. η_R and η_J are the DLFs for a pedestrian running and jumping. When the initial four DLFs for running and jumping are modeled using cubic polynomial regression, the Equations (18) and (19) are obtained for running and jumping pedestrians, respectively, as depicted by the solid lines in Figure 9.

$$\begin{aligned} \eta_{1R} &= -4.66 + 5.562\, f_p - 1.69(f_p)^2 + 0.1692(f_p)^3 \\ \eta_{2R} &= 4.791 - 2.688\, f_p + 0.5\, (f_p)^2 - 0.0295(f_p)^3 \\ \eta_{3R} &= 0.148 - 0.027 f_p + 0.0032\, (f_p)^2 - 0.000006(f_p)^3 \\ \eta_{4R} &= -2.790 + 1.326 f_p - 0.1223\, (f_p)^2 + 0.0047(f_p)^3 \end{aligned} \tag{18}$$

$$\begin{aligned} \eta_{1J} &= -0.776 + 2.533\, f_p - 0.8047(f_p)^2 + 0.077(f_p)^3 \\ \eta_{1J} &= -0.8647 + 0.7567\, f_p - 0.0879(f_p)^2 + 0.00132(f_p)^3 \\ \eta_{1J} &= 1.2552 - 0.6367\, f_p + 0.1194(f_p)^2 - 0.0068(f_p)^3 \\ \eta_{4J} &= 0.398 - 0.052 f_p - 0.0044\, (f_p)^2 + 0.0006(f_p)^3 \end{aligned} \tag{19}$$

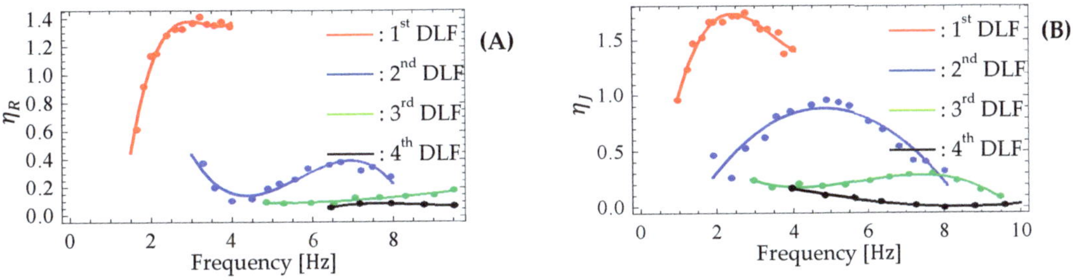

Figure 9. The initial four DLFs for (**A**) running pedestrian, and (**B**) jumping pedestrian.

In this study, the efficiency of a linear DVA optimized using the numerical deflection method is evaluated against analytical optimization techniques such as Den Hartog [51], Tigli [52], and Asami's H_∞ [53], as shown in Table 4. The primary goal of the H_∞ optimization criterion is to reduce the highest amplification factor based on [53]. The main goal of H_2 optimization is to reduce the squared area under the response curve of the main system. The results indicate that the maximum deflection of the footbridge during pedestrian activities is reduced when employing the numerical optimization approach used in this study, compared to the results from analytical approaches for the attached DVA. Table 4 demonstrates that the mechanical properties of the DVA vary under different types of excitations. Consequently, by utilizing a semi-active DVA that adjusts to surrounding conditions and excitation levels, significant reductions in bridge vibrations can be achieved. Notably, the optimization methods used in previous studies by Asami [53] (H_2 *and* H_∞), Tigli [52], and Den Hartog [51] focused on linear DVAs. Therefore, only the linear format of the DVA for the numerical optimization approach, is considered in Table 4.

Table 4. Comparison of different optimization results under different types of pedestrian excitations.

Case	Attached DVA	Optimization Approach	Type of Excitation	Maximum Deflection [mm]	Deflection Reduction vs. a Bare Footbridge %	Deflection Reduction Concerning Tigli's %	Deflection Reduction Concerning Den Hartog's %	Optimized Stiffness $k[\frac{kN}{m}]$	Optimized Damping $\lambda[\frac{kNs}{m}]$
1	×	–	Walking	10.30	–	–	–	–	–
2	✓	Numerical *	Walking	0.96	91	9	11	180	5.60
3	✓	Tigli	Walking	1.05	90	–	–	172	4.80
4	✓	Asami H_2	Walking	1.07	90	–	–	172	4.47
5	✓	Asami H_∞	Walking	1.09	90	–	–	163	5.30
6	✓	Den Hartog	Walking	1.08	90	–	–	164	5.29
7	×	–	Running	27.87	–	–	–	–	–
8	✓	Numerical *	Running	1.39	95	34	38	240	3.80
9	✓	Tigli	Running	2.11	92	–	–	172	4.80
10	✓	Asami H_2	Running	2.16	92	–	–	172	4.47
11	✓	Asami H_∞	Running	2.25	92	–	–	163	5.30
12	✓	Den Hartog	Running	2.24	92	–	–	164	5.29
13	×	–	Jumping	43.99	–	–	–	–	–
14	✓	Numerical *	Jumping	1.86	96	37	42	235	3.40
15	✓	Tigli	Jumping	2.95	93	–	–	172	4.80
16	✓	Asami H_2	Jumping	3.00	93	–	–	172	4.47
17	✓	Asami H_∞	Jumping	3.20	93	–	–	163	5.30
18	✓	Den Hartog	Jumping	3.18	93	–	–	164	5.29

Numerical *: considering the maximum deflection optimization approach by using Equations (1)–(12) in this study.

4.3. Review of Some Nonlinear DVAs

The parameters k and λ depend on the bridge's fundamental frequency, ω_1. Canter et al. [54] demonstrated that the natural frequencies of vehicle-bridge systems change with vehicle position, primarily due to a mass effect. This also applies to lightweight footbridges with pedestrians. Environmental factors affect structural stiffness and bridge frequency; Abdel-Wahab and Guido [55] observed that natural frequencies tend to increase as temperature decreases. Consequently, a passive vibration absorber may detune over time, therefore a variable damping and stiffness should be retuned automatically [56]. Additionally, Van Nimmen et al. [15] noted that, predicting a bridge's dynamic behavior is difficult due to uncertainties in parameters like stiffness of the supports of the bridge. They demonstrated that a deviation of 10% in the bridge's natural frequency can be expected compared to the predictions made by the finite element model. Temperature changes and long-term mechanical property variations also affect footbridge dynamics, as fluctuations can shift the modulus of elasticity for structural steel from 195 GPa to 205 GPa [57,58].

The aforementioned uncertainties are the motivation for introducing a new adjustable dashpot designed for use in a DVA, it is equipped with an actuator and motor and can be classified as a semi-active DVA.

As the nonlinearity can arise due to various reasons, such as the arrangement of the elements, which may be linear when considered individually, the structure of the element, and so on. In this work we propose two types of nonlinearities: geometric cubic nonlinearity and quadratic nonlinear damping.

4.3.1. Geometry Nonlinearity of Cubic Type

The nonlinear vibration absorber designed for the bridge is depicted in Figure 10.

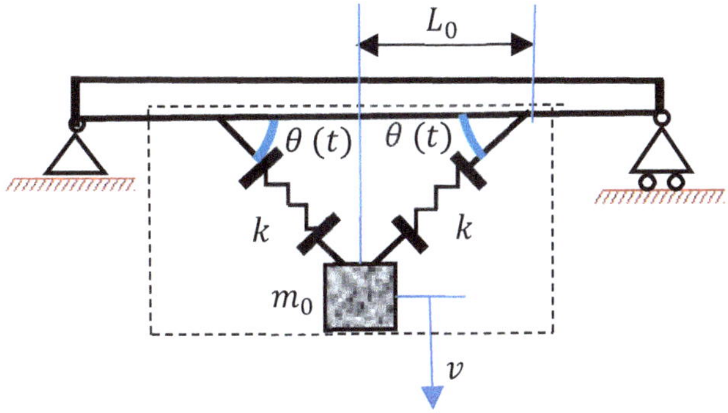

Figure 10. A DVA with geometric nonlinearity.

To determine the degree of nonlinearity in the specific nonlinear configuration of the system depicted in Figure 10, we take advantages from a previous study, Ref. [9], which results in cubic stiffness nonlinearity, while each connected spring is linear, the overall system connected exhibits cubic nonlinearity, the restoring force reads:

$$F = \frac{k}{{L_0}^2}v^3 + O\left(v^5\right) = Kv^3 + O\left(v^5\right) \tag{20}$$

Moreover, Minaei and Ghorbani [47] developed a variable stiffness element that can be incorporated into a DVA, transforming it into a semi-active device. Their work demonstrates the ability to change θ(t), as shown in Figure 10, which allows the stiffness element to be variable, thereby enabling the DVA to function as a semi-active nonlinear system with adjustable stiffness. Although cubic stiffness has been introduced here, there was no significant improvement for a footbridge subjected to pedestrian loads compared to an attached linear or quadratic stiffness. It was presented primarily to demonstrate how cubic nonlinearity can function in practice; for more information, refer to Table 3.

4.3.2. New Nonlinear Damper of Quadratic Type

This section describes a structurally nonlinear dashpot, accompanied by a schematic diagram that illustrates its main components. It can be classified as a semi-active quadratic variable damping dashpot. This type of dashpot can be used in a DVA as a quadratic damping element, enabling the adjustment of its parameters according to optimized values calculated to reduce bridge vibrations; see Table 3. As illustrated in Figure 11, the variable damping viscous damper (VDVD) comprises an outer cylinder, steel rods, an upper plate, and a truncated conical valve controlled by a handle threaded from inside. The main components of the dashpot are outlined here. The outer cylinder has a cylinder, five rods, and an upper plate. Each steel rod is connected to both the outer cylinder and the upper plate, forming a unit. A truncated conical valve slides along the rods to manage fluid flow. It has an internally threaded handle that passes through a hole in the upper plate. Inside the handle, an adjusting screw can rotate axially, and a motor on the inner cylinder turns this screw, moving the valve up or down. O-rings and bellows are used to prevent hydraulic oil leaks, ensuring the device is sealed.

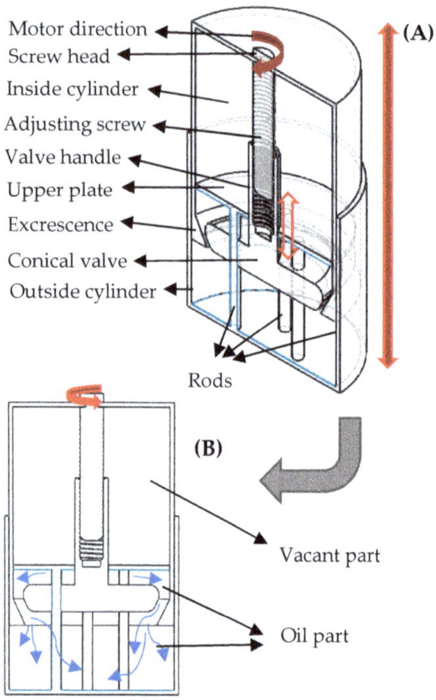

Figure 11. The VDVD is represented by a schematic diagram; (**A**) 3D model; (**B**) flowing of oil.

The benefits of the proposed nonlinear variable damping system in comparison to the orifice type include: (1) the system can handle a wide range of fluid flow rates and allows for variability in damping constants based on specific conditions; (2) unlike the orifice type, which can experience high-pressure drops and corrosion of thin plates leading to inaccuracies, the proposed system offers a more reliable and accurate solution for variable damping. The researchers studied how the damping force of the dashpot's two cylinders correlated with their relative velocity to identify the nonlinearity of the damper. The fluid moves through the channel as the cylinders are in motion, references [59,60] describe the equation for the fluid's volume flow rate Q through an orifice:

$$Q = \alpha(\Delta p)^{\frac{1}{2}} \tag{21}$$

$$Q = \rho\ V\ A \tag{22}$$

The equation in Figure 11B incorporates the experimental constant α specific to the fluid, the base area of both the conical valve and excrescence, along with the oil channel area. It relates to the pressure drop (Δp) between points 1 and 2. Equation (22) represents the fluid's volume flow rate through the channel, where the fluid's density is denoted as ρ, the relative velocity of the two cylinders is identified as V, and A is the surface area of the conical valve exposed to the fluid. By using Equations (21) and (22), it can be stated that:

$$V = \alpha(\Delta p)^{\frac{1}{2}}/\rho\ A \tag{23}$$

The external force exerted on the upper cylinder in Figure 11B results in a pressure variation between points 1 and 2. Hence, the total force acting on the conical valve and the excrescence can be calculated using the formula: $F = \Delta p A$; thus:

$$F = \frac{\rho^2 A^3}{\alpha^2} V^2 = c\, V^2 \tag{24}$$

As presented in Equation (24), the damping force of the dashpot in Figure 11 is proportional to the square of the velocity, making it a quadratic nonlinear element. The damping constant, c, signifies this relationship. An actuator can control the motor's rotation, allowing the dashpot to provide various damping constants. This adaptability enables effective use of this nonlinear element in passive vibration absorbers, enhancing efficiency across a wide range of frequencies and highlighting a key advantage of nonlinear energy sinks.

5. Results and Discussion

This paper focuses on a case study involving bridge properties derived from Caprani et al. [61], who based their findings on Fujino et al.'s experimental research [62]. We consider a DVA attached to the bridge, emphasizing that its mechanical parameters should be tailored to the bridge type to ensure the model's adaptability across various structures. Furthermore, the response of the footbridge does not exhibit a linear relationship with the number of pedestrians. In the cases of marching troops, where nearly full synchronization occurs, the footbridge's response can be estimated by multiplying the response of a single pedestrian by $\sqrt{N}$. This suggests that in random crowds, pedestrians dampen each other's resonance effects, leading to reduced dynamic vibrations compared to scenarios with either a single pedestrian or a fully synchronized group.

Figure 12 represents a convergence analysis carried out using 1, 5 and 20 modal expansions, for the footbridge displacement field, with nonlinear DVA. For the sake of brevity, only two DVAs are selected: (1) quadratic damping and stiffness, and (2) quadratic stiffness and linear damping. In Figure 12A,B, the continuous red line indicates the footbridge response with five-mode expansion, while the black dotted line represents 20 modes. The results reveal no significant difference between the two expansions, indicating that modal interactions due to nonlinearity do not occur for excitation frequencies in the 1.5–2.5 Hz range. Frequencies above 3 Hz or below 1.25 Hz, are not investigated because they are outside typical walking excitation frequencies.

Furthermore, Sections 4.1–4.3 of this paper explore interesting findings about different types of nonlinear dampers using energy and deflection approach methods. It is worth noting that the specific results are presented in Table 3. Figure 7A presents the nonlinear DVA with quadratic stiffness and linear damping, showcasing a notable decrease in energy at point C, potentially due to superharmonic resonance. In Figure 7B, it is demonstrated that employing a DVA with quadratic stiffness and linear damping optimized through the deflection method leads to reduced deflection of the footbridge, outperforming a footbridge with a linearly attached DVA, across 92% of the frequency spectrum ranging from 1.5–2.5 Hz. The nonlinear DVA with quadratic damping and stiffness depicted by the dashed black line in Figure 8B performs better than the linear DVA with Den Hartog values in the entire frequency range analyzed, except for the intervals [1.78 Hz–1.83 Hz] and [2.3 Hz–2.4 Hz]. As a result, the deflection of the footbridge within the investigated frequency range of 1.5 to 2.5 Hz is lower in more than 86% of the frequency range, compared to the footbridge with the optimized linear DVA. The decrease in the absorbed energy at frequencies below 1.75 Hz is not due to resonance or superharmonic resonance, but rather to the optimization method and the associated mechanical values. To facilitate the comparison, Figure 13 illustrates the maximum deflection of the footbridge equipped with an attached DVA, highlighting various types of nonlinearities. The effectiveness of the different types of nonlinear DVAs examined in this study on the maximum deflection of the footbridge is represented by distinct lines.

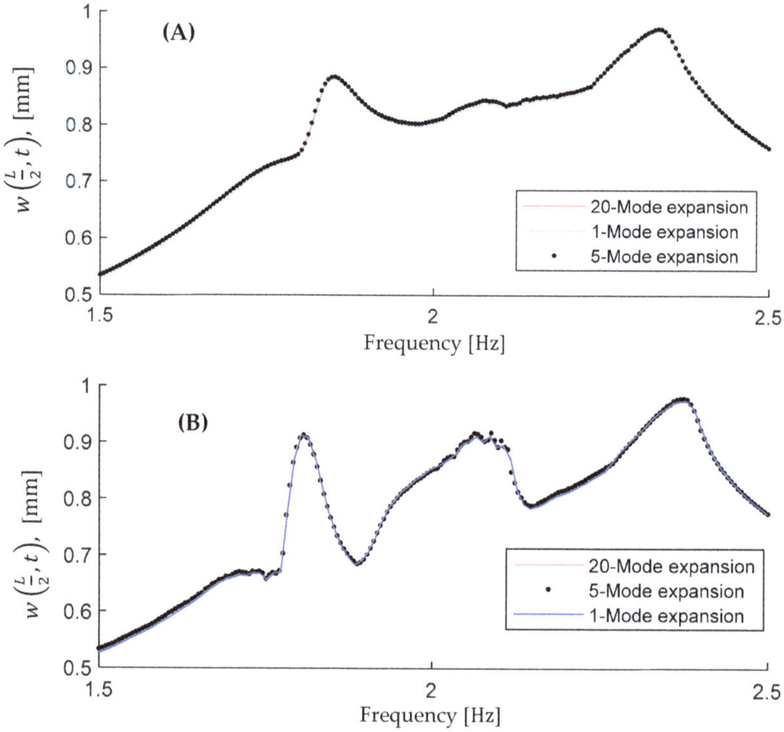

Figure 12. Evaluation of the nonlinearity of the DVAs on higher modes; (**A**): DVA with quadratic stiffness and linear damping elements; (**B**): DVA with both quadratic stiffness damping elements.

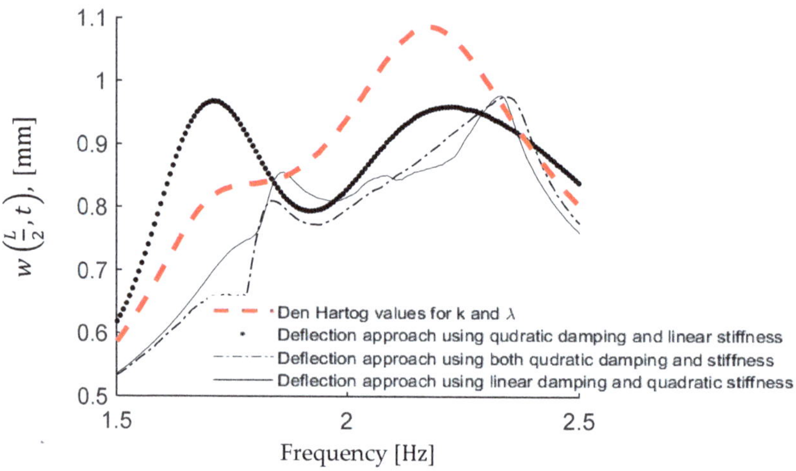

Figure 13. Comparison of a footbridge deflection equipped with various types of DVAs.

The results indicate that the optimal parameters for minimizing deflection and maximizing absorbed energy may be not similar. It is important to define the objective of using DVA and then select appropriate parameters; using a nonlinear DVA dampens the bridge's deflection over a wider range of frequencies versus a linear one. Note that, reference [2] suggests that increasing the power of nonlinear stiffness results in a more efficient reduction of beam deflection caused by vehicles. This study demonstrates that quadratic nonlinearities perform better when the beam is excited by pedestrians. Higher-order nonlinearities in stiffness and damping, are also studied, but no improvement was observed.

6. Conclusions

In this study, we explored the effectiveness of nonlinear semi-active dynamic vibration absorbers in mitigating vibrations of light bridges subjected to moving loads. The recent results show that those traditional passive absorbers are often weak in adjusting the damping and stiffness parameters of the DVA required for optimal performance in real-time conditions. Therefore, the introduction of nonlinear DVAs, particularly those with variable damping capabilities, presents a significant advancement in vibration control technology compared to traditional linear passive DVAs.

The main conclusion points of this research are listed as follow:

- The nonlinear DVAs, especially those with quadratic stiffness and linear damping, and DVA with both quadratic damping and stiffness elements, significantly reduce bridge deflections in a wider frequency range, compared to linear DVAs.
- The optimization of DVA parameters is pivotal for achieving the performant results in vibration reduction. In this study the two goal functions including, minimizing of the bridge displacement and maximizing of the amount of absorbed energy is considered.
- In the following, some of the challenges proposed for the future research, are listed:
- Exploring the design and implementation of active nonlinear dynamic vibration absorbers to enhance vibration control performance.
- Investigating the application of nonlinear quadratic stiffnesses to improve the effectiveness and responsiveness of vibration absorption systems.
- Investigating other types of nonlinear vibration absorbers attached to light footbridges, including piecewise linear stiffness or damping.
- Focus on developing semi-active or active control strategies that aim to minimize the damping time of vibrations and maximize the energy absorbed.
- The effects of various types of human activities specially the synchronized activities on the vibrations of the footbridges.

In conclusion, this study emphasizes the importance of selecting appropriate DVA parameters based on the desired objective, such as minimizing deflection or maximizing energy dissipation. Furthermore, Table 4 shows that by utilizing certain types of nonlinear DVAs, such as a numerically optimized DVA with both quadratic damping and stiffness, can reduce the vibrations of the bridge by approximately 40%.

Author Contributions: Conceptualization, F.P. and F.S.S.; methodology, F.P. and F.S.S.; software, H.S. and M.M.; validation, H.S. and F.S.S.; investigation, H.S., F.S.S. and F.P.; writing—original draft preparation, H.S., A.Z. and M.M.; writing—review and editing, H.S., F.S.S., A.Z. and F.P.; visualization, H.S. and M.M.; supervision, A.Z. and F.P.; project administration, A.Z. All authors have read and agreed to the published version of the manuscript.

Funding: This research received no external funding.

Data Availability Statement: The data that support the findings of this study are available from the corresponding author, [A.Z.], upon reasonable request.

Conflicts of Interest: The authors declare no conflict of interest.

Nomenclature

The following symbols are used in this paper:

W	weight of the pedestrian, [N]
m_p	pedestrian body mass, [kg]
g	gravity acceleration, [N/kg]
f_p	pedestrian pacing rate (pedestrian frequency), [Hz]
v_p	pedestrian velocity, [m/s]
l_p	step length of the pedestrian, [m]
η_k	coefficient of Fourier series named as "dynamic load factor (DLF)"
φ_k	harmonic phase angle
h	the number of harmonics
m_0	the mass of the dynamic vibration absorber (DVA), [kg]
$z(t)$	position of the DVA's mass
$w(x,t)$	vertical displacement of the beam
$u(t)$	the relative displacement of the DVA's mass and the footbridge mid-span
$G(t)$	passing pedestrian amplitude
$F(x,t)$	moving pedestrian-induced load
L	the length of the footbridge, [m]
E	modulus of elasticity of the footbridge, [GPa]
ξ_r	the damping ratio of the footbridge
$f(u)$	the force exerted by the DVA's spring, [N]
$g(u_{,t})$	viscous damping force, [N]
A	cross-section area, [m^2]
m	the footbridge mass per unit length, [m/kg]
I	moment of inertia, [m^4]
λ	damping coefficient, [kNs/m]
k	stiffness coefficient, [kN/m]
d	the location of the damper, [m]
ρ	the density of the footbridge material, [kg/m^3]
$q_r(t)$	modal coordinates
$\varphi_r(x)$	normalized eigenfunctions
N	the number of modes
ω_r	natural frequencies of the rth mode of the footbridge, [rad/s]
m_e	footbridge equivalent mass, [kg]
μ	mass ratio

References

1. Samani, F.S.; Pellicano, F. Vibration reduction on beams subjected to moving loads using linear and nonlinear dynamic absorbers. *J. Sound Vib.* **2009**, *325*, 742. [CrossRef]
2. Samani, F.S.; Pellicano, F.; Masoumi, A. Performances of dynamic vibration absorbers for beams subjected to moving loads. *Nonlinear Dyn.* **2013**, *73*, 1065. [CrossRef]
3. Gatti, G. Fundamental insight on the performance of a nonlinear tuned mass damper. *Meccanica* **2018**, *53*, 111. [CrossRef]
4. Liu, P.; Zhu, H.-X.; Moaveni, B.; Yang, W.-G.; Huang, S.-Q. Vibration Monitoring of Two Long-Span Floors Equipped with Tuned Mass Dampers. *Int. J. Struct. Stab. Dyn.* **2019**, *19*, 1950101. Available online: https://worldscientific.com/doi/abs/10.1142/S0219455419501013 (accessed on 23 December 2024). [CrossRef]
5. Samani, F.S.; Pellicano, F. Vibration reduction of beams under successive traveling loads by means of linear and nonlinear dynamic absorbers. *J. Sound Vib.* **2012**, *331*, 2272. [CrossRef]
6. Saber, H.; Samani, F.S.; Pellicano, F. Vibration reduction of footbridges subjected to walking, running, and jumping pedestrian. *J. Vib. Control* **2023**, *29*, 3227. [CrossRef]

7. Chen, Z.; Chen, Z.; Li, G.; Zhang, W.; Zhang, X.; Huang, S.; Chen, Z. Dynamic Response Analysis and Vibration Reduction of Steel Truss Corridor Pedestrian Bridge Under Pedestrian Load. *Front. Mater.* **2022**, *9*, 839265. [CrossRef]
8. Bassoli, E.; Vincenzi, L. Parameter calibration of a social force model for the crowd-induced vibrations of footbridges. *Front. Built Environ.* **2021**, *7*, 656799. [CrossRef]
9. Saber, H.; Samani, F.S.; Pellicano, F. Nonlinear vibration absorbers applied on footbridges. *Meccanica* **2021**, *56*, 23. [CrossRef]
10. Caprani, C.C.; Ahmadi, E. Formulation of human–structure interaction system models for vertical vibration. *J. Sound Vib.* **2016**, *377*, 346. [CrossRef]
11. Ao, W.K.; Reynolds, P. (Eds.) Analytical and experimental study of eddy current damper for vibration suppression in a footbridge structure. In *Dynamics of Civil Structures*; Springer: Berlin/Heidelberg, Germany, 2017; Volume 2. [CrossRef]
12. Ao, W.K.; Reynolds, P. Analysis and numerical evaluation of H∞ and H2 optimal design schemes for an electromagnetic shunt damper. *J. Vib. Acoust.* **2020**, *142*, 021003. [CrossRef]
13. Pedersen, L.; Frier, C. Stochastic Load Models and Footbridge Response. *Dyn. Civ. Struct.* **2015**, *2*, 75. [CrossRef]
14. Lievens, K.; Lombaert, G.; De Roeck, G.; Van den Broeck, P. Robust design of a TMD for the vibration serviceability of a footbridge. *Eng. Struct.* **2016**, *123*, 408. [CrossRef]
15. Van Nimmen, K.; Lombaert, G.; De Roeck, G.; Van den Broeck, P. Vibration serviceability of footbridges: Evaluation of the current codes of practice. *Eng. Struct.* **2014**, *59*, 448. [CrossRef]
16. Ding, H.; Chen, L.-Q. Designs, analysis, and applications of nonlinear energy sinks. *Nonlinear Dyn.* **2020**, *100*, 3061. [CrossRef]
17. Gourdon, E.; Lamarque, C.-H.; Pernot, S. Contribution to efficiency of irreversible passive energy pumping with a strong nonlinear attachment. *Nonlinear Dyn.* **2007**, *50*, 793. [CrossRef]
18. Ferreira, F.; Moutinho, C.; Cunha, Á.; Caetano, E. Use of semi-active tuned mass dampers to control footbridges subjected to synchronous lateral excitation. *J. Sound Vib.* **2019**, *446*, 176. [CrossRef]
19. Maślanka, M. Optimised semi-active tuned mass damper with acceleration and relative motion feedbacks. *Mech. Syst. Signal Process.* **2019**, *130*, 707. [CrossRef]
20. Saber, H.; Samani, F.S.; Pellicano, F. A novel nonlinear variable damping device and its application for the systems with uncertain parameters. *Proc. Inst. Mech. Eng. Part K J. Multi-Body Dyn.* **2022**, *236*, 660. [CrossRef]
21. Chen, J.; Han, Z.; Xu, R. Effects of human-induced load models on tuned mass damper in reducing floor vibration. *Adv. Struct. Eng.* **2019**, *22*, 2449. [CrossRef]
22. Nguyen, K.; Soria, J.M.; Díaz, I.M.; Goicolea, J.M. Exploring the potential of the semi-active inertial absorber in control resonant effects for short-to-medium span high-speed railway bridges. *Struct. Infrastruct. Eng.* **2023**, 1–16. [CrossRef]
23. Kumar, J.; Bhushan, G. Modelling of a semi-active vibration absorber featuring variable stiffness and variable damping using magnetorheological materials. *Mater. Today Proc.* **2023**, in press. [CrossRef]
24. Barrera-Vargas, C.A.; Naranjo-Pérez, J.; Díaz, I.M.; García-Palacios, J.H. Design of a Semiactive TMD for Lightweight Pedestrian Structures Considering Human–Structure–Actuator Interaction. *Actuators* **2022**, *11*, 101. [CrossRef]
25. Wang, J.; Zhang, X.; Liu, Y.; Qin, Z.; Ma, L.; Hong, F.; Chu, F. Dynamic analysis of magnetorheological damper incorporating elastic ring in coupled multi-physical fields. *Mech. Syst. Signal Process.* **2024**, *208*, 111040. [CrossRef]
26. Javani, M.; Eslami, M.R.; Kiani, Y. Active control of thermally induced vibrations of temperature-dependent FGM circular plate with piezoelectric sensor/actuator layers. *Aerosp. Sci. Technol.* **2024**, *146*, 108997. [CrossRef]
27. Jiang, X.; McFarland, D.M.; Bergman, L.A.; Vakakis, A.F. Steady state passive nonlinear energy pumping in coupled oscillators: Theoretical and experimental results. *Nonlinear Dyn.* **2003**, *33*, 87. [CrossRef]
28. Yang, Y.; Wang, X. Investigation into the linear velocity response of cantilever beam embedded with impact damper. *J. Vib. Control* **2019**, *25*, 1365. [CrossRef]
29. Wang, J.; Wang, B.; Liu, Z.; Zhang, C.; Li, H. Experimental and numerical studies of a novel asymmetric nonlinear mass damper for seismic response mitigation. *Struct. Control Health Monit.* **2020**, *27*, e2513. [CrossRef]
30. Wang, L.; Zhou, Y.; Shi, W. Random crowd-induced vibration in footbridge and adaptive control using semi-active TMD including crowd-structure interaction. *Eng. Struct.* **2024**, *306*, 117839. [CrossRef]
31. Wu, J.-J. Study on the inertia effect of helical spring of the absorber on suppressing the dynamic responses of a beam subjected to a moving load. *J. Sound Vib.* **2006**, *297*, 981. [CrossRef]
32. Zienkiewicz, O.C. RLTaJZZ. In *The Finite Element Method: Its Basis and Fundamentals*; Elsevier: Amsterdam, The Netherlands, 2013.
33. Reddy, J.N. *An Introduction to the Finite Element Method*; McGraw-Hill: New York, NY, USA, 2005.
34. Khurshudyan, A.; Ohanyan, S. (Eds.) Vibrations of geometrically nonlinear beam subjected to two oppositely moving loads and supported by three equidistant visco-elastic dampers. *J. Phys. Conf. Ser.* **2018**, *991*, 012046. [CrossRef]
35. Szafrański, M. Vibration of the bridge under moving singular loads-theoretical formulation and numerical solution. *J. Appl. Math. Comput. Mech.* **2016**, *15*, 169. [CrossRef]
36. Vakakis, A.F.; Manevitch, L.; Gendelman, O.; Bergman, L. Dynamics of linear discrete systems connected to local, essentially non-linear attachments. *J. Sound Vib.* **2003**, *264*, 559. [CrossRef]

37. Sayyad, F.; Gadhave, N. Variable stiffness type magnetic vibration absorber to control the vibration of beam structure. *J. Vib. Control* **2014**, *20*, 1960. [CrossRef]
38. Pedersen, L.; Frier, C. Sensitivity of footbridge vibrations to stochastic walking parameters. *J. Sound Vib.* **2010**, *329*, 2683. [CrossRef]
39. Fujino, Y.; Siringoringo, D.M. A conceptual review of pedestrian-induced lateral vibration and crowd synchronization problem on footbridges. *J. Bridge Eng.* **2016**, *21*, C4015001. [CrossRef]
40. Racic, V.; Brownjohn, J.M.W. Stochastic model of near-periodic vertical loads due to humans walking. *Adv. Eng. Inform.* **2011**, *25*, 259. [CrossRef]
41. Young, P. Improved floor vibration prediction methodologies. In Proceedings of the Arup Vibration Seminar on Engineering for Structural Vibration—Current Developments in Research and Practice, London, UK, 1 October 2001.
42. Kim, S.-H.; Cho, K.-I.; Choi, M.-S.; Lim, J.-Y. Development of human body model for the dynamic analysis of footbridges under pedestrian induced excitation. *Steel Struct.* **2008**, *8*, 333.
43. Wu, Q.; Kitahara, Y.; Takahashi, K.; Chen, B. Dynamic characteristics of Megami cable-stayed bridge: A comparison of experimental and analytical results. *Int. J. Steel Struct.* **2008**, *8*, 1–9.
44. Rainer, J.; Pernica, G.; Allen, D.E. Dynamic loading and response of footbridges. *Can. J. Civ. Eng.* **1988**, *15*, 66. [CrossRef]
45. Živanović, S.; Pavic, A.; Reynolds, P. Vibration serviceability of footbridges under human-induced excitation: A literature review. *J. Sound Vib.* **2005**, *279*, 1–74. [CrossRef]
46. Starosvetsky, Y.; Gendelman, O. Vibration absorption in systems with a nonlinear energy sink: Nonlinear damping. *J. Sound Vib.* **2009**, *324*, 916. [CrossRef]
47. Minaei, A.; Ghorbani-Tanha, A. Optimal step-by-step tuning method for variable stiffness semiactive tuned mass dampers. *J. Eng. Mech.* **2019**, *145*, 04019037. [CrossRef]
48. Nayfeh, A.H.; Mook, D.T. *Nonlinear Oscillations*; John Wiley & Sons: Hoboken, NJ, USA, 2024.
49. Vakakis, A.F.; Gendelman, O.V.; Bergman, L.A.; McFarland, D.M.; Kerschen, G.; Lee, Y.S. *Nonlinear Targeted Energy Transfer in Mechanical and Structural Systems*; Springer Science & Business Media: Berlin/Heidelberg, Germany, 2008.
50. Ye, X.; Ni, Y.-Q.; Ao, W.K.; Yuan, L. Modeling of the hysteretic behavior of nonlinear particle damping by Fourier neural network with transfer learning. *Mech. Syst. Signal Process.* **2024**, *208*, 111006. [CrossRef]
51. Den Hartog, J.P. *Mechanical Vibrations*; Courier Corporation: Chelmsford, MA, USA, 1985.
52. Tigli, O.F. Optimum vibration absorber (tuned mass damper) design for linear damped systems subjected to random loads. *J. Sound Vib.* **2012**, *331*, 3035. [CrossRef]
53. Asami, T.; Nishihara, O. Closed-form exact solution to H∞ optimization of dynamic vibration absorbers (application to different transfer functions and damping systems). *J. Vib. Acoust.* **2003**, *125*, 398. [CrossRef]
54. Cantero, D.; McGetrick, P.; Kim, C.-W.; OBrien, E. Experimental monitoring of bridge frequency evolution during the passage of vehicles with different suspension properties. *Eng. Struct.* **2019**, *187*, 209. [CrossRef]
55. Wahab, M.A.; De Roeck, G. Effect of temperature on dynamic system parameters of a highway bridge. *Struct. Eng. Int.* **1997**, *7*, 266. [CrossRef]
56. Zhang, L.; Hong, L.; Dhupia, J.S.; Johnson, S.; Qaiser, Z.; Zhou, Z. (Eds.) A novel semi-active tuned mass damper with tunable stiffness. In Proceedings of the IEEE/ASME International Conference on Advanced Intelligent Mechatronics (AIM), Auckland, New Zealand, 9–12 July 2018; IEEE: Piscataway, NJ, USA, 2018. [CrossRef]
57. Ledbetter, H. Stainless-steel elastic constants at low temperatures. *J. Appl. Phys.* **1981**, *52*, 1587. [CrossRef]
58. Wagner, D.; Cavalieri, F.J.; Bathias, C.; Ranc, N. Ultrasonic fatigue tests at high temperature on an austenitic steel. *Propuls. Power Res.* **2012**, *1*, 29. [CrossRef]
59. Munson, B.R.; Young, D.F.; Okiishi, T.H.; Huebsch, W.W. *Fundamentals of Fluid Mechanics*; John Wiley & Sons, Inc.: Hoboken, NJ, USA, 2006.
60. Rao, S.S. *Mechanical Vibrations*; Pearson Education: Singapore, 2011.
61. Caprani, C.C.; Keogh, J.; Archbold, P.; Fanning, P. Enhancement factors for the vertical response of footbridges subjected to stochastic crowd loading. *Comput. Struct.* **2012**, *102*, 87. [CrossRef]
62. Fujino, Y.; Pacheco, B.M.; Nakamura, S.I.; Warnitchai, P. Synchronization of human walking observed during lateral vibration of a congested pedestrian bridge. *Earthq. Eng. Struct. Dyn.* **1993**, *22*, 741. [CrossRef]

Mathematical and Computational Applications

MDPI

Article

Mode Shape Projection for Damage Detection of Laminated Composite Plates

Morteza Saadatmorad [1], Mohammad-Hadi Pashaei [1,*], Ramazan-Ali Jafari-Talookolaei [1,2] and Samir Khatir [3,*]

1 School of Mechanical Engineering, Babol Noshirvani University of Technology, Babol 47148-71167, Iran; eng.saadatmorad@gmail.com (M.S.); ramazanali@gmail.com (R.-A.J.-T.)
2 Department of Engineering, University of Business and Science, Gavhar Street, Chilanzar District, Tashkent 100000, Uzbekistan
3 Center for Engineering Application & Technology Solutions, Ho Chi Minh City Open University, Ho Chi Minh City 700000, Vietnam
* Correspondence: mpashaei@nit.ac.ir (M.-H.P.); khatir_samir@hotmail.fr (S.K.)

Abstract: The wavelet technique has limitations in detecting damage at the edges of two-dimensional signals. This weakness arises from the nature of the wavelet transform procedure, which shifts the signal by differencing the signal's pair arrays in the neighborhood. This study introduces the mode shape projection method as an efficient technique for detecting damages in two-dimensional signals in rectangular laminated composite plates to eliminate the weakness of damage detection by the wavelet method. In other words, this paper proposes creating two one-dimensional waves containing information about damages or faults in signals from vibration amplitude signals of composite plates to have an efficient damage detection method. Results show that the proposed method acts much better than wavelet transform and detects damages in numerical and experimental investigations with high performance for various damage scenarios.

Keywords: mode shape projection; laminated composite plates; damage detection; signal processing

1. Introduction

Damage detection of composite structures has been widely studied as one of the most critical activities in the field of structural health monitoring in recent decades [1–3]. One of the most commonly used damage detection techniques is the vibration-based damage detection technique since it is a global non-destructive test [4]. In vibration-based damage detection techniques, modal characteristics of the composite structures, such as natural frequencies and mode shapes, are acquired to use for localizing damages [5–8]. Among the vibration-based damage detection techniques, those that use mode shapes are very popular due to their simplicity [9].

Wavelet transform-based damage detection techniques can use the mode shapes of the structures to detect damages [10]. Thus, they may be considered mode shape-based damage detection methods. Two types of wavelet transforms can be used based on the dimension of structures' signals. For structures such as cables, bars, and beam-like structures, signals have one dimension; thus, the one-dimensional wavelet transform is used for their damage detection [11]. Also, in terms of types of continuity or discontinuity of transform, wavelet transform can be divided into two main types: continuous wavelet transform and discrete wavelet transform. Katunin et al. [10] used the modal rotation differences signal for damage

 https://doi.org/10.3390/mca30010018

detection of the beam structures. They used one-dimensional continuous wavelet analysis for damage detection. In [12], a quasi-Pearson correlation signal was suggested for damage detection in beam structures using wavelet transform. The wavelet transform used in this study was the one-dimensional discrete wavelet transform. Kumar et al. [13] used the one-dimensional continuous wavelet analysis for crack detection near the ends of the beams. The signal used in their study was one-dimensional. For damage detection of polymer composite beams, Janeliukstis et al. [14] investigated spatial continuous wavelet transform.

For plate structures, the signal acquired is a two-dimensional signal, and thus, the two-dimensional wavelet transform is used for damage detection. Similar to the one-dimensional wavelet transform, the two-dimensional wavelet transform can be either continuous or discrete. Rucka et al. [15] used continuous wavelet transform for damage detection of steel plates. Damage detection of a rectangular plate by a spatial wavelet-based approach was studied by Chang et al. [16]. The two-dimensional wavelet transform is powerful and, at the same time, a simple method for damage detection of plate structures; however, it has several weaknesses. One of the most critical weaknesses is the dependency on the accuracy of the wavelet transform to select the wavelet function and its vanishing moment. Ashory et al. [17] investigated damage detection in laminated composite plates using an optimal wavelet selection criterion. Zhou et al. [18] studied damage detection of composite plates with cutouts based on continuous wavelet transform. In [19], the abilities of the two-dimensional discrete wavelet transform and artificial neural network were combined for damage detection of laminated composite plate structures. The optimal wavelet function was selected based on trial-and-error efforts. Saadatmorad et al. [20] used the convolutional neural network (CNN) to select the best wavelet function to detect damages in rectangular laminated composite plates. Rucka et al. [21] presented a Neuro-wavelet damage detection technique for plate structures. The selection of the wavelet family function was based on trial-and-error simulations. Another weakness of the two-dimensional wavelet transform for damage detection in plate structures is that for low-level damages, several locations may be detected for a single damage. The results of wavelet transform in low-level damage may contain noises. Also, in order to detect damages in laminated composite plates, other advanced methods have been proposed by various researchers. For example, Qiao et al. [22] investigated damage detection in laminated composite plates using curvature mode shapes. The method detected a relative size of delamination in the composite plates. Oliver et al. [23] studied delamination detection in laminated composites via artificial neural networks. The method used natural frequency data from finite element analysis for predicting damage level and location. The neural network for severity prediction achieved 95% accuracy, while the location prediction network significantly narrowed down the search area. This approach relied solely on natural frequency, making it practical and easily implementable. However, in practical damage detection, obtaining such big data is very difficult. Ardebili et al. [24] investigated delamination detection in multi-layer GFRP composite patches bonded to aluminum plates. The study analyzed the influence of thermal intensity and size difference percentage on defect identification, finding that all defects were detectable in both 4- and 8-layer laminates. Notably, 8-layer patches exhibited 30% higher dimensional accuracy in defect size determination due to reduced heat reflection to the IR camera. A disadvantage of such thermography-based methods is that they are local, non-destructive tests. Katunin [25] proposed directional wavelet transforms (DWTs) for identifying damage in composite structures. The study compared the effectiveness of dual-tree, double-density, and dual-tree double-density DWTs against the standard discrete wavelet transform using shearographic experimental data. Results indicated that DWTs, especially those with directional characteristics, are superior to the standard DWT in damage detection. Additionally, the paper introduced a method employing entropic weights to selectively emphasize the most informative detail coefficients, significantly enhancing the accuracy and sensitivity of the damage identification process even in noisy conditions. Saadatmorad et al. [26] proposed a convolutional neural network (CNN) to select the optimum wavelet function for detecting damage in rectangular laminated composite plates (RLCPs). They used damaged mode shape images as the input of the CNN and the wavelet function name as the output label of the CNN. They named this damage detection technique WT-CNN. The findings indicated that the proposed WT-CNN accurately predicted and localized damages in RLCPs, eliminating the need for trial-and-error simulations for future input signals of damaged RLCPs. This paper proposes a novel method for damage detection of plate structure by focusing on the laminated composite plates. The novelty of this work lies in projecting the two-dimensional mode shape signal of the plate structures onto two different one-dimensional signals in the x and y directions using successive derivatives. In the current paper, a comparative study is presented to prove the advantages of the proposed method over wavelet transform. Also, in addition to numerical investigations, experimental investigations are conducted on a damaged glass-epoxy laminated composite plate to evaluate the efficiency of the proposed method for real damage detection scenarios. Section 2 presented the mathematical formulation of the wavelet transform. In Section 3, the proposed mode shape projection method is presented. Section 4 deals with the numerical and experimental results in different damage scenarios. Finally, Section 5 concludes the paper.

2. Wavelet Transform

The one-dimensional discretized wavelet function (1D-DWT) is obtained according to the following equation [27]:

$$\psi_{j,k} = \int_{-\infty}^{+\infty} 2^{-\frac{j}{2}} \psi\left(\frac{x-2^j k}{2^j}\right) dx = \int_{-\infty}^{+\infty} 2^{-\frac{j}{2}} \psi(2^{-j}x - k) dx \tag{1}$$

One-dimensional discrete wavelet transform (1D-DWT) in the real space x for the signal $f(x)$ is applied as follows [28]:

$$cD_{j,k} = \int_{-\infty}^{+\infty} f(x) 2^{-\frac{j}{2}} \psi_{j,k}\left(\frac{x-2^j k}{2^j}\right) dx = \int_{-\infty}^{+\infty} f(x) 2^{-\frac{j}{2}} \psi_{j,k}(2^{-j}x - k) dx \tag{2}$$

$$cA_{j,k} = \int_{-\infty}^{+\infty} f(x) 2^{-\frac{j}{2}} \phi_{j,k}\left(\frac{x-2^j k}{2^j}\right) dx = \int_{-\infty}^{+\infty} f(x) 2^{-\frac{j}{2}} \phi_{j,k}(2^{-j}x - k) dx \tag{3}$$

where $cD_{j,k}$ is the detail wavelet coefficient in the data sample with scale j and shift k, also, $cA_{j,k}$ is the approximate wavelet coefficient in the data sample with scale j and shift k.

From another point of view, 1D-DWT decomposes arbitrary one-dimensional signal $f(x)$ as follows:

$$f(x) = A_j(x) + \sum_{j<J} D_j(x) \tag{4}$$

where A_j represents the approximation signal at level j, and D_j represents the detail signals at level j. Approximation signals at level j are defined as follows [29]:

$$A_j(x) = \sum_{k=-\infty}^{+\infty} cA_{j,k} \phi_{j,k}(x) \tag{5}$$

where $\phi_{j,k}(x)$ are the scaling functions at level j and $\phi_{j,k}(x) = 2^{-\frac{j}{2}} \phi(2^{-j}x - k)$ and has the property $\int_{-\infty}^{+\infty} \phi_{0,0}(x) = 1$. Also, $\phi_{0,0}(x) = 0$ is also called the scaling function or father wavelet function.

Also, detail signals at level j are defined as follows:

$$D_j(x) = \sum_{k\epsilon Z} cD_{j,k}\psi_{j,k}(x) \quad (6)$$

where $cD_{j,k}$ are the detail wavelet coefficients at level j, and $\psi_{j,k}(x)$ is called wavelet function or mother wavelet function. j is the level or scale, and k is the shifting parameter. Z is an integer. It should be noted that A_j, which includes the scaling function $\phi_{j,k}(x)$, acts as a low-pass filter, and D_j, which includes the wavelet function $\psi_{j,k}(x)$, acts as a high-pass filter works, and in wavelet-based damage identification, usually high transient and local frequencies are identified by using a low-pass filter.

One of the most essential and effective parameters for identifying singularities or local jumps in signals is vanishing moments. When a wavelet has n number of vanishing moments, the following relation is satisfied:

$$\int_{-\infty}^{+\infty} x^i\psi(x)dx = 0\,,\ i = 1,\ 2,\ \ldots,\ n-1 \quad (7)$$

The mentioned above wavelet transform, described from Equations (6)–(12), is the one-dimensional discrete wavelet transform. It can identify very small discontinuities and sudden singularities in one-dimensional signals.

Equations (1)–(7) can be expanded for a specific two-dimensional signal $f(x,y)$ because two-dimensional wavelets can be expressed as a tensor product of two one-dimensional wavelets, as follows:

$$\begin{aligned} \phi(x,y) &= \phi(x)\phi(y) \\ \psi^H(x,y) &= \psi(x)\,\phi(y) \\ \psi^V(x,y) &= \phi(y)\psi(x) \\ \psi^D(x,y) &= \psi(x)\,\psi(y) \end{aligned} \quad (8)$$

where $\phi(x,y)$ is a two-dimensional scaling function and $\psi^H(x,y)$, $\psi^V(x,y)$, $\psi^D(x,y)$ are horizontal, vertical, and diagonal two-dimensional wavelet functions, respectively. In addition, they are diagonal. Therefore, the two-dimensional signal $f(x,y)$ is divided into four images: W_ϕ as approximate image, W_ψ^H as horizontal detail image, W_ψ^V as vertical detail image, and W_ψ^D as diagonal detail image.

By discretizing the wavelet functions and the scaling function, one can write:

$$\begin{aligned} \phi_{j,m,n}(x,y) &= 2^{-\frac{j}{2}}\phi(2^{-j}x - m,\ 2^{-j}y - n) \\ {\psi^H}_{j,m,n}(x,y) &= 2^{\frac{-j}{2}}\psi^H(2^{-j}x - m,\ 2^{-j}y - n) \\ {\psi^V}_{j,m,n}(x,y) &= 2^{\frac{-j}{2}}\psi^V(2^{-j}x - m,\ 2^{-j}y - n) \\ {\psi^D}_{j,m,n}(x,y) &= 2^{-\frac{j}{2}}\psi^D(2^{-j}x - m,\ 2^{-j}y - n) \end{aligned} \quad (9)$$

Therefore, the discrete wavelet transform of the function $f(x,y)$ with $M \times N$ dimensions is expressed as follows:

$$A\phi_{j,m,n}(x,y) = \frac{1}{\sqrt{MN}}\sum_{x=0}^{M-1}\sum_{y=0}^{N-1} f(x,y)\phi_{j,m,n}(x,y)$$

$${D^H}_{j,m,n}(x,y) = \frac{1}{\sqrt{MN}}\sum_{x=0}^{M-1}\sum_{y=0}^{N-1} f(x,y){\psi^H}_{j,m,n}(x,y)$$

$$D^V{}_{j,m,n}(x,y) = \frac{1}{\sqrt{MN}} \sum_{x=0}^{M-1} \sum_{y=0}^{N-1} f(x,y) \psi^V{}_{j,m,n}(x,y) \tag{10}$$

$$D^D{}_{j,m,n}(x,y) = \frac{1}{\sqrt{MN}} \sum_{x=0}^{M-1} \sum_{y=0}^{N-1} f(x,y) \psi^D{}_{j,m,n}(x,y)$$

Thus:

$$A\phi_{j,m,n}(x,y) = \frac{1}{\sqrt{MN}} \sum_{x=0}^{M-1} \sum_{y=0}^{N-1} f(x,y) 2^{\frac{-j}{2}} \phi(2^{-j}x - m,\ 2^{-j}y - n)$$

$$D^H{}_{j,m,n}(x,y) = \frac{1}{\sqrt{MN}} \sum_{x=0}^{M-1} \sum_{y=0}^{N-1} f(x,y) 2^{\frac{-j}{2}} \psi(2^{-j}x - m,\ 2^{-j}y - n)$$

$$D^V{}_{j,m,n}(x,y) = \frac{1}{\sqrt{MN}} \sum_{x=0}^{M-1} \sum_{y=0}^{N-1} f(x,y) 2^{\frac{-j}{2}} \psi(2^{-j}x - m,\ 2^{-j}y - n) \tag{11}$$

$$D^D{}_{j,m,n}(x,y) = \frac{1}{\sqrt{MN}} \sum_{x=0}^{M-1} \sum_{y=0}^{N-1} f(x,y) 2^{\frac{-j}{2}} \psi(2^{-j}x - m,\ 2^{-j}y - n)$$

Having $A\phi_{jo,m,n}(x,y)$, $D^H{}_{j,m,n}(x,y)$, $D^V{}_{j,m,n}(x,y)$ and $D^D{}_{j,m,n}(x,y)$ which are, respectively, approximation functions, horizontal details, vertical details and diagonal details of the two-dimensional discrete wavelet transform, one can write:

$$f(x,y) = \frac{1}{\sqrt{MN}} \sum_m \sum_n A\phi_{j,m,n}(x,y) \phi_{j,m,n}(x,y) + \frac{1}{\sqrt{MN}} \sum_{i=H,V,D} \sum_{j=1}^{\infty} \sum_m \sum_n D^i{}_{j,m,n}(x,y) \psi^i{}_{j,m,n}(x,y) \tag{12}$$

3. Mode Shape Projection Method

In this paper, a novel mode shape projection method is introduced to detect discontinuity in two-dimensional signals (i.e., images). The main idea of this method is to convert a two-dimensional signal $f(x,y)$ containing discontinuity into two one-dimensional signals, $f(x)$ and $f(y)$, which are contained the discontinuity. The discontinuous functions $f(x)$ and $f(y)$ are waves created by differentiating the signal $f(x,y)$ in directions of x and y, respectively. This method provides a tremendous advantage for discontinuity detection of two-dimensional signals compared with the other local signal processing methods, such as the wavelet method. The final results of discontinuity detection based on wavelet for two-dimensional signals containing discontinuity at edges are very difficult to detect and usually fail to detect them. In addition, there are noises at the edges of a two-dimensional signal processed by wavelet transform in many applications. The mode shape projection method fixes this problem and ensures an efficient and reliable discontinuity detection result. Consider the two-dimensional digital signal $f(x,y)$ containing one discontinuity (Figure 1). Thus, in the mode shape projection method, given a two-dimensional signal with dimensions n by m, first we take the derivative $n-1$ times of this signal in the x direction (where n is the number of signal sampling points in the x direction) to project it into a curve in the y direction. Then, we take the derivative $m-1$ times of this signal in the x direction (where m is the number of signal sampling points in the y direction) to project it onto a curve in the x direction.

Assume the size of this signal is 3×3, as follows:

$$f_{3\times3} = \begin{bmatrix} f_{1\,1} & f_{1\,2} & f_{1\,3} \\ f_{2\,1} & f_{2\,2} & f_{2\,3} \\ f_{3\,1} & f_{3\,2} & f_{3\,3} \end{bmatrix} \tag{13}$$

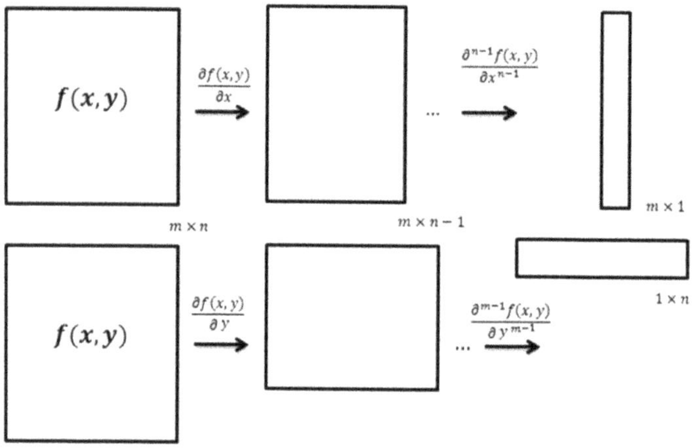

Figure 1. Projection of two two-dimensional mode shapes for creating two one-dimensional signals.

For obtaining the one-dimensional wave along x (i.e., $f_{1\times3}$) the following operation is performed:

$$f_{2\times3} = \begin{bmatrix} f_{2\,1}-f_{1\,1} & f_{2\,2}-f_{1\,2} & f_{2\,3}-f_{1\,3} \\ f_{3\,1}-f_{2\,1} & f_{3\,2}-f_{2\,2} & f_{3\,3}-f_{2\,3} \end{bmatrix} \tag{14}$$

$$f_{1\times3} = \left[(f_{3\,1}-f_{2\,1})-(f_{2\,1}-f_{1\,1}) \quad (f_{3\,2}-f_{2\,2})-(f_{2\,2}-f_{1\,2}) \quad (f_{3\,3}-f_{2\,3})-(f_{2\,3}-f_{1\,3}) \right] \tag{15}$$

For obtaining the one-dimensional wave along y (i.e., $f_{3\times1}$) the following operation is performed:

$$f_{3\times2} = \begin{bmatrix} f_{1\,2}-f_{1\,1} & f_{1\,3}-f_{1\,2} \\ f_{2\,2}-f_{2\,1} & f_{2\,3}-f_{2\,2} \\ f_{3\,2}-f_{3\,1} & f_{3\,3}-f_{3\,2} \end{bmatrix} \tag{16}$$

and:

$$f_{3\times1} = \left[(f_{1\,3}-f_{1\,2})-(f_{1\,2}-f_{1\,1}) \quad (f_{2\,3}-f_{2\,2})-(f_{2\,2}-f_{2\,1}) \quad (f_{3\,3}-f_{3\,2})-(f_{3\,2}-f_{3\,1}) \right]^{T} \tag{17}$$

This mathematical operation can be expanded for the signal $f_{m\times n}$ to have:

$$f_{m\times n} = \begin{bmatrix} f_{1\,1} & f_{1\,2} & f_{1\,3} & \cdots & f_{1\,n-2} & f_{1\,n-1} & f_{1\,n} \\ f_{2\,1} & f_{2\,2} & f_{2\,3} & \cdots & f_{2\,n-2} & f_{2\,n-1} & f_{2\,n} \\ f_{3\,1} & f_{3\,2} & f_{3\,3} & & f_{3\,n-2} & f_{3\,n-1} & f_{3\,n} \\ & \vdots & & \ddots & & \vdots & \\ f_{m-2\,1} & f_{m-2\,2} & f_{m-2\,3} & & f_{m-2\,n-2} & f_{m-2\,n-1} & f_{m-2\,n} \\ f_{m-1\,1} & f_{m-1\,2} & f_{m-1\,3} & \cdots & f_{m-1\,n-2} & f_{m-1\,n-1} & f_{m-1\,n} \\ f_{m\,1} & f_{m\,2} & f_{m\,3} & & f_{m\,n-2} & f_{m\,n-1} & f_{mn} \end{bmatrix} \tag{18}$$

$$\begin{aligned} f_{1\times n} = [\,(f_{m\,1} &- f_{m-1\,1}) - (f_{m-1\,1} - f_{m-2\,1}) - \ldots - (f_{3\,1} - f_{2\,1}) \\ &-(f_{2\,1} - f_{1\,1}) \ldots (f_{mn} - f_{m-1\,n}) - (f_{m-1\,n} - f_{m-2\,n}) \\ &- \ldots - (f_{3\,n} - f_{2\,n}) - (f_{2\,n} - f_{1\,n})] \end{aligned} \tag{19}$$

$$\begin{aligned} f_{m\times1} = [(f_{1\,n} - {} & f_{1\,n-1}) - (f_{1\,n-1} - f_{1n-2}) - \ldots - (f_{1\,3} - f_{1\,2}) - (f_{1\,2} \\ & -f_{1\,1}) \ldots (f_{mn} - f_{m\,n-1}) - (f_{m\,n-1} - f_{m\,n-2}) - \ldots \\ & -(f_{m\,3} - f_{m\,2}) - (f_{m\,2} - f_{m\,1})]^{T} \end{aligned} \tag{20}$$

This paper suggests that if the signal $f_{m \times n}$ contains a sudden jump at a data point, it will detect waves in $f_{1 \times n}$ and $f_{m \times 1}$. This is proved in the result section numerically and experimentally.

Also, the differentiation thresholds depend on the number of nodes in the finite element model or the number of sampling points in the experimental modal analysis to obtain the mode shape. Therefore, the greater the number of sampling points of the part, the higher the differentiation order is required to identify the damage. Also, according to the formulation of the proposed method, it can be mentioned that the number of differentiation orders in a direction (i.e., x or y) as the differentiation order (threshold) is equal to the number of sampling points that form the mode shape in the same direction minus one.

4. Results

4.1. Numerical Results

In this section, the proposed mode shape projection method is evaluated for a numerical digital signal obtained for the finite element modeling of a vibrating rectangular laminated composite plate with the general properties listed in Table 1. According to Table 2, finite element modeling is performed for six different damage scenarios that create six different sudden jumps in the obtained signals. Table 3 shows results from the two-dimensional wavelet transform for the six considered damage scenarios. These values are obtained from the diagonal detail signal shown in Figure 2. As seen in Table 3 and Figure 2, the wavelet transform detects the location of damage or a sudden jump in signals obtained from six different scenarios (Figures 3 and 4) with noises. Therefore, the proposed mode shape projection method is used to fix this problem and detect the exact location of damages or sudden jumps in these signals.

Table 1. General properties of the rectangular laminated composite plate.

Parameter	Description or Value
Number of layers	2
Layups configuration	[0, 45]
Plate's Length (a)	0.2 m
Plate's Width (b)	0.2 m
Plate's Thickness	$h = 0.1a$
Discretizing	30 × 30
Shear Correction Factor	$k_s = 5/6$
Young's modulus	$E_{22} = 9.65$ GPa, $E_{11} = 25 \times E_{22}$
Shear modulus	$G_{12} = G_{13} = 0.5E_{22}$, $G_{13} = 0.2E_{22}$
Poisson's ratios	$\nu_{12} = 0.25$, $\nu_{21} = \frac{E_{22}}{E_{11}}\nu_{12}$

Table 2. Six different damage scenarios that create six different sudden jumps in the obtained signals.

Scenario No.	Location of Damage		Level of Damage
	x	y	
1	3	13	70%
2	17	15	50%
3	19	21	30%
4	26	9	9%
5	3	13	40%
6	16	16	15%

Table 3. Results from two-dimensional wavelet transform for the six considered damage scenarios.

Scenario No.	Actual Location of Damage		Location of Damage Detected by Wavelet Transform	
	x	y	x	y
1	3	13	1–5, 24–30	14–20, 24–27, 30
2	17	15	1–3, 15–22, 27–30	15–20, 25–30
3	19	21	1–3, 5, 16, 22, 25, 29, 30	17–22, 29, 30
4	26	9	1, 2, 4, 25–26	1, 2, 4, 9, 10
5	3	13	1, 2, 7, 9, 10, 12	1–6
6	16	16	2–4, 18, 27–30	2–4, 18, 27–30

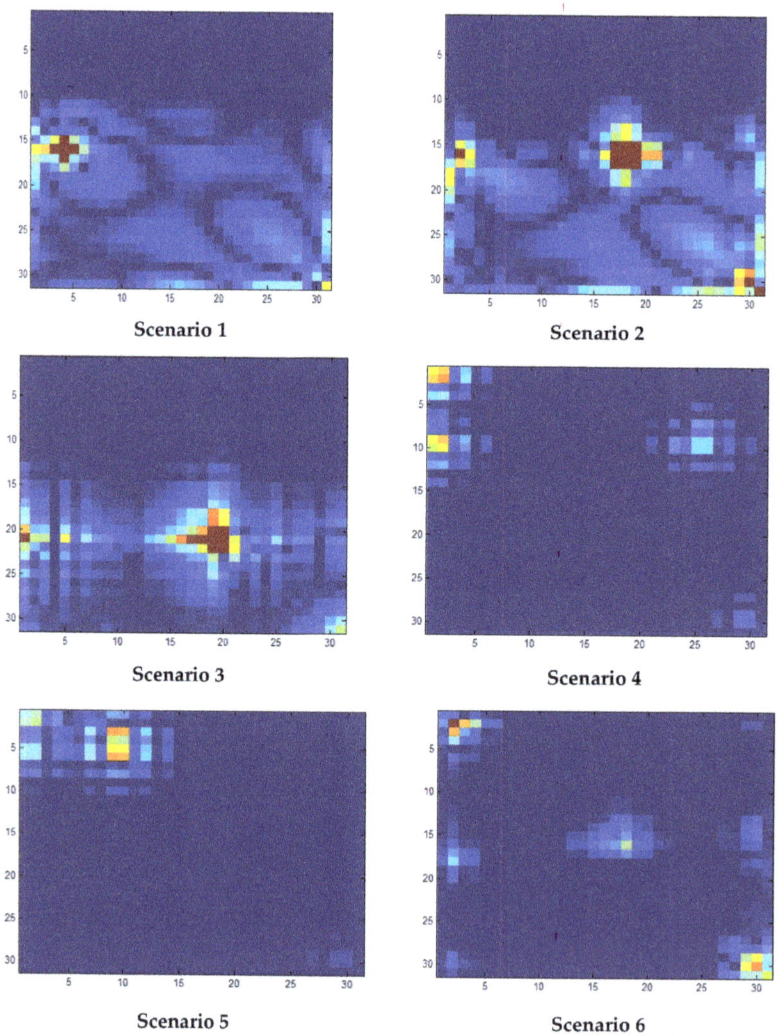

Figure 2. Results from two-dimensional wavelet transform for the six considered damage scenarios.

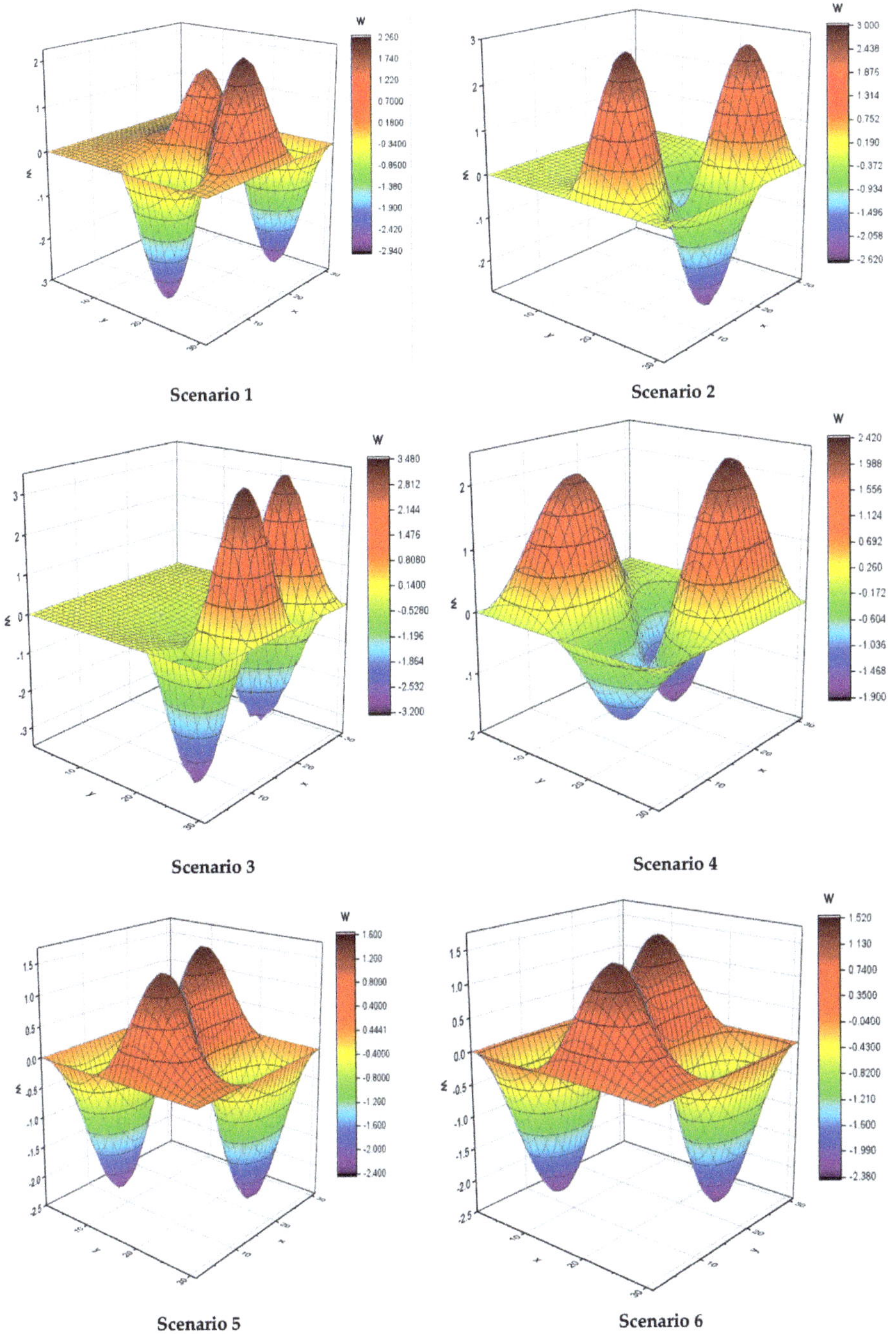

Figure 3. Two-dimensional signals were obtained for the six damage scenarios in the three-dimensional distribution.

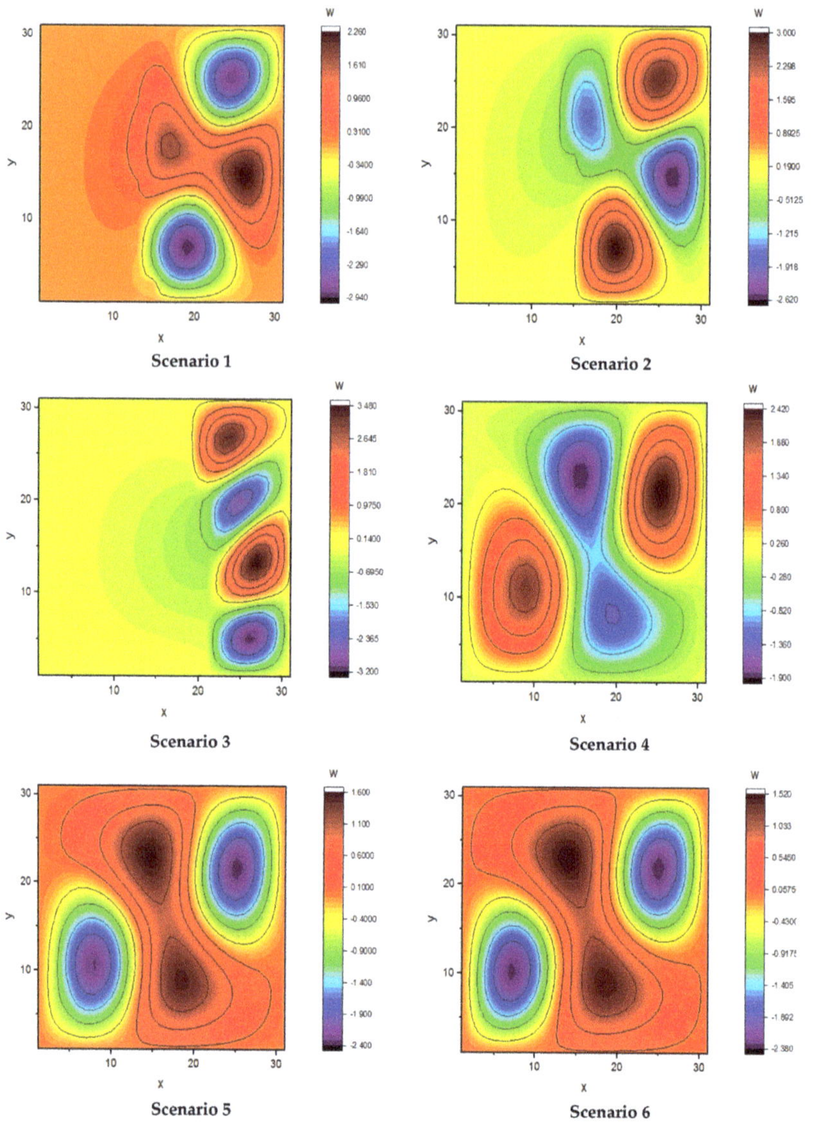

Figure 4. Two-dimensional signals were obtained for the six damage scenarios in the two-dimensional distribution.

Figure 5 shows the results of the proposed mode shape projection method for Scenarios 1–6.

Table 4 lists the results of the proposed mode shape projection method for scenarios 1–6. As seen in Figure 5 and Table 4, the proposed mode shape projection method can detect damages or sudden jumps in signals with high accuracy, and it has better performance than wavelet transform. The results in Figure 5 demonstrate that the proposed methodology effectively addresses the edge effect limitations of the wavelet transform. It successfully identifies all damage positions across various locations and percentages while also reducing the number of sampling points by one. Notably, in scenario 1, this method can detect damage in the signal corners, an area where the wavelet transform fell short due to edge effects.

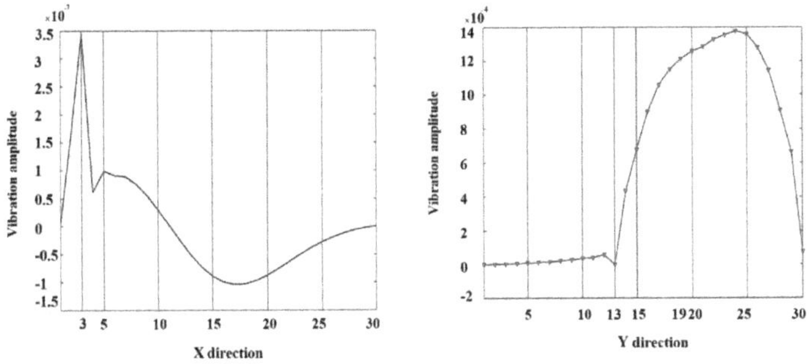

Scenario 1

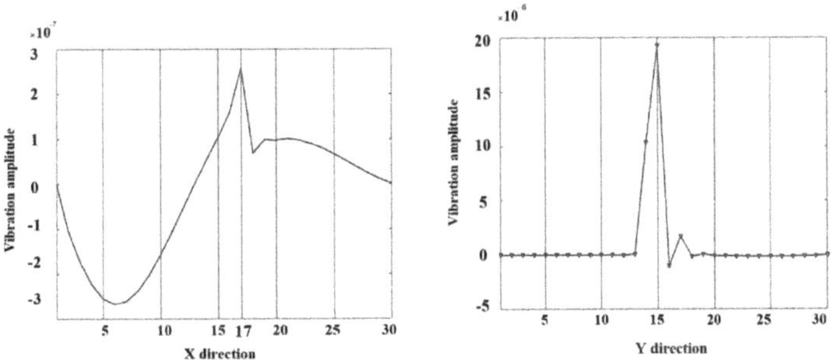

Scenario 2

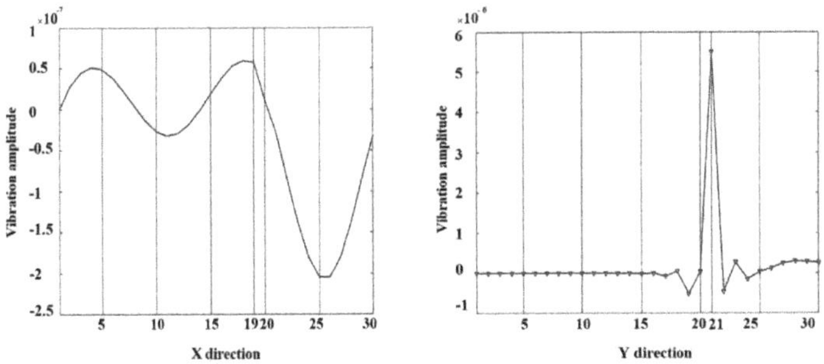

Scenario 3

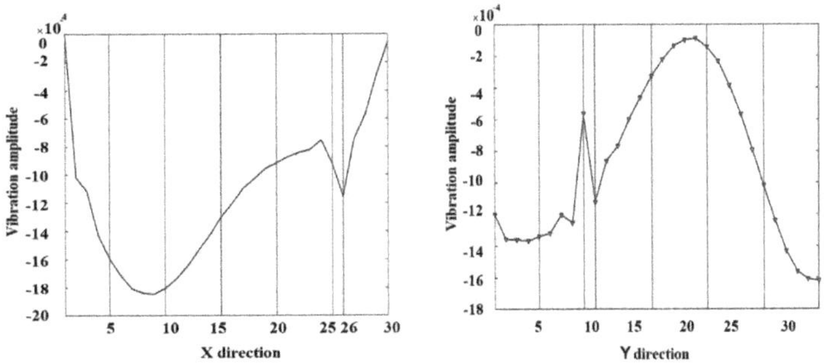

Scenario 4

Figure 5. *Cont.*

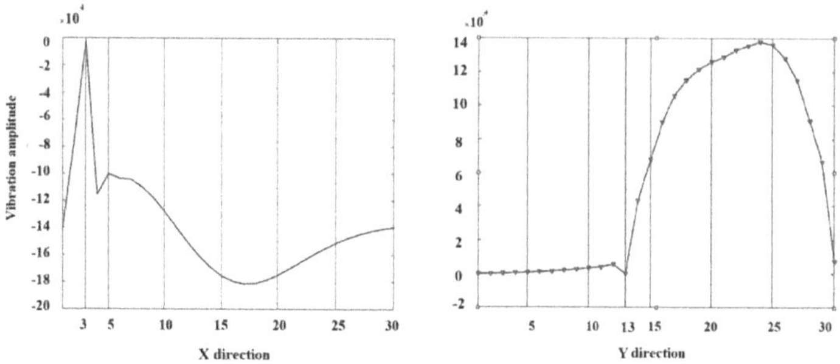

Scenario 5

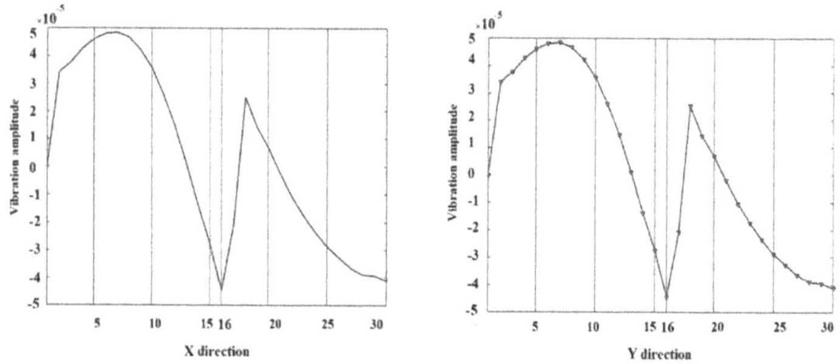

Scenario 6

Figure 5. Result of the proposed mode shape projection method for Scenarios 1 to 6.

Table 4. Results of the proposed mode shape projection method for Scenarios 1–6.

Scenario No.	Actual Location of Damage		Location of Damage Detected by the Proposed Creation Method	
	x	y	x	y
1	3	13	3	13
2	17	15	17	15
3	19	21	19	21
4	26	9	26	9
5	3	13	3	13
6	16	16	16	16

4.2. The Effect of Noise

This section presents examples of damage detection under noisy conditions, presenting a sensitivity analysis with the proposed method. We apply Gaussian noise as a noise characterized by the Gaussian probability density function. Four noisy damage scenarios are considered in this section. Algorithm 1 shows the Pseudo code of the mode shape projection method for noisy scenarios. Damage is applied at the location $(X,Y) = (9,9)$, and the damage level is 50%.

Figure 6 shows a two-dimensional image of four noise mode shapes corresponding to four noise damage scenarios. As can be seen, the increase in noise level is noticeable in the mode shapes; however, the damage location cannot be identified in any of the four mode shapes.

Algorithm 1. Pseudo Code of the Mode Shape Projection Method for Noisy Scenarios

```
% Noise Level
Noisy scenario 1: Noise level = 0.1
Noisy scenario 1: Noise level = 0.11
Noisy scenario 1: Noise level = 0.25
Noisy scenario 1: Noise level = 5.0
 % Choose Noise Type
noise_type = 'gaussian'; % Options: 'gaussian', 'salt_and_pepper', 'uniform'
% W is the mode shape signal
% Add Noise
 W_noisy = W + noise_level * randn(size(W));
 Xd = diff(W_noisy, 30); % Mode shape projection along X direction
Yd = diff(W_noisy', 30); % Mode shape projection along Y direction
```

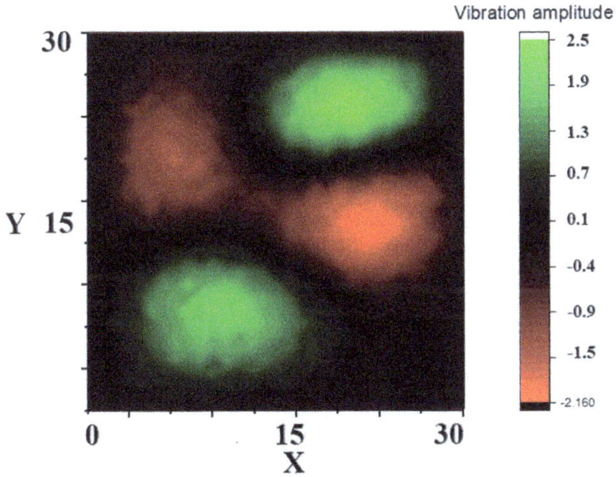

Noisy scenario 1

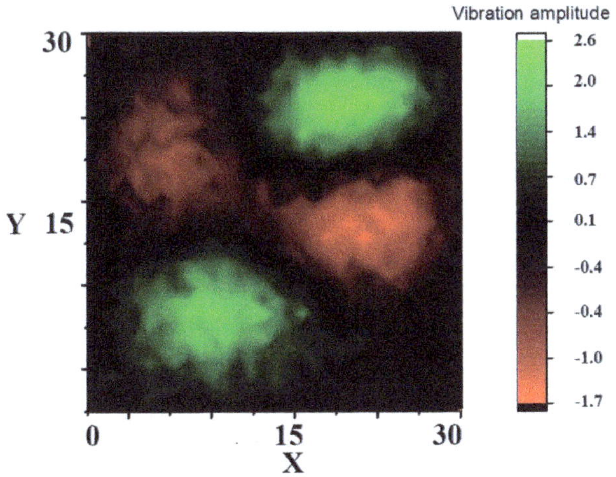

Noisy scenario 2

Figure 6. *Cont.*

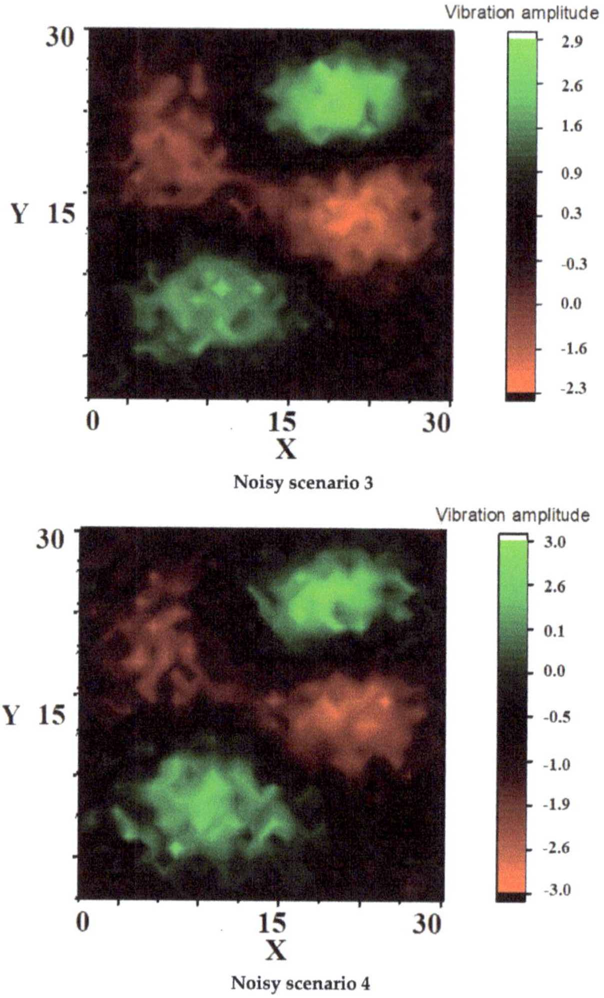

Figure 6. Mode shapes corresponding to the four noisy scenarios.

Figure 7 presents the results of damage detection under noisy conditions using the mode shape projection method. In scenarios one to three, the proposed methodology effectively identifies the damage location despite the noise. However, when the noise level surpasses 0.5, damage detection becomes impossible, as the amplitude difference between two sampling points near the damage is smaller than that between two other points at that noise level.

4.3. Experimental Results

In order to verify the efficiency of the proposed mode shape projection method in practical damage detection, this section applies the method for experimental signals obtained from a rectangular laminated composite plate made of glass epoxy. The vacuum infusion process (VIP) is used to manufacture a rectangular laminated glass-epoxy composite plate. Then, the manufactured composite plate is graded in 15×15 elements to measure the vibration amplitude of its mode shape signal. After manufacturing the composite plate shown in Figure 8, U-shaped damage, 4 mm deep (equal to the plate's thickness), is imposed at the location $(x,y) = (7,7)$, resulting in a jump in the experimental signal.

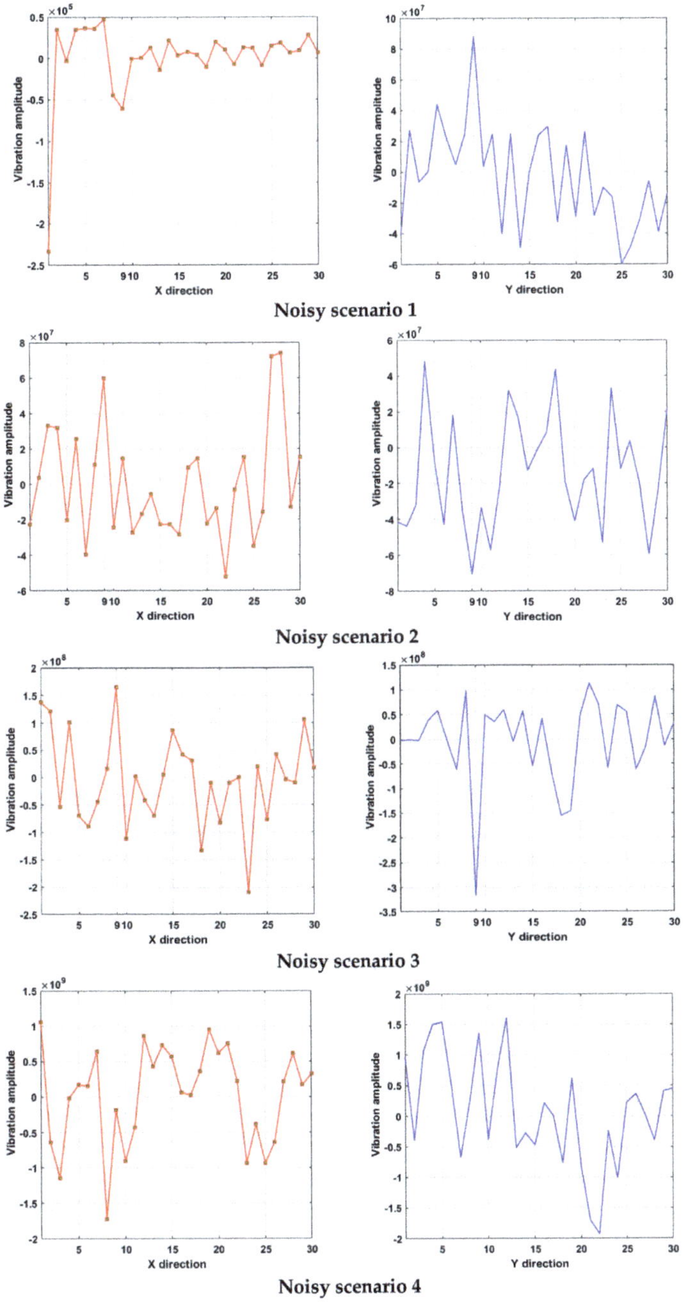

Figure 7. Result of damage detection for the four considered noisy scenarios using the proposed mode shape projection method.

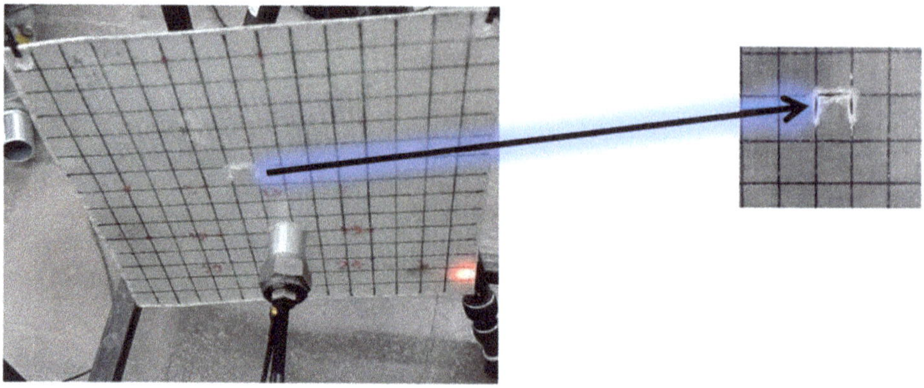

Figure 8. Damage created in the composite plate.

According to Figure 9, the Laser Doppler vibrometer (LDV) (manufacturer of the device: B&K Precision Corporation) shaker is used to measure the vibration mode shape amplitude signal. In order to apply force to the structure, a vibration shaker equipped with an 8200BK force transducer was used. Also, a 2647 A amplifier was used to convert the force signal. The shaker was fixed at point $(x,y) = (8,11)$, and the response was measured by laser at all points. This test was performed for a damaged composite sheet. The experimental vibration mode shape amplitude signal from the LDV shaker is presented in Figure 10.

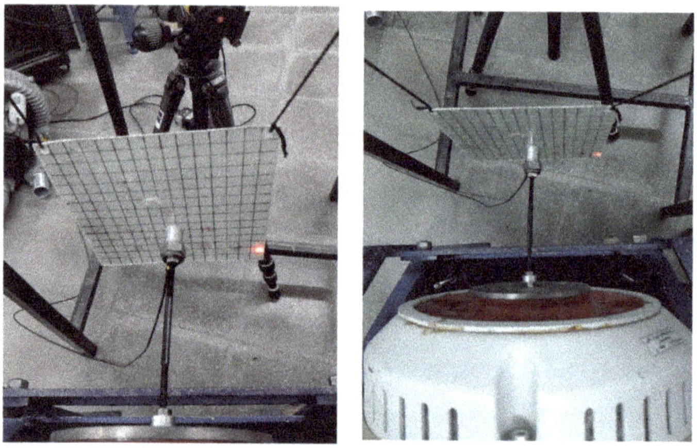

Figure 9. Laser Doppler vibrometer (LDV) shaker experimental setup for measuring the experimental vibration mode shape amplitude signal.

Figure 11 shows the results of the proposed mode shape projection method for the experimental damage scenario. As seen in Figure 11, the location of the damage is detected with high accuracy. This proves that the proposed mode shape projection method is highly efficient for numerical and experimental damage detection processes.

Comparing the results from the numerical and experimental sections reveals that the mode shapes from the numerical analysis are smoother than those from the experimental test. This discrepancy is likely due to environmental noise and limited measurement accuracy in the experimental mode shapes. Consequently, it is crucial to assess the impact of noise on the performance of numerical damage detection methods. Additionally, while numerical damage detection can utilize a high number of sampling points, increasing sampling points in experimental setups is both time-consuming and costly. Since the accuracy of damage detection relies on the number of sampling points, it is essential to determine an appropriate number for practical applications. Future investigations should focus on identifying suitable sampling points for different structures and types of damage identification.

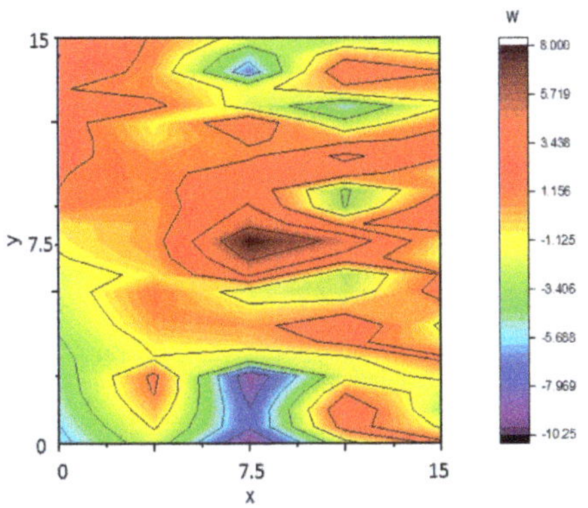

Figure 10. Experimental vibration mode shape amplitude signal from the LDV shaker.

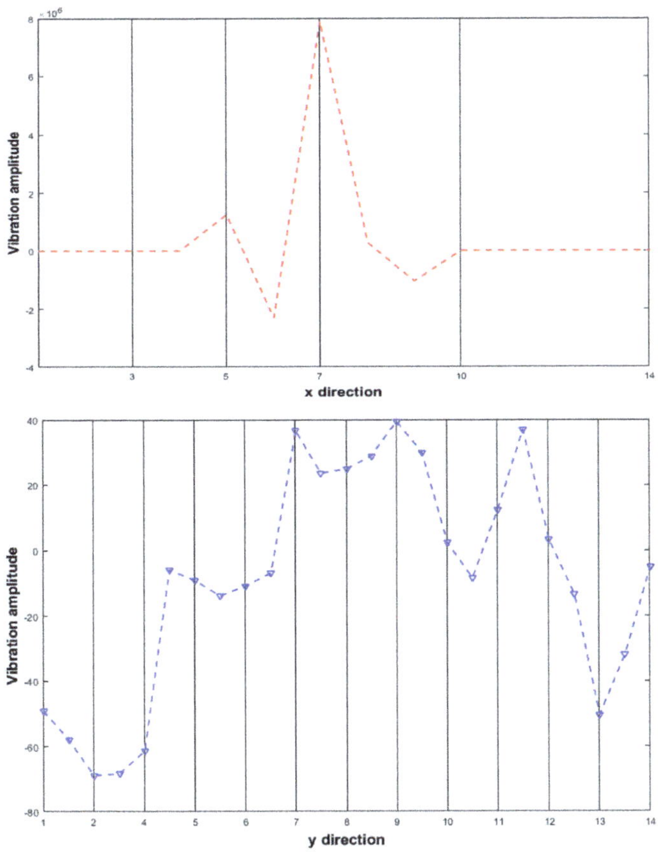

Figure 11. Results of the proposed mode shape projection method for the experimental damage scenario.

5. Conclusions

This paper presents a promising and straightforward approach called the mode shape projection method for damage detection in composite plate structures. The proposed method is suggested to eliminate weaknesses in the traditional popular methods, such as wavelet transform, that many times cannot detect damages with high accuracy because their results are based on the selection of the proper wavelet family and vanishing moments. Findings demonstrate that the wavelet transform can detect damage, but its results contain noises that may lead to inaccurate damage detection. Also, in addition to this high performance, this method is straightforward and has no complexities of the conventional method, such as wavelet transformation for implementation. Findings show that in contrast to wavelet transformation, the results obtained from the proposed method show that the proposed mode shape projection method eliminates noises, and the two final one-dimensional waves along the x and y axes contain no noises. Also, this paper shows that the mathematical implementation of the proposed mode shape projection method is much simpler than the wavelet transform. The findings suggest that the proposed method is effective for noisy signals with noise levels of 0.1, 0.11, and 0.25. However, at a damage level of 5.0, detecting damage is difficult due to confusion between damage-related disturbances and noise. Future research should focus on enhancing the distinction between noise and damage disturbances. This method avoids the undesirable edge effects of the wavelet transform from incomplete convolution. However, the derivative operation subtracts one sample from the original signal, identifying the damage location with a difference unit, which is more desired than the edge effects in the results.

Author Contributions: Conceptualization, M.S.; methodology, M.S.; software, M.S. and R.-A.J.-T.; validation, S.K., R.-A.J.-T. and M.-H.P.; formal analysis, M.S. and R.-A.J.-T.; investigation, M.S.; resources, S.K.; data curation, M.S.; writing—original draft preparation, M.S.; writing—review and editing, S.K. and R.-A.J.-T.; visualization, M.S.; supervision, S.K.; project administration, M.-H.P. All authors have read and agreed to the published version of the manuscript.

Funding: This research received no external funding.

Data Availability Statement: The original contributions presented in this study are included in the article. Further inquiries can be directed to the corresponding author.

Conflicts of Interest: The authors declare no conflict of interest.

References

1. Heshmati, A.; Jafari-Talookolaei, R.-A.; Valvo, P.S.; Saadatmorad, M. Free and forced vibration analysis of laminated composite beams with through-the-width delamination by considering the in-plane and out-of-plane deformations. *Mech. Adv. Mater. Struct.* **2024**, *31*, 5953–5972. [CrossRef]
2. Civera, M.; Boscato, G.; Fragonara, L.Z. Treed gaussian process for manufacturing imperfection identification of pultruded GFRP thin-walled profile. *Compos. Struct.* **2020**, *254*, 112882. [CrossRef]
3. Boscato, G.; Civera, M.; Zanotti Fragonara, L. Recursive partitioning and Gaussian process regression for the detection and localization of damages in pultruded glass fiber reinforced polymer material. *Struct. Control Health Monit.* **2021**, *28*, e2805. [CrossRef]
4. Xie, H.; Fang, H.; Li, X.; Wan, L.; Wu, P.; Yu, Y. Low-velocity impact damage detection and characterization in composite sandwich panels using infrared thermography. *Compos. Struct.* **2021**, *269*, 114008. [CrossRef]
5. Heshmati, A.; Jafari-Talookolaei, R.A.; Valvo, P.S.; Saadatmorad, M. A novel damage detection technique for laminated composite beams under the action of a moving load. *Mech. Syst. Signal Process.* **2023**, *202*, 110692. [CrossRef]
6. Jafari-Talookolaei, R.A.; Attar, M.; Valvo, P.S.; Lotfinejad-Jalali, F.; Shirsavar, S.F.G.; Saadatmorad, M. Flapwise and chordwise free vibration analysis of a rotating laminated composite beam. *Compos. Struct.* **2022**, *292*, 115694. [CrossRef]
7. Saadatmorad, M.; Shahavi, M.H.; Gholipour, A. Damage Detection in Laminated Composite Beams Reinforced with Nanoparticles Using Covariance of Vibration Mode Shape and Wavelet Transform. *J. Vib. Eng. Technol.* **2024**, *12*, 2865–2875. [CrossRef]

8. Abdushkour, H.A.; Saadatmorad, M.; Khatir, S.; Benaissa, B.; Al Thobiani, F.; Khawaja, A.U. Structural Damage Detection by Derivative-Based Wavelet Transforms. *Arab. J. Sci. Eng.* **2024**, *49*, 15701–15709. [CrossRef]
9. Khomarian, N.; Jafari-Talookolaei, R.A.; Saadatmorad, M.; Haghani, R. Damage Detection of the Pipes Conveying Fluid on the Pasternak Foundation Using the Matching Pursuit Method. *J. Mar. Sci. Appl.* **2025**, 1–19. [CrossRef]
10. Katunin, A.; Araújo dos Santos, J.V.; Lopes, H. Damage identification by wavelet analysis of modal rotation differences. *Structures* **2021**, *30*, 1–10. [CrossRef]
11. Saadatmorad, M.; Jafari-Talookolaei, R.A.; Pashaei, M.H.; Khatir, S.; Abdel Wahab, M. Application of multilayer perceptron neural network for damage detection in rectangular laminated composite plates based on vibrational analysis. In Proceedings of the 2nd International Conference on Structural Damage Modelling and Assessment (SDMA 2021), Ghent, Belgium, 4–5 August 2021; Springer: Singapore, 2021; pp. 163–178.
12. Saadatmorad, M.; Talookolaei, R.A.J.; Pashaei, M.H.; Khatir, S.; Wahab, M.A. Pearson Correlation and Discrete Wavelet Transform for Crack Identification in Steel Beams. *Mathematics* **2022**, *10*, 2689. [CrossRef]
13. Kumar, R.; Singh, S.K. Crack detection near the ends of a beam using wavelet transform and high resolution beam deflection measurement. *Eur. J. Mech. A/Solids* **2021**, *88*, 104259. [CrossRef]
14. Janeliukstis, R.; Rucevskis, S.; Wesolowski, M.; Kovalovs, A.; Chate, A. Damage identification in polymer composite beams based on spatial continuous wavelet transform. *IOP Conf. Ser. Mater. Sci. Eng.* **2016**, *111*, 012005. [CrossRef]
15. Rucka, M.; Wilde, K. Application of continuous wavelet transform in vibration based damage detection method for beams and plates. *J. Sound Vib.* **2006**, *297*, 536–550. [CrossRef]
16. Chang, C.C.; Chen, L.W. Damage detection of a rectangular plate by spatial wavelet based approach. *Appl. Acoust.* **2004**, *65*, 819–832. [CrossRef]
17. Ashory, M.R.; Ghasemi-Ghalebahman, A.; Kokabi, M.J. Damage detection in laminated composite plates via an optimal wavelet selection criterion. *J. Reinf. Plast. Compos.* **2016**, *35*, 1761–1775. [CrossRef]
18. Zhou, J.; Li, Z.; Chen, J. Damage identification method based on continuous wavelet transform and mode shapes for composite laminates with cutouts. *Compos. Struct.* **2018**, *191*, 12–23. [CrossRef]
19. Saadatmorad, M.; Jafari-Talookolaei, R.A.; Pashaei, M.H.; Khatir, S. Damage Detection in Rectangular Laminated Composite Plate Structures using a Combination of Wavelet Transforms and Artificial Neural Networks. *J. Vib. Eng. Technol.* **2022**, *20*, 1647–1664. [CrossRef]
20. Rucka, M.; Wilde, K. Neuro-wavelet damage detection technique in beam, plate and shell structures with experimental validation. *J. Theor. Appl. Mech.* **2010**, *48*, 579–604.
21. Qiao, P.; Lu, K.; Lestari, W.; Wang, J. Curvature mode shape-based damage detection in composite laminated plates. *Compos. Struct.* **2007**, *80*, 409–428. [CrossRef]
22. Oliver, G.A.; Ancelotti, A.C.; Gomes, G.F. Neural network-based damage identification in composite laminated plates using frequency shifts. *Neural Comput. Appl.* **2021**, *33*, 3183–3194. [CrossRef]
23. Ardebili, A.; Alaei, M.H. Non-destructive testing of delamination defects in GFRP patches using step heating thermography. *NDT Int.* **2022**, *128*, 102617. [CrossRef]
24. Katunin, A. Performance of Damage Identification Based on Directional Wavelet Transforms and Entopic Weights Using Experimental Shearographic Testing Results. *Sensors* **2021**, *21*, 714. [CrossRef] [PubMed]
25. Saadatmorad, M.; Jafari-Talookolaei, R.A.; Pashaei, M.H.; Khatir, S. Damage detection on rectangular laminated composite plates using wavelet based convolutional neural network technique. *Compos. Struct.* **2021**, *278*, 114656. [CrossRef]
26. Burnes, S.; Villa, J.; Moreno, G.; de la Rosa, I.; González, E.; Alaniz, D. 3D shape measurement with temporal phase unwrapping and 1-D continuous wavelet transform. In *Photonic Instrumentation Engineering VIII*; SPIE: Bellingham, WA, USA, 2021; Volume 11693, pp. 203–210.
27. Kathuria, L.; Goel, S.; Khanna, N. Fourier–Boas-Like Wavelets and Their Vanishing Moments. *J. Math.* **2021**, *2021*, 6619551. [CrossRef]
28. Knitter-Piątkowska, A.; Pozorski, Z.; Garstecki, A. Application of discrete wavelet transformation in damage detection. Part I: Static and dynamic experiments. *Comput. Assist. Methods Eng. Sci.* **2006**, *13*, 21–38.
29. Ziopaja, K.; Pozorski, Z.; Garstecki, A. Damage detection using thermal experiments and wavelet transformation. *Inverse Prob. Sci. Eng.* **2011**, *19*, 127–153. [CrossRef]

Mathematical and Computational Applications

MDPI

Article

Nonlinear Finite Element Model for FGM Porous Circular and Annular Micro-Plates Under Thermal and Mechanical Loads Using Modified Couple Stress-Based Third-Order Plate Theory

Enrique Nava and Jinseok Kim *

Department of Mechanical and Aerospace Engineering, Western Michigan University, Kalamazoo, MI 49008-5343, USA; enrique.navamunoz@wmich.edu

* Correspondence: jinseok.kim@wmich.edu

Abstract: A nonlinear finite element model for circular and annular micro-plates under thermal and mechanical loading was developed using a third-order shear deformation theory. In the kinematic assumptions, a change in plate thickness is allowed, and no transverse shear strains are considered on the top and bottom surfaces. A power-law distribution was utilized to account for variations in two constituents through the thickness of the plate. Three different types of porosity distributions are considered. The strain gradient effect in micro-scale structures is accounted for by using the modified couple stress theory. Hamilton's principle is used to obtain the equations of motion, and conforming plate elements are used in the development of the finite element model. The developed finite element model was verified against the available literature and analytical solutions. The effects of the material and porosity distribution, microstructure-dependency, geometric nonlinearity, and various boundary conditions on the bending response of functionally graded and porous circular and annular micro-plates were studied using the developed nonlinear finite element model.

Keywords: nonlinear finite element analysis; circular/annular plates; third-order theory; functionally graded porous materials; modified couple stress theory

1. Introduction

Novel composite materials have recently been a subject of interest in the scientific community because of their many advantages over traditional materials. Functionally graded porous materials (FGPMs) represent one type of such materials, with potential applications in the aerospace sector and micro-electro-mechanical systems field. The concept of functionally graded materials first appeared [1] in Japan (1984) as a material for thermal barriers developed for aerospace missions that could reduce thermal stresses that occur predominantly at the interface of the metallic structure and the ceramic thermal shield during hypersonic flight. The review articles [2–5] provide context for the development of functionally graded materials.

Functionally graded materials (FGMs) are composite materials that have a gradual variation in their constituents instead of an abrupt change of composition, like in traditional laminated composite materials. This results in an inhomogeneous material that can be tailored to specific applications. A commonly studied type of FGM structure is plates with ceramic and metal as their constituents. Figure 1 shows a representation of an FGM under external thermal load. The ceramic provides excellent thermal characteristics to withstand extreme thermal environments, and the metal provides ductility and fracture resistance (since ceramics are commonly brittle). The current study focuses on FGM plates with a volumetric fraction variation along the thickness direction of the plates. The properties of the FGMs are given by

$$P(z) = [(P_c - P_m)(\frac{1}{2} + \frac{z}{h})^n + P_m] \tag{1}$$

where $P(z)$ is any material property, P_c is the ceramic property, P_m is the metallic property, z is the coordinate perpendicular to the plate, h is the height of the plate, and n is the power-law index. Figure 2 shows the variation in the volume fraction of the material on the top surface with different values for the power-law index n.

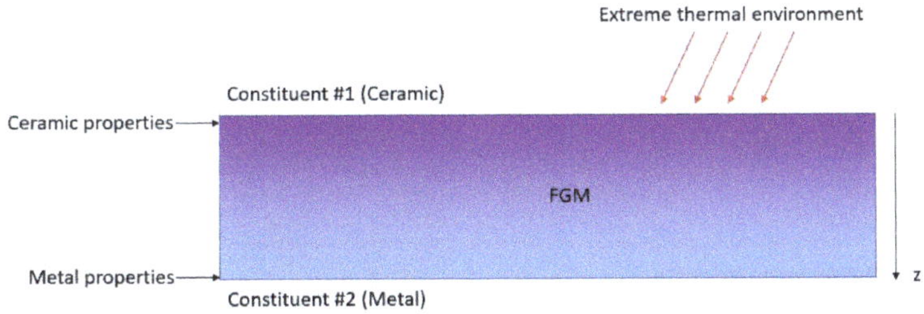

Figure 1. Functionally graded material.

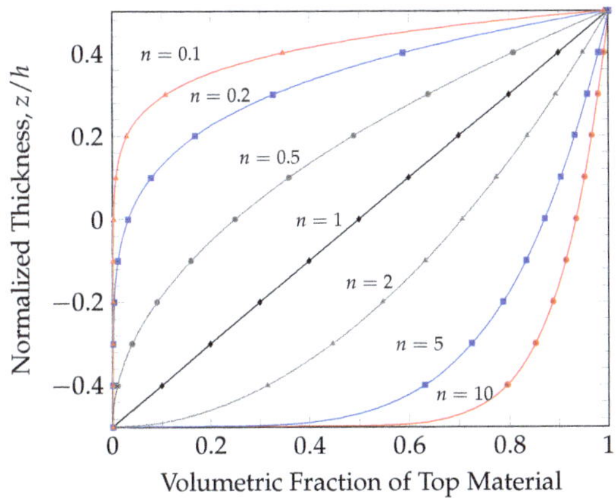

Figure 2. Volumetric distribution of a functionally graded material.

Other potential fields of application for FGPMs are micro-electro-mechanical systems (MEMSs) [6] and nano-electro-mechanical systems (NEMSs). At their core, these systems depend on the behavior of micro-beams and micro-plates [7]. At such length scales, structures have been observed [8] to be size-dependent, which cannot be accounted for by conventional continuum mechanics [9]. To correctly model these length scale effects, couple stress theories [8,10,11], the Eringen nonlocal elasticity theory [12], and the strain gradient elasticity theories [13–15] have been developed. The modified couple stress theory by Yang [8] requires only one length scale parameter, which facilitates formulations and parametric studies.

To predict the behavior of FGM micro-plates, multiple finite element models (FEMs) that include size-dependent effects have been derived [16–29]. These FEMs require a plate theory, the simplest of which is classical plate theory (CPT). CPT neglects transverse shear deformation effects. This model is efficient and accurate for thin plates but becomes inaccurate for thick plates, where shear deformation is critical. Shear deformation theories have been developed to address these shortcomings.

First-order shear deformation theory (FSDT) has been used to model functionally graded plates in several studies [30–33]. FSDT requires a shear correction factor, which reduces its usefulness. Higher-order theories were developed in order to forego the correction factor and improve accuracy. The third-order shear deformation theory (TSDT) presented by Reddy [34] in 1984 considers the cubic variation of in-plane displacements and constant transverse displacement through thickness. It was used by Reddy [29] and, later on, by Najafizadeh et al. [35] on circular plates to investigate thermal buckling behavior. A general third-order plate theory (GTPT) was later presented by Reddy and Kim [36], which describes thickness stretch using a quadratic variation in order to obtain a parabolic variation in transverse shear strains. Kim and Reddy [37] presented the analytical solutions for the general third-order theory. Shear deformation theories have been used to study FGM plates [23,38–43]. Vinh [44] presented a comprehensive analysis of bending, free vibration, and buckling behaviors of functionally graded nanoplates using a modified nonlocal strain gradient theory. Wang et al. [45] studied the bending and buckling behavior of porous, functionally graded curved nano-beams using a size-dependent, quasi-3D beam model that accounts for a thickness-stretching effect.

Engineering structures commonly employ circular and annular plates. Although they are less common than rectangular plates [46], several studies have investigated the behavior of circular FG plates [20,33,46–49]. The analytical solutions for the full plate bending behavior of circular and annular plates under asymmetric loads were presented by Reddy [34] for several boundary conditions. The work by Duda [50] examined 3D heat transfer problems for annular plates using both Cartesian and polar finite element discretizations. The results demonstrate the advantages of using a cylindrical mesh to describe circular (or cylindrical) geometries. For the heat conduction problem to be solved, the relative error of the Cartesian finite element model was found to be 11%, and for the cylindrical finite element model, it was only 1%.

After a review of the available literature, it is evident that no existing nonlinear finite element model for porous circular/annular micro-plates incorporates higher-order shear deformations in cylindrical coordinates. This study makes a significant contribution by developing such a model, which not only solves circular/annular plate problems but also takes advantage of the increased accuracy provided by cylindrical formulations. Moreover, the model accounts for moderate rotations and stretches in the thickness direction, which is crucial for accurately capturing the behavior of thick plates under thermal and mechanical loads.

This study utilizes C_1 conforming elements, which are specifically employed to ensure the continuity condition in the context of strain gradient theory. These elements ensure that the displacement field and its gradients remain continuous across element boundaries, thereby improving the model's accuracy in capturing the complex behavior of functionally graded porous materials. This approach allows for a more accurate representation of the plate's bending response and thermal-mechanical behavior, which is essential for the design of advanced engineering structures.

Additionally, the study incorporates temperature-dependent behavior and porosity, which are critical factors in the typical applications of FGM plates. The temperature-dependent properties found in the literature [51] have been used in the work by Reddy and Chin [30]. Furthermore, this research considers the effect of porosity on material properties, as observed in numerous studies [42,52–54]. Three cosine functions have been used to prescribe the volumetric distribution of porosity on FGM plates to illustrate the effects of porosity distribution [17,23,55,56]. The expressions for the porosity distributions used in this study are

$$\text{Type 1} : \Phi(z) = \phi \cos\left[\pi\frac{z}{h}\right]$$
$$\text{Type 2} : \Phi(z) = \phi \cos\left[\frac{\pi}{2}(\pi\frac{z}{h}+\frac{1}{2})\right]$$
$$\text{Type 3} : \Phi(z) = \phi \cos\left[\frac{\pi}{2}(\pi\frac{z}{h}-\frac{1}{2})\right] \tag{2}$$

where Φ is the porosity at a given location along the thickness of the plate, and ϕ is the maximum porosity value.

Since the variation in Poisson's ratio with plate thickness is considered to have a minor impact on the behavior of the plate, many studies [17,20,33,36,37,49,57] consider it constant. Other studies consider its variation to be like any other FGM property [39,47,48,58,59]. In the current work, Poisson's ratio is considered constant.

2. Model Development

2.1. Displacement Field and Strain Definition

Reddy and Kim [36] presented a general third-order displacement field by considering a cubic expansion of in-plane displacements and quadratic variation in transverse displacement. It can be written in the cylindrical coordinate system as

$$U_r(r,\theta,z,t) = U_o(r,\theta,t) + z\beta_r(r,\theta,t) + z^2\phi_x(r,\theta,t) + z^3\psi_r(r,\theta,t) \tag{3}$$
$$U_\theta(r,\theta,z,t) = V_o(r,\theta,t) + z\beta_\theta(r,\theta,t) + z^2\phi_\theta(r,\theta,t) + z^3\psi_\theta(r,\theta,t)$$
$$U_z(r,\theta,z,t) = W_o(r,\theta,t) + z\beta_z(r,\theta,t) + z^2\phi_z(r,\theta,t)$$

where U_o, V_o, and W_o are the displacements at $z = 0$. β_r, β_θ, and β_z are the linear components of their respective displacements. ϕ_r, ϕ_θ, and ϕ_z are the quadratic components. Similarly, ψ_r and ψ_θ are the cubic components.

With zero transverse shear enforced on the upper and lower surfaces, we have (4)

$$\sigma_{z\theta} = Q_{55}\gamma_{z\theta} = 0, \qquad \sigma_{rz} = Q_{66}\gamma_{rz} = 0, \qquad \text{at } z = \pm\frac{h}{2} \tag{4}$$

the displacements in the radial direction, U_r, and angular direction, U_θ, contain the cubic terms of the thickness coordinate, z, and the displacement along the thickness direction, U_z, contains quadratic terms of z:

$$U_r = U_o + z\beta_r - z^2\frac{1}{2}\frac{\partial\beta_z}{\partial r} - \frac{4z^3}{3h^2}\left(\beta_r + \frac{\partial\lambda}{\partial r}\right) \tag{5}$$
$$U_\theta = V_o + z\beta_\theta - z^2\frac{1}{2r}\frac{\partial\beta_z}{\partial\theta} - \frac{4z^3}{3h^2}\left(\beta_\theta + \frac{1}{r}\frac{\partial\lambda}{\partial\theta}\right)$$
$$U_z = W_o + z\beta_z + z^2\phi_z$$

where the grouping $\lambda = W_o + \frac{h^2}{4}\phi_z$ was used to simplify the manipulation of the equations.

The proposed strain field is based on von Kármán strain definition in cylindrical coordinates:

$$\begin{Bmatrix} \varepsilon_{rr} \\ \varepsilon_{\theta\theta} \\ \varepsilon_{zz} \\ \gamma_{r\theta} \\ \gamma_{\theta z} \\ \gamma_{zr} \end{Bmatrix} = \begin{Bmatrix} \frac{\partial U_o}{\partial r} + \frac{1}{2}\left(\frac{\partial W_o}{\partial r}\right)^2 \\ \frac{1}{r}U_o + \frac{1}{r}\frac{\partial V_o}{\partial \theta} + \frac{1}{2r^2}\left(\frac{\partial W_o}{\partial \theta}\right)^2 \\ \beta_z \\ \frac{1}{r}\frac{\partial U_o}{\partial \theta} + \frac{\partial V_o}{\partial r} - \frac{V_o}{r} + \frac{1}{r}\frac{\partial W_o}{\partial \theta}\frac{\partial W_o}{\partial r} \\ \beta_\theta + \frac{1}{r}\frac{\partial W_o}{\partial \theta} \\ \beta_r + \frac{\partial W_o}{\partial r} \end{Bmatrix} + z \begin{Bmatrix} \frac{\partial \beta_r}{\partial r} \\ \frac{1}{r}\beta_r + \frac{1}{r}\frac{\partial \beta_\theta}{\partial \theta} \\ 2\phi_z \\ \frac{1}{r}\frac{\partial \beta_r}{\partial \theta} + \frac{\partial \beta_\theta}{\partial r} - \frac{1}{r}\beta_\theta \\ 0 \\ 0 \end{Bmatrix}$$

$$+ z^2 \begin{Bmatrix} -\frac{1}{2}\frac{\partial^2 \beta_z}{\partial r^2} \\ -\frac{1}{2r}\frac{\partial \beta_z}{\partial r} - \frac{1}{2r^2}\frac{\partial^2 \beta_z}{\partial \theta^2} \\ 0 \\ -\frac{1}{r}\frac{\partial^2 \beta_z}{\partial \theta \partial r} + \frac{1}{r^2}\frac{\partial \beta_z}{\partial \theta} \\ -\frac{4}{h^2}\left(\beta_\theta + \frac{1}{r}\frac{\partial \lambda}{\partial \theta}\right) + \frac{1}{r}\frac{\partial \phi_z}{\partial \theta} \\ -\frac{4}{h^2}\left(\beta_r + \frac{\partial \lambda}{\partial r}\right) + \frac{\partial \phi_z}{\partial r} \end{Bmatrix} + z^3 \begin{Bmatrix} \frac{4}{3h^2}\left(\frac{\partial \beta_r}{\partial r} + \frac{\partial^2 \lambda}{\partial r^2}\right) \\ \frac{-4}{3rh^2}\left(\beta_r + \frac{\partial \lambda}{\partial r} + \frac{\partial \beta_\theta}{\partial \theta} + \frac{1}{r}\frac{\partial^2 \lambda}{\partial \theta^2}\right) \\ 0 \\ \frac{-4}{3h^2}\left\{\frac{1}{r}\frac{\partial \beta_r}{\partial \theta} + \frac{\partial \beta_\theta}{\partial r} + \frac{2}{r}\frac{\partial^2 \lambda}{\partial \theta \partial r} - \frac{1}{r}\beta_\theta - \frac{2}{r^2}\frac{\partial \lambda}{\partial \theta}\right\} \\ 0 \\ 0 \end{Bmatrix}.$$

Based on von Kármán strains (i.e., small strains and moderate rotation), equal to or higher than the square of the strains is neglected, and the following assumptions are made:

$$\left(\frac{\partial U_z}{\partial r}\right)^2 \approx \left(\frac{\partial W_o}{\partial r}\right)^2, \left(\frac{1}{r}\frac{\partial U_z}{\partial \theta}\right)^2 \approx \left(\frac{1}{r}\frac{\partial W_o}{\partial \theta}\right)^2, \text{ and} \left(\frac{\partial U_z}{\partial \theta}\frac{\partial U_z}{\partial r}\right) \approx \left(\frac{\partial W_o}{\partial \theta}\frac{\partial W_o}{\partial r}\right).$$

2.2. Hamilton's Principle and Equations of Motion

The derivation of the equations of motion for the model begins with Hamilton's principle, which is the dynamic form of the principle of virtual displacements:

$$0 = \int_0^t (\delta U + \delta V + \delta K) dT \tag{6}$$

where δU denotes virtual strain energy, δV denotes the virtual work carried out by external forces, and δK denotes virtual kinetic energy.

To account for size-dependent material behavior, the modified couple stress theory by Yang et al. [8] was included in the model. The theory starts with a definition for virtual strain energy:

$$\delta U = \int_v (\sigma_{ij}\delta\varepsilon_{ij} + m_{ij}\delta\chi_{ij}) dV \tag{7}$$

where σ_{ij} represents Cauchy stresses, ε_{ij} represents strains, m_{ij} are the deviatoric part of the symmetric couple stress tensor, and χ_{ij} represents the components of the curvature tensor.

The components of the curvature tensor, organized by the order of plate thickness direction and the notation in the work by Reddy and Kim [36], will take the form

$$\begin{aligned} \chi_{rr} &= \chi_{rr}^{(0)} + z\chi_{rr}^{(1)} + z^2\chi_{rr}^{(2)} \\ \chi_{\theta\theta} &= \chi_{\theta\theta}^{(0)} + z\chi_{\theta\theta}^{(1)} + z^2\chi_{\theta\theta}^{(2)} \\ \chi_{zz} &= \chi_{zz}^{(0)} + z^2\chi_{zz}^{(2)} \\ \chi_{r\theta} &= \chi_{r\theta}^{(0)} + z\chi_{r\theta}^{(1)} + z^2\chi_{r\theta}^{(2)} \\ \chi_{\theta z} &= \chi_{\theta z}^{(0)} + z\chi_{\theta z}^{(1)} + z^3\chi_{\theta z}^{(3)} \\ \chi_{zr} &= \chi_{zr}^{(0)} + z\chi_{zr}^{(1)} + z^3\chi_{zr}^{(3)} \end{aligned} \tag{8}$$

where the terms $\chi_{ij}^{(k)}$ are obtained using the displacement field in Equation (5) so that the curvature tensor can be expressed in terms of the generalized displacements.

$$
\begin{aligned}
\chi_{rr}^{(0)} &= \frac{1}{2r}\frac{\partial^2 W_o}{\partial\theta\partial r} - \frac{1}{2r^2}\frac{\partial W_o}{\partial\theta} - \frac{1}{2}\frac{\partial\beta_\theta}{\partial r} \\
\chi_{rr}^{(1)} &= \frac{1}{r}\frac{\partial^2\beta_z}{\partial\theta\partial r} - \frac{1}{r^2}\frac{\partial\beta_z}{\partial\theta} \\
\chi_{rr}^{(2)} &= \frac{1}{2r}\frac{\partial^2\phi_z}{\partial\theta\partial r} - \frac{1}{2r^2}\frac{\partial\phi_z}{\partial\theta} + \frac{2}{h^2}\left(\frac{\partial\beta_\theta}{\partial r} + \frac{1}{r}\frac{\partial^2\lambda}{\partial\theta\partial r} - \frac{1}{r^2}\frac{\partial\lambda}{\partial\theta}\right) \\
\chi_{\theta\theta}^{(0)} &= \frac{1}{2r}\frac{\partial\beta_r}{\partial\theta} - \frac{1}{2r}\frac{\partial^2 W_o}{\partial r\partial\theta} + \frac{1}{2r^2}\frac{\partial W_o}{\partial\theta} - \frac{1}{2r}\beta_\theta \\
\chi_{\theta\theta}^{(1)} &= \frac{1}{r}\frac{\partial^2\beta_z}{\partial r\partial\theta} - \frac{1}{r^2}\frac{\partial\beta_z}{\partial\theta} \\
\chi_{\theta\theta}^{(2)} &= \frac{1}{2r^2}\frac{\partial\phi_z}{\partial\theta} + \frac{2}{h^2 r}\left(\beta_\theta + \frac{1}{r}\frac{\partial\lambda}{\partial\theta}\right) - \frac{2}{h^2 r}\left(\frac{\beta_\theta}{\partial\theta} + \frac{\partial^2\lambda}{\partial r\partial\theta}\right) - \frac{1}{2r}\frac{\partial^2\phi_z}{\partial r^2} \\
\chi_{zz}^{(0)} &= \frac{1}{2r}\beta_\theta + \frac{1}{2}\frac{\partial\beta_\theta}{\partial r} - \frac{1}{2r}\frac{\partial\beta_r}{\partial\theta} \\
\chi_{zz}^{(2)} &= \frac{2}{h^2}\left(\frac{1}{r}\frac{\partial\beta_r}{\partial\theta} - \frac{\beta_\theta}{r} - \frac{\partial\beta_\theta}{\partial r}\right) \\
\chi_{r\theta}^{(0)} &= \frac{1}{2}\left[\frac{1}{4}\frac{\partial\beta_r}{\partial r} - \frac{1}{2}\frac{\partial^2 W_o}{\partial r^2} + \frac{1}{2r^2}\frac{\partial^2 W_o}{\partial\theta^2} - \frac{1}{2r}\frac{\partial\beta_\theta}{\partial\theta} - \frac{1}{2r}\beta_r + \frac{1}{2r}\frac{\partial W_o}{\partial r}\right] \\
\chi_{r\theta}^{(1)} &= \frac{1}{2}\left[-\frac{\partial^2\beta_z}{\partial r^2} + \frac{1}{r^2}\frac{\partial^2\beta_z}{\partial\theta^2} + \frac{1}{r}\frac{\partial\beta_z}{\partial r}\right] \\
\chi_{r\theta}^{(2)} &= \frac{1}{2}\left[-\frac{2}{h^2}\left(\frac{\partial\beta_r}{\partial r} + \frac{\partial^2\lambda}{\partial r^2}\right) - \frac{1}{2}\frac{\partial^2\phi_z}{\partial r^2} + \frac{1}{2r^2}\frac{\partial^2\phi_z}{\partial\theta} + \frac{2}{h^2 r}\left(\frac{\partial\beta_\theta}{\partial\theta} + \frac{1}{r}\frac{\partial^2\lambda}{\partial\theta^2}\right)\right. \\
&\quad \left. + \frac{2}{h^2 r}\left(\beta_r + \frac{\partial\lambda}{\partial r}\right) + \frac{1}{2r}\frac{\partial\phi_z}{\partial r}\right] \\
\chi_{\theta z}^{(0)} &= \frac{1}{2}\left[\frac{1}{2r^2}\frac{\partial^2 V_o}{\partial\theta} + \frac{1}{2r}\frac{\partial^2 U_o}{\partial r\partial\theta} - \frac{1}{4r^2}\frac{\partial^2 U_o}{\partial\theta^2} - \frac{\partial\beta_z}{\partial r}\right] \\
\chi_{\theta z}^{(1)} &= \frac{1}{2}\left[\frac{1}{2r^2}\frac{\partial\beta_\theta}{\partial\theta} + \frac{1}{2r}\frac{\partial^2\beta_\theta}{\partial r\partial\theta} - \frac{1}{2r^2}\frac{\partial^2\beta_r}{\partial_\theta^2} - \frac{4}{h^2}\left(\beta_r + \frac{\partial\lambda}{\partial r}\right) - \frac{\partial\phi_z}{\partial r}\right] \\
\chi_{\theta z}^{(3)} &= \frac{1}{2}\left[-\frac{2}{3h^2 r}\left(\frac{1}{r}\frac{\partial\beta_\theta}{\partial\theta} + \frac{\partial^2\beta_\theta}{\partial r\partial\theta} - \frac{1}{r}\frac{\partial^2\beta_r}{\partial\theta^2}\right)\right] \\
\chi_{zr}^{(0)} &= \frac{1}{2}\left[\frac{1}{2r}\frac{\partial V_o}{\partial r} - \frac{1}{2r^2}V_o + \frac{1}{2}\frac{\partial^2 V_o}{\partial r^2} - \frac{1}{2r}\frac{\partial^2 U_o}{\partial\theta\partial r} + \frac{1}{2r^2}\frac{\partial U_o}{\partial\theta} + \frac{1}{r}\frac{\partial\beta_z}{\partial\theta}\right] \\
\chi_{zr}^{(1)} &= \frac{1}{2}\left[\frac{1}{2r}\frac{\partial\beta_\theta}{\partial r} - \frac{1}{2r^2}\beta_\theta + \frac{1}{2}\frac{\partial^2\beta_\theta}{\partial r^2} - \frac{1}{2r}\frac{\partial^2\beta_r}{\partial\theta\partial r} + \frac{1}{2r^2}\frac{\partial\beta_r}{\partial\theta} + \frac{1}{r}\frac{\partial\phi_z}{\partial\theta} + \frac{4}{h^2}\left(\beta_\theta + \frac{1}{r}\frac{\partial\lambda}{\partial\theta}\right)\right] \\
\chi_{zr}^{(3)} &= \frac{1}{2}\left[\frac{2}{3h^2}\left(-\frac{1}{r}\frac{\partial\beta_\theta}{\partial r} + \frac{1}{r^2}\beta_\theta - \frac{\partial^2\beta_\theta}{\partial r^2} + \frac{1}{r}\frac{\partial^2\beta_r}{\partial_\theta\partial_r} - \frac{1}{r^2}\frac{\partial\beta_r}{\partial\theta}\right)\right]
\end{aligned}
$$

The virtual strain energy can then be rewritten using the definitions in Equation (10):

$$
\begin{aligned}
\delta U = \int_\Omega \Bigg\{ & \sum_{i=0}^{3} M_{rr}^i \delta\varepsilon_{rr}^i + \sum_{i=0}^{3} M_{\theta\theta}^i \delta\varepsilon_{\theta\theta}^i + \sum_{i=0}^{3} M_{zz}^i \delta\varepsilon_{zz}^i + \sum_{i=0}^{3} M_{r\theta}^i \delta\gamma_{r\theta}^i \\
& + \sum_{i=0}^{3} M_{\theta z}^i \delta\gamma_{\theta z}^i + \sum_{i=0}^{3} M_{zr}^i \delta\gamma_{zr}^i + \sum_{i=0}^{3} \mu_{rr}^i \delta\chi_{rr}^i + \sum_{i=0}^{3} \mu_{\theta\theta}^i \delta\chi_{\theta\theta} \\
& + \sum_{i=0}^{3} \mu_{zz}^i \delta\chi_{zz}^i + \sum_{i=0}^{3} \mu_{r\theta}^i \delta\chi_{r\theta}^i + \sum_{i=0}^{3} \mu_{\theta z}^i \delta\chi_{\theta z}^i + \sum_{i=0}^{3} \mu_{zr}^i \delta\chi_{zr}^i \Bigg\} r dr d\theta
\end{aligned} \tag{9}
$$

where

$$M_{ij}^{k} = \int_{\frac{-h}{2}}^{\frac{h}{2}} (z)^k \sigma_{ij} dz, \qquad \mu_{ij} = 2\int_{\frac{-h}{2}}^{\frac{h}{2}} (z)^k m_{ij} dz. \tag{10}$$

Virtual kinetic energy is defined in cylindrical coordinates as

$$\delta K = \int_{\Omega} \left\{ \int_{\frac{-h}{2}}^{\frac{h}{2}} \rho\left[\dot{U}_r \delta \dot{U}_r + \dot{U}_\theta \delta \dot{U}_\theta + \dot{U}_z \delta \dot{U}_z\right] dz \right\} r dr d\theta \tag{11}$$

where ρ is the mass density. By using the displacement field in Equation (5), virtual kinetic energy becomes

$$\begin{aligned}
\delta K = \int_{\Omega} \Bigg\{ & \left[m_0 \dot{U}_o + m_1 \dot{\beta} r - m_2 \frac{1}{2}\frac{\partial \dot{\beta}_z}{\partial r} - m_3 \frac{4}{3h^2}\left(\dot{\beta}_r + \frac{\partial \dot{\lambda}}{\partial r}\right)\right]\left[\delta \dot{U}_o\right] \\
& + \left[m_1 \dot{U}_o + m_2 \dot{\beta}_r - m_3 \frac{1}{2}\frac{\partial \dot{\beta}_z}{\partial r} - m_4 \frac{4}{3h^2}\left(\dot{\beta}_r + \frac{\partial \lambda}{\partial r}\right)\right]\left[\delta \dot{\beta}_r\right] \\
& + \left[m_2 \dot{U}_o + m_3 \dot{\beta}_r - m_4 \frac{1}{2}\frac{\partial \dot{\beta}_z}{\partial r} - m_5 \frac{4}{3h^2}\left(\dot{\beta}_r + \frac{\partial \lambda}{\partial r}\right)\right]\left[-\frac{1}{2}\frac{\partial \delta \dot{\beta}_z}{\partial r}\right] \\
& + \left[m_3 \dot{U}_o + m_4 \dot{\beta}_r - m_5 \frac{1}{2}\frac{\partial \dot{\beta}_z}{\partial r} - m_6 \frac{4}{3h^2}\left(\dot{\beta}_r + \frac{\partial \lambda}{\partial r}\right)\right]\left[-\frac{4}{3h^2}\left(\delta \dot{\beta}_r + \frac{\partial \delta \lambda}{\partial r}\right)\right] \\
& + \left[m_o \dot{V}_o + m_1 \dot{\beta}_\theta - m_2 \frac{1}{2r}\frac{\partial \dot{\beta}_z}{\partial \theta} - m_3 \frac{4}{3h^2}\left(\dot{\beta}_\theta + \frac{1}{r}\frac{\partial \lambda}{\partial \theta}\right)\right]\left[\delta \dot{V}_o\right] \\
& + \left[m_1 \dot{V}_o + m_2 \dot{\beta}_\theta - m_3 \frac{1}{2r}\frac{\partial \dot{\beta}_z}{\partial \theta} - m_4 \frac{4}{3h^2}\left(\dot{\beta}_\theta + \frac{1}{r}\frac{\partial \lambda}{\partial \theta}\right)\right]\left[\delta \dot{\beta}_\theta\right] \\
& + \left[m_2 \dot{V}_o + m_3 \dot{\beta}_\theta - m_4 \frac{1}{2r}\frac{\partial \dot{\beta}_z}{\partial \theta} - m_5 \frac{4}{3h^2}\left(\dot{\beta}_\theta + \frac{1}{r}\frac{\partial \lambda}{\partial \theta}\right)\right]\left[-\frac{1}{2r}\frac{\partial \delta \dot{\beta}_z}{\partial \theta}\right] \\
& + \left[m_3 \dot{V}_o + m_4 \dot{\beta}_\theta - m_5 \frac{1}{2r}\frac{\partial \dot{\beta}_z}{\partial \theta} - m_6 \frac{4}{3h^2}\left(\dot{\beta}_\theta + \frac{1}{r}\frac{\partial \lambda}{\partial \theta}\right)\right]\left[-\frac{4}{3h^2}\left(\delta \dot{\beta}_\theta + \frac{1}{r}\frac{\partial \delta \dot{\lambda}}{\partial \theta}\right)\right] \\
& + \left[m_o \dot{W}_o + m_1 \dot{\beta}_z + m_2 \dot{\phi}_z\right]\left[\delta \dot{W}_o\right] \\
& + \left[m_1 \dot{W}_o + m_2 \dot{\beta}_z + m_3 \dot{\phi}_z\right]\left[\delta \dot{\beta}_z\right] \\
& + \left[m_2 \dot{W}_o + m_3 \dot{\beta}_z + m_4 \dot{\phi}_z\right]\left[\delta \dot{\phi}_z\right] \Bigg\} r dr d\theta
\end{aligned} \tag{12}$$

We use the following definition, which is nonzero for any value of i for functionally graded materials.

$$m_i = \int_{\frac{-h}{2}}^{\frac{h}{2}} \rho(z)^i dz. \tag{13}$$

The virtual work carried out by external forces is defined by

$$\begin{aligned}
\delta V = & -\int_{v} (f_r \delta U_r + f_\theta \delta U_\theta + f_z \delta U_z + c_r \delta \omega_r + c_\theta \delta \omega_\theta + c_z \delta \omega_z) dV \\
& - \int_{\Omega^t} (q_r^t \delta U_r + q_\theta^t \delta U_\theta + q_z^t \delta U_z) r dr d\theta \\
& - \int_{\Omega^-} \left(q_r^b \delta U_r + q_\theta^b \delta U_\theta + q_z^b \delta U_z\right) r dr d\theta \\
& - \int_{s} (t_r \delta U_r + t_\theta \delta U_\theta + t_z \delta U_z) ds
\end{aligned} \tag{14}$$

where f_i denotes body forces, c_i is body couples, t_i is surface tractions, and q_i^t and q_i^b denote distributed loads on the upper and lower surface, respectively, for $i = z, r, \theta$. Figure 3 presents surfaces where external forces are applied, and the integration is carried out over the upper surface Ω^+, lower surface Ω^-, or lateral surface S to compute the virtual work carried out.

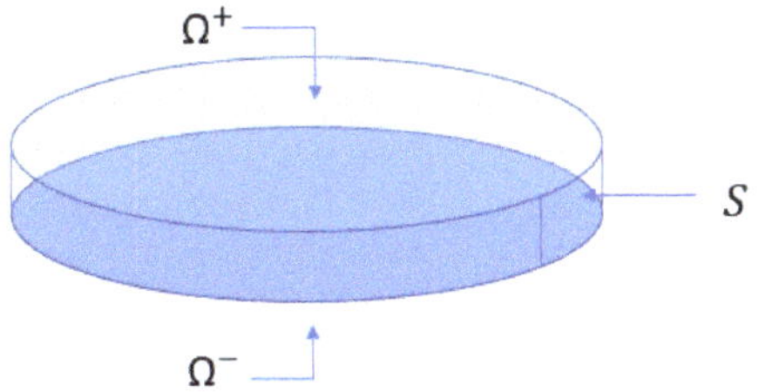

Figure 3. Plate surfaces.

By using the displacement field in Equation (14), we obtain

$$
\begin{aligned}
\delta V = \int_\Omega \Big\{ & F_r^0 \delta U_o + F_r \delta\beta_r + F_r^2\left(-\frac{1}{2}\frac{\partial\delta\beta_z}{\partial r}\right) + F_r^3\left(-\frac{4}{3h^2}\left(\delta\beta_r + \frac{\partial\delta\phi}{\partial r}\right)\right) + \\
& + F_\theta^0\delta V_o + F_\theta^1 \delta\beta_\theta + F_\theta^2\left(-\frac{1}{2r}\frac{\partial\delta\beta_z}{\partial r}\right) + F_\theta^3\left(-\frac{4}{3h^2}\left(\delta\beta_\theta+\frac{1}{r}\frac{\partial\delta\phi}{\partial\theta}\right)\right) + F_z^{(0)}\delta W_o \\
& + F_z^1\delta\beta_z + F_z^2\delta\phi_z + C_r^0\left[\frac{1}{2r}\frac{\partial\delta W_o}{\partial\theta} - \frac{1}{2}\frac{\partial\delta W_o}{\partial\theta} - \frac{1}{2}\delta\beta_\theta\right] + C_r^1\left[\frac{1}{r}\frac{\partial\delta\beta_z}{\partial\theta}\right] \\
& + C_r^2\left[\frac{1}{2r}\frac{\partial\delta\phi_z}{\partial\theta} + \frac{2}{h^2}\left(\delta\beta_\theta+\frac{1}{r}\frac{\partial\delta\phi}{\partial\theta}\right)\right] + C_\theta^0\left[\frac{1}{2}\delta\beta_r - \frac{1}{2}\delta\beta_r - \frac{1}{2}\frac{\partial\delta W_o}{\partial r}\right] + C_\theta^1\left[-\frac{\partial\delta\beta_z}{\partial r}\right] \\
& + C_\theta^2\left[-\frac{2}{h^2}\left(\delta\beta r + \frac{\partial\delta\beta_r}{\partial r}\right) - \frac{1}{2}\frac{\partial\delta\phi_z}{\partial r}\right] + C_z^0\left[\frac{1}{2r}\delta V_o + \frac{1}{2}\frac{\partial\delta W_o}{\partial r} - \frac{1}{2r}\frac{\partial\delta U_o}{\partial\theta}\right] \\
& + C_z^1\left[\frac{1}{2r}\delta\beta_\theta + \frac{1}{2}\frac{\partial\delta\beta_\theta}{\partial r} - \frac{1}{2r}\frac{\partial\delta\beta_r}{\partial\theta}\right] + C_z^3\left[-\frac{2}{3h^2}\left(\frac{1}{r}\delta\beta_\theta + \frac{\partial\delta\beta_\theta}{\partial r} - \frac{1}{r}\frac{\partial\delta\beta_r}{\partial\theta}\right)\right]\Big\} r dr d\theta \\
& + \int_\Gamma\Big\{ t_r^0\delta U_o + t_r^1\delta\beta_r + t_r^2\left(-\frac{1}{2}\frac{\delta\delta\beta_z}{\partial r}\right) + t_r^3\left(-\frac{4}{3h^2}\left(\delta\beta_r+\frac{\partial\delta\phi}{\partial r}\right)\right) + t_\theta^0\delta V_o + t_\theta^1\delta\beta_\theta \\
& + t_\theta^2\left(-\frac{1}{2r}\frac{\partial\delta\beta_z}{\partial\theta}\right) + t_\theta^3\left(-\frac{4}{3h^2}\left(\delta\beta_\theta+\frac{1}{r}\frac{\partial\delta\phi}{\partial\theta}\right)\right) + +t_z^0\delta W_o + T_z^1\delta\beta_z + t_z^2\delta\phi_z\Big\} d\Gamma
\end{aligned}
\tag{15}
$$

with the following definitions:

$$
f_\varsigma^{(i)} = \int_{-\frac{h}{2}}^{\frac{h}{2}}(z)^i f_\varsigma dz,\ \ t_\varsigma^i = \int_{\frac{-h}{2}}^{\frac{h}{2}}(z)^i t_\varsigma dz,\ \ C_\varsigma^i = \int_{\frac{-h}{2}}^{\frac{h}{2}}(z)^i C_\varsigma dz,\ \ F_\varsigma^i = f_\varsigma^i + \left(\frac{h}{2}\right)^i\left[q_\varsigma^t + (-1)q_\varsigma^b\right]
\tag{16}
$$

By grouping all the terms in Equations (9), (12) and (15) using variational generalized displacements, we obtain the equations of motion:

$$
\begin{aligned}
\delta U_o : & -\frac{\partial}{\partial r}\left(rM_{rr}^0\right) + M_{\theta\theta}^0 - \frac{\partial}{\partial\theta}\left(M_{r\theta}^0\right) + \frac{\partial^2}{\partial\theta\partial r}\left(-M_{zr}^0\frac{1}{4}\right) - \frac{\partial}{\partial\theta}\left(M_{zr}^0\frac{1}{4r}\right) + rFr^0 + \frac{\partial}{\partial\theta}\left(\frac{1}{2}C_z^0\right) \\
& = -vm_o\ddot{U}_o - m_1\ddot{\beta}_r + m_2\frac{1}{2}\frac{\partial\ddot{\beta}_z}{\partial r} + m_3\frac{4}{3h^2}\left(\ddot{\beta}_r + \frac{\partial\ddot{W}_o}{\partial r}\frac{h^2}{4}\frac{\partial\ddot{\phi}_z}{\partial r}\right)
\end{aligned}
\tag{17}
$$

$$
\begin{aligned}
\delta V_o : & -\frac{\partial}{\partial\theta}\left(M_{\theta\theta}^0\right) - \frac{\partial}{\partial r}\left(rM_{r\theta}^0\right) - M_{r\theta}^0 - \frac{\partial}{\partial\theta}\left(\mu_{\theta z}^0\frac{1}{4r}\right) + \frac{\partial^2}{\partial r\partial\theta}\left(\mu_{\theta z}^0\frac{1}{4}\right) + \frac{\partial^2}{\partial\theta^2}\left(-\mu_{\theta z}\frac{1}{4}\right) \\
& - \frac{\partial}{\partial r}\left(\mu_{zr}^0\frac{1}{4}\right) - \mu_{zr}^0\frac{1}{4r} + \frac{\partial^2}{\partial r^2}\left(\mu_{zr}^0\frac{r}{4}\right) + rF_{(\theta)}^0 + \frac{1}{2}C_z^0 \\
& = -rm_o\ddot{V}_o - rm_1\ddot{\beta}_\theta + \frac{1}{2} + \frac{1}{2}m_2\frac{\partial\ddot{\beta}_z}{\partial\theta} + m_3\frac{4}{3h^2}\left(r\ddot{\beta}_\theta + \frac{\partial\ddot{W}_o}{\partial r} + \frac{h^2}{4}\frac{\partial\ddot{\phi}_z}{\partial r}\right)
\end{aligned}
\tag{18}
$$

$$\delta W_o: -\frac{\partial}{\partial r}\left(rM_{rr}^0\frac{\partial W_o}{\partial r}\right)+\frac{\partial^2}{\partial r^2}\left(\frac{-4r}{3h^2}M_{rr}^3\right)-\frac{\partial}{\partial\theta}\left(\frac{1}{r}\frac{\partial W_o}{\partial\theta}M_{\theta\theta}^0\right)-\frac{\partial}{\partial r}\left(\frac{-4r}{3h^2}M_{\theta\theta}^3\right)$$
$$+\frac{\partial^2}{\partial\theta^2}\left(\frac{-4r}{3h^2r^2}M_{\theta\theta}^3\right)+\frac{-\partial}{\partial r}\left(\frac{\partial W_o}{\partial\theta}M_{r\theta}^0\right)-\frac{\partial}{\partial\theta}\left(\frac{\partial W_o}{\partial r}M_{r\theta}o\right)-\frac{4}{3h^2}\frac{\partial^2}{\partial\theta\partial r}\left(2rM_{r\theta}^3\right)$$
$$+\frac{\partial}{\partial\theta}\left(M_{r\theta}^3\right)\frac{8}{3h^2r^2}-\frac{\partial}{\partial\theta}M_{\theta z}^0+\frac{\partial}{\partial\theta}\left(\frac{4}{h^2}M_{\theta z}^2\right)-\frac{\partial}{\partial r}\left(rM_{zr}^0\right)+\frac{\partial}{\partial r}\left(\frac{4r}{h^2}M_{zr}^2\right)+\frac{\partial^2}{\partial\theta\partial r}\left(\frac{1}{2}\mu_{rr}^0\right)$$
$$+\frac{\partial}{\partial\theta}\left(\frac{1}{2r}\mu_{rr}^0\right)+\frac{\partial^2}{\partial\theta\partial r}\left(\frac{2}{h^2}\mu_{rr}^2\right)+\frac{\partial}{\partial\theta}\left(\frac{2}{h^2r}\mu_{rr}^2\right)+\frac{\partial^2}{\partial rd\theta}\left(-\mu_{\theta\theta}^0\frac{1}{2}\right)-\frac{\partial}{\partial\theta}\left(\mu_{\theta\theta}^0\frac{1}{2r}\right)$$
$$+\frac{\partial^2}{\partial\theta^2}\left(\mu_{\theta\theta}^2\frac{2}{h^2r}\right)+\frac{\partial}{\partial r}\left(\mu_{\theta\theta}^2\frac{2}{h^2}\right)+\frac{\partial^2}{\partial r^2}\left(-\mu_{r\theta}\frac{r}{4}\right)+\frac{\partial^2}{\partial\theta^2}\left(\mu_{r\theta}o\frac{1}{4r}\right)-\frac{\partial}{\partial r}\left(\mu_{r\theta}^0\frac{1}{4}\right)-\frac{\partial^2}{\partial r^2}\left(\mu_{r\theta}^2\frac{r}{h^2}\right)$$
$$+\frac{\partial^2}{\partial\theta^2}\left(\mu_{r\theta}^2\frac{1}{h^2r}\right)-\frac{\partial}{\partial r}\left(\mu_{r\theta}^2\frac{1}{h}\right)+\frac{\partial}{\partial r}\left(\mu_{\theta z}^1\frac{2r}{h^2}\right)-\frac{\partial}{\partial\theta}\left(\mu_{zr}^1\frac{2}{h^2}\right)+\frac{\partial}{\partial r}\left(\frac{4r}{3h^2}F_r^3\right)+\frac{\partial}{\partial\theta}\left(\frac{4}{3h^2}F_\theta^3\right)$$
$$+rF_z^0-\frac{\partial}{\partial\theta}\left(\frac{1}{2}C_r^0\right)-\frac{\partial}{\partial\theta}\left(\frac{2}{h^2}C_r^2\right)+\frac{\partial}{\partial r}\left(\frac{r}{2}C_\theta^0\right)+\frac{\partial}{\partial r}\left(\frac{2r}{h^2}C_\theta^2\right)-\frac{\partial}{\partial r}\left(\frac{r}{2}C_z^0\right)$$
$$=\frac{\partial}{\partial r}\left[\frac{-4}{3h^2}\left\{rm_3\ddot{U}_o+rm_4\ddot{\beta}_r-m_5\frac{r}{2}\frac{\partial\ddot{\beta}_z}{\partial r}-m_6\frac{4r}{3h^2}\left(\ddot{\beta}_r+\frac{\partial\ddot{W}_o}{\partial r}+\frac{h^2}{4}\frac{\partial\ddot{\phi}_z}{\partial r}\right)\right\}\right]+m_3\ddot{V}_o+m_4\ddot{\beta}_\theta$$
$$-m_5\frac{1}{2r}\frac{\partial\ddot{\beta}_z}{\partial\theta}-m_6\frac{4}{3h^2r}\left(r\ddot{\beta}_\theta+\frac{\partial\ddot{W}_o}{\partial r}+\frac{h^2}{4}\frac{\partial\ddot{\phi}_z}{\partial r}\right)+rm_o\ddot{W}_o+rm_1\ddot{\beta}_z+rm_2\ddot{\phi}_z \quad (19)$$

$$\delta\beta_r: -\frac{\partial}{\partial r}\left(rM_{rr}^1\right)-\frac{\partial}{\partial r}\left(-\frac{4r}{3h^2}M_{rr}^3\right)+M_{\theta\theta}^1-\frac{4}{3h^2}M_{\theta\theta}^3-\frac{\partial}{\partial\theta}\left(M_{r\theta}^1\right)+\frac{4}{3h^2}\frac{\partial}{\partial\theta}\left(M_{r\theta}^3\right)$$
$$+rM_{rz}^0-\frac{4r}{h^2}M_{zr}^2-\frac{\partial}{\partial\theta}\left(\frac{1}{2}\mu_{\theta\theta}^0\right)-\mu_{\theta\theta}^2\frac{2}{h^2}+\frac{\partial}{\partial\theta}\left(\mu_{zz}^0\frac{1}{2}\right)-\frac{\partial}{\partial\theta}\left(\mu_{zz}^2\frac{2}{h^2}\right)-\frac{\partial}{\partial\theta}\left(\mu_{r\theta}^0\frac{1}{4}\right)-\mu_{r\theta}^0\frac{1}{4}$$
$$+\frac{\partial}{\partial r}\left(\mu_{r\theta}^2\frac{r}{h^2}\right)-\frac{\partial^2}{\partial\theta^2}\left(\mu_{\theta z}^1\frac{1}{4r}\right)-\mu_{\theta z}^1\frac{2r}{h^2}+\frac{\partial^2}{\partial\theta^2}\left(\mu_{\theta z}^3\frac{1}{3h^2r}\right)+\frac{\partial^2}{\partial\theta\partial r}\left(-\mu_{zr}^1\frac{1}{4}\right)+\frac{\partial}{\partial\theta}\left(\mu_{zr}^1\frac{1}{4r}\right)$$
$$+\frac{\partial^2}{\partial\theta\partial r}\left(-\mu_{zr}^3\frac{1}{3h^2}\right)-\frac{\partial}{\partial\theta}\left(\mu_{zr}^3\frac{2}{3h^2r}\right)-\frac{4r}{3h^2}F_r^3+\frac{v}{2}C_\theta^0-\frac{2r}{h^2}C_\theta^2-\frac{1}{2}\frac{\partial}{\partial\theta}C_z^{(1)}+\frac{\partial}{\partial\theta}\left(\frac{2}{3h^2}C_z^3\right)$$
$$=-rm_1\ddot{U}_o-rm_2\ddot{\beta}_r+m_3\frac{v}{2}\frac{\partial\ddot{\beta}_z}{\partial r}+m_4\frac{4r}{3h^2}\left(\ddot{\beta}_r+\frac{\partial\ddot{W}_o}{\partial r}+\frac{h^2}{4}\frac{\partial\ddot{\phi}_z}{\partial r}\right)-rFr^{(1)}\left\{-rm_3\ddot{U}_o-rm_4\ddot{\beta}_r\right.$$
$$\left.+m_5\frac{r}{2}\frac{\partial\ddot{\beta}_z}{\partial r}+m_6\frac{4r}{3h^2}\left(\ddot{\beta}_r+\frac{\partial\ddot{W}_o}{\partial r}+\frac{h^2}{\frac{\partial\ddot{\phi}_z}{\partial r}}\right)\right\}\left(\frac{-4}{3h^2}\right) \quad (20)$$

$$\delta\beta_\theta: -\frac{\partial}{\partial\theta}\left(\mu_{\theta\theta}^1\right)-\frac{\partial}{\partial\theta}\left(-\frac{4}{3h^2}\mu_{\theta\theta}^3\right)-\frac{\partial}{\partial r}\left(r\mu_{t\theta}^1\right)-\mu_{r\theta}^1+\frac{4}{3h^2}\frac{\partial}{\partial r}\left(r\mu_{r\theta}^3\right)+1$$
$$+\frac{\partial}{\partial r}\left(\frac{r}{2}\mu_{rr}^0\right)+\mu_{\theta z}^0r-\frac{4r}{h^2}\mu_{\theta z}^2-\frac{\partial}{\partial r}\left(\frac{2r}{h^2}\mu_{rr}^2\right)+\mu_{\theta\theta}^0\frac{1}{2}-\frac{\partial}{\partial\theta}\left(\mu_{\theta\theta}^2\frac{2}{h^2}\right)+\frac{1}{2}\mu_{zz}^0$$
$$-\frac{\partial}{\partial r}\left(\mu_{zz}^0\frac{r}{2}\right)m\mu_{zz}^2\frac{2}{h^2}+\frac{\partial}{\partial r}\left(\mu_{zz}^2\frac{2}{h^2r}\right)+\frac{\partial}{\partial\theta}\left(\mu_{r\theta}^0\frac{1}{4}\right)-\frac{\partial}{\partial\theta}\left(\mu_{r\theta}^2\frac{1}{h^2}\right)-\frac{\partial}{\partial\theta}\left(\mu_{\theta z}^1\frac{1}{4r}\right)$$
$$+\frac{\partial^2}{\partial rd\theta}\left(\mu_{\theta z}^1\frac{1}{4}\right)+\frac{\partial}{\partial\theta}\left(\mu_{\theta z}^3\frac{1}{3h^2r}\right)-\frac{\partial^2}{\partial rd\theta}\left(\mu_{\theta z}^3\frac{1}{3h^2}\right)210-\frac{\partial}{\partial r}\left(\mu_{zr}^1\frac{1}{4}\right)-\mu_{zr}^1\frac{1}{4r}+\frac{\partial^2}{\partial r^2}\left(\mu_{zr}^1\frac{r}{4}\right)$$
$$+\mu_{zr}^1\frac{2r}{h^2}-\frac{\partial}{\partial r}\left(-\mu_{zr}^3\frac{1}{3h^2}\right)+\mu_{zr}^3\frac{1}{3h^2r}+\frac{\partial^2}{\partial r^2}\left(-\mu_{zr}^3\frac{r}{3h^2}\right)+rF_\theta^{(1)}-\frac{4r}{3h^2}F_\theta^3-\frac{r}{2}C_r^0+\frac{2r}{h^2}C_r^2$$
$$+\frac{1}{2}C_z^{(1)}-\frac{\partial}{\partial r}\left(\frac{r}{2}C_z^{(1)}\right)-\frac{2}{3h^2}C_z^3+\frac{\partial}{\partial r}\left(\frac{2r}{3h^2}C_z^3\right)$$
$$=\left\{-rm_1\ddot{V}_o-rm_2\ddot{\beta}_\theta+m_3\frac{1}{2}\frac{\partial\ddot{\beta}_z}{\partial\theta}+m_4\frac{4}{3h^2}\left(r\ddot{\beta}_\theta+\frac{\partial\ddot{W}_o}{\partial r}+\frac{h^2}{4}\frac{\partial\ddot{\phi}_z}{\partial r}\right)\right\}+rm_3\ddot{V}_\theta+rm_4\ddot{\beta}_\theta-m_5 \quad (21)$$

$$\delta\beta_z : \frac{-\partial^2}{\partial r^2}\left(\frac{1}{2}r\mu_{rr}^2\right) + \frac{\partial}{\partial r}\left(\mu_{\theta\theta}^2\frac{1}{2}\right) - \frac{\partial^2}{\partial r^2}\left(-\mu_{\theta\theta}^2\frac{1}{2r}\right) + \mu_{zz}^0 - \frac{\partial^2}{\partial\theta\partial r}\left(\mu_{r\theta}^2\right) - \frac{\partial}{pa\theta}\left(\frac{\mu_{r\theta}^2}{r}\right)$$
$$+ \frac{\partial^2}{\partial\theta\partial r}\left(\mu_{rr}^1\right) + \frac{\partial}{\partial\theta}\left(\mu_{rr}^1\frac{1}{r}\right) + \frac{\partial^2}{\partial r d\theta}\left(-\mu_{\theta\theta}^1\right) - \frac{\partial}{\partial\theta}\left(\mu_{\theta\theta}^1\frac{1}{r}\right) + \frac{\partial^2}{\partial r^2}\left(-\mu_{r\theta}^1\frac{r}{2}\right) + \frac{\partial^2}{\partial\theta^2}\left(\mu_{r\theta}^1\frac{1}{2r}\right)$$
$$- \frac{\partial}{\partial r}\left(\mu_{r\theta}^1\frac{1}{2}\right) + \frac{\partial}{\partial r}\left(\mu_{\theta z}^0\frac{1}{2r}\right) + \frac{\partial}{\partial r}\left(\frac{r}{2}F_r^2\right) - \frac{\partial}{\partial\theta}\left(\frac{1}{2}F_\theta^2\right) + rF_z^{(1)} - \frac{\partial}{\partial\theta}\left(C_r^{(1)}\right) + \frac{\partial}{\partial r}\left(rC_\theta^{(1)}\right)$$
$$= \frac{-1}{2}\frac{\partial}{\partial r}\left\{rm_2\ddot{U}_o + rm_3\ddot{\beta}_r - m_4\frac{r}{2}\frac{\partial\ddot{\beta}_z}{\partial r} - m_5\frac{4r}{3h^2}\left(\ddot{\beta}_r + \frac{\partial\ddot{W}_o}{\partial r} + \frac{h^2}{4}\frac{\partial\ddot{\phi}_z}{\partial r}\right)\right\} - \frac{1}{2r}\frac{\partial}{\partial\theta}\{rm_2\ddot{V}_o$$
$$+rm_3\ddot{\beta}_\theta - m_4\frac{1}{2}\frac{\partial\ddot{\beta}_z}{\partial\theta} - m_5\frac{4}{3h^2}\left(r\ddot{\beta}_o + \frac{\partial\ddot{W}_o}{\partial r} + \frac{h^2}{4}\frac{\partial\ddot{\phi}_z}{\partial r}\right)\Big\} - rm_1\ddot{W}_o - rm_2\ddot{\beta}_z - rm_3\ddot{\phi}_z \tag{22}$$

$$\delta\phi_z : -\frac{1}{3}\frac{\partial^2}{\partial r^2}\left(r\mu_{rr}^3\right) + \frac{\partial}{\partial r}\left(\frac{1}{3}\mu_{\theta\theta}^3\right) + \frac{\partial^2}{\partial\theta^2}\left(-\frac{1}{3r}\mu_{\theta\theta}^3\right) + \mu_{zz}^1 2 - \frac{2}{3}\frac{\partial^2}{\partial\theta\partial r}\left(r\mu_{r\theta}^3\right) + \frac{2}{3r^2}\frac{\partial}{\partial\theta}\left(\mu_{r\theta}^3\right)$$
$$+ \frac{\partial}{\partial\theta\partial r}\left(\frac{1}{2}\mu_{rr}^2\right) + \frac{\partial}{\partial\theta}\left(\mu_{rr}^2\frac{1}{2r}\right) + \frac{\partial^2}{\partial\theta\partial r}\left(\frac{1}{2}\mu_{rr}^2\right) + \frac{\partial}{\partial\theta}\left(\frac{1}{2}\mu_{rr}^2\right) + \frac{\partial^2}{\partial\theta^2}\left(\mu_{\theta\theta}^2\frac{1}{2r}\right) + \frac{\partial^2}{\partial\theta^2}\left(\mu_{\theta\theta}^2\frac{1}{2r}\right)$$
$$+ \frac{\partial}{\partial r}\left(\mu\theta\theta^2\frac{1}{2}\right) + \frac{\partial}{\partial r}\left(\frac{1}{r}\mu_{\theta\theta}^2\right) - \frac{\partial^2}{\partial r}\left(\mu_{r\theta}\frac{r}{2}\right) + \frac{\partial^2}{\partial\theta^2}\left(\mu_{r\theta}^2\frac{1}{4r}\right) + \frac{\partial^2}{\partial\theta^2}\left(\mu_{r\theta}^2\frac{1}{4r}\right) - \frac{\partial}{\partial r}\left(\mu_{r\theta}^2\frac{h}{4}\right) - \frac{\partial}{\partial r}\left(\mu_{r\theta}^2\frac{1}{4}\right)$$
$$= \frac{h^2}{4}\frac{\partial}{\partial r}\left[\frac{-4}{3h^2}\left\{rm_3\ddot{U}_o + rm_4\ddot{\beta}_r - m_5\frac{r}{2}\frac{\partial\ddot{\beta}_z}{\partial r} - m_6\frac{4r}{3h^2}\left(\ddot{\beta}_r + \frac{\partial\ddot{W}_o}{\partial r} + \frac{h^2}{4}\frac{\partial\ddot{\phi}_z}{\partial r}\right)\right\}\right] + \frac{h^2}{4}m_3\ddot{V}_o$$
$$+ \frac{h^2}{4}m_4\ddot{\beta}_\theta - \frac{h^2}{4}m_5\frac{1}{2r}\frac{\partial\ddot{\beta}_z}{\partial\theta} - \frac{h^2}{4}m_6\frac{4}{3h^2 r}\left(r\ddot{\beta}_\theta + \frac{\partial\ddot{W}_o}{\partial r} + \frac{h^2}{4}\frac{\partial\ddot{\phi}_z}{\partial r}\right) + \frac{h^2}{4}rm_o\ddot{W}_o$$
$$+ \frac{h^2}{4}rm_1\ddot{\beta}_z + \frac{h^2}{4}rm_2\ddot{\phi}_z. \tag{23}$$

2.3. Constitutive Relations

The functionally graded materials in this work are considered to have linearly elastic isotropic behavior, and therefore, the constitutive relations can be expressed as

$$\sigma_{ij} = 2\hat{\mu}\varepsilon_{ij} + \hat{\lambda}\delta_{ij}\varepsilon_{kk} \tag{24}$$

$$m_{ij} = 2\hat{\mu}l^2\chi_{ij} \tag{25}$$

where $\hat{\lambda}$ and $\hat{\mu}$ are the lame parameters defined as

$$\hat{\lambda} = \frac{\nu E}{(1+\nu)(1-2\nu)}, \qquad \hat{\mu} = \frac{E}{2(1+\nu)}. \tag{26}$$

The porous functionally graded material properties are a function of the position in the transverse direction, the porosity, and the temperature. Therefore, the elastic modulus, E, and other material properties have the form of

$$P(z,T,\phi) = [(P_c(T) - P_m(T))(\frac{1}{2} + \frac{z}{h})^n + P_m](1 - \Phi(z)) \tag{27}$$

where P indicates the material property of the functionally graded material, $P_c(T)$ indicates the property of the ceramic constituent, $P_m(T)$ indicates the material property of the metallic constituent, ϕ indicates the maximum porosity, Φ the porosity distribution function, and n indicates the power-law index. The porosity distribution functions are defined in Equation (2).

2.4. Finite Element Model

A C_1 continuity conforming element was utilized to develop the finite element model. The utilized interpolation function of the C_1 conforming element was developed by Bogner et al. [60], with u, $\frac{\partial u}{\partial r}$, $\frac{\partial u}{\partial \theta}$, and $\frac{\partial^2 u}{\partial r \partial \theta}$ being the degrees of freedom per node. Note that u and its derivatives are a nodal value and its derivatives. All seven generalized displacements were approximated with the same interpolation functions, with the form

$$u \approx U_h(\xi, \eta) = \sum_{j=1}^{16} \hat{\Delta}_j \psi_j(\xi, \eta) \tag{28}$$

where $\hat{\Delta}_j$ and $\psi_j(\xi, \eta)$ nodal variables and their derivatives are in a four-node element and the interpolation functions. ξ and η are normalized coordinates with respect to the size of an element, where the interpolation functions are

$$\psi_j^e = g_{i1}(i = 1,5,9,13), \qquad \psi_j^e = g_{i2}(i = 2,6,10,14)$$

$$\psi_j^e = g_{i3}(i = 3,7,11,15), \qquad \psi_j^e = g_{i4}(i = 4,8,12,16)$$

$$g_{i1} = \frac{1}{16}(\xi + \xi_i)^2(\xi_i\xi - 2)(\eta + \eta_i)^2(\eta_i\eta - 2)$$

$$g_{i2} = \frac{1}{16}a\xi_i(\xi + \xi_i)^2(1 - \xi_i\xi)(\eta + \eta_i)^2(\eta_i\eta - 2)$$

$$g_{i3} = \frac{1}{16}b\eta_i(\xi + \xi_i)^2(\xi_i\xi - 2)(\eta + \eta_i)^2(1 - \eta_i\eta)$$

$$g_{i4} = \frac{1}{16}ab\xi_i\eta_i(\xi + \xi_i)^2(1 - \xi_i\xi)(\eta + \eta_i)^2(1 - \eta_i\eta)$$

where i is the number of degrees of freedom per generalized displacement in a four-node element. g_{i1}, g_{i2}, g_{i3}, and g_{i4} are interpolation functions associated with u, $\frac{\partial u}{\partial r}$, $\frac{\partial u}{\partial \theta}$, and $\frac{\partial^2 u}{\partial r \partial \theta}$, respectively.

The mesh was defined in polar coordinates, with a value for the radius and another for the angle, using four nodes at the vertices. If the modeled plate is circular, the elements at the center of the plate have a pair of nodes at the origin of the plate ($r = 0$), which share physical position since their different angular coordinates (θ) do not translate into a different position (given that the value of the radius is zero). The model behaved well given this mesh definition, and therefore, no three-node element was implemented.

The seven generalized displacements, then, are

$$U^{(k)} \approx \sum_{j=1}^{16} \hat{\Delta}_j^k \psi_j^k(\xi, \eta)$$

where $U^{(k)}$ are the seven generalized displacements: $U^{(1)} = U_o$, $U^{(2)} = V_o$, $U^{(3)} = W_o$, $U^{(4)} = \beta_r$, $U^{(5)} = \beta_\theta$, $U^{(6)} = \beta_z$, and $U^{(7)} = \phi_z$. The finite element equations will adopt the form

$$[M]^e\{\ddot{U}\}^e + [K]^e\{U\}^e = \{F\}^e + \{F^T\}^e \tag{31}$$

where U is a displacement vector (note that it should be distinct from the virtual strain energy in Equation (7)), the superscript e indicates an element, $\{F\}^e$ is the mechanical force vector, $\{F^T\}^e$ is the thermal force vector, and $[K]^e$ and $[M]^e$ are the stiffness and mass matrices. $[K]^e$ and $[M]^e$ are 112 by 112 matrices, the components of which are shown in Appendices A.1 and A.2, respectively. Note that a four-node element has seven generalized displacements per node and four degrees of freedom (nodal value and its derivatives) for each generalized displacement per node.

2.5. Computational Considerations

Newton iteration was selected as the iterative solution method, which obtains the solution increment ΔU for each iteration and adds it to the previous solution rather than finding the solution vector, U, itself. This is conducted through the following equation:

$$\Delta U = -\left[T\left(U^{(r-1)}\right)\right]^{-1} R^{r-1} \tag{32}$$

where r is the iteration number, and T is the tangent matrix. A large number of iterations were necessary to converge on a solution in the work by Reddy et al. [20], which used FSDT and a formulation made in the cylindrical coordinate system. Given that the current model is of a higher order, a large number of iterations to converge is expected.

The tangent matrix T is defined by

$$T_{ij}^{\alpha\beta} = \frac{\partial R_i^{\alpha}}{\partial \Delta_j^{\beta}} \tag{33}$$

where Δ_j^{β} represents the generalized displacements. After some manipulations, the expression in terms of the stiffness matrix elements can be obtained:

$$T_{IJ} = K_{IJ} + \sum_{m=1}^{N} \frac{\partial K_{Im}}{\partial \Delta_J^{\beta}} \Delta_m^{\beta} \tag{34}$$

where K_{IJ} represents the stiffness matrix elements. Since the second term of Equation (34) requires the stiffness matrix elements to be functions of the generalized displacements in order to be nonzero, the only components of T that are different from K are shown in Appendix A.3.

The numerical values of the matrices K_{ij}, M_{ij}, and T_{ij} were obtained via Gauss-Legendre quadrature formulas, which are of the form

$$\int_{\Omega} F_{ij}(\xi, \eta) d\xi\eta \approx \sum_{I=1}^{M} \sum_{J=1}^{N} F_{IJ}(\xi, \eta) W_I W_J \tag{35}$$

where ξ and η are local normalized coordinates, W_I and W_J are Gauss weights, and F is a function, typically the stiffness matrix K, in terms of master element coordinates. The number of integration points was 2×2 for all nonlinear, couple stress, and transverse shear terms and 3×3 for all other terms in order to reduce shear-locking-like effects.

To accelerate the convergence of the iterative solver, acceleration parameters were implemented for static problems. This method uses a weighted average of the two previous solutions to obtain the solution increment instead of just using the last iteration's solution. This weighted average adopts the form

$$\hat{U} = \beta U^{r-2} + (1 - \beta) U^{r-1} \tag{36}$$

where β is the acceleration parameter, which must be a value from 0 to 1.

For the time approximation schemes, the Newmark constant average acceleration method was employed. Newmark's method consists of approximating the solution and its first and second derivatives based on their previous values. This is achieved by using the approximation

$$U_{s+1} = U_s + \Delta t \dot{u}_s + \frac{1}{2}(\Delta t)^2\left[(1-\gamma)\ddot{U}_{s+1}\right] \tag{37}$$

$$\dot{U}_{s+1} = \dot{U}_s + [\Delta t(1-\alpha)]\ddot{U}_s + \alpha\Delta t\ddot{U}_{s+1} \tag{38}$$

where α and γ are constants that depend on the method that is being implemented. For the constant-average acceleration method, the values are $\alpha = 0.5$ and $\gamma = 0.5$.

The constrained generalized displacements for clamped and simply supported boundary conditions used in this work are defined in Table 1. The clamped outer edge boundary condition constrains the displacements, rotations, and thickness-wise stretch along the outer edge of the plate, and in the case of an annular plate, it leaves the inner edge free. For the clamped inner edge, the displacements, rotations, and thickness-wise stretch along the inner edge are constrained, and the outer edge is free. For the simply supported boundary condition, the outer edge displacements are stretched and constrained, but the rotations are released. In the case of annular plates, the simply supported case leaves the inner edge free.

Table 1. Boundary condition definitions.

Boundary Condition	Edge Definition	Constrained Generalized Displacements						
Clamped outer edge	$r = a$	U_o	V_o	$W_o, \frac{\partial W_o}{\partial r}, \frac{\partial W_o}{\partial \theta}$	β_r	β_θ	$\beta_z, \frac{\partial \beta_z}{\partial r}, \frac{\partial \beta_z}{\partial \theta}$	$\phi_z, \frac{\partial \phi_z}{\partial r}, \frac{\partial \phi_z}{\partial \theta}$
Clamped inner edge (Only annular plates)	$r = b$	U_o	V_o	$W_o, \frac{\partial W_o}{\partial r}, \frac{\partial W_o}{\partial \theta}$	β_r	β_θ	$\beta_z, \frac{\partial \beta_z}{\partial r}, \frac{\partial \beta_z}{\partial \theta}$	$\phi_z, \frac{\partial \phi_z}{\partial r}, \frac{\partial \phi_z}{\partial \theta}$
Simply supported	$r = a$	U_o	V_o	W_o			β_z	ϕ_z

2.6. Steady State Heat Conduction

The steady-state heat conduction problem was solved using a 1D finite element model. The effective thermal conductivity, $k_{eff}(z,T)$, was obtained using the Maxwell-Eucken model, as presented by Deng et al. [61].

$$k_{eff}(z,T) = k_s(z,T)\left[\frac{k_f + 2k_s(z,T) + 2\Phi(z)(k_f - k_s(z,T))}{k_f + 2k_s(z,T) - \Phi(z)(k_f - k_s(z,T))}\right] \tag{39}$$

where $k_s(z,T)$ is the thermal conductivity of the solid, k_f is the thermal conductivity of the fluid, and Φ is the porosity. The thermal conductivity of the solid, $k_s(z,T)$, needs to be calculated using Equation (1). The finite element model approximation is

$$T \approx \sum_{i}^{N} T_i^e \psi_i \tag{40}$$

where T_i^e represents the nodal temperatures of the element, and ψ_i represents the quadratic Lagrange interpolation functions. Since thermal conductivity is considered a function of temperature, the Newton iteration method was used in order to model nonlinearity.

3. Model Validation

3.1. Static Load

The behavior of circular and annular plates under uniformly distributed mechanical loads was modeled using the first shear deformation theory by Reddy et al. [20]. The numerical results were compared with the current model. The following nondimensionalized parameters were used:

$$h = 0.1, \quad L = 10h, \quad \nu = 0.25, \quad E_c = 10^6, \quad E_m = 10^5.$$

Figure 4 shows a mesh convergence study. The center deflection at $z = 0$ associated with the load parameter is plotted.

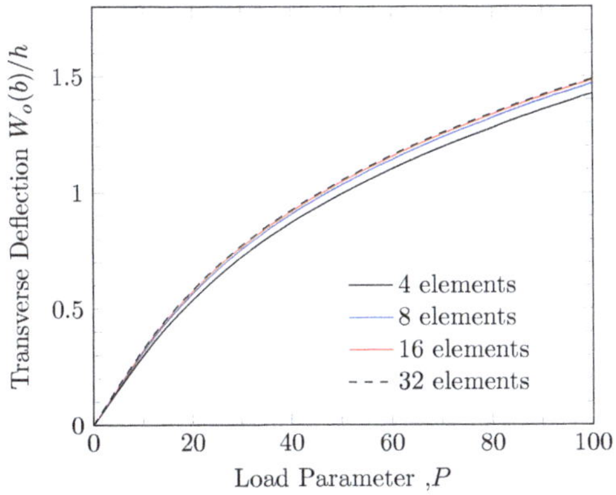

Figure 4. Mesh convergence study.

A 16 by 1 mesh was used to model the circular and annular plates with a clamped outer edge. For the maximum deflection at $z = 0$, W_o is plotted against the load parameter in Figure 5.

There is good agreement between the current model and the one developed by Reddy et al. [20], both with and without length scale parameters. Clear nonlinear behavior is observed. The effect of a higher power-law index is to soften the material since the behavior becomes dominated by the softer material with elastic modulus, E_m. Small discrepancies between the models can be attributed to the allowed change in thickness and the enforcement of zero traction at the upper and lower surfaces in the current model.

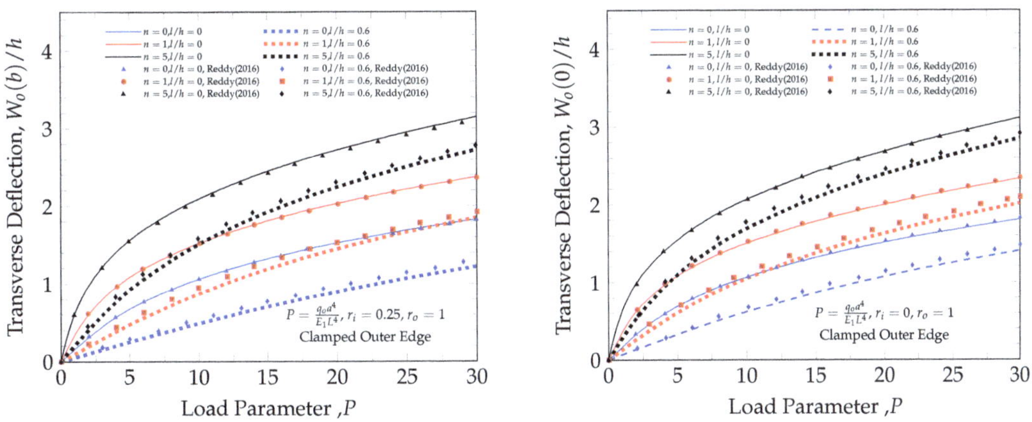

(**a**) (**b**)

Figure 5. Load deflection curves for clamped annular and circular plates. (**a**) Anular plate with clamped outer edge. (**b**) Circular plate with clamped outer edge.

3.2. Asymmetric Load

The analytical solution for a circular plate under asymmetrical loads, as shown in Figure 6, was obtained by Reddy [34] using the infinitesimal strain definition. To validate the asymmetric behavior of the model, different loads were applied to a circular plate. Figure 7a,b show deflection along the load symmetry line. The linear and nonlinear solutions from the current model and the analytical solution from Reddy [34] are shown in the same plot.

The linear solution agrees very well with the analytical solution; this is expected given the strain definition used by Reddy [34]. The clamped case does not show much nonlinearity, and the linear, nonlinear, and analytical solutions all give virtually the same results.

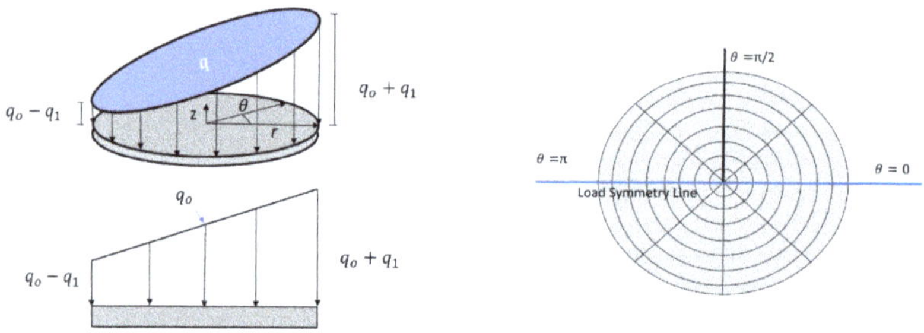

(a) (b)

Figure 6. Asymmetric load. (**a**) Asymmetric load form. (**b**) An 8 × 8 mesh.

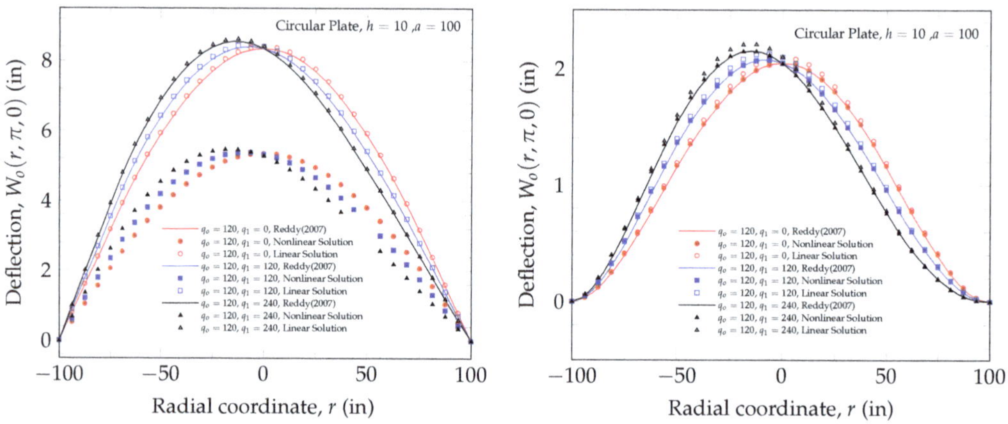

(a) (b)

Figure 7. Deflection along the symmetry line. (**a**) Simply supported. (**b**) Clamped.

3.3. Transient Response

The transient response of a circular plate clamped on the outer edge under a uniformly distributed load was analyzed by Reddy [62] using the first shear deformation theory (FSDT). The modeled plate has a radius of 100 in and a thickness of 2 in, and the numerical results for a uniformly distributed load of 1, 2, and 5 psi were obtained. A model verification study was conducted using the same geometry and loading cases as the current model. To ensure that the results are not mesh-dependent, a mesh convergence study was conducted using 6, 12, 24, 48, 96, and 192 elements in the radial direction and a single element in the angular direction, taking advantage of the polar coordinate formulation to establish symmetric boundary conditions.

Figure 8a shows that a mesh of 96 elements gives essentially the same results as a mesh of 192. The difference with respect to FSDT is less than 3% at the peaks for 96 elements. The small stiffening effect may be attributed to zero traction enforcement and the higher-order model.

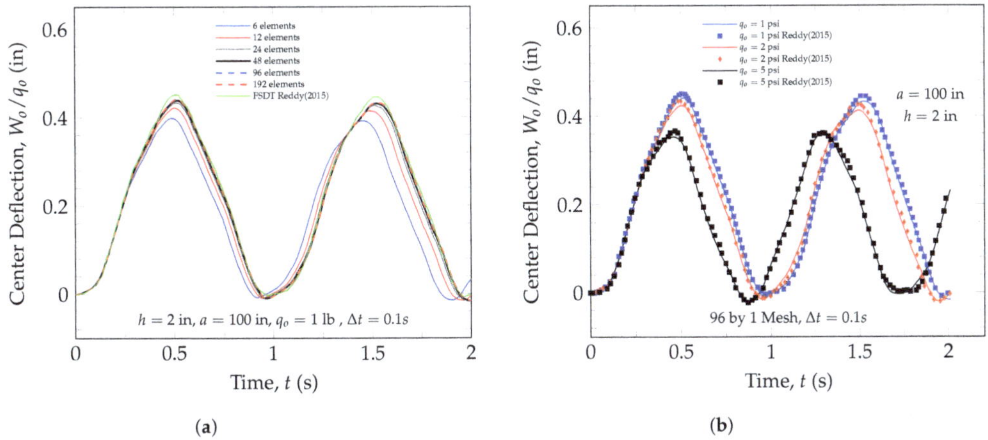

Figure 8. Transient response validation. (**a**) Mesh convergence study of transient response for circular plate clamped in the outer edge. (**b**) Transient response for three different uniformly distributed loads for a clamped circular plate.

The transient response with 96 elements shows a clear match between the behavior of the plate using the present model and the behavior of the FSDT plate modeled by Reddy [62], as shown in Figure 8b. The increase in the uniformly distributed load affects both the amplitude and the frequency of the response, having a slightly smaller amplitude and higher frequency for higher loads.

3.4. Temperature Distribution

The temperature distribution of a functionally graded porous material was reported by Yapor et al. [17]. The constituents of the plate were zirconia and Ti-6Al-4 V, and their properties were considered to be temperature-dependent, adopting the polynomial presented by Reddy et al. [30]

$$P(T) = P_0(1 + P_1T + P_2T^2 + P_3T^3) \tag{41}$$

Figure 9a shows the temperature distribution for the three porosity distributions considered and for no porosity. The plot shows remarkable agreement between the current model and the work of Yapor et al. [17]. The effect of different maximum porosity values with the symmetric porosity distribution (Type 1) is explored in Figure 9b, which also shows agreement between the models.

The small differences in the temperature distributions may be due to the use of different numbers of elements and element types since the current study used 100 linear elements, and the work carried out by Yapor et al. [17] used only 10 higher-order elements.

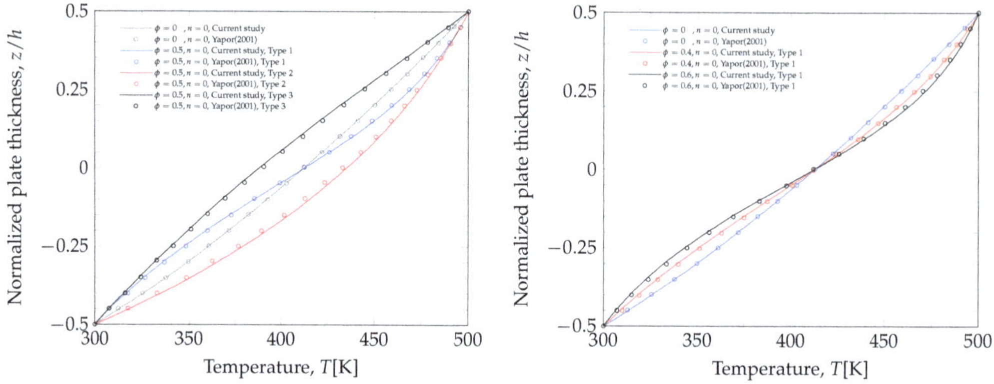

(a) (b)

Figure 9. Temperature distribution validation. (**a**) Temperature distribution for different porosity types. (**b**) Temperature distribution for Type 1 with different porosity values.

3.5. Thermo-Mechanical LOAD

The thermo-mechanical behavior of functionally graded plates was studied by Fallah et al. [48], and their results were validated against a previous study carried out by Ma et al. [33]. The same study was used to validate the work by Nosier et al. [47].

The materials chosen for this study were aluminum and zirconia, with the following material properties:

$$E_m = 151 \text{ GPa}, \quad E_c = 70 \text{ GPa}, \quad \nu = 0.3, \quad K_m = 204 \text{ W/mk}, \tag{42}$$

$$K_c = 2.09 \text{ W/mk}, \quad \alpha_m = 23 \times 10^6 \frac{1}{^\circ\text{C}}, \quad \alpha_c = 10 \times 10^6 \frac{1}{^\circ\text{C}} \tag{43}$$

The mechanical load applied varied for different values of the load parameter, Q, from 0 to 300. The load parameter Q is defined as

$$Q = \frac{qb^4}{D_c H}$$

where q is the mechanical, uniformly distributed load, b is the radius of the plate, D_c is plate stiffness, and H is the thickness of the plate.

Thermal load was applied by holding the top and bottom surfaces at constant temperatures so that $T_m = 15T_c$. The thermal and mechanical loads were applied gradually at the same time, as opposed to first applying the thermal load and then the mechanical load.

A mesh convergence test was conducted to ensure the results were not mesh-dependent. The displacement solutions were obtained using different numbers of elements. A 16×1 element mesh is enough for axisymmetric cases since a 32×1 version shows no significant improvement in the solution.

It was noted by Ma et al. [33] that pure thermal loading does not produce displacements in the case of clamped circular plates in a model, but it does produce displacements for simply supported plates. The current model predicts a very small displacement for pure thermal loading due to the allowed change in thickness, which the work by Ma [33] did not consider.

Good agreement between the models can be appreciated in Figure 10a. Slightly stiffer behavior by the current model may be explained by the higher-order model used, allowing for displacement along the thickness direction. As shown in the previous section, a higher power-law index corresponds to softer behavior, as the material properties become dominated by the metallic material.

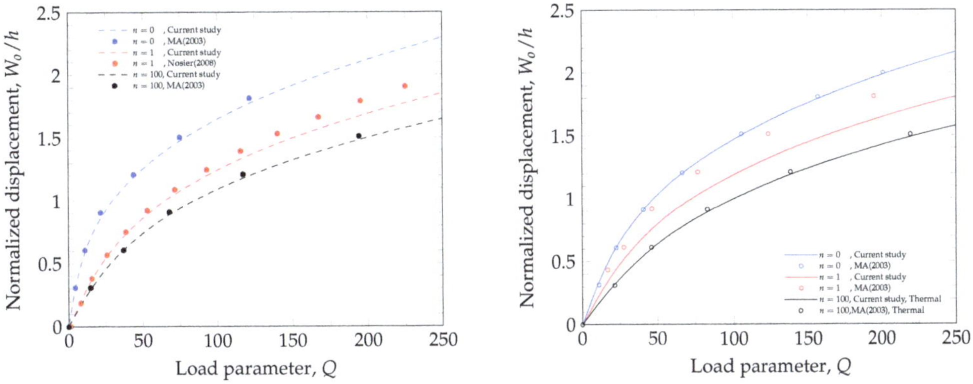

(a) (b)

Figure 10. Thermo-mechanical validation on circular clamped plates. (**a**) Thermo-mechanical load deflection curves. (**b**) Mechanical load deflection curves.

4. Numerical Examples

4.1. Dynamic Response

Dynamic response was studied using a thin plate of 100 inches in radius and 2 inches in thickness. The load applied was a uniformly distributed load of 1 psi, and no dampening was considered. Simply supported and clamped at the outer edge boundary conditions were used. The selected materials were zirconia and Ti-6Al-4V, the properties of which are shown in Tables 2 and 3. A time step of 0.2 s and the constant-average acceleration method time scheme were used.

Table 2. Temperature-dependent properties of zirconia.

Zirconia	P_0	$P_1 \times 10^4$	$P_2 \times 10^8$	$P_3 \times 10^{10}$
Density, ρ (kg/m^3)	5700	0	0	0
Thermal conductivity, k (W/m K)	1.7	1.276	0.6485	0
Coefficient of thermal expansion, α (K)	12.7657×10^{-6}	−14.4	0.0001	−0.0678
Poison's ratio, ν	0.2882	1.1335	0	0
Specific heat, C_v (J/kg K)	487.3428	3.0491	−6.0372	0
Young's Modulus, E (Pa)	244.266×10^9	−13.707	121.393	−3.6814

Table 3. Temperature-dependent properties of Ti-6Al-4V.

Ti-6Al-4V	P_0	$P_1 \times 10^4$	$P_2 \times 10^8$	$P_3 \times 10^{10}$
Density, ρ (kg/m^3)	4429	0	0	0
Thermal conductivity, k (W/m K)	1.2095	139.375	0	0
Coefficient of thermal expansion, α (K)	7.5788×10^{-6}	6.5	31.467	0
Poison's ratio, ν	0.2884	1.1214	0	0
Specific heat, C_v (J/kg K)	625.2969	−4.2239	71.7865	0
Young's Modulus, E (Pa)	122.5568×10^9	−4.5864	0	−3.6814

Figure 11a shows the expected behavior of a plate with and without length scale parameters. The effect of including the length scale parameter of the couple stress theory is to reduce amplitude and increase frequency across all power-law index numbers. The stiffening effect in micro-scale structures is clearly captured when utilizing the length scale parameter. The purely metallic plate at $n = 0$ is the soft material configuration, and it shows a higher amplitude and lower frequency than the mostly ceramic plate at $n = 100$, which is mostly the stiffer material. The linearly varying material properties at $n = 1$ represent a mixture of soft and stiff materials, showing behavior that is in between the previous two.

When comparing Figure 11a and Figure 11b, it can be observed that boundary conditions play a big role in frequency and amplitude. The simply supported plate, which has a softer boundary condition than the clamped plate, shows a larger frequency than the case with the clamped boundary condition and a much larger amplitude. The trends regarding the index number and length scale parameters are similar in both cases. However, the clamped plates are more sensitive to material variations and the length scale parameters.

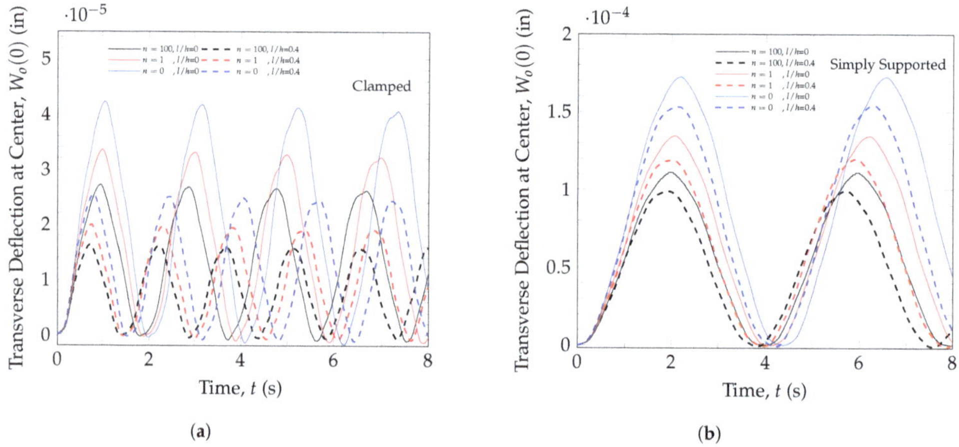

Figure 11. Dynamic response for different material index numbers. (**a**) Clamped circular plate. (**b**) Simply supported circular plate.

4.2. Static Response Under Symmetric Thermo-Mechanical Loads

For the static behavior under symmetric thermo-mechanical loads, a geometry of $a = 1$ m, $b = 0.25$ m, and $h = 0.1$ m was used with the same FGM used in the dynamic study. The parameters a, b, and h are shown in Figure 12. The mechanical load was varied up to a load parameter of 30, as defined by Reddy et al. [20]. The thermal load was applied by holding the metallic surface at 300 degrees and the ceramic surface at 400 degrees. Cases of purely mechanical and thermo-mechanical loads were analyzed.

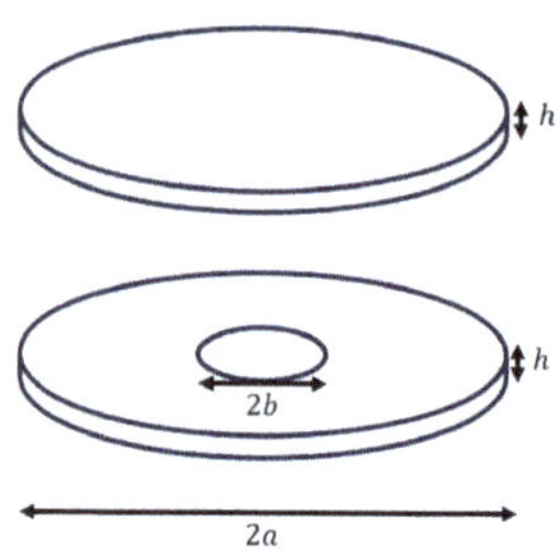

Figure 12. Circular and annular plates.

The impact of thermal load on deflection diminishes as the load parameter increases, as shown in Figure 13a,b, where the thermo-mechanical case gives a very similar result to the purely mechanical load at load parameter 30; however, the curvature is higher in the thermo-mechanical case, and its effect is more noticeable at lower load parameter values. It can also be noted that the length scale parameters have a strong stiffening effect on both purely mechanical and thermo-mechanical cases. In the case of the thermo-mechanical load, the thermal load makes the plates stiffer, with compressive thermal stresses. This stiffening also noticeably reduces the nonlinear behavior of the plate. The stresses generated by the thermo-mechanical load close to the clamped edge of an annular plate clamped on the outer edge are shown in Figure 14a,b. The effect of the length scale parameter clearly results in a reduction in stress for all cases. Unlike homogeneous materials, the bending stress distribution of FGMs is not a linear variation. This shows that we can design the stress variation in FGM by controlling material variation.

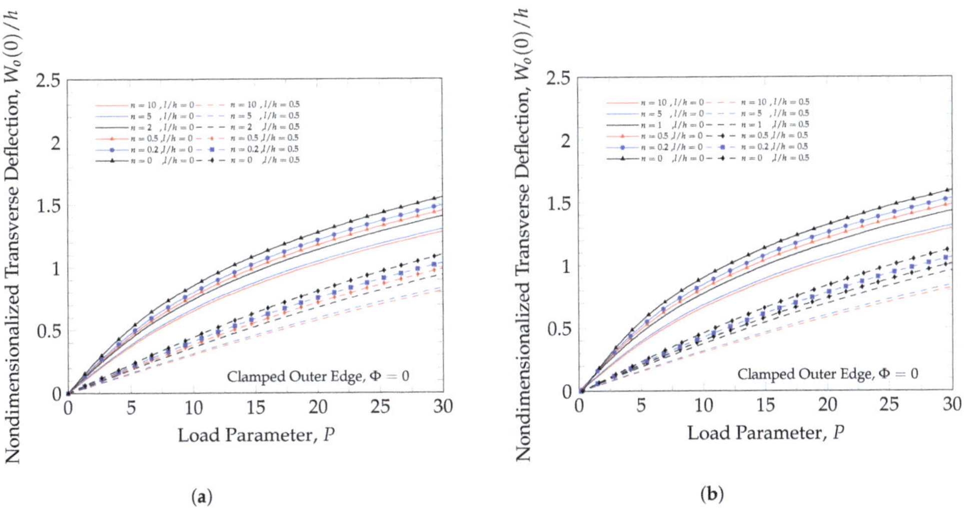

Figure 13. Annular plate static response. (**a**) Mechanical load. (**b**) Thermo-mechanical load.

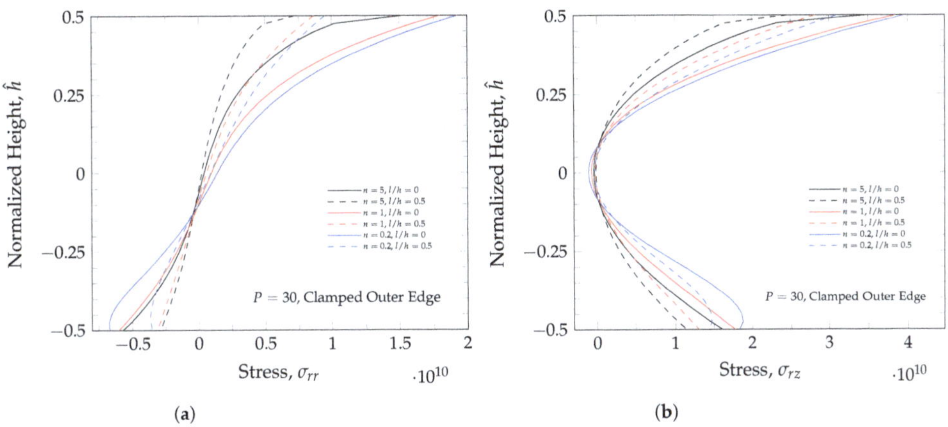

Figure 14. Stresses for clamped circular plate under static thermo-mechanical load. (**a**) Radial stress. (**b**) Transverse shear stress.

4.3. Static Response Under Asymmetric Loads

Asymmetric cases were solved to assess the model's full plate-modeling capabilities using the same geometry and loads as the asymmetric model verification cases, as well as the same FGM used in the other parametric study cases. Figure 15b shows the elastic curve for the same three FG plates under the same symmetric load and under two different asymmetric loads. The observed behavior corresponds with what was expected and the previous results. The stiffest behavior corresponds with the mostly ceramic plate, and the softest behavior is shown by the metallic plate, and the linear distribution ($n = 1$) shows intermediate behavior. The different asymmetric loads change the magnitude of the maximum deflection of the plate but do not affect the deflection at the center, $W(0)$.

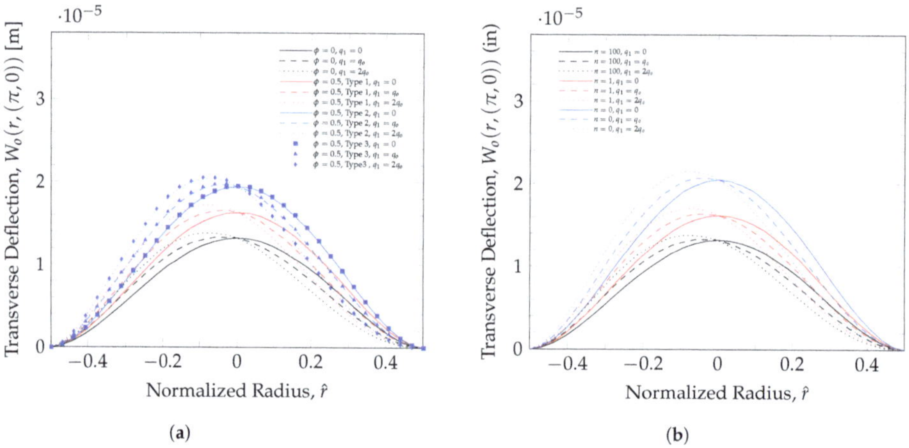

Figure 15. Behavior at symmetry line for clamped circular plate. (**a**) Porosity effect under asymmetric loads. (**b**) Power-law index effect under asymmetric loads

The porosity effect on full-plate behavior was explored using the three different porosity types and a maximum porosity of 0.5. Figure 15a shows the effect of the three different porosity distributions and compares this to the solid plate for a mostly ceramic plate ($n = 100$). The stiffest plate is the solid plate. Porosity distribution Type 1 is much stiffer than the Type 2 and 3 porosity distributions, as expected. In the considered examples, the Type 2 and Type 3 porosity distributions are symmetric to each other about the middle plane of plates, and the plate bending stiffness of homogeneous materials with these two porosity distributions are the same. As expected, the differences between porosity Types 2 and 3 are negligible. Therefore, distribution Type 3 can be omitted in the case of homogenous materials without loss of information.

5. Conclusions

A nonlinear finite element model for functionally graded porous micro-plates was developed for circular and annular micro-plates in cylindrical coordinates. In order to obtain a quadratic variation of transverse shear strains, the displacement field was expanded in the transverse direction with second-order transverse displacement and third-order in-plane displacements. Von Kármán strains were used to enable the model to capture moderate rotations. To account for length scale effects, the modified couple stress theory was implemented. The variation in material properties via the thickness of the plate was modeled using a power-law volumetric distribution. Three different porosity distributions were prescribed for the material.

The equations of motion for the proposed model were obtained using the principle of virtual displacements. The finite element model was obtained using a conforming four-node plate element with 112 degrees of freedom. The tangent matrix was derived to implement the Newton iteration method. Gauss-Legendre quadrature was utilized to numerically integrate the element matrices.

The model was validated against analytical solutions and numerical studies from the literature. The static response under a uniformly distributed load with and without length scale parameters was validated for various power-law index numbers. The temperature distribution matched the results available in the literature. Static response under an asymmetric load, dynamic response, and thermo-mechanical behavior all showed good agreement with the analytical solutions and available literature.

The numerical results for annular and circular plates under different loads and boundary conditions are presented; a parametric study was conducted. The study shows the following:

- A stiffening effect of the length scale parameter in the modified couple stress theory was observed for all boundary conditions and loads;
- Boundary conditions play an important role in the nonlinear behavior of the plate;
- The variation in the power-law index makes the plate softer or stiffer as it transitions from metallic- to ceramic-dominated properties;
- The model is able to capture nonlinear behavior and material variations in plate thickness. The proposed model was validated against other models in the literature, and it could be useful to study cases where these effects are expected to be significant;
- The proposed model has been found to be computationally expensive. This was expected due to the higher-order terms, and it is in line with the observations made by Reddy et al. [20] for their model, which also operates in cylindrical coordinates.

Author Contributions: Conceptualization, J.K.; Methodology, J.K.; Software, E.N.; Validation, J.K. and E.N.; Formal analysis, E.N.; Investigation, E.N.; Resources, J.K.; Writing—original draft, E.N.; Writing—review & editing, J.K.; Visualization, E.N.; Supervision, J.K. All authors have read and agreed to the published version of the manuscript.

Funding: This research received no external funding.

Data Availability Statement: The original contributions presented in this study are included in the article. Further inquiries can be directed to the corresponding author.

Conflicts of Interest: The authors declare no conflicts of interest.

Appendix A

Appendix A.1. Stiffness Matrix Elements

$$
\begin{aligned}
K_{11} = \int_{\Omega} \Bigg\{ & \frac{\partial \psi_i^1}{\partial r} \left[A_{11}^0 \frac{\partial \psi_j^1}{\partial r} + A_{12}^0 \frac{1}{r} \psi_j^1 \right] + \frac{1}{r} \psi_i^1 \left[A_{21}^0 \frac{\partial \psi_j^1}{\partial r} + A_{22}^0 \frac{1}{r} \psi_j^1 \right] + \frac{1}{r^2} A_{44}^0 \frac{\partial \psi_i^1}{\partial \theta} \frac{\partial \psi_j^1}{\partial \theta} \\
& - \frac{1}{16 r^4} T_{55}^0 \frac{\partial^2 \psi_i^1}{\partial \theta^2} \frac{\partial^2 \psi_j^1}{\partial \theta^2} + \left(\frac{1}{4r^2} \frac{\partial \psi_i^1}{\partial \theta} - \frac{1}{4r} \frac{\partial^2 \psi_i^1}{\partial \theta \partial r} \right) \left[T_{66}^0 \left(-\frac{1}{4r} \frac{\partial^2 \psi_j^1}{\partial \theta \partial r} + \frac{1}{4r^2} \frac{\partial \psi_j^1}{\partial \theta} \right) \right] \Bigg\} r dr d\theta
\end{aligned}
\tag{A1}
$$

$$K_{12} = \int_\Omega \left\{ A_{12}^0 \frac{1}{r} \frac{\partial \psi_i^1}{\partial r} \frac{\partial \psi_j^2}{\partial \theta} + A_{22}^0 \frac{1}{r^2} \psi_i^1 \frac{\partial \psi_j^2}{\partial \theta} + \frac{1}{r} \frac{\partial \psi_i^1}{\partial \theta} \left[A_{44}^0 \left(\frac{\partial \psi_j^1}{\partial r} - \frac{\psi_j^2}{r} \right) \right] \right.$$
$$- \frac{1}{4r^2} \frac{d^2 \psi_i^1}{\partial \theta^2} \left[T_{55}^0 \left(\frac{1}{4r^2} \frac{\partial \psi_j^2}{\partial \theta} + \frac{1}{4r} \frac{\partial^2 \psi_j^2}{\partial r \partial \theta} \right) \right]$$
$$\left. + \left(\frac{1}{4r^2} \frac{\partial \psi_i^1}{\partial \theta} - \frac{1}{4r} \frac{\partial^2 \psi_i^1}{\partial \theta \partial r} \right) \left[T_{66}^0 \left(\frac{1}{4r} \frac{\partial \psi_j^2}{\partial r} - \frac{1}{4r^2} \psi_j^2 + \frac{1}{4} \frac{\partial^2 \psi_j^2}{\partial r^2} \right) \right] \right\} r dr d\theta \tag{A2}$$

$$K_{13} = \int_\Omega \left\{ \frac{\partial \psi_i^1}{\partial r} \left[A_{11}^0 \frac{1}{2} \frac{\partial W_o}{\partial r} \frac{\partial \psi_j^3}{\partial r} + A_{12}^0 \frac{1}{2r} \frac{\partial W_o}{\partial \theta} \frac{\partial \psi_j^3}{\partial \theta} - A_{11}^3 \frac{4}{3h^2} \frac{\partial^2 \psi_j^3}{\partial r^2} - A_{12}^3 \frac{4}{3h^2 r^2} \frac{\partial^2 \psi_j^3}{\partial \theta^2} \right. \right.$$
$$\left. - A_{12}^3 \frac{4}{3h^2 r} \frac{\partial \psi_j^3}{\partial r} \right] + \frac{1}{r} \psi_i^1 \left[A_{21}^0 \frac{1}{2} \frac{\partial W_o}{\partial r} \frac{\partial \psi_j^3}{\partial r} + A_{22}^0 \frac{1}{2r^2} \frac{\partial W_o}{\partial \theta} \frac{\partial \psi_j^3}{\partial \theta} - A_{21}^3 \frac{4}{3h^2} \frac{\partial^2 Wo}{\partial r^2} \right.$$
$$\left. - A_{22}^3 \frac{4}{3r^2 h^2} \frac{\partial^2 \psi_j^3}{\partial \theta^2} - A_{22}^3 \frac{4}{3rh^2} \frac{\partial \psi_j^3}{\partial r} \right] + \frac{1}{r} \frac{\partial \psi_i^1}{\partial \theta} \left[A_{44}^0 \frac{1}{r} \frac{\partial \psi_j^3}{\partial \theta} \frac{\partial \psi_j^3}{\partial r} - A_{44}^3 \frac{8}{3h^2} \frac{\partial^2 \psi_j^3}{\partial \theta \partial r} \right]$$
$$\left. + T_{55}^1 \frac{2}{4r^2 h^2} \frac{\partial \psi_i^1}{\partial \theta^2} \frac{\partial \psi_j^3}{\partial r} + \left(\frac{1}{4r^2} \frac{\partial \psi_i^1}{\partial \theta} - \frac{1}{4r} \frac{\partial^2 \psi_i^1}{\partial \theta \partial r} \right) T_{66}^1 \frac{2}{h^2} \frac{\partial \psi_j^3}{\partial \theta} + A_{44}^3 \frac{8}{3h^2 r^3} \frac{\partial \psi_i^1}{\partial \theta} \frac{\partial \psi_j^3}{\partial \theta} \right\} r dr d\theta \tag{A3}$$

$$K_{14} = \int_\Omega \left\{ \frac{\partial \psi_i^1}{\partial r} \left[A_{11}^1 \frac{\partial \psi_j^4}{\partial r} + \frac{1}{r} A_{12}^1 \psi_j^4 - \frac{4}{3h^2} A_{11}^3 \frac{\partial \psi_j^4}{\partial r} - \frac{4}{3rh^2} A_{12}^3 \psi_j^4 \right] + \frac{1}{r} \psi_i^1 \left[A_{21}^1 \frac{\partial \psi_j^4}{\partial r} + A_{22}^1 \frac{1}{r} \psi_j^4 \right. \right.$$
$$\left. - A_{21}^3 \frac{4}{3h^2} \frac{\partial \psi_j^4}{\partial r} - A_{22}^3 \frac{4}{3rh^2} \psi_j^4 \right] + \frac{1}{r} \frac{\partial \psi_i^1}{\partial \theta} \left[A_{44}^1 \frac{1}{r} \frac{\partial \psi_j^4}{\partial \theta} - A_{44}^3 \frac{4}{3h^2 r} \frac{\partial \psi_j^4}{\partial \theta} \right]$$
$$+ \frac{1}{4r^2} \frac{\partial \psi_i^1}{\partial \theta^2} \left[T_{55}^1 \frac{2}{4h^2 r^2} \frac{\partial^2 \psi_j^4}{\partial \theta^2} \psi_j^4 - T_{55}^3 \frac{1}{3h^2 r^2} \frac{\partial^2 \psi_j^4}{\partial \theta^2} \right]$$
$$+ \left(\frac{1}{4r^2} \frac{\partial \psi_i^1}{\partial \theta} - \frac{1}{4r} \frac{\partial^2 \psi_i^1}{\partial \theta \partial r} \right) \left[T_{66}^1 \left(-\frac{1}{4r} \frac{\partial^2 \psi_j^4}{\partial \theta \partial r} + \frac{1}{4r^2} \frac{\partial \psi_j^4}{\partial \theta} \right) \right.$$
$$\left. \left. + T_{66}^3 \left(-\frac{1}{3h^2 r} \frac{\partial^2 \psi_j^4}{\partial \theta \partial r} + \frac{1}{3h^2 r^2} \frac{\partial \psi_j^4}{\partial \theta} \right) \right] \right\} r dr d\theta \tag{A4}$$

$$K_{15} = \int_\Omega \left\{ \frac{\partial \psi_i^1}{\partial r} \left[A_{12}^1 \frac{1}{r} \frac{\partial \psi_j^5}{\partial \theta} - \frac{4}{3rh^2} A_{12}^3 \frac{\partial \psi_j^5}{\partial \theta} \right] + \frac{1}{r} \psi_i^1 \left[A_{22}^1 \frac{1}{r} \frac{\partial \psi_j^5}{\partial \theta} - A_{22}^3 \frac{4}{3h^2 r} \frac{\partial \psi_j^5}{\partial \theta} \right] \right.$$
$$+ \frac{1}{r} \frac{\partial \psi_i^1}{\partial \theta} \left[A_{44}^1 \left(\frac{\partial \psi_j^5}{\partial r} - \frac{1}{r} \psi_j^5 \right) - A_{44}^3 \left(\frac{4}{3h^2} \frac{\partial \psi_j^5}{\partial r} + \frac{4}{3h^2 r} \psi_j^5 \right) \right]$$
$$- \frac{1}{4r^2} \frac{\partial^2 \delta Uo}{\partial \theta^2} \left[T_{55}^1 \left(\frac{1}{4r^2} \frac{\partial \psi_j^5}{\partial \theta} + \frac{1}{4r} \frac{\partial^2 \psi_j^5}{\partial r \partial \theta} \right) - T_{55}^3 \left(\frac{1}{3h^2 r^2} \frac{\partial \psi_j^5}{\partial \theta} + \frac{1}{3h^2 r} \frac{\partial^2 \psi_j^5}{\partial r \partial \theta} \right) \right]$$
$$+ \left(\frac{1}{4r^2} \frac{\partial \psi_i^1}{\partial \theta} - \frac{1}{4r} \frac{\partial^2 \psi_i^1}{\partial \theta \partial r} \right) \left[T_{66}^1 \left(\frac{1}{4r} \frac{\partial \psi_j^5}{\partial r} - \frac{1}{4r^2} \psi_j^5 + \frac{1}{4} \frac{\partial^2 \psi_j^5}{\partial r^2} + \frac{2}{h^2} \psi_j^5 \right) \right.$$
$$\left. \left. + T_{66}^3 \left(-\frac{1}{3h^2 r} \frac{\partial \psi_j^5}{\partial r} + \frac{1}{3h^2 r^2} \psi_j^5 - \frac{1}{3h^2} \frac{\partial^2 \psi_j^5}{\partial r^2} \right) \right] \right\} r dr d\theta \tag{A5}$$

$$K_{16}=\int_{\Omega}\left\{\frac{\partial\psi_i^1}{\partial r}\left[A_{13}^0\psi_j^6-A_{11}^2\frac{1}{2}\frac{\partial^2\psi_j^6}{\partial r^2}-A_{12}^2\left(\frac{1}{2r}\frac{\partial\psi_j^6}{\partial r}+\frac{1}{2r^2}\frac{\partial^2\psi_j^6}{\partial\theta^2}\right)\right]+\frac{1}{r}\psi_i^1\left[A_{23}^0\psi_j^6\right.\right.$$
$$\left.-A_{21}^2\frac{1}{2}\frac{\partial^2\psi_j^6}{\partial r^2}-A_{22}^2\left(\frac{1}{2r}\frac{\partial\psi_j^6}{\partial r}+\frac{1}{2r^2}\frac{\partial^2\psi_j^6}{d\theta^2}\right)\right]-\frac{1}{r}\frac{\partial\psi_i^1}{\partial\theta}\left[A_{44}^2\left(-\frac{1}{r}\frac{\partial^2\psi_j^6}{\partial\theta\partial r}+\frac{1}{r^2}\frac{\partial\psi_j^6}{\partial\theta}\right)\right]$$
$$\left.+T_{55}^0\frac{1}{8r^2}\frac{\partial^2\psi_i^1}{\partial\theta^2}\frac{\partial\beta}{\partial r}+\left(\frac{1}{4r^2}\frac{\partial\psi_i^1}{\partial\theta}-\frac{1}{4r}\frac{\partial\psi_i^1}{\partial\theta\partial r}\right)T_{66}^0\frac{1}{2r}\frac{\partial\psi_j^6}{\partial\theta}\right\}rdrd\theta \tag{A6}$$

$$K_{17}=\int_{\Omega}\left\{\frac{\partial\psi_i^1}{\partial r}\left[A_{13}^1 2\psi_j^7-A_{11}^3\frac{1}{3}\frac{\partial^2\psi_j^7}{\partial r^2}-A_{12}^3\frac{1}{3r}\frac{\partial\psi_j^7}{\partial r}-A_{12}^3\frac{1}{3r^2}\frac{\partial^2\psi_j^7}{\partial\theta^2}\right]+\frac{1}{r}\psi_i^1\left[A_{23}^1 2\psi_j^7-A_{21}^3\frac{1}{3}\frac{\partial^2\psi_j^7}{\partial r^2}\right.\right.$$
$$\left.-A_{22}^3\frac{1}{3r^2}\frac{\partial^2\psi_j^7}{\partial\theta^2}-A_{22}^3\frac{1}{3}\frac{\partial\psi_j^7}{\partial r}\right]-A_{44}^3\frac{2}{3r}\frac{\partial\psi_i^1}{\partial\theta}\frac{\partial^2\psi_j^7}{\partial\theta\partial r}+T_{55}^1\frac{3}{8r^2}\frac{\partial^2\psi_i^1}{\partial\theta}\frac{\partial\psi_j^7}{\partial r}$$
$$\left.+\left(\frac{1}{4r^2}\frac{\partial\psi_i^1}{\partial\theta}-\frac{1}{4r}\frac{\partial^2\psi_i^1}{\partial\theta\partial r}\right)T_{66}^1\frac{1}{r}\frac{\partial\psi_j^7}{\partial\theta}+A_{44}^3\frac{2}{3r^3}\frac{\partial\psi_i^1}{\partial\theta}\frac{\partial\psi_j^7}{\partial\theta}\right\}rdrd\theta \tag{A7}$$

$$K_{21}=\int_{\Omega}\left\{\frac{1}{r}\frac{\partial\psi_i^2}{\partial\theta}\left[A_{21}^0\frac{\partial\psi_j^1}{\partial r}+A_{22}^0\frac{1}{r}\psi_j^1\right]+\left(\frac{\partial\psi_i^2}{\partial r}-\frac{1}{r}\psi_i^2\right)A_{44}^0\frac{1}{r}\frac{\partial\psi_j^1}{\partial\theta}+\left(\frac{1}{4r^2}\frac{\partial\psi_i^2}{\partial\theta}\right.\right.$$
$$\left.+\frac{1}{4r}\frac{\partial^2\psi_i^2}{\partial r\partial\theta}\right)\left[-T_{56}^0\frac{1}{4r^2}\frac{\partial^2\psi_j^1}{\partial\theta^2}\right]+\left(\frac{1}{4r}\frac{\partial\psi_i^2}{\partial r}-\frac{1}{4r^2}\psi_i^2+\frac{1}{4}\frac{\partial^2\psi_i^1}{\partial r^2}\right)\left[T_{66}^0\left(\frac{-1}{4r}\frac{\partial^2\psi_j^1}{\partial\theta\partial r}\right.\right.$$
$$\left.\left.\left.+\frac{1}{4r^2}\frac{\partial\psi_j^1}{\partial\theta}\right)\right]\right\}rdrd\theta \tag{A8}$$

$$K_{22}=\int_{\Omega}\left\{A_{22}^0\frac{1}{r^2}\frac{\partial\psi_i^2}{\partial\theta}\frac{\partial\psi_j^2}{\partial\theta}+\left(\frac{\partial\psi_i^2}{\partial r}-\frac{1}{r}\psi_i^2\right)\left[A_{44}^0\left(\frac{\partial\psi_j^2}{\partial r}-\frac{\psi_j^2}{r}\right)\right]+\left(\frac{1}{4r^2}\frac{\partial\psi_j^2}{\partial\theta}\right.\right.$$
$$\left.+\frac{1}{4r}\frac{\partial^2\psi_i^2}{\partial r\partial\theta}\right)\left[T_{55}^0\left(\frac{1}{4r^2}\frac{\partial\psi_j^2}{\partial\theta}+\frac{1}{4r}\frac{\partial^2\psi_j^2}{\partial r\partial\theta}\right)\right]+\left(\frac{1}{4r}\frac{\partial\psi_i^2}{\partial r}-\frac{1}{4r^2}\psi_i^2+\frac{1}{4}\frac{\partial^2\psi_i^2}{\partial r^2}\right)\left[T_{66}^0\left(\frac{1}{4r}\frac{\partial\psi_j^2}{\partial r}\right.\right.$$
$$\left.\left.\left.-\frac{1}{4r^2}\psi_j^2+\frac{1}{4}\frac{\partial^2\psi_j^2}{\partial r-2}\right)\right]\right\}rdrd\theta \tag{A9}$$

$$K_{23}=\int_{\Omega}\left\{\frac{1}{r}\frac{\partial\psi_i^2}{\partial\theta}\left[A_{21}^0\frac{1}{2}\frac{\partial W_o}{\partial r}\frac{\partial\psi_j^3}{\partial r}+A_{22}^0\frac{1}{2r^2}\frac{\partial W_o}{\partial\theta}\frac{\partial\psi_j^3}{\partial\theta}-A_{21}^3\frac{4}{3h^2}\frac{\partial^2\psi_j^3}{\partial r^2}-A_{22}^3\frac{4}{3r^2h^2}\frac{\partial^2\psi_j^3}{\partial r^2}-A_{22}^3\frac{4}{3rh^2}\frac{\partial\psi_j^3}{\partial r}\right]\right.$$
$$+\left(\frac{\partial\psi_i^2}{\partial r}-\frac{1}{r}\psi_i^2\right)\left[A_{44}^0\frac{1}{2r}\frac{\partial W_o}{\partial r}\frac{\partial\psi_j^3}{\partial\theta}+\frac{1}{2}\frac{\partial W_o}{\partial\theta}\frac{\partial\psi_j^3}{\partial r}-A_{44}^3\frac{8}{3h^2}\frac{\partial^2\psi_j^3}{\partial\theta\partial r}\right]$$
$$-\left(\frac{1}{4r^2}\frac{\partial\psi_i^2}{\partial\theta}+\frac{1}{4r}\frac{\partial^2\psi_i^2}{\partial\theta\partial r}\right)T_{55}^1\frac{2}{h^2}\frac{\partial\psi_j^3}{\partial r}+\left(\frac{1}{4r}\frac{\partial\psi_i^2}{\partial r}-\frac{1}{4r^2}\psi_i^2\right.$$
$$\left.\left.+\frac{1}{4}\frac{\partial^2\psi_i^2}{\partial r^2}\right)T_{66}^1\frac{2}{h^2}\frac{\partial\psi_j^3}{\partial\theta}+\left(\frac{\partial\psi_i^2}{\partial r}-\frac{1}{r}\psi_i^2\right)\left[A_{44}^3\frac{8}{3h^2r^2}\frac{\partial\psi_j^3}{\partial\theta}\right]\right\}rdrd\theta \tag{A10}$$

$$K_{24} = \int_{\Omega}\left\{\frac{1}{r}\frac{\partial\psi_i^2}{\partial\theta}\left[A_{21}^1\frac{\partial\psi_j^4}{\partial r} + A_{22}^1\frac{1}{r}\psi_j^4 - A_{21}^3\frac{4}{3h^2}\frac{\partial\psi_j^4}{\partial r} - A_{22}^3\frac{4}{3rh^2}\psi_j^4\right] + \left(\frac{\partial\psi_i^2}{\partial r} - \frac{1}{r}\psi_i^2\right)\left[A_{44}^1\frac{1}{r}\frac{\partial\psi_j^4}{\partial\theta}\right.\right.$$
$$\left. - A_{44}^3\frac{4}{3h^2r}\frac{\partial\psi_j^4}{\partial\theta}\right] + \left(\frac{1}{4r^2}\frac{\partial\psi_i^2}{\partial\theta} + \frac{1}{4r}\frac{\partial^2\psi_i^2}{\partial\theta\partial r}\right)\left[T_{55}^1\left(-\frac{1}{4r^2}\frac{\partial^2\psi_j^4}{\partial\theta^2} - \frac{2}{h^2}\psi_j^4\right) + T_{55}^3\frac{1}{3h^2r^2}\frac{\partial^2\psi_j^4}{\partial\theta^2}\right]$$
$$+ \left(\frac{1}{4r}\frac{\partial\psi_i^2}{\partial r} - \frac{1}{4r^2}\psi_i^2 + \frac{1}{4}\frac{\partial^2\psi_i^2}{\partial r^2}\right)\left[T_{66}^1\left(\frac{-1}{4r}\frac{\partial^2\psi_j^4}{\partial\theta\theta r} + \frac{1}{4r^2}\frac{\partial\psi_j^4}{\partial\theta}\right)\right.$$
$$\left.\left. + T_{66}^3\left(\frac{-1}{3h^2r}\frac{\partial^2\psi_j^4}{\partial\theta\partial r} + \frac{1}{3h^2r^2}\frac{\partial\psi_j^4}{\partial\theta}\right)\right]\right\} r dr d\theta \quad \text{(A11)}$$

$$K_{25} = \int_{\Omega}\left\{\frac{1}{r}\frac{\partial\psi_i^2}{\partial\theta}\left[A_{22}^1\frac{1}{r}\frac{\partial\psi_j^5}{\partial\theta} + A_{22}^3\frac{(-4)}{3h^2r}\frac{\partial\psi_j^5}{\partial\theta}\right] + \left(\frac{\partial\psi_i^2}{dr} - \frac{1}{r}\psi_i^2\right)\left[A_{44}^1\left(\frac{\partial\psi_j^5}{\partial r} - \frac{1}{r}\psi_j^5\right)\right.\right.$$
$$\left. - A_{44}^3\left(\frac{4}{3h^2}\frac{\partial\psi_j^5}{\partial r} + \frac{4}{3h^2r}\psi_j^5\right)\right] + \left(\frac{1}{4r^2}\frac{\partial\psi_i^2}{\partial\theta} + \frac{1}{4r}\frac{\partial^2\psi_i^2}{\partial\theta\partial r}\right)\left[T_{55}^1\left(\frac{1}{4r^2}\frac{\partial\psi_j^5}{\partial\theta} + \frac{1}{4r}\frac{\partial^2\psi_j^5}{\partial r d\theta}\right)\right.$$
$$\left. - T_{55}^3\left(\frac{1}{3h^2r^2}\frac{\partial\psi_j^5}{\partial\theta} + \frac{1}{3h^2r}\frac{\partial\psi_j^5}{\partial r d\theta}\right)\right] + \left(\frac{1}{4r}\frac{\partial\psi_i^2}{\partial r} - \frac{1}{4r^2}\psi_i^2 + \frac{1}{4}\frac{\partial^2\psi_i^2}{\partial r^2}\right)\left[T_{66}^1\left(\frac{1}{4r}\frac{\partial\psi_j^5}{\partial r} - \frac{1}{4r^2}\psi_j^5\right.\right.$$
$$\left.\left.\left. + \frac{1}{4}\frac{\partial^2\psi_j^5}{\partial r^2} + \frac{2}{h^2}\psi_j^5\right) + T_{66}^3\left(-\frac{1}{3h^2r}\frac{\partial\psi_j^5}{\partial r} + \frac{1}{3h^2r^2}\psi_j^5 - \frac{1}{3h^2}\frac{\partial^2\psi_j^5}{\partial r^2}\right)\right]\right\} r dr d\theta \quad \text{(A12)}$$

$$K_{26} = \int_{\Omega}\left\{\frac{1}{r}\frac{\partial\psi_i^2}{\partial\theta}\left[A_{23}^0\psi_j^6 - A_{21}^2\frac{1}{2}\frac{\partial^2\psi_j^6}{\partial r^2} - A_{22}^2\left(\frac{1}{2r}\frac{\partial\psi_j^6}{\partial r} + \frac{1}{2r^2}\frac{\partial^2\psi_j^6}{\partial\theta^2}\right)\right]\right.$$
$$+ \left(\frac{\delta d\psi_j^2}{\partial r} - \frac{1}{r}\psi_i^2\right)\left[A_{44}^2\left(\frac{-1}{r}\frac{\partial^2\psi_j^6}{\partial\theta\partial r} + \frac{1}{r^2}\frac{\partial\beta_z}{\partial\theta}\right)\right] - \left(\frac{1}{4r^2}\frac{\partial\psi_i^2}{\partial\theta} + \frac{1}{4r}\frac{\partial^2\psi_i^2}{\partial\theta\partial r}\right)T_{55}^0\frac{1}{2}\frac{\partial\psi_j^6}{\partial r}$$
$$\left. + \left(\frac{1}{4r}\frac{\partial\psi_i^2}{\partial r} - \frac{1}{4r^2}\psi_i^2 + \frac{1}{4}\frac{\partial^2\psi_i^2}{\partial r^2}\right)T_{66}^0\frac{1}{2r}\frac{\partial\psi_j^6}{\partial\theta}\right\} r dr d\theta \quad \text{(A13)}$$

$$K_{27} = \int_{\Omega}\left\{\frac{1}{r}\frac{\partial\psi_i^2}{\partial\theta}\left[A_{23}^1 2\psi_j^7 - A_{21}^3\frac{1}{3}\frac{\partial\psi_j^7}{\partial r^2} - A_{22}^3\left(\frac{1}{3r^2}\frac{\partial^2\psi_j^7}{\partial\theta^2} + \frac{1}{3r}\frac{\partial\psi_j^7}{\partial r}\right)\right]\right.$$
$$- \left(\frac{d\psi_i^2}{\partial r} - \frac{1}{r}\psi_i^2\right)\left[A_{44}^3\left(\frac{2}{3}\frac{\partial^2\psi_j^7}{\partial\theta\partial r}\right)\right] - \left(\frac{1}{4r^2}\frac{\partial\psi_i^2}{\partial\theta} + \frac{1}{4r}\frac{\partial^2\psi_i^2}{\partial\theta\partial r}\right)T_{55}^1\frac{3}{2}\frac{\partial\psi_j^7}{\partial r}$$
$$\left. + \left(\frac{1}{4r}\frac{\partial\psi_i^2}{\partial r} - \frac{1}{4r^2}\psi_i^2 + \frac{1}{4}\frac{\partial\psi_i^2}{\partial r^2}\right)T_{66}^1\frac{1}{r}\frac{\partial\psi_j^6}{\partial\theta} + \left(\frac{\psi_i^2}{\partial r} - \frac{1}{r}\psi_i^2\right)A_{44}^3\frac{8}{3h^2r^2}\frac{\psi_i^7}{d\theta}\right\} r dr d\theta \quad \text{(A14)}$$

$$K_{31} = \int_{\Omega} \left\{ \frac{\partial W_o}{\partial r} \frac{\partial \psi_i^3}{\partial r} \left[A_{11}^0 \frac{\partial \psi_j^1}{\partial r} + A_{12}^0 \frac{1}{r} \psi_j^1 \right] - \frac{4}{3h^2} \frac{\partial^2 \psi_i^3}{\partial r^2} \left[\frac{\partial \psi_j^1}{\partial r} A_{11}^3 + A_{12}^3 \frac{1}{r} \psi_j^1 \right] \right.$$
$$+ \frac{1}{r^2} \frac{\partial W_o}{\partial \theta} \frac{\partial \psi_i^3}{\partial \theta} \left[A_{21}^0 \frac{\partial \psi_j^1}{\partial r} + A_{22}^0 \frac{1}{r} \psi_j^1 \right] - \frac{4}{3rh^2} \left(\frac{\partial \psi_i^3}{\partial r} + \frac{1}{r} \frac{\partial^2 \psi_i^3}{\partial \theta^2} \right)$$
$$\left[A_{21}^3 \frac{\partial \psi_j^1}{\partial r} + A_{21}^3 \frac{1}{r} \psi_j^1 \right] + \left(\frac{1}{r} \frac{\partial \psi_i^3}{\partial \theta} \frac{\delta W_o}{\partial r} + \frac{1}{r} \frac{\partial \psi_i^3}{\partial r} \frac{\delta W_o}{\partial \theta} \right) A_{44}^0 \frac{1}{r} \frac{\partial \psi_j^1}{\partial \theta}$$
$$+ \left(\frac{-8}{3h^2 r^2} \frac{\partial \psi_i^3}{d\theta} + \frac{-8}{3h^2} \frac{\partial^2 \psi_i^3}{\partial \theta \partial r} \right) A_{44}^6 \left(\frac{\partial \psi_j^2}{\partial r} - \frac{\psi_j^2}{r} \right) + T_{55}^1 \frac{2}{4r^2 h^2} \frac{\partial \psi_i^3}{\partial r} \frac{\partial^2 \psi_j^1}{\partial \theta^2}$$
$$\left. + \frac{2}{h^2} \frac{\partial \psi_i^3}{\partial \theta} T_{66}^1 \left[-\frac{1}{4r} \frac{\partial^2 \psi_j^1}{de \partial \theta \partial r} + \frac{1}{4r^2} \frac{\partial \psi_j^1}{\partial \theta} \right] - A_{44}^3 \frac{8}{3h^2 r^2} \frac{\partial \psi_i^3}{\partial \theta} \frac{\partial \psi_j^1}{d\theta} \right\} r dr d\theta \tag{A15}$$

$$K_{32} = \int_{\Omega} \left\{ A_{12}^0 \frac{1}{r} \frac{\partial W_o}{\partial \theta} \frac{\partial \psi_i^3}{\partial r} \frac{\partial \psi_j^2}{d\theta} - A_{12}^3 \frac{4}{3rh^2} \frac{\partial^2 \psi_i^3}{\partial r^2} \frac{\partial \psi_j^2}{\partial \theta} + A_{22}^0 \frac{1}{r^3} \frac{\partial W_o}{\partial \theta} \frac{\partial \psi_i^3}{\partial \theta} \frac{\partial \psi_j^2}{\partial \theta} \right.$$
$$+ \frac{-4}{3rh^2} \left(\frac{\partial \psi_i^3}{\partial r} + \frac{1}{r} \frac{\partial^2 \psi_i^3}{\partial \theta^2} \right) \left[A_{22}^3 \frac{1}{r} \frac{\partial \psi_j^2}{\partial \theta} \right] + \left(\frac{1}{r} \frac{\partial W_o}{\partial \theta} \frac{\partial \psi_i^3}{\partial r} + \frac{1}{r} \frac{\partial W_o}{\partial r} \frac{\partial \psi_i^3}{\partial \theta} \right) \left[A_{44}^0 \left(\frac{\partial \psi_j^2}{\partial r} \right. \right.$$
$$\left. \left. - \frac{\psi_j^2}{r} \right) \right] - \left[\frac{8}{3h^2 r^2} \frac{\partial \psi_i^3}{d\theta} + \frac{8}{3h^2} \frac{\partial^2 \psi_i^3}{\partial \theta \partial r} \right] \left[A_{44}^3 \left(\frac{\partial \psi_j^2}{\partial r} - \frac{\psi_j^2}{r} \right) \right] + \left(\frac{-2}{h^2} \frac{\partial \psi_i^3}{\partial r} \right) \left[\left(\frac{1}{4r^2} \frac{\partial \psi_j^2}{\partial \theta} \right. \right.$$
$$\left. \left. + \frac{1}{4r} \frac{\partial^2 \psi_j^2}{\partial r \partial \theta} \right) T_{55}^1 \right] + \frac{2}{h^2} \frac{\partial \psi_i^3}{\partial \theta} \left[T_{66}^1 \left(\frac{1}{4r} \frac{\partial \psi_j^2}{\partial r} - \frac{1}{4r^2} \psi_j^2 + \frac{1}{4} \frac{\partial^2 \psi_j^2}{\partial r^2} \right) \right]$$
$$\left. + \frac{-8}{3h^2 r^2} \frac{\partial \psi_i^3}{\partial \theta} \left[A_{44} \left(\frac{\partial \psi_j^2}{dr} - \frac{\psi_j^2}{r} \right) \right] \right\} r dr d\theta \tag{A16}$$

$$
\begin{aligned}
K_{33} = \int_{\Omega} \Bigg\{ & \frac{\partial W_o}{\partial r}\frac{\partial \psi_i^3}{\partial r}\left[A_{11}^0 \frac{1}{2}\frac{\partial \psi_j^3}{\partial r} + A_{12}^0 \frac{1}{2r^2}\frac{\partial W_o}{\partial \theta}\frac{\partial \psi_j^3}{\partial \theta} - A_{11}^3 \frac{4}{3h^2}\frac{\partial^2 \psi_j^3}{\partial r^2} - A_{12}^3\left(\frac{4}{3h^2 r^2}\frac{\partial^2 \psi_j^3}{\partial \theta^2}\right.\right. \\
& \left.\left. - \frac{4}{3h^2 r}\frac{\partial \psi_j^3}{\partial r}\right)\right] - \frac{4}{3h^2}\frac{\partial^2 \psi_i^3}{\partial r^2}\left[A_{11}^3 \frac{\partial \psi_j^3}{\partial r} + A_{12}^3 \frac{1}{2r}\frac{\partial W_o}{\partial \theta}\frac{\partial \psi_j^3}{\partial \theta} - A_{11}^6 \frac{4}{3h^2}\frac{\partial^2 \psi_j^3}{\partial r^2}\right. \\
& \left. - A_{12}^6\left(\frac{4}{3h^2 r^2}\frac{\partial^2 \psi_j^3}{\partial \theta^2} + \frac{4}{3h^2 r}\frac{\partial \psi_j^3}{\partial r}\right)\right] + \frac{1}{r^2}\frac{\partial \psi_j^3}{\partial \theta}\frac{\partial \psi_i^3}{\partial \theta}\left[A_{21}^0 \frac{1}{2}\frac{\partial W_o}{\partial r}\frac{\partial \psi_j^3}{\partial r} + A_{22}^0 \frac{1}{2r^2}\frac{\partial W_o}{\partial \theta}\frac{\partial \psi_j^3}{\partial \theta}\right. \\
& \left. - A_{21}^3 \frac{4}{3r^2 h^2}\frac{\partial^2 \psi_j^3}{\partial r^2} - A_{22}^3\left(\frac{4}{3r^2 h^2}\frac{\partial^2 \psi_j^3}{\partial \theta^2} + \frac{4}{3rh^2}\frac{\partial \psi_j^3}{\partial r}\right)\right] - \frac{4}{3rh^2}\left(\frac{\partial \psi_i^3}{\partial r} + \frac{1}{r}\frac{\partial^2 \psi_i^3}{\partial \theta^2}\right)\left[A_{21}^3 \frac{1}{2}\frac{\partial \psi_j^3}{\partial r}^2\right. \\
& \left. + A_{22}^3 \frac{1}{2r^2}\frac{\partial W_o}{\partial \theta}\frac{\partial \psi_j^3}{\partial \theta} - A_{21}^6 \frac{4}{3r^2 h^2}\frac{\partial^2 \psi_j^3}{\partial r^2} - A_{22}^6\left(\frac{4}{3r^2 h^2}\frac{\partial^2 \psi_j^3}{\partial \theta^2} + \frac{4}{3rh^2}\frac{\partial \psi_j^3}{\partial r}\right)\right] \\
& + \left(\frac{1}{r}\frac{\partial W_o}{\partial \theta}\frac{\partial \psi_i^3}{\partial r} + \frac{1}{r}\frac{\partial W_o}{\partial r}\frac{\partial \psi_i^3}{\partial \theta}\right)\left[A_{44}^0 \frac{1}{r}\frac{\partial \psi_j^3}{\partial \theta}\frac{\partial W_o}{\partial r} - A_{44}^3 \frac{8}{3h^2}\frac{\partial^2 \psi_j^3}{\partial \theta \partial r}\right] \\
& - \left[\frac{8}{3h^2 r^2}\frac{\partial \psi_i^3}{d\theta} + \frac{8}{3h^2}\frac{\partial^2 \psi_i^3}{\partial \theta \partial r}\right]\left[A_{44}^3 \frac{1}{r}\frac{\partial \psi_j^3}{\partial \theta}\frac{\partial W_o}{\partial r} - A_{44}^6 \frac{8}{3h^2}\frac{\partial^2 \psi_j^3}{\partial \theta \partial r}\right] + \frac{\partial \psi_i^3}{\partial r}\left[A_{66}^0 \frac{\partial \psi_j^3}{\partial r} - A_{66}^2 \frac{4}{h^2}\frac{\partial \psi_j^3}{\partial r}\right] \\
& + \frac{1}{r}\frac{\partial \psi_i^3}{\partial \theta}\left[A_{55}^0 \frac{1}{r}\frac{\partial \psi_j^3}{\partial \theta} - A_{55}^2 \frac{4}{h^2 r}\frac{\partial \psi_j^3}{\partial \theta}\right] - \frac{4}{h^2 r}\frac{\partial \psi_j^3}{\partial \theta}\left[A_{55}^2 \frac{1}{r}\frac{\partial \psi_j^3}{\partial \theta} - A_{55}^4 \frac{4}{h^2 r}\frac{\partial \psi_j^3}{\partial \theta}\right] \\
& - \frac{4}{h^2}\frac{\partial \psi_i^3}{\partial r}\left[A_{66}^2 \frac{\partial \psi_j^3}{\partial r} - A_{66}^4 \frac{4}{h^2}\frac{\partial \psi_j^3}{\partial r}\right] + \left(\frac{1}{2r}\frac{\partial^2 \psi_i^3}{\partial \theta \partial r} - \frac{1}{2r^2}\frac{\partial \psi_i^3}{\partial \theta}\right)\left[T_{11}^0\left(\frac{1}{2r}\frac{\partial^2 \psi_j^3}{\partial \theta \partial r} - \frac{1}{2r^2}\frac{\partial \psi_j^3}{\partial \theta}\right)\right. \\
& \left. - T_{11}^2\left(\frac{2}{h^2 r}\frac{\partial^2 \psi_i^3}{\partial \theta \partial r} + \frac{2}{h^2 r^2}\frac{\partial \psi_i^3}{\partial \theta}\right)\right] + \left(\frac{2}{h^2 r}\frac{\partial^2 \psi_i^3}{\partial \theta \partial r} - \frac{2}{h^2 r^2}\frac{\partial \psi_i^3}{\partial \theta}\right)\left[T_{11}^2\left(\frac{1}{2r}\frac{\partial^2 \psi_j^3}{\partial \theta \partial r} - \frac{1}{2r^2}\frac{\partial \psi_j^3}{\partial \theta}\right)\right. \\
& \left. - T_{11}^4\left(\frac{2}{hr}\frac{\partial^2 \psi_i^3}{d\theta dr} + \frac{2}{h^2 r^2}\frac{d\psi_i^3}{d\theta}\right)\right] + \left(\frac{1}{2r^2}\frac{\partial \psi_i^3}{\partial \theta} - \frac{1}{2r}\frac{\partial^2 \psi_i^3}{\partial r \partial \theta}\right)\left[T_{22}^0\left(-\frac{1}{2r}\frac{\partial^2 \psi_j^3}{\partial r d\theta} + \frac{1}{2r^2}\frac{\partial \psi_j^3}{\partial \theta}\right)\right. \\
& \left. + T_{22}^2\left(\frac{2}{h^2 r^2}\frac{\partial^2 \psi_j^3}{\partial \theta^3} - \frac{2}{h^2 r}\frac{\partial \psi_j^3}{\partial r}\right)\right]\left(\frac{2}{h^2 r^2}\frac{\partial^2 \psi_i^3}{\partial \theta^2} - \frac{2}{h^2 r}\frac{\partial \psi_i^3}{\partial r}\right)\left[T_{22}^2\left(-\frac{1}{2r}\frac{\partial^2 \psi_j^3}{\partial r \partial \theta} + \frac{1}{2r^2}\frac{\partial \psi_j^3}{\partial \theta}\right)\right. \\
& \left. + T_{22}^4\left(\frac{2}{h^2 r^2}\frac{\partial^2 \psi_j^3}{\partial \theta^2} - \frac{2}{h^2 r}\frac{\partial \psi_j^3}{\partial r}\right)\right] + \left(\frac{1}{4r^2}\frac{\partial^2 \psi_i^3}{\partial \theta^2} - \frac{1}{4}\frac{\partial^2 \psi_i^3}{\partial r^2} + \frac{1}{4r}\frac{\partial \psi_i^3}{\partial r}\right)\left[T_{44}^0\left(-\frac{1}{4}\frac{\partial^2 \psi_j^3}{\partial r^2}\right.\right. \\
& \left.\left. + \frac{1}{4r^2}\frac{\partial^2 \psi_j^3}{\partial \theta^2} + \frac{1}{4r}\frac{\partial \psi_j^3}{\partial r}\right) + T_{44}^2\left(\frac{-1}{h^2}\frac{\partial^2 \psi_j^3}{\partial r^2} + \frac{1}{h^2 r^2}\frac{\partial^2 \psi_j^3}{\partial \theta^2} + \frac{1}{h^2 r}\frac{\partial \psi_j^3}{\partial r}\right)\right] + \left(\frac{-1}{h^2}\frac{\partial^2 \psi_i^3}{\partial r^2} + \frac{1}{h^2 r^2}\frac{\partial^2 \psi_i^3}{\partial \theta^2}\right. \\
& \left. + \frac{1}{h^2 r}\frac{\partial \psi_i^3}{\partial r}\right)\left[T_{44}^2\left(\frac{-1}{4}\frac{\partial^2 \psi_i^3}{\partial r^2} + \frac{1}{4r^2}\frac{\partial^2 \psi_j^3}{\partial \theta^2} + \frac{1}{4r}\frac{\partial \psi_j^3}{\partial r}\right) T_{44}^4\left(\frac{-1}{h^2}\frac{\partial^2 \psi_j^3}{\partial r^2} + \frac{1}{h^2 r^2}\frac{\partial^2 \psi_j^3}{\partial \theta^2} + \frac{1}{h^2 r}\frac{\partial \psi_j^3}{\partial r}\right)\right] \\
& + T_{55}^2 \frac{4}{h^4}\frac{\partial \psi_i^3}{\partial r}\frac{\partial \psi_j^3}{\partial r} + T_{66}^2 \frac{4}{h^4}\frac{\partial \psi_i^3}{\partial \theta}\frac{\partial \psi_j^3}{\partial \theta} + \left(\frac{1}{r}\frac{\partial \psi_j^3}{\partial \theta}\frac{\partial \psi_i^3}{\partial r} + \frac{1}{r}\frac{\partial \psi_j^3}{\partial r}\frac{\partial \psi_i^3}{\partial \theta}\right) A_{44}^3 \frac{8}{3h^2 r^2}\frac{\partial \psi_j^3}{d\theta} \\
& - A_{44}^6 \frac{64}{9h^4 r^2}\frac{\partial^2 \psi_i^7}{\partial \theta \partial r}\frac{\partial \psi_j^7}{\partial \theta} - \frac{8}{3h^2 r^2}\frac{\partial \psi_i^7}{\partial \theta}\left[A_{44}^3 \frac{1}{r}\frac{\partial^2 \psi_j^7}{\partial \theta \partial r} - A_{44}^6 \frac{8}{3h^2}\frac{\partial \psi_j^7}{\partial r}\right]\Bigg\} r dr d\theta
\end{aligned}
\tag{A17}
$$

$$
\begin{aligned}
K_{34} = \int_{\Omega} \Bigg\{ & \frac{\partial W_o}{\partial r}\frac{\partial \psi_i^3}{\partial r}\left[A_{11}^1 \frac{\partial \psi_j^4}{\partial r} + A_{12}^1 \psi_j^4 - \frac{4}{3h^2} A_{11}^3 \frac{\partial \psi_j^4}{\partial r} - \frac{4}{3rh^2} A_{12}^3 \psi_j^4\right] - \frac{4}{3h^2}\frac{\partial^2 \psi_i^3}{\partial r^2}\left[A_{11}^4 \frac{\partial \psi_j^4}{\partial r} A_{12}^4 \psi_j^4\right. \\
& \left. - \frac{4}{3h^2} A_{11}^6 \frac{\partial \psi_j^4}{\partial r} - \frac{4}{3h^2 r} A_{12}^6 \psi_j^4\right] + \frac{1}{r^2}\frac{\partial W_o}{\partial \theta}\frac{\partial \psi_i^3}{\partial \theta}\left[A_{21}^1 \frac{\partial \psi_j^4}{\partial r} + A_{22}^1 \frac{1}{r}\psi_j^4 - A_{21}^3 \frac{4}{3h^2}\frac{\partial \psi_j^4}{\partial r} - A_{22}^3 \frac{4}{3rh^2}\psi_j^4\right] \\
& - \frac{4}{3rh^2}\left(\frac{\partial \psi_i^3}{\partial r} + \frac{1}{r}\frac{\partial^2 \psi_i^3}{\partial \theta^2}\right)\left[A_{21}^4 \frac{\partial \psi_j^4}{\partial r} + A_{22}^4 \frac{1}{r}\psi_j^4 - A_{21}^6 \frac{4}{3h^2}\frac{\partial \psi_j^4}{\partial r} - A_{22}^3 \frac{4}{3rh^2}\psi_j^4\right] + \left(\frac{1}{r}\frac{\partial W_o}{\partial \theta}\frac{\partial \psi_i^3}{\partial r}\right. \\
& \left. + \frac{1}{r}\frac{\partial W_o}{\partial r}\frac{\partial \psi_i^3}{\partial \theta}\right)\left[A_{44}^1 \frac{1}{r}\frac{\partial \psi_j^4}{\partial \theta} - A_{44}^3 \frac{4}{3h^2 r}\frac{\partial \psi_j^4}{\partial \theta}\right] - \frac{8}{3h^2}\frac{\partial^2 \psi_i^3}{\partial \theta \partial r}\left[A_{44}^4 \frac{1}{r}\frac{\partial \psi_j^4}{\partial \theta} - A_{44}^6 \frac{4}{3h^2 r}\frac{\partial \psi_j^4}{\partial \theta}\right] \\
& + \delta \psi_j^4\left[A_{66}^0 \psi_j^4 - A_{66}^2 \frac{4}{h^2}\psi_j^4\right] - \frac{4}{h^2}\psi_j^4\left[A_{66}^2 \psi_j^4 - A_{66}^4 \frac{4}{h^2 \psi_j^4}\right] + \left(\frac{1}{2r^2}\frac{\partial \psi_i^3}{\partial \theta}\right. \\
& \left. - \frac{1}{2r}\frac{\partial^2 \psi_i^3}{\partial r \partial \theta}\right)\left[T_{22}^0 \frac{1}{2r}\frac{\partial \psi_j^4}{\partial \theta} - T_{22}^2 \frac{2}{h^2 r}\psi_j^4\right] + \left(\frac{2}{h^2 r^2}\frac{\partial^2 \psi_i^3}{\delta \theta^2} - \frac{2}{h^2 r}\frac{\partial \psi_i^3}{\partial r}\right)\left[T_{22}^2 \frac{1}{2r}\frac{\partial \psi_j^4}{\partial \theta}\right. \\
& \left. + T_{22}^4 \frac{-2}{h^2 r}\psi_j^4\right] + \left(\frac{1}{4r^2}\frac{\partial^2 \psi_i^3}{\partial \theta^2} - \frac{1}{4}\frac{\partial^2 \psi_i^3}{\partial r^2} + \frac{1}{4r}\frac{\partial \psi_i^3}{\partial r}\right)\left[T_{44}^0 \left(\frac{1}{4}\frac{\partial \psi_j^4}{\partial \theta} - \frac{1}{4r}\psi_j^4\right)\right. \\
& \left. + T_{44}^2 \left(\frac{-1}{h^2}\frac{\partial \psi_j^4}{\partial r} + \frac{1}{h^2 r}\psi_j^4\right)\right] + \left(\frac{-1}{h^2}\frac{\partial^2 \psi_i^3}{\partial r^2} + \frac{1}{h^2 r^2}\frac{\partial^2 \psi_i^3}{\partial \theta^2} + \frac{1}{h^2 r}\frac{d\psi_i^3}{\partial r}\right)\left[T_{44}^2 \left(\frac{1}{4}\frac{\partial \psi_j^4}{\partial \theta}\right.\right. \\
& \left.\left. - \frac{1}{4r}\psi_j^4\right) + T_{44}^4 \left(-\frac{1}{h^2}\frac{\partial \psi_j^4}{\partial r} + \frac{1}{h^2}\psi_j^4\right)\right] + \frac{2}{h^2}\frac{\partial \psi_i^3}{\partial r}\left[T_{55}^2 \left(\frac{1}{4r^2}\frac{\partial^2 \psi_j^4}{\partial \theta^2} + \frac{2}{h^2}\psi_j^4\right)\right. \\
& \left. + T_{55}^4 \frac{1}{3h^2 r^2}\frac{\partial^2 \psi_j^4}{\partial \theta^2}\right] + \frac{2}{h^2}\frac{\partial \psi_i^3}{\partial r}\left[T_{66}^2 \left(\frac{-1}{4r}\frac{\partial^2 \psi_j^4}{\partial \theta \partial r} + \frac{1}{4r^2}\frac{\partial \psi_j^4}{\partial \theta}\right)\right. \\
& \left. + T_{66}^4 \left(\frac{-1}{3h^2 r}\frac{\partial^2 \psi_j^4}{\partial \theta \partial r} + \frac{1}{3h^2 r^2}\frac{\partial \psi_j^4}{\partial \theta}\right)\right] - \frac{8}{3h^2 r^\theta}\frac{\partial \psi_i^3}{\partial \theta}\left[A_{44}^4 \frac{1}{r}\frac{\partial \psi_j^4}{\partial \theta} - A_{44}^6 \frac{4}{3h^2}\frac{\partial \psi_j^4}{\partial \theta}\right]\Bigg\} r dr d\theta
\end{aligned}
\tag{A18}
$$

$$
\begin{aligned}
K_{35} = \int_{\Omega} \Bigg\{ & \frac{\partial W_o}{\partial r}\frac{\partial \psi_i^1}{\partial r}\left[A_{12}^1\frac{1}{r}\frac{\partial \psi_j^5}{\partial \theta} - \frac{4}{3rh^2}A_{12}^3\frac{\partial \psi_j^5}{\partial \theta}\right] - \frac{4}{3h^2}\frac{\partial \psi_i^1}{\partial r^2}\left[A_{12}^4\frac{1}{r}\frac{\partial \psi_j^5}{\partial \theta} - \frac{4}{3rh^2}A_{12}^6\frac{\partial \psi_j^5}{\partial \theta}\right] \\
& + \frac{1}{r^2}\frac{\partial W_o}{\partial \theta}\frac{\partial \psi_i^1}{\partial \theta}\left[A_{22}^1\frac{1}{r}\frac{\partial \psi_j^5}{\partial \theta} - A_{22}^3\frac{4}{3h^2 r}\frac{\partial \psi_j^5}{\partial \theta}\right] - \frac{4}{3rh^2}\left(\frac{\partial \psi_i^1}{\partial r} + \frac{1}{r}\frac{\partial^2 \psi_i^1}{\partial \theta^2}\right)\Bigg[A_{22}^4\frac{1}{r}\frac{\partial \psi_j^5}{\partial \theta} \\
& - A_{22}^6\frac{4}{3h^2 r}\frac{\partial \psi_j^5}{\partial \theta}\Bigg] + \left(\frac{1}{r}\frac{\partial W_o}{\partial \theta}\frac{\partial \psi_i^1}{\partial r} + \frac{1}{r}\frac{\partial W_o}{\partial V}\frac{\partial \psi_i^1}{\partial \theta}\right)\Bigg[A_{44}^1\left(\frac{\partial \psi_j^5}{\partial r} - \frac{1}{r}\psi_j^5\right) - A_{44}^3\Bigg(\frac{4}{3h^2}\frac{\partial \psi_j^5}{\partial r} \\
& + \frac{4}{3h^2 r}\psi_j^5\Bigg)\Bigg] - \left[\frac{8}{3h^2 r^2}\frac{\partial \psi_i^1}{d\theta} + \frac{8}{3h^2}\frac{\partial^2 \psi_i^1}{\partial \theta \partial r}\right]\left[A_{44}^4\left(\frac{\partial \psi_j^5}{\partial r} - \frac{1}{r}\psi_j^5\right) - A_{44}^6\left(\frac{4}{3h^2}\frac{\partial \psi_j^5}{\partial r} + \frac{4}{3h^2 r}\psi_j^5\right)\right] \\
& + \frac{1}{r}\frac{\partial \psi_i^1}{\partial \theta}\left[A_{55}^0\psi_j^5 - A_{55}^2\frac{4}{h^2}\psi_j^5\right] - \frac{4}{h^2 r}\frac{\partial \psi_j^1}{\partial \theta}\left[A_{55}^2\psi_j^5 - A_{55}^4\frac{4}{h^2}\psi_j^5\right] \\
& + \left(\frac{1}{2r}\frac{\partial^2 \psi_i^1}{\partial \theta \partial r} - \frac{1}{2r^2}\frac{\partial \psi_i^1}{\partial \theta}\right)\left[-T_{11}^0\frac{1}{2}\frac{\partial \psi_j^5}{\partial r} + T_{11}^2\frac{2}{h^2}\frac{\partial \psi_j^5}{\partial r}\right] + \Bigg(\frac{1}{r}\frac{\partial^2 \psi_i^1}{\partial \theta \partial r} \\
& - \frac{1}{r^2}\frac{\partial \psi_i^1}{\partial \theta}\Bigg)\left[T_{11}^2 - \frac{1}{2}\frac{\partial \psi_j^5}{\partial r} + T_{11}^4\frac{2}{h^2}\frac{\partial \psi_j^5}{\partial r}\right] + \left(\frac{1}{2r^2}\frac{\partial \psi_i^1}{\partial \theta} - \frac{1}{2r}\frac{\partial^2 \psi_i^1}{\partial r \partial \theta}\right)\Bigg[T_{22}^0\frac{1}{2r}\psi_j^5 \\
& + T_{22}^2\frac{2}{h^2 r}\frac{\partial \psi_j^5}{\partial r}\Bigg] + \left(\frac{2}{h^2 r^2}\frac{\partial^2 \psi_i^1}{\partial \theta^2} - \frac{2}{h^2 r}\frac{\partial \psi_i^1}{\partial r}\right)\left[T_{22}^2\frac{1}{2r}\psi_j^5 + T_{22}^4\frac{2}{h^2 r}\frac{\partial \psi_j^5}{\partial r}\right] \\
& + \left(\frac{1}{4r^2}\frac{\partial^2 \psi_i^1}{\partial \theta^2} - \frac{1}{4}\frac{\partial^2 \psi_i^1}{\partial r^2} + \frac{1}{4r}\frac{\partial \psi_i^1}{\partial r}\right)\left[-T_{44}^0\frac{1}{4r}\frac{\partial \psi_i^5}{\partial \theta} + T_{44}^2\frac{1}{h^2 r}\frac{\partial \psi_j^5}{\partial \theta}\right] + \Bigg(\frac{-1}{h^2}\frac{\partial^2 \psi_i^1}{\partial r^2} \\
& + \frac{1}{h^2 r^2}\frac{\partial^2 \psi_i^1}{\partial \theta^2} + \frac{1}{h^2 r}\frac{\partial \psi_i^1}{\partial r}\Bigg)\left[-T_{44}^2\frac{1}{4r}\frac{\partial \psi_i^5}{\partial \theta} + T_{44}^4\frac{1}{h^2 r}\frac{\partial \psi_j^5}{\partial \theta}\right] - \frac{2}{h^2}\frac{\partial \psi_i^1}{\partial r}\Bigg[T_{55}^2\left(\frac{1}{4r^2}\frac{\partial \psi_j^5}{\partial \theta} + \frac{1}{4r}\frac{\partial^2 \psi_j^5}{\partial \theta \partial r}\right) \\
& - T_{55}^4\left(\frac{1}{3h^2 r^2}\frac{\partial \psi_j^5}{\partial \theta} + \frac{1}{3h^2 r}\frac{\partial^2 \psi_j^5}{\partial r \partial \theta}\right)\Bigg] + \frac{2}{h^2}\frac{\partial \psi_i^1}{\partial \theta}\Bigg[T_{66}^2\left(\frac{1}{4r}\frac{\partial \psi_j^5}{\partial r} - \frac{1}{4r^2} - \frac{1}{4r^2}\psi_j^5 + \frac{1}{4}\frac{\partial^2 \psi_j^5}{\partial r^2} + \frac{2}{h^2}\psi_j^5\right) \\
& + T_{66}^4\left(\frac{-1}{3h^2 r}\frac{\partial \psi_j^5}{\partial r} + \frac{1}{3h^2 r^2}\psi_j^5 - \frac{1}{3h^2}\frac{\partial^2 \psi_j^5}{\partial r^2}\right)\Bigg]\Bigg\} r dr d\theta
\end{aligned}
\tag{A19}
$$

$$
\begin{aligned}
K_{36} = \int_{\Omega} \Bigg\{ & \frac{\partial W_o}{\partial r}\frac{\partial \psi_i^3}{\partial r}\left[A_{13}o\psi_j^6 - A_{11}^2\frac{1}{2}\frac{\partial^2 \psi_j^6}{\partial r^2} - A_{12}^2\left(\frac{1}{2r}\frac{\partial \psi_j^6}{\partial r} + \frac{1}{2r^2}\frac{\partial^2 \psi_j^6}{\partial \theta^2}\right)\right] - \frac{4}{3h^2}\frac{\partial^2 \psi_i^3}{\partial r^2}\Big[A_{13}^3\psi_j^6 \\
& - A_{11}^5\frac{1}{2}\frac{\partial^2 \psi_j^6}{\partial r^2} - A_{12}^5\left(\frac{1}{2r}\frac{\partial \psi_j^6}{\partial r} + \frac{1}{2r^2}\frac{\partial^2 \psi_j^6}{\partial \theta^2}\right)\Big] + \frac{1}{r^2}\frac{\partial W_o}{\partial \theta}\frac{\partial \psi_i^3}{\partial \theta}\Big[A_{23}^0\psi_j^6 - A_{21}^2\frac{1}{2}\frac{\partial^2 \psi_j^6}{\partial r^2} \\
& - A_{22}^2\left(\frac{1}{2r}\frac{\partial \psi_j^6}{\partial r} + \frac{1}{2r^2}\frac{\partial^2 \psi_j^6}{\partial \theta^2}\right)\Big] - \frac{4}{3rh^2}\left(\frac{\partial \psi_i^3}{\partial r} + \frac{1}{r}\frac{\partial^2 \psi_i^3}{\partial \theta^2}\right)\Big[A_{23}^3\psi_j^6 - A_{21}^5\frac{1}{2}\frac{\partial^2 \psi_j^6}{\partial r^2} \\
& - A_{22}^5\left(\frac{1}{2r}\frac{\partial \psi_j^6}{\partial r} + \frac{1}{2r^2}\frac{\partial^2 \psi_j^6}{\partial \theta^2}\right)\Big] + \left(\frac{1}{r}\frac{\partial \psi_j^3}{\partial \theta}\frac{\partial \psi_i^3}{\partial r} + \frac{1}{r}\frac{\partial \psi_j^3}{\partial r}\frac{\partial \psi_i^3}{\partial \theta}\right)\left[A_{44}^2\left(\frac{-1}{r}\frac{\partial^2 \psi_j^6}{\partial \theta \partial r} + \frac{1}{r^2}\frac{\partial \psi_j^6}{\partial \theta}\right)\right] \\
& - \left[\frac{8}{3h^2 r^2}\frac{\partial \psi_i^3}{d\theta} + \frac{8}{3h^2}\frac{\partial^2 \psi_i^3}{\partial \theta \partial r}\right]\left[A_{44}^5\left(\frac{-1}{r}\frac{\partial^2 \psi_j^6}{\partial \theta \partial r} + \frac{1}{r^2}\frac{\partial \psi_j^6}{\partial \theta}\right)\right] \\
& + \left(\frac{1}{2r}\frac{\partial^2 \psi_i^3}{\partial \theta \partial r} - \frac{1}{2r^2}\frac{\partial \psi_i^3}{\partial \theta}\right)\left[T_{11}^1\left(\frac{1}{r}\frac{\partial^2 \psi_j^6}{\partial \theta \partial r} + \frac{1}{r^2}\frac{\partial \psi_j^6}{\partial \theta}\right)\right] \\
& + \left(\frac{1}{r}\frac{\partial \psi_i^3}{\partial \theta \partial r} - \frac{1}{r^2}\frac{\partial \psi_i^3}{\partial \theta}\right)\left[T_{11}^3\left(\frac{1}{r}\frac{\partial^2 \psi_j^6}{\partial \theta \partial r} - \frac{1}{r^2}\frac{\partial \psi_j^6}{\partial \theta}\right)\right] \\
& + \left(\frac{1}{2r^2}\frac{\partial \psi_i^3}{\partial \theta} - \frac{1}{2r}\frac{\partial^2 \psi_i^3}{\partial r \partial \theta}\right)\left[T_{22}^1\left(\frac{-1}{r}\frac{\partial^2 \psi_j^6}{\partial r \partial \theta} + \frac{1}{r^2}\frac{\partial \psi_j^6}{\partial \theta}\right)\right] \\
& + \left(\frac{2}{h^2 r^2}\frac{\partial^2 \psi_i^3}{\partial \theta^2} - \frac{2}{h^2 r}\frac{\partial \psi_i^3}{\partial r}\right)\left[T_{22}^3\left(\frac{-1}{r}\frac{\partial^2 \psi_j^6}{\partial r \partial \theta} + \frac{1}{r^2}\frac{\partial \psi_j^6}{\partial \theta}\right)\right] + \Bigg(\frac{1}{4r^2}\frac{\partial^2 \psi_i^3}{\partial \theta^2} - \frac{1}{4}\frac{\partial^2 \psi_i^3}{\partial r^2} \\
& + \frac{1}{4r}\frac{\partial \psi_i^3}{\partial r}\Bigg)\left[T_{44}^1\left(\frac{-1}{2}\frac{\partial^2 \psi_j^6}{\partial r^2} + \frac{1}{2r^2}\frac{\partial^2 \psi_j^6}{\partial \theta^2} + \frac{1}{r}\frac{\partial \psi_j^6}{\partial r}\right)\right] + \Bigg(\frac{-1}{h^2}\frac{\partial^2 \psi_i^3}{\partial r^2} + \frac{1}{h^2 r^2}\frac{\partial^2 \psi_i^3}{\partial \theta} \\
& + \frac{1}{h^2 r}\frac{\partial \psi_i^3}{\partial r}\Bigg)\left[T_{44}^3\left(\frac{-1}{2}\frac{\partial^2 \psi_j^6}{\partial r^2} + \frac{1}{2r^2}\frac{\partial^2 \psi_j^6}{\partial \theta^2} + \frac{1}{r}\frac{\partial \psi_j^6}{\partial r}\right)\right] + T_{55}^1\frac{1}{h^2}\frac{\partial \psi_i^3}{\partial r}\frac{\partial \psi_j^6}{\partial r} \\
& + T_{66}^1\frac{1}{rh^2}\frac{\partial \psi_i^3}{\partial \theta}\frac{\partial \psi_j^6}{\partial \theta}\Bigg\} r dr d\theta
\end{aligned} \tag{A20}
$$

$$
\begin{aligned}
K_{37} = \int_{\Omega} \Bigg\{ & \frac{\partial W_o}{\partial r}\frac{\partial \psi_i^3}{\partial r}\left[A_{13}^1 2\psi_j^7 - A_{11}^3 \frac{1}{3}\frac{\partial^2 \psi_j^7}{\partial r^2} + A_{12}^3 \frac{1}{3r^2}\frac{\partial^2 \psi_j^7}{\partial r^2} - A_{12}^3\left(\frac{1}{3r^2}\frac{\partial^2 \psi_j^7}{\partial \theta^2} + \frac{1}{3r}\frac{\partial \psi_j^7}{\partial r}\right)\right] \\
& - \frac{4}{3h^2}\frac{\partial^2 \psi_i^3}{\partial r^2}\left[A_{13}^4 2\psi_j^7 - A_{11}^6 \frac{1}{3}\frac{\partial^2 \psi_j^7}{\partial r^2} + A_{12}^6 \frac{1}{3r^2}\frac{\partial^2 \psi_j^7}{\partial r^2} - A_{12}^6\left(\frac{1}{3r^2}\frac{\partial^2 \psi_j^7}{\partial \theta^2} + \frac{1}{3r}\frac{\partial \psi_j^7}{\partial r}\right)\right] \\
& + \frac{1}{r^2}\frac{\partial W_o}{\partial \theta}\frac{\partial \psi_i^3}{\partial \theta}\left[A_{23}^1 2\psi_j^7 - A_{21}^3 \frac{1}{3}\frac{\partial^2 \psi_j^7}{\partial r^2} - A_{22}^3\left(\frac{1}{3r^2}\frac{\partial^2 \psi_j^7}{\partial \theta^2} + \frac{1}{3r}\frac{\partial \psi_j^7}{\partial r}\right)\right] \\
& + \left(\frac{1}{r^2}\frac{\partial \psi_j^3}{\partial \theta} + \frac{\partial \psi_i^3}{\partial \theta}\right)\left[A_{23}^4 2\psi_j^7 - A_{21}^6 \frac{1}{3}\frac{\partial^2 \psi_j^7}{\partial r^2} - A_{22}^6\left(\frac{1}{3r^2}\frac{\partial^2 \psi_j^7}{\partial \theta^2} + \frac{1}{3r}\frac{\partial \psi_j^7}{\partial r}\right)\right] \\
& + \left(\frac{1}{r}\frac{\partial \psi_j^3}{\partial \theta}\frac{\partial \psi_i^3}{\partial r} - \frac{1}{r}\frac{\partial \psi_j^3}{\partial r}\frac{\partial \psi_i^3}{\partial \theta}\right)A_{44}^3 \frac{2}{3}\frac{\partial^2 \psi_j^7}{\partial \theta \partial r} + \left[\frac{8}{3h^2 r^2}\frac{\partial \psi_i^3}{d\theta} + \frac{8}{3h^2}\frac{\partial^2 \psi_i^3}{\partial \theta \partial r}\right]A_{44}^6 \frac{2}{3}\frac{\partial^2 \psi_j^7}{\partial \theta \partial r} \\
& + \left(\frac{1}{2r}\frac{\partial^2 \psi_i^3}{\partial \theta \partial r} - \frac{1}{2r^2}\frac{\partial \psi_i^3}{\partial \theta}\right)\left[T_{11}^2\left(\frac{1}{r^2}\frac{\partial^2 \psi_j^7}{\partial \theta \partial r} - \frac{1}{r^2}\frac{\partial \psi_j^7}{\partial \theta} + \frac{1}{2r}\frac{\partial^2 \psi_j^7}{\partial \theta \partial r}\right)\right] \\
& + \left(\frac{1}{r}\frac{\partial^2 \psi_i^3}{\partial \theta \partial r} - \frac{1}{r^2}\frac{\partial \psi_i^3}{\partial \theta}\right)\left[T_{11}^4\left(\frac{1}{2r}\frac{\partial^2 \psi_j^7}{\partial \theta \partial r} - \frac{1}{r^2}\frac{\partial \psi_j^7}{\partial \theta} + \frac{1}{2r}\frac{\partial^2}{\psi}{}^7_j \partial \theta \partial r\right)\right] + \left(\frac{1}{2r^2}\frac{\partial \psi_i^3}{\partial \theta}\right. \\
& \left. - \frac{1}{2r}\frac{\partial^2 \psi_i^3}{\partial r \partial \theta}\right)\left[T_{22}^2\left(\frac{1}{r^2}\frac{\partial^2 \psi_j^7}{\partial \theta^2} - \frac{1}{r}\frac{\partial \psi_j^7}{\partial r}\right)\right] + \left(\frac{2}{h^2 r^2}\frac{\partial^2 \psi_i^3}{\partial \theta^2} - \frac{2}{h^2 r}\frac{\partial \psi_i^3}{\partial r}\right)\left[T_{22}^4\left(\frac{1}{r^2}\frac{\partial^2 \psi_j^7}{\partial \theta^2}\right.\right. \\
& \left.\left. - \frac{1}{r}\frac{\partial \psi_j^7}{\partial r}\right)\right] + \left(\frac{1}{4r^2}\frac{\partial^2 \psi_i^3}{\partial \theta^2} - \frac{1}{4}\frac{\partial^2 \psi_i^3}{\partial r^2} + \frac{1}{4r}\frac{\partial \psi_i^3}{\partial r}\right)\left[T_{44}^2\left(-\frac{1}{2}\frac{\partial^2 \psi_j^7}{\partial r^2} + \frac{1}{2r^2}\frac{\partial^2 \psi_j^7}{\partial \theta^2} + \frac{1}{2r}\frac{\partial \psi_j^7}{\partial r}\right)\right] \\
& + \left(\frac{-1}{h^2}\frac{\partial^2 \psi_i^3}{\partial r^2} + \frac{1}{h^2 r^2}\frac{\partial^2 \psi_i^3}{\partial \theta^2} + \frac{1}{h^2 r}\frac{\partial \psi_i^3}{\partial r}\right)\left[T_{44}^4\left(\frac{-1}{2}\frac{\partial^2 \psi_j^7}{\partial r^2} + \frac{1}{2r^2}\frac{\partial^2 \psi_j^7}{\partial \theta^2} + \frac{1}{2r}\frac{\partial \psi_j^7}{\partial r}\right)\right] \\
& + T_{66}^2 \frac{2}{rh^2}\frac{\partial \psi_i^3}{\partial \theta}\frac{\partial \psi_j^7}{\partial \theta} - \left(\frac{1}{r}\frac{\partial W_o}{\partial \theta}\frac{\partial \psi_i^3}{\partial r} + \frac{1}{r}\frac{\partial \psi_j^7}{\partial r}\frac{\partial \delta W_o}{\partial \theta}\right)A_{44}^3 \frac{2}{3r^2}\frac{\partial \psi_j^7}{\partial \theta} \\
& + T_{55}^2 \frac{3}{h^2}\frac{\partial \psi_i^3}{\partial r}\frac{\partial \psi_j^7}{\partial r} - A_{44}^6 \frac{16}{9r^2 h^2}\frac{\partial^2 \psi_i^7}{\partial \theta \partial r}\frac{\partial \psi_j^7}{\partial \theta}\Bigg\} r dr d\theta
\end{aligned}
\tag{A21}
$$

$$
\begin{aligned}
K_{41} = \int_{\Omega} \Bigg\{ & \frac{\partial \delta \psi_j^4}{\partial r}\left[\frac{\partial \psi_j^1}{\partial r}A_{11}^1 + \frac{1}{r}\psi_j^1 A_{12}^1\right] - \frac{4}{2h^2}\frac{\partial \psi_i^4}{\partial r}\left[\frac{\partial \psi_j^1}{\partial r}A_{11}^3 + \frac{1}{r}A_{12}^3 \psi_j^1\right] + \frac{1}{r}\delta \psi_j^4\left[A_{21}^1 \frac{\partial \psi_j^1}{\partial r} + A_{22}^1 \frac{1}{r}\psi_j^1\right] \\
& - \frac{4}{3rh^2}\delta \psi_j^4\left[A_{21}^3 \frac{\partial \psi_j^1}{\partial r} + A_{22}^3 \frac{1}{r}\psi_j^1\right] + A_{44}^1 \frac{1}{r^2}\frac{\partial \psi_i^4}{\partial \theta}\frac{\partial \psi_j^1}{\partial \theta} - A_{44}^3 \frac{4}{3h^2 r^2}\frac{\partial \psi_i^4}{\partial \theta}\frac{\partial \psi_j^1}{\partial \theta} \\
& + \left(\frac{1}{4r^2}\frac{\partial^2 \psi_i^4}{\partial \theta^2} + \frac{2}{h^2}\psi_i^4\right)t_{55}^1 \frac{1}{4r^2}\frac{\partial^2 \psi_j^1}{\partial \theta^2} - T_{55}^3 \frac{1}{12h^2 r^4}\frac{\partial^2 \delta \psi_j^4}{\partial \theta^2}\frac{\partial^2 \psi_j^1}{\partial \theta^2} \\
& + \left(-\frac{1}{4r}\frac{\partial^2 \psi_i^4}{\partial \theta \partial r} + \frac{1}{4r^2}\frac{\partial \psi_i^4}{\partial \theta}\right)\left[T_{66}^1\left(\frac{-1}{4r}\frac{\partial^2 \psi_j^1}{\partial \theta \partial r} + \frac{1}{4r^2}\frac{\partial \psi_j^1}{\partial \theta}\right)\right] \\
& + \left(-\frac{1}{3h^2 r}\frac{\partial^2 \psi_i^4}{\partial \theta \partial r} + \frac{1}{3h^2 r^2}\frac{\partial \psi_i^4}{\partial \theta}\right)\left[T_{66}^3\left(\frac{-1}{4r}\frac{\partial^2 \psi_j^1}{\partial \theta \partial r} + \frac{1}{4r^2}\frac{\partial \psi_j^1}{\partial \theta}\right)\right]\Bigg\} r dr d\theta
\end{aligned}
\tag{A22}
$$

$$K_{42} = \int_{\Omega} \left\{ A_{12}^{1} \frac{1}{r} \frac{\partial \psi_i^4}{\partial r} \frac{\partial \psi_j^2}{\partial \theta} - A_{12}^{3} \frac{4}{3rh^2} \frac{\partial \psi_i^4}{\partial r} \frac{\partial \psi_j^2}{\partial \theta} + A_{22}^{1} \frac{1}{2r} \psi_i^4 \frac{\partial \psi_j^2}{\partial \theta} - A_{22}^{3} \frac{4}{3r^2h^2} \psi_i^4 \frac{\partial \psi_j^2}{\partial \theta} \right.$$
$$+ \frac{1}{r} \frac{\partial \psi_i^4}{\partial \theta} A_{44}^{1} \left(\frac{\partial \psi_j^2}{\partial r} - \frac{\psi_j^2}{r} \right) - \frac{4}{3h^2 r} \frac{\partial \psi_i^4}{\partial \theta} A_{44}^{3} \left(\frac{\partial \psi_j^2}{\partial r} - \frac{\psi_j^2}{r} \right)$$
$$- \left(\frac{1}{4r^2} \frac{\partial^2 \psi_i^4}{\partial \theta^2} + \frac{2}{h^2} \psi_i^4 \right) \left[T_{55}^{1} \left(\frac{1}{4r^2} \frac{\partial \psi_j^2}{\partial \theta} + \frac{1}{4r} \frac{\partial^2 \psi_j^2}{\partial r d\theta} \right) \right]$$
$$+ \frac{1}{3h^2r^2} \frac{\partial^2 \psi_i^4}{\partial \theta^2} \left[T_{55}^{3} \left(\frac{1}{4r^2} \frac{\partial \psi_j^2}{\partial \theta} + \frac{1}{4r} \frac{\partial^2 \psi_j^2}{\partial r \partial \theta} \right) \right]$$
$$+ \left(-\frac{1}{4r} \frac{\partial^2 \psi_i^4}{\partial \theta \partial r} + \frac{1}{4r^2} \frac{\partial \psi_i^4}{\partial \theta} \right) \left[T_{66}^{1} \left(\frac{1}{4r} \frac{\partial \psi_j^2}{\partial r} - \frac{1}{4r^2} \psi_j^2 + \frac{1}{4} \frac{\partial^2 \psi_j^2}{\partial r^2} \right) \right]$$
$$\left. + \left(\frac{-1}{3h^2 r} \frac{\partial^2 \psi_i^4}{\partial \theta \partial r} + \frac{1}{3h^2r^2} \frac{\partial \psi_i^4}{\partial \theta} \right) T_{66}^{3} \frac{1}{4r} \frac{\partial \psi_j^2}{\partial r} - \frac{1}{4r^2} \psi_j^2 + \frac{1}{4} \frac{\partial^2 \psi_j^2}{\partial r^2} \right\} r dr d\theta \tag{A23}$$

$$K_{43} = \int_{\Omega} \left\{ \frac{\partial \psi_i^4}{\partial r} \left[A_{11}^{1} \frac{1}{2} \frac{\partial W_o}{\partial r} \frac{\partial \psi_j^3}{\partial r} + A_{12}^{1} \frac{1}{2r^2} \frac{\partial W_o}{\partial \theta} \frac{\partial \psi_j^3}{\partial \theta} - A_{11}^{4} \frac{4}{3h^2} \frac{\partial^2 \psi_j^3}{\partial r^2} - A_{12}^{4} \left(\frac{4}{3h^2r^2} \frac{\partial^2 \psi_j^3}{\partial \theta^2} \right. \right. \right.$$
$$\left. \left. + \frac{4}{3h^2 r} \frac{\partial \psi_j^3}{\partial r} \right) \right] - \frac{4}{3h^2} \frac{\partial \psi_i^4}{\partial r} \left[A_{11}^{3} \frac{1}{2} \frac{\partial W_o}{\partial r} \frac{\partial \psi_j^3}{\partial r} + A_{12}^{3} \frac{1}{2r^2} \frac{\partial W_o}{\partial \theta} \frac{\partial \psi_j^3}{\partial \theta} - A_{11}^{6} \frac{4}{3h^2} \frac{\partial \psi_j^3}{\partial r^2} \right.$$
$$\left. - A_{12}^{6} \left(\frac{4}{3h^2r^2} \frac{\partial^2 \psi_j^3}{\partial \theta^2} + \frac{4}{3h^2 r} \frac{\partial \psi_j^3}{\partial r} \right) \right] + \frac{1}{r} \psi_i^4 \left[A_{21}^{1} \frac{1}{2} \frac{\partial W_o}{\partial r} \frac{\partial \psi_j^3}{\partial r} + A_{22}^{1} \frac{1}{2r^2} \frac{\partial W_o}{\partial \theta} \frac{\partial \psi_j^3}{\partial \theta} \right.$$
$$\left. - A_{21}^{4} \frac{4}{3h^2} \frac{\partial^2 \psi_j^3}{\partial r^2} - A_{22}^{4} \left[\frac{4}{3r^2h^2} \frac{\partial^2 \psi_j^3}{\partial \theta^2} + \frac{4}{3rh^2} \frac{\partial \psi_j^3}{\partial r} \right] \right] - \frac{4}{3rh^2} \psi_i^4 \left[A_{21}^{3} \frac{1}{2} \frac{\partial W_o}{\partial r} \frac{\partial \psi_j^3}{\partial r} \right.$$
$$\left. + A_{22}^{3} \frac{1}{2r^2} \frac{\partial W_o}{\partial \theta} \frac{\partial \psi_j^3}{\partial \theta} - A_{21}^{6} \frac{4}{3h^2} \frac{\partial^2 \psi_j^3}{\partial r^2} - A_{22}^{6} \left(\frac{4}{3r^2h^2} \frac{\partial^2 \psi_j^3}{\partial \theta} + \frac{4}{3rh} \frac{\partial \psi_j^3}{\partial r} \right) \right]$$
$$+ \frac{1}{r} \frac{\partial \delta \psi_j^4}{\partial \theta} \left[A_{44}^{1} \frac{1}{r} \frac{\partial \psi_j^3}{\partial \theta} \frac{\partial \psi_j^3}{\partial r} - A_{44}^{4} \frac{8}{3h^2} \frac{\partial^2 \psi_j^3}{\partial \theta \partial r} \right] - \frac{4}{3h^2 r} \frac{\partial \psi_i^4}{\partial \theta} \left[A_{44}^{3} \frac{1}{r} \frac{\partial \psi_j^3}{\partial \theta} \frac{\partial \psi_j^3}{\partial r} + A_{44}^{6} \frac{-8}{3h^2} \frac{\partial^2 \psi_j^3}{\partial \theta \partial r} \right]$$
$$+ \psi_i^4 \left[A_{66}^{0} \frac{\partial \psi_j^3}{\partial r} - A_{66}^{2} \frac{4}{h^2} \frac{\partial \psi_j^3}{\partial r} \right] - \frac{4}{h^2} \psi_i^4 \left[A_{66}^{2} \frac{\partial \psi_j^3}{\partial r} - A_{66}^{4} \frac{4}{h^2} \frac{\partial \psi_j^3}{\partial r} \right] + \frac{1}{2r} \frac{\partial \psi_i^4}{\partial \theta} \left[T_{22}^{0} \left(-\frac{1}{2r} \frac{\partial^2 \psi_j^3}{\partial r \partial \theta} \right. \right.$$
$$\left. \left. + \frac{1}{2r^2} \frac{\partial \psi_j^3}{\partial \theta} \right) + A_{22}^{2} \left(\frac{2}{h^2r^2} \frac{\partial^2 \psi_j^3}{\partial \theta^2} - \frac{2}{h^2 r} \frac{\partial \psi_j^3}{\partial r} \right) \right] - \frac{2}{h^2 r} \psi_i^4 \left[T_{22}^{2} \left(-\frac{1}{2r} \frac{\partial^2 \psi_j^3}{\partial r \partial \theta} + \frac{1}{2r^2} \frac{\partial \psi_j^3}{\partial \theta} \right) \right.$$
$$\left. + T_{22}^{4} \left(\frac{2}{h^2r^2} \frac{\partial^2 \psi_j^3}{\partial \theta^2} - \frac{2}{h^2 r} \frac{\partial \psi_j^3}{\partial r} \right) \right] + \left(\frac{1}{4} \frac{\partial \psi_i^4}{\partial \theta} - \frac{1}{4r} \psi_i^4 \right) \left[T_{44}^{0} \left(-\frac{1}{4} \frac{\partial^2 \psi_j^3}{\partial r^2} + \frac{1}{4r^2} \frac{\partial^2 \psi_j^3}{\partial \theta^2} + \frac{1}{4r} \frac{\partial \psi_j^3}{\partial r} \right) \right.$$
$$\left. + T_{44}^{2} \left(\frac{-1}{h^2} \frac{\partial^2 \psi_j^3}{\partial r^2} + \frac{1}{h^2r^2} \frac{\partial^2 \psi_j^3}{\partial \theta^2} + \frac{1}{h^2 r} \frac{\partial \psi_j^3}{\partial r} \right) \right] - \frac{1}{h^2} \left(\frac{\partial \psi_i^4}{\partial r} - \frac{1}{r} \psi_i^4 \right) \left[T_{44}^{2} \left(\frac{-1}{4} \frac{\partial^2 \psi_j^3}{\partial r^2} + \frac{1}{4r^2} \frac{\partial^2 \psi_j^3}{\partial \theta^2} \right. \right.$$
$$\left. \left. + \frac{1}{4r} \frac{\partial \psi_j^3}{\partial r} \right) + T_{44}^{4} \left(\frac{-1}{h^2} \frac{\partial \psi_j^3}{\partial r^2} + \frac{1}{h^2r^2} \frac{\partial^2 \psi_j^3}{\partial \theta^2} + \frac{1}{h^2 r} \frac{\partial \psi_j^3}{\partial r} \right) \right] + \left(\frac{1}{4r^2} \frac{\partial^2 \psi_i^4}{\partial \theta^2} + \frac{2}{h^2} \psi_i^4 \right) T_{55}^{2} \frac{2}{h^2} \frac{\partial \psi_j^3}{\partial r}$$
$$- T_{55}^{4} \frac{2}{3h^4r^2} \frac{\partial^2 \psi_j^4}{\partial \theta^2} \frac{\partial \psi_j^3}{\partial r} + \left(-\frac{1}{4r} \frac{\partial^2 \psi_i^4}{\partial \theta \partial r} + \frac{1}{4r^2} \frac{\partial \psi_i^4}{\partial \theta} \right) T_{66}^{2} \frac{2}{h^2} \frac{\partial \psi_j^3}{\partial \theta} + \left(\frac{-1}{3h^2 r} \frac{\partial^2 \psi_i^4}{\partial \theta \partial r} \right.$$
$$\left. \left. + \frac{1}{3h^2r^2} \frac{\partial \psi_i^4}{\partial \theta} \right) T_{66}^{4} \frac{2}{h^2} \frac{\partial \psi_j^3}{\partial \theta} - A_{44}^{6} \frac{32}{3h^4r^3} \frac{\partial \psi_i^4}{\partial \theta} \frac{\partial \psi_j^7}{\partial \theta} + A_{44}^{4} \frac{8}{3h^2r^3} \frac{\partial \psi_i^4}{\partial \theta} \frac{\partial \psi_j^7}{\partial \theta} \right\} r dr d\theta \tag{A24}$$

$$
\begin{aligned}
K_{44} = \int_{\Omega} \Bigg\{ & \frac{\partial \psi_i^4}{\partial r}\left[A_{11}^2 \frac{\partial \psi_j^4}{\partial r} + A_{12}^2 \frac{1}{r}\psi_j^4 - A_{11}^4 \frac{4}{3h^2}\frac{\partial \psi_j^4}{\partial r} - A_{12}^4 \frac{4}{3rh^2}\psi_j^4\right] - \frac{4}{3h^2}\frac{\partial \psi_i^4}{\partial r}\left[A_{11}^4 \frac{\partial \psi_j^4}{\partial r} + A_{12}^4 \frac{1}{r}\psi_j^4\right. \\
& \left. - A_{11}^6 \frac{4}{3h^2}\frac{\partial \psi_j^4}{\partial r} - A_{12}^6 \frac{4}{3h^2}\psi_j^4\right] + \frac{1}{r}\psi_i^4\left[A_{21}^2 \frac{\partial \psi_j^4}{\partial r} + A_{22}^2 \frac{1}{r}\psi_j^4 - A_{21}^4 \frac{4}{3h^2}\frac{\partial \psi_j^4}{\partial r} - A_{22}^4 \frac{4}{3rh^2}\psi_j^4\right] \\
& - \frac{4}{3rh^2}\psi_i^4\left[A_{21}^4 \frac{\partial \psi_j^4}{\partial r} + A_{22}^4 \frac{1}{r}\psi_j^4 - A_{21}^6 \frac{4}{3h^2}\frac{\partial \psi_j^4}{\partial r} - A_{22}^6 \frac{4}{3h^2}\psi_j^4\right] + \psi_i^4\left[A_{66}^0 \psi_j^4 - A_{66}^2 \frac{4}{h^2}\psi_j^4\right] \\
& + \frac{1}{r}\frac{\partial \psi_i^4}{\partial \theta}\left[A_{44}^2 \frac{1}{r}\frac{\partial \psi_j^4}{\partial \theta} - A_{44}^4 \frac{4}{3h^2 r}\frac{\partial \psi_j^4}{\partial \theta}\right] - \frac{4}{3h^2 r}\frac{\partial \psi_i^4}{\partial \theta}\left[A_{44}^4 \frac{1}{r}\frac{\partial \psi_j^4}{\partial \theta} - A_{44}^6 \frac{4}{3h^2 r}\frac{\partial \psi_j^4}{\partial \theta}\right] \\
& - \frac{4}{h^2}\psi_i^4\left[A_{66}^2 \psi_j^4 - A_{66}^4 \frac{4}{h^2}\psi_j^4\right] + \frac{1}{2r}\frac{\partial \psi_i^4}{\partial \theta}\left[T_{22}^0 \frac{1}{2r}\frac{\partial \psi_j^4}{\partial \theta} - T_{22}^2 \frac{2}{h^2 r}\psi_j^4\right] \\
& - \frac{2}{h^2 r}\psi_i^4\left[T_{22}^2 \frac{1}{2r}\frac{\partial \psi_j^4}{\partial \theta} + T_{22}^4 - \frac{2}{h^2 r}\psi_j^4\right] + \frac{1}{2r}\frac{\partial \psi_i^4}{\partial \theta}\left[T_{33}^0 \frac{1}{2r}\frac{\partial \psi_j^4}{\partial \theta} - T_{33}^2 \frac{2}{h^2 r}\frac{\partial \psi_j^4}{\partial \theta}\right] \\
& + \frac{2}{h^2 r}\frac{\partial \psi_i^4}{\partial \theta}\left[-T_{33}^2 \frac{1}{2r}\frac{\partial \psi_j^4}{\partial \theta} + T_{33}^4 \frac{2}{h^2 r}\frac{\partial \psi_j^4}{\partial \theta}\right] \\
& + \left(\frac{1}{4}\frac{\partial \psi_i^4}{\partial \theta} - \frac{1}{4r}\psi_i^4\right)\left[T_{44}^0\left(\frac{1}{4}\frac{\partial \psi_j^4}{\partial \theta} - \frac{1}{4r}\psi_j^4\right) + T_{44}^2\left(\frac{-1}{h^2}\frac{\partial \psi_j^4}{\partial r} + \frac{1}{h^2 r \psi_j^4}\right)\right] \\
& + \left(\frac{-1}{h^2}\frac{\partial \psi_i^4}{\partial r} + \frac{1}{h^2 r}\psi_i^4\right)\left[T_{44}^2\left(\frac{1}{4}\frac{\partial \psi_j^4}{\partial \theta} - \frac{1}{4r}\psi_j^4\right) + T_{44}^4\left(\frac{-1}{h^2}\frac{\partial \psi_j^4}{\partial r} + \frac{1}{h^2 r}\psi_j^4\right)\right] \\
& + \left(\frac{-1}{4r^2}\frac{\partial^2 \psi_i^4}{\partial \theta^2} - \frac{2}{h^2}\psi_i^4\right)\left[T_{55}^2\left(\frac{-1}{4r^2}\frac{\partial^2 \psi_j^4}{\partial \theta^2} - \frac{2}{h^2}\psi_j^4\right) + T_{55}^4 \frac{1}{3h^2 r^2}\frac{\partial^2 \psi_j^4}{\partial \theta^2}\right] \\
& + \frac{1}{3h^2 r^2}\frac{\partial^2 \psi_j^4}{\partial \theta^2}\left[T_{55}^2\left(\frac{-1}{4r^2}\frac{\partial^2 \psi_j^4}{\partial \theta^2} - \frac{2}{h^2}\psi_j^4\right) + T_{55}^6 \frac{1}{3h^2 r^2}\frac{\partial^2 \psi_j^4}{\partial \theta^2}\right] + \left(\frac{-1}{4r}\frac{\partial^2 \psi_i^4}{\partial \theta \partial r} + \frac{1}{4r^2}\frac{\partial \psi_i^4}{\partial \theta}\right)\Bigg[T_{66}^2 \\
& \left(\frac{-1}{4r}\frac{\partial^2 \psi_j^4}{\partial \theta \partial r} + \frac{1}{4r^2}\frac{\partial \psi_j^4}{\partial \theta}\right) + T_{66}^4\left(\frac{-1}{3h^2 r}\frac{\partial^2 \psi_j^4}{\partial \theta \partial r} + \frac{1}{3h^2 r^2}\frac{\partial \psi_j^4}{\partial \theta}\right)\Bigg] + \left(\frac{-1}{3h^2 r}\frac{\partial^2 \psi_i^4}{\partial \theta \partial r} + \frac{1}{3h^2 r^2}\frac{\partial \psi_i^4}{\partial \theta}\right) \\
& \left[T_{66}^4\left(\frac{-1}{4r}\frac{\partial^2 \psi_j^4}{\partial \theta \partial r} + \frac{1}{4r^2}\frac{\partial \psi_j^4}{\partial \theta}\right) + T_{66}^6\left(\frac{-1}{3h^2 r}\frac{\partial^2 \psi_j^4}{\partial \theta \partial r} + \frac{1}{3h^2 r^2}\frac{\partial \psi_j^4}{\partial \theta}\right)\right]\Bigg\} r dr d\theta
\end{aligned}
\tag{A25}
$$

$$
\begin{aligned}
K_{45} = \int_{\Omega} \Bigg\{ & \frac{\partial \psi_i^4}{\partial r}\left[A_{12}^2 \frac{1}{r}\frac{\partial \psi_j^5}{\partial \theta} - \frac{4}{3rh^2}A_{12}^4 \frac{\partial \psi_j^5 - \theta}{\partial \theta}\right] - \frac{4}{3h^2}\frac{\partial \psi_i^4}{\partial r}\left[A_{12}^4 \frac{1}{r}\frac{\partial \psi_j^5}{\partial \theta} - \frac{4}{3rh^2}A_{12}^6 \frac{\psi_j^5}{\partial \theta}\right] \\
& + \frac{1}{r}\psi_i^4\left[A_{22}^2 \frac{1}{r}\frac{\partial \psi_j^5}{\partial \theta} - A_{22}^4 \frac{4}{3h^2 r}\frac{\partial \psi_j^5}{\partial \theta}\right] - \frac{4}{3rh^2}\psi_i^4\left[A_{22}^4 \frac{1}{r}\frac{\partial \psi_j^5}{\partial} - \frac{4}{3rh^2}A_{22}^6 \frac{\partial \psi_j^5}{\partial \theta}\right] \\
& + \frac{1}{r}\frac{\partial \psi_i^4}{\partial \theta}\left[A_{44}^2\left(\frac{\partial \psi_j^5}{\partial r} - \frac{1}{r}\psi_j^5\right) - A_{44}^4\left(\frac{4}{d3h^2}\frac{\partial \psi_j^5}{\partial r} + \frac{4}{3h^2 r}\psi_j^5\right)\right] \\
& - \frac{4}{3h^2 r}\frac{\partial \psi_i^4}{\partial \theta}\left[A_{44}^4\left(\frac{\partial \psi_j^5}{\partial r} - \frac{1}{r}\psi_j^5\right) - A_{44}^6\left(\frac{4}{3h^2}\frac{\partial \psi_j^5}{\partial r} + \frac{4}{3h^2 r}\psi_j^5\right)\right] \\
& + \frac{1}{2r}\frac{\partial \psi_i^4}{\partial \theta}\left[T_{22}^0 \frac{1}{2r}\psi_j^5 + T_{22}^2 \frac{2}{h^2 r}\frac{\partial \psi_j^5}{\partial r}\right] - \frac{2}{h^2 r}\psi_i^4\left[T_{22}^2 \frac{1}{2r}\psi_j^5 + T_{22}^4 \frac{2}{h^2 r}\frac{\partial \psi_j^5}{\partial r}\right] \\
& - \frac{1}{2r}\frac{\partial \psi_i^4}{\partial \theta}\left[T_{33}^0\left(\frac{1}{2r}\psi_j^5 + \frac{1}{2}\frac{\partial \psi_j^5}{\partial r}\right) - T_{33}^2\left(2\frac{\psi_j^5}{h^2 r} + \frac{2}{h^2}\frac{\partial \psi_j^5}{\partial r}\right)\right] + \frac{2}{h^2 r}\frac{\partial \psi_i^4}{\partial \theta}\Bigg[T_{33}^2\Bigg(\frac{1}{2r}\psi_j^5 \\
& + \frac{1}{2}\frac{\partial \psi_j^5}{\partial r}\Bigg) - T_{33}^4\left(2\frac{\psi_j^5}{h^2 r} + \frac{2}{h^2}\frac{\partial \psi_j^5}{\partial r}\right)\Bigg] + \left(\frac{1}{4}\frac{\partial \psi_i^4}{\partial \theta} - \frac{1}{4r}\psi_i^4\right)\Bigg[T_{44}^0 \frac{-1}{4r}\frac{\partial \psi_j^5}{\partial \theta} \\
& + T_{44}^2 \frac{1}{h^2 r}\frac{\partial \psi_j^5}{\partial \theta}\Bigg] + \left(\frac{-1}{h^2}\frac{\partial \psi_i^4}{\partial r} + \frac{1}{h^2 r}\psi_i^4\right)\left[-T_{44}^2 \frac{1}{4r}\frac{\partial \psi_j^5}{\partial \theta} + T_{44}^4 \frac{1}{h^2 r}\frac{\partial \psi_j^5}{\partial \theta}\right] - \Bigg(\frac{1}{4r^2}\frac{\partial^2 \psi_i^4}{\partial \theta} \\
& + \frac{2}{h^2}\psi_i^4\Bigg)\left[T_{55}^2\left(\frac{1}{4r^2}\frac{\partial \psi_j^5}{\partial \theta} + \frac{1}{4r}\frac{\partial^2 \psi_j^5}{\partial r \partial \theta}\right) - T_{55}^4\left(\frac{1}{3h^2 r^2}\frac{\partial \psi_j^5}{\partial \theta} + \frac{1}{3h^2 r}\frac{\partial^2 \psi_j^5}{\partial r \partial \theta}\right)\right] + \frac{1}{3h^2 r^2}\frac{\partial^2 \psi_j^4}{\partial \theta^2} \\
& \left[T_{55}^4\left(\frac{1}{4r^2}\frac{\partial \psi_j^5}{\partial \theta} + \frac{1}{4r}\frac{\partial^2 \psi_j^5}{\partial r \partial \theta}\right) - T_{55}^6\left(\frac{1}{3h^2 r^2}\frac{\partial \psi_j^5}{\partial \theta} + \frac{1}{3h^2 r}\frac{\partial^2 \psi_j^5}{\partial \theta \partial r}\right)\right] + \left(\frac{-1}{4r}\frac{\partial^2 \psi_i^4}{\partial \theta \partial r} + \frac{1}{4r^2}\frac{\partial \psi_i^4}{\partial \theta}\right) \\
& \left[T_{66}^2\left(\frac{1}{4r}\frac{\partial \psi_j^5}{\partial r} - \frac{1}{4r^2}\psi_j^5 + \frac{1}{4}\frac{\partial^2 \psi_j^5}{\partial r^2} + \frac{2}{h^2}\psi_j^5\right) + T_{66}^4\left(\frac{-1}{3h^2 r}\frac{\partial \psi_j^5}{\partial r} + \frac{1}{3h^2 r^2}\psi_j^5 - \frac{1}{3h^2}\frac{\partial^2 \psi_j^5}{\partial r^2}\right)\right] \\
& + \left(\frac{-1}{3h^2 r}\frac{\partial^2 \psi_i^4}{\partial \theta \partial r} + \frac{1}{3h^2 r^2}\frac{\partial \psi_i^4}{\partial \theta}\right)\Bigg[T_{66}^4\left(\frac{1}{4r}\frac{\partial \psi_j^5}{\partial r} - \frac{1}{4r^2}\psi_j^5 + \frac{1}{4}\frac{\partial^2 \psi_j^5}{\partial r^2} + \frac{2}{h^2}\psi_j^5\right) \\
& + T_{66}^6\left(\frac{-1}{3h^2 r}\frac{\partial \psi_j^5}{\partial r} + \frac{1}{3h^2 r^2}\psi_j^5 - \frac{1}{3h^2}\frac{\partial^2 \psi_j^5}{\partial r^2}\right)\Bigg]\Bigg\} r dr d\theta
\end{aligned} \tag{A26}
$$

$$
\begin{aligned}
K_{46} = \int_{\Omega} \Bigg\{ & \frac{\partial \psi_i^4}{\partial r}\left[A_{13}^1 \psi_j^6 - A_{11}^3 \frac{1}{2}\frac{\partial^2 \psi_j^6}{\partial r^2} - A_{12}^3\left(\frac{1}{2r}\frac{\partial \psi_j^6}{\partial r} + \frac{1}{2r^2}\frac{\partial^2 \psi_j^6}{\partial \theta^2}\right)\right] - \frac{4}{3h^2}\frac{\partial \psi_i^4}{\partial r}\Big[A_{13}^3 \psi_j^6 \\
& - A_{11}^5 \frac{1}{2}\frac{\partial^2 \psi_j^6}{\partial r^2} - A_{12}^5\left(\frac{1}{2r}\frac{\partial \psi_j^6}{\partial r} + \frac{1}{2r^2}\frac{\partial^2 \psi_j^6}{\partial \theta^2}\right)\Big] + \frac{1}{r}\psi_i^4\Big[A_{23}^1 \psi_j^6 + A_{21}^3 \frac{-1}{2}\frac{\partial^2 \psi_j^6}{\partial r^2} - A_{22}^3\Big(\frac{1}{2r}\frac{\partial \psi_j^6}{\partial r} \\
& + \frac{1}{2r^2}\frac{\partial^2 \psi_j^6}{\partial \theta^2}\Big)\Big] - \frac{4}{3rh^2}\psi_i^4\left[A_{23}^3 \psi_j^6 - A_{21}^5 \frac{1}{2}\frac{\partial^2 \psi_j^6}{\partial r} - A_{22}^5\left(\frac{1}{2r}\frac{\partial \psi_j^6}{\partial r} + \frac{1}{2r^2}\frac{\partial^2 \psi_j^6}{\partial \theta^2}\right)\right] \\
& + \frac{1}{r}\frac{\partial \psi_i^4}{\partial \theta}\left[A_{44}^3\left(\frac{-1}{r}\frac{\partial^2 \psi_j^6}{\partial \theta \partial r} + \frac{1}{r^2}\frac{\partial \psi_j^6}{\partial \theta}\right)\right] - \frac{4}{3h^2 r}\frac{\partial \psi_i^4}{\partial \theta}\left[A_{44}^5\left(\frac{-1}{r}\frac{\partial^2 \psi_j^6}{\partial \theta \partial r} + \frac{1}{r^2}\frac{\partial \psi_j^6}{\partial \theta}\right)\right] \\
& + \frac{1}{2r}\frac{\partial \psi_i^4}{\partial \theta}\left[T_{22}^1\left(\frac{-1}{r}\frac{\partial^2 \psi_j^6}{drd\theta} + \frac{1}{r}\frac{\partial \psi_j^6}{\partial \theta}\right)\right] + \frac{-2}{h^2 r}\psi_i^4\left[T_{22}^3\left(\frac{-1}{r}\frac{\partial^2 \psi_j^6}{\partial rd\theta} + \frac{1}{r}\frac{\partial \psi_j^6}{\partial \theta}\right)\right] \\
& + \left(\frac{1}{4}\frac{\partial \psi_i^4}{\partial \theta} - \frac{1}{4r}\psi_j^4\right)\left[T_{44}^1\left(\frac{-1}{2}\frac{\partial^2 \psi_j^6}{\partial r^2} + \frac{1}{2r^2}\frac{\partial^2 \psi_j^6}{\partial \theta^2} + \frac{1}{r}\frac{\partial \psi_j^6}{\partial r}\right)\right] \\
& + \left(\frac{-1}{h^2}\frac{\partial \psi_i^4}{\partial r} + \frac{1}{h^2}\psi_i^4\right)\left[\frac{-1}{2}\frac{\partial^2 \psi_j^6}{\partial r^2} + \frac{1}{2r^2}\frac{\partial^2 \psi_j^6}{\partial \theta^2} + \frac{1}{r}\frac{\partial \psi_j^6}{\partial r}T_{44}^3\right] \\
& + \left(\frac{1}{4r^2}\frac{\partial^2 \psi_i^4}{\partial \theta} + \frac{2}{h^2}\psi_i^4\right)T_{55}^1 \frac{1}{2}\frac{\partial \psi_j^6}{\partial r} - T_{55}^3 \frac{1}{6h^2 r^2}\frac{\partial^2 \psi_j^4}{\partial \theta^2}\frac{\partial \psi_j^6}{\partial r} \\
& + \left(\frac{-1}{4r}\frac{\partial^2 \psi_i^4}{\partial \theta \partial r} + \frac{1}{4r^2}\frac{\partial \psi_i^4}{\partial \theta}\right)T_{66}^1 \frac{1}{2r}\frac{\partial \psi_j^6}{\partial \theta} + \left(\frac{-1}{3h^2 r}\frac{\partial^2 \psi_i^4}{d\theta \partial r} + \frac{1}{3h^2 r^2}\frac{\partial \psi_i^4}{\partial \theta}\right)T_{66}^3 \frac{1}{2r}\frac{\partial \psi_j^6}{\partial \theta}\Bigg\} r dr d\theta \qquad \text{(A27)}
\end{aligned}
$$

$$
\begin{aligned}
K_{47} = \int_{\Omega} \Bigg\{ & \frac{\partial \psi_i^4}{\partial r}\left[A_{13}^2 2\psi_j^7 - A_{11}^4 \frac{1}{3}\frac{\partial^2 \psi_j^7}{\partial r^2} - A_{12}^4\left(\frac{1}{3r^2}\frac{\partial^2 \psi_j^7}{\partial \theta^2} + \frac{1}{3r}\frac{\partial \psi_j^7}{\partial r}\right)\right] - \frac{4}{3h^2}\frac{\partial \psi_i^4}{\partial r}\Bigg[A_{13}^4 2\psi_j^7 \\
& - A_{11}^6 \frac{1}{3}\frac{\partial^2 \psi_j^7}{\partial r^2} - A_{12}^6\left(\frac{1}{3r}\frac{\partial^2 \psi_j^7}{\partial \theta^2} + \frac{1}{3r}\frac{\partial \partial_z}{\partial r}\right)\Bigg] \\
& + \frac{1}{r}\psi_i^4\left[A_{23}^2 2\psi_j^7 - A_{21}^4 \frac{1}{3}\frac{\partial^2 \psi_j^7}{\partial r^2} - A_{22}^4\left(\frac{1}{3r^2}\frac{\partial^2 \psi_j^7}{\partial \theta^2} + \frac{1}{3r}\frac{\partial \psi_j^7}{\partial r}\right)\right] \\
& - \frac{4}{3rh^2}\psi_i^4\left[A_{23}^4 2\psi_j^7 + A_{21}^6 \frac{-1}{3}\frac{\partial^2 \psi_j^7}{\partial r^2} - A_{22}^6\left(\frac{1}{3r}\frac{\partial^2 \psi_j^7}{\partial \theta^2} + \frac{1}{3r}\frac{\partial \partial_z}{\partial r}\right)\right] - A_{44}^4 \frac{2}{3r}\frac{\partial \psi_i^5}{\partial \theta}\frac{\partial^2 \psi_j^7}{\partial \theta \partial r} \\
& + A_{44}^6 \frac{8}{9h^2 r}\frac{\partial \psi_i^4}{\partial \theta}\frac{\partial^2 \psi_j^7}{\partial \theta \partial r} + \frac{1}{2r}\frac{\partial \psi_i^4}{\partial \theta}\left[T_{22}^2\left(\frac{1}{r^2}\frac{\partial^2 \psi_j^7}{\partial \theta^2} + \frac{-1}{r}\frac{\partial \psi_j^7}{\partial r}\right)\right] \\
& - \frac{2}{h^2 r}\psi_i^4\left[T_{22}^4\left(\frac{1}{r^2}\frac{\partial^2 \psi_j^7}{\partial \theta^2} + \frac{-1}{r}\frac{\partial \psi_j^7}{\partial r}\right)\right] \\
& + \left(\frac{1}{4}\frac{\partial \psi_i^4}{\partial \theta} - \frac{1}{4r}\psi_j^4\right)\left[T_{44}^2\left(-\frac{1}{2}\frac{\partial^2 \psi_j^7}{\partial r^2} + \frac{1}{2r^2}\frac{\partial^2 \psi_j^7}{\partial \theta^2} + \frac{1}{2r}\frac{\partial \psi_j^7}{\partial r}\right)\right] \\
& + \left(\frac{-1}{h^2}\frac{\partial \psi_i^4}{\partial r} + \frac{1}{h^2 r}\delta\beta\right)\left[T_{44}^4\left(-\frac{1}{2}\frac{\partial^2 \psi_j^7}{\partial r^2} + \frac{1}{2r^2}\frac{\partial^2 \psi_j^7}{\partial \theta^2} + \frac{1}{2r}\frac{\partial \psi_j^7}{\partial r}\right)\right] \\
& + \left(\frac{1}{4r^2}\frac{\partial^2 \psi_i^4}{\partial \theta} + \frac{2}{h^2}\psi_i^4\right)T_{55}^2 \frac{3}{2}\frac{\partial \psi_j^7}{\partial r} - T_{55}^4 \frac{1}{2h^2 r^2}\frac{\partial^2 \psi_j^4}{\partial \theta}\frac{\partial \psi_j^7}{\partial r} \\
& + \left(\frac{-1}{4r}\frac{\partial^2 d\psi_j^4}{\partial \theta \partial r} + \frac{1}{4r^2}\frac{\partial d\psi_j^4}{\partial \theta}\right)T_{66}^2 \frac{1}{r}\frac{\partial \psi_j^7}{\partial \theta} + \left(\frac{-1}{3h^2 r}\frac{\partial^2 \psi_i^4}{\partial \theta \partial r} + \frac{1}{3h^2 r^2}\frac{\partial \psi_i^4}{\partial \theta}\right)T_{66}^4 \frac{1}{r}\frac{\partial \psi_j^7}{\partial \theta} \\
& - A_{44}^6 \frac{8}{9h^2 r^3}\frac{\partial \psi_i^4}{d\theta}\frac{\partial \psi_j^7}{\partial \theta} + A_{44}^4 \frac{2}{3r^3 r}\frac{\partial \psi_i^4}{d\theta}\frac{\partial \psi_j^7}{d\theta}\Bigg\} r dr d\theta
\end{aligned} \tag{A28}
$$

$$
\begin{aligned}
K_{51} = \int_{\Omega} \Bigg\{ & \frac{1}{r}\frac{\partial \psi_i^5}{\partial \theta}\left[A_{21}^1 \frac{\partial \psi_j^1}{\partial r} + A_{22}^1 \frac{1}{r}\psi_j^1\right] - \frac{4}{3rh^2}\frac{\partial \psi_i^5}{\partial \theta}\left[A_{21}^3 \frac{\partial \psi_j^1}{\partial r} + A_{22}^3 \frac{1}{r}\psi_j^1\right] \\
& + \left(\frac{\partial \psi_i^5}{\partial r} - \frac{1}{r}\psi_i^5\right) A_{44}^1 \frac{1}{r}\frac{\partial \psi_j^1}{\partial \theta} - \frac{4}{3h^2}\left(\frac{\partial \psi_i^5}{\partial r} + \frac{1}{r}\delta\beta\theta\right) A_{44}^3 \frac{1}{r}\frac{\partial \psi_j^1}{\partial \theta} \\
& - \left(\frac{1}{4r^2}\frac{\partial \psi_i^5}{\partial \theta} + \frac{1}{4r}\frac{\partial^2 \psi_i^5}{\partial r \partial \theta}\right)\frac{1}{4r^2}\frac{\partial^2 \psi_j^1}{\partial \theta^2} T_{55}^1 + \left(\frac{1}{3h^2 r^2}\frac{\partial \psi_i^5}{\partial \theta} + \frac{1}{3h^2 r}\frac{\partial^2 \psi_i^5}{\partial \theta \partial r}\right) T_{55}^3 \frac{1}{4r^2}\frac{\partial^2 \psi_j^1}{\partial \theta^2} \\
& + \left(\frac{1}{4r}\frac{\partial \psi_i^5}{\partial r} - \frac{1}{4r^2}\psi_i^5 + \frac{1}{4}\frac{\partial^2 \psi_i^5}{\partial r^2} + \frac{2}{h^2}\psi_i^5\right)\left[T_{66}^1\left(\frac{-1}{4r}\frac{\partial^2 \psi_j^1}{\partial \theta \partial r} + \frac{1}{4r^2}\frac{\partial \psi_j^1}{\partial \theta}\right)\right] \\
& + \left(\frac{-1}{3h^2 r}\frac{\partial \psi_i^5}{\partial r} + \frac{1}{3h^2 r^2}\psi_i^5 - \frac{1}{3h^2}\frac{\partial^2 \psi_i^5}{\partial r^2}\right)\left[T_{66}^3\left(\frac{1}{4r}\frac{\partial^2 \psi_j^1}{\partial \theta \partial r} + \frac{1}{4r^2}\frac{\partial \psi_j^1}{\partial \theta}\right)\right]\Bigg\} r dr d\theta
\end{aligned}
\quad \text{(A29)}
$$

$$
\begin{aligned}
K_{52} = \int_{\Omega} \Bigg\{ & \frac{1}{r^2}\frac{\partial \psi_i^5}{\partial \theta} A_{22}^1 \frac{\partial \psi_j^2}{\partial \theta} - A_{22}^3 \frac{4}{3r^2 h^2}\frac{\partial \psi_i^5}{\partial \theta}\frac{\partial \psi_j^2}{\partial \theta} + \left(\frac{\partial \psi_i^5}{\partial r} - \frac{1}{r}\psi_i^5\right)\left[A_{44}^1\left(\frac{\partial \psi_j^2}{\partial r} - \frac{\psi_j^2}{r}\right)\right] \\
& + \left(\frac{1}{4r^2}\frac{\partial \psi_i^5}{\partial \theta} + \frac{1}{4r}\frac{\partial^2 \psi_i^5}{\partial r d\theta}\right)\left[T_{55}^1\left(\frac{1}{4r^2}\frac{\partial \psi_j^2}{\partial \theta} + \frac{1}{4r}\frac{\partial^2 \psi_j^2}{\partial r \partial \theta}\right)\right] \\
& - \left(\frac{1}{3h^2 r^2}\frac{\partial \psi_i^5}{\partial \theta} + \frac{1}{3h^2 r}\frac{\partial^2 \psi_i^5}{d\theta dr}\right)\left[T_{55}^3\left(\frac{1}{4r^2}\frac{\partial \psi_j^2}{\partial \theta} + \frac{1}{4r}\frac{\partial^2 \psi_j^2}{\partial r d\theta}\right)\right] \\
& + \left(\frac{1}{4r}\frac{\partial \psi_i^5}{\partial r} - \frac{1}{4r^2}\psi_i^5 + \frac{1}{4}\frac{\partial^2 \psi_i^5}{\partial r^2} + \frac{2}{h^2}\psi_i^5\right)\left[T_{66}^1\left(\frac{1}{4r}\frac{\partial \psi_j^2}{\partial r} - \frac{1}{4r^2}\psi_j^2 + \frac{1}{4}\frac{\partial^2 \psi_j^2}{\partial r^2}\right)\right] \\
& + \left(\frac{-1}{3h^2 r}\frac{\partial \psi_i^5}{\partial r} + \frac{1}{3h^2 r^2}\psi_i^5 - \frac{1}{3h^2}\frac{\partial^2 \psi_i^5}{\partial r^2}\right)\left[T_{66}^3\left(\frac{1}{4r}\frac{\partial \psi_j^2}{\partial r} - \frac{1}{4r^2}\psi_j^2 + \frac{1}{4}\frac{\partial^2 \psi_j^2}{\partial r^2}\right)\right] \\
& - \frac{4}{3h^2}\left(\frac{\partial \psi_i^5}{\partial r} + \frac{1}{r}\psi_i^5\right)\left[A_{44}^3\left(\frac{\partial \psi_j^2}{\partial r}\frac{-\psi_j^2}{r}\right)\right]\Bigg\} r dr d\theta
\end{aligned}
\quad \text{(A30)}
$$

$$K_{53} = \int_{\Omega}\left\{\frac{1}{r}\frac{\partial\psi_i^5}{\partial\theta}\left[A_{21}^1\frac{1}{2}\frac{\partial W_o}{\partial r}\frac{\partial\psi_j^3}{\partial r} + A_{22}^1\frac{1}{2r^2}\frac{\partial W_o}{d\theta}\frac{\partial\psi_j^3}{d\theta} - A_{21}^4\frac{4}{3h^2}\frac{\partial^2\psi_j^3}{\partial r^2} - A_{22}^4\left(\frac{4}{3r^2h^2}\frac{\partial^2\psi_j^3}{\partial\theta^2} + \right.\right.\right.$$
$$\left.\left. + \frac{4}{3rh^2}\frac{\partial\psi_j^3}{\partial r}\right)\right] - \frac{4}{3rh^2}\frac{\partial\psi_i^5}{\partial\theta}\left[A_{21}^3\frac{1}{2}\frac{\partial W_o}{\partial r}\frac{\partial\psi_j^3}{\partial r} + A_{22}^3\frac{1}{2r^2}\frac{\partial W_o}{\partial\theta}\frac{\partial\psi_j^3}{\partial\theta} - A_{21}^6\frac{4}{3h^2}\frac{\partial^2\psi_j^3}{\partial r^2}\right.$$
$$\left. - A_{22}^6\left(\frac{4}{3r^2h^2}\frac{\partial^2\psi_j^3}{\partial\theta^2} + \frac{4}{3rh^2}\frac{\partial\psi_j^3}{\partial r}\right)\right]$$
$$+ \left(\frac{\partial\psi_i^5}{\partial r} - \frac{1}{r}\psi_i^5\right)\left[A_{44}^1\left(\frac{1}{2r}\frac{\partial W_o}{\partial r}\frac{\partial\psi_j^3}{\partial\theta} + \frac{1}{2}\frac{\partial W_o}{\partial\theta}\frac{\partial\psi_j^3}{\partial r}\right) - A_{44}^4\left(\frac{8}{3h^2}\frac{\partial^2\psi_j^3}{\partial\theta\partial r}\right)\right]$$
$$- \frac{4}{3h^2}\left(\frac{\partial\psi_i^5}{\partial r} + \frac{1}{r}\psi_i^5\right)\left[A_{44}^3\frac{1}{r}\frac{\partial\psi_j^3}{\partial r}\frac{\partial\psi_j^3}{\partial\theta} - A_{44}^6\frac{8}{3h^2}\frac{\partial^2\psi_j^3}{\partial\theta\partial r}\right] + \psi_i^5\left[A_{55}^0\frac{1}{r}\frac{\partial\psi_j^3}{\partial\theta}\right.$$
$$\left. - A_{55}^2\frac{4}{h^2 r}\frac{\partial\psi_j^3}{\partial\theta}\right] - \frac{4}{h^2}\psi_i^5\left[A_{55}^2\frac{1}{r}\frac{\partial\psi_j^3}{\partial\theta} - A_{55}^4\frac{4}{h^2 r}\frac{\partial\psi_j^3}{\partial\theta}\right] - \frac{1}{2}\frac{\partial\psi_i^5}{\partial r}\left[T_{11}^0\left(\frac{1}{2r}\frac{\partial^2\psi_j^3}{\partial\theta\partial r}\right.\right.$$
$$\left.\left. - \frac{1}{2r^2}\frac{\partial\psi_j^3}{\partial\theta}\right) - T_{11}^2\left(\frac{2}{h^2 r}\frac{\partial^2\psi_j^3}{\partial\theta\partial r} + \frac{2}{h^2r^2}\frac{\partial\psi_j^3}{\partial\theta}\right)\right] + \frac{2}{h^2}\frac{\partial\psi_i^5}{\partial r}\left[T_{11}^2\left(\frac{1}{2r}\frac{\partial^2\psi_j^3}{\partial\theta\partial r} - \frac{1}{2r^2}\frac{\partial\psi_j^3}{\partial\theta}\right)\right.$$
$$\left. - T_{11}^4\left(\frac{2}{h^2 r}\frac{\partial^2\psi_j^3}{\partial\theta\partial r} + \frac{2}{h^2r^2}\frac{\partial\psi_j^3}{\partial\theta}\right)\right] + \frac{1}{2r}\psi_i^5\left[T_{22}^0\left(-\frac{1}{2r}\frac{\partial^2\psi_j^3}{\partial r\partial\theta} + \frac{1}{2r^2}\frac{\partial\psi_j^3}{\partial\theta}\right) + T_{22}^2\left(\frac{2}{h^2r^2}\frac{\partial\psi_j^3}{\partial\theta^2}\right.\right.$$
$$\left.\left. - \frac{2}{h^2 r}\frac{\partial\psi_j^3}{\partial r}\right)\right] + \frac{2}{h^2 r}\frac{\partial\psi_i^5}{\partial\theta}\left[T_{22}^2\left(\frac{-1}{2r}\frac{\partial^2\psi_j^3}{\partial r\partial\theta} + \frac{1}{2r^2}\frac{\partial\psi_j^3}{\partial\theta}\right) + T_{22}^4\left(\frac{2}{h^2r^2}\frac{\partial^2\psi_j^3}{\partial\theta^2} - \frac{2}{h^2 r}\frac{\partial\psi_j^3}{\partial r}\right)\right]$$
$$- \frac{1}{4r}\frac{\partial\psi_i^5}{\partial\theta}\left[T_{44}^0\left(\frac{-1}{4}\frac{\partial^2\psi_j^3}{\partial r^2} + \frac{1}{4r^2}\frac{\partial^2\psi_j^3}{\partial\theta^2} + \frac{1}{4r}\frac{\partial\psi_j^3}{\partial r}\right) + T_{44}^2\left(\frac{-1}{h^2}\frac{\partial^2\psi_j^3}{\partial r^2} + \frac{1}{h^2r^2}\frac{\partial^2\psi_j^3}{\partial\theta^2}\right.\right.$$
$$\left.\left. + \frac{1}{h^2 r}\frac{\partial\psi_j^3}{\partial r}\right)\right] + \frac{1}{h^2 r}\frac{\partial\psi_i^5}{\partial\theta}\left[T_{44}^2\left(-\frac{1}{4}\frac{\partial^2\psi_j^3}{\partial r^2} + \frac{1}{4r^2}\frac{\partial^2\psi_j^3}{\partial\theta^2} + \frac{1}{4r}\frac{\partial\psi_j^3}{\partial r}\right) + T_{44}^4\left(\frac{-1}{h^2}\frac{\partial^2\psi_j^3}{\partial r^2}\right.\right.$$
$$\left.\left. + \frac{1}{h^2r^2}\frac{\partial^2\psi_j^3}{\partial\theta^2} + \frac{1}{h^2 r}\frac{\partial\psi_j^3}{\partial r}\right)\right] - \left(\frac{1}{4r^2}\frac{\partial\psi_i^5}{\partial\theta} + \frac{1}{4r}\frac{\partial^2\delta\beta\_\theta}{\partial r\partial\theta}\right)T_{55}^2\frac{2}{h^2}\frac{\partial\psi_j^3}{\partial r} + \left(\frac{1}{3h^2r^2}\frac{\partial\psi_i^5}{\partial\theta}\right.$$
$$\left. + \frac{1}{3h^2 r}\frac{\partial^2\psi_i^5}{\partial\theta\partial r}\right)T_{55}^4\frac{2}{h^2}\frac{\partial\psi_j^3}{\partial r} + \left(\frac{1}{4r}\frac{\partial\psi_i^5}{\partial r} - \frac{1}{4r}\delta\beta\theta + \frac{1}{4}\frac{\partial^2\delta\beta\theta}{\partial r^2} + \frac{2}{h^2}\psi_i^5\right)T_{66}^2\frac{2}{h^2}\frac{\partial\psi_j^3}{\partial\theta}$$
$$+ \left(\frac{-1}{3h^2 r}\frac{\partial\psi_i^5}{\partial r} + \frac{1}{3h^2r^2}\psi_i^5 - \frac{1}{3h^2}\frac{\partial^2\psi_i^5}{\partial r^2}\right)T_{66}^4\frac{2}{h^2}\frac{\partial\psi_j^3}{\partial\theta} + \left(\frac{1}{r}\frac{\partial\psi_i^5}{\partial r} - \frac{1}{r}\psi_i^5\theta\right)A_{44}^4\frac{8}{3h^2r^2}\frac{\partial\psi_j^7}{\partial\theta}$$
$$\left. + \left(\frac{-4}{3h^2}\frac{\partial\psi_i^5}{\partial r} + \frac{4}{3h^2 r}\psi_i^5\right)A_{44}^6\frac{8}{3h^2r^2}\frac{\partial\psi_j^7}{\partial\theta}\right\}rdrd\theta \quad \text{(A31)}$$

$$
\begin{aligned}
K_{54} = \int_{\Omega} \bigg\{ & \frac{1}{r}\frac{\partial\psi_i^5}{\partial\theta}\bigg[A_{21}^2\frac{\partial\psi_j^4}{\partial r} + A_{22}^2\frac{1}{r}\psi_j^4 - A_{21}^4\frac{4}{3h^2}\frac{\partial\psi_j^4}{\partial r} - A_{22}^4\frac{4}{3rh^2}\psi_j^4\bigg] - \frac{4}{3rh^2}\frac{\partial\psi_i^5}{\partial\theta}\bigg[A_{21}^4\frac{\partial\psi_j^4}{\partial r} \\
& + A_{22}^2\frac{1}{r}\psi_j^4 - A_{21}^4\frac{4}{3h^2}\frac{\partial\psi_j^4}{\partial r} - A_{22}^4\frac{4}{3rh^2}\psi_j^4\bigg] + \bigg(\frac{\partial\psi_i^5}{\partial r} - \frac{1}{r}\delta\psi_i^5\bigg)\bigg[A_{44}^2\frac{1}{r}\frac{\partial\psi_j^4}{\partial\theta} - A_{44}^4\frac{4}{3h^2r}\frac{\partial\psi_j^4}{\partial\theta}\bigg] \\
& - \frac{4}{3h^2}\bigg(\frac{\partial\psi_i^5}{\partial r} + \frac{1}{r}\psi_i^5\bigg)\bigg[A_{44}^4\frac{1}{r}\frac{\partial\psi_j^4}{\partial\theta} - A_{44}^6\frac{4}{3h^2r}\frac{\partial\psi_j^4}{\partial\theta}\bigg] \\
& + \frac{1}{2r}\psi_i^5\bigg[T_{22}^0\frac{1}{2r}\frac{\partial\psi_j^4}{\partial\theta} - T_{22}^2\frac{2}{h^2r}\psi_j^4\bigg] + \frac{2}{h^2r}\frac{\partial\psi_i^5}{\partial\theta}\bigg[T_{22}^2\frac{1}{2r}\frac{\partial\psi_j^4}{\partial\theta} - T_{22}^4\frac{2}{hr}\psi_j^4\bigg] \\
& + \bigg(\frac{1}{2r}\psi_i^5 + \frac{1}{2}\frac{\partial\psi_i^5}{\partial r}\bigg)\bigg[T_{33}^0\frac{-1}{2r}\frac{\partial\psi_j^4}{\partial\theta} + T_{33}^2\frac{2}{h^2r}\frac{\partial\psi_j^4}{\partial\theta}\bigg] \\
& + \frac{2}{h^2}\bigg(\frac{\partial\psi_i^5}{\partial r} + \frac{\psi_i^5}{v}\bigg)\bigg[T_{33}^2\frac{1}{2r}\frac{\partial\psi_j^4}{\partial\theta} - T_{33}^4\frac{2}{h^2r}\frac{\partial\psi_j^4}{\partial\theta}\bigg] \\
& + \frac{-1}{4}\frac{\partial\psi_i^5}{\partial\theta}\bigg[T_{44}^0\bigg(\frac{1}{4}\frac{\partial\psi_j^4}{\partial\theta} - \frac{1}{4r}\psi_j^4\bigg) + T_{44}^2\bigg(-\frac{1}{h^2}\frac{\partial\psi_j^4}{\partial r} + \frac{1}{h^2r}\psi_j^4\bigg)\bigg] \\
& + \frac{1}{h^2r}\frac{\partial\psi_i^5}{\partial\theta}\bigg[T_{44}^2\bigg(\frac{1}{4}\frac{\partial\psi_j^4}{\partial\theta} - \frac{1}{4r}\psi_j^4\bigg) + T_{44}^4\bigg(-\frac{1}{h^2}\frac{\partial\psi_j^4}{\partial r} + \frac{1}{h^2r}\psi_j^4\bigg)\bigg] \\
& + \bigg(\frac{1}{4r^2}\frac{\partial\psi_i^5}{\partial\theta} + \frac{1}{4r}\frac{\partial^2\psi_i^5}{\partial r\partial\theta}\bigg)\bigg[T_{55}^2\bigg(\frac{-1}{4r^2}\frac{\partial^2\psi_j^4}{\partial\theta^2} - \frac{2}{h2}\psi_j^4\bigg) + T_{55}^4\frac{1}{3h^2r^2}\frac{\partial^2\psi_j^4}{\partial\theta^2}\bigg] \\
& + \bigg(\frac{1}{3h^2r^2}\frac{\partial\psi_i^5}{\partial\theta} + \frac{1}{3h^2r}\frac{\partial^2\psi_i^5}{\partial\theta\partial r}\bigg)\bigg[T_{55}^4\bigg(\frac{1}{4r^2}\frac{\partial^2\psi_j^4}{\partial\theta^2} + \frac{2}{h^2}\psi_j^4\bigg) + T_{55}^6\frac{1}{3h^2r^2}\frac{\partial^2\psi_j^4}{\partial\theta^2}\bigg] \\
& + \bigg(\frac{1}{4r}\frac{\partial\psi_i^5}{\partial r} - \frac{1}{4r}\psi_i^5 + \frac{1}{4}\frac{\partial^2\psi_i^5}{\partial r^2} + \frac{2}{h^2}\psi_i^5\bigg)\bigg[T_{66}^2\bigg(\frac{-1}{4r}\frac{\partial^2\psi_j^4}{\partial\theta\partial r} + \frac{1}{4r^2}\frac{\partial\psi_j^4}{\partial\theta}\bigg) \\
& + T_{66}^4\bigg(\frac{-1}{3h^2r}\frac{\partial^2\psi_j^4}{d\theta dr} + \frac{1}{3h^2r^2}\frac{\partial\psi_j^4}{d\theta}\bigg)\bigg] + \bigg(\frac{-1}{3h^2r}\frac{\partial\psi_i^5}{\partial r} + \frac{1}{3h^2r^2}\psi_i^5 - \frac{1}{3h^2}\frac{\partial^2\psi_i^5}{\partial r^2}\bigg) \\
& \bigg[T_{66}^4\bigg(\frac{-1}{4r}\frac{\partial^2\psi_j^4}{\partial\theta\partial r} + \frac{1}{4r^2}\frac{\partial\psi_j^4}{\partial\theta}\bigg) + T_{66}^6\bigg(\frac{-1}{3h^2r}\frac{\partial\psi_j^4}{\partial\theta\partial r} + \frac{1}{3h^2r^2}\frac{\partial\psi_j^4}{\partial\theta}\bigg)\bigg]\bigg\} r dr d\theta
\end{aligned}
\tag{A32}
$$

$$
\begin{aligned}
K_{55} = \int_{\Omega} \Bigg\{ & \frac{1}{r}\frac{\partial \delta\psi_j^5}{\partial\theta}\left[A_{22}^2 \frac{1}{r}\frac{\partial\psi_j^5}{\partial\theta} - A_{22}^4 \frac{4}{3h^2 r}\frac{\partial\psi_j^5}{\partial\theta}\right] - \frac{4}{3rh^2}\frac{\partial\psi_i^5}{\partial\theta}\left[A_{22}^4 \frac{1}{r}\frac{\partial\psi_j^5}{\partial\theta} - A_{22}^6 \frac{4}{3h^2 r}\frac{\partial\psi_j^5}{\partial\theta}\right] \\
& + \left(\frac{\partial\psi_i^5}{\partial r} - \frac{1}{r}\psi_i^5\right)\left[A_{44}^2\left(\frac{\partial\psi_j^5}{\partial r} - \frac{1}{r}\psi_j^5\right) + A_{44}^4\left(\frac{-4}{3h^2}\frac{\partial\psi_j^5}{\partial r} + \frac{4}{3h^2 r}\psi_j^5\right)\right] \\
& - \frac{4}{3h^2}\left(\frac{\partial\psi_i^5}{\partial r} + \frac{1}{r}\psi_i^5\right)\left[A_{44}^4\left(\frac{\partial\psi_j^5}{\partial r} - \frac{1}{r}\psi_j^5\right) + A_{44}^6\left(\frac{-4}{3h^2}\frac{\partial\psi_j^5}{\partial r} + \frac{4}{3h^2 r}\psi_j^5\right)\right] \\
& + \psi_i^5\left[A_{55}^0\psi_j^5 - A_{55}^2\frac{4}{h^2}\psi_j^5\right] - \frac{4}{h^2}\psi_i^5\left[A_{55}^2\psi_j^5 - A_{55}^4\frac{4}{h^2}\psi_j^5\right] \\
& + \frac{1}{2}\frac{\partial\psi_i^5}{\partial r}\left[T_{11}^0\frac{1}{2}\frac{\partial\psi_j^5}{\partial r} - T_{11}^2\frac{2}{h^2}\frac{\partial\psi_j^5}{\partial r}\right] + \frac{2}{h^2}\frac{\partial\psi_i^5}{\partial r}\left[T_{11}^2\frac{-1}{2}\frac{\partial\psi_j^5}{\partial r} + T_{11}^4\frac{2}{h^2}\frac{\partial\psi_j^5}{\partial r}\right] \\
& + \frac{1}{2r}\psi_i^5\left[T_{22}^0\frac{1}{2r}\psi_j^5 + T_{22}^2\frac{2}{h^2 r}\frac{\partial\psi_j^5}{\partial r}\right] + \frac{2}{h^2 r}\frac{\partial\psi_i^5}{\partial\theta}\left[T_{22}^2\frac{1}{2r}\psi_j^5 + T_{22}^4\frac{2}{h^2 r}\frac{\partial\psi_i^5}{\partial r}\right] \\
& + \left(\frac{1}{2r}\psi_i^5 + \frac{1}{2}\frac{\partial\psi_i^5}{\partial r}\right)\left[T_{33}^0\left(\frac{1}{2r}\psi_j^5 + \frac{1}{2}\frac{\partial\psi_j^5}{\partial r}\right) - T_{33}^2\left(\frac{2\psi_j^5}{h^2 r} + \frac{2}{h^2}\frac{\partial\psi_j^5}{\partial r}\right)\right] \\
& - \frac{2}{h^2}\left(\frac{\partial\psi_i^5}{\partial r} + \frac{\psi_i^5}{r}\right)\left[T_{33}^2\left(\frac{1}{2r}\psi_j^5 + \frac{1}{2}\frac{\partial\psi_j^5}{\partial r}\right) - T_{33}^4\left(\frac{2\psi_j^5}{h^2 r} + \frac{2}{h^2}\frac{\partial\psi_j^5}{\partial r}\right)\right] \\
& - \frac{1}{4r}\frac{\partial\psi_i^5}{\partial\theta}\left[T_{44}^0\frac{-1}{4r}\frac{\partial\psi_i^5}{\partial\theta} + T_{44}^2\frac{1}{h^2 r}\frac{\partial\psi_j^5}{\partial\theta}\right] + \frac{1}{h^2 r^2}\frac{\partial\psi_i^5}{\partial\theta}\left[-T_{44}^2\frac{1}{4r}\frac{\partial\psi_i^5}{\partial\theta} + T_{44}^4\frac{1}{h^2 r}\frac{\partial\psi_j^5}{d\theta}\right] \\
& + \left(\frac{1}{4r^2}\frac{\partial\psi_i^5}{\partial\theta} + \frac{1}{4r}\frac{\partial^2\psi_i^5}{\partial r\partial\theta}\right)\left[T_{55}^2\left(\frac{1}{4r^2}\frac{\partial\psi_j^5}{\partial\theta} + \frac{1}{4r}\frac{\partial^2\psi_j^5}{\partial r\partial\theta}\right) - T_{55}^4\left(\frac{1}{3h^2 r^2}\frac{\partial\psi_j^5}{\partial\theta} + \frac{1}{3h^2 r}\frac{\partial^2\psi_j^5}{\partial r\partial\theta}\right)\right] \\
& - \left(\frac{1}{3h^2 r^2}\frac{\partial\psi_i^5}{\partial\theta} + \frac{1}{3h^2 r}\frac{\partial^2\psi_i^5}{\partial\theta\partial r}\right)\left[T_{55}^4\left(\frac{1}{4r^2}\frac{\partial\psi_j^5}{\partial\theta} + \frac{1}{4r}\frac{\partial^2\psi_j^5}{\partial r d\theta}\right) - T_{55}^6\left(\frac{1}{3h^2 r^2}\frac{\partial\psi_j^5}{\partial\theta} + \frac{1}{3h^2 r}\frac{\partial^2\psi_j^5}{\partial r\partial\theta}\right)\right] \\
& + \left(\frac{1}{4r}\frac{\partial\psi_i^5}{\partial r} - \frac{1}{4r}\psi_i^5 + \frac{1}{4}\frac{\partial^2\psi_i^5}{\partial r^2} + \frac{2}{h^2}\psi_i^5\right)\left[T_{66}^2\left(\frac{1}{4r}\frac{\partial\psi_j^5}{\partial r} - \frac{1}{4r^2}\psi_j^5 + \frac{1}{4}\frac{\partial^2\psi_j^5}{\partial r^2} + \frac{2}{h^2}\psi_j^5\right)\right. \\
& \left. + T_{66}^4\left(\frac{-1}{3h^2 r}\frac{\partial\psi_j^5}{\partial r} + \frac{1}{3h^2 r^2}\psi_j^5 - \frac{1}{3h^2}\frac{\partial^2\psi_j^5}{\partial r^2}\right)\right] \\
& + \left(\frac{-1}{3h^2 r}\frac{\partial\psi_i^5}{\partial r} + \frac{1}{3h^2 r^2}\psi_i^5 - \frac{1}{3h^2}\frac{\partial^2\psi_i^5}{\partial r^2}\right)\left[T_{66}^4\left(\frac{1}{4r}\frac{\partial\psi_j^5}{\partial r} - \frac{1}{4r^2}\psi_j^5 + \frac{1}{4}\frac{\partial^2\psi_j^5}{\partial r^2} + \frac{2}{h^2}\psi_j^5\right)\right. \\
& \left. - T_{66}^6\left(\frac{1}{3h^2 r}\frac{\partial\psi_j^5}{\partial r} + \frac{1}{3h^2 r^2}\psi_j^5 + \frac{1}{3h^2}\frac{\partial^2\psi_j^5}{\partial r^2}\right)\right]\Bigg\} r dr d\theta
\end{aligned}
\tag{A33}
$$

$$
\begin{aligned}
K_{56} = \int_{\Omega} \Bigg\{ & \frac{1}{r}\frac{\partial \psi_i^5}{\partial \theta}\left[A_{23}^1 \psi_j^6 - A_{21}^3 \frac{1}{2}\frac{\partial^2 \psi_j^6}{\partial r^2} - A_{22}^3\left(\frac{1}{2r}\frac{\partial \psi_j^6}{\psi_j^4} + \frac{1}{2r^2}\frac{\partial^2 \psi_j^6}{\partial \theta^2}\right)\right] - \frac{4}{3rh^2}\frac{\partial \psi_i^5}{\partial \theta}\Big[A_{23}^3 \psi_j^6 \\
& - A_{21}^5 \frac{1}{2}\frac{\partial^2 \psi_j^6}{\partial r^2} - A_{22}^5\left(\frac{1}{2r}\frac{\partial \psi_j^6}{\partial r} + \frac{1}{2r^2}\frac{\partial^2 \psi_j^6}{\partial \theta^2}\right)\Big] + \left(\frac{\partial \psi_i^5}{\partial r} - \frac{1}{r}\psi_i^5\right)\left[A_{44}^3\left(\frac{-1}{r}\frac{\partial^2 \psi_j^6}{\partial \theta \partial r} + \frac{1}{r^2}\frac{\partial \psi_j^6}{\partial \theta}\right)\right] \\
& - \frac{4}{3h^2}\left(\frac{\partial \psi_i^5}{\partial r} + \frac{1}{r}\psi_i^5\right)\left[A_{44}^5\left(\frac{-1}{r}\frac{\partial^2 \psi_j^6}{\partial \theta \partial r} + \frac{1}{r^2}\frac{\partial \psi_j^6}{\partial \theta}\right)\right] - \frac{1}{2}\frac{\partial \psi_i^5}{\partial r}\left[T_{11}^1\left(\frac{1}{r}\frac{\partial^2 \psi_j^6}{\partial \theta \partial r} - \frac{1}{r^2}\frac{\partial \psi_j^6}{\partial \theta}\right)\right] \\
& + \left(\frac{2}{h^2}\frac{\partial \psi_i^5}{\partial r}\right)\left[T_{11}^3\left(\frac{1}{r}\frac{\partial^2 \psi_j^6}{\partial \theta \partial r} - \frac{1}{r^2}\frac{\partial \psi_j^6}{\partial \theta}\right)\right] + \frac{1}{2r}\psi_i^5\left[T_{22}^1\left(\frac{-1}{r}\frac{\partial^2 \psi_j^6}{\partial r d\theta} + \frac{1}{r^2}\frac{\partial \psi_j^6}{\partial \theta}\right)\right] \\
& + \frac{2}{h^2 r}\frac{\partial \psi_i^5}{\partial \theta}\left[T_{22}^3\left(\frac{-1}{r}\frac{\partial^2 \psi_j^6}{\partial r d\theta} + \frac{1}{r^2}\frac{\partial \psi_j^6}{\partial \theta}\right)\right] - \frac{1}{4r}\frac{\partial \psi_i^5}{\partial \theta}\left[T_{44}^1\left(\frac{-1}{2}\frac{\partial^2 \psi_j^6}{\partial r^2} + \frac{1}{2r^2}\frac{\partial^2 \psi_j^6}{\partial \theta^2} + \frac{1}{r}\frac{\partial \psi_j^6}{\partial r}\right)\right] \\
& + \frac{1}{h^2 r^2}\frac{\partial \psi_i^5}{\partial \theta}\left[T_{44}^3\left(-\frac{1}{2}\frac{\partial^2 \psi_j^6}{\partial r^2} + \frac{1}{2r^2}\frac{\partial^2 \psi_j^6}{\partial \theta^2} + \frac{1}{r}\frac{\partial \psi_j^6}{\partial r}\right)\right] - \left(\frac{1}{4r^2}\frac{\partial \psi_i^5}{\partial \theta} + \frac{1}{4r}\frac{\partial^2 \psi_i^5}{\partial r \partial \theta}\right)T_{55}^1 \frac{1}{2}\frac{\partial \psi_j^6}{\partial r} \\
& + \left(\frac{1}{3h^2 r^2}\frac{\partial \psi_i^5}{\partial \theta} + \frac{1}{3h^2 r}\frac{\partial \psi_i^5}{\partial \theta \partial r}\right)T_{55}^3 \frac{1}{2}\frac{\partial \psi_j^6}{\partial r} + \left(\frac{1}{4r}\frac{\partial \psi_i^5}{\partial r} - \frac{1}{4r}\psi_i^5 + \frac{1}{4}\frac{\partial^2 \psi_i^5}{\partial r^2} + \frac{2}{h^2}\psi_i^5\right)T_{66}^1 \frac{1}{2r}\frac{\partial \psi_j^6}{\partial \theta} \\
& - \left(\frac{1}{3h^2 r}\frac{\partial \psi_i^5}{\partial r} + \frac{1}{3h^2 r^2}\psi_i^5 + \frac{1}{3h^2}\frac{\partial^2 \psi_i^5}{\partial r^2}\right)T_{66}^3 \frac{1}{2r}\frac{\partial \psi_j^6}{\partial \theta} - \left(\frac{\partial \psi_i^5}{\partial r} - \frac{1}{r}\psi_i^5\right)A_{44}^4 \frac{2}{3r^2}\frac{\partial \psi_j^7}{\partial \theta} \\
& + \left(\frac{4}{3h^2}\frac{\partial \psi_i^5}{\partial r} + \frac{-4}{3h^2 r}\psi_i^5\right)\left[A_{44}^6 \frac{2}{3r^2}\frac{\partial \psi_j^7}{\partial \theta}\right]\Bigg\} r dr d\theta
\end{aligned}
\quad \text{(A34)}
$$

$$
\begin{aligned}
K_{57} = \int_{\Omega} \Bigg\{ & \frac{1}{r}\frac{\partial \psi_i^5}{\partial \theta}\left[A_{23}^2 2\psi_j^7 - A_{21}^4 \frac{1}{3}\frac{\partial^2 \psi_j^7}{\partial r^2} - A_{22}^4\left(\frac{1}{3r^2}\frac{\partial^2 \psi_j^7}{\partial \theta} + \frac{1}{3r}\frac{\partial \psi_j^7}{\partial r}\right)\right] - \frac{4}{3rh^2}\frac{\partial \psi_i^5}{\partial \theta}\Big[A_{23}^4 2\psi_j^7 \\
& - A_{21}^6 \frac{1}{3}\frac{\partial^2 \psi_j^7}{\partial r^2} - A_{22}^6\left(\frac{1}{3r^2}\frac{\partial^2 \psi_j^7}{\partial \theta^2} + \frac{1}{3r}\frac{\partial \psi_j^7}{\partial r}\right)\Big] - \left(\frac{\partial \psi_i^5}{\partial r} - \frac{1}{r}\psi_i^5\right)A_{44}^4 \frac{2}{3}\frac{\partial^2 \psi_j^7}{\partial \theta \partial r} \\
& + \frac{8}{9h^2}\left(\frac{\partial \psi_i^5}{\partial r} + \frac{1}{r}\psi_i^5\right)A_{44}^6 \frac{\partial^2 \psi_j^7}{\partial \theta \partial r} - \frac{1}{2}\frac{\partial \psi_i^5}{\partial r}\left[T_{11}^2\left(\frac{1}{r}\frac{\partial^2 \psi_j^7}{\partial \theta \partial r} + \frac{-1}{r^2}\frac{\partial \psi_j^7}{\partial \theta}\right)\right] \\
& + \frac{2}{h^2}\frac{\partial \psi_i^5}{\partial r}\left[T_{11}^4\left(\frac{1}{r}\frac{\partial^2 \psi_j^7}{\partial \theta \partial r} - \frac{1}{r^2}\frac{\partial \psi_j^7}{\partial \theta}\right)\right] + \frac{1}{2r}\psi_i^5\left[T_{22}^2\left(\frac{1}{r^2}\frac{\partial \psi_j^7}{\partial \theta^2} - \frac{1}{r}\frac{\partial \psi_j^7}{\partial r}\right)\right] \\
& + \frac{2}{h^2 r}\frac{\partial \psi_i^5}{\partial \theta}\left[T_{22}^4\left(\frac{1}{r^2}\frac{\partial^2 \psi_j^7}{\partial \theta^2} - \frac{1}{r}\frac{\partial \psi_j^7}{\partial r}\right)\right] - \frac{1}{4r}\frac{\partial \psi_i^5}{\partial \theta}\left[T_{44}^2\left(\frac{-1}{2}\frac{\partial \psi_j^7}{\partial r^2} + \frac{1}{2r^2}\frac{\partial^2 \psi_j^7}{\partial \theta^2} + \frac{1}{2r}\frac{\partial \psi_j^7}{\partial r}\right)\right] \\
& + \frac{1}{h^2 r^2}\frac{\partial \psi_i^5}{\partial \theta}\left[T_{44}^4\left(-\frac{1}{2}\frac{\partial^2 \psi_j^7}{\partial r^2} + \frac{1}{2r^2}\frac{\partial^2 \psi_j^7}{\partial \theta^2} + \frac{1}{2r}\frac{\partial \psi_j^7}{\partial r}\right)\right] - \left(\frac{1}{4r^2}\frac{\partial \psi_i^5}{\partial \theta} + \frac{1}{4r}\frac{\partial^2 \psi_i^5}{\partial r d\theta}\right)T_{55}^2 \frac{3}{2}\frac{\partial \psi_j^7}{\partial r} \\
& + \left(\frac{1}{3h^2 r^2}\frac{\partial \psi_i^5}{\partial \theta} + \frac{1}{3h^2 r}\frac{\partial^2 \psi_i^5}{\partial \theta \partial r}\right)T_{55}^4 \frac{3}{2}\frac{\partial \psi_j^7}{\partial r} + \left(\frac{1}{4r}\frac{\partial \psi_i^5}{\partial r} - \frac{1}{4r}\psi_i^5 + \frac{1}{4}\frac{\partial^2 \psi_i^5}{\partial r^2} + \frac{2}{h^2}\psi_i^5\right)T_{66}^2 \frac{1}{r}\frac{\partial \psi_j^7}{\partial \theta} \\
& + \left(\frac{-1}{3h^2 r}\frac{\partial \delta \beta \theta}{\partial r} + \frac{1}{3h^2 r^2}\psi_i^5 - \frac{1}{3h^2}\frac{\partial^2 \psi_i^5}{\partial r^2}\right)T_{66}^4 \frac{1}{r}\frac{\partial \psi_j^7}{\partial \theta} \\
& + \left(\frac{\partial \psi_i^5}{\partial r} - \frac{1}{r}\psi_i^5\right)A_{44}^2 \frac{2}{3r^2}\frac{\partial \psi_j^7}{d\theta} + \frac{-8}{9r^2 h^2}\left(\frac{\partial \psi_i^5}{\partial r} + \frac{1}{r}\psi_i^5\right)A_{44}^6 \frac{\partial \psi_j^7}{\partial \theta}\Bigg\} r dr d\theta
\end{aligned}
\quad \text{(A35)}
$$

$$K_{61} = \int_{\Omega} \left\{ \frac{1}{2} \frac{\partial^2 \psi_i^6}{\partial r^2} \left[A_{11}^2 \frac{\partial \psi_j^1}{\partial r} + A_{12}^2 \frac{1}{r} \psi_j^1 \right] - \left(\frac{1}{r} \frac{\partial \psi_i^6}{\partial r} + \frac{1}{2r^2} \frac{\partial^2 \psi_i^6}{\partial r^2} \right) \left[A_{21}^2 \frac{\partial \psi_j^1}{\partial r} + A_{22}^2 \frac{1}{r} \psi_j^1 \right] \right.$$
$$+ \psi_i^6 r \left[A_{31}^0 \frac{\partial \psi_j^1}{\partial r} + A_{32}^0 \frac{1}{r} \psi_j^1 \right] + \left(\frac{-1}{r} \frac{\partial^2 \psi_i^6}{\partial \theta \partial r} + \frac{1}{r^2} \frac{\partial \psi_i^6}{\partial \theta} \right) A_{44}^2 \frac{1}{r} \frac{\partial \psi_j^1}{d \partial \theta}$$
$$\left. + T_{55}^0 \frac{1}{8r^2} \frac{\partial \psi_i^6}{\partial r} \frac{\partial^2 \psi_j^1}{\partial \theta^2} + \frac{1}{2r} \frac{\partial \psi_i^6}{\partial \theta} \left[T_{66}^0 \left(-\frac{1}{4r} \frac{\partial^2 \psi_j^1}{\partial \theta \partial r} - \frac{1}{4r^2} \frac{\partial \psi_j^1}{\partial \theta} \right) \right] \right\} r dr d\theta \tag{A36}$$

$$K_{62} = \int_{\Omega} \left\{ -A_{12}^2 \frac{1}{2r} \frac{\partial^2 \psi_i^6}{\partial r^2} \frac{\partial \psi_j^2}{\partial \theta} - \left(\frac{1}{2r} \frac{\partial \psi_i^6}{\partial r} + \frac{1}{2r^2} \frac{\partial^2 \psi_j^6}{\partial r^2} \right) A_{22}^2 \frac{1}{r} \frac{\partial \psi_j^2}{\partial \theta} + \partial \psi_i^6 A_{32}^0 \frac{1}{r} \frac{\partial \psi_j^2}{\partial \theta} \right.$$
$$- \left(\frac{1}{r} \frac{\partial^2 \psi_i^6}{\partial \theta} + \frac{1}{r^2} \frac{\partial \psi_i^6}{\partial \theta} \right) \left[A_{44}^2 \left(\frac{\partial \psi_j^2}{\partial r} - \frac{\psi_j^2}{r} \right) \right] - \frac{1}{2} \frac{\partial \psi_i^6}{\partial r} \left[T_{55}^0 \left(\frac{1}{4r^2} \frac{\partial \psi_j^2}{\partial \theta} + \frac{1}{4r} \frac{\partial^2 \psi_j^2}{\partial r \partial \theta} \right) \right]$$
$$\left. + \frac{1}{2r} \frac{\partial \psi_i^6}{\partial \theta} \left[T_{66}^0 \left(\frac{1}{4r} \frac{\partial \psi_j^2}{\partial r} - \frac{1}{4r^2} \psi_j^2 + \frac{1}{4} \frac{\partial^2 \psi_j^2}{\partial r^2} \right) \right] \right\} r dr d\theta \tag{A37}$$

$$K_{63} = \int_{\Omega} \left\{ \frac{-1}{2} \frac{\partial^2 \psi_i^6}{\partial r^2} \left[A_{11}^2 \frac{1}{2} \frac{\partial W_o}{\partial r} \frac{\partial \psi_j^3}{\partial r} + A_{12}^2 \frac{1}{2r^2} \frac{\partial W_o}{\partial \theta} \frac{\partial \psi_j^3}{\partial \theta} - A_{11}^5 \frac{4}{3h^2} \frac{\partial^2 \psi_j^3}{\partial r^2} \right. \right.$$
$$\left. - A_{12}^5 \left(\frac{4}{3h^2 r^2} \frac{\partial^2 \psi_j^3}{\partial \theta^2} + \frac{4}{3h^2 r} \frac{\partial \psi_j^3}{\partial r} \right) \right] - \left(\frac{1}{2r} \frac{\partial \psi_i^6}{\partial r} + \frac{1}{2r^2} \frac{\partial^2 \psi_j^6}{\partial \theta^2} \right) \left[A_{21}^2 \frac{1}{2} \frac{\partial W_o}{\partial r} \frac{\partial \psi_j^3}{\partial r} \right.$$
$$\left. + A_{22}^2 \frac{1}{2r^2} \frac{\partial W_o}{\partial \theta} \frac{\partial \psi_j^3}{\partial \theta} - A_{21}^5 \frac{4}{3h^2} \frac{\partial^2 \psi_j^3}{\partial r^2} - A_{22}^5 \left(\frac{4}{3r^2 h^2} \frac{\partial^2 \psi_j^3}{\partial \theta} + \frac{4}{3rh^2} \frac{\partial \psi_j^3}{\partial r} \right) \right]$$
$$+ \partial \psi_i^6 \left[A_{31}^0 \frac{1}{2} \frac{\partial W_o}{\partial r} \frac{\partial \psi_j^3}{\partial r} + A_{32}^0 \frac{1}{2r^2} \frac{\partial W_o}{\partial \theta} \frac{\partial \psi_j^3}{\partial \theta} - A_{31}^3 \frac{4}{3h^2} \frac{\partial^2 \psi_j^3}{\partial r^2} - A_{32}^3 \left(\frac{4}{3h^2 r^2} \frac{\partial^2 \psi_j^3}{\partial \theta^2} + \frac{4}{3h^2 r} \frac{\partial \psi_j^3}{\partial r} \right) \right]$$
$$+ \left(\frac{-1}{r} \frac{\partial^2 \psi_i^6}{\partial \theta \partial r} + \frac{1}{r^2} \frac{\partial \psi_i^6}{\partial \theta} \right) \left[A_{44}^2 \frac{1}{r} \frac{\partial \psi_j^3}{\partial \theta} \frac{\partial \psi_j^3}{\partial r} - A_{44}^5 \frac{8}{3h^2} \frac{\partial^2 \psi_j^3}{\partial \theta \partial r} \right]$$
$$+ \left(\frac{1}{r} \frac{\partial^2 \psi_i^6}{\partial \theta \partial r} - \frac{1}{r^2} \frac{\partial \psi_i^6}{\partial \theta} \right) \left[T_{11}^1 \left(\frac{1}{2r} \frac{\partial^2 \psi_j^3}{\partial \theta dr} - \frac{1}{2r^2} \frac{\partial \psi_j^3}{\partial \theta} \right) - T_{11}^3 \left(\frac{2}{h^2 r} \frac{\partial^2 \psi_j^3}{\partial \theta dr} + \frac{2}{h^2 r^2} \frac{\partial \psi_j^3}{\partial \theta} \right) \right]$$
$$+ \left(\frac{-1}{r} \frac{\partial^2 \psi_i^6}{\partial r d\theta} + \frac{1}{r^2} \frac{\partial \psi_i^6}{\partial \theta} \right) \left[T_{22}^1 \left(\frac{-1}{2r} \frac{\partial^2 \psi_j^3}{\partial r \partial \theta} + \frac{1}{2r^2} \frac{\partial \psi_j^3}{\partial \theta} \right) + T_{22}^3 \left(\frac{2}{h^2 r^2} \frac{\partial^2 \psi_j^3}{\partial \theta^2} - \frac{2}{h^2 r} \frac{\partial \psi_j^3}{\partial r} \right) \right]$$
$$+ \left(\frac{-1}{2} \frac{\partial^2 \psi_i^6}{\partial r^2} + \frac{1}{2r^2} \frac{\partial^2 \psi_i^6}{\partial \theta^2} + \frac{1}{2r} \frac{\partial \psi_i^7}{\partial r} \right)$$
$$\left[T_{44}^1 \left(-\frac{1}{4} \frac{\partial^2 \psi_j^3}{\partial r^2} + \frac{1}{4r^2} \frac{\partial^2 \psi_j^3}{\partial \theta^2} + \frac{1}{4r} \frac{\partial \psi_j^3}{\partial r} \right) + T_{44}^3 \left(\frac{-1}{h^2} \frac{\partial^2 \psi_j^3}{\partial r^2} + \frac{1}{h^2 r^2} \frac{\partial^2 \psi_j^3}{\partial \theta^2} + \frac{1}{h^2 r} \frac{\partial \psi_j^3}{\partial r} \right) \right]$$
$$\left. + T_{55}^1 \frac{1}{h^2} \frac{\partial \psi_i^6}{\partial r} \frac{\partial \psi_j^3}{\partial r} + T_{66}^1 \frac{1}{h^2 r} \frac{\partial \psi_i^6}{\partial \theta} \frac{\partial \psi_j^3}{\partial \theta} + \left(\frac{-1}{r} \frac{\partial^2 \psi_i^6}{\partial \theta \partial r} + \frac{1}{r^2} \frac{\partial \psi_i^6}{\partial \theta} \right) A_{44}^5 \frac{8}{3h^2 r^2} \frac{\partial \psi_j^7}{\partial \theta} \right\} r dr d\theta \tag{A38}$$

$$K_{64} = \int_{\Omega} \left\{ \frac{-1}{2} \frac{\partial^2 \psi_i^6}{\partial r^2} \left[A_{11}^3 \frac{\partial \psi_j^4}{\partial r} + \frac{1}{r} A_{12}^3 \psi_j^4 - \frac{4}{3h^2} A_{11}^5 \frac{\partial \psi_j^4}{\partial r} - \frac{4}{3rh^2} A_{12}^5 \psi_j^4 \right] \right.$$
$$- \left(\frac{1}{2r} \frac{\partial \psi_i^6}{\partial r} + \frac{1}{2r^2} \frac{\partial^2 \psi_j^6}{\partial r^2} \right) \left[A_{21}^3 \frac{\partial \psi_j^4}{\partial r} + \frac{1}{r} A_{22}^3 \psi_j^4 - \frac{4}{3h^2} A_{21}^5 \frac{\partial \psi_j^4}{\partial r} - \frac{4}{3rh^2} A_{22}^5 \psi_j^4 \right]$$
$$+ \partial \psi_i^6 \left[A_{31}^1 \frac{\partial \psi_j^4}{\partial r} + A_{32}^1 \frac{1}{r} \psi_j^4 - A_{31}^3 \frac{4}{3h^2} \frac{\partial \psi_j^4}{\partial r} - A_{32}^3 \frac{4}{3rh^2} \psi_j^4 \right]$$
$$+ \left(\frac{-1}{r} \frac{\partial^2 \psi_i^6}{\partial \theta \partial r} + \frac{1}{r^2} \frac{\partial \psi_i^6}{d\theta} \right) \left[A_{44}^3 \frac{1}{r} \frac{\partial \psi_j^4}{\partial \theta} - A_{44}^5 \frac{4}{3h^2 r} \frac{\partial \psi_j^4}{\partial \theta} \right] + \frac{1}{r} \frac{\partial^2 \psi_i^6}{\partial r} \left[T_{55}^1 \left(\frac{1}{4r^2} \frac{\partial^2 \psi_j^4}{\partial \theta^2} \right. \right.$$
$$\left. \left. + \frac{2}{h^2} \psi_j^4 \right) + T_{55}^3 \frac{1}{3h^2 r^2} \frac{\partial^2 \psi_j^4}{\partial \theta^2} \right] + \frac{1}{2r} \frac{\partial \psi_i^6}{\partial \theta} \left[T_{66}^1 \left(\frac{-1}{4r} \frac{\partial^2 \psi_j^4}{\partial \theta \partial r} + \frac{1}{4r^2} \frac{\partial \psi_j^4}{\partial \theta} \right) \right.$$
$$\left. \left. + T_{66}^3 \left(\frac{-1}{3h^2 r} \frac{\partial^2 \psi_j^4}{\partial \theta \partial r} + \frac{1}{3h^2 r^2} \frac{\partial \psi_j^4}{\partial \theta} \right) \right] \right\} r dr d\theta \tag{A39}$$

$$K_{65} = \int_{\Omega} \left\{ \frac{-1}{2} \frac{\partial^2 \psi_i^6}{\partial r^2} \left[A_{12}^3 \frac{1}{r} \frac{\partial \psi_j^5}{\partial \theta} - A_{12}^5 \frac{4}{3rh^2} \frac{\partial \psi_j^5}{\partial \theta} \right] - \left(\frac{1}{2r} \frac{\partial \psi_i^6}{\partial r} + \frac{1}{2r^2} \frac{\partial^2 \psi_j^6}{\partial r^2} \right) \left[A_{22}^3 \frac{1}{r} \frac{\partial \psi_j^5}{\partial \theta} \right. \right.$$
$$\left. - A_{22}^5 \frac{4}{3rh^2} \frac{\partial \psi_j^5}{\partial \theta} \right] + \partial \psi_i^6 \left(A_{32}^1 \frac{1}{r} \frac{\partial \psi_j^5}{\partial \theta} - A_{32}^2 \frac{4}{3rh^2} \frac{\partial \psi_j^5}{\partial \theta} \right) + \left(\frac{1}{r} \frac{\partial^2 \psi_i^6}{\partial \theta \partial r} + \frac{1}{r^2} \frac{\partial \psi_i^6}{\partial \theta} \right) \left[A_{44}^3 \left(\frac{\partial \psi_j^5}{\partial r} \right. \right.$$
$$\left. \left. - \frac{1}{r} \psi_j^5 \right) - A_{44}^5 \left(\frac{4}{3h^2} \frac{\partial \psi_j^5}{\partial r} + \frac{4}{3h^2 r} \psi_j^5 \right) \right] + \left(\frac{1}{r} \frac{\partial^2 \psi_i^6}{\partial \theta \partial r} - \frac{1}{r^2} \frac{\partial \psi_i^6}{d\theta} \right) \left[T_{11}^1 \frac{-1}{2} \frac{\partial \psi_j^5}{\partial r} \right.$$
$$\left. + T_{11}^3 \frac{2}{h^2} \frac{\partial \psi_j^5}{\partial r} \right] - \left(\frac{1}{r} \frac{\partial^2 \psi_i^6}{\partial r \partial \theta} - \frac{1}{r^2} \frac{\partial \psi_i^6}{\partial \theta} \right) \left[T_{22}^1 \frac{1}{2r} \psi_j^5 + T_{22}^3 \frac{2}{h^2 r} \frac{\partial \psi_j^5}{\partial r} \right] + \left(\frac{-1}{2} \frac{\partial^2 \psi_i^6}{\partial r^2} \right.$$
$$\left. + \frac{1}{2r^2} \frac{\partial \psi_i^6}{d\theta^2} + \frac{1}{2r} \frac{\partial \psi_i^6}{\partial r} \right) \left[-T_{44}^1 \frac{1}{4r} \frac{\partial \psi_i^5}{\partial \theta} + T_{44}^3 \frac{1}{h^2 r} \frac{\partial \psi_j^5}{\partial \theta} \right] - \frac{1}{2} \frac{\partial \psi_i^6}{\partial r} \left[T_{55}^1 \left(\frac{1}{4r^2} \frac{\partial \psi_j^5}{\partial \theta} \right. \right.$$
$$\left. \left. + \frac{1}{4r} \frac{\partial^2 \psi_j^5}{\partial r \partial \theta} \right) - T_{55}^3 \left(\frac{1}{3h^2 r^2} \frac{\partial \psi_j^5}{\partial \theta} + \frac{1}{3h^2 r} \frac{\partial^2 \psi_j^5}{\partial r \partial \theta} \right) \right] + \frac{1}{2r} \frac{\partial \psi_i^6}{\partial \theta} \left[T_{66}^1 \left(\frac{1}{4r} \frac{\partial \psi_j^5}{\partial r} - \frac{1}{4r^2} \psi_j^5 \right. \right.$$
$$\left. \left. \left. + \frac{1}{4} \frac{\partial^2 \psi_j^5}{\partial r^2} + \frac{2}{h^2} \psi_j^5 \right) + T_{66}^3 \left(\frac{-1}{3h^2 r} \frac{\partial \psi_j^5}{\partial r} + \frac{1}{3h^2 r^2} \psi_j^5 - \frac{1}{3h^2} \frac{\partial \psi_j^5}{\partial r^2} \right) \right] \right\} r dr d\theta \tag{A40}$$

$$K_{66} = \int_{\Omega} \left\{ \frac{-1}{2} \frac{\partial^2 \psi_i^6}{\partial r^2} \left[A_{13}^2 \psi_j^6 - A_{11}^4 \frac{1}{2} \frac{\partial^2 \psi_j^6}{\partial r^2} - A_{12}^4 \left(\frac{1}{2r} \frac{\partial \psi_j^6}{\partial r} + \frac{1}{2r^2} \frac{\partial^2 \psi_j^6}{\partial \theta^2} \right) \right] \right.$$
$$- \left(\frac{1}{2r} \frac{\partial \psi_i^6}{\partial r} + \frac{1}{2r^2} \frac{\partial^2 \psi_j^6}{\partial r^2} \right) \left[A_{23}^2 \psi_j^6 - A_{21}^4 \frac{1}{2} \frac{\partial^2 \psi_j^6}{\partial r^2} - A_{22}^4 \left(\frac{1}{2r} \frac{\partial \psi_j^6}{\partial r} + \frac{1}{2r^2} \frac{\partial^2 \psi_j^6}{\partial \theta^2} \right) \right]$$
$$+ \partial \psi_i^6 \left[A_{33}^0 \psi_j^6 - A_{31}^2 \frac{1}{2} \frac{\partial^2 \psi_j^6}{\partial r^2} - A_{32}^2 \left(\frac{1}{2r} \frac{\partial \psi_j^6}{\partial r} + \frac{1}{2r^2} \frac{\partial^2 \psi_j^6}{\partial \theta^2} \right) \right]$$
$$+ \left(\frac{1}{r} \frac{\partial^2 \psi_i^6}{d\theta dr} + \frac{1}{r^2} \frac{\partial \psi_i^6}{\partial \theta} \right) \left[A_{44}^4 \left(\frac{-1}{r} \frac{\partial^2 \psi_j^6}{\partial \theta \partial r} + \frac{1}{r^2} \frac{\partial \psi_j^6}{\partial \theta} \right) \right]$$
$$+ \left(\frac{1}{r} \frac{\partial^2 \psi_i^6}{\partial \theta \partial r} - \frac{1}{r^2} \frac{\partial \psi_i^6}{\partial \theta} \right) \left[T_{11}^2 \left(\frac{1}{r} \frac{\partial^2 \psi_j^6}{\partial \theta dr} - \frac{1}{r^2} \frac{\partial \psi_j^6}{\partial \theta} \right) \right] + \left(\frac{-1}{r} \frac{\partial^2 \psi_i^6}{\partial r d\theta} + \frac{1}{r^2} \frac{\partial \psi_i^6}{\partial \theta} \right) \left[T_{22}^2 \left(\frac{-1}{r} \frac{\partial^2 \psi_j^6}{\partial r d\theta} \right. \right.$$
$$\left. \left. + \frac{1}{r^2} \frac{\partial \psi_j^6}{\partial \theta} \right) \right] + \left(\frac{-1}{2} \frac{\partial^2 \psi_i^6}{\partial r^2} + \frac{1}{2r^2} \frac{\partial \psi_i^6}{\partial \theta^2} + \frac{1}{2r} \frac{\partial \psi_i^6}{\partial r} \right) \left[T_{44}^2 \left(\frac{-1}{2} \frac{\partial^2 \psi_j^6}{\partial r^2} + \frac{1}{2r^2} \frac{\partial^2 \psi_j^6}{\partial \theta^2} + \frac{1}{r} \frac{\partial \psi_j^6}{\partial r} \right) \right]$$
$$\left. + T_{55}^0 \frac{1}{4} \frac{\partial \psi_i^6}{\partial r} \frac{\partial \psi_j^6}{\partial r} + T_{66}^0 \frac{1}{4r^2} \frac{\partial \psi_i^6}{\partial \theta} \frac{\partial \psi_j^6}{\partial \theta} \right\} r dr d\theta \tag{A41}$$

$$K_{67} = \int_{\Omega} \left\{ \frac{-1}{2} \frac{\partial^2 \psi_i^6}{\partial r^2} \left[A_{13}^3 2 \psi_j^7 - A_{11}^5 \frac{1}{3} \frac{\partial^2 \psi_j^7}{\partial r^2} + A_{12}^5 \left(\frac{1}{3r^2} \frac{\partial^2 \psi_j^7}{\partial \theta^2} + \frac{1}{3r^2} \frac{\partial \psi_j^7}{\partial r} \right) \right] + \left(- \frac{1}{2r} \frac{\partial \psi_i^6}{dr} \right. \right.$$
$$\left. - \frac{1}{2r^2} \frac{\partial \psi_j^6}{\partial r^2} \right) \left[A_{23}^3 2 \psi_j^7 + A_{21}^5 \frac{-1}{3} \frac{\partial^2 \psi_j^7}{\partial r^2} + A_{12}^5 \left(\frac{1}{3r^2} \frac{\partial^2 \psi_j^7}{\partial \theta^2} + \frac{1}{3r^2} \frac{\partial \psi_j^7}{\partial r} \right) \right] + \psi_i^6 \left[A_{33}^1 2 \psi_j^7 \right.$$
$$\left. + A_{31}^3 \frac{-1}{3} \frac{\partial^2 \psi_j^7}{\partial r^2} + A_{32}^3 \left(\frac{-1}{3r^2} \frac{\partial^2 \psi_j^7}{\partial \theta^2} + \frac{-1}{3r} \frac{\partial \psi_j^7}{dr} \right) \right] - \left(\frac{1}{r} \frac{\partial^2 \psi_i^6}{\partial \theta \partial r} + \frac{1}{r^2} \frac{\partial \psi_i^6}{\partial \theta} \right) A_{44}^5 \frac{2}{3} \frac{\partial^2 \psi_j^7}{\partial \theta \partial r}$$
$$+ \left(\frac{1}{r} \frac{\partial^2 \psi_i^6}{\partial \theta \partial r} - \frac{1}{r^2} \frac{\partial \psi_i^6}{\partial \theta} \right) \left[T_{11}^3 \left(\frac{1}{r} \frac{\partial^2 \psi_j^7}{\partial \theta \partial r} - \frac{1}{r} \frac{\partial \psi_j^7}{\partial \theta} \right) \right] + \left(\frac{-1}{r} \frac{\partial^2 \psi_i^6}{\partial r \partial \theta} + \frac{1}{r^2} \frac{\partial \psi_i^6}{\partial \theta} \right) \left[T_{22}^3 \left(\frac{1}{r^2} \frac{\partial^2 \psi_j^7}{\partial \theta^2} \right. \right.$$
$$\left. \left. - \frac{1}{r} \frac{\partial \psi_j^7}{dr} \right) \right] + \left(\frac{-1}{2} \frac{\partial^2 \psi_i^6}{\partial r^2} + \frac{1}{2r^2} \frac{\partial \psi_i^6}{d\theta^2} + \frac{1}{2r} \frac{\partial \psi_i^6}{\partial r} \right) \left[T_{44}^3 \left(\frac{-1}{2} \frac{\partial^2 \psi_j^7}{\partial r^2} + \frac{1}{2r^2} \frac{\partial^2 \psi_j^7}{\partial \theta^2} + \frac{1}{2r} \frac{\partial \psi_j^7}{\partial r} \right) \right]$$
$$\left. + T_{55}^1 \frac{3}{4} \frac{\partial \psi_i^6}{\partial r} \frac{\partial \psi_j^7}{\partial r} + T_{66}^1 \frac{1}{2r^2} \frac{\partial \psi_i^6}{\partial \theta} \frac{\partial \psi_j^7}{\partial \theta} + \left(\frac{-1}{r} \frac{\partial^2 \psi_j^6}{\partial \theta \partial r} + \frac{1}{r^2} \frac{\partial \psi_i^6}{\partial \theta} \right) A_{44}^5 \frac{2}{3r^2} \frac{\partial \psi_j^7}{d\theta} \right\} r dr d\theta \tag{A42}$$

$$K_{71} = \int_{\Omega} \left\{ \frac{h^2}{4} \frac{\partial^2 \psi_i^7}{\partial r^2} \left[A_{11}^3 \frac{\partial \psi_j^1}{\partial r} + A_{12}^3 \frac{1}{r} \psi_j^1 \right] + \left(\frac{h^2}{4} \frac{\partial \psi_i^7}{\partial r} + \frac{h^2}{4r} \frac{\partial^2 \psi_j^7}{\partial \theta^2} \right) \left[A_{21}^3 \frac{\partial \psi_j^1}{\partial r} + A_{22}^3 \frac{1}{r} \psi_j^1 \right] \right.$$
$$+ 2 \partial \psi_i^7 \left[A_{31}^1 \frac{\partial \psi_j^1}{\partial r} + A_{32}^1 \frac{1}{r} \psi_j^1 \right] - A_{44}^3 \frac{2}{3r} \frac{\partial^2 \psi_i^7}{\partial \theta \partial r} \frac{\partial \psi_j^1}{\partial \theta} + T_{55}^1 \frac{3}{8r^2} \frac{\partial \psi_i^7}{\partial r} \frac{\partial^2 \psi_j^1}{\partial \theta^2}$$
$$\left. + \frac{1}{r} \frac{\partial \psi_i^7}{\partial \theta} \left[T_{66}^1 \left(\frac{-1}{4r} \frac{\partial^2 \psi_j^1}{\partial \theta \partial r} + \frac{1}{4r^2} \frac{\partial \psi_j^1}{\partial \theta} \right) \right] \right\} r dr d\theta \tag{A43}$$

$$K_{72} = \int_{\Omega} \left\{ A_{12}^{3} \frac{h^2}{4r} \frac{\partial^2 \psi_i^7}{\partial r^2} \frac{\partial \psi_j^2}{\partial \theta} + \left(\frac{h^2}{4} \frac{\partial \psi_i^7}{\partial r} + \frac{h^2}{4r} \frac{\partial^2 \psi_j^7}{\partial \theta^2} \right) A_{22}^{3} \frac{1}{r} \frac{\partial \psi_j^2}{\partial \theta} + A_{32}^{1} \frac{2}{r} \psi_i^7 \frac{\partial \psi_j^2}{\partial \theta} \right.$$
$$- \frac{2}{3} \frac{\partial^2 \psi_i^7}{\partial \theta \partial r} \left[A_{44}^{3} \left(\frac{\partial \psi_j^2}{\partial r} - \frac{\psi_j^2}{r} \right) \right] - \frac{3}{2} \frac{\partial \psi_i^7}{\partial r} \left[T_{55}^{1} \left(\frac{1}{4r^2} \frac{d \psi_j^2}{\partial \theta} + \frac{1}{4r} \frac{\partial \psi_j^2}{\partial r \partial \theta} \right) \right]$$
$$\left. + \frac{1}{r} \frac{\partial \psi_i^7}{\partial \theta} \left[T_{66}^{1} \left(\frac{1}{4r} \frac{\partial \psi_j^2}{\partial r} - \frac{1}{4r^2} \psi_j^2 + \frac{1}{4} \frac{\partial^2 \psi_j^2}{\partial r^2} \right) \right] \right\} r dr d\theta \tag{A44}$$

$$K_{73} = \int_{\Omega} \left\{ \frac{-1}{3} \frac{\partial^2 \psi_i^7}{\partial r^2} \left[A_{11}^{3} \frac{1}{2} \frac{\partial W_o}{\partial r} \frac{\partial \psi_j^3}{\partial r} + A_{12}^{3} \frac{1}{2r^2} \frac{\partial W_o}{\partial \theta} \frac{\partial \psi_j^3}{\partial \theta} - A_{11}^{6} \frac{4}{3h^2} \frac{\partial^2 \psi_j^3}{\partial r^2} \right. \right.$$
$$\left. - A_{12}^{3} \left(\frac{4}{3h^2 r^2} \frac{\partial^2 \psi_j^3}{\partial \theta} + \frac{4}{3h^2 r} \frac{\partial \psi_j^3}{\partial r} \right) \right]$$
$$- \left(\frac{1}{3r} \frac{\partial \psi_i^7}{\partial r} + \frac{1}{3r^2} \frac{\partial^2 \psi_j^7}{\partial \theta^2} \right) \left[A_{21}^{3} \frac{1}{2} \frac{\partial W_o}{\partial r} \frac{\partial \psi_j^3}{\partial r} + A_{22}^{3} \frac{1}{2r^2} \frac{\partial W_o}{\partial \theta} \frac{\partial \psi_j^3}{\partial \theta} \right.$$
$$\left. - A_{21}^{6} \frac{4}{3h^2} \frac{\partial^2 \psi_j^3}{\partial r^2} - A_{22}^{6} \left(\frac{4}{3r^2 h^2} \frac{\partial^2 \psi_j^3}{\partial \theta^2} + \frac{4}{3rh^2} \frac{\partial \psi_j^3}{\partial \theta^2} + \frac{4}{3rh^2} \frac{\partial \psi_j^3}{\partial r} \right) \right]$$
$$+ 2\psi_i^7 \left[A_{31}^{1} \frac{1}{2} \frac{\partial W_o}{\partial r} \frac{\partial \psi_j^3}{\partial r} + A_{32}^{1} \frac{1}{2r^2} \frac{\partial W_o}{\partial \theta} \frac{\partial \psi_j^3}{\partial \theta} - A_{31}^{3} \frac{4}{3h^2} \frac{\partial^2 \psi_j^3}{\partial r^2} - A_{32}^{3} \left(\frac{4}{3h^2 r^2} \frac{\partial^2 \psi_j^3}{\partial \theta^2} + \frac{4}{3h^2 r} \frac{\partial \psi_j^3}{\partial r} \right) \right]$$
$$- \frac{2}{3} \frac{\partial^2 \psi_i^7}{\partial \theta \partial r} \left[A_{44}^{3} \frac{1}{r} \frac{\partial \psi_j^3}{\partial \theta} \frac{\partial \psi_j^3}{\partial r} - A_{44}^{6} \frac{8}{3h^2} \frac{\partial \psi_j^3}{\partial \theta \partial r} \right]$$
$$+ \left(\frac{3}{2r} \frac{\partial^2 \psi_i^7}{\partial r \partial d} - \frac{1}{r^2} \frac{\partial \psi_i^7}{\partial \theta} \right) \left[T_{11}^{2} \left(\frac{1}{2r} \frac{\partial^2 \psi_j^3}{\partial \theta \partial r} - \frac{1}{2r^2} \frac{\partial \psi_j^3}{\partial \theta} \right) - T_{11}^{4} \left(\frac{2}{h^2 r} \frac{\partial^2 \psi_j^3}{\partial \theta \partial r} + \frac{2}{h^2 r^2} \frac{\partial \psi_j^3}{\partial \theta} \right) \right]$$
$$+ \left(\frac{1}{r^2} \frac{\partial^2 \psi_i^7}{\partial \theta^2} - \frac{1}{r} \frac{\partial \psi_i^7}{\partial r} \right) \left[T_{22}^{2} \left(\frac{-1}{2r} \frac{\partial^2 \psi_j^3}{\partial r \partial \theta} + \frac{1}{2r^2} \frac{\partial \psi_j^3}{\partial \theta} \right) + T_{22}^{4} \left(\frac{2}{h^2 r 2} \frac{\partial^2 \psi_j^3}{\partial \theta^2} - \frac{2}{h^2 r} \frac{\partial \psi_j^3}{\partial r} \right) \right]$$
$$+ \left(\frac{-1}{2} \frac{\partial^2 \psi_i^7}{\partial r^2} + \frac{1}{2r} \frac{\partial^2 \psi_i^7}{\partial \theta^2} + \frac{1}{2r} \frac{\partial \psi_i^7}{\partial r} \right)$$
$$\left[T_{44}^{2} \left(\frac{-1}{4} \frac{\partial^2 \psi_j^3}{\partial r^2} + \frac{1}{4r^2} \frac{\partial^2 \psi_j^3}{\partial \theta^2} + \frac{1}{4r} \frac{\partial \psi_j^3}{\partial \theta} \right) + T_{44}^{4} \left(\frac{-1}{h^2} \frac{\partial^2 \psi_j^3}{\partial r^2} + \frac{1}{h^2 r^2} \frac{\partial^2 \psi_j^3}{\partial \theta^2} + \frac{1}{h^2 r} \frac{\partial \psi_j^3}{\partial r} \right) \right]$$
$$\left. + T_{55}^{2} \frac{3}{h^2} \frac{\partial \psi_i^7}{\partial r} \frac{\partial \psi_j^3}{\partial r} + T_{66}^{2} \frac{1}{r} \frac{\partial \psi_i^7}{\partial \theta} \frac{2}{h^2} \frac{\partial \psi_j^3}{\partial \theta} - \left(\frac{2}{3} \frac{\partial^2 \psi_i^7}{d \theta \partial r} + \frac{2}{3r^2} \frac{\psi_i^7}{\partial \theta} \right) A_{44}^{6} \frac{8}{3h^2 r^2} \frac{\partial \psi_j^7}{\partial \theta} \right\} r dr d\theta \tag{A45}$$

$$
\begin{aligned}
K_{74} = \int_{\Omega} \Bigg\{ & \frac{-1}{3}\frac{\partial^2\psi_i^7}{\partial r^2}\left[A_{11}^4\frac{\partial\psi_j^4}{\partial r} + \frac{1}{r}A_{12}^4\psi_j^4 - \frac{4}{3h^2}A_{11}^6\frac{\partial\psi_j^4}{\partial r} - \frac{4}{3rh^2}A_{12}^6\psi_j^4\right] \\
& - \left(\frac{1}{3r}\frac{\partial\psi_i^7}{\partial r} + \frac{1}{3r^2}\frac{\partial^2\psi_j^7}{\partial\theta^2}\right)\left[A_{21}^4\frac{\partial\psi_j^6}{\partial r} + A_{22}^4\frac{1}{r}\psi_j^4 - A_{21}^6\frac{4}{3h^2}\frac{\partial\psi_j^4}{dr} - A_{22}^6\frac{4}{3rh^2}\psi_j^4\right] \\
& + 2\psi_i^7\left[A_{31}^2\frac{\partial\psi_j^4}{\partial r} + A_{32}^2\frac{1}{r}\psi_j^4 - A_{31}^4\frac{4}{3h^2}\frac{\partial\psi_j^4}{\partial r} - A_{32}^4\frac{4}{3rh^2}\psi_j^4\right] \\
& - \frac{2}{3}\frac{\partial^2\psi_i^7}{\partial\theta\partial r}\left[A_{44}^4\frac{1}{r}\frac{\partial\psi_j^4}{\partial\theta} - A_{44}^6\frac{4}{3h^2r}\frac{\partial\psi_j^4}{\partial\theta}\right] \\
& + \left(\frac{1}{r^2}\frac{\partial^2\psi_i^7}{\partial\theta^2} - \frac{1}{r}\frac{\partial\psi_i^7}{\partial r}\right)\left[T_{22}^2\frac{1}{2r}\frac{\partial\psi_j^4}{\partial\theta} - T_{22}^4\frac{2}{h^2r}\psi_j^4\right] \\
& + \left(\frac{-1}{2}\frac{\partial^2\psi_i^7}{\partial r^2} + \frac{1}{2r}\frac{\partial^2\psi_i^7}{\partial\theta^2} + \frac{1}{2r}\frac{\partial\psi_i^7}{\partial r}\right)\left[T_{44}^2\left(\frac{1}{4}\frac{\partial\psi_j^4}{\partial\theta} - \frac{1}{4r}\psi_j^4\right) + T_{44}^4\left(\frac{-1}{h^2}\frac{\partial\psi_j^4}{\partial r} + \frac{1}{h^2r}\psi_j^4\right)\right] \\
& + \frac{3}{2}\frac{\partial\psi_i^7}{\partial r}\left[T_{55}^2\left(\frac{1}{4r^2}\frac{\partial^2\psi_j^4}{\partial\theta^2} + \frac{2}{h^2}\psi_j^4\right) - T_{55}^4\frac{1}{3h^2r^2}\frac{\partial^2\psi_j^4}{\partial\theta^2}\right] \\
& + \frac{1}{r}\frac{\partial\psi_i^7}{\partial\theta}\left[T_{66}^2\left(\frac{-1}{4r}\frac{\partial^2\psi_j^4}{\partial\theta\partial r} + \frac{1}{4r^2}\frac{\partial\psi_j^4}{\partial\theta}\right) + T_{66}^4\left(\frac{-1}{3h^2r}\frac{\partial^2\psi_j^4}{d\theta dr} + \frac{1}{3h^2r^2}\frac{\partial\psi_j^4}{\partial\theta}\right)\right]\Bigg\} r dr d\theta
\end{aligned} \tag{A46}
$$

$$
\begin{aligned}
K_{75} = \int_{\Omega} \Bigg\{ & \frac{h^2}{3}\frac{\partial^2\psi_i^7}{\partial r^2}\left[A_{12}^4\frac{1}{r}\frac{\partial\psi_j^5}{\partial\theta} - A_{12}^6\frac{4}{3rh^2}\frac{\partial\psi_j^5}{\partial\theta}\right] + \left(\frac{h^2}{4}\frac{\partial\psi_i^7}{\partial r} + \frac{h^2}{4r}\frac{\partial^2\psi_j^7}{\partial\theta^2}\right)\left[A_{22}^4\frac{1}{r}\frac{\partial\psi_j^5}{\partial\theta}\right. \\
& \left. - A_{22}^6\frac{4}{3h^2r}\frac{\partial\psi_j^5}{\partial\theta}\right] + 2\psi_i^7\left[A_{32}^2\frac{1}{r}\frac{\partial\psi_j^5}{\partial\theta} - A_{32}^3\frac{4}{3rh^2}\frac{\partial\psi_j^5}{\partial\theta}\right] - \frac{2}{3}\frac{\partial^2\psi_i^7}{\partial\theta\partial r}\left[A_{44}^4\left(\frac{\partial\psi_j^5}{\partial r} - \frac{1}{r}\psi_j^5\right)\right. \\
& \left. - A_{44}^6\left(\frac{4}{3h^2}\frac{\partial\psi_j^5}{\partial r} + \frac{4}{3h^2r}\psi_j^5\right)\right] + \left(\frac{3r}{2}\frac{\partial^2\psi_i^7}{drd\theta} - \frac{1}{r^2}\frac{\partial\psi_i^7}{\partial\theta}\right)\left[-T_{11}^2\frac{1}{2}\frac{\partial\psi_j^5}{\partial r} + T_{11}^4\frac{2}{h^2}\frac{\partial\psi_j^5}{\partial r}\right] \\
& + \left(\frac{1}{r^2}\frac{\partial^2\psi_i^7}{\partial\theta} - \frac{1}{r}\frac{\partial\psi_i^7}{\partial r}\right)\left[T_{22}^2\frac{1}{2r}\psi_j^5 + T_{22}^4\frac{2}{h^2r}\frac{\partial\psi_j^5}{\partial r}\right] + \left(\frac{-1}{2}\frac{\partial^2\psi_i^7}{\partial r^2} + \frac{1}{2r}\frac{\partial^2\psi_i^7}{\partial\theta^2}\right. \\
& \left. + \frac{1}{2r}\frac{\partial\psi_i^7}{dr}\right)\left[T_{44}^2\frac{-1}{4r}\frac{\partial\psi_j^5}{d\theta} + T_{44}^4\frac{1}{h^2r}\frac{\partial\psi_j^5}{d\theta}\right] - \frac{3}{2}\frac{\partial\psi_i^7}{\partial r}\left[T_{55}^2\left(\frac{1}{4r^2}\frac{\partial\psi_j^5}{\partial\theta} + \frac{1}{4r}\frac{\partial^2\psi_j^5}{\partial rd\theta}\right)\right. \\
& \left. - T_{55}^4\left(\frac{1}{3h^2r^2}\frac{\partial\psi_j^5}{\partial\theta} + \frac{1}{3h^2r}\frac{\partial^2\psi_j^5}{\partial rd\partial\theta}\right)\right] + \frac{1}{r}\frac{\partial\psi_i^7}{\partial\theta}\left[T_{66}^2\left(\frac{1}{4r}\frac{\partial\psi_j^5}{\partial r} - \frac{1}{4r^2}\psi_j^5 + \frac{1}{4}\frac{\partial^2\psi_j^5}{\partial r^2} + \frac{2}{h^2}\psi_j^5\right)\right. \\
& \left. + T_{66}^4\left(\frac{-1}{3h^2r}\frac{\partial\psi_j^5}{\partial r} + \frac{1}{3h^2r^2}\psi_j^5 - \frac{1}{3h^2}\frac{\partial^2\psi_j^5}{\partial r^2}\right)\right]\Bigg\} r dr d\theta
\end{aligned} \tag{A47}
$$

$$K_{76} = \int_{\Omega} \left\{ \frac{h^2}{3}\frac{\partial^2 \psi_j^7}{\partial r^2}\left[A_{13}^3 \psi_j^6 - A_{11}^5 \frac{1}{2}\frac{\partial^2 \psi_j^6}{\partial r^2} - A_{12}^5 \left(\frac{1}{2r}\frac{\partial \psi_j^6}{\partial r} + \frac{1}{2r^2}\frac{\partial^2 \psi_j^6}{\partial \theta^2} \right) \right] \right.$$
$$+ \left(\frac{h^2}{4}\frac{\partial \psi_i^7}{\partial r} + \frac{h^2}{4r}\frac{\partial^2 \psi_j^7}{d\theta^2} \right)\left[A_{23}^3 \psi_j^6 - A_{21}^5 \frac{1}{2}\frac{\partial^2 \psi_j^6}{\partial r^2} - A_{22}^5 \left(\frac{1}{2r}\frac{\partial \psi_j^6}{\partial r} + \frac{1}{2r^2}\frac{\partial^2 \psi_j^6}{d\theta^2} \right) \right]$$
$$+ 2\psi_i^7 \left[A_{33}^1 \psi_j^6 - A_{31}^3 \frac{1}{2}\frac{\partial \psi_j^6}{\partial r^2}. - A_{32}^3 \left(\frac{1}{2r}\frac{\partial \psi_j^6}{\partial r} + \frac{1}{2r^2}\frac{\partial^2 \psi_j^6}{\partial \theta^2} \right) \right]$$
$$- \frac{2}{3}\frac{\partial^2 \psi_i^7}{\partial \theta \partial r}\left[A_{44}^5 \left(\frac{-1}{r}\frac{\partial^2 \psi_j^6}{d\theta \partial r} + \frac{1}{r^2}\frac{\partial \psi_j^6}{\partial \theta} \right) \right] + \left(\frac{3}{2} r \frac{\partial^2 \psi_i^7}{\partial e d\theta} - \frac{1}{r^2}\frac{\partial \psi_i^7}{\partial \theta} \right)\left[T_{11}^3 \left(\frac{1}{r}\frac{\partial^2 \psi_j^6}{\partial \theta dr} - \frac{1}{r^2}\frac{\partial \psi_j^6}{d\theta} \right) \right]$$
$$+ \left(\frac{1}{r^2}\frac{\partial^2 \psi_i^7}{\partial \theta^2} + \frac{-1}{r}\frac{\partial \psi_i^7}{\partial r} \right)\left[T_{22}^3 \left(\frac{-1}{r}\frac{\partial^2 \psi_j^6}{\partial r d\theta} + \frac{1}{r^2}\frac{\partial \psi_j^6}{\partial \theta} \right) \right]$$
$$+ \left(-\frac{1}{2}\frac{\partial^2 \psi_i^7}{\partial r^2} + \frac{1}{2r}\frac{\partial^2 \psi_i^7}{\partial \theta^2} + \frac{1}{2r}\frac{\partial \psi_i^7}{\partial r} \right)\left[T_{44}^3 \left(\frac{-1}{2}\frac{\partial^2 \psi_j^6}{\partial r^2} + \frac{1}{2r^2}\frac{\partial^2 \psi_j^6}{\partial \theta^2} + \frac{1}{r}\frac{\partial \psi_j^6}{\partial r} \right) \right]$$
$$\left. + T_{56}^1 \frac{3}{4}\frac{\partial \psi_i^7}{\partial r}\frac{\partial \psi_j^6}{\partial r} + T_{66}^1 \frac{1}{2r^2}\frac{\partial \psi_i^7}{\partial \theta}\frac{\partial \psi_j^6}{\partial \theta} \right\} r dr d\theta \tag{A48}$$

$$K_{77} = \int_{\Omega} \left\{ \frac{h^2}{3}\frac{\partial^2 \psi_j^7}{\partial r^2}\left[A_{13}^4 2\psi_j^7 - A_{11}^6 \frac{1}{3}\frac{\partial^2 \psi_j^7}{\partial r^2} - A_{12}^6 \left(\frac{1}{3r^2}\frac{\partial \psi_j^6}{\partial \theta^2} + \frac{1}{3r}\frac{2\psi_j^7}{\partial r} \right) \right] \right.$$
$$+ \left(\frac{h^2}{4}\frac{\partial \psi_i^7}{\partial r} + \frac{h^2}{4r}\frac{\partial^2 \psi_j^7}{\partial \theta^2} \right)\left[A_{23}^4 2\psi_j^7 - A_{21}^6 \frac{1}{3}\frac{\partial^2 \psi_j^7}{\partial r^2} - A_{22}^6 \left(\frac{1}{3r^2}\frac{\partial \psi_j^7}{\partial \theta} + \frac{1}{3r}\frac{\partial \psi_j^7}{\partial r} \right) \right]$$
$$+ 2\psi_i^7 \left[A_{33}^2 2\psi_j^7 - A_{31}^4 \frac{1}{3}\frac{\partial^2 \psi_j^7}{\partial r^2} - A_{32}^4 \left(\frac{1}{3r^2}\frac{\partial^2 \psi_j^7}{\partial \theta^2} + \frac{1}{3r}\frac{\partial \psi_j^7}{\partial r} \right) \right]$$
$$+ A_{44}^6 \frac{4}{9}\frac{\partial^2 \psi_i^7}{d\theta \partial r}\frac{d^2 \psi_j^7}{\partial \theta \partial r} + \left(\frac{3}{2} r \frac{\partial^2 \psi_i^7}{\partial r d\theta} - \frac{1}{r^2}\frac{\partial \psi_i^7}{\partial \theta} \right)\left[T_{11}^4 \left(\frac{1}{r}\frac{\partial^2 \psi_j^7}{\partial \theta \partial r} - \frac{1}{r^2}\frac{\partial \psi_j^7}{\partial \theta} \right) \right]$$
$$+ \left(\frac{1}{r^2}\frac{\partial^2 \psi_i^7}{\partial \theta^2} + \frac{-1}{r}\frac{\partial \psi_i^7}{\partial r} \right)\left[T_{22}^4 \left(\frac{1}{r^2}\frac{\partial^2 \psi_j^7}{d\theta^2} + \frac{-1}{r}\frac{\partial \psi_j^7}{\partial r} \right) \right]$$
$$+ \left(\frac{-1}{2}\frac{\partial^2 \psi_i^7}{\partial r^2} + \frac{1}{2r}\frac{\partial^2 \psi_i^7}{\partial \theta^2} + \frac{1}{2r}\frac{\partial \psi_i^7}{dr} \right)\left[T_{44}^4 \left(\frac{-1}{2}\frac{\partial^2 \psi_j^7}{\partial r^2} + \frac{1}{2r^2}\frac{\partial^2 \psi_j^7}{\partial \theta^2} + \frac{1}{2r}\frac{\partial \psi_j^7}{\partial r} \right) \right]$$
$$\left. + T_{55}^2 \frac{9}{4}\frac{\partial \psi_i^7}{\partial r}\frac{\partial \psi_j^7}{\partial r} + T_{66}^2 \frac{1}{r}\frac{\partial \psi_i^7}{\partial \theta}\frac{1}{r}\frac{\partial \psi_j^7}{\partial \theta} + \left(\frac{2}{3}\frac{\partial^2 \psi_i^7}{\partial \theta \partial r} + \frac{2}{3r^2}\frac{\psi_i^7}{\partial \theta} \right) A_{44}^6 \frac{2}{3r^2}\frac{\partial \psi_j^7}{d\theta} \right\} r dr d\theta \tag{A49}$$

Appendix A.2. Mass Matrix Elements

$$M_{11} = \int_{\Omega} \left\{ -m_o \psi_j^1 \psi_i^1 \right\} r dr d\theta \tag{A50}$$

$$M_{12} = 0 \tag{A51}$$

$$M_{13} = \int_{\Omega} \left\{ m_3 \frac{4}{3h^2}\frac{\partial \psi_j^3}{\partial r}\psi_i^1 \right\} r dr d\theta \tag{A52}$$

$$M_{14} = \int_{\Omega} \left\{ -m_1 \psi_j^4 \psi_i^1 + m_3 \frac{4}{3h^2}\psi_j^4 \psi_i^1 \right\} r dr d\theta \tag{A53}$$

$$M_{15} = 0 \tag{A54}$$

$$M_{16} = \int_{\Omega} \left\{ m_2 \frac{1}{2} \frac{\partial \psi_j^6}{\partial r} \psi_i^1 \right\} r dr d\theta \tag{A55}$$

$$M_{17} = \int_{\Omega} \left\{ m_3 \frac{1}{3} \frac{\partial \psi_j^7}{\partial r} \psi_i \right\} r dr d\theta \tag{A56}$$

$$M_{21} = 0 \tag{A57}$$

$$M_{22} = \int_{\Omega} \left\{ -m_o \psi_j^2 \psi_i^2 \right\} r dr d\theta \tag{A58}$$

$$M_{23} = \int_{\Omega} \left\{ m_3 \frac{4}{3rh^2} \frac{\partial \psi_j^3}{\partial \theta} \psi^2 \right\} r dr d\theta \tag{A59}$$

$$M_{24} = 0 \tag{A60}$$

$$M_{25} = \int_{\Omega} \left\{ -m_1 \psi_j^5 \psi_i^2 + m_3 \frac{4}{3h^2} \psi_j^5 \psi_i^2 \right\} r dr d\theta \tag{A61}$$

$$M_{26} = \int_{\Omega} \left\{ m_2 \frac{1}{2r} \frac{\partial \psi_j}{\partial \theta} \psi_i^2 \right\} r dr d\theta \tag{A62}$$

$$M_{27} = \int_{\Omega} \left\{ m_3 \frac{1}{3r} \frac{\partial \psi_j^7}{\partial \theta} \psi_i^2 \right\} r dr d\theta \tag{A63}$$

$$M_{31} = \int_{\Omega} \left\{ m_3 \frac{4}{3h^2} \psi_j^1 \frac{\partial \psi_i^3}{\partial r} \right\} r dr d\theta \tag{A64}$$

$$M_{32} = \int_{\Omega} \left\{ m_3 \frac{4}{3rh^2} \psi_j^2 \frac{\partial \psi_i^3}{\partial \theta} \right\} r dr d\theta \tag{A65}$$

$$M_{33} = \int_{\Omega} \left\{ m_o \psi_j^3 \psi_i^3 - m_6 \frac{16}{9h^4} \frac{\partial \psi_j^3}{\partial r} \frac{\partial \psi_i^3}{\partial r} - m_6 \frac{16}{9h^4 r^4} \frac{\partial \psi_j^3}{\partial \theta} \frac{\partial \psi_i^3}{\partial \theta} \right\} r dr d\theta \tag{A66}$$

$$M_{34} = \int_{\Omega} \left\{ m_4 \frac{4}{3h^2} \psi_j^4 \frac{\partial \psi_i^3}{\partial r} - m_6 \frac{16}{9h^4} \psi_j^4 \frac{\partial \psi_i^3}{\partial r} \right\} r dr d\theta \tag{A67}$$

$$M_{35} = \int_{\Omega} \left\{ m_4 \frac{4}{3rh^2} \psi_j^5 \frac{\partial \psi_i^3}{\partial \theta} - m_6 \frac{16}{9rh^4} \psi_j^5 \frac{\partial \psi_i^3}{\partial \theta} \right\} r dr d\theta \tag{A68}$$

$$M_{36} = \int_{\Omega} \left\{ -m_1 \psi_j^6 \psi_i^3 - m_5 \frac{2}{3h^2} \frac{\partial \psi_j^6}{\partial r} \frac{\partial \psi_i^3}{\partial r} - m_5 \frac{2}{3r^2 h^2} \frac{\partial \psi_j^6}{\partial \theta} \frac{\partial \psi_i^3}{\partial \theta} \right\} r dr d\theta \tag{A69}$$

$$M_{37} = \int_{\Omega} \left\{ -m_2 \psi_j^7 \psi_i^3 - m_6 \frac{4}{9h^2} \frac{\partial \psi_j^7}{\partial r} \frac{\partial \psi_i^3}{\partial r} - m_6 \frac{4}{9r^2 h^2} \frac{\partial \psi_j^7}{\partial \theta} \frac{\partial \psi_i^3}{\partial \theta} \right\} r dr d\theta \tag{A70}$$

$$M_{41} = \int_{\Omega} \left\{ -m_1 \psi_j^1 \psi_i^4 + m_3 \frac{4}{3h^2} \psi_j^1 \psi_i^4 \right\} r dr d\theta \tag{A71}$$

$$M_{42} = 0 \tag{A72}$$

$$M_{43} = \int_{\Omega} \left\{ m_4 \frac{4}{3h^2} \frac{\partial \psi_j^3}{\partial r} \psi_i^4 - m_6 \frac{16}{9h^4} \frac{\partial \psi_j}{\partial r} \psi_i^4 \right\} r dr d\theta \tag{A73}$$

$$M_{44} = \int_{\Omega} \left\{ -m_2 \psi_j^4 \psi_i^4 + m_4 \frac{4}{3^2} \psi_j^4 \psi_i^4 + m_4 \frac{4}{3h^2} \psi_j^4 \psi_i^4 - m_6 \frac{16}{9h^4} \psi_j^4 \psi_i^4 \right\} r dr d\theta \tag{A74}$$

$$M_{45} = 0 \tag{A75}$$

$$M_{46} = \int_{\Omega} \left\{ m_3 \frac{1}{2} \frac{\partial \psi_j^6}{\partial r} \psi_i^4 - m_5 \frac{2}{3h^2} \frac{\partial \psi_j^6}{\partial r} \psi_i^4 \right\} r dr d\theta \quad \text{(A76)}$$

$$M_{47} = \int_{\Omega} \left\{ m_4 \frac{1}{3} \frac{\partial \psi_j^7}{\partial r} \psi_i^4 - m_6 \frac{4}{9h^2} \frac{\partial \psi_j^7}{\partial r} \psi_i^4 \right\} r dr d\theta \quad \text{(A77)}$$

$$M_{51} = 0 \quad \text{(A78)}$$

$$M_{52} = \int_{\Omega} \left\{ -m_1 \psi_j^2 \psi_i^5 + m_3 \frac{4}{3h^2} \psi_j^2 \psi_i^5 \right\} r dr d\theta \quad \text{(A79)}$$

$$M_{53} = \int_{\Omega} \left\{ m_4 \frac{4}{3rh^2} \frac{\partial \psi_j^3}{\partial \theta} \psi_i^5 - m_6 \frac{16}{9rh^4} \frac{\partial \psi_j^3}{\partial \theta} \psi_i^5 \right\} r dr d\theta \quad \text{(A80)}$$

$$M_{54} = 0 \quad \text{(A81)}$$

$$M_{55} = \int_{\Omega} \left\{ m_2 \psi_j^5 \psi_i^5 + m_4 \frac{4}{3h^2} \psi_j^5 \psi_i^5 + m_4 \frac{4}{3h^2} \psi_j^5 \psi_i^5 - m_6 \frac{16}{9h^4} \psi_j^5 \psi_i^5 \right\} r dr d\theta \quad \text{(A82)}$$

$$M_{56} = \int_{\Omega} \left\{ m_3 \frac{1}{2r} \frac{\partial \psi_j^6}{\partial \theta} \psi_i^5 - m_5 \frac{2}{3rh^2} \frac{\partial \psi_j^6}{\partial \theta} \psi_i^5 \right\} r dr d\theta \quad \text{(A83)}$$

$$M_{57} = \int_{\Omega} \left\{ m_4 \frac{1}{3} \frac{1}{r} \frac{\partial \psi_j^7}{\partial \theta} \psi_i^5 - m_6 \frac{4}{9rh^2} \frac{\partial \psi_j^7}{\partial \theta} \psi_i^5 \right\} r dr d\theta \quad \text{(A84)}$$

$$M_{61} = \int_{\Omega} \left\{ m_2 \psi_j^1 \frac{1}{2} \frac{\partial \psi_i^6}{\partial r} \right\} r dr d\theta \quad \text{(A85)}$$

$$M_{62} = \int_{\Omega} \left\{ m_2 \psi_j^2 \frac{1}{2r} \frac{\partial \psi_i^6}{\partial \theta} \right\} r dr d\theta \quad \text{(A86)}$$

$$M_{63} = \int_{\Omega} \left\{ -m_5 \frac{2}{3h^2} \frac{\partial \psi_j^3}{\partial r} \frac{\partial \psi_i^7}{\partial r} - m_5 \frac{2}{3r^2h^2} \frac{\partial \psi_j^3}{\partial \theta} \frac{\partial \psi_i^6}{\partial \theta} - m_1 \psi_j^3 \psi_i^6 \right\} r dr d\theta \quad \text{(A87)}$$

$$M_{64} = \int_{\Omega} \frac{1}{2} \left\{ m_3 \psi_j^4 \frac{\partial \psi_i^6}{\partial r} - m_5 \frac{2}{3h^2} \psi_j^4 \frac{\partial \psi_i^6}{\partial r} \right\} r dr d\theta \quad \text{(A88)}$$

$$M_{65} = \int_{\Omega} \left\{ m_3 \psi_j^3 \frac{1}{2r} \frac{\partial \psi_i^6}{\partial r} - m_5 \frac{2}{3rh^2} \psi_j^5 \frac{\partial \psi_i^6}{\partial \theta} \right\} r dr d\theta \quad \text{(A89)}$$

$$M_{66} = \int_{\Omega} \left\{ -m_4 \frac{1}{4} \frac{\partial \psi_j^6}{\partial r} \frac{\partial \psi_i^6}{\partial r} - m_4 \frac{1}{4r^4} \frac{\partial \psi_j^6}{\partial \theta} \frac{\partial \psi_i^6}{\partial \theta} - m_2 \psi_j^6 \psi_i^6 \right\} r dr d\theta \quad \text{(A90)}$$

$$M_{67} = \int_{\Omega} \left\{ -m_5 \frac{1}{6} \frac{\partial \psi_j^7}{\partial r} \frac{\partial \psi_i^7}{\partial r} - m_5 \frac{1}{6r^2} \frac{\partial \psi_j^7}{\partial \theta} \frac{\partial \psi_i^6}{\partial \theta} - m_3 \psi_j^7 \psi_i^6 \right\} r dr d\theta \quad \text{(A91)}$$

$$M_{71} = \int_{\Omega} \left\{ m_3 \frac{1}{3} \psi_j^1 \frac{\partial \psi_i^7}{\partial r} \right\} r dr d\theta \quad \text{(A92)}$$

$$M_{72} = \int_{\Omega} \left\{ m_3 \frac{1}{3r} \psi_j^2 \frac{\partial \psi_i^7}{\partial \theta} \right\} r dr d\theta \quad \text{(A93)}$$

$$M_{73} = \int_{\Omega} \left\{ -m_2 \psi_j^3 \psi_i^7 - m_6 \frac{4}{9h^2} \frac{\partial \psi_j^3}{\partial r} \frac{\psi_i^7}{\partial r} - m_6 \frac{4}{9r^2h^2} \frac{\partial \psi_j^3}{\partial \theta} \frac{\partial \psi_i^7}{\partial \theta} \right\} r dr d\theta \quad \text{(A94)}$$

$$M_{74} = \int_{\Omega} \left\{ m_4 \frac{1}{3} \psi_j^4 \frac{\partial \psi_i^7}{\partial r} - m_6 \frac{4}{9h^2} \psi_j^4 \frac{\partial \psi_i^7}{\partial r} \right\} r dr d\theta \tag{A95}$$

$$M_{75} = \int_{\Omega} \left\{ m_4 \frac{1}{3r} \psi_j \frac{\partial \psi_i^7}{\partial \theta} - m_6 \frac{4}{9rh^2} \psi_j^5 \frac{\partial \psi_i^7}{\partial \theta} \right\} r dr d\theta \tag{A96}$$

$$M_{76} = \int_{\Omega} \left\{ -m_3 \psi_j^6 \psi_i^7 - m_5 \frac{1}{6} \frac{\partial \psi_j^6}{\partial r} \frac{\partial \psi_i^7}{\partial r} - m_5 \frac{1}{6r^2} \frac{\partial \psi_j^6}{\partial \theta} \frac{\partial \psi_i^7}{\partial \theta} \right\} r dr d\theta \tag{A97}$$

$$M_{77} = \int_{\Omega} \left\{ -m_4 \psi_j^7 \psi_i^7 - m_6 \frac{1}{9} \frac{\partial \psi_j^7}{\partial r} \frac{\partial \psi_i^7}{\partial r} - m_6 \frac{1}{3^2 r^2} \frac{\partial \psi_j^7}{\partial \theta} \frac{\partial \psi_i^7}{\partial \theta} \right\} r dr d\theta \tag{A98}$$

Appendix A.3. Tangent Matrix Elements

$$\begin{aligned} T_{ij}^{13} = \int_{\Omega} \Bigg\{ & \frac{1}{2} A_{11}^0 \frac{\partial \psi_i}{\partial r}^1 \frac{\partial \psi_j}{\partial r}^3 \frac{\partial W_o}{\partial r} + \frac{1}{2r^2} A_{12}^0 \frac{\partial \psi_i}{\partial r}^1 \frac{\partial \psi_j}{\partial \theta}^3 \frac{\partial W_o}{\partial \theta} + A_{21}^0 \frac{1}{2r} \psi_i^1 \frac{\partial \psi_j}{\partial r}^3 \frac{\partial W_o}{\partial r} + \\ & + A_{22}^0 \frac{1}{2r^3} \psi_i^1 \frac{\partial \psi_j}{\partial \theta}^3 \frac{\partial W_o}{\partial \theta} + A_{44}^0 \frac{1}{2r^2} \frac{\partial \psi_i^1}{\partial \theta} \frac{\partial \psi_j^3}{\partial \theta} \frac{\partial W_o}{\partial r} + A_{44}^0 \frac{1}{2r^2} \frac{\partial \psi_i^1}{\partial \theta} \frac{\partial \psi_j^3}{\partial r} \frac{\partial W_o}{\partial \theta} \Bigg\} r dr d\theta \\ & + K_{13} \end{aligned} \tag{A99}$$

$$\begin{aligned} T_{ij}^{23} = \int_{\Omega} \Bigg\{ & \frac{1}{2r} A_{21}^0 \frac{\partial \psi_i}{\partial \theta}^2 \frac{\partial \psi_i}{\partial r}^3 \frac{\partial W_o}{\partial r} + \frac{1}{2r^3} A_{22}^0 \frac{\partial \psi_i}{\partial \theta}^2 \frac{\partial \psi_j}{\partial \theta}^3 \frac{\partial W_o}{\partial \theta} + \frac{1}{2r} A_{44}^0 \frac{\partial \psi_i}{\partial r}^2 \frac{\partial \psi_j}{\partial \theta}^3 \frac{\partial W_o}{\partial r} \\ & + \frac{1}{2r} A_{44}^0 \frac{\partial \psi_i}{\partial r}^2 \frac{\partial \psi_j}{\partial r}^3 \frac{\partial W_o}{\partial \theta} - \frac{1}{2r^2} A_{44}^0 \psi_i^2 \frac{\partial \psi_j}{\partial \theta}^3 \frac{\partial W_o}{\partial r} - \frac{1}{2r^2} A_{44}^0 \psi_i^2 \frac{\partial \psi_j}{\partial r}^3 \frac{\partial W_o}{\partial \theta} \Bigg\} r dr d\theta \\ & + K_{23} \end{aligned} \tag{A100}$$

$$
\begin{aligned}
T_{ij}^{33} = \int_{\Omega} \Bigg\{ & A_{11}^{0} {\frac{\partial \psi_i}{\partial r}}^{3} {\frac{\partial \psi_j}{\partial r}}^{3} \frac{\partial U_o}{\partial r} + \frac{1}{r} A_{12}^{0} {\frac{\partial \psi_i}{\partial r}}^{3} {\frac{\partial \psi_j}{\partial r}}^{3} U_o + \frac{1}{r^2} A_{21}^{0} {\frac{\partial \psi_i}{\partial \theta}}^{3} {\frac{\partial \psi_j}{\partial \theta}}^{3} \frac{\partial U_o}{\partial r} \\
& + \frac{1}{r^2} A_{22}^{0} {\frac{\partial \psi_i}{\partial \theta}}^{3} {\frac{\partial \psi_j}{\partial \theta}}^{3} U_o + \frac{1}{r^2} A_{44}^{0} {\frac{\partial \psi_i}{\partial r}}^{3} {\frac{\partial \psi_j}{\partial \theta}}^{3} \frac{\partial U_o}{\partial r} + \frac{1}{r^2} A_{44}^{0} {\frac{\partial \psi_i}{\partial \theta}}^{3} {\frac{\partial \psi_j}{\partial r}}^{3} \frac{\partial U_o}{\partial \theta} \\
& + \frac{1}{r} A_{12}^{0} {\frac{\partial \psi_i}{\partial r}}^{3} {\frac{\partial \psi_j}{\partial r}}^{3} \frac{\partial V_o}{\partial \theta} + \frac{1}{r^3} A_{22}^{0} {\frac{\partial \psi_i}{\partial \theta}}^{3} {\frac{\partial \psi_j}{\partial \theta}}^{3} \frac{\partial V_o}{\partial \theta} + \frac{1}{r} A_{44}^{0} {\frac{\partial \psi_i}{\partial r}}^{3} {\frac{\partial \psi_j}{\partial \theta}}^{3} \frac{\partial V_o}{\partial r} \\
& + \frac{1}{r} A_{44} o {\frac{\partial \psi_i}{\partial \theta}}^{3} {\frac{\partial \psi_j}{\partial r}}^{3} \frac{\partial V_o}{\partial r} - \frac{1}{r^2} A_{44}^{0} {\frac{\partial \psi_i}{\partial r}}^{3} {\frac{\partial \psi_j}{\partial \theta}}^{3} V_o - \frac{1}{r^2} A_{44} o {\frac{\partial \psi_i}{\partial \theta}}^{3} {\frac{\partial \psi_j}{\partial r}}^{3} V_o \\
& + A_{11}^{0} \left(\frac{\partial W_o}{\partial r}\right)^2 \frac{\partial \psi_i}{\partial r} \frac{\partial \psi_j}{\partial r} + A_{12}^{0} \frac{1}{2r} \frac{\partial W_o}{\partial r} \frac{\partial W_o}{\partial \theta} \frac{\partial \psi_i^3}{\partial r} \frac{\partial \psi_j^3}{\partial \theta} + A_{12}^{0} \frac{1}{2r} \left(\frac{\partial W_o}{\partial \theta}\right)^2 \frac{\partial \psi_i^3}{\partial r} \frac{\partial \psi_j^3}{\partial r} \\
& - A_{11}^{3} \frac{4}{3h^2} \frac{\partial^2 W_o}{\partial r^2} \frac{\partial \psi_i^3}{\partial r} \frac{\partial \psi_j}{\partial r} - A_{12}^{3} \frac{4}{3h^2 r^2} \frac{\partial^2 W_o}{\partial \theta^2} \frac{\partial \psi_j^3}{\partial r} \frac{\partial \psi_i}{\partial r} \\
& - A_{12}^{3} \frac{4}{3h^2 r} \frac{\partial W_o}{\partial r} \frac{\partial \psi_i^3}{\partial r} \frac{\partial \psi_j^3}{\partial r} - A_{11}^{3} \frac{2}{3h^2} \frac{\partial W_o}{\partial r} \frac{\partial \psi_i}{\partial r^2} \frac{\partial \psi_j}{\partial r} - A_{12}^{3} \frac{4}{6rh^2} \frac{\partial W_o}{\partial \theta} \frac{\partial^2 \psi_i^3}{\partial r^2} \frac{\partial \psi_j^3}{\partial \theta} \\
& + A_{21}^{0} \frac{1}{2r^2} \left(\frac{\partial W_o}{\partial r}\right)^2 \frac{\partial \psi_i}{\partial \theta} \frac{\partial \psi_j}{\partial \theta} + A_{21}^{0} \frac{1}{2r^2} \frac{\partial W_o}{\partial \theta} \frac{\partial W_o}{\partial r} \frac{\partial \psi_i}{\partial \theta} \frac{\partial \psi_j}{\partial r} + A_{22}^{0} \frac{1}{r^4} \left(\frac{\partial W_o}{\partial \theta}\right)^2 \frac{\partial \psi_i^3}{\partial \theta} \frac{\partial \psi_j^3}{\partial \theta} \\
& - A_{21}^{3} \frac{4}{3r^4 h^2} \frac{\partial^2 W_o}{\partial r^2} \frac{\partial \psi_i^3}{\partial \theta} \frac{\partial \psi_j^3}{\partial \theta} - A_{22}^{3} \frac{4}{3r^4 h^2} \frac{\partial^2 W_o}{\partial \theta^2} \frac{\partial \psi_i^3}{\partial \theta} \frac{\partial \psi_j^3}{\partial \theta} - A_{22}^{3} \frac{4}{3r^3 h^2} \frac{\partial W_o}{\partial r} \frac{\partial \psi_i^3}{\partial \theta} \frac{\partial \psi_j^3}{\partial \theta} \\
& - A_{21}^{3} \frac{2}{3rh^2} \frac{\partial W_o}{\partial r} \frac{\partial \psi_i^3}{\partial r} \frac{\partial \psi_j^3}{\partial r} - A_{21}^{3} \frac{2}{3r^2 h^2} \frac{\partial W_o}{\partial r} \frac{\partial^2 \psi_i^3}{\partial \theta^2} \frac{\partial \psi_j^3}{\partial r} - A_{22}^{3} \frac{2}{3r^3 h^2} \frac{\partial W_o}{\partial \theta} \frac{\partial \psi_i^3}{\partial r} \frac{\partial \psi_j^3}{\partial \theta} \\
& - A_{22}^{3} \frac{2}{3r^4 h^2} \frac{\partial W_o}{\partial \theta} \frac{\partial^2 \psi_i^3}{\partial \theta^2} \frac{\partial \psi_j^3}{\partial \theta} + A_{44}^{0} \frac{1}{r^2} \frac{\partial W_o}{\partial \theta} \frac{\partial W_o}{\partial r} \frac{\partial \psi_i^3}{\partial r} \frac{\partial \psi_j^3}{\partial \theta} + A_{44}^{0} \frac{1}{2r^2} \frac{\partial W_o}{\partial \theta} \frac{\partial W_o}{\partial r} \frac{\partial \psi_i^3}{\partial r} \frac{\partial \psi_j}{\partial \theta} \\
& + A_{44}^{0} \frac{1}{r^2} \left(\frac{\partial W_o}{\partial \theta}\right)^2 \frac{\partial \psi_i^3}{\partial r} \frac{\partial \psi_j^3}{\partial r} - A_{44}^{3} \frac{8}{3rh^2} \frac{\partial^2 W_o}{\partial \theta \partial r} \frac{\partial \psi_i^3}{\partial r} \frac{\partial \psi_j^3}{\partial \theta} + A_{44}^{0} \frac{1}{r^2} \frac{\partial W_o}{\partial r} \frac{\partial W_o}{\partial \theta} \frac{\partial \psi_i^3}{\partial \theta} \frac{\partial \psi_j^3}{\partial r} \\
& + A_{44}^{0} \frac{1}{2r^2} \left(\frac{\partial W_o}{\partial r}\right)^2 \frac{\partial \psi_i^3}{\partial \theta} \frac{\partial \psi_j}{\partial \theta} + A_{44}^{0} \frac{1}{2r^2} \frac{\partial W_o}{\partial r} \frac{\partial W_o}{\partial \theta} \frac{\partial \psi_i^3}{\partial \theta} \frac{\partial \psi_j^3}{\partial r} - A_{44}^{3} \frac{8}{3h^2 r} \frac{\partial^2 W_o}{\partial \theta \partial r} \frac{\partial \psi_i^3}{\partial \theta} \frac{\partial \psi_j^3}{\partial r} \\
& - A_{44}^{3} \frac{4}{3h^2 r} \frac{\partial W_o}{\partial r} \frac{\partial^2 \psi_i^3}{\partial \theta \partial r} \frac{\partial \psi_j^3}{\partial \theta} - A_{44}^{3} \frac{4}{3h^2 r} \frac{\partial W_o}{\partial \theta} \frac{\partial^2 \psi_i^3}{\partial \theta \partial r} \frac{\partial \psi_j^3}{\partial r} - A_{44}^{3} \frac{4}{3h^2 r^2} \frac{\partial \beta_r}{\partial \theta} \frac{\partial \psi_i}{\partial \theta} \frac{\partial \psi_j}{\partial r} \\
& + A_{11}^{1} \frac{\partial \beta r}{\partial r} \frac{\partial \psi_i^3}{\partial r} \frac{\partial \psi^3}{\partial r} + A_{12}^{1} \beta_r \frac{\partial \psi_i^3}{\partial r} \frac{\partial \psi_j^3}{\partial r} - A_{11}^{3} \frac{4}{3h^2} \frac{\partial \beta_r}{\partial r} \frac{\partial \psi_i^3}{\partial r} \frac{\partial \psi_j^3}{\partial r} - A_{12}^{3} \frac{4}{3rh^2} \beta_r \frac{\partial \psi_i^3}{\partial r} \frac{\partial \psi_j^3}{\partial r} \\
& + A_{21}^{1} \frac{1}{r^2} \frac{\partial \beta_r}{\partial r} \frac{\partial \psi_i^3}{\partial \theta} \frac{\partial \psi_j^3}{\partial \theta} + A_{22}^{1} \frac{1}{r^3} \beta_r \frac{\partial \psi_i^3}{\partial \theta} \frac{\partial \psi_j^3}{\partial \theta} - A_{21}^{3} \frac{4}{3h^2 r^2} \frac{\partial \beta_r}{\partial r} \frac{\partial \psi_i^3}{\partial \theta} \frac{\partial \psi_j^3}{\partial \theta} - A_{22}^{3} \frac{4}{3r^3 h^2} \beta_r \frac{\partial \psi_i}{\partial \theta} \frac{\partial \psi_j}{\partial \theta} \\
& + A_{44}^{1} \frac{1}{r^2} \frac{\partial \beta_r}{\partial \theta} \frac{\partial \psi_i}{\partial r} \frac{\partial \psi_j}{\partial \theta} + A_{44}^{1} \frac{1}{r^2} \frac{\partial \beta_r}{\partial \theta} \frac{\partial \psi_i}{\partial \theta} \frac{\partial \psi_j}{\partial r} - A_{44}^{3} \frac{4}{3h^2 r^2} \frac{\partial \beta_r}{\partial \theta} \frac{\partial \psi_i}{\partial r} \frac{\partial \psi_j}{\partial \theta} \\
& - \Bigg\{ \frac{8}{3h^2 r^2} \left(\frac{\partial^2 W_o}{\partial \theta \partial r} \frac{\partial \psi_i^3}{\partial r} \frac{\partial \psi_j}{\partial \theta} + \frac{\partial W_o}{\partial \theta} \frac{\partial \psi_i^3}{\partial r} \frac{\partial \psi_j^3}{\partial \theta} - \frac{\partial^2 W_o}{\partial \theta \partial r} \frac{\partial \psi_i^3}{\partial \theta} \frac{\partial \psi_j^3}{\partial r} + \frac{1}{r} \frac{\partial W_o}{\partial \theta} \frac{\partial \psi_i^3}{\partial \theta} \frac{\partial \psi_j^3}{\partial r} \right) \\
& + \frac{4}{3h^2 r^2} \left(- \frac{\partial W_o}{\partial r} \frac{\partial^2 \psi_i^3}{\partial \theta dr} \frac{\partial \psi_j^3}{d\theta} - \frac{\partial W_o}{\partial \theta} \frac{\partial^2 \psi_i^3}{\partial \theta \partial r} \frac{\partial \psi_j^3}{\partial r} + \frac{1}{r} \frac{\partial W_o}{\partial r} \frac{\partial \psi_i^3}{\partial \theta} \frac{\partial \psi_j^3}{\partial \theta} + \frac{1}{r} \frac{\partial W_o}{\partial \theta} \frac{\partial \psi_i^3}{\partial \theta} \frac{\partial \psi_j^3}{\partial r} \right) \Bigg\} A_{44}^{3} \\
& + A_{12}^{1} \frac{1}{r} \frac{\partial \beta_\theta}{\partial \theta} \frac{\partial \psi_i^3}{\partial r} \frac{\partial \psi_j^3}{\partial r} - A_{12}^{3} \frac{4}{3rh^2} \frac{\partial \beta_\theta}{\partial \theta} \frac{\partial \psi_i^3}{\partial r} \frac{\partial \psi_j^3}{\partial r} + A_{22}^{1} \frac{1}{r^3} \frac{\partial \beta_\theta}{\partial \theta} \frac{\partial \psi_i^3}{\partial \theta} \frac{\partial \psi_j^3}{\partial \theta} + A_{44}^{3} \frac{4}{3h^2 r^2} \beta_\theta \frac{\partial \psi_i^3}{\partial \theta} \frac{\partial \psi_j^3}{\partial r} \\
& - A_{22}^{3} \frac{4}{3h^2 r^3} \frac{\partial \beta_\theta}{\partial \theta} \frac{\partial \psi_i^3}{\partial \theta} \frac{\partial \psi_j^3}{\partial \theta} + A_{44}^{1} \frac{1}{r} \frac{\partial \beta_\theta}{\partial r} \frac{\partial \psi_i^3}{\partial r} \frac{\partial \psi_j^3}{\partial \theta} - A_{44}^{1} \frac{1}{r^2} \beta_\theta \frac{\partial \psi_i^3}{\partial r} \frac{\partial \psi_j^3}{\partial \theta} + A_{44}^{1} \frac{1}{r} \frac{\partial \beta_\theta}{\partial r} \frac{\partial \psi_i^3}{\partial \theta} \frac{\partial \psi_j^3}{\partial r} \\
& - A_{44}^{1} \frac{1}{r^2} \beta_\theta \frac{\partial \psi_i}{\partial \theta} \frac{\partial \psi_j}{\partial r} - A_{44}^{3} \frac{4}{3h^2 r} \frac{\partial \beta_\theta}{\partial r} \frac{\partial \psi_i^3}{\partial r} \frac{\partial \psi_j^3}{\partial \theta} + A_{44}^{3} \frac{4}{3h^2 r^2} \beta_\theta \frac{\partial \psi_i^3}{\partial r} \frac{\partial \psi_j^3}{\partial \theta} - A_{44}^{3} \frac{4}{3h^2 r} \frac{\partial \beta_\theta}{\partial r} \frac{\partial \psi_i^3}{\partial \theta} \frac{\partial \psi_j^3}{\partial r} \\
& + A_{13}^{0} \beta_z \frac{\partial \psi_i^3}{\partial r} \frac{\partial \psi_j^3}{\partial r} - A_{11}^{2} \frac{1}{2} \frac{\partial^2 \beta_z}{\partial r^2} \frac{\partial \psi_i^3}{\partial r} \frac{\partial \psi_j^3}{\partial r} - A_{12} \frac{1}{2r} \frac{\partial \beta_z}{\partial r} \frac{\partial \psi_i^3}{\partial r} \frac{\partial \psi_j}{\partial r} - A_{12}^{2} \frac{1}{2r^2} \frac{\partial^2 \beta_z}{\partial \theta^2} \frac{\partial \psi_i^3}{\partial r} \frac{\partial \psi_j^2}{\partial r} \\
& + A_{23}^{0} \beta_z \frac{1}{r^2} \frac{\partial \psi_i^3}{\partial \theta} \frac{\partial \psi_j^3}{\partial \theta} - A_{21}^{2} \frac{1}{2r^2} \frac{\partial^2 \beta_z}{\partial r^2} \frac{\partial \psi_i^3}{\partial \theta} \frac{\partial \psi_j^3}{\partial \theta} - A_{22}^{2} \frac{1}{2r^3} \frac{\partial \beta_z}{\partial r} \frac{\partial \psi_i^3}{\partial \theta} \frac{\partial \psi_j^3}{\partial \theta} - A_{22}^{2} \frac{1}{2r4} \frac{\partial \beta_z}{\partial \theta^2} \frac{\partial \psi_i^3}{\partial \theta} \frac{\partial \psi_j^3}{\partial \theta} \\
& - A_{44}^{2} \frac{1}{r^2} \frac{\partial \beta_z}{\partial \theta \partial r} \frac{\partial \psi_i^3}{\partial r} \frac{\partial \psi_j^3}{\partial \theta} - A_{44}^{2} \frac{1}{r^2} \frac{\partial^2 \beta_z}{\partial \theta \partial r} \frac{\partial \psi_i^3}{\partial \theta} \frac{\partial \psi_j^3}{\partial r} + A_{44}^{2} \frac{1}{r^3} \frac{\partial \beta_z}{\partial \theta} \frac{\partial \psi_i^3}{\partial r} \frac{\partial \psi_j^3}{\partial \theta} + A_{44}^{2} \frac{1}{r^3} \frac{\partial \beta_z}{\partial \theta} \frac{\partial \psi_i^3}{\partial \theta} \frac{\partial \psi_j^3}{\partial r} \\
& + A_{13}^{1} 2\phi_z \frac{\partial \psi_i^3}{\partial r} \frac{\partial \psi_j^3}{\partial r} - A_{11}^{3} \frac{1}{2} \frac{\partial^2 \phi_z}{\partial r^2} \frac{\partial \psi_i^3}{\partial r} \frac{\partial \psi_j^3}{\partial r} + A_{12}^{3} \frac{1}{3r^2} \frac{\partial^2 \phi_z}{\partial r^2} \frac{\partial \psi_i^3}{\partial r} \frac{\partial \psi_j^3}{\partial r} - A_{12}^{3} \frac{1}{3r^2} \frac{\partial^2 \phi_z}{\partial \theta^2} \frac{\partial \psi_i^3}{\partial r} \frac{\partial \psi_j^3}{\partial r} \\
& - A_{12}^{3} \frac{1}{3r} \frac{\partial \phi_z}{\partial r} \frac{\partial \psi_i^3}{\partial r} \frac{\partial \psi_j^3}{\partial r} + A_{23}^{1} \frac{2}{r^2} \phi_z \frac{\partial \psi_i^3}{\partial \theta} \frac{\partial \psi_j^3}{\partial \theta} - A_{21}^{3} \frac{1}{3r^2} \frac{\partial^2 \phi_z}{\partial r^2} \frac{\partial \psi_i^3}{\partial \theta} \frac{\partial \psi_j^3}{\partial \theta} - A_{22}^{3} \frac{1}{3r^4} \frac{\partial^2 \phi_z}{\partial \theta^2} \frac{\partial \psi_i^3}{\partial \theta} \frac{\partial \psi_j^3}{\partial \theta} \\
& - A_{22}^{3} \frac{1}{3r^3} \frac{\partial \phi_z}{\partial r} \frac{\partial \psi_i^3}{\partial \theta} \frac{\partial \psi_j^3}{\partial \theta} - A_{44}^{3} \frac{2}{3r} \frac{\partial^2 \phi_z}{\partial r \partial \theta} \frac{\partial \psi_i^3}{\partial r} \frac{\partial \psi_j^3}{\partial \theta} - A_{44}^{3} \frac{2}{3r} \frac{\partial^2 \phi_z}{\partial r \partial \theta} \frac{\partial \psi_i^3}{\partial r} \frac{\partial \psi_j^3}{\partial \theta} \Bigg\} r dr d\theta + K_{ij}^{33}
\end{aligned}
\quad \text{(A101)}
$$

$$
\begin{aligned}
T_{ij}^{43} = \int_{\Omega} \Bigg\{ & A_{11}^{1}\frac{1}{2}\frac{\partial \psi_i^4}{\partial r}\frac{\partial \psi_j^3}{\partial r}\frac{\partial W_o}{\partial r} + A_{12}^{1}\frac{1}{2r^2}\frac{\partial W_o}{\partial \theta}\frac{\partial \psi_i^4}{\partial r}\frac{\partial \psi_j^3}{\partial \theta} - A_{11}^{3}\frac{2}{3h^2}\frac{\partial W_o}{\partial r}\frac{\partial \psi_i^4}{\partial r}\frac{\partial \psi_j^3}{\partial r} \\
& - A_{12}^{3}\frac{2}{3h^2r^2}\frac{\partial W_o}{\partial \theta}\frac{\partial \psi_i^4}{\partial r}\frac{\partial \psi_j^3}{\partial \theta}. + A_{21}^{1}\frac{1}{2r}\frac{\partial W_o}{\partial r}\psi_i^4\frac{\partial \psi_j^3}{\partial r} + A_{22}^{1}\frac{1}{2r^3}\frac{\partial W_o}{\partial \theta}\psi_i^4\frac{\partial \psi_j^3}{\partial \theta} \\
& - A_{21}^{3}\frac{2}{3rh^2}\frac{\partial W_o}{\partial r}\psi_i^4\frac{\partial \psi_j}{\partial r} - A_{22}^{3}\frac{2}{3r^3h^2}\frac{\partial W_o}{\partial \theta}\psi_i^4\frac{\partial \psi_j^3}{\partial \theta} + A_{44}^{1}\frac{1}{2r^2}\frac{\partial W_o}{\partial r}\frac{\partial \psi_i^4}{\partial \theta}\frac{\partial \psi_j^3}{\partial \theta} \\
& + A_{44}^{1}\frac{1}{2r^2}\frac{\partial W_o}{\partial \theta}\frac{\partial \psi_i^4}{\partial \theta}\frac{\partial \psi_j^3}{\partial r} - A_{44}^{3}\frac{2}{3h^2r^2}\frac{\partial \psi_i^4}{\partial \theta}\frac{\partial \psi_j^3}{\partial \theta}\left(\frac{\partial W_o}{\partial \theta} + \frac{\partial W_o}{\partial r}\right)\Bigg\} r dr d\theta + K_{ij}^{43}
\end{aligned} \quad \text{(A102)}
$$

$$
\begin{aligned}
T_{ij}^{53} = \int_{\Omega} \Bigg\{ & A_{21}^{1}\frac{1}{2r}\frac{\partial W_o}{\partial r}\frac{\partial \psi_i^5}{\partial \theta}\frac{\partial \psi_j^3}{\partial r} + A_{22}^{1}\frac{1}{2r^3}\frac{\partial W_o}{\partial \theta}\frac{\partial \psi_i^5}{\partial \theta}\frac{\partial \psi_j^3}{\partial \theta} - A_{21}^{3}\frac{2}{3rh^2}\frac{\partial W_o}{\partial r}\frac{\partial \psi_i^5}{\partial \theta}\frac{\partial \psi_j^3}{\partial r} \\
& - A_{22}^{3}\frac{2}{3r^2h^2}\frac{\partial W_o}{\partial \theta}\frac{\partial \psi_i^5}{\partial \theta}\frac{\partial \psi_j^3}{\partial \theta} + A_{44}^{1}\frac{1}{2r}\frac{\partial W_o}{\partial r}\frac{\partial \psi_i^5}{\partial r}\frac{\partial \psi_j^3}{\partial \theta} + A_{44}^{1}\frac{1}{2r}\frac{\partial W_o}{\partial \theta}\frac{\partial \psi_i^5}{\partial r}\frac{\partial \psi_j^3}{\partial r} \\
& - A_{44}^{1}\frac{1}{2r^2}\psi_i^5\frac{\partial W_o}{\partial r}\frac{\partial \psi_j^3}{\partial \theta} - A_{44}^{1}\frac{1}{2r^2}\psi_i^5\frac{\partial W_o}{\partial \theta}\frac{\partial \psi_j^3}{\partial r} - A_{44}^{3}\frac{2}{3rh^2}\frac{\partial W_o}{\partial r}\frac{\partial \psi_i^5}{\partial r}\frac{\partial \psi_j^3}{\partial \theta} \\
& - A_{44}^{3}\frac{2}{3rh^2}\frac{\partial W_o}{\partial \theta}\frac{\partial \psi_i^5}{\partial r}\frac{\partial \psi_j^3}{\partial r} - A_{44}^{3}\frac{2}{3r^2h^2}\left(\frac{\partial W_o}{\partial \theta}\psi_i^5\frac{\partial \psi_j^3}{\partial r} - \frac{\partial W_o}{\partial r}\psi_i^5\frac{\partial \psi_j^3}{\partial \theta}\right)\Bigg\} r dr d\theta + K_{ij}^{53}
\end{aligned} \quad \text{(A103)}
$$

$$
\begin{aligned}
T_{ij}^{63} = \int_{\Omega} \Bigg\{ & -A_{11}^{2}\frac{1}{4}\frac{\partial W_o}{\partial r}\frac{\partial^2 \psi_i^6}{\partial r^2}\frac{\partial \psi_j^3}{\partial r} - A_{12}^{2}\frac{1}{4r^2}\frac{\partial W_o}{\partial \theta}\frac{\partial^2 \psi_i^6}{\partial r^2}\frac{\partial \psi_j^3}{\partial \theta} - A_{21}^{2}\frac{1}{4r}\frac{\partial W_o}{\partial r}\frac{\partial \psi_i^6}{\partial r}\frac{\partial \psi_j^3}{\partial r} \\
& - A_{22}^{2}\frac{1}{4r^3}\frac{\partial W_o}{\partial \theta}\frac{\partial \psi_i^5}{\partial r}\frac{\partial \psi_j^3}{\partial \theta} - A_{22}^{2}\frac{1}{4r^4}\frac{\partial W_o}{\partial \theta}\frac{\partial^2 \psi_i^5}{\partial \theta^2}\frac{\partial \psi_j^3}{\partial \theta} + A_{31}^{0}\frac{1}{2}\frac{\partial W_o}{\partial r}\psi_i^6\frac{\partial \psi_j}{\partial r} \\
& + A_{32}^{0}\frac{1}{2r^2}\frac{\partial W_o}{\partial \theta}\psi^6\frac{\partial \psi_j}{\partial \theta} - A_{44}^{2}\frac{1}{2r^2}\frac{\partial W_o}{\partial \theta}\frac{\partial^2 \psi_i^6}{\partial \theta \partial r}\frac{\partial \psi_j^3}{\partial r} - A_{44}^{2}\frac{1}{2r^2}\frac{\partial W_o}{\partial r}\frac{\partial^2 \psi_i^6}{\partial \theta \partial r}\frac{\partial \psi_j^3}{\partial \theta} \\
& + A_{44}^{2}\frac{1}{2r^3}\left(\frac{\partial W_o}{\partial \theta}\frac{\partial \psi_i^6}{\partial \theta}\frac{\partial \psi_j^3}{\partial r} + \frac{\partial W_o}{\partial r}\frac{\partial \psi_i^6}{\partial \theta}\frac{\partial \psi_j^3}{\partial \theta}\right) - A_{21}^{2}\frac{1}{4r^2}\frac{\partial W_o}{\partial r}\frac{\partial^2 \psi_i^6}{\partial \theta^2}\frac{\partial \psi_j^3}{\partial r}\Bigg\} r dr d\theta + K_{ij}^{63}
\end{aligned} \quad \text{(A104)}
$$

$$
\begin{aligned}
T_{ij}^{73} = \int_{\Omega} \Bigg\{ & -A_{11}^{3}\frac{1}{6}\frac{\partial W_o}{\partial r}\frac{\partial^2 \psi_i^7}{\partial r^2}\frac{\partial \psi_j^3}{\partial r} - A_{12}^{3}\frac{1}{6r^2}\frac{\partial W_o}{\partial \theta}\frac{\partial^2 \psi_i^7}{\partial r^2}\frac{\partial \psi_j^3}{\partial \theta} - A_{21}^{3}\frac{1}{6r}\frac{\partial W_o}{\partial r}\frac{\partial \psi_i^7}{\partial r}\frac{\partial \psi_j^3}{\partial r} \\
& - A_{22}^{3}\frac{1}{6r^3}\frac{\partial W_o}{\partial G}\frac{\partial \psi_i^7}{\partial r}\frac{\partial \psi_j^3}{\partial \theta} - A_{21}^{3}\frac{1}{6r^2}\frac{\partial W_o}{\partial r}\frac{\partial^2 \psi_i^7}{\partial \theta^2}\frac{\partial \psi_j^3}{\partial r} - A_{22}^{3}\frac{1}{6r^4}\frac{\partial W_o}{\partial \theta}\frac{\partial^2 \psi_i^7}{\partial \theta^2}\frac{\partial \psi_j^3}{\partial \theta} \\
& + A_{31}^{1}\frac{\partial W_o}{\partial r}\psi_i^7\frac{\partial \psi_j^3}{\partial r} + A_{32}^{1}\frac{1}{r^2}\frac{\partial W_o}{\partial \theta}\psi_i^7\frac{\partial \psi_j^3}{\partial \theta} - A_{44}^{3}\frac{1}{3r^2}\frac{\partial W_o}{\partial r}\frac{\partial^2 \psi_i^7}{\partial \theta \partial r}\frac{\partial \psi_j^3}{\partial \theta} \\
& - A_{44}^{3}\frac{1}{3r^2}\left(\frac{\partial W_o}{\partial \theta}\frac{\partial^2 \psi_i^7}{\partial \theta \partial r}\frac{\partial \psi_j^3}{\partial r} + \frac{1}{r}\frac{\partial W_o}{\partial r}\frac{\partial \psi_i^7}{\partial \theta}\frac{\partial \psi_j^3}{\partial \theta} + \frac{1}{r}\frac{\partial W_o}{\partial \theta}\frac{\partial \psi_i^7}{\partial \theta}\frac{\partial \psi_j^3}{\partial r}\right)\Bigg\} r dr d\theta + K_{ij}^{73}
\end{aligned} \quad \text{(A105)}
$$

References

1. Koizumi, M. FGM activities in Japan. *Compos. Part B Eng.* **1997**, *28*, 1–4. [CrossRef]
2. Birman, V.; Byrd, L.W. Modeling and Analysis of Functionally Graded Materials and Structures. *Appl. Mech. Rev.* **2007**, *60*, 195–216. [CrossRef]
3. Mahamood, R.; Akinlabi, E.; Shukla, D.M.; Pityana, S. Functionally graded material: An overview. In Proceedings of the World Congress on Engineering, London, UK, 4–6 July 2012; Volume III.
4. Jha, D.; Kant, T.; Singh, R. A critical review of recent research on functionally graded plates. *Compos. Struct.* **2013**, *96*, 833–849. [CrossRef]
5. Swaminathan, K.; Sangeetha, D. Thermal analysis of FGM plates—A critical review of various modeling techniques and solution methods. *Compos. Struct.* **2017**, *160*, 43–60. [CrossRef]

6. Judy, J.W. Microelectromechanical systems (MEMS): Fabrication, design and applications. *Smart Mater. Struct.* **2001**, *10*, 1115. [CrossRef]
7. Tahani, M.; Askari, A.R.; Mohandes, Y.; Hassani, B. Size-dependent free vibration analysis of electrostatically pre-deformed rectangular micro-plates based on the modified couple stress theory. *Int. J. Mech. Sci.* **2015**, *94–95*, 185–198. [CrossRef]
8. Yang, F.; Chong, A.; Lam, D.; Tong, P. Couple stress based strain gradient theory for elasticity. *Int. J. Solids Struct.* **2002**, *39*, 2731–2743. [CrossRef]
9. Ma, Q.; Clarke, D. Size dependent hardness of silver single crystals. *J. Mater. Res.* **1995**, *10*, 853–863. [CrossRef]
10. Toupin, R.A. Elastic materials with couple-stresses. *Arch. Ration. Mech. Anal.* **1962**, *11*, 385–414. [CrossRef]
11. Mindlin, R.D.; Tiersten, H.F. Effects of couple-stresses in linear elasticity. *Arch. Ration. Mech. Anal.* **1962**, *11*, 415–448. [CrossRef]
12. Eringen, A. Nonlocal polar elastic continua. *Int. J. Eng. Sci.* **1972**, *10*, 1–16. [CrossRef]
13. Fleck, N.; Muller, G.; Ashby, M.; Hutchinson, J. Strain gradient plasticity: Theory and experiment. *Acta Metall. Mater.* **1994**, *42*, 475–487. [CrossRef]
14. Lam, D.; Yang, F.; Chong, A.; Wang, J.; Tong, P. Experiments and theory in strain gradient elasticity. *J. Mech. Phys. Solids* **2003**, *51*, 1477–1508. [CrossRef]
15. Fleck, N.; Hutchinson, J. A Reformulation of Strain Gradient Plasticity. *J. Mech. Phys. Solids* **2001**, *49*, 2245–2271. [CrossRef]
16. Shu, J.Y.; King, W.E.; Fleck, N.A. Finite elements for materials with strain gradient effects. *Int. J. Numer. Methods Eng.* **1999**, *44*, 373–391. [CrossRef]
17. Yapor Genao, F.; Kim, J.; Żur, K.K. Nonlinear finite element analysis of temperature-dependent functionally graded porous micro-plates under thermal and mechanical loads. *Compos. Struct.* **2021**, *256*, 112931. [CrossRef]
18. Aghababaei, R.; Reddy, J. Nonlocal third-order shear deformation plate theory with application to bending and vibration of plates. *J. Sound Vib.* **2009**, *326*, 277–289. [CrossRef]
19. Ke, L.L.; Yang, J.; Kitipornchai, S.; Bradford, M.A. Bending, buckling and vibration of size-dependent functionally graded annular microplates. *Compos. Struct.* **2012**, *94*, 3250–3257. [CrossRef]
20. Reddy, J.; Romanoff, J.; Loya, J.A. Nonlinear finite element analysis of functionally graded circular plates with modified couple stress theory. *Eur. J. Mech.—A/Solids* **2016**, *56*, 92–104. [CrossRef]
21. Reddy, J.; Berry, J. Nonlinear theories of axisymmetric bending of functionally graded circular plates with modified couple stress. *Compos. Struct.* **2012**, *94*, 3664–3668. [CrossRef]
22. Tadi Beni, Y.; Mehralian, F.; Razavi, H. Free vibration analysis of size-dependent shear deformable functionally graded cylindrical shell on the basis of modified couple stress theory. *Compos. Struct.* **2015**, *120*, 65–78. [CrossRef]
23. Kim, J.; Żur, K.K.; Reddy, J. Bending, free vibration, and buckling of modified couples stress-based functionally graded porous micro-plates. *Compos. Struct.* **2019**, *209*, 879–888. [CrossRef]
24. Eshraghi, I.; Dag, S.; Soltani, N. Bending and free vibrations of functionally graded annular and circular micro-plates under thermal loading. *Compos. Struct.* **2016**, *137*, 196–207. [CrossRef]
25. Hosseini-Hashemi, S.; Bedroud, M.; Nazemnezhad, R. An exact analytical solution for free vibration of functionally graded circular/annular Mindlin nanoplates via nonlocal elasticity. *Compos. Struct.* **2013**, *103*, 108–118. [CrossRef]
26. Chi, S.H.; Chung, Y.L. Mechanical behavior of functionally graded material plates under transverse load—Part I: Analysis. *Int. J. Solids Struct.* **2006**, *43*, 3657–3674. [CrossRef]
27. Chi, S.H.; Chung, Y.L. Mechanical behavior of functionally graded material plates under transverse load—Part II: Numerical results. *Int. J. Solids Struct.* **2006**, *43*, 3675–3691. [CrossRef]
28. Nguyen, T.K.; Sab, K.; Bonnet, G. First-order shear deformation plate models for functionally graded materials. *Compos. Struct.* **2008**, *83*, 25–36. [CrossRef]
29. Reddy, J. Analysis of functionally graded plates. *Int. J. Numer. Methods Eng.* **2000**, *47*, 663–684.
30. Reddy, J.; Chin, C. Thermomechanical analysis of functionally graded cylinders and plates. *J. Therm. Stress.* **1998**, *21*, 593–626.
31. Praveen, G.; Reddy, J. Nonlinear transient thermoelastic analysis of functionally graded ceramic-metal plates. *Int. J. Solids Struct.* **1998**, *35*, 4457–4476. [CrossRef]
32. Reddy, J.; Wang, C.; Kitipornchai, S. Axisymmetric bending of functionally graded circular and annular plates. *Eur. J. Mech.–A/Solids* **1999**, *18*, 185–199. [CrossRef]
33. Ma, L.; Wang, T. Nonlinear bending and post-buckling of a functionally graded circular plate under mechanical and thermal loadings. *Int. J. Solids Struct.* **2003**, *40*, 3311–3330. [CrossRef]
34. Reddy, J. *Theory and analysis of Elastic Plates and Shells*; CRC Press: Boca Raton, FL, USA, 2007.
35. Najafizadeh, M.; Heydari, H. Thermal buckling of functionally graded circular plates based on higher order shear deformation plate theory. *Eur. J. Mech.—A/Solids* **2004**, *23*, 1085–1100. [CrossRef]
36. Reddy, J.; Kim, J. A nonlinear modified couple stress-based third-order theory of functionally graded plates. *Compos. Struct.* **2012**, *94*, 1128–1143. [CrossRef]

37. Kim, J.; Reddy, J. Analytical solutions for bending, vibration, and buckling of FGM plates using a couple stress-based third-order theory. *Compos. Struct.* **2013**, *103*, 86–98. [CrossRef]
38. Prakash, T.; Ganapathi, M. Asymmetric flexural vibration and thermoelastic stability of FGM circular plates using finite element method. *Compos. Part B Eng.* **2006**, *37*, 642–649. [CrossRef]
39. Efraim, E.; Eisenberger, M. Exact vibration analysis of variable thickness thick annular isotropic and FGM plates. *J. Sound Vib.* **2007**, *299*, 720–738. [CrossRef]
40. Żur, K. Free vibration analysis of discrete-continuous functionally graded circular plates via Neumann series method. *Appl. Math. Model.* **2019**, *73*, 166–189. [CrossRef]
41. Rahmat Talabi, M.; Saidi, A. An explicit exact analytical approach for free vibration of circular/annular functionally graded plates bonded to piezoelectric actuator/sensor layers based on Reddy's plate theory. *Appl. Math. Model.* **2013**, *37*, 7664–7684. [CrossRef]
42. Zhao, J.; Xie, F.; Wang, A.; Shuai, C.; Tang, J.; Wang, Q. Dynamics analysis of functionally graded porous (FGP) circular, annular and sector plates with general elastic restraints. *Compos. Part B Eng.* **2019**, *159*, 20–43. [CrossRef]
43. Talha, M.; Singh, B. Static response and free vibration analysis of FGM plates using higher order shear deformation theory. *Appl. Math. Model.* **2010**, *34*, 3991–4011. [CrossRef]
44. Vinh, P.V. A novel modified nonlocal strain gradient theory for comprehensive analysis of functionally graded nanoplates. *Acta Mech.* **2025**, *236*, 173–204.
45. Wang, S.; Ding, W.; Li, Z.; Xu, B.; Zhai, C.; Kang, W.; Yang, W.; Li, Y. A size-dependent quasi-3D model for bending and buckling of porous functionally graded curved nanobeam. *Int. J. Eng. Sci.* **2023**, *193*, 103962.
46. Nosier, A.; Fallah, F. Non-linear analysis of functionally graded circular plates under asymmetric transverse loading. *Int. J.-Non-Linear Mech.* **2009**, *44*, 928–942. [CrossRef]
47. Nosier, A.; Fallah, F. Reformulation of Mindlin–Reissner governing equations of functionally graded circular plates. *Acta Mech.* **2008**, *198*, 209–233.
48. Fallah, F.; Nosier, A. Nonlinear behavior of functionally graded circular plates with various boundary supports under asymmetric thermo-mechanical loading. *Compos. Struct.* **2012**, *94*, 2834–2850. [CrossRef]
49. Kim, J.; Nava, E.; Rakici, S. Nonlinear Finite Element Model for Bending Analysis of Functionally-Graded Porous Circular/Annular Micro-Plates under Thermomechanical Loads Using Quasi-3D Reddy Third-Order Plate Theory. *Materials* **2023**, *16*, 3505. [CrossRef] [PubMed]
50. Piotr, D. Finite element method formulation in polar coordinates for transient heat conduction problems. *J. Therm. Sci.* **2016**, *25*, 188–194. [CrossRef]
51. Touloukian, Y.S. *Thermophysical Properties of High Temperature Solid Materials. Volume 4. Oxides and Their Solutions and Mixtures*; Defense Technical Information Center: Fort Belvoir, VA, USA, 1966.
52. Nguyen, L.B.; Thai, C.H.; Zenkour, A.; Nguyen-Xuan, H. An isogeometric Bézier finite element method for vibration analysis of functionally graded piezoelectric material porous plates. *Int. J. Mech. Sci.* **2019**, *157–158*, 165–183. [CrossRef]
53. Carranza, J.C.; Pérez, L.; Ganesan, R.; Casas, B.Y.; Drew, R.A.L.; Ruiz-Aguilar, C.; Figueroa, I.A.; Alfonso, I. Effect of fractal distribution of the porosity on mechanical properties of Al foams manufactured by infiltration. *J. Braz. Soc. Mech. Sci. Eng.* **2019**, *41*, 379. [CrossRef]
54. Gao, K.; Li, R.; Yang, J. Dynamic characteristics of functionally graded porous beams with interval material properties. *Eng. Struct.* **2019**, *197*, 109441.
55. Coskun, S.; Kim, J.; Toutanji, H. Bending, Free Vibration, and Buckling Analysis of Functionally Graded Porous Micro-Plates Using a General Third-Order Plate Theory. *J. Compos. Sci.* **2019**, 3, 15. [CrossRef]
56. Mota, A.F.; Loja, M.A.R.; Barbosa, J.I.; Rodrigues, J.A. Porous Functionally Graded Plates: An Assessment of the Influence of Shear Correction Factor on Static Behavior. *Math. Comput. Appl.* **2020**, *25*, 25. [CrossRef]
57. Kim, J.; Reddy, J. A general third-order theory of functionally graded plates with modified couple stress effect and the von Kármán nonlinearity: Theory and finite element analysis. *Acta Mech.* **2015**, *226*, 1973–2998. [CrossRef]
58. Golmakani, M.; Kadkhodayan, M. Nonlinear bending analysis of annular FGM plates using higher-order shear deformation plate theories. *Composite Structures* **2011**, *93*, 973–982. [CrossRef]
59. Mognhod Bezzie, Y.; Woldemichael, D. Effects of graded-index and Poisson's ratio on elastic-solutions of a pressurized functionally graded material thick-walled cylinder. *Forces Mech.* **2021**, *4*, 100032. [CrossRef]
60. Bogner, F. The generation of interelement compatible stiffness and mass matrices by the use of interpolation formulae. In Proceedings of the Conference on Matrix Methods in Structural Mechanics, Wright-Patterson Air Force Base, Fairborn, OH, USA, 26–28 October 1965.

61. Deng, Z.; Huang, Y.; Zhang, C.; Chen, Y. Heat Conduction in Porous Media Characterized by Fractal Geometry. *Energies* **2017**, *10*, 1230. [CrossRef]
62. Reddy, J. *An Introduction to Nonlinear Finite Element Analysis*, 2nd ed.; Oxford University Press: Oxford, UK, 2015.

Mathematical and Computational Applications

MDPI

Article

A New Fractional Boundary Element Model for the 3D Thermal Stress Wave Propagation Problems in Anisotropic Materials

Mohamed Abdelsabour Fahmy [1,2,*] and Moncef Toujani [1]

[1] Department of Mathematics, Adham University College, Umm Al-Qura University, Adham, Makkah 28653, Saudi Arabia; aatoujani@uqu.edu.sa
[2] Faculty of Computers and Informatics, Suez Canal University, New Campus, Ismailia 41522, Egypt
* Correspondence: maselim@uqu.edu.sa; Tel.: +966-537930306

Abstract: The primary purpose of this work is to provide a new fractional boundary element method (BEM) formulation to solve thermal stress wave propagation problems in anisotropic materials. In the Laplace domain, the fundamental solutions to the governing equations can be identified. Then, the boundary integral equations are constructed. The Caputo fractional time derivative was used in the formulation of the considered heat conduction equation. The three-block splitting (TBS) iteration approach was used to solve the resulting BEM linear systems, resulting in fewer iterations and less CPU time. The new TBS iteration method converges rapidly and does not involve complicated computations; it performs better than the two-dimensional double successive projection method (2D-DSPM) and modified symmetric successive overrelaxation (MSSOR) for solving the resultant BEM linear system. We only studied a special case of our model to compare our findings to those of other articles in the literature. Because the BEM results are so consistent with the finite element method (FEM) findings, the numerical results demonstrate the validity, accuracy, and efficiency of our proposed BEM formulation for solving three-dimensional thermal stress wave propagation problems in anisotropic materials.

Keywords: boundary element method; fractional order; three-dimensional; thermal stress wave propagation; anisotropic materials

1. Introduction

Within the discipline of continuum mechanics, thermoelasticity studies the relationship between mechanical memory and thermodynamics in the behavior of solid bodies. There are various options for doing this. The most general method is to try to put thermodynamic constraints on the constitutive equations, with deformation and temperature as dependent variables [1–3]. In some materials, these constraints are so specific that, among the infinite ways of coupling mechanics and thermodynamics, certain closed sets of equations can be obtained that characterize the unknown driving forces of the coupled field. The most typical sets of linked equations appear to be very simplified versions of what can be obtained using a more generic approach [4]. However, when a non-quadratic elastic energy function is considered, the simplifying feature required to distinguish one theory from others may not always be reduced to the property of meeting a set of equilibrium equations and a temperature equation [5,6].

Fractional calculus is the study of the properties and results of the derivative of a function of order a. It provides tools to understand phenomena and processes that evolve in time in a more accurate way than those offered by classical integral and differential calculus, considering long memories in their internal evolution [7,8]. Moreover, fractional calculus is naturally used to model processes with unique and non-local effects, which are considered highly complex. Indeed, phenomena described by models based on non-integer order integrals and derivatives have attracted the attention of the scientific community and have been applied in several areas not only as mathematical models but also as theoretical tools for the study of other physical phenomena [9–11]. The rapid development of computational and theoretical techniques to efficiently deal with mathematical models based on fractional calculus, as well as the success of these models in solving mathematical problems, has naturally motivated several scientific researchers to investigate the potential of these models in solving various engineering problems, with positive and significant complex effects. Consequently, fractional calculus models began to spread into distinct traditional fields of engineering like control and power systems, becoming a major topic of investigation in all other fields. Fractional calculus is undoubtedly a very valuable tool for the study of complex media and has a considerable impact in many different fields, both theoretical and experimental. Nevertheless, the physico-mathematical aspect perceived in the theory of rate-type constitutive models for the specific formulation of the stress tensor in linear and nonlinear thermoelasticity cannot be completely established until the physical meaning of the fractional order and the causality principle are well understood [12,13].

Another important topic in modern engineering is anisotropy. Anisotropic materials comprise most materials in a solid-state body. Beams and plates in a cross-section can be, and in some cases must be, modeled as anisotropic. It is difficult to define the category of anisotropic materials in a convenient manner. However, this term is usually used to describe materials that are neither isotropic nor transversely isotropic. Anisotropy occurs in materials such as single crystals, rolled pentagonal structures, etc. Anisotropic materials have 4 elastic constants, so there are 21 independent elastic constants for general materials. The permissible anisotropic qualities are determined by the symmetry of the coefficients of the elastic component in the formulation of the deformation equilibrium equation [14,15]. If symmetry conditions on each component's elastic coefficients are considered, then the strain energy function can identify numerous types of anisotropy and their associations [16,17].

The concept of generalized thermoelasticity theories was introduced separately in 1972 and 1970. The reasons for generalizing the theory originated from the fact that the mathematical opponent of the simple theory was faced while solving the problem of the relative size of the thermal field and the premise upon which the theory was founded [18,19]. The mechanical portion of the thermodynamic surface of elastic materials, as well as the first full set of thermodynamic balances that offer motion equations, extended Hooke's law, the energy equation, and other results, serves as the foundation for classical thermoelasticity theory [20–22]. The thermal field enters only the second rank of the dissipation functional through entropy and entropy balance, which is determined by the dissipation functional's local extreme. To address the issue, a full thermodynamic functional incorporating the thermal field was constructed. The presence of the thermodynamic principle and the entire thermodynamic functional in characterizing the thermal behavior of a solid has been discussed [23,24].

To address the first problem in the classical thermo-elasticity (CTE) theory proposed by Duhamel [25] and Neumann [26], which predicts two occurrences that contradict empirical facts, Biot [27] proposed the classical coupled thermo-elasticity (CCTE) theory. Most methods for overcoming the classical theory's unwanted prediction are based on the non-Fourier effect. Lord and Shulman [28] proposed an extended thermoelasticity (ETE) theory with a single relaxation time. Green and Lindsay [29] proposed the temperature rate-dependent thermoelasticity (TRDTE) theory, which incorporates temperature rate as a constitutive variable. Green and Naghdi [30,31] made substantial theoretical advances in the field, developing three models for the generalized thermoelasticity of homogeneous isotropic materials. Chen and Gurtin [32] and Chen et al. [33,34] proposed heat conduction theory based on conductive and thermodynamic temperatures. Quintanilla [35] conducted extensive research on the two-temperature thermoelasticity theory. Youssef [36] introduced the two-temperature generalized thermoelasticity theory, which has been applied to solve several engineering problems [37–40].

The thermoelastic problem has been studied since the fundamental equations that govern it were deduced. Problems involving a heating source and with or without external forces have been the subject of many analyses. It is difficult to identify the analytical solution for such problems; thus, several numerical methods exist for estimating solutions to these problems [41–45]. In recent years, new methods have proven to be useful when used to thermoelasticity problems [46–49]. All these methods are based on solid mathematical principles and can be automated; however, they often require software to achieve the result. Because not all natural phenomena can be characterized by integer-order partial differential equations, some are represented by fractional partial differential equations (FPDEs). Most fractional differential equations do not have explicit analytical solutions; hence, several researchers have devised numerical solution methodologies for time-fractional partial differential equations (TFPDEs). The boundary element method (BEM) is a numerical technique for solving partial differential equations (PDEs) with time-fractional order. This technique combines boundary integral equations with numerical approximation of boundary integrals. These equations can be obtained from the fundamental solutions to PDEs' differential operators. The most significant advantage of the BEM is that the needed discretization of the domain is one less than that of other numerical approaches. It has significant advantages over traditional methods like the finite element method (FEM) and the finite difference method (FDM). One of the key advantages of the BEM is that it is a boundary-only approach, which means that only the issue's boundary must be discretized, resulting in a one-dimensional problem [50–52]. A two-dimensional problem, for example, requires two dimensions of discretization in the FEM or FDM, whereas the BEM just requires one. This is useful for boundary layer problems, which demand tighter grids in locations with large gradients. The BEM has an even greater advantage for problems with infinite or semi-infinite domains, as it is usually necessary to truncate the domain in the FEM or FDM and introduce artificial boundaries with associated treatments such as adding boundary conditions, whereas this is not the case with the BEM because only the boundary is discretized. Domain discretization in the FEM or FDM also requires mesh production, which can frequently be challenging and a time-consuming task [53–55]. This is especially difficult for complex domains or problems whose domain geometry changes over time. With recent computer improvements, numerical approaches based on boundary integral equations have garnered significant attention due to their success in addressing a variety of two-dimensional issues. The boundary element method (BEM) is a popular numerical technique that has applications in a variety of engineering fields, including fluid mechanics, magnetohydrodynamics, and electrodynamics. Recent advances in the BEM have made it possible to apply this method to increasingly complex issues, such as multi-regions [56–58].

Although the boundary element method (BEM) is widely acknowledged for its best-use scenario in tackling high-dimensional issues, one impediment remains to be overcome to make it more accessible and easier to use [59–61]. This impediment is the need for remedies for low-frequency situations in prospective issues; otherwise, numerical instability will be introduced. In recent decades, several initiatives have been made to address this issue, with most of them focused on the concept of transitioning from the original domains to new ones [62–64]. However, those existing translation methods either rely on operator solutions or generate several integral types for a single state variable. As a result, in practice, they continue to make BEM deployment more challenging. As a result, it is important and meaningful to develop a transformation method that keeps the benefits of simple boundary-type methods while addressing the numerical instability difficulties of low-frequency instances [65–68]. The scaled coordinate transformation (SCT) is purely a mathematical operation that, like the original coordinate transformation, requires only discretization on the structure's surface while remaining analytical in the radial direction, eliminating the need for half-domain discretization and second derivative computations. The scaled coordinate transformation boundary element method (SCTBEM) uses the same integral types and operations on discretized boundary elements as the conventional BEM. However, with the newly devised coordinate transformation, there is no need to be concerned about low-frequency situations in prospective difficulties. Numerical findings demonstrate that the SCTBEM is robust and accurate, even when dealing with very low wave numbers or very huge structures. In addition, the SCTBEM provides a research topic that is not confined to the BEM. Coordinate transformation is a purely mathematical technique that modifies domain integrals in potential problems while leaving boundary integrals untouched. As a result, the SCTBEM can be used for other domain-type methods that use integrals for state variables that are comparable in form [68,69].

Three-block splitting (TBS) is an FFT-based iterative method for solving the three-dimensional time–domain boundary integral equation of the wave equation that is formulated with respect to the boundary magnetic field. In this equation, the time derivative of the boundary magnetic field appears with minus sign, and thus, it has the time-delayed exponential integrator (TDEI) type. The TBS approximately splits this boundary integral equation into three blocks with respect to the wave number components. The convergence of the TBS iteration depends on the value of the time step. For a large time step, the TBS iteration does not converge. To overcome this difficulty, the TBS iteration is applied first with a coarse time step for a few iterations, and then it is applied with the original time step [70].

In the present paper, we investigated the fundamental solutions of fractional order coupled with anisotropic thermoelasticity in the Laplace domain. The fractional boundary element technique was then formulated using a suitable reciprocal connection to solve the considered problem. The boundary was discretized at the collocation nodes. The original problem's boundary integral equations at these collocation points were then solved using the point collocation method. Finally, we presented the results of the suggested BEM model, which better explained our formulation for 3D thermal stress wave propagation in anisotropic materials.

2. Formulation of the Problem

Based on Cattaneo [71] and Vernotte's [72,73] heat conduction equation and definition of the Caputo derivative, Sherief et al. [74] proposed the following fractional heat conduction equation:

$$-k\nabla T = q(x,\tau) + \overline{\tau}\frac{\partial^a q}{\partial \tau^a},\ 0 < a < 1 \tag{1}$$

In Cartesian coordinates, the governing equations for 3D thermal stress wave propagation in anisotropic materials are [28]

$$C_{ijkl}e_{kl} + \rho F_i - \gamma_{ij}T_{,i} = \rho\ddot{u}_i, \gamma_{ij} = C_{ijkl}\alpha_{kl} \tag{2}$$

$$\begin{aligned} k\bar{T}_{,kk} = \rho C_e\left(\dot{T} + \tau_0\tfrac{\partial^a}{\partial\tau^a}\dot{T}\right) + \gamma_{ij}T_0\left(\dot{e} + \tau_0\tfrac{\partial^a}{\partial\tau^a}\dot{e}\right) \\ -\rho C_e\left(Q + \tau_0\tfrac{\partial^a}{\partial\tau^a}Q\right), \end{aligned} \tag{3}$$

$$\sigma_{ij} = C_{ijkl}e_{kl} - \gamma_{ij}T, \tag{4}$$

where

$$Q = Q(x,\tau) = \frac{1-R}{x_0} e^{\left(-\frac{x_a}{x_0}\right)J(\tau)}, J(\tau) = \frac{J_0 \tau}{t_1^2} e^{-\frac{\tau}{t_1}}, \mathrm{a} = 1,2,3 \tag{5}$$

$$e_{ij} = \tfrac{1}{2}\left(u_{i,j} + u_{j,i}\right). \tag{6}$$

$$t_i = \sigma_{ij} n_j, \tag{7}$$

Now, we assume the following conditions:

$$\sigma_{ij} n_j = p_{i0}(x,\tau) \text{ on } \mathbb{C}_1, \tag{8}$$

$$u_i = u_{i0}(x,\tau) \text{ on } \mathbb{C}_2, \mathbb{C}_1 \cup \mathbb{C}_2 = \mathbb{C}, \mathbb{C}_1 \cap \mathbb{C}_2 = \phi \tag{9}$$

$$T = T_0(x,\tau) \text{ on } \mathbb{C}_3, \tag{10}$$

$$T_{,n} = T_{n0}(x,\tau) \text{ on } \mathbb{C}_4, \quad \mathbb{C}_3 \cup \mathbb{C}_4 = \mathbb{C}, \mathbb{C}_3 \cap \mathbb{C}_4 = \phi \tag{11}$$

By applying Equation (4), the traction vector can be represented as follows:

$$t_i(x,\tau) = \left[C_{ijkl} e_{kl} - \gamma_{ij} T\right] n_j(x) \tag{12}$$

3. Boundary Element Implementation

Function $f(\tau)$ has the following Laplace transform:

$$\bar{f}(t) = \int_0^{+\infty} e^{-t\tau} f(\tau) d\tau. \tag{13}$$

Via the application of the Laplace transform to Equations (2)–(4), we obtain

$$C_{ijkl}\bar{\varepsilon}_{kl} + \rho \bar{F}_i - \gamma_{ij}\bar{T}_{,i} = \rho t^2 \bar{u}_i, \tag{14}$$

$$k\bar{T}_{,kk} = \rho C_e t(1+\tau_0 t^\alpha)\left(\bar{T} + \tfrac{\gamma_{ij} T_0}{\rho C_e}\bar{u}_{,kk} - \tfrac{\bar{Q}}{t}\right), \tag{15}$$

$$\bar{\sigma}_{ij} = C_{ijkl}\bar{\varepsilon}_{kl} - \gamma_{ij}\bar{T}. \tag{16}$$

We now present the vectors of displacement and body force as follows:

$$u_i = \phi_{,i} + \epsilon_{ijk}\psi_{k,j}, \tag{17}$$

$$\psi_{i,i} = 0, \tag{18}$$

$$F_i = X_{,i} + \epsilon_{ijk} Y_{k,j}, \tag{19}$$

$$Y_{i,i} = 0. \tag{20}$$

To obtain the fundamental solutions in the Laplace transform domain, we consider the following two cases:

3.1. Case 1: $Q = Q(x,\tau), F_i = 0$

Based on [75], we obtain

$$\left(\nabla^2 - k_1^2\right)\left(\nabla^2 - k_2^2\right)\bar{\phi}' = -m\frac{\rho C_e}{k}(1+\tau_0 t^\alpha) Q(x,\tau), \tag{21}$$

where k_1^2, k_2^2 are the solutions of the following characteristic equation:

$$kv^4 - \left[(\rho C_e + mak)t(1+\tau_0 t^\alpha) + t^{\alpha+1}\frac{k}{c_1^2}\right]v^2 + t^{\alpha+2}\rho C_e\frac{(1+\tau_0 t^\alpha)}{c_1^2} = 0. \tag{22}$$

Equation (21) has the following solution:

$$\bar{\phi}'(x,t) = -m\rho C_e\frac{(1+\tau_0 t^\alpha)}{(\nabla^2 - k_1^2)(\nabla^2 - k_2^2)}Q(x,\tau). \tag{23}$$

which can be written using the Helmholtz equation $\frac{1}{(\nabla^2-k^2)}\delta(r) = -\frac{1}{4\pi r}e^{-kr}$ as follows:

$$\bar{\phi}'(x,t) = \frac{m\rho C_e}{4\pi k(k_1^2 - k_2^2)}(1+\tau_0 t^\alpha)\left(e^{-k_1 r} - e^{-k_2 r}\right). \tag{24}$$

Thus, Equations (17) and (24) yield

$$\overline{u}_i'(x,t) = -\frac{\rho C_e}{kr}\frac{m(1+\tau_0 p^\alpha)}{4\pi(k_1^2-k_2^2)}\left[e^{-k_1 r}\left(1+\frac{k_1}{r}\right) - e^{-k_2 r}\left(1+\frac{k_2}{r}\right)\right]r_{,i}\,, \tag{25}$$

and

$$\overline{T}'(x,t) = \frac{\rho C_e}{kr}\frac{m(1+\tau_0 t^\alpha)}{4\pi(k_1^2-k_2^2)}\left[e^{-k_1 r}\left(k_1^2 - \frac{t^2}{c_1^2}\right) - e^{-k_2 r}\left(k_2^2 - \frac{t^2}{c_2^2}\right)\right]. \tag{26}$$

The Laplace transform was successfully applied to the traction vector to yield (see Appendix A)

$$\bar{t}_l'(x,t) = \frac{\rho C_e\, C_{ijkl}}{kr}\left\{n_k\left[r_{,l}\, r_{,k}\,(g_3 + 3\tfrac{g_1}{r})\tfrac{\delta_{lk}}{r}\right] + n_l\left[r_{,k}\, r_{,k}(g_3 + 3\tfrac{g_1}{r}) - \tfrac{3}{r}\right]\right\}. \tag{27}$$

3.2. Case 2: $Q = 0, \bar{F}_i^{(j)} = \delta_{ij}\delta(x-y)$

By using the Helmholtz equation, we obtain (see Appendix B)

$$\bar{\phi}^{(j)} = \frac{1}{4\pi c_1^2}\frac{r_{,i}}{r^2}\frac{\delta_{ij}}{(k_1^2 - k_2^2)}\left[\sum_{n=1}^{2}(-1)^{n-1}E(1+k_n r)e^{-k_n r}\right] + \delta_{ij}\frac{r_i}{r^2}\frac{1}{4\pi t^2} \tag{28}$$

$$E = \frac{\left[k_n^2 - \frac{\rho C_e t(1+\tau_0 t^\alpha)}{k}\right]}{k_n^2}, \tag{29}$$

$$\bar{\psi}_l^{(j)} = \epsilon_{ijl}\left(\frac{r_{,i}}{4\pi t^2 r^2}\right)\left[\left(1+\frac{tr}{c_2}\right)e^{-\frac{tr}{c_2}} - 1\right], \tag{30}$$

$$\bar{u}_l^{(j)} = \frac{U_1\delta_{ij}}{r} + \frac{U_2 r_{,i}\, r_{,j}}{r}, \tag{31}$$

$$U_1 = \frac{1}{4\pi t^2}\left(\frac{t^2}{c_2^2} + \frac{t}{rc_2} + \frac{1}{r^2}\right)e^{-\frac{tr}{c_2}} + \sum_{n=1}^{2}(-1)^{n-1}\frac{B_n}{r^2}(1+k_n r)e^{-k_n r}, \tag{32}$$

$$U_2 = \left[-\frac{1}{4\pi t^2}\left(\frac{t^2}{c_2^2} + 3\frac{t}{rc_2} + 3\frac{1}{r^2}\right)e^{-\frac{tr}{c_2}}\right] + \sum_{n=1}^{2}(-1)^{n-1}\frac{B_n}{r^2}\left(k_n^2 + 3\frac{k_n}{r} + \frac{3}{r^2}\right)e^{-k_n r}, \tag{33}$$

$$B_n = \frac{1}{k_n^2 c_1^2}\frac{1}{(k_1^2-k_2^2)}\left(k_n^2 - \frac{\rho C_e t(1+\tau_0 t^\alpha)}{k}\right). \tag{34}$$

In the absence of a heat source, we find

$$\bar{T}^{(j)} = G\sum_{n=1}^{2} (-1)^{n-1} e^{-k_n r}(1 + k_n r)\frac{r_{,i}}{r^2}, \tag{35}$$

where

$$G = \frac{\delta_{ij}}{4\pi c_1^2}\frac{t(1+\tau_0 t^{\alpha})}{(k_2^2 - k_1^2)}.$$

Now, we establish that the temperature in Case 2 is proportional to the displacement in Case 1 as follows:

$$\bar{T}^{(j)} = \frac{\rho t \epsilon}{m\gamma} u'_j, \tag{36}$$

where

$$\epsilon = \frac{mak}{\rho C_e}.$$

The traction vector is then obtained in a manner like that used in Case 1

$$\bar{t}_l^{(j)}(x,t) = C_{ijkl}\, n_k\Big[\Big(\bar{u}_{l,k}^{(j)} + \bar{u}_{k,l}^{(j)}\Big) + n_l\Big(\bar{u}_{k,k}^{(j)} - \gamma_{ij}\bar{T}^{(j)}\Big)\Big], \tag{37}$$

where

$$\bar{u}_{i,k}^{(j)} = \frac{U_{1,k}}{r}\delta_{ij} - \frac{U_1\delta_{ij}}{r^2} + \frac{U_{2,k}}{r^2}r_{,i}r_{,j} - \frac{U_2}{r^2}r_{,i}r_{,j}\,r_{,k} + \frac{U_2}{r}r_{,ik}r_{,j} + \frac{U_2}{r}r_{,i}r_{,jk}\,, \tag{38}$$

$$\begin{aligned} U_{1,k} = {} & \sum_{n=1}^{2} (-1)^{n-1} B_n e^{-k_n r}\frac{r_{,k}}{r}\left[-k_n^2 - 2\frac{(1+k_n r)}{r^2}\right] \\ & + \frac{r_{,k}}{4\pi t^2} e^{\frac{-tr}{c_2}}\left[-\frac{t^3}{c_2^3} - 2\frac{t}{r^2 c_2} - \frac{2}{r^3} - \frac{t^2}{c_2^2 r}\right], \end{aligned} \tag{39}$$

$$\begin{aligned} U_{2,k} = {} & -\frac{r_{,k}}{4\pi t^2} e^{\frac{-tr}{c_2}}\left[-\frac{t^3}{c_2^3} - 6\frac{t}{r^2 c_2} - \frac{6}{r^2} - 3\frac{t^2}{c_2^2 r}\right] \\ & + \sum_{n=1}^{2} (-1)^{n-1} B_n e^{-k_n r} r_{,k}\left[-k_n^2 - 6\frac{k_n}{r^2} - 3\frac{k_n^2}{r} - \frac{6}{r^3}\right]. \end{aligned} \tag{40}$$

Sherief et al. [74] introduced the following reciprocal relation:

$$\begin{aligned} & \tfrac{\rho T_0 p(1+\tau_0 p^{\alpha})}{k}\int_{\mathbb{R}} \Big[\bar{F}_i^{(1)}\bar{u}_i^{(2)} - \bar{F}_i^{(2)}\bar{u}_i^{(1)}\Big]\mathrm{d}\mathbb{R} \\ & - \tfrac{\rho C_e(1+\tau_0 p^{\alpha})}{k}\int_{\mathbb{R}} \Big[\bar{Q}^{(1)}\bar{T}^{(2)} - \bar{Q}^{(2)}\bar{T}^{(1)}\Big]\mathrm{d}\mathbb{R} \\ & = \int_{\mathbb{C}_3} \Big[\bar{T}^{(1)}\bar{T}_n^{(2)} - \bar{T}^{(2)}\bar{T}_{,n}^{(1)}\Big]\mathrm{d}\mathbb{C} \\ & + \int_{\mathbb{C}_4} \Big[\bar{T}^{(1)}\bar{T}_n^{(2)} - \bar{T}^{(2)}\bar{T}_n^{(1)}\Big]\mathrm{d}\mathbb{C} - \tfrac{T_0 p(1+\tau_0 p^{\alpha})}{k} \\ & \times\Bigg\{\int_{\mathbb{C}_1} \Big[\bar{\sigma}_{ij}^{(1)}\bar{u}_i^{(2)} - \bar{\sigma}_{ij}^{(2)}\bar{u}_i^{(1)}\Big]n_j\,\mathrm{d}\mathbb{C} \\ & + \int_{\mathbb{C}_2} \Big[\bar{\sigma}_{ij}^{(1)}\bar{u}_i^{(2)} - \bar{\sigma}_{ij}^{(2)}\bar{u}_i^{(1)}\Big]n_j\,\mathrm{d}\mathbb{C}\Bigg\}. \end{aligned} \tag{41}$$

To describe the displacement and temperature integral equation with respect to the specified functions $\bar{t}_{i0}, \bar{u}_{i0}, \bar{T}_0, \bar{T}_{n0}$, fundamental solutions $\bar{u}'_i$, $\bar{T}'$, $\bar{u}_i^{(j)}$, $\bar{T}(j)$ and their values $\bar{u}'_{i0}, \bar{T}'_0$, $\bar{u}_{i0}^{(j)}$, $\bar{T}_0^{(j)}$ on $\mathbb{C}$, we consider Case 1 ($\bar{F}_i = 0$ and $\bar{Q} = \delta(x-y)$) and Case 2 ($\bar{F}_i = \delta_{ij}\delta(x-y)$ and $\bar{Q} = 0$) below.

For case 1, Equation (41) becomes

$$\begin{aligned}&(1+\tau_0 t^a)\Delta(x)\bar{T}(x,t)\\&=\tfrac{k}{\rho C_e}\left\{\int\limits_{\mathbb{C}_3}[\bar{T}_0'\bar{T}_n-\bar{T}_0\bar{T}_{n0}']\mathrm{d}\mathbb{C}+\int\limits_{\mathbb{C}_4}[\bar{T}'\bar{T}_{n0}-\bar{T}\bar{T}_{,n}']\mathrm{d}\mathbb{C}\right\}-\tfrac{T_0}{\rho C_e}t(1+\tau_0 t^a)\\&\times\left\{\int\limits_{\mathbb{C}_1}[t_{i0}\bar{u}_i'-\bar{t}_{i0}'\bar{u}_i]\mathrm{d}\mathbb{C}+\int\limits_{\mathbb{C}_2}\left[\bar{\sigma}_{ij}\bar{u}_{i0}'-\bar{\sigma}_{ij}'\bar{u}_{i0}\right]n_j\mathrm{d}\mathbb{C}\right\}\\&-\tfrac{T_0}{C_e}(t+\tau_0 t^\alpha)\int\limits_{\mathbb{R}}\bar{F}_i\bar{u}_i'\mathrm{d}\mathbb{R}+(1+\tau_0 t^a)\int\limits_{\mathbb{R}}\bar{Q}'\bar{T}'\mathrm{d}\mathbb{R}\end{aligned}\tag{42}$$

where

$$\int\limits_{\mathbb{R}}\delta(x-y)\mathrm{d}\mathbb{R}(y)=\Delta(x)=\begin{cases}1, x\in\mathbb{R}\\0,\ x\notin(\mathbb{R}\cup\mathbb{C}),\\\frac{1}{2}, x\in\mathbb{C}\end{cases}$$

For Case II, Equation (41) can be expressed as

$$\begin{aligned}&p(1+\tau_0 p^\alpha)\Delta(x)\bar{u}_j(x,p)=\tfrac{k}{\rho T_0}\left\{\int\limits_{\mathbb{C}_3}\left[\bar{T}_0\bar{T}_{,n}^{(j)}-\bar{T}_0^{(j)}\bar{T}_{,n}\right]\mathrm{d}\mathbb{C}\right.\\&\left.+\int\limits_{\mathbb{C}_4}\left[\bar{T}\bar{T}_{n0}^{(j)}-\bar{T}^{(j)}\bar{T}_{n0}\right]\mathrm{d}\mathbb{C}\right\}+\tfrac{1}{\rho}p(1+\tau_0 p^\alpha)\left\{\int\limits_{\mathbb{C}_1}\left[\bar{p}_{i0}\bar{u}_i^{(j)}-\bar{p}_{i0}^{(j)}\bar{u}_{i0}\right]\mathrm{d}\mathbb{C}\right.\\&\left.+\int\limits_{\mathbb{C}_2}\left[\bar{\sigma}_{il}\bar{u}_{i0}^{(j)}-\bar{\sigma}_{il}^{(j)}\bar{u}_{i0}\right]n_j\mathrm{d}\mathbb{C}\right\}-p(1+\tau_0 p^\alpha)\int\limits_{\mathbb{R}}\bar{F}_i\bar{u}_i^{(j)}\mathrm{d}\mathbb{R}-\tfrac{C_e}{T_0}(1+\tau_0 p^\alpha)\int\limits_{\mathbb{R}}\bar{Q}\bar{T}^{(j)}\mathrm{d}\mathbb{R}\end{aligned}\tag{43}$$

Equation (42) can be solved by using the inverse Laplace transform as follows:

$$L^{-1}(\bar{F}_1(t)\bar{F}_2(t))=\int\limits_0^t F_1(\overline{\tau})F_2(\overline{\tau})d\tau,$$

we arrive at

$$\Delta(x)\left[T(x,\tau)+\tau_0\frac{\partial^a}{\partial\tau^a}T(x,\tau)\right]=M_1(x,\tau),\tag{44}$$

where

$$\begin{aligned}&M_1(x,\tau)=\tfrac{k}{\rho C_e}\int\limits_0^\tau\left\{\int\limits_{\mathbb{C}_3}[T_0'(y,\tau-\overline{\tau})T_{,n}(y,x,\overline{\tau})-T_0(y,x,\overline{\tau})T_{,n}'(y,\tau-\overline{\tau})]\mathrm{d}\mathbb{C}\right.\\&\left.+\int\limits_{\mathbb{C}_4}[T'(y,\tau-\overline{\tau})T_{n0}(y,x,\overline{\tau})-T(y,x,\overline{\tau})T_{n0}'(y,\tau-\overline{\tau})]\mathrm{d}\mathbb{C}\right\}d\overline{\tau}\\&+\tfrac{T_0}{\rho C_e}\int\limits_0^\tau\left\{\int\limits_{\mathbb{C}_1}\left[p_{i0}(y,x,\overline{\tau})\left(\tfrac{\partial}{\partial\overline{\tau}}+\tau_0\tfrac{\partial^{a+1}}{\partial\overline{\tau}^{a+1}}\right)u_i'(y,\tau-\overline{\tau})\right]\mathrm{d}\mathbb{C}\right.\\&\left.\times\int\limits_{\mathbb{C}_2}\left[\sigma_{ij}(y,\tau-\overline{\tau})\left(\tfrac{\partial}{\partial\overline{\tau}}+\tau_0\tfrac{\partial^{a+1}}{\partial\overline{\tau}^{a+1}}\right)u_{i0}'(y,x,\overline{\tau})\right]\mathrm{d}\mathbb{C}\right\}d\overline{\tau}\\&-\tfrac{T_0}{\rho C_e}\int\limits_0^\tau\left\{\int\limits_{\mathbb{C}_1}u_i(y,x,\overline{\tau})\left(\tfrac{\partial}{\partial\overline{\tau}}+\tau_0\tfrac{\partial^{a+1}}{\partial\overline{\tau}^{a+1}}\right)p_{i0}'(y,\tau-\overline{\tau})\mathrm{d}\mathbb{C}\right.\\&\left.+\int\limits_{\mathbb{C}_2}u_{i0}(y,\tau-\overline{\tau})\left(\tfrac{\partial}{\partial\overline{\tau}}+\tau_0\tfrac{\partial^{a+1}}{\partial\overline{\tau}^{a+1}}\right)\sigma_{ij}'(y,x,\overline{\tau})\mathrm{d}\mathbb{C}\right\}d\overline{\tau}\\&+\tfrac{T_0}{C_e}\int\limits_0^\tau\int\limits_{\mathbb{R}}F_i(y,\tau-\overline{\tau})\left(\tfrac{\partial}{\partial\overline{\tau}}+\tfrac{\partial^{a+1}}{\partial\overline{\tau}^{a+1}}\right)u_i'(y,x,\overline{\tau})\mathrm{d}\mathbb{R}d\overline{\tau}\\&+\int\limits_0^\tau\int\limits_{\mathbb{R}}Q(y,\tau-\overline{\tau})\left(1+\tfrac{\partial^a}{\partial\overline{\tau}^a}\right)T'(y,x,\overline{\tau})\mathrm{d}\mathbb{R}d\overline{\tau}.\end{aligned}\tag{45}$$

The solution of (44) yields

$$T(x,\tau) = \frac{1}{\Delta x \tau_0}\left[\int_0^{\overline{\tau}} E_{\alpha,\alpha}\left(-\frac{1}{\tau_0}\overline{\tau}^{a}\right) M_1(x,\tau-\overline{\tau})d\overline{\tau}\right], \tag{46}$$

Where Mittag–Leffler function $E_{\alpha,\alpha}(z)$ is defined as follows [76]:

$$E_{\alpha,\beta}(z) = \sum_{k=0}^{\infty}\frac{z^k}{\Gamma(\alpha k+\beta)}. \tag{47}$$

Similarly, from Equation (43), we obtain

$$\Delta(x)\left[u_j(x,\tau) + \tau_0 \frac{\partial^{\alpha}}{\partial t^{\alpha}} u_j(x,\tau)\right] = M_2(x,\tau), \tag{48}$$

where

$$\begin{aligned}
M_2(x,\tau) = {} & \tfrac{k}{\rho T_0}\int_0^{\tau}\left\{\int_{\mathbb{C}_3}\left[T_0(y,x,\overline{\tau})\tfrac{\partial u_j'(y,\tau-\overline{\tau})}{\partial n} - u_j'(y,\tau-\overline{\tau})\tfrac{\partial T(y,x,\overline{\tau})}{\partial n}\right]d\mathbb{C}\right.\\
&+\int_{\mathbb{C}_4}\left[T(y,x,\overline{\tau})\tfrac{\partial u_j'(y,\tau-\overline{\tau})}{\partial n} - u_j'(y,\tau-\overline{\tau})T_{n0}(y,x,\overline{\tau})\right]d\mathbb{C}\Big\}d\overline{\tau}\\
&-u_j'(y,\tau-\overline{\tau})T_{n0}(y,x,\overline{\tau})\Big]d\mathbb{C}\Big\}d\overline{\tau} + \tfrac{1}{\rho}\int_0^{\tau}\left\{\int_{\mathbb{C}_1}\left[p_{i0}(y,x,\overline{\tau})\left(1+\tau_0\tfrac{\partial^a}{\partial\overline{\tau}^a}\right)u_i^{(j)}(y,\tau-\overline{\tau})d\mathbb{C}\right]\right.\\
&+\int_{\mathbb{C}_2}\left[\sigma_{il}(y,\tau-\overline{\tau})\left(1+\tau_0\tfrac{\partial^a}{\partial\overline{\tau}^a}\right)u_{i0}^{(j)}(y,x,\overline{\tau})n_l d\mathbb{C}\right]\Big\}d\overline{\tau}\\
&-\tfrac{1}{\rho}\left\{\int_0^{\tau}\int_{\mathbb{C}_1} u_i(y,x,\overline{\tau})\left(1+\tfrac{\partial^a}{\partial\overline{\tau}^a}\right)p_{i0}^{(j)}(y,\tau-\overline{\tau})d\mathbb{C}\right.\\
&+\int_{\mathbb{C}_2} u_{i0}(y,\tau-\overline{\tau})\left(1+\tfrac{\partial^a}{\partial\overline{\tau}^a}\right)\sigma_{il}^{(j)}(y,x,\overline{\tau})n_l d\mathbb{C}\Big\}d\overline{\tau}\\
&+\int_{\mathbb{R}} F_i(y,\tau-\overline{\tau})\left(1+\tau_0\tfrac{\partial^a}{\partial\overline{\tau}^a}\right)u_i^{(j)}(y,x,\tau-\overline{\tau})d\mathbb{R}d\overline{\tau}\\
&-\int_0^{\tau}\int_{\mathbb{R}} Q(y,\tau-\overline{\tau})\left(1+\tau_0\tfrac{\partial^a}{\partial\overline{\tau}^a}\right)u_j'(y,x,\tau-\overline{\tau})d\mathbb{R}d\overline{\tau}
\end{aligned} \tag{49}$$

By solving Equation (48), we obtain

$$u_j(x,\tau) = \frac{1}{\Delta x \tau_0}\left[\int_0^{\tau} E_{\alpha,\alpha}\left(-\frac{1}{\tau_0}\overline{\tau}^{\alpha}\right) M_2(x,\tau-\overline{\tau})d\overline{\tau}\right] \tag{50}$$

Consider the $\lim\limits_{x\to\xi} T(x,\tau)$ of (46) and $\lim\limits_{x\to\xi} u_j(x,\tau)$ of (50). Thus, we have

$$T(\xi,\tau) = \tfrac{2}{\tau_0}\left[\int_0^{\tau} E_{\alpha,\alpha}\left(-\tfrac{1}{\tau_0}\overline{\tau}^{\alpha}\right) M_1(\xi,\tau-\overline{\tau})d\overline{\tau}\right],\ \xi\in\mathbb{C} \tag{51}$$

$$u_j(\xi,\tau) = \tfrac{2}{\tau_0}\left[\int_0^{\tau} E_{\alpha,\alpha}\left(-\tfrac{1}{\tau_0}\overline{\tau}^{\alpha}\right) M_2(\xi,\tau-\overline{\tau})d\overline{\tau}\right]\ .\xi\in\mathbb{C} \tag{52}$$

The resulting linear systems were solved using the iteration approach of three-block splitting (TBS) [77].

Figure 1 shows the proposed BEM algorithm flowchart.

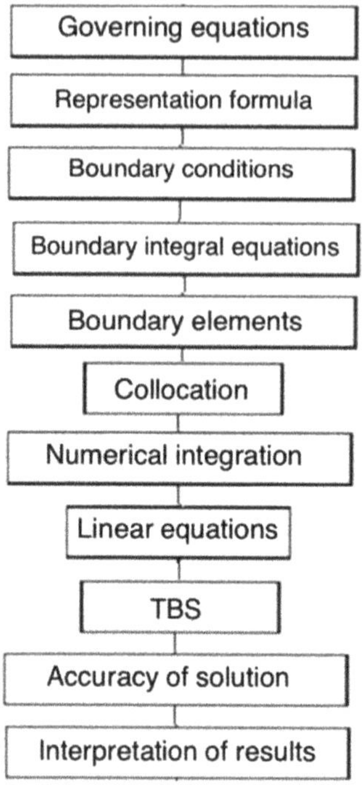

Figure 1. Flowchart of the considered BEM model.

This study focuses on the computational domain, which has 40 boundary nodes and 81 interior nodes, as indicated in Figure 2.

Figure 2. BEM model of the considered problem.

4. Numerical Results and Discussion

To exemplify the numerical findings provided by the proposed methodology, an anisotropic alumina (Al_2O_3) was studied, which had the following properties [14]:

Anisotropic elasticity tensor

$$C = \begin{pmatrix} 576.985 & 75.162 & 132.224 & 47.259 & -37.651 & -1.616 \\ 75.162 & 583373 & 57.046 & -29.680 & -32.710 & 83.907 \\ 132.224 & 57.046 & 519.778 & -12.175 & 85.817 & -54.890 \\ 47.259 & -29.680 & -12.175 & 113.191 & -33.962 & -20.906 \\ -37.651 & -32.710 & 85.817 & -33.962 & 240.907 & 51.386 \\ -1.616 & 83.907 & -54.890 & -20.906 & 51.386 & 188.834 \end{pmatrix} \quad (53)$$

Thermal moduli

$$\begin{aligned} &\gamma_{11} = 2.143(\mathrm{Pa}/^{\circ}\mathrm{C}), \gamma_{22} = 4.049(\mathrm{Pa}/^{\circ}\mathrm{C}) \\ &\gamma_{33} = 4.072(\mathrm{Pa}/^{\circ}\mathrm{C}), \\ &\gamma_{12} = -0.414(\mathrm{Pa}/^{\circ}\mathrm{C}), \gamma_{13} = -0.024(\mathrm{Pa}/^{\circ}\mathrm{C}) \end{aligned} \quad (54)$$

Figure 3 shows the distribution of thermal stress σ_{11} wave propagation throughout the x-axis for various fractional parameter values ($a = 0.25$, 0.50, 0.75, and 1.00). The figure shows that the thermal stress σ_{11} waves grow nonlinearly at $0 \leq x \leq 1.5$, then decline linearly and quickly converge to zero at $x = 3$. It is also recognized that when fractional parame a increases, so does σ_{11}. This figure depicts the way the fractional parameter affects the propagation of the thermal stress σ_{12} wave in anisotropic materials.

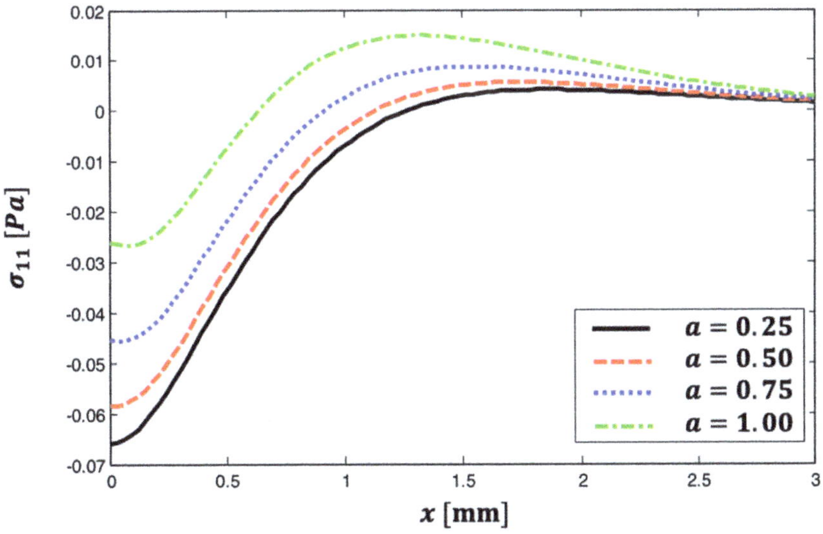

Figure 3. The distribution of thermal stress σ_{11} wave propagation throughout the x-axis for various fractional parameter values.

Figure 4 shows the distribution of thermal stress σ_{12} wave propagation throughout the x-axis for various fractional parameter values ($a = 0.25$, 0.50, 0.75, and 1.00). The image shows that all curves begin at $x = 0$ and rise nonlinearly until they reach a maximum at $0.25 \leq x \leq 0.50$. The function reduces nonlinearly until it reaches a minimal value at $1.0 \leq x \leq 1.5$. The curves then expand linearly until they meet at approximately $x = 3$. It is also noted that σ_{12} diminishes with an increase in fractional parameter a. The figure depicts the way the fractional parameter affects the propagation of the thermal stress σ_{12} wave in anisotropic materials.

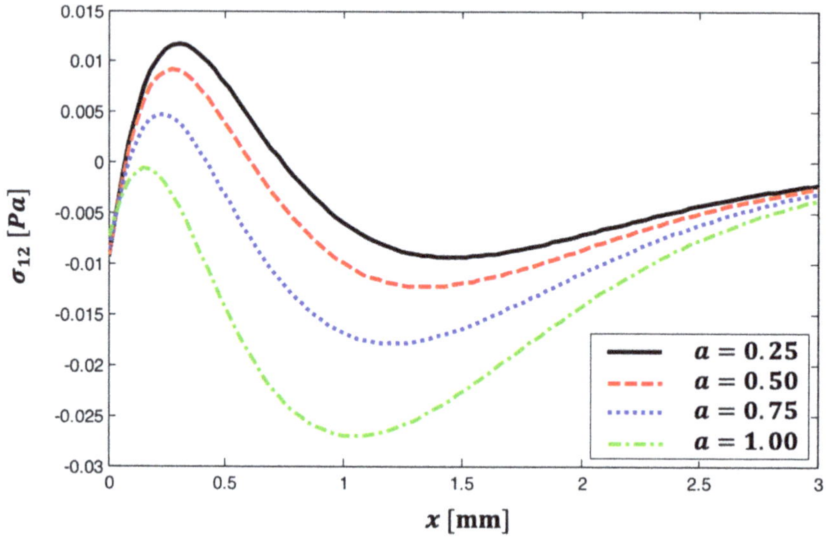

Figure 4. The distribution of thermal stress σ_{12} wave propagation throughout the x-axis for various fractional parameter values.

Figure 5 shows the distribution of thermal stress σ_{22} wave propagation throughout the x-axis for various fractional parameter values ($a = 0.25$, 0.50, 0.75, and 1.00). This graphic shows that all curves begin at $x = 0$ and subsequently drop nonlinearly until they reach a minimum at $x = 0.55$. Then, they increase nonlinearly until they meet at around $x = 3$. It is also noted that when the fractional parameter grows, so does σ_{22}. This figure depicts the way the fractional parameter affects the propagation of the thermal stress σ_{22} wave in anisotropic materials.

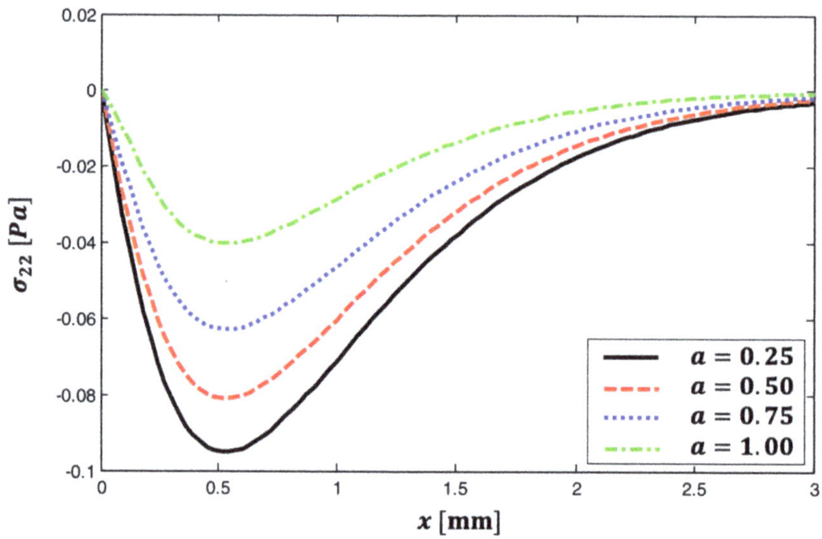

Figure 5. The distribution of thermal stress σ_{22} wave propagation throughout the x-axis for various fractional parameter values.

Figure 6 shows the distribution of thermal stress σ_{13} wave propagation throughout the x-axis for various fractional parameter values ($a = 0.25$, 0.50, 0.75, and 1.00). This graphic shows that all curves begin with a maximum value at $x = 0$, and as the distance increases, these values decrease to practically zero at $x = 3$. Additionally, as the fractional parameter grows, so does σ_{13}. This figure depicts the way the fractional parameter affects the propagation of the thermal stress σ_{13} wave in anisotropic materials.

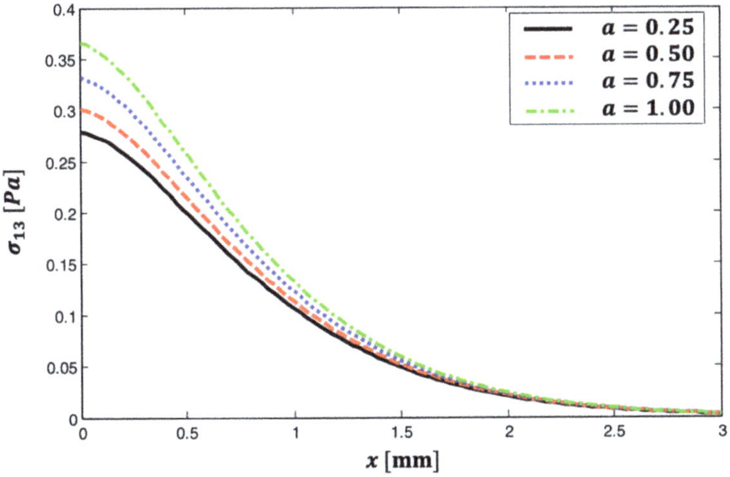

Figure 6. The distribution of thermal stress σ_{13} wave propagation throughout the x-axis for various fractional parameter values.

Figure 7 shows the distribution of thermal stress σ_{23} wave propagation throughout the x-axis for various fractional parameter values ($a = 0.25$, 0.50, 0.75, and 1.00). This image shows that all curves decrease nonlinearly until they reach a minimal value at $0.45 \leq x \leq 0.65$, after which, σ_{23} climbs nonlinearly to approach zero at $x = 3$. Additionally, as the fractional parameter increases, σ_{23} diminishes. The fractional parameter has a substantial impact on thermal stress σ_{23} wave propagation in thermoelastic materials, as illustrated in this figure.

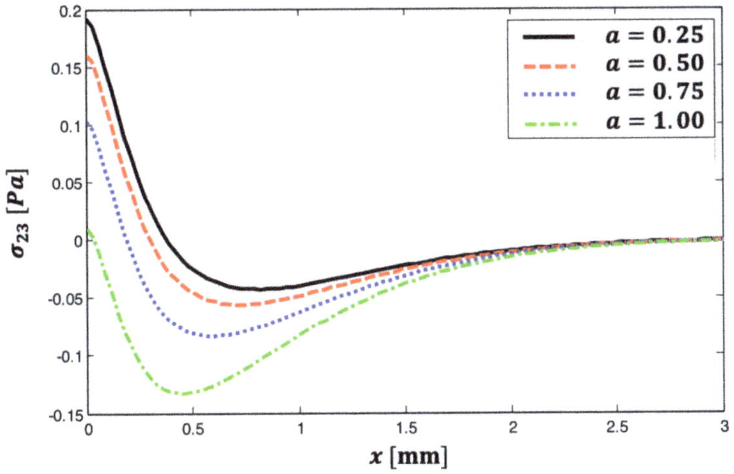

Figure 7. The distribution of thermal stress σ_{23} wave propagation throughout the x-axis for various fractional parameter values.

Figure 8 shows the distribution of thermal stress σ_{33} wave propagation throughout the x-axis for various fractional parameter values ($a = 0.25, 0.50, 0.75,$ and 1.00). This image shows that the curves begin with separate values at $x = 0$, then change and coincide until they reach zero at $x = 3$. It is also noted that when the fractional parameter grows, so does σ_{33}. This graphic illustrates how the fractional parameter affects thermal stress σ_{33} wave propagation in thermoelastic materials.

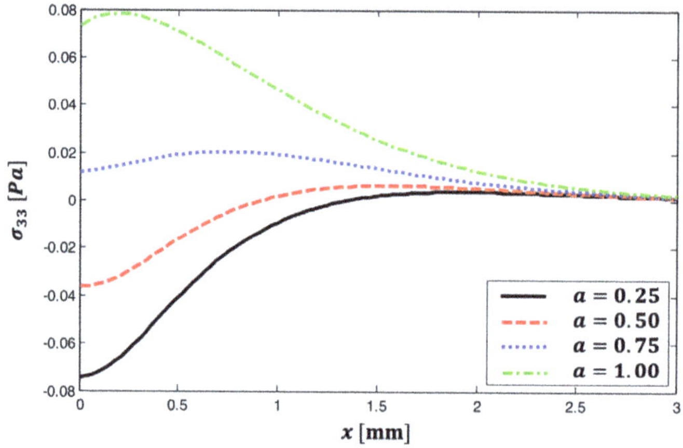

Figure 8. The distribution of thermal stress σ_{33} wave propagation throughout the x-axis for various fractional parameter values.

For validation, we used a particular example of our model and compared our BEM results to Marin et al.'s FEM results [78] and Sharifi's analytical results [79].

Figures 9–11 depict the distributions of thermal stress σ_{11}, σ_{12} and σ_{22} waves propagating throughout the x-axis using BEM, FEM [78] and analytical [79] models. These figures show that the BEM is in excellent agreement with the FEM and analytical methods demonstrating the validity and accuracy of our proposed technique. Matlab R2022a was utilized to generate the computation results for the problem at hand. The proposed fractional boundary element technique in this study is applicable to a wide range of thermal stress wave propagation problems in thermoelastic materials.

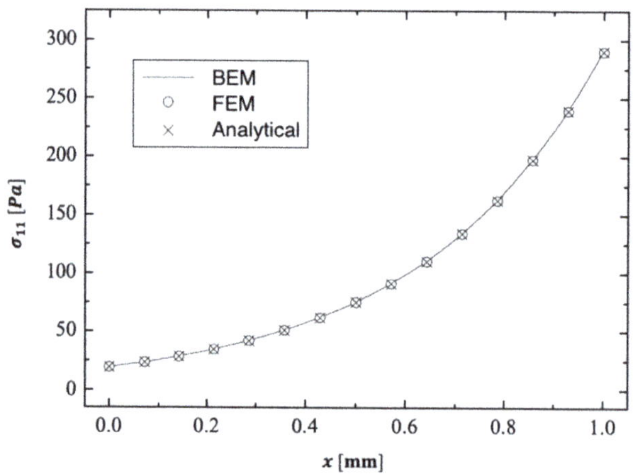

Figure 9. The distribution of thermal stress σ_{11} wave propagation throughout the x-axis using BEM, FEM and analytical methods.

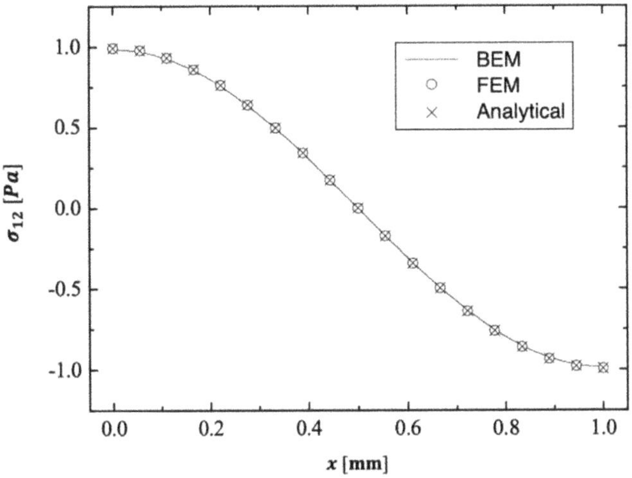

Figure 10. The distribution of thermal stress σ_{12} wave propagation throughout the x-axis using BEM, FEM and analytical methods.

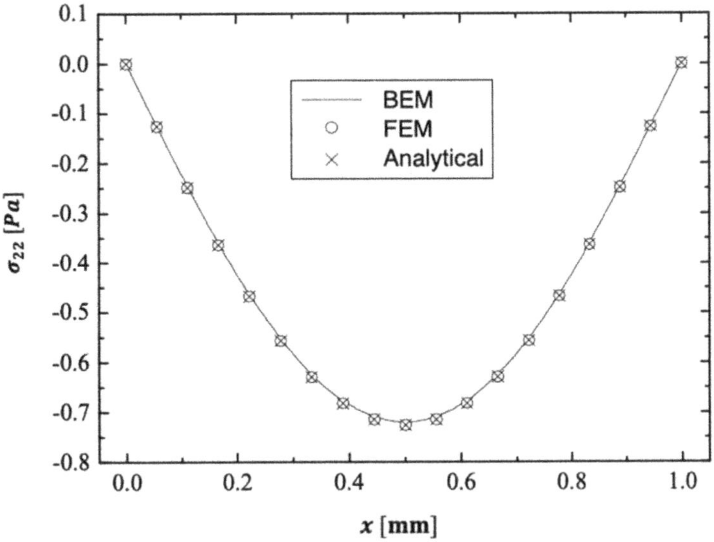

Figure 11. The distribution of thermal stress σ_{22} wave propagation throughout the x-axis using BEM, FEM and analytical methods.

Table 1 displays the CPU time and iteration count for the two-dimensional double successive projection method (2D-DSPM) of Jing and Huang [80], modified symmetric successive overrelaxation (MSSOR) of Darvishi and Hessari [81] and three-block splitting (TBS) of Li et al. [77] iterative methods at each discretization level, with equation numbers in brackets. This table demonstrates that the TBS strategy exceeds both the 2D-DSPM and MSSOR methods.

Table 2 compares the computational requirements for modeling thermal stress wave propagation problems in anisotropic materials using current BEM and FEM approaches [78]. This table demonstrates the efficacy of our proposed BEM approach.

Table 1. CPU timings and iterations for different iterative methods.

Discretization Level	Preconditioning Level	2D-DSPM CPU Time	2D-DSPM Iteration Number	2D-DSPM Error	MSSOR CPU Time	MSSOR Iteration Number	MSSOR Error	TBS CPU Time	TBS Iteration Number	TBS Error
1 (36)	0	0.07	8	0.0099	0.08	8	0.0098	0.05	8	0.0098
2 (72)	0	0.19	9	0.0098	0.23	9	0.0097	0.16	8	0.0094
	1	0.16	7	0.0097	0.19	7	0.0096	0.11	7	0.0090
3 (144)	0	0.52	10	0.0095	0.62	11	0.0091	0.42	10	0.0085
	1	0.47	8	0.0092	0.52	9	0.0087	0.34	6	0.0080
	2	0.44	6	0.0088	0.48	7	0.0084	0.30	4	0.0078
4 (288)	0	2.42	13	0.0090	2.52	17	0.0086	1.88	11	0.0084
	1	1.90	11	0.0084	2.10	15	0.0080	1.58	7	0.0078
	2	1.62	7	0.0080	1.82	11	0.0078	1.42	5	0.0076
	3	1.42	5	0.0078	1.52	7	0.0076	1.38	3	0.0074
5 (576)	0	9.98	15	0.0088	12.04	19	0.0084	7.84	13	0.0082
	1	9.12	11	0.0084	10.12	17	0.0082	6.82	9	0.0080
	2	8.20	9	0.0082	9.32	15	0.0076	6.12	7	0.0075
	3	7.26	7	0.0080	8.48	11	0.0074	5.84	5	0.0073
	4	6.46	5	0.0078	7.01	7	0.0072	5.20	3	0.0070
6 (1152)	0	40.4	19	0.0086	46.6	21	0.0082	34.4	15	0.0080
	1	36.3	17	0.0084	43.0	19	0.0080	32.6	11	0.0078
	2	33.9	15	0.0082	41.0	17	0.0078	30.8	9	0.0076
	3	29.0	11	0.0080	34.9	13	0.0076	29.0	7	0.0074
	4	26.8	9	0.0076	32.8	11	0.0074	22.9	5	0.0072
	5	24.9	7	0.0074	29.0	9	0.0072	21.1	3	0.0070

Table 2. Study of computational power requirements for modeling thermal stress wave propagation problems in anisotropic materials utilizing current BEM and FEM.

	BEM	FEM
Number of nodes	54	56,000
Number of elements	18	9000
CPU time [min]	2	200
Memory [Mbyte]	1	140
Disk space [Mbyte]	0	260
Accuracy of results [%]	1.0	2.3

5. Conclusions

The primary goal of this paper was to present a novel fractional boundary element method (BEM) formulation for solving thermal stress wave propagation problems in anisotropic materials. In the Laplace domain, the fundamental solutions to the governing equations could be found. The boundary integral equations were then built. The heat conduction equation under consideration was formulated using the Caputo fractional time derivative. The resulting BEM linear systems were solved using the three-block splitting (TBS) iteration strategy, which required fewer iterations and consumed less CPU time. The new TBS iteration approach converged quickly and did not require complex computations. It outperformed the two-dimensional double successive projection method (2D-DSPM) and modified symmetric successive overrelaxation (MSSOR) in solving the resultant BEM linear system. We only looked at one specific scenario of our model to compare our results to those of other publications in the literature. Because the BEM results were so compatible with the finite element method (FEM) and analytical findings, the numerical results showed that our proposed BEM formulation was valid, accurate, and efficient in handling three-dimensional thermal stress wave propagation problems in anisotropic materials. The current research has several applications, including nuclear physical science, biophysics, geothermal engineering, pressure vessels, econophysics, biochemistry, robotics and control theory, food engineering, signal and image processing, aviation, electronics, and many more.

Author Contributions: Conceptualization, M.A.F.; Methodology, M.A.F.; Software, M.A.F.; Validation, M.A.F.; Formal analysis, M.A.F.; Investigation, M.A.F.; Resources, M.A.F. and M.T.; Data curation, M.A.F.; Writing—original draft, M.A.F. and M.T.; Writing—review & editing, M.A.F. and M.T. All authors have read and agreed to the published version of the manuscript.

Funding: This research received no external funding.

Data Availability Statement: All data generated or analyzed during this study are included in this published article.

Conflicts of Interest: The authors declare no conflicts of interest.

Nomenclature

α_{kl}	Coefficients of thermal expansion
γ_{ij}	$= C_{ijkl}\alpha_{kl}$ thermal moduli
δ_{ij}	Kronecker delta
e_{ij}	Strains
σ_{ij}	Stress
τ	Time
a	Fractional-order parameter
C_{ijkl}	Elastic constants
C_e	Specific heat at constant strain
$\mathbb{C}$	$= \mathbb{C}_1 \cup \mathbb{C}_2 = \mathbb{C}_3 \cup \mathbb{C}_4$ boundary
e	$= e_{kk}$ dilatation
F_i	Body force vector
$J(\tau)$	Non-Gaussian temporal profile
J_0	Total energy intensity
k	Thermal conductivity
n_j	Outward normal components
$Q(x,\tau)$	Heat source intensity
R	Irradiated surface absorptivity
r	$= \sqrt{(x_i - y_i)(x_i - y_i)}$ radial distance
$r_{,i}$	$= \frac{(x_i - y_i)}{r}$
T	Temperature
$\bar{T}^{(j)}$	Temperature fundamental solutions
T_0	Reference temperature
t_1	Laser pulse time characteristic
u_j	Displacement vector
$\bar{u}_i^{(j)}$	Displacement fundamental solutions
x	$= (x_1, x_2, x_3)$

Appendix A. Laplace Transform Implementation

The traction vector on $\mathbb{C}$ can be expressed as

$$t_i(x,\tau) = \left[C_{ijkl}e_{kl} - \gamma_{ij}T\right]n_j(x) \tag{A1}$$

The Laplace transform was successfully applied to the traction vector (A1) to yield

$$\bar{t}_i(x,\tau) = \left[C_{ijkl}\bar{e}_{kl} - \gamma_{ij}\bar{T}\right]n_i(x). \tag{A2}$$

$$\overline{u}'_i(x,t) = -\frac{\rho C_e}{kr}\frac{m(1+\tau_0 p^\alpha)}{4\pi\left(k_1^2-k_2^2\right)}\left[e^{-k_1 r}\left(1+\frac{k_1}{r}\right) - e^{-k_2 r}\left(1+\frac{k_2}{r}\right)\right]r_{,i}, \tag{A3}$$

The derivative of Equation (A3) gives

$$\bar{u}'_{i,j} = -\frac{\rho C_e}{k}\left[\frac{r_{,i}}{r} g_{1,j} - \frac{(r_{,j}\, r_{,i}\, g_1 - r\, r_{,ij} g_1)}{r^2}\right], \quad \text{(A4)}$$

where

$$g_1 = \frac{m(1+\tau_0 t^\alpha)}{4\pi(k_1^2-k_2^2)}\left[e^{-k_1 r}\left(1+\frac{k_1}{r}\right) - e^{-k_2 r}\left(1+\frac{k_2}{r}\right)\right], \quad \text{(A5)}$$

and

$$g_{1,j} = \frac{m(1+\tau_0 t^\alpha)}{4\pi(k_1^2-k_2^2)}\left[-k_1 e^{-k_1 r} r_{,j}\left(1+\frac{1}{r^2}\right)\right.$$
$$\left. -k_1^2 e^{-k_1 r}\frac{r_{,j}}{r} + k_2 e^{-k_2 r} r_{,j}\left(1+\frac{1}{r^2}\right) - k_2^2 e^{-k_2 r}\frac{r_{,j}}{r}\right]. \quad \text{(A6)}$$

Equation (A4) may be expressed as

$$\bar{u}'_{i,j} = \frac{m(1+\tau_0 t^\alpha)}{4\pi(k_1^2-k_2^2)}\left[r_{,i} r_{,j}\frac{g_3}{r} - \frac{1}{r^2}(\delta_{ij} - 3r_{,i}\, r_{,j})g_1\right], \quad \text{(A7)}$$

where

$$g_3 = \frac{(1+\tau_0 t^\alpha)}{4\pi(k_1^2-k_2^2)}\left[k_1^2 e^{-k_1 r} - k_2^2 e^{-k_2 r}\right], \quad \text{(A8)}$$

Thus, using Equations (A2) and (A7), we obtain

$$\bar{t}'_l(x,t) = \frac{\rho C_e\, C_{ijkl}}{kr}\left\{n_k\left[r_{,l}\, r_{,k}\left(g_3 + 3\frac{g_1}{r}\right)\frac{\delta_{lk}}{r}\right]\right.$$
$$\left. + n_l\left[r_{,k}\, r_{,k}\left(g_3 + 3\frac{g_1}{r}\right) - \frac{3}{r}\right]\right\}. \quad \text{(A9)}$$

Appendix B. Helmholtz Theorem Implementation

The Helmholtz theorem is applied to vectors $u_i^{(j)}$ and $F_i^{(j)}$ to obtain

$$\bar{u}_i^{(j)} = \bar{\phi}_{,i}^{(j)} + \epsilon_{ilk}\bar{\psi}_{l,k}^{(j)}, \quad \text{(A10)}$$

$$\bar{F}_i^{(j)} = \bar{P}_{,i}^{(j)} + \epsilon_{ilk}\bar{R}_{l,k}^{(j)}. \quad \text{(A11)}$$

where the potentials $\bar{\phi}^{(j)}$, $\bar{P}^{(j)}$, $\bar{\psi}_l^{(j)}$, and $\bar{R}_i^{(j)}$ satisfy the following relations:

$$(\nabla^2 - k_1^2)(\nabla^2 - k_2^2)\bar{\phi}^{(j)} = -\frac{1}{c_1^2}\left[\nabla^2 - \frac{\rho C_e}{k} t(1+\tau_0 t^\alpha)\right]\bar{P}^{(j)}, \quad \text{(A12)}$$

$$\bar{\theta}^{(j)} = \frac{1}{m}\left[\left(\nabla^2 - \frac{t^2}{c_1^2}\right)\bar{\phi}^{(j)} + \frac{\bar{P}^{(j)}}{c_1^2}\right], \quad \text{(A13)}$$

$$\left(\nabla^2 - \frac{t^2}{c_1^2}\right)\bar{\psi}_l^{(j)} = -\frac{1}{c_2^2}\bar{R}_i^{(j)}, \quad \text{(A14)}$$

The Helmholtz decomposition theorem is used to determine

$$\bar{P}^{(j)} = -\frac{1}{4\pi}\left(\frac{\delta_{ij}}{r}\right)_{,i}, \quad \text{(A15)}$$

$$\bar{R}_l^{(j)} = \frac{1}{4\pi}\epsilon_{ilk}\left(\frac{\delta_{ij}}{r}\right)_{,k}. \quad \text{(A16)}$$

References

1. Ezzat, M.; Zakaria, M.; Shaker, O.; Barakat, F. State space formulation to viscoelastic fluid flow of magnetohydrodynamic free convection through a porous medium. *Acta Mech.* **1996**, *119*, 147–164. [CrossRef]
2. Ezzat, M.A. Free convection effects on perfectly conducting fluid. *Int. J. Eng. Sci.* **2001**, *39*, 799–819. [CrossRef]
3. Fahmy, M.A. Thermoelastic stresses in a rotating non-homogeneous aniso-tropic body. *Numer. Heat Transf. Part A* **2008**, *53*, 1001–1011. [CrossRef]
4. Abouelregal, A.E.; Mohammed, W.W. Effects of nonlocal thermoelasticity on nanoscale beams based on couple stress theory. *Math. Methods Appl. Sci.* **2020**. [CrossRef]
5. Othman, M.I.A.; Abd-Elaziz, E.M. Dual-phase-lag model on micropolar thermoelastic rotating medium under the effect of thermal load due to laser pulse. *Indian J. Phys.* **2020**, *94*, 999–1008. [CrossRef]
6. Othman, M.I.A.; Zidan, M.E.M.; Mohamed, I.E.A. Dual-phase-lag model on thermo-microstretch elastic solid under the effect of initial stress and temperature-dependent. *Steel Compos. Struct.* **2021**, *38*, 355–363.
7. Bagley, R.L.; Torvik, P.J. On the fractional calculus model of viscoelastic behavior. *J. Rheol.* **1986**, *30*, 133–155. [CrossRef]
8. Machado, J.A.T. Analysis and design of fractional-order digital control systems. *SAMS J. Syst. Anal. Model. Simul.* **1997**, *27*, 107–122.
9. Oldham, K.B.; Spanier, J. *The Fractional Calculus: Theory and Applications of Differentiation and Integration to Arbitrary Order*, 1st ed.; Dover Publication: Mineola, NY, USA, 2006; Volume 111, pp. 1–64.
10. Kilbas, A.A.; Srivastava, H.M.; Trujillo, J.J. *Theory and Applications of Fractional Differential Equations*, 1st ed.; Elsevier Science: Amsterdam, The Netherlands, 2006; Volume 204, pp. 449–463.
11. Sabatier, J.; Agrawal, O.P.; Machado, J.A.T. *Advances in Fractional Calculus: Theoretical Developments and Applications in Physics and Engineering*, 1st ed.; Springer: Dordrecht, The Netherlands, 2007; Volume 1, pp. 169–302.
12. Wang, J.L.; Li, H.F. Surpassing the fractional derivative: Concept of the memory-dependent derivative. *Comput. Math. Appl.* **2011**, *62*, 1562–1567. [CrossRef]
13. Yu, Y.J.; Zhao, L.J. Fractional thermoelasticity revisited with new definitions of fractional derivative. *Eur. J. Mech.—A/Solids* **2020**, *84*, 104043. [CrossRef]
14. Shiah, Y.C.; Tuan, N.A.; Hematiyan, M.R. Direct transformation of the volume integral in the boundary integral equation for treating three-dimensional steady-state anisotropic thermoelasticity involving volume heat source. *Int. J. Solids Struct.* **2018**, *143*, 287–297. [CrossRef]
15. Fahmy, M.A. Boundary element algorithm for nonlinear modeling and simulation of three temperature anisotropic generalized micropolar piezothermoelasticity with memory-dependent derivative. *Int. J. Appl. Mech.* **2020**, *12*, 2050027. [CrossRef]
16. Fahmy, M.A. Boundary element modeling of fractional nonlinear generalized photothermal stress wave propagation problems in FG anisotropic smart semiconductors. *Eng. Anal. Bound. Elem.* **2022**, *134*, 665–679. [CrossRef]
17. Fahmy, M.A.; Shaw, S.; Mondal, S.; Abouelregal, A.E.; Lotfy, K.; Kudinov, I.A.; Soliman, A.H. Boundary Element Modeling for Simulation and Optimization of Three-Temperature Anisotropic Micropolar Magneto-thermoviscoelastic Problems in Porous Smart Structures Using NURBS and Genetic Algorithm. *Int. J. Thermophys.* **2021**, *42*, 29. [CrossRef]
18. Othman, M.I.A.; Atwa, S.Y.; Farouk, R.M. Generalized magneto-thermoviscoelastic plane waves under the effect of rotation without energy dissipation. *Int. J. Eng. Sci.* **2008**, *46*, 639–653. [CrossRef]
19. Othman, M.I.A.; Song, Y. Effect of rotation on plane waves of generalized electro magneto-thermoviscoelasticity with two relaxation times. *Appl. Math. Model.* **2008**, *32*, 811–825. [CrossRef]
20. Ezzat, M.A.; Awad, E.S. Micropolar generalized magneto-thermoelasticity with modified Ohm's and Fourier's laws. *J. Math. Anal. Appl.* **2009**, *353*, 99–113. [CrossRef]
21. Ezzat, M.A.; Youssef, H.M. Generalized magneto-thermoelasticity in a perfectly conducting medium. *Int. J. Solids Struct.* **2005**, *42*, 6319–6334. [CrossRef]
22. Othman, M.I.A.; Eraki, E.E.M. Effect of gravity on generalized thermoelastic diffusion due to laser pulse using dual-phase-lag model. *Multidiscip. Model. Mater. Struct.* **2018**, *14*, 457–481. [CrossRef]
23. Fahmy, M.A. A Nonlinear Fractional BEM Model for Magneto-Thermo-Visco-Elastic Ultrasound Waves in Temperature-Dependent FGA Rotating Granular Plates. *Fractal Fract.* **2023**, *7*, 214. [CrossRef]
24. Fahmy, M.A. A New Boundary Element Strategy for Modeling and Simulation of Three Temperatures Nonlinear Generalized Micropolar-Magneto-Thermoelastic Wave Propagation Problems in FGA Structures. *Eng. Anal. Bound. Elem.* **2019**, *108*, 192–200. [CrossRef]
25. Duhamel, J. Some memoire sur les phenomenes thermo-mechanique. *J. L'école Polytech.* **1837**, *15*, 1–57.
26. Neumann, F. *Vorlesungen Uber die Theorie der Elasticitat*; Meyer: Brestau, Germany, 1885.
27. Biot, M. Thermoelasticity and irreversible thermo-dynamics. *J. Appl. Phys.* **1956**, *27*, 249–253. [CrossRef]
28. Lord, H.W.; Shulman, Y. A generalized dynamical theory of thermoelasticity. *J. Mech. Phys. Solids* **1967**, *15*, 299–309. [CrossRef]
29. Green, A.E.; Lindsay, K.A. Thermoelasticity. *J. Elast.* **1972**, *2*, 1–7. [CrossRef]

30. Green, A.E.; Naghdi, P.M. On undamped heat waves in an elastic solid. *J. Therm. Stress.* **1992**, *15*, 253–264. [CrossRef]
31. Green, A.E.; Naghdi, P.M. Thermoelasticity without energy dissipation. *J. Elast.* **1993**, *31*, 189–208. [CrossRef]
32. Chen, P.J.; Gurtin, M.E. On a theory of heat conduction involving two temperatures. *Z. Angew. Math. Phys. ZAMP* **1968**, *19*, 614–627. [CrossRef]
33. Chen, P.J.; Gurtin, M.E.; Williams, W.O. A note on non-simple heat conduction. *Z. Angew. Math. Phys. ZAMP* **1968**, *19*, 969–970. [CrossRef]
34. Chen, P.J.; Gurtin, M.E.; Williams, W.O. On the thermodynamics of non-simple elastic materials with two temperatures. *Z. Angew. Math. Phys. ZAMP* **1969**, *20*, 107–112. [CrossRef]
35. Quintanilla, R. On existence, structural stability, convergence and spatial behavior in thermoelasticity with two-temperatures. *Acta Mech.* **2004**, *168*, 61–73. [CrossRef]
36. Youssef, H.M. Theory of two-temperature generalized thermoelasticity. *IMA J. Appl. Math.* **2006**, *71*, 383–390. [CrossRef]
37. Youssef, H.M.; Al-Lehaibi, E.A. State-space approach of two-temperature generalized thermoelasticity of one dimensional problem. *Int. J. Solids Struct.* **2007**, *44*, 1550–1562. [CrossRef]
38. Bassiouny, E.; Youssef, H.M. Two-temperature generalized thermopiezoelasticity of finite rod subjected to different types of thermal loading. *J. Therm. Stress.* **2008**, *31*, 233–245. [CrossRef]
39. Youssef, H.M. Two-dimensional problem of two-temperature generalized thermoelastic half-space subjected to ramp-type heating. *Comput. Math. Model.* **2008**, *19*, 201–216. [CrossRef]
40. Fahmy, M.A. Shape design sensitivity and optimization for two-temperature generalized magneto-thermoelastic problems using time-domain DRBEM. *J. Therm. Stress.* **2018**, *41*, 119–138. [CrossRef]
41. Rizzo, F.J.; Shippy, D.J. An advanced boundary integral equation method for three-dimensional thermoelasticity. *Int. J. Numer. Methods Eng.* **1977**, *11*, 1753–1768. [CrossRef]
42. Brebbia, C.A. *The Boundary Element Method for Engineers*; Pentech Press: London, UK, 1978.
43. Brebbia, C.A.; Walker, S. *Boundary Element Method Techniques in Engineering*; Newness-Butterworths: London, UK, 1980.
44. Banerjee, P.K.; Butterfield, R. *Boundary Element Methods in Engineering Science*; McGraw-Hill: London, UK, 1981.
45. Fenner, R.T. Boundary element for stress problems. In *Seminar on Finite Elements or Boundary Elements*; Institution of Mechanical Engineers: London, UK, 1982.
46. Brebbia, C.A.; Tells, J.C.F.; Wrobel, L.C. *Boundary Element Techniques: Theory and Applications in Engineering*; Springer: Heidelberg, Germany, 1984.
47. Sladek, V.; Sladek, J. Boundary integral equation method in two-dimensional thermoelasticity. *Eng. Anal.* **1984**, *1*, 135–148. [CrossRef]
48. Sladek, V.; Sladek, J. Boundary integral equation method in thermoelasticity Part III: Uncoupled thermoelasticity. *Appl. Math. Model.* **1984**, *8*, 413–418. [CrossRef]
49. Cruse, T.A.; Rizzo, F.J. Boundary integral equation methods-computational applications. In *Applied Mechanics, Proceedings of the ASME Conference on Boundary Integral Equation Methods*; ASME: New York, NY, USA, 1985; pp. 118–123.
50. Cao, G.; Yu, B.; Chen, L.; Yao, W. Isogeometric dual reciprocity BEM for solving non-Fourier transient heat transfer problems in FGMs with uncertainty analysis. *Int. J. Heat Mass Transf.* **2022**, *203*, 123783. [CrossRef]
51. Sladek, J.; Sladek, V.; Markechova, I. Boundary element method analysis of stationary thermoelasticity problems in non-homogeneous media. *Int. J. Numer. Methods Eng.* **1990**, *30*, 505–516. [CrossRef]
52. Zhang, S.; Yu, B.; Chen, L. Non-iterative reconstruction of time-domain sound pressure and rapid prediction of large-scale sound field based on IG-DRBEM and POD-RBF. *J. Sound Vib.* **2024**, *573*, 118226. [CrossRef]
53. Tanaka, M.; Matsumoto, T.; Moradi, M. Application of boundary element method to 3-D problems of coupled thermoelasticity. *Eng. Anal. Boundary. Elem.* **1995**, *16*, 297–303. [CrossRef]
54. Ang, W.T.; Clements, D.L.; Cooke, T. A Complex Variable Boundary Element Method for a Class of Boundary Value Problems in Anisotropic Thermoelasticity. *Int. J. Comput. Math.* **1999**, *70*, 571–586. [CrossRef]
55. Shiah, Y.C.; Tan, C.L. Exact boundary integral transformation of the thermoelastic domain integral in BEM for general 2D anisotropic elasticity. *Comput. Mech.* **1999**, *23*, 87–96. [CrossRef]
56. Kogl, M.; Gaul, L. A boundary element method for anisotropic coupled thermoelasticity. *Arch. Appl. Math.* **2003**, *73*, 377–398.
57. El-Naggar, A.M.; Abd-Alla, A.M.; Fahmy, M.A. The propagation of thermal stresses in an infinite elastic slab. *Appl. Math. Comput.* **2004**, *157*, 307–312. [CrossRef]
58. Fahmy, M.A.; Jeli, R.A.A. A New Fractional Boundary Element Model for Anomalous Thermal Stress Effects on Cement-Based Materials. *Fractal Fract.* **2024**, *8*, 753. [CrossRef]
59. Abd-Alla, A.M.; Fahmy, M.A.; El-Shahat, T.M. Magneto-thermo-elastic problem of a rotating non-homogeneous anisotropic solid cylinder. *Arch. Appl. Mech.* **2008**, *78*, 135–148. [CrossRef]
60. Fahmy, M.A. A time-stepping DRBEM for nonlinear fractional sub-diffusion bio-heat ultrasonic wave propagation problems during electromagnetic radiation. *J. Umm Al-Qura Univ. Appl. Sci.* **2024**. [CrossRef]

61. Fahmy, M.A.; Almehmadi, M.M. Fractional Dual-Phase-Lag Model for Nonlinear Viscoelastic Soft Tissues. *Fractal Fract.* **2023**, *7*, 66. [CrossRef]
62. Zhang, S.; Yu, B.; Chen, L.; Lian, H.; Bordas, S.P.A. Isogeometric dual reciprocity BEM for solving time-domain acoustic wave problems; Non-iterative reconstruction of time-domain sound pressure and rapid prediction of large-scale sound field based on IG-DRBEM and POD-RBF. *Comput. Math. Appl.* **2024**, *160*, 125–141. [CrossRef]
63. Fahmy, M.A.; Alzubaidi, M.H.M. A boundary element analysis of quasi-potential inviscid incompressible flow in multiply connected airfoil wing. *J. Umm Al-Qura Univ. Eng. Archit.* **2024**, *15*, 398–402. [CrossRef]
64. Fahmy, M.A.; Toujani, M. Fractional Boundary Element Solution for Nonlinear Nonlocal Thermoelastic Problems of Anisotropic Fibrous Polymer Nanomaterials. *Computation* **2024**, *12*, 117. [CrossRef]
65. Fahmy, M.A.; Alsulami, M.O.; Abouelregalm, A.E. Three-Temperature Boundary Element Modeling of Ultrasound Wave Propagation in Anisotropic Viscoelastic Porous Media. *Axioms* **2023**, *12*, 473. [CrossRef]
66. Fahmy, M.A. Fractional Temperature-Dependent BEM for Laser Ultrasonic Thermoelastic Propagation Problems of Smart Nanomaterials. *Fractal Fract.* **2023**, *7*, 536. [CrossRef]
67. Fahmy, M.A. BEM Modeling for Stress Sensitivity of Nonlocal Thermo-Elasto-Plastic Damage Problems. *Computation* **2024**, *12*, 87. [CrossRef]
68. Yu, B.; Jing, R. SCTBEM: A scaled coordinate transformation boundary element method with 99-line MATLAB code for solving Poisson's equation. *Comput. Phys. Commun.* **2024**, *300*, 109185. [CrossRef]
69. Jing, R.; Yu, B.; Ren, S.; Yao, W. A novel SCTBEM with inversion-free Padé series expansion for 3D transient heat transfer analysis in FGMs. *Comput. Methods Appl. Mech. Eng.* **2025**, *433*, 117546. [CrossRef]
70. Takahashi, T.; Tanigawa, M.; Miyazawa, N. An enhancement of the fast time-domain boundary element method for the three-dimensional wave equation. *Comput. Phys. Commun.* **2022**, *271*, 108229. [CrossRef]
71. Cattaneo, C. A form of heat conduction equation which eliminates the paradox of instantaneous propagation. *Comptes Rendus* **1958**, *247*, 431–433.
72. Vernotte, P. Les paradoxes de la theorie continue de l'equation de la chaleur. *Comptes Rendus* **1958**, *246*, 3154–3155.
73. Vernotte, P. Some possible complications in the phenomena of thermal conduction. *Comptes Rendus* **1961**, *252*, 2190–2191.
74. Sherief, H.H.; El Sayed, A.; El-Latief, A. Fractional Order Theory of Thermoelasticity. *Int. J. Solids Struct.* **2010**, *47*, 269–275. [CrossRef]
75. Tiwari, R.; Mukhopadhyay, S. Boundary integral equations formulation for fractional order thermoelasticity. *Comput. Methods Sci. Eng. CMST* **2014**, *20*, 49–58. [CrossRef]
76. Podlubny, I. *Fractional Differential Equations. An Introduction to Fractional Order Derivatives, Fractional Differential Equations, to Methods of Their Solutions and Some of Their Applications*; Academic Press: Cambridge, MA, USA, 1999; Volume 198.
77. Li, Y.R.; Shao, X.F.; Li, S.Y. New Preconditioned Iteration Method Solving the Special Linear System from the PDE-Constrained Optimal Control Problem. *Mathematics* **2021**, *9*, 510. [CrossRef]
78. Marin, M.; Hobiny, A.; Abbas, I. The Effects of Fractional Time Derivatives in Porothermoelastic Materials Using Finite Element Method. *Mathematics* **2021**, *9*, 1606. [CrossRef]
79. Sharifi, H. Analytical Solution for Thermoelastic Stress Wave Propagation in an Orthotropic Hollow Cylinder. *Eur. J. Comput. Mech.* **2022**, *31*, 239–274. [CrossRef]
80. Jing, Y.F.; Huang, T.Z. On a new iterative method for solving linear systems and comparison results. *J. Comput. Appl. Math.* **2008**, *220*, 74–84. [CrossRef]
81. Darvishi, M.T.; Hessari, P. A modified symmetric successive overrelaxation method for augmented systems. *Comput. Math. Appl.* **2011**, *61*, 3128–3135. [CrossRef]

Mathematical and Computational Applications

MDPI

Article

Forced Vibration Behaviour of Elastically Constrained Graphene Origami-Enabled Auxetic Metamaterial Beams

Behrouz Karami * and Mergen H. Ghayesh

School of Electrical and Mechanical Engineering, University of Adelaide, Adelaide, SA 5005, Australia; mergen.ghayesh@adelaide.edu.au
* Correspondence: behrouz.karami@adelaide.edu.au

Abstract: This paper explores the vibration behaviour of an elastically constrained graphene origami-enabled auxetic metamaterial beam subject to a harmonic external force. The effective mechanical properties of the metamaterial are approximated using a micromechanical model trained via a genetic algorithm provided in the literature. The three coupled equations of motion are solved numerically; a set of trigonometric functions is used to approximate the displacement components. The accuracy of the proposed model is confirmed by comparing it with the natural frequencies of a simplified non-metamaterial structure available in the literature. Following this validation, the investigation extends to investigate the forced vibration response of the metamaterial beam, examining the influence of the graphene origami distribution pattern and content, graphene folding degree, linear and shear layer stiffness, and geometrical parameters on the dynamic behaviour of the structure. The results generally highlight the considerable effect of the shear layer, modelled as a Pasternak foundation, on the vibration behaviour of the elastically constrained metamaterial beams.

Keywords: metamaterial beam; Winkler–Pasternak foundation; forced vibrations; graphene origami

1. Introduction

Beams, which are fundamental components in many engineering designs, often experience various vibrational loads due to environmental or operational conditions. To ensure safety and performance, it is essential to analyse their vibration behaviour [1–4].

The recent advent of metamaterials has provided an opportunity for better vibration design of systems. These structures, designed with properties not usually found in conventional structures, are becoming highly valuable in engineering because they can be tailored to display unique behaviours, for instance in vibration isolation, through their unique characteristics such as negative thermal expansion, negative Poisson's ratio, etc. [5–8]. Such characteristics make metamaterials particularly useful for improving how structures respond to vibrations. By using metamaterial beams, we can achieve better control over vibration frequencies and improve the overall performance of engineering systems [9–13].

External constraints on beams and plates are often modelled as elastic foundations. The Winkler and Pasternak models are two of the most well-known methods for representing elastic foundations. The Winkler model treats the foundation as a series of independent springs, where each point reacts only to the local deflection of the beam. The Pasternak model improves this by introducing shear interaction between points, offering a more realistic representation of how elastic media behave in real-world conditions. Together, these models allow for more accurate analysis of structures on elastic supports, making them particularly useful for studying vibration. Kacar et al. [14], for example, studied the free vibration behaviour of beams resting on a variable Winkler elastic foundation via the differential transform method. Kumar [15] examined the free vibration analysis of composite beams resting on a variable Pasternak foundation using the Rayleigh–Ritz method. Avcar and Mohammed [16] presented the free vibration analysis of functionally graded beams resting on a Winkler–Pasternak foundation using the separation of variables method. The forced vibrations of an elastically constrained cracked double-beam system interconnected by a viscoelastic layer were studied by Cehn et al. [17] via the development of a closed-form solution. A comprehensive study for the bending, buckling, and free vibration behaviours of materially imperfect beams resting on elastic foundation was performed in [18].

The integration of metamaterial beams with Winkler–Pasternak elastic constraints subject to external dynamic loads represents a promising fundamental research. While beams on elastic foundations have been studied extensively, metamaterial beams on elastic foundations remain largely unexplored. This presents a gap in the current understanding, particularly when it comes to forced vibrations, which are highly relevant in many practical applications; the forced vibration of beams supported by elastic foundations is of great importance in engineering fields such as civil and mechanical engineering. Metamaterials are also increasingly being used in advanced engineering sectors such as automotive and civil engineering due to their ability to control vibrations and improve the resilience of structures [19–21].

The aim of this paper is to address this research gap by conducting an in-depth analysis of the forced vibration behaviour of metamaterial beams constrained by a Winkler–Pasternak foundation. The metamaterial beam model has been adopted from our previous study [10] and is modified to take into account the effect of the Winkler–Pasternak foundation and a harmonic external force. Then, it is used to study how the properties of the metamaterial beam and the stiffness of the foundation influence key vibration characteristics and the time-dependent central deflection under the excitation force. The Winkler–Pasternak foundation is modelled as an elastic support, and a range of parametric studies are conducted to investigate the effects of varying foundation stiffness, metamaterial properties, and external forcing on the vibration behaviour of the beam.

2. Forced Vibration Metamaterial Beam Model

Metamaterial Beam

Consider an elastically constrained graphene origami-enabled auxetic metamaterial beam as shown in Figure 1. The multilayer system is characterised by a length L, a width b, and a thickness h. In the current study, the concentration of graphene origami is distributed with respect to two different patterns, Pattern-U and Pattern-A, with an even number of layers, mathematically, where [22]

$$\text{U}-\text{Pattern}: V_{\text{Gr}}^{(k)} = V_{\text{Gr}}, \tag{1}$$

$$\text{A}-\text{Pattern}: V_{\text{Gr}}^{(k)} = V_{\text{Gr}}(2k-1)/N_{\text{L}}, \tag{2}$$

where the volume fraction of the graphene origami is $V_{\text{Gr}}^{(k)}$, and N_{L} is the total layer number. The V_{Gr} (total volume fraction of the graphene origami) is defined by [22]

$$V_{\text{Gr}} = \frac{W_{\text{Gr}}}{W_{\text{Gr}} + (\rho_{\text{Gr}}/\rho_{\text{Cu}})(1-W_{\text{Gr}})}, \tag{3}$$

where $[W_{\text{Gr}}, \rho_{\text{Gr}}]$ is the [weight fraction, density] of nanofiller, and ρ_{Cu} is the matrix density. The effective mechanical properties of metamaterial are determined by [23]

$$\rho_i = (\rho_{\text{Gr}} V_{\text{Gr}} + \rho_{\text{Cu}} V_{\text{Cu}}) \times f_\rho(V_{\text{Gr}}, T), \tag{4}$$

$$\nu_i = (\nu_{\text{Gr}} V_{\text{Gr}} + \nu_{\text{Cu}} V_{\text{Cu}}) \times f_\nu(H_{\text{Gr}}, V_{\text{Gr}}, T), \tag{5}$$

$$E_i = \frac{1 + \xi \eta V_{\text{Gr}}}{1 - \eta V_{\text{Gr}}} E_{\text{Cu}} \times f_E(H_{\text{Gr}}, V_{\text{Gr}}, T), \tag{6}$$

where $[\rho_i, \nu_i, E_i]$ is [mass density, Poisson's ratio, Young's modulus] of the graphene origami-enabled auxetic metamaterial, and the modification functions are denoted by $f_\nu, f_\rho,$ and f_E. Geometrical parameters $(\eta; \xi)$ are formulated as [23]

$$\eta = \frac{(E_{\text{Gr}}/E_{\text{Cu}}) - 1}{(E_{\text{Gr}}/E_{\text{Cu}}) + \xi}, \tag{7}$$

$$\xi = 2\left(\frac{\ell_{\text{Gr}}}{t_{\text{Gr}}}\right), \tag{8}$$

in which Young's moduli of the matrix and the graphene are shown by E_{Cu} and E_{Gr}, respectively; ℓ_{Gr} and t_{Gr} are the length and the thickness of the graphene, and [23]

$$\begin{aligned} f_\nu(H_{\text{Gr}}, V_{\text{Gr}}, T) &= 1.01 - 1.43V_{\text{Gr}} + 0.165\left(\tfrac{T}{T_0}\right) - 16.8H_{\text{Gr}}V_{\text{Gr}} \\ &-1.1H_{\text{Gr}}V_{\text{Gr}}\left(\tfrac{T}{T_0}\right) + 16H_{\text{Gr}}^2 V_{\text{Gr}}^2, \end{aligned} \tag{9}$$

$$f_\rho(V_{\text{Gr}}, T) = 1.01 - 2.01V_{\text{Gr}}^2 - 0.0131\left(\frac{T}{T_0}\right), \tag{10}$$

$$\begin{aligned} f_E(H_{\text{Gr}}, V_{\text{Gr}}, T) &= 1.11 - 1.22V_{\text{Gr}} - 0.134\left(\tfrac{T}{T_0}\right) + 0.559V_{\text{Gr}}\left(\tfrac{T}{T_0}\right) \\ &-5.5H_{\text{Gr}}V_{\text{Gr}} + 38H_{\text{Gr}}V_{\text{Gr}}^2 - 20.6H_{\text{Gr}}^2 V_{\text{Gr}}^2, \end{aligned} \tag{11}$$

where $T/T_0 = 1$, which is assumed to represent room temperature (300 K), and H_{Gr} denotes the folding degree of graphene origami.

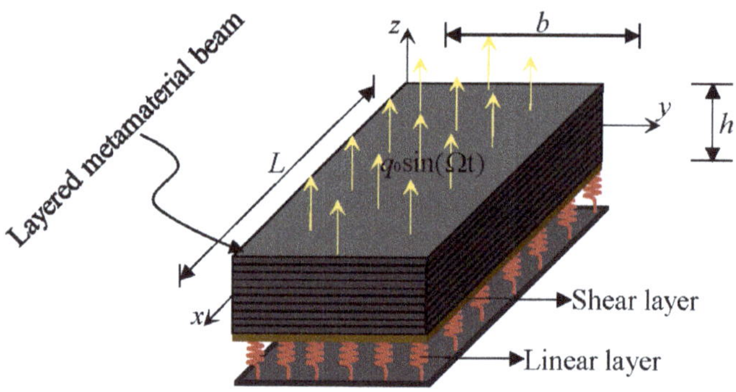

Figure 1. Schematic of an elastically constrained graphene origami-enabled auxetic metamaterial beam.

The equations of motion used in this paper have been adopted from our previous study [10] and have been modified to account for the effect of the Winkler–Pasternak foundation and a harmonic external force; this gives

$$
\begin{aligned}
&\left\{ \sum_{k=1}^{N_L} \int_{z_k}^{z_{k+1}} \frac{E_i(k)}{1-\nu_i^2(k)} dz \right\} \frac{\partial^2 u}{\partial x^2} + \left\{ \sum_{k=1}^{N_L} \int_{z_k}^{z_{k+1}} \frac{E_i(k)}{1-\nu_i^2(k)} z dz \right\} \frac{\partial^2 \varphi}{\partial x^2} \\
&-c_1 \left\{ \sum_{k=1}^{N_L} \int_{z_k}^{z_{k+1}} \frac{E_i(k)}{1-\nu_i^2(k)} z^3 dz \right\} \frac{\partial^2 \varphi}{\partial x^2} - c_1 \left\{ \sum_{k=1}^{N_L} \int_{z_k}^{z_{k+1}} \frac{E_i(k)}{1-\nu_i^2(k)} z^3 dz \right\} \frac{\partial^3 w}{\partial x^3} \\
&= \left\{ \sum_{k=1}^{N_L} \int_{z_k}^{z_{k+1}} \rho(k) dz \right\} \frac{\partial^2 u}{\partial t^2} + \left\{ \sum_{k=1}^{N_L} \int_{z_k}^{z_{k+1}} \rho(k) z dz \right\} \frac{\partial \varphi}{\partial t^2} \\
&-c_1 \left\{ \sum_{k=1}^{N_L} \int_{z_k}^{z_{k+1}} \rho(k) z^3 dz \right\} \frac{\partial \varphi}{\partial t^2} - c_1 \left\{ \sum_{k=1}^{N_L} \int_{z_k}^{z_{k+1}} \rho(k) z^3 dz \right\} \frac{\partial^3 w}{\partial x \partial t^2},
\end{aligned}
\tag{12}
$$

$$
\begin{aligned}
&\left\{ \sum_{k=1}^{N_L} \int_{z_k}^{z_{k+1}} \frac{E_i(k)}{2+2\nu_i(k)} dz \right\} \frac{\partial \varphi}{\partial x} - c_2 \left\{ \sum_{k=1}^{N_L} \int_{z_k}^{z_{k+1}} \frac{E_i(k)}{2+2\nu_i(k)} z^2 dz \right\} \frac{\partial \varphi}{\partial x} \\
&-c_2 \left\{ \sum_{k=1}^{N_L} \int_{z_k}^{z_{k+1}} \frac{E_i(k)}{2+2\nu_i(k)} z^2 dz \right\} \frac{\partial^2 w}{\partial x^2} + \left\{ \sum_{k=1}^{N_L} \int_{z_k}^{z_{k+1}} \frac{E_i(k)}{2+2\nu_i(k)} dz \right\} \frac{\partial^2 w}{\partial x^2} \\
&-c_2 \left\{ \sum_{k=1}^{N_L} \int_{z_k}^{z_{k+1}} \frac{E_i(k)}{2+2\nu_i(k)} z^2 dz \right\} \frac{\partial \varphi}{\partial x} + c_2^2 \left\{ \sum_{k=1}^{N_L} \int_{z_k}^{z_{k+1}} \frac{E_i(k)}{2+2\nu_i(k)} z^4 dz \right\} \frac{\partial \varphi}{\partial x} \\
&+c_2^2 \left\{ \sum_{k=1}^{N_L} \int_{z_k}^{z_{k+1}} \frac{E_i(k)}{2+2\nu_i(k)} z^4 dz \right\} \frac{\partial^2 w}{\partial x^2} - c_2 \left\{ \sum_{k=1}^{N_L} \int_{z_k}^{z_{k+1}} \frac{E_i(k)}{2+2\nu_i(k)} z^2 dz \right\} \frac{\partial^2 w}{\partial x^2} \\
&+c_1 \left\{ \sum_{k=1}^{N_L} \int_{z_k}^{z_{k+1}} \frac{E_i(k)}{1-\nu_i^2(k)} z^3 dz \right\} \frac{\partial^3 u}{\partial x^3} + c_1 \left\{ \sum_{k=1}^{N_L} \int_{z_k}^{z_{k+1}} \frac{E_i(k)}{1-\nu_i^2(k)} z^4 dz \right\} \frac{\partial^3 \varphi}{\partial x^3} \\
&-c_1^2 \left\{ \sum_{k=1}^{N_L} \int_{z_k}^{z_{k+1}} \frac{E_i(k)}{1-\nu_i^2(k)} z^6 dz \right\} \frac{\partial^3 \varphi}{\partial x^3} - c_1^2 \left\{ \sum_{k=1}^{N_L} \int_{z_k}^{z_{k+1}} \frac{E_i(k)}{1-\nu_i^2(k)} z^6 dz \right\} \frac{\partial^4 w}{\partial x^4} \\
&-k_W w + k_P \frac{\partial^2 w}{\partial x^2} + q = \left\{ \sum_{k=1}^{N_L} \int_{z_k}^{z_{k+1}} \rho(k) dz \right\} \frac{\partial^2 w}{\partial t^2} + c_1 \left\{ \sum_{k=1}^{N_L} \int_{z_k}^{z_{k+1}} \rho(k) z^3 dz \right\} \frac{\partial^3 u}{\partial x \partial t^2} \\
&+c_1 \left\{ \sum_{k=1}^{N_L} \int_{z_k}^{z_{k+1}} \rho(k) z^4 dz \right\} \frac{\partial^3 \varphi}{\partial x \partial t^2} - c_1^2 \left\{ \sum_{k=1}^{N_L} \int_{z_k}^{z_{k+1}} \rho(k) z^6 dz \right\} \frac{\partial^3 \varphi}{\partial x \partial t^2} \\
&-c_1^2 \left\{ \sum_{k=1}^{N_L} \int_{z_k}^{z_{k+1}} \rho(k) z^6 dz \right\} \frac{\partial^4 w}{\partial x^2 \partial t^2},
\end{aligned}
\tag{13}
$$

$$
\begin{aligned}
&\left\{ \sum_{k=1}^{N_L} \int_{z_k}^{z_{k+1}} \frac{E_i(k)}{1-\nu_i^2(k)} z dz \right\} \frac{\partial^2 u}{\partial x^2} + \left\{ \sum_{k=1}^{N_L} \int_{z_k}^{z_{k+1}} \frac{E_i(k)}{1-\nu_i^2(k)} z^2 dz \right\} \frac{\partial^2 \varphi}{\partial x^2} \\
&-c_1 \left\{ \sum_{k=1}^{N_L} \int_{z_k}^{z_{k+1}} \frac{E_i(k)}{1-\nu_i^2(k)} z^4 dz \right\} \frac{\partial^2 \varphi}{\partial x^2} - c_1 \left\{ \sum_{k=1}^{N_L} \int_{z_k}^{z_{k+1}} \frac{E_i(k)}{1-\nu_i^2(k)} z^4 dz \right\} \frac{\partial^3 w}{\partial x^3} \\
&-\left\{ \sum_{k=1}^{N_L} \int_{z_k}^{z_{k+1}} \frac{E_i(k)}{2+2\nu_i(k)} dz \right\} \varphi + c_2 \left\{ \sum_{k=1}^{N_L} \int_{z_k}^{z_{k+1}} \frac{E_i(k)}{2+2\nu_i(k)} z^2 dz \right\} \varphi \\
&+c_2 \left\{ \sum_{k=1}^{N_L} \int_{z_k}^{z_{k+1}} \frac{E_i(k)}{2+2\nu_i(k)} z^2 dz \right\} \frac{\partial w}{\partial x} - \left\{ \sum_{k=1}^{N_L} \int_{z_k}^{z_{k+1}} \frac{E_i(k)}{2+2\nu_i(k)} dz \right\} \frac{\partial w}{\partial x} \\
&+c_2 \left\{ \sum_{k=1}^{N_L} \int_{z_k}^{z_{k+1}} \frac{E_i(k)}{2+2\nu_i(k)} z^2 dz \right\} \varphi - c_2^2 \left\{ \sum_{k=1}^{N_L} \int_{z_k}^{z_{k+1}} \frac{E_i(k)}{2+2\nu_i(k)} z^4 dz \right\} \varphi \\
&-c_2^2 \left\{ \sum_{k=1}^{N_L} \int_{z_k}^{z_{k+1}} \frac{E_i(k)}{2+2\nu_i(k)} z^4 dz \right\} \frac{\partial w}{\partial x} + c_2 \left\{ \sum_{k=1}^{N_L} \int_{z_k}^{z_{k+1}} \frac{E_i(k)}{2+2\nu_i(k)} z^2 dz \right\} \frac{\partial w}{\partial x} \\
&-c_1 \left\{ \sum_{k=1}^{N_L} \int_{z_k}^{z_{k+1}} \frac{E_i(k)}{1-\nu_i^2(k)} z^3 dz \right\} \frac{\partial^2 u}{\partial x^2} - c_1 \left\{ \sum_{k=1}^{N_L} \int_{z_k}^{z_{k+1}} \frac{E_i(k)}{1-\nu_i^2(k)} z^4 dz \right\} \frac{\partial^2 \varphi}{\partial x^2} \\
&+c_1^2 \left\{ \sum_{k=1}^{N_L} \int_{z_k}^{z_{k+1}} \frac{E_i(k)}{1-\nu_i^2(k)} z^6 dz \right\} \frac{\partial^2 \varphi}{\partial x^2} + c_1^2 \left\{ \sum_{k=1}^{N_L} \int_{z_k}^{z_{k+1}} \frac{E_i(k)}{1-\nu_i^2(k)} z^6 dz \right\} \frac{\partial^3 w}{\partial x^3} \\
&= \left\{ \sum_{k=1}^{N_L} \int_{z_k}^{z_{k+1}} \rho(k) z dz \right\} \frac{\partial^2 u}{\partial t^2} + \left\{ \sum_{k=1}^{N_L} \int_{z_k}^{z_{k+1}} \rho(k) z^2 dz \right\} \frac{\partial^2 \varphi}{\partial t^2} - c_1 \left\{ \sum_{k=1}^{N_L} \int_{z_k}^{z_{k+1}} \rho(k) z^3 dz \right\} \frac{\partial^2 u}{\partial t^2} \\
&-2c_1 \left\{ \sum_{k=1}^{N_L} \int_{z_k}^{z_{k+1}} \rho(k) z^4 dz \right\} \frac{\partial^2 \varphi}{\partial t^2} - c_1 \left\{ \sum_{k=1}^{N_L} \int_{z_k}^{z_{k+1}} \rho(k) z^4 dz \right\} \frac{\partial^3 w}{\partial x \partial t^2} \\
&+c_1^2 \left\{ \sum_{k=1}^{N_L} \int_{z_k}^{z_{k+1}} \rho(k) z^6 dz \right\} \frac{\partial^2 \varphi}{\partial t^2} + c_1^2 \left\{ \sum_{k=1}^{N_L} \int_{z_k}^{z_{k+1}} \rho(k) z^6 dz \right\} \frac{\partial^3 w}{\partial x \partial t^2},
\end{aligned}
\tag{14}
$$

where k_W and k_P are the linear layer (spring) stiffness and shear layer stiffness, respectively, and q is the dynamic force; the rest of the coefficients are given in [10]. The foundation parameters are presented in the following dimensionless form:

$$K_W = \frac{k_W D}{L^4} \text{ and } K_P = \frac{k_P D}{L^2} \text{ for } D = \frac{E_{Cu} h^3}{12(1 - \nu_{Cu}^2)}. \tag{15}$$

3. Solution Procedure

To date, numerous numerical and analytical methods have been proposed for the static and dynamic analyses of different continuous systems [24–28]. This section details the solution procedure for the forced vibration problem introduced in Section 2.

The solution to the forced vibration problem is formulated via a set of trigonometric functions; these series are utilised to approximate the displacement components while ensuring that the boundary conditions for all simply supported edges are satisfied.

$$u(x,t) = \sum_{m=1}^{\infty} U_m \cos\frac{m\pi x}{L} \sin(\Omega t), \tag{16}$$

$$w(x,t) = \sum_{m=1}^{\infty} W_m \sin\frac{m\pi x}{L} \sin(\Omega t), \tag{17}$$

$$\varphi(x,t) = \sum_{m=1}^{\infty} \Phi_m \cos\frac{m\pi x}{L} \sin(\Omega t), \tag{18}$$

where Ω denotes the excitation frequency. The dynamic load is given by the following expression:

$$q = \sum_{m=1}^{\infty} Q_m \sin\frac{m\pi x}{L} \sin(\Omega t), \tag{19}$$

where

$$Q_m = q_0, \tag{20}$$

with q_0 being distributed-load intensity. The utilisation of trigonometric series provides an efficient and systematic approach to representing displacement components, offering reduced computational complexity compared to methods such as the finite element or finite difference techniques. However, the methodology also has limitations. The use of trigonometric series inherently restricts their application to problems with boundary conditions that align with the assumed series. For more complex geometries or boundary conditions, alternative numerical techniques may be required.

4. Numerical Results

For validation, the natural frequencies obtained from our simulations for a simplified version of the current model (excluding the metamaterial and multilayered effects, the external force, and the elastic foundation) are compared with the results reported in Ref. [29]. As illustrated in Figure 2, the comparison demonstrates excellent agreement.

In the present study, the auxetic metamaterial beam is fabricated using a copper (Cu) matrix, characterised by a Young's modulus E_{Cu} = 65.79 GPa, Poisson's ratio ν_{Cu} = 0.387, and mass density ρ_{Cu} = 8800 kg/m^3 at room temperature; graphene has material properties with a Young's modulus E_{Gr} = 929.57 GPa, Poisson's ratio ν_{Gr} = 0.220, and mass density ρ_{Gr} = 1800 kg/m^3 at room temperature. The graphene layers used in this study have a length of ℓ_{Gr} = 8.376 nm and a thickness of t_{Gr} = 0.34 nm, as detailed in Refs. [23,30].

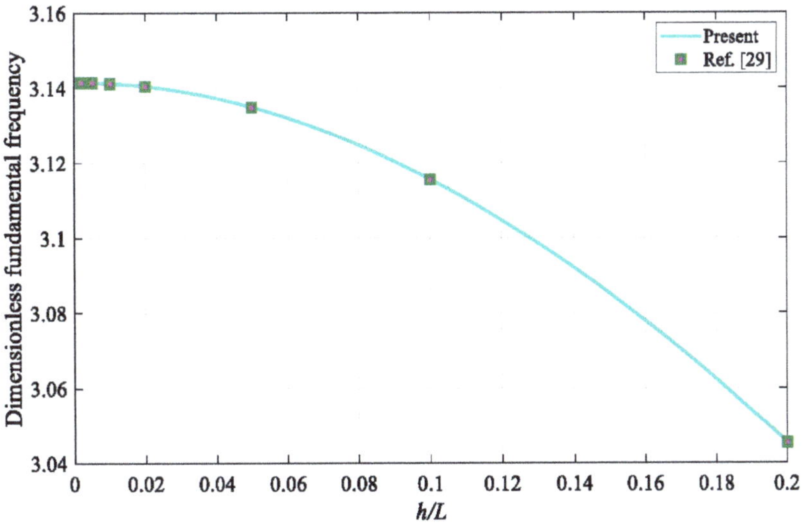

Figure 2. The non-dimensional fundamental frequency of a homogenous beam for various length-to-thickness ratios, showing an excellent agreement between the current study and that given in Ref. [29].

Depicted in Figure 3 are the phase plots of the beam (the centre point) subject to a harmonic force for (a) a metallic matrix (non-metamaterial), (b) a metamaterial with Pattern-U, and (c) a metamaterial with Pattern-A; each panel displays three phase plots: namely, with no foundation ($K_W = K_P = 0.0$), with a Winkler foundation ($K_W = 10.0$, $K_P = 0.0$), and with a Pasternak foundation ($K_W = 10.0$, $K_P = 1.0$). The results show that the addition of the elastic foundations, specifically the Winkler and Pasternak types, reduces the transverse deflection compared to the case without any foundation. This reduction occurs because the elastic foundations provide additional stiffness and resistance to deformation, effectively suppressing larger deflections. This phenomenon aligns with the theoretical predictions, where the elastic foundation parameters enhance the beam's rigidity, thereby suppressing deflections under harmonic loading. The maximum deflection difference between the no-foundation and Winkler-foundation (panel (a)) cases is larger than those of the metamaterial ones (panels (b) and (c)). Comparing panels (b) and (c), i.e., the metamaterial cases, highlights that the effect of the Winkler foundation on the maximum deflection for Pattern-U is larger (when compared to Pattern-A).

Figure 4 depicts the time history response of a graphene origami-enabled auxetic metamaterial beam for different degrees of graphene folding (H_{Gr}) for a fixed graphene weight fraction ($W_{Gr} = 2.5$ wt%). For $H_{Gr} = 20\%$ (a), both Pattern-U and Pattern-A exhibit similar amplitudes and harmonic behaviour, indicating slight differences in the responses. At $H_{Gr} = 50\%$ (b), Pattern-A shows a lower amplitude compared to Pattern-U; this trend becomes more visible for $H_{Gr} = 100\%$, as seen in panel (c). Furthermore, normalised transverse deflection, in general, increases with the graphene folding degree.

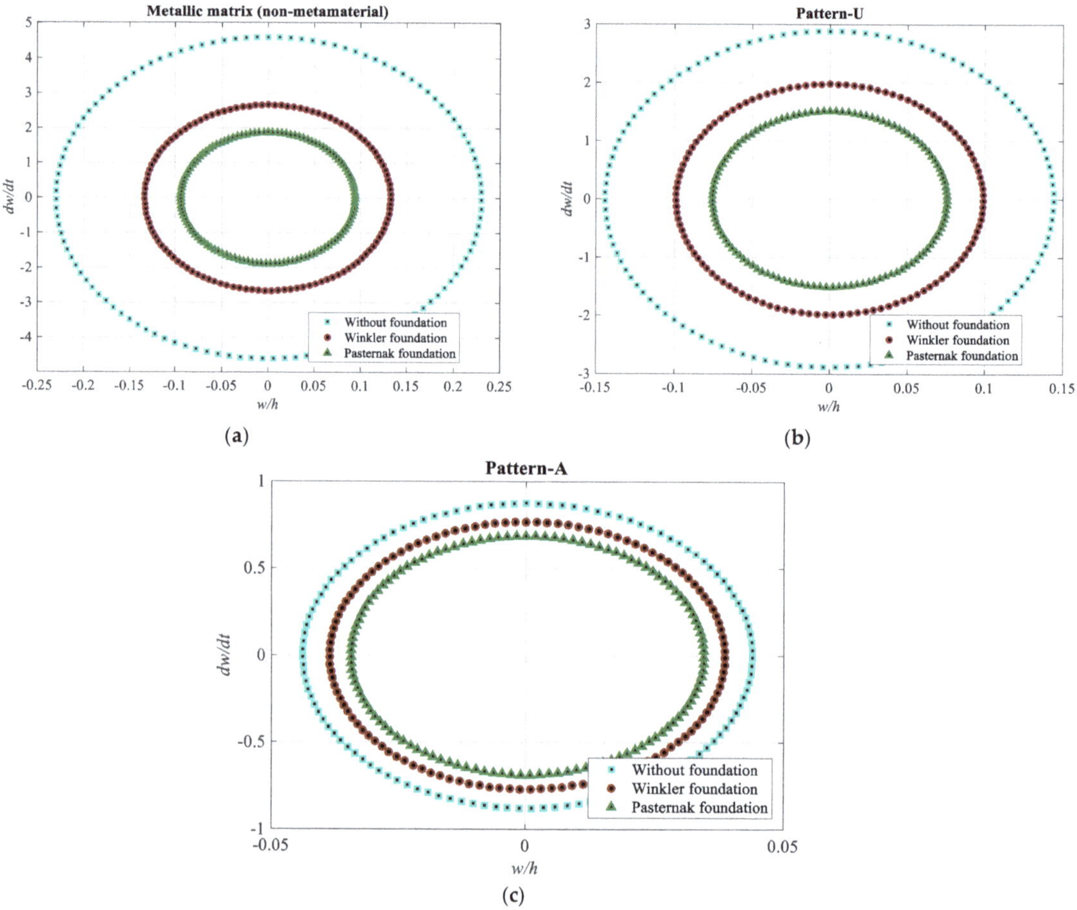

Figure 3. Phase plot diagram of graphene origami-enabled auxetic metamaterial beam versus two-parameter elastic foundation (h = 0.01 m, L = 0.20 m, $\Omega = 2 \times 10^3$ rad·s^{-1}). (**a**) Metallic matrix; (**b**) Pattern-U; (**c**) Pattern-A.

Figure 5 shows the phase diagrams plotted for various graphene weight fractions (W_{Gr}) for different values of the graphene folding degree (H_{Gr}): (a) H_{Gr} = 10%, (b) H_{Gr} = 30%, (c) H_{Gr} = 60%, and (d) H_{Gr} = 100%. For smaller values of the graphene folding degree ($H_{Gr} \leq 60\%$), in general, the transverse deflection decreases as the graphene weight fraction increases. However, in panel (d), where the folding degree is H_{Gr} = 100%, the normalised transverse deflection initially increases with W_{Gr}, reaching a maximum at W_{Gr} = 0.25 wt%, before decreasing at higher weight fractions, as seen by the closed-loop trajectories. This behaviour suggests an optimal graphene weight fraction at which the transverse deflection is maximised, likely due to the interplay between the material stiffness and flexibility, where the concentration of graphene initially enhances flexibility, leading to larger deflections, while higher concentrations lead to an increased stiffness, reducing the deflection amplitude.

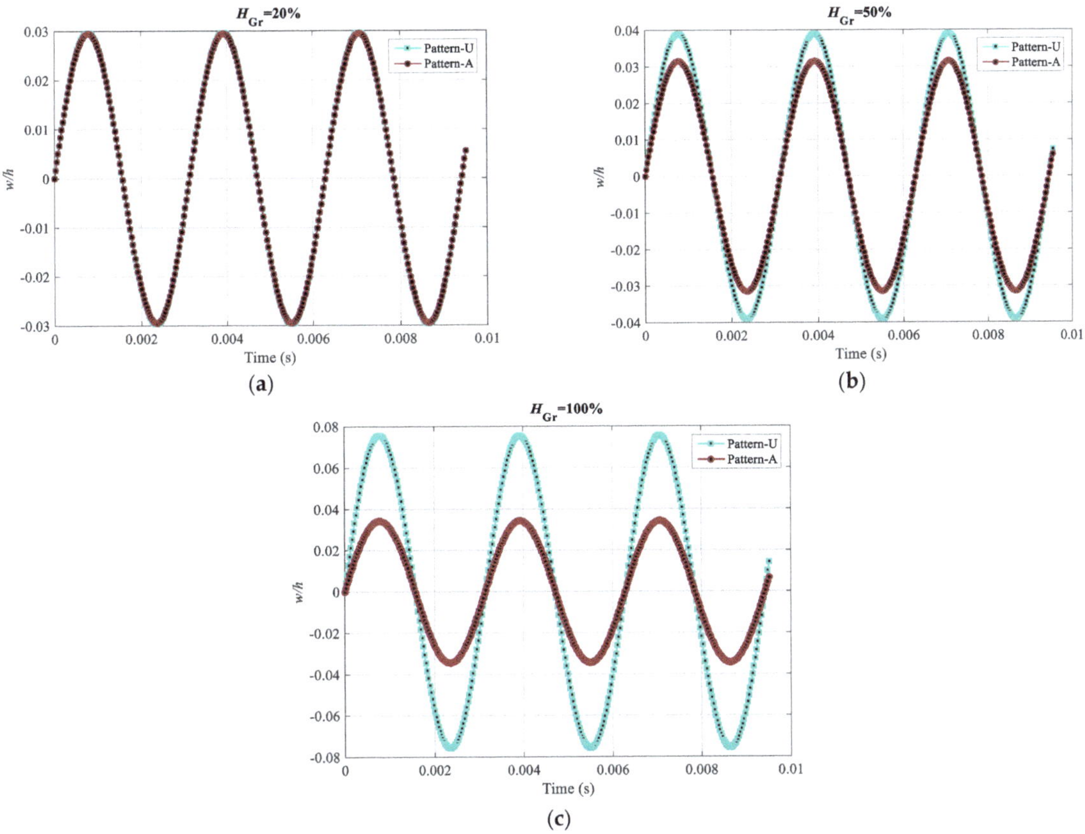

Figure 4. Time history of the graphene origami-enabled auxetic metamaterial beam versus graphene folding degree (h = 0.01 m, L = 0.20 m, $\Omega = 2 \times 10^3$ rad·s^{-1}, W_{Gr} = 2.5 wt%, K_W = 10.0, K_P = 1.0). (**a**) H_{Gr} = 20%; (**b**) H_{Gr} = 50%; (**c**) H_{Gr} = 100%.

Depicted in Figure 6 are the time history responses of the graphene origami-enabled auxetic metamaterial beam, illustrating the influences of the two-parameter elastic foundation coefficients on its forced dynamic behaviour. Panel (a) presents the normalised transverse deflection of the beam versus the linear layer stiffness (K_W). The results indicate that increasing the linear layer stiffness generally reduces the normalised transverse vibration amplitude. Panel (b) shows the normalised transverse deflection against the shear layer stiffness (K_P), with K_W fixed at 10. Similarly, the normalised transverse deflection decreases as the shear layer stiffness increases.

The dynamic response of an elastically constrained graphene origami-enabled auxetic metamaterial beam under different excitation frequencies is depicted in Figure 7 for both Pattern-U and Pattern-A. An increase in the excitation frequency, in general, leads to a rise in the amplitude of the oscillations. As the forcing frequency approaches the linear resonant fundamental frequency (ω_1), the transverse vibration amplitude becomes larger.

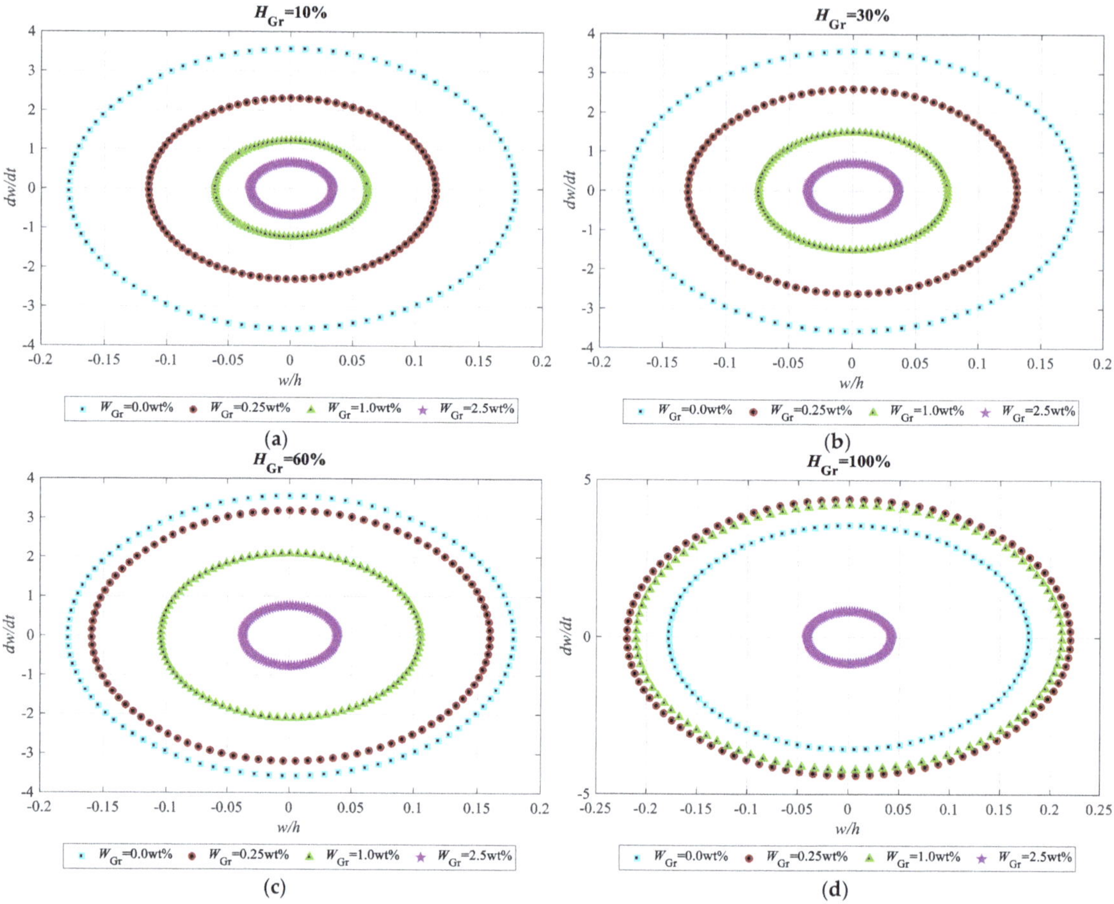

Figure 5. Phase-plot diagrams of graphene origami-enabled auxetic metamaterial beam versus weight fraction of graphene (Pattern-A, h = 0.01 m, L = 0.20 m, $\Omega = 2 \times 10^3$ rad·s^{-1}, K_W = 2.0, K_P = 0.2). (**a**) H_{Gr} = 10%; (**b**) H_{Gr} = 30%; (**c**) H_{Gr} = 60%; (**d**) H_{Gr} = 100%.

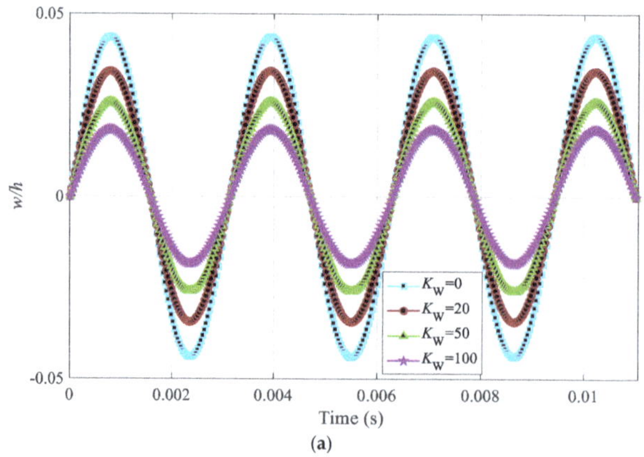

(a)

Figure 6. *Cont.*

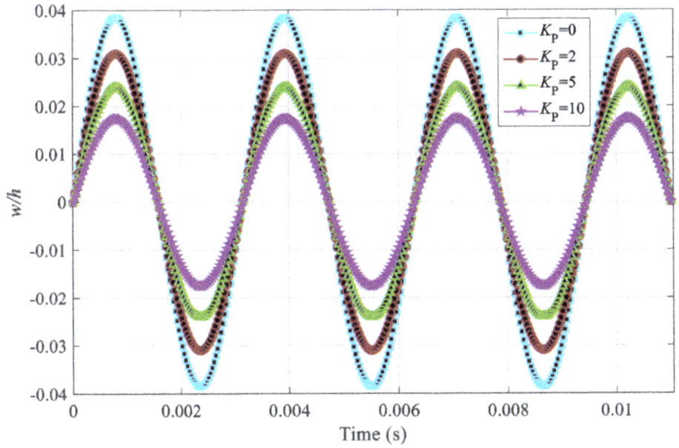

(**b**)

Figure 6. Time history of elastically constrained graphene origami-enabled auxetic metamaterial beam versus elastic foundation parameters. (**a**) Versus linear layer (spring) stiffness; (**b**) versus shear layer stiffness. (Pattern-A, h = 0.01 m, L = 0.20 m, $\Omega = 2 \times 10^3$ rad·s^{-1}, W_{Gr} = 2.5 wt%, H_{Gr} = 100%).

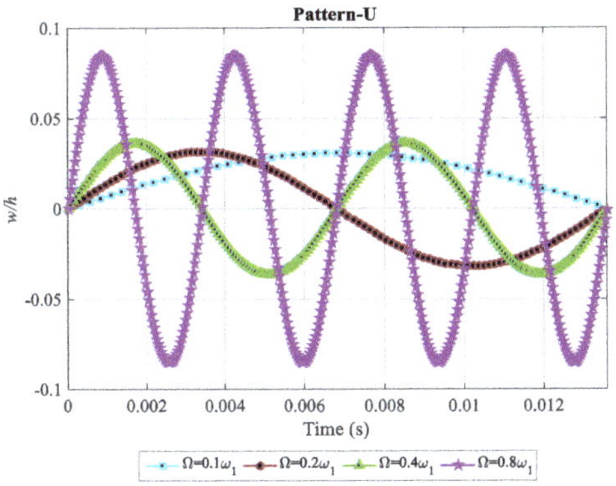

(**a**)

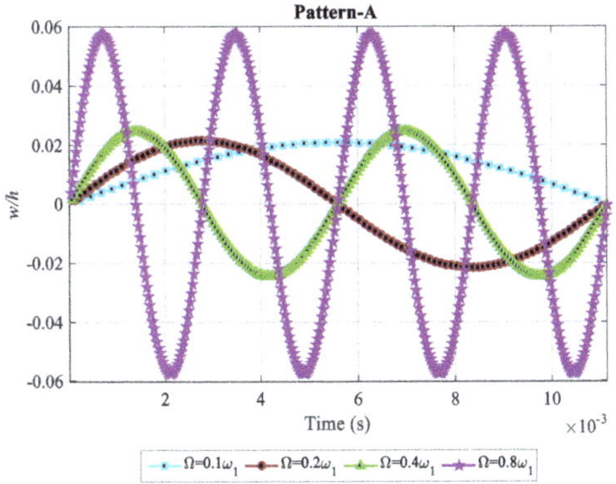

(**b**)

Figure 7. Time history of elastically constrained graphene origami-enabled auxetic metamaterial beam versus excitation frequency (h = 0.01 m, L = 0.20 m, W_{Gr} = 2.5 wt%, H_{Gr} = 100%, K_W = 2.0, K_P = 0.2). (**a**) Pattern-U; (**b**) Pattern-A.

5. Conclusions

The forced vibrational behaviour of elastically constrained graphene origami-enabled auxetic metamaterial beams subjected to harmonic external forces has been investigated. The three coupled equations of motion were adopted from the literature and were modified to take into account external forcing and constraint effects. These equations were numerically solved using a set of trigonometric functions and then validated by comparing the natural frequencies with those of non-metamaterial beams available in the literature. Extensive numerical simulations were subsequently performed to analyse the forced vibration response of the metamaterial beam under harmonic excitations, focusing on the influence of the graphene origami content, distribution patterns, folding degree, and the elastic foundation linear and shear-layer stiffnesses. For the elastically constrained metamaterial beam studied in this study, the following conclusions have been reached:

- Similar to non-metamaterial beams, in general, having elastic constraints reduces the forced vibration amplitude of the metamaterial beam.
- At a fixed graphene weight fraction (W_{Gr} = 2.5 wt%), both Pattern-U and Pattern-A exhibit similar amplitudes with a minor difference and harmonic behaviour for H_{Gr} = 20%. However, for H_{Gr} = 50%, Pattern-A shows a lower amplitude compared to Pattern-U, and this difference becomes more dominant as H_{Gr} increases to 100%.
- For graphene folding degrees $\leq$ 60% (for the H_{Gr} cases studied in this paper), the transverse deflection generally decreases as the graphene weight fraction (W_{Gr}) increases. However, for H_{Gr} = 100%, the transverse vibration amplitude initially increases with W_{Gr}, and then starts decreasing thereafter.
- For the excitation frequencies lower than the fundamental linear frequency, the amplitude increases with the forcing frequency; however, no phase-shift is observed.

Author Contributions: Conceptualization, B.K. and M.H.G.; methodology, B.K. and M.H.G.; software, B.K.; validation: B.K.; formal analysis, B.K. and M.H.G.; investigation, B.K. and M.H.G.; writing—original draft, B.K.; writing—review and editing, M.H.G.; supervision, M.H.G. All authors have read and agreed to the published version of the manuscript.

Funding: This research received no external funding.

Data Availability Statement: This paper is part of an ongoing study and hence the data cannot be shared at this stage.

Acknowledgments: The Higher Degree by Research support of the University of Adelaide, and the Faculty of Sciences, Engineering, and Technology at the University of Adelaide, is acknowledged.

Conflicts of Interest: The authors declare that they have no known competing financial interests or personal relationships that could have appeared to influence the work reported in this paper.

References

1. Beards, C. *Engineering Vibration Analysis with Application to Control Systems*; Elsevier: Amsterdam, The Netherlands, 1995.
2. Norton, M.P.; Karczub, D.G. *Fundamentals of Noise and Vibration Analysis for Engineers*; Cambridge University Press: Cambridge, UK, 2003.
3. De Silva, C.W. *Vibration: Fundamentals and Practice*; CRC Press: Boca Raton, FL, USA, 2006.
4. Tornabene, F.; Fantuzzi, N.; Bacciocchi, M. Refined shear deformation theories for laminated composite arches and beams with variable thickness: Natural frequency analysis. *Eng. Anal. Bound. Elem.* **2019**, *100*, 24–47. [CrossRef]
5. Nicolaou, Z.G.; Motter, A.E. Mechanical metamaterials with negative compressibility transitions. *Nat. Mater.* **2012**, *11*, 608–613. [CrossRef] [PubMed]
6. Chen, J.; Hu, L.; Deng, J.; Xing, X. Negative thermal expansion in functional materials: Controllable thermal expansion by chemical modifications. *Chem. Soc. Rev.* **2015**, *44*, 3522–3567. [CrossRef] [PubMed]
7. Huang, C.; Chen, L. Negative Poisson's ratio in modern functional materials. *Adv. Mater.* **2016**, *28*, 8079–8096. [CrossRef]

8. Tan, X.; Chen, S.; Wang, B.; Tang, J.; Wang, L.; Zhu, S.; Yao, K.; Xu, P. Real-time tunable negative stiffness mechanical metamaterial. *Extrem. Mech. Lett.* **2020**, *41*, 100990. [CrossRef]
9. Karampour, S.; Ghavanloo, E.; Fazelzadeh, S.A. Free vibration analysis of elastic metamaterial circular curved beams with locally resonant microstructures. *Arch. Appl. Mech.* **2023**, *93*, 323–333. [CrossRef]
10. Karami, B.; Ghayesh, M.H. Dynamics of graphene origami-enabled auxetic metamaterial beams via various shear deformation theories. *Int. J. Eng. Sci.* **2024**, *203*, 104123. [CrossRef]
11. Zhao, S.; Zhang, Y.; Zhang, Y.; Yang, J.; Kitipornchai, S. A functionally graded auxetic metamaterial beam with tunable nonlinear free vibration characteristics via graphene origami. *Thin-Walled Struct.* **2022**, *181*, 109997. [CrossRef]
12. Murari, B.; Zhao, S.; Zhang, Y.; Yang, J. Graphene origami-enabled auxetic metamaterial tapered beams in fluid: Nonlinear vibration and postbuckling analyses via physics-embedded machine learning model. *Appl. Math. Model.* **2023**, *122*, 598–613. [CrossRef]
13. Ebrahimi, F.; Parsi, M. Wave propagation analysis of functionally graded graphene origami-enabled auxetic metamaterial beams resting on an elastic foundation. *Acta Mech.* **2023**, *234*, 6169–6190. [CrossRef]
14. Kacar, A.; Tan, H.T.; Kaya, M.O. Free vibration analysis of beams on variable winkler elastic foundation by using the differential transform method. *Math. Comput. Appl.* **2011**, *16*, 773–783. [CrossRef]
15. Kumar, S. Free vibration analysis on axially graded beam resting on variable Pasternak foundation. *IOP Conf. Ser. Mater. Sci. Eng.* **2021**, *1206*, 012016. [CrossRef]
16. Avcar, M.; Mohammed, W.K.M. Free vibration of functionally graded beams resting on Winkler-Pasternak foundation. *Arab. J. Geosci.* **2018**, *11*, 232. [CrossRef]
17. Chen, B.; Lin, B.; Zhao, X.; Zhu, W.; Yang, Y.; Li, Y. Closed-form solutions for forced vibrations of a cracked double-beam system interconnected by a viscoelastic layer resting on Winkler–Pasternak elastic foundation. *Thin-Walled Struct.* **2021**, *163*, 107688. [CrossRef]
18. Nguyen, N.-D.; Nguyen, T.-N.; Nguyen, T.-K.; Vo, T.P. A Legendre-Ritz solution for bending, buckling and free vibration behaviours of porous beams resting on the elastic foundation. In *Structures*; Elsevier: Amsterdam, The Netherlands, 2023; pp. 1934–1950.
19. Al Rifaie, M.; Abdulhadi, H.; Mian, A. Advances in mechanical metamaterials for vibration isolation: A review. *Adv. Mech. Eng.* **2022**, *14*, 16878132221082872. [CrossRef]
20. Kumar, R.; Kumar, M.; Chohan, J.S.; Kumar, S. Overview on metamaterial: History, types and applications. *Mater. Today Proc.* **2022**, *56*, 3016–3024. [CrossRef]
21. Hamzehei, R.; Bodaghi, M.; Wu, N. Mastering the art of designing mechanical metamaterials with quasi-zero stiffness for passive vibration isolation: A review. *Smart Mater. Struct.* **2024**, *33*, 083001. [CrossRef]
22. Murari, B.; Zhao, S.; Zhang, Y.; Ke, L.; Yang, J. Vibrational characteristics of functionally graded graphene origami-enabled auxetic metamaterial beams with variable thickness in fluid. *Eng. Struct.* **2023**, *277*, 115440. [CrossRef]
23. Zhao, S.; Zhang, Y.; Zhang, Y.; Zhang, W.; Yang, J.; Kitipornchai, S. Genetic programming-assisted micromechanical models of graphene origami-enabled metal metamaterials. *Acta Mater.* **2022**, *228*, 117791. [CrossRef]
24. Karami, B.; Janghorban, M.; Fahham, H. On the stress analysis of anisotropic curved panels. *Int. J. Eng. Sci.* **2022**, *172*, 103625. [CrossRef]
25. Avey, M.; Fantuzzi, N.; Sofiyev, A. Vibration of laminated functionally graded nanocomposite structures considering the transverse shear stresses and rotary inertia. *Compos. Struct.* **2022**, *301*, 116209. [CrossRef]
26. Ouyang, Q.; Kang, G.; Zhuang, X.; Rabczuk, T.; Chen, P. Development of crack surface tracking algorithm for explosive fracture simulation with three-dimensional numerical manifold method. *Eng. Fract. Mech.* **2024**, *313*, 110645. [CrossRef]
27. Moghadasi, K.; Ghayesh, M.H.; Hu, E.; Li, J. Nonlinear biomechanics of diseased carotid arteries. *Int. J. Eng. Sci.* **2024**, *199*, 104070. [CrossRef]
28. Karami, B.; Ghayesh, M.H. Wave propagation characteristics of quasi-3D graphene origami-enabled auxetic metamaterial plates. *Int. J. Eng. Sci.* **2025**, *207*, 104185. [CrossRef]
29. Şimşek, M.; Kocatürk, T. Free vibration analysis of beams by using a third-order shear deformation theory. *Sadhana* **2007**, *32*, 167–179. [CrossRef]
30. Zhao, S.; Zhang, Y.; Zhang, Y.; Yang, J.; Kitipornchai, S. Graphene origami-enabled auxetic metallic metamaterials: An atomistic insight. *Int. J. Mech. Sci.* **2021**, *212*, 106814. [CrossRef]

Mathematical and Computational Applications

MDPI

Article

A Mathematical Approach to the Buckling Problem of Axially Loaded Laminated Nanocomposite Cylindrical Shells in Various Environments

Abdullah H. Sofiyev [1,2,3,*], Mahmure Avey [4,5] and Nigar M. Aslanova [6]

1 Department of Mathematics, Istanbul Ticaret University, 34445 Istanbul, Turkey
2 Scientific Research Department, Azerbaijan University of Architecture and Construction, Baku AZ1073, Azerbaijan
3 Scientific Research Centers, Odlar Yurdu University, Baku AZ1073, Azerbaijan
4 Application and Research Center, Istanbul Ticaret University, 34445 Istanbul, Turkey; mahmureavey@gmail.com
5 Analytical Information Resources Center, UNEC-Azerbaijan State Economic University, Baku AZ1001, Azerbaijan
6 Department of Mathematics, Azerbaijan University of Architecture and Construction, Baku AZ1073, Azerbaijan; nigar.aslanova@yahoo.com
* Correspondence: aavey@ticaret.edu.tr

Abstract: In this study, the solution of the buckling problem of axially loaded laminated cylindrical shells consisting of functionally graded (FG) nanocomposites in elastic and thermal environments is presented within extended first-order shear deformation theory (FOST) for the first time. The effective material properties and thermal expansion coefficients of nanocomposites in the layers are computed using the extended rule of mixture method and molecular dynamics simulation techniques. The governing relations and equations for laminated cylindrical shells consisting of FG nanocomposites on the two-parameter elastic foundation and in thermal environments are mathematically modeled and solved to find the expression for the axial buckling load. The numerical results of the current analytical approach agree well with the existing literature results obtained using a different methodology. Finally, some new results and interpretations are provided by investigating the influences of different parameters such as elastic foundations, thermal environments, FG nanocomposite models, shear stress, and stacking sequences on the axial buckling load.

Keywords: FG nanocomposite orthotropic material; cross-ply cylindrical shells; stability; thermal environment; two-parameter elastic foundation; axial buckling load

MSC: 74E05; 74E10; 74H55; 74K25; 74F05; 74G10

1. Introduction

The use of laminated cylindrical structural elements on elastic foundations and in thermal environments is frequently encountered in advanced technologies. For the correct formulation of engineering problems regarding structural elements consisting of new or traditional composites on elastic soils, the accurate and realistic mathematical modeling of their interactions is very important. There are various models in the literature that describe the interaction between the behavior of structural elements on the ground and the behavior of the ground itself. The first mathematical model for elastic soil was proposed by Winkler, and the theoretical principles of one-parameter elastic soil were determined [1]. Since the Winkler foundation model was inadequate in some cases, researchers developed various foundation models such as the Hetenyi model, Vlassov and Leontev model, Kerr model, Filonenko–Borodich model, and the Pasternak model to describe the ground continuous environment more realistically [2–5]. One of the most realistic and useful of those models was suggested by Pasternak, and that model will be used in this study. In the Pasternak model, the shear layer, consisting of elements that can only perform vertical displacement and are not compressed, was considered on the springs in the Winkler model [6].

Laminated cylindrical shells used in various branches of contemporary engineering may be exposed to axial compressive loads when operating in elastic and thermal environments. Since the load-carrying capacity of cylindrical shells is determined mainly by buckling, determining the optimal value of the mechanical loads acting on them in elastic and thermal environments is very important in terms of design [7]. Comprehensive and fundamental studies on the theory and applications of laminated homogeneous shells are included in the books of Ambartsumian [8] and Reddy [9]. The first studies on the buckling behavior of axially loaded laminated homogeneous orthotropic composite cylindrical shells were performed without considering the effects of the ground and thermal environments [10–13]. There are some studies on the buckling behavior of axially loaded laminated homogeneous orthotropic composite cylindrical shells in elastic and/or thermal environments [14,15].

The discovery of carbon nanotubes (CNTs) has led to the formation of polymer, metal, ceramic, and other matrix-based nanocomposites. In the last two decades, great attention has been paid to the development of polymer nanocomposites in which at least one of the filler dimensions is in the nanometer range. There are many studies focusing on the modeling of polymer-based nanocomposites via molecular dynamics simulation techniques [16–19]. The mentioned studies have shown that molecular modeling techniques are effective in predicting both the structure and elastic mechanical properties of polymer-based nanocomposites. Polymer-based nanocomposites have outstanding mechanical, thermal, chemical, and physical properties proven by numerous studies [20–25]. In those studies, a comprehensive review of the basic concepts, synthesis, technologies, and applications of polymer nanocomposites is presented. A more effective way to improve the buckling capacity of CNT-reinforced structures in different environments is to use CNTs in FG, with the idea of including it in the concept. Shen [26] introduced the concept of FG-CNT-reinforced composite material, which is obtained by functionally dispersing aligned and flat single-walled CNTs in an isotropic polymer matrix. This study has led to new scientific research [27–34]. Nevertheless, the number of publications on the buckling problem of laminated nanocomposite unconstrained structural elements in thermal environments is limited [35–37], and the number of similar studies considering both soil and thermal effects is also quite limited [38–40]. In recent years, 3D non-local solution methods have been developed for multilayer functionally graded shells with a layer-based approach and the differential quadrature method (DQM) [41–43]. These studies will lead to more realistic results in the future investigation of the behavior of new-generation multilayer heterogeneous structural elements.

Based on the literature review and the authors' knowledge, the buckling behavior of axially loaded cross-ply laminated cylindrical shells consisting of nanocomposite plies subjected to elastic and thermal media has not been sufficiently investigated in the framework of the extended FOST so far. The shear deformation shell theory for homogeneous orthotropic materials [8], which was extended to laminated functionally graded nanocomposite orthotropic shells by Sofiyev [35], is used in this study. The extended FOST can accurately predict the structural responses (buckling and vibration) of laminated shells prepared from layers of FG nanocomposite materials. Generally, one of the most important advantages of this theory is that it does not require the use of shear correction factors.

The surrounding elastic soil is modeled as the two-parameter elastic foundation or the Pasternak-type elastic foundation. The material of each lay-up is assumed to be linearly elastic, orthotropic, reinforced with CNTs, and vary with temperature. The buckling behavior of cross-ply laminated cylindrical shells made of FG nanocomposite material plies is based on the extended ST. Numerical examples demonstrate the buckling response of axially loaded laminated anisotropic cylindrical nanocomposite shells on elastic foundations and in thermal environments. The analysis of shells resting on elastic soil is carried out by three-stage modeling. First, the appropriate soil model that best represents the mutual behavior of the shell and the soil is selected, the characteristic quantities of the soil and the shell are determined realistically, and then the problem is solved by mathematical modeling using the data obtained.

The structure of this paper is as follows: Section 2 is on the mathematical modeling of soil and thermo-mechanical properties of nanocomposite layers. In Section 3, the governing equations of laminated FG nanocomposite cylindrical shells are introduced. Section 4 includes the boundary conditions and solution procedure. Section 5 covers the numerical analyses and their interpretations, and Section 6 covers the conclusions.

2. Mathematical Modeling

Consider a moderately thick laminated cylindrical shell with a total thickness h consisting of N functionally graded nanocomposite orthotropic plies of identical thickness $t = h/N$, subjected to an axial load $N_{11}^0 = -N_0$, $N_{22}^0 = N_{12}^0 = 0$, where $N_{pq}^0(p,q = 1,2)$ are the pre-buckling load resultants. The dimensions and coordinate system of the laminated cylindrical shell on the elastic foundation are plotted in Figure 1. The displacement (u, v and w) coordinates are x, y, and z, respectively, for axial, circumferential, and thickness directions (Figure 1). The laminated cylindrical shell has dimensions L and r, which specify the length and radius, respectively. ϕ_x and ϕ_y are the rotations of normal to the mid-surface versus the y- and x-axes, respectively. The elastic foundation represented by the two-parameter foundation model, i.e., reaction of the foundation, is assumed to be [2–6]

$$R = K_w w - K_p\left(w_{,xx} + w_{,yy}\right) \tag{1}$$

where commas indicate partial derivatives with respect to coordinates, R indicates the force per unit area, and K_w and K_p indicate the Winkler foundation stiffness and the shearing layer coefficient of the foundation, respectively. Let Φ be the stress function for forced defined by [8,9]

$$(N_{11}, N_{22}, N_{12}) = h\left(\Phi_{,yy},\ \Phi_{,xx},\ -\Phi_{,xy}\right) \tag{2}$$

The distribution scheme of CNTs along the shell thickness is either uniformly distributed (referred to U) or in the form of linear functions (referred to as $\diamond$ and X). As shown in Figure 2, for the uniformly distributed CNT layer type (U), the CNTs are evenly distributed throughout the entire thickness; for the functionally graded CNT layer scheme X, the CNTs are concentrated in both the top and bottom regions; while for the functionally graded CNT layer scheme $\diamond$, the CNTs are concentrated in the center regions. The dispersion schemes of CNTs in the layers visually presented in Figure 2 are mathematically defined as follows [26,35–38]:

$$V_{CN}^{(i)} = \begin{cases} V_{CN}^{*(i)} & (U) \\ 2V_{CN}^{*(i)}\left(1 - 2\frac{|z|}{t}\right) & (\diamond) \\ 2V_{CN}^{*(i)}\frac{2|z|}{t} & (X) \end{cases} \tag{3}$$

where $V_{CN}^{*(i)}$ is the volume fraction of the ith-ply and computed as

$$\frac{1}{V_{CN}^{*(i)}} = \frac{\rho_m^{(i)} - \rho_{CN}^{(i)}}{\rho_m^{(i)}} + \frac{\rho_{CN}^{(i)}}{w_{CN}^{(i)} \rho_m^{(i)}} \tag{4}$$

in which $w_{CN}^{(i)}, \rho_{CN}^{(i)}$, and $\rho_m^{(i)}$ are the mass fraction of CNTs and the densities of CNTs and the polymer phase in the ith-ply, respectively.

The material properties and thermal expansion coefficients of the FG nanocomposite orthotropic material in the ith layer are defined by [35–38]

$$\begin{aligned} &E_{11(Z,T)}^{(i)} = \eta_1^{(i)} V_{CN}^{(i)} E_{11(T)}^{CN(i)} + V_m^{(i)} E_{m(T)}^{(i)}, \quad \frac{\eta_2^{(i)}}{E_{22(Z,T)}^{(i)}} = \frac{V_{CN}^{(i)}}{E_{22(T)}^{CN(i)}} + \frac{V_m^{(i)}}{E_{m(T)}^{(i)}}, \quad \frac{\eta_3^{(i)}}{G_{12(Z,T)}^{(i)}} = \frac{V_{CN}^{(i)}}{G_{12(T)}^{CN(i)}} + \frac{V_m^{(i)}}{G_{m(T)}^{(i)}}, \\ &G_{13(Z,T)}^{(i)} = G_{12(Z,T)}^{(i)}, \quad G_{23(Z,T)}^{(i)} = 1.2 G_{12(Z,T)}^{(i)}, \alpha_{11(Z,T)}^{(i)} = \frac{V_{CN}^{(i)} E_{11(T)}^{CN(i)} \alpha_{11(T)}^{CN(i)} + V_m^{(i)} E_{m(T)}^{(i)} \alpha_{(T)}^{m(i)}}{V_{CN}^{(i)} E_{11(T)}^{CN(i)} + V_m^{(i)} E_{m(T)}^{(i)}}, \\ &V_{CN}^{(i)} + V_m^{(i)} = 1, \quad \alpha_{22(Z,T)}^{(i)} = (1 + \nu_{12}^{CN(i)}) V_{CN}^{(i)} \alpha_{22(T)}^{CN(i)} + (1 + \nu_m^{(i)}) V_m^{(i)} \alpha_{m(T)}^{(i)} - \nu_{12}^{(i)} \alpha_{11(Z,T)}^{(i)}. \end{aligned} \tag{5}$$

where $E_{pp(T)}^{CN(i)}, G_{pq(T)}^{CN(i)}, \alpha_{pp(Z,T)}^{CN(i)} (p = 1,2, q = 1,2,3)$, and $E_{m(T)}^{(i)}, G_{m(T)}^{(i)}, \alpha_{m(T)}^{(i)}$ are the Young and shear moduli and the thermal expansion coefficients of the CNT and polymer, respectively. In Equation (3), $\eta_q^{(i)}$ denotes the efficiency parameters of CNT in the ith lay-up, which draw the scale-dependent material properties of CNTs. Their evaluation is achieved by matching the Young modulus of FG nanocomposite plies observed from the molecular dynamic simulations [16–19].

According to the extended rule of mixture, the Poisson ratio and density of the layers are assumed to be constant since they are weakly dependent on the temperature change and location, calculated as follows [26,35–38]:

$$\nu_{12}^{(i)} = V_{CN}^{*(i)} \nu_{12}^{CN(i)} + V_m^{(i)} \nu^{m(i)}, \quad \rho_t^{(i)} = V_{CN}^{*(i)} \rho_{CN}^{(i)} + V_m^{(i)} \rho_m^{(i)} \tag{6}$$

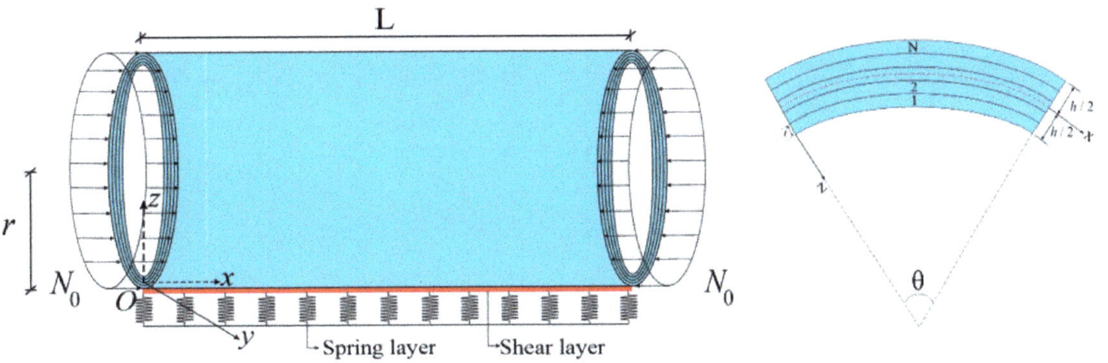

(**a**) (**b**)

Figure 1. Notation: (**a**) axially loaded cross-ply laminated cylindrical shell on the elastic foundation and coordinate system; (**b**) staking sequences.

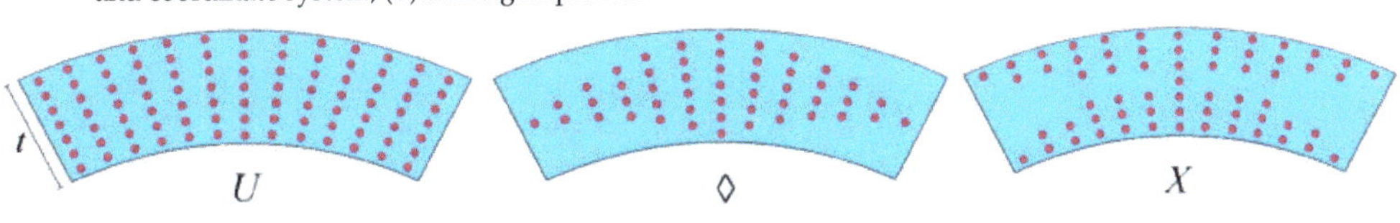

Figure 2. Dispersion schemes of CNTs in the layers.

3. Governing Equations

In this study, the buckling analysis of the cylindrical shells is discussed within the framework of the FOST. According to the FOST, the displacement components may be represented by [9]

$$u_1 = u(x,y) + z\phi_1(x,y),\ u_2 = v(x,y) + z\phi_2(x,y),\ \ u_3 = w(x,y) \tag{7}$$

where the displacements at the mid-surface are denoted by u, v, and w, and the rotations of a normal to the reference in the y and x directions are denoted by $\phi_1(x,y)$ and $\phi_2(x,y)$, respectively.

The constitutive relationships for FG nanocomposite layers, which are functions of location and temperature together, used in the construction of the basic equations on the FOST basis are expressed as follows [35]:

$$\begin{bmatrix} \sigma_{11}^{(i)} \\ \sigma_{22}^{(i)} \\ \sigma_{12}^{(i)} \\ \sigma_{13}^{(i)} \\ \sigma_{23}^{(i)} \end{bmatrix} = \begin{bmatrix} U_{11(Z,T)}^{(i)} & U_{12(Z,T)}^{(i)} & 0 & 0 & 0 \\ U_{21(Z,T)}^{(i)} & U_{22(Z,T)}^{(i)} & 0 & 0 & 0 \\ 0 & 0 & U_{66(Z,T)}^{(i)} & 0 & 0 \\ 0 & 0 & 0 & U_{55(Z,T)}^{(i)} & 0 \\ 0 & 0 & 0 & 0 & U_{44(Z,T)}^{(i)} \end{bmatrix} \begin{bmatrix} e_{11} \\ e_{22} \\ \gamma_{12} \\ \gamma_{13} \\ \gamma_{23} \end{bmatrix} + \begin{bmatrix} \sigma_{11(T)}^{(i)} \\ \sigma_{22(T)}^{(i)} \\ 0 \\ 0 \\ 0 \end{bmatrix} \tag{8}$$

where

$$\begin{aligned} \sigma_{11(T)}^{(i)} &= -\left[U_{11(Z,T)}^{(i)}\alpha_{11(Z,T)}^{(i)} + U_{12(Z,T)}^{(i)}\alpha_{22(Z,T)}^{(i)}\right]T(Z) \\ \sigma_{22(T)}^{(i)} &= -\left[U_{21(Z,T)}^{(i)}\alpha_{11(Z,T)}^{(i)} + U_{22(Z,T)}^{(i)}\alpha_{22(Z,T)}^{(i)}\right]T(Z) \end{aligned} \tag{9}$$

in which $\sigma_{pq}^{(i)}(p = 1,2, q = 1,2,3)$, e_{pp}, and γ_{pq} are the stresses and strains of the ith-ply consisting of FG nanocomposite materials, and $U_{pq(Z,T)}^{(i)}$ is defined by

$$\begin{aligned} & U_{11(Z,T)}^{(i)} = \frac{E_{11(Z,T)}^{(i)}}{1-\nu_{12}^{(i)}\nu_{21}^{(i)}},\ U_{22(Z,T)}^{(i)} = \frac{E_{22(Z,T)}^{(i)}}{1-\nu_{12}^{(i)}\nu_{21}^{(i)}},\ U_{12(Z,T)}^{(i)} = \frac{\nu_{21}^{(i)}E_{11(Z,T)}^{(i)}}{1-\nu_{12}^{(i)}\nu_{21}^{(i)}}, \\ & U_{21(Z,T)}^{(i)} = \frac{\nu_{12}^{(i)}E_{22(Z,T)}^{(i)}}{1-\nu_{12}^{(i)}\nu_{21}^{(i)}},\ U_{44(Z,T)}^{(i)} = G_{23(Z,T)}^{(i)},\ U_{55(Z,T)}^{(i)} = G_{13(Z,T)}^{(i)},\ U_{66(Z,T)}^{(i)} = G_{12(Z,T)}^{(i)} \end{aligned} \tag{10}$$

The variation in shear stresses along the thickness direction of the ith-ply consisting of the FG nanocomposites within the ST can be defined by [8,35]

$$\sigma_z^{(i)} = 0,\ \sigma_{13}^{(i)} = \frac{dJ^{(i)}}{dz}\phi_1(x,y),\ \sigma_{23}^{(i)} = \frac{dJ^{(i)}}{dz}\phi_2(x,y) \tag{11}$$

where $J^{(i)}$ represents the shear stress shape functions on the piles.

The following expressions are obtained for the strains after the mathematical operations performed on Equations (8), (9) and (11) [35]:

$$\begin{bmatrix} e_{11} \\ e_{22} \\ \gamma_{12} \end{bmatrix} = \begin{bmatrix} e_{11}^0 - zw_{,xx} + \Pi_{1(z,T)}^{(i)}\phi_{1,x} \\ e_{22}^0 - zw_{,yy} + \Pi_{2(z,T)}^{(i)}\phi_{2,y} \\ \gamma_{12}^0 - 2zw_{,xy} + \Pi_{1(z,T)}^{(i)}\phi_{1,y} + \Pi_{2(z,T)}^{(i)}\phi_{2,x} \end{bmatrix} \tag{12}$$

where e^0_{11}, e^0_{22}, γ^0_{12} represent strains on the mid-surface and $\Pi^{(i)}_{p(z,T)}$, defined as follows:

$$\Pi^{(i)}_{1(z,T)} = \int_0^z \frac{1}{U^{(i)}_{55(Z,T)}} \frac{dJ^{(i)}}{dz} dz, \quad \Pi^{(i)}_{2(z,T)} = \int_0^z \frac{1}{U^{(i)}_{44(Z,T)}} \frac{dJ^{(i)}}{dz} dz. \tag{13}$$

The relation of resultant forces and moments of laminated shells consisting of FG nanocomposite materials can be represented as follows [8–10]:

$$(N_{pq}, Q_{p3}, M_{pq}) = \sum_{i=1}^{N} \int_{z_{i-1}}^{z_i} \left[\sigma^{(i)}_{pq}, \sigma^{(i)}_{q3}, z\sigma^{(i)}_{pq}\right] dz. \tag{14}$$

The relation for resultant thermal forces $(N_{pp(T)})$ and moments $M_{pp(T)}$, $(p = 1,2)$ used in the derivation of the basic equations is determined as follows [26,35]:

$$\begin{aligned}
(N_{11(T)}, M_{11(T)}) &= \sum_{i=1}^{N} \int_{z_{i-1}}^{z_i} \begin{bmatrix} U^{(k)}_{11(Z,T)} & 0 \\ 0 & U^{(k)}_{12(Z,T)} \end{bmatrix} \begin{bmatrix} \alpha^{(i)}_{11(Z,T)} \\ \alpha^{(i)}_{22(Z,T)} \end{bmatrix} [1, z](T - T_0) dz, \\
(N_{22(T)}, M_{22(T)}) &= \sum_{i=1}^{N} \int_{z_{i-1}}^{z_i} \begin{bmatrix} U^{(i)}_{21(Z,T)} & 0 \\ 0 & U^{(i)}_{22(Z,T)} \end{bmatrix} \begin{bmatrix} \alpha^{(i)}_{11(Z,T)} \\ \alpha^{(i)}_{22(Z,T)} \end{bmatrix} [1, z](T - T_0) dz.
\end{aligned} \tag{15}$$

where T_0 is the reference temperature at which thermal strains do not yet exist, and T represents the temperature rise from $T_0(\mathrm{K}) = 300$.

Based on extended Ambartsumian's shear deformation theory [8,35], including shell–foundation interaction and thermal effects, the stability and compatibility equations for axially loaded laminated cylindrical shell consisting of FG nanocomposite plies resting on the two-parameter elastic foundation can be derived in terms of the stress function Φ, two rotations ϕ_1 and ϕ_2, and transverse displacement w as follows:

$$\begin{aligned}
& h\left[(\Lambda_{11} - \Lambda_{31})\Phi_{,xxyy} + \Lambda_{12}\Phi_{,xxxx}\right] - \Lambda_{13}w_{,xxxx} - (\Lambda_{14} + \Lambda_{32})w_{,xxyy} + \Lambda_{15}\phi_{1,xxx} + \Lambda_{35}\phi_{1,xyy} \\
& -\Pi_3\phi_{1,x} + (\Lambda_{18} + \Lambda_{38})\phi_{2,xxy} = 0, \\
& h\left[\Lambda_{21}\Phi_{,yyyy} + (\Lambda_{22} - \Lambda_{31})\Phi_{,xxyy}\right] - (\Lambda_{32} + \Lambda_{23})w_{,xxyy} - \Lambda_{24}w_{,yyyy} + (\Lambda_{35} + \Lambda_{25})\phi_{1,xyy} + \Lambda_{38}\phi_{2,yyx} \\
& +\Lambda_{28}\phi_{2,yyy} - \Pi_4\phi_{2,y} = 0, \\
& h\left[\Gamma_{11}\Phi_{,yyyy} + (\Gamma_{12} + \Gamma_{21} + \Gamma_{31})\Phi_{,xxyy} + \Gamma_{22}\Phi_{,xxxx}\right] + \tfrac{1}{r}w_{,xx} - (\Gamma_{24} + \Gamma_{13} - \Gamma_{32})w_{,xxyy} \\
& -\Gamma_{14}w_{,yyyy} - \Gamma_{23}w_{,xxxx} + \Gamma_{25}\phi_{1,xxx} + (\Gamma_{15} + \Gamma_{35})\phi_{1,xyy} + (\Gamma_{28} + \Gamma_{38})\phi_{2,xxy} + \Gamma_{18}\phi_{2,xxx} = 0, \\
& \tfrac{h}{r}\Phi_{,xx} - N_0 w_{,xx} - K_w w + K_p(w_{,xx} + w_{,yy}) + \Pi_3\phi_{1,x} + \Pi_4\phi_{2,y} = 0.
\end{aligned} \tag{16}$$

For more details about the coefficients Π_3, Π_4, Λ_{pq}, and Γ_{pq}, the reader is referred to Appendix A.

4. Solution Procedure

The axially loaded simply supported laminated FG nanocomposite cylindrical shell corresponding boundary conditions are defined mathematically as follows [8,9]:

$$w = \Phi_{,yy} = \phi_2 = M_{11} = 0, \ at \ x = 0, \ L \tag{17}$$

In order to satisfy the simply supported boundary conditions in Equation (16), the airy stress function, displacements, and rotations are mathematically sought as follows [8,9,35]:

$$\Phi = C_1 \sin(\overline{m}x)\sin(\overline{n}y),\ w = C_2 \sin(\overline{m}x)\sin(\overline{n}y),\ \phi_1 = C_3 \cos(\overline{m}x)\sin(\overline{n}y),\ \phi_2 = C_4 \sin(\overline{m}x)\cos(\overline{n}y). \quad (18)$$

where C_i denotes unknown amplitudes, and $\overline{m} = \frac{m\pi}{L}$ and $\overline{n} = \frac{n}{r}$, in which (m, n) are wave numbers.

By substituting (18) into (16) and then applying the Galerkin method, one obtains the following:

$$[Q_{pq}]_{4\times4}[C_i]_{4\times1} = [0]_{4\times1} \quad (19)$$

where $Q_{pq}(p, q = 1, 2, \ldots, 4)$ are given in Appendix B.

The non-trivial solutions of homogenous algebraic Equation (19) are determined by equating the determinant of algebraic equations to zero as follows:

$$Q_{41}S_1 - \left[N_0\overline{m}^2 - K_w - K_P\left(\overline{m}^2 + \overline{n}^2\right)\right]S_2 + Q_{43}S_3 + Q_{44}S_4 = 0 \quad (20)$$

where

$$S_1 = -\begin{vmatrix} Q_{12} & Q_{13} & Q_{14} \\ Q_{22} & Q_{23} & Q_{24} \\ Q_{32} & Q_{33} & Q_{34} \end{vmatrix},\ S_2 = \begin{vmatrix} Q_{11} & Q_{13} & Q_{14} \\ Q_{21} & Q_{23} & Q_{24} \\ Q_{31} & Q_{33} & Q_{34} \end{vmatrix},\ S_3 = -\begin{vmatrix} Q_{11} & Q_{12} & Q_{14} \\ Q_{21} & Q_{22} & Q_{24} \\ Q_{31} & Q_{32} & Q_{34} \end{vmatrix},\ S_4 = \begin{vmatrix} Q_{11} & Q_{12} & Q_{13} \\ Q_{21} & Q_{22} & Q_{23} \\ Q_{31} & Q_{32} & Q_{33} \end{vmatrix} \quad (21)$$

From Equation (20), the expression for the axial buckling load (N_{0ST}^{bucwp}) on the two-parameter elastic foundation in thermal environments within the ST is as follows:

$$N_{0ST}^{bucwp} = \frac{Q_{41}S_1 + Q_{43}S_3 + Q_{44}S_4}{S_2\overline{m}^2} + \frac{K_w + K_p(\overline{m}^2 + \overline{n}^2)}{\overline{m}^2} \quad (22)$$

The expression for the nondimensional axial buckling load ($\overline{N}_{0ST}^{bucwp}$) on the two-parameter elastic foundation in thermal environments within FOST is defined by

$$\overline{N}_{0ST}^{bucwp} = \frac{N_{0ST}^{bucwp}}{hE_{m(T_0)}^{(1)}} \quad (23)$$

where $E_{m(T_0)}^{(1)}$ is the elasticity modulus of the matrix forming the single-layer cylindrical shell at $T_0 = 300\,\mathrm{K}$.

In this special case, by ignoring the effect of transverse shear strains from the basic relations and following the similar solution procedure, the expression for the nondimensional axial buckling load ($\overline{N}_{0CT}^{bucwp}$) on the two-parameter elastic foundation and in thermal environments in the framework of the classical theory (CT) can be obtained:

$$\begin{aligned} \overline{N}_{0CT}^{bucwp} &= \frac{1}{E_{m(T_0)}^{(1)}\overline{m}^2 h}\Big\{K_w + K_p(\overline{m}^2 + \overline{n}^2) + \left[\Lambda_{13}\overline{m}^4 + (\Lambda_{14} + 2\Lambda_{32} + \Lambda_{23})\overline{m}^2\overline{n}^2 + \Lambda_{24}\overline{n}^4\right] \\ &+ \left[\frac{\overline{m}^2}{r} - \Lambda_{12}\overline{m}^4 - (\Lambda_{11} - 2\Lambda_{31} + \Lambda_{22})\overline{m}^2\overline{n}^2 - \Lambda_{21}\overline{n}^4\right] \times \frac{\left[\overline{m}^2/r + \Gamma_{23}\overline{m}^4 + (\Gamma_{13} - \Gamma_{32} + \Gamma_{24})\overline{m}^2\overline{n}^2 + \Gamma_{14}\overline{n}^4\right]}{\Gamma_{22}\overline{m}^4 + (\Gamma_{12} + \Gamma_{31} + \Gamma_{21})\overline{m}^2\overline{n}^2 + \Gamma_{11}\overline{n}^4}\Big\} \end{aligned} \quad (24)$$

The expressions for the nondimensional axial buckling load in the soilless case from Formulas (22) and (24) are obtained as $K_w = K_p = 0$.

5. Numerical Analyses

5.1. Initial Data

This section aims to explain the stability behavior of axially loaded cylindrical shells consisting of FG nanocomposite layers resting on the two-parameter elastic foundation and in thermal environments within the FOST and CT based on numerical analysis and interpretations.

The effective material properties of two-phase composites consisting of the mixture of CNTs and PMMA, whose short name is poly (methyl methacrylate), are estimated according to the modified extended rule of the mixture rule method. The PMMA properties in each layer are as follows: $\nu_m = 0.34$, $\alpha_{m(T)} = [45 + 0.0225(T - T_0)] \times 10^{-6}/\text{K}$ and $E_{m(T)} = (3.52 - 0.0034T) \times 10^9\,(\text{Pa})$. At the reference temperature, $\alpha_{m(T)} = \alpha_m = 45 \times 10^{-6}/\text{K}$ [26,33]. (10, 10) armchair single-walled carbon nanotubes (SWCNTs), with properties $a^{CN} = 9.26 \times 10^{-9}$ m, $r^{CN} = 6.8 \times 10^{-10}$ m, $h^{CN} = 6.7 \times 10^{-11}$ m, $\nu_{12}^{CN} = 0.175$ in each layer, are used as reinforcements, and the temperature-dependent material properties in the layers are evaluated as follows:

$$
\begin{aligned}
E_{11(T)}^{(i)CN} &= 6.18387 - 2.86 \times 10^{-3} \times T + 4.22867 \times 10^{-6} \times T^2 - 2.2724 \times 10^{-9} \times T^3\,(\text{TPa}) \\
E_{22(T)}^{(i)CN} &= 7.75348 - 3.58 \times 10^{-3} \times T + 5.30057 \times 10^{-6} \times T^2 - 2.84868 \times 10^{-9} \times T^3\,(\text{TPa}) \\
G_{12(T)}^{(i)CN} &= 1.80126 + 0.77845 \times 10^{-3} \times T - 1.1279 \times 10^{-6} \times T^2 + 4.93484 \times 10^{-10} \times T^3\,(\text{TPa}) \\
\alpha_{11(T)}^{(i)CN} &= (-1.12148 + 2.289 \times 10^{-2} \times T - 2.88155 \times 10^{-5} \times T^2 + 1.13253 \times 10^{-8} \times T^3) \times 10^{-6}(1/\text{K}) \\
\alpha_{22(T)}^{(i)CN} &= (5.43874 - 9.95498 \times 10^{-4} \times T + 3.13525 \times 10^{-7} \times T^2 - 3.56332 \times 10^{-12} \times T^3) \times 10^{(-6)}(1/\text{K})
\end{aligned}
\tag{25}
$$

The magnitudes of the material properties and thermal expansion coefficients for $T(\text{K}) = T_0, T_0 + 200, T_0 + 400$ of (10, 10) SWCNTs using Equation (25) are tabulated in Table 1.

The efficiency parameters $\eta_j^{(i)}\,(j = 1,2,3)$ are determined from the extended rule of the mixture method, and molecular dynamics simulation techniques were taken from the studies of [16–19], which are tabulated in Table 2. Since both PMMA/CNT and poly{(*m*-phenylenevinylene)-*co*-[(2,5-dioctoxy-*p*-phenylene) vinylene]} (PmPV)/CNT nanocomposites are used in the comparisons, the efficiency parameters of both are given in Table 2. At $T_0(\text{K}) = 300$, the Young modulus of PmPV is $E_{m(T_0)}^{(i)} = 2.1 \times 10^9$ (Pa), and other properties are the same as PMMA. The posteriori specified shape functions are defined by $J^{(i)}(z) = z\left(1 - \frac{4z^2}{3t^2}\right)$ [8].

Table 1. Temperature-dependent material properties of (10, 10) SWCNTs.

T (K)	$E_{11(T)}^{(i)CN}$ **(TPa)**	$E_{22(T)}^{(i)CN}$ **(TPa)**	$G_{12(T)}^{(i)CN}$ **(TPa)**	$\alpha_{11(T)}^{(i)CN} \times$ **10^{-6}/K**	$\alpha_{22(T)}^{(i)CN} \times$ **10^{-6}/K**
T_0	5.6465	7.0800	1.9445	3.4584	5.1641
$T_0 + 100$	5.5679	6.9814	1.9703	4.1496	5.0849
$T_0 + 200$	5.5308	6.9348	1.9643	4.5361	5.0120
$T_0 + 400$	5.4744	6.8641	1.9644	4.6677	4.8846

Table 2. Magnitudes of efficiency parameters for two sets of $V_{CN}^{*(i)}$.

$V_{CN}^{*(i)}$	$\eta_1^{(i)}$	$\eta_2^{(i)}$	$\eta_3^{(i)}$
	PMMA/CNT		
12%	0.137	1.626	0.715
17%	0.142	1.626	1.138
28%	0.141	1.585	1.109
	PmPV/CNT		
11%	0.149	0.150	0.149
14%	0.934	0.941	1.381
17%	0.934	0.941	1.381

5.2. Validation and Verification

In this subsection, the accuracy of the formulas obtained analytically is verified by comparing them with the results obtained using different theories and solution methodologies. The magnitudes of the axial buckling load of unconstrained single-layer cylindrical shells modeled with U- and X-shaped CNTs are listed in Table 3 for a comparison with the results of Shen [26] in thermal environments. It should be emphasized that in Shen's study [26], Reddy's higher-order shear deformation theory (HOST) is used [9]. A comparison was made with Shen's study [26]. Since the axial buckling load in thermal environment is used as $N_{Shen}^{STbuc} = 2\pi r N_{0ST}^{buc}$ in Ref. [26], expression (24) in our study is multiplied by $2\pi r$ at $K_w = K_p = 0$. The shell characteristics are $r = 6$ cm, $h = 0.2$ cm, $L = 19.87$ cm, $V_{CN}^{*(1)} = 17\%$ [26]. The elastic and thermal properties of the nanocomposite containing PMMA/CNT at different temperatures are presented in Tables 1 and 2. As can be seen from Table 3, the minimum values of the axial buckling load of the U- and X-shaped CNT cylindrical shells within FOST obtained in our study at T(K) = 300, 500, and 700 are in good agreement with the results of Shen [26]. The numbers in parentheses (m, n) are the wave numbers.

The axial buckling load of the single-layer cylindrical shell panels consisting of FG nanocomposite material with the X shape on the elastic foundation and in thermal environments within the ST is compared with the results of Shen and Xiang [36] who used the HOST proposed by Reddy [9] in Table 4. The dimensionless ground coefficients are defined as

$$k_w = K_w b^4 / E_m^{(1)} h^3, \; k_p = K_p b^2 / E_m^{(1)} h^3$$

and geometric data are $a = 0.98b$, $r = 2a$, $b = 20h$, $h = 0.1$ cm, and $(m, n) = (1, 1)$ [36]. Since the axial buckling load on the elastic foundation and in thermal environments is used as $N_{Shen}^{STbuc} = \left[b^2/(2h\pi^2)\right] N_{0ST}^{buc}$ in Ref. [36], expression (22) in our study is multiplied by $\left[b^2/(2h\pi^2)\right]$. The elastic and thermal properties of the nanocomposite containing PMMA/CNT at T(K) = 300, 400, and 500 are presented in Table 1. A comparative assessment of the results is presented in Table 4. The good agreement between our results and the predictions in the literature confirms the robustness and accuracy of the proposed formulation.

Table 5 compares the nondimensional axial buckling load ($\widetilde{N}_{0ST}^{buc} = N_{0ST}^{buc} b^2 / E_m^{(1)} h^3$) of the uniaxially loaded laminated flat panel consisting of U nanocomposite material (PmPV/CNT) plies with the $(0°/90°/90°/0°)$ stacking sequence without elastic foundation with the results of Lei et al. [37] and Chakraborty et al. [38] using different solution methodologies for different $V_{CN}^{*(i)}$ $(i = 4)$, and the necessary parameters are set to be $(a/b = 1$, $a/h = 10$, $r \to \infty$, $h = 2$ mm, $K_w = K_p = 0$, $(m, n) = (1, 1)$, $T_0(\mathrm{K}) = 300)$. It is seen that our results are in good agreement with the results of Lei et al. [37], who used the

FOST and the meshless kp-Ritz method, and with the results of Chakraborty et al. [38], who used the HOST proposed by Reddy [9].

Table 3. Comparison of axial buckling load of single-layer cylindrical shells with U and X schemes within ST.

	$N_{Shen}^{STbuc}=2\pi r N_{0ST}^{buc}(in\ kN),\ (m,n)$			
	U	**X**	**U**	**X**
***T*(K)**	**Shen [26]**		**Present Study**	
$T=T_0$	122.25	148.06	121.80 (2,4)	150.33 (1,3)
T_0+200	97.56	113.56	96.84 (2,4)	113.98 (1,3)
T_0+400	68.96	76.49	70.31 (1,3)	76.74 (1,3)

Table 4. Comparisons of axial buckling load (in KN) for monolayer cylindrical panels consisting of FG nanocomposite orthotropic material with the X shape resting on the elastic foundation and in thermal environments.

		Shen and Xiang [36]	**Present Study**	**Shen and Xiang [36]**	**Present Study**
		$(k_w,k_p)=(0,0)$		$(k_w,k_p)=(100,0)$	
***T*(K)**	$V_{CN}^{*(1)}$	**FG Nanocomposite with X Shape**			
$T=T_0$	12%	5.74	5.73	6.91	6.96
	17%	8.76	8.94	9.93	10.17
	28%	12.74	12.21	13.91	13.44
T_0+100	12%	5.34	5.31	6.59	6.54
	17%	8.14	8.28	9.43	9.52
	28%	11.94	11.26	13.15	12.49
T_0+200	12%	4.96	4.87	6.27	6.10
	17%	7.50	7.61	8.94	8.84
	28%	11.17	10.26	12.38	11.49

Table 5. Comparisons of nondimensional axial buckling load (in kN) for unconstrained laminated flat panels consisting of U nanocomposite orthotropic material (PmPV/CNT) with (0°/90°/90°/0°) tacking sequence at $T(\mathrm{K})=T_0$.

	Chakabarty et al. [38]	**Lei et al. [37]**	**Present Study**
$V_{CN}^{*(1)}$	$\tilde{N}_{0ST}^{buc}=N_{0ST}^{buc}b^2/E_m^{(1)}h^3$ for (0°/90°/90°/0°)		
11%	20.1225	19.8435	19.8591
14%	23.2158	22.6416	22.7128
17%	31.2920	30.9592	30.9764

The unique micromechanical model developed for laminated FG nanocomposite (PMMA/CNT) cylindrical shells is applied to investigate the nondimensional axial buckling load values depending on the variation in parameters such as soil, material, shear stress, temperature, stacking sequences, and geometry together and separately:

$$\left(\frac{\overline{N}_{0FG}^{bucwp}-\overline{N}_{0U}^{bucwp}}{\overline{N}_{0U}^{bucwp}},\ \frac{\overline{N}_{0CT}^{bucwp}-\overline{N}_{0ST}^{bucwp}}{\overline{N}_{0CT}^{bucwp}},\ \frac{\overline{N}_{0T}^{bucwp}-\overline{N}_{0T_0}^{bucwp}}{\overline{N}_{0T_0}^{bucwp}},\ \frac{\overline{N}_{0Lam}^{bucwp}-\overline{N}_{0SL}^{bucwp}}{\overline{N}_{0SL}^{bucwp}},\ \frac{\overline{N}_{0}^{bucwp}-\overline{N}_{0}^{buc}}{\overline{N}_{0}^{buc}}\right)\times 100\%.$$

Since the wave number in the x direction is equal to one ($m=1$), it is not included in the tables. The shells with (0°) or SL_1, (0°/90°/0°) or L_{31}, (90°/0°/90°) or

L_{32}, (0°/90°/90°/0°) or L_{41}, or (90°/0°/0°/90°) or the L_{42} array are used in the next step (Figure 3).

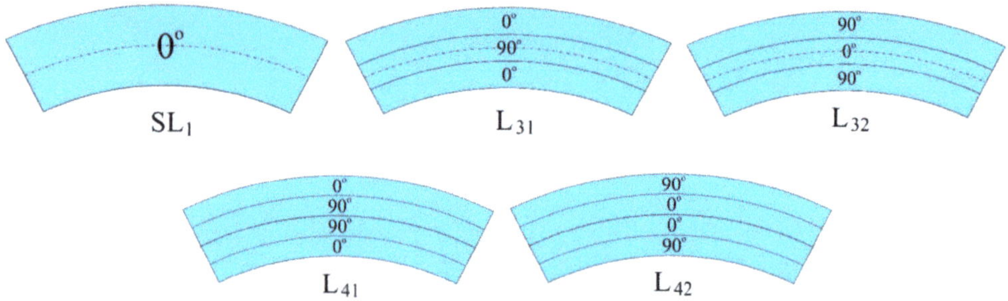

Figure 3. Cross-section of total thickness of cross-ply laminated cylindrical shells and their stacking sequences.

5.3. Parametric Study

In this subsection, the influences of various factors such as layer arrangement and number, pattern models in each layer, thermal environment, and elastic foundation on the axial buckling load in the framework of classical and shear deformation theories are discussed. Tables 6–8 and Figures 4–7 represent the influence of the r/h on the magnitudes of the $\overline{N}_0^{buc}$ and corresponding circumferential wave number (n_{cr}) for four types of laminated cylindrical shells with U-, ◇-, and X-shaped layers with and without elastic foundations in thermal environments within the FOST and CT. In this parametric study, the ST is used instead of the FOST. The necessary parameters are set to be $h = 2$ mm, $r = 20h$, $L/r = 1$, $V_{cnt}^{*(k)} = 28\%$, $K_w(N/m^3) = 6 \times 10^8$, $K_p(N/m) = 8 \times 10^4$. The values of the nondimensional axial buckling load reduce as the r/h and T(K) increase with and without an elastic foundation. In all r/h (=20, 30, 40, 50) ratios, as the values of the nondimensional axial buckling load in the grounded and groundless cases are compared at T(K) = 300, 500, and 700, the presence of the ground significantly weakens the influence of the patterns on the nondimensional axial buckling load values within the ST and CT. In addition, when we examine the groundless and grounded cases within themselves for the fixed r/h and $T(\mathrm{K}) = T_0$, T_0 + 200 and T_0 + 400, the influences of the ◇ and X shapes on the nondimensional axial buckling load values generally weaken with the increase in T(K).

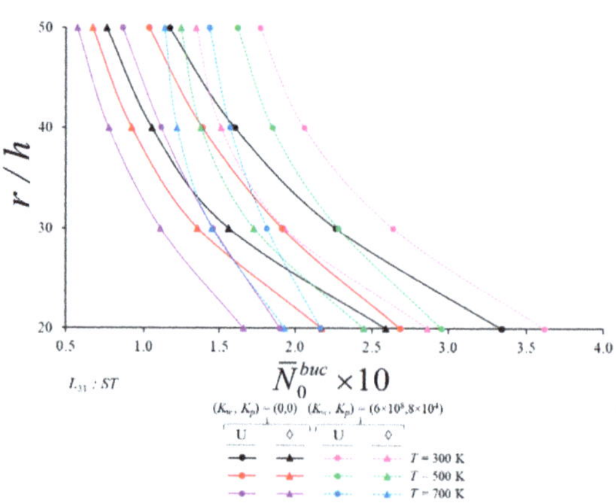

(a)

Figure 4. *Cont.*

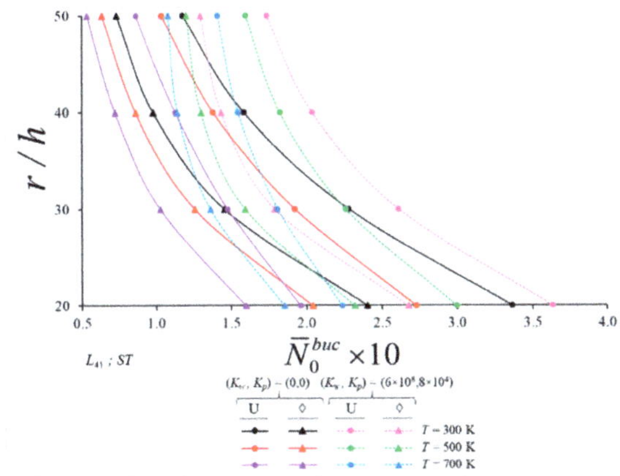

(**b**)

Figure 4. Distribution of the nondimensional axial buckling load of cross-ply laminated cylindrical shells with (**a**) L_{31} and (**b**) L_{41} lay-up consisting of U and ◇ schemes as the function of r/h within ST with and without elastic foundation in thermal environments.

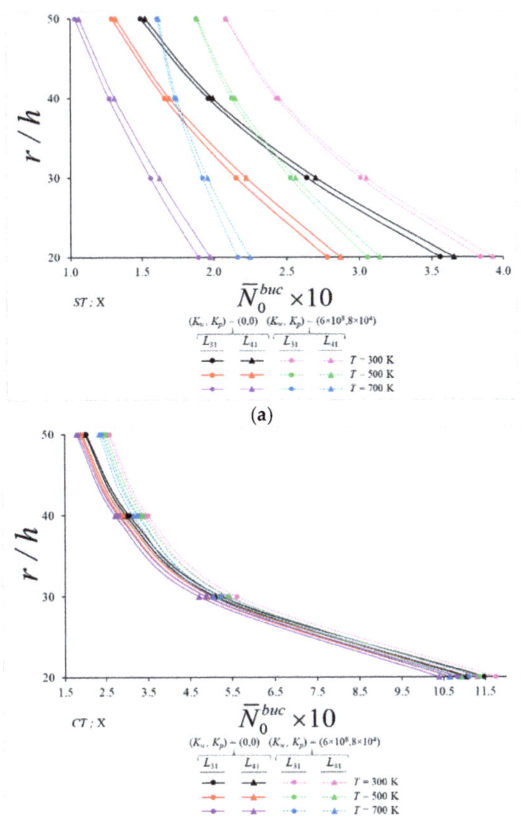

(**b**)

Figure 5. Distribution of the nondimensional axial buckling load of laminated cylindrical shells with L_{31} and L_{41} lay-up consisting of X scheme as the function of r/h within (**a**) ST and (**b**) CT with and without elastic foundation in thermal environments.

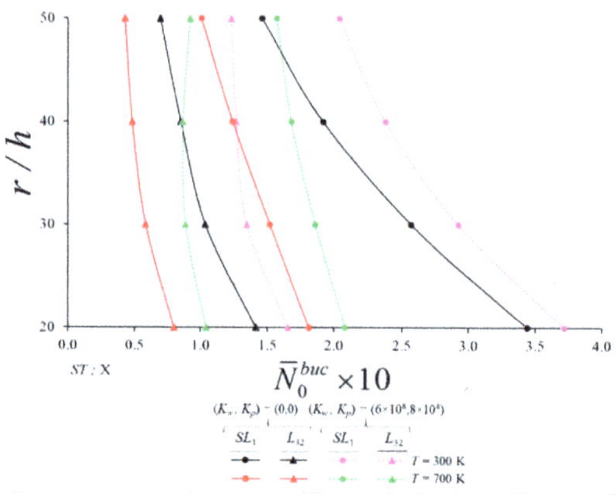

(a)

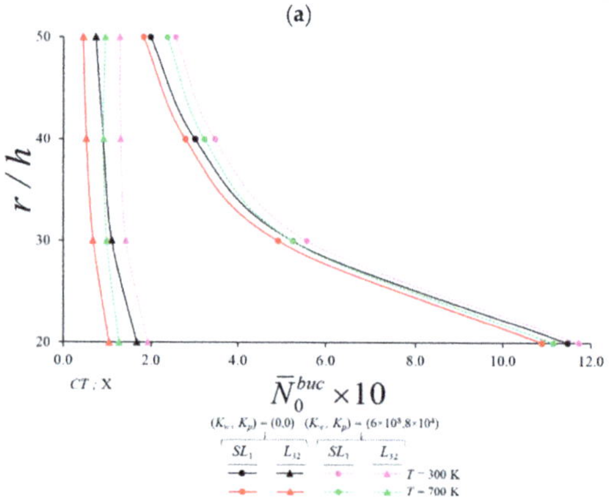

(b)

Figure 6. Distribution of the nondimensional axial buckling load of laminated cylindrical shells with SL_1 and L_{32} lay-up consisting of X scheme as the function of r/h within (**a**) ST and (**b**) CT with and without elastic foundation in thermal environments.

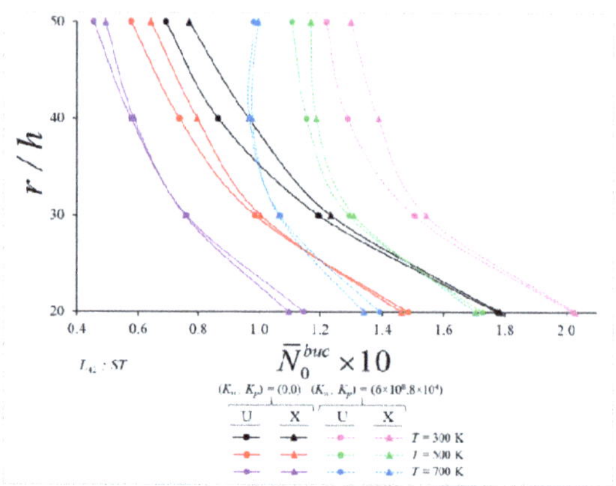

Figure 7. Distribution of the nondimensional axial buckling load of laminated cylindrical shells with L_{42} lay-up consisting of U and X schemes as the function of r/h within ST with and without elastic foundation in thermal environments.

Table 6. Distribution of the nondimensional axial buckling load and n_{cr} of laminated cylindrical shells with FG nanocomposite plies against the r/h with $T(\mathrm{K}) = T_0$ within ST and CT with and without elastic foundation.

r/h	Staking Sequences	$\overline{N}_0^{bucwp} \times 10,\ (n_{cr})$ for $(K_w,\ K_p) = (6 \times 10^8,\ 8 \times 10^4)$ and $T(\mathrm{K}) = T_0$					
		U		◇		X	
		ST	CT	ST	CT	ST	CT
20	SL_1	3.483 (4)	8.029 (3)	2.814 (4)	4.385 (3)	3.715 (4)	11.715 (3)
	L_{31}	3.619 (4)	7.950 (4)	2.864 (4)	4.193 (4)	3.840 (4)	11.74 (4)
	L_{32}	1.592 (3)	1.743 (3)	1.590 (3)	1.671 (3)	1.652 (3)	1.905 (3)
	L_{41}	3.635 (4)	7.423 (4)	2.675 (4)	3.586 (4)	3.926 (4)	11.30 (4)
	L_{42}	2.021 (3)	2.339 (3)	2.059 (3)	2.334 (3)	2.029 (3)	2.420 (3)
30	SL_1	2.550 (4)	3.912 (4)	1.890 (4)	2.294 (4)	2.922 (4)	5.563 (4)
	L_{31}	2.636 (5)	3.930 (5)	1.930 (5)	2.272 (5)	3.009 (5)	5.616 (5)
	L_{32}	1.282 (3)	1.312 (3)	1.210 (4)	1.240 (4)	1.341 (3)	1.402 (3)
	L_{41}	2.610 (4)	3.704 (4)	1.791 (4)	2.010 (4)	3.050 (4)	5.436 (4)
	L_{42}	1.501 (3)	1.572 (3)	1.426 (4)	1.501 (4)	1.540 (3)	1.631 (3)
40	SL_1	2.003 (4)	2.528 (4)	1.480 (5)	1.623 (4)	2.373 (4)	3.461 (4)
	L_{31}	2.059 (5)	2.555 (5)	1.509 (5)	1.628 (5)	2.432 (5)	3.504 (5)
	L_{32}	1.154 (4)	1.203 (4)	1.108 (4)	1.088 (4)	1.264 (3)	1.290 (3)
	L_{41}	2.040 (5)	2.461 (5)	1.438 (5)	1.519 (5)	2.450 (5)	3.431 (5)
	L_{42}	1.286 (4)	1.334 (4)	1.206 (4)	1.231 (4)	1.384 (4)	1.418 (3)
50	SL_1	1.714 (5)	1.955 (5)	1.312 (5)	1.375 (5)	2.036 (5)	2.558 (5)
	L_{31}	1.764 (5)	1.988 (5)	1.349 (5)	1.400 (5)	2.087 (5)	2.597 (5)
	L_{32}	1.126 (4)	1.156 (4)	1.101 (4)	1.088 (4)	1.224 (4)	1.262 (4)
	L_{41}	1.740 (5)	1.929 (5)	1.296 (5)	1.330 (5)	2.089 (5)	2.553 (5)
	L_{42}	1.218 (4)	1.239 (4)	1.166 (4)	1.176 (4)	1.297 (4)	1.337 (4)
r/h		$\overline{N}_0^{buc} \times 10,\ (n_{cr})$ for $(K_w,\ K_p) = (0,0)$ and $T(\mathrm{K}) = T_0$					
20	SL_1	3.209 (4)	7.777 (4)	2.540 (4)	4.120 (4)	3.441 (4)	11.47 (3)
	L_{31}	3.346 (4)	7.677 (4)	2.590 (4)	3.920 (4)	3.561 (5)	11.46 (4)
	L_{32}	1.353 (3)	1.498 (3)	1.343 (3)	1.424 (3)	1.413 (3)	1.659 (3)
	L_{41}	3.361 (4)	7.150 (4)	2.401 (4)	3.313 (4)	3.653 (4)	11.03 (4)
	L_{42}	1.776 (3)	2.094 (3)	1.814 (3)	2.089 (3)	1.784 (3)	2.174 (3)
30	SL_1	2.196 (5)	3.571 (5)	1.533 (5)	1.944 (5)	2.570 (5)	5.228 (4)
	L_{31}	2.265 (5)	3.559 (5)	1.559 (5)	1.901 (5)	2.638 (5)	5.245 (5)
	L_{32}	0.973 (3)	1.005 (3)	0.867 (4)	0.905 (4)	1.038 (3)	1.096 (3)
	L_{41}	2.276 (4)	3.370 (4)	1.457 (4)	1.676 (4)	2.698 (5)	5.101 (4)
	L_{42}	1.195 (3)	1.266 (3)	1.091 (4)	1.167 (4)	1.234 (3)	1.325 (3)
40	SL_1	1.545 (6)	2.079 (5)	1.015 (6)	1.163 (6)	1.919 (6)	3.016 (5)
	L_{31}	1.598 (6)	2.099 (5)	1.053 (5)	1.172 (5)	1.964 (6)	3.047 (6)
	L_{32}	0.744 (4)	0.784 (4)	0.656 (4)	0.668 (4)	0.853 (4)	0.899 (3)
	L_{41}	1.585 (5)	2.005 (5)	0.982 (5)	1.063 (5)	1.994 (5)	2.975 (5)
	L_{42}	0.866 (4)	0.915 (4)	0.787 (4)	0.812 (4)	0.965 (4)	1.027 (3)
50	SL_1	1.132 (6)	1.376 (6)	0.727 (6)	0.791 (6)	1.456 (6)	1.983 (6)
	L_{31}	1.172 (6)	1.400 (6)	0.760 (6)	0.814 (6)	1.492 (6)	2.007 (6)
	L_{32}	0.610 (4)	0.627 (4)	0.553 (5)	0.558 (4)	0.695 (4)	0.733 (4)
	L_{41}	1.175 (5)	1.364 (5)	0.731 (5)	0.765 (5)	1.524 (5)	1.988 (5)
	L_{42}	0.690 (4)	0.710 (4)	0.617 (5)	0.633 (5)	0.768 (4)	0.808 (4)

Table 7. Distribution of the nondimensional axial buckling load and n_{cr} of laminated cylindrical shells with FG nanocomposite plies against r/h with $T(\mathrm{K}) = T_0 + 200$ within ST and CT with and without elastic foundation.

r/h	Staking Sequences	$\overline{N}_0^{bucwp} \times 10$, (n_{cr}) for $(K_w, K_p) = (6\times10^8, 8\times10^4)$ and $T(\mathrm{K}) = T_0 + 200$					
		U		◇		X	
		ST	CT	ST	CT	ST	CT
20	SL_1	2.840 (4)	7.756 (3)	2.400 (4)	4.180 (3)	2.951 (4)	11.36 (3)
	L_{31}	2.958 (4)	7.652 (4)	2.448 (4)	3.966 (4)	3.057 (4)	11.36 (4)
	L_{32}	1.339 (3)	1.501 (3)	1.343 (3)	1.434 (3)	1.361 (3)	1.634 (3)
	L_{41}	2.999 (4)	7.132 (4)	2.318 (4)	3.368 (4)	3.143 (4)	10.93 (4)
	L_{42}	1.726 (3)	2.090 (3)	1.778 (3)	2.097 (3)	1.704 (3)	2.141 (3)
30	SL_1	2.197 (4)	3.758 (4)	1.686 (4)	2.170 (4)	2.445 (4)	5.370 (4)
	L_{31}	2.282 (5)	3.754 (4)	1.724 (4)	2.124 (4)	2.526 (5)	5.404 (4)
	L_{32}	1.077 (3)	1.114 (3)	1.057 (4)	1.093 (3)	1.119 (3)	1.187 (3)
	L_{41}	2.259 (4)	3.524 (4)	1.595 (4)	1.859 (4)	2.560 (4)	5.217 (4)
	L_{42}	1.289 (3)	1.373 (3)	1.272 (4)	1.362 (4)	1.307 (3)	1.412 (3)
40	SL_1	1.789 (4)	2.415 (4)	1.350 (4)	1.525 (4)	2.068 (4)	3.325 (4)
	L_{31}	1.846 (5)	2.436 (5)	1.379 (5)	1.525 (5)	2.127 (5)	3.364 (5)
	L_{32}	1.029 (3)	1.042 (3)	0.953 (4)	0.967 (4)	1.070 (3)	1.094 (3)
	L_{41}	1.829 (4)	2.325 (4)	1.302 (4)	1.395 (4)	2.152 (5)	3.281 (4)
	L_{42}	1.153 (4)	1.186 (3)	1.082 (4)	1.112 (4)	1.185 (3)	1.221 (3)
50	SL_1	1.571 (4)	1.863 (4)	1.220 (4)	1.297 (4)	1.831 (4)	2.449 (4)
	L_{31}	1.617 (5)	1.891 (5)	1.248 (5)	1.312 (5)	1.880 (5)	2.486 (5)
	L_{32}	1.024 (4)	1.044 (4)	0.970 (4)	0.976 (4)	1.095 (4)	1.121 (3)
	L_{41}	1.600 (5)	1.832 (5)	1.201 (5)	1.243 (5)	1.887 (5)	2.440 (5)
	L_{42}	1.102 (4)	1.127 (4)	1.054 (4)	1.067 (4)	1.166 (4)	1.202 (3)
r/h		$\overline{N}_0^{bucwp} \times 10$, (n_{cr}) for $(K_w, K_p) = (0, 0)$ and $T(\mathrm{K}) = T_0 + 200$					
20	SL_1	2.567 (4)	7.506 (4)	2.127 (4)	3.921 (4)	2.677 (4)	11.11 (3)
	L_{31}	2.684 (4)	7.379 (4)	2.175 (4)	3.692 (4)	2.780 (5)	11.09 (4)
	L_{32}	1.094 (3)	1.256 (3)	1.098 (3)	1.189 (3)	1.116 (3)	1.389 (3)
	L_{41}	2.725 (4)	6.859 (4)	2.044 (4)	3.095 (4)	2.870 (4)	10.65 (4)
	L_{42}	1.481 (3)	1.845 (3)	1.533 (3)	1.852 (3)	1.459 (3)	1.896 (3)
30	SL_1	1.848 (5)	3.419 (5)	1.335 (5)	1.824 (5)	2.096 (5)	5.035 (4)
	L_{31}	1.911 (5)	3.394 (5)	1.359 (5)	1.767 (5)	2.156 (5)	5.042 (5)
	L_{32}	0.771 (3)	0.808 (3)	0.722 (4)	0.766 (4)	0.813 (3)	0.881 (3)
	L_{41}	1.925 (4)	3.190 (4)	1.260 (4)	1.525 (4)	2.224 (5)	4.883 (4)
	L_{42}	0.983 (3)	1.067 (3)	0.938 (4)	1.027 (4)	1.001 (3)	1.106 (3)
40	SL_1	1.341 (6)	1.975 (5)	0.896 (6)	1.077 (6)	1.622 (6)	2.887 (5)
	L_{31}	1.390 (5)	1.980 (5)	0.923 (5)	1.070 (5)	1.663 (6)	2.908 (5)
	L_{32}	0.614 (4)	0.651 (3)	0.533 (4)	0.548 (4)	0.679 (3)	0.703 (3)
	L_{41}	1.384 (5)	1.887 (5)	0.864 (5)	0.962 (5)	1.696 (5)	2.833 (5)
	L_{42}	0.734 (4)	0.792 (4)	0.663 (4)	0.693 (4)	0.794 (3)	0.830 (3)
50	SL_1	1.000 (6)	1.297 (6)	0.644 (6)	0.723 (6)	1.261 (6)	1.886 (6)
	L_{31}	1.036 (6)	1.313 (6)	0.672 (6)	0.738 (6)	1.293 (6)	1.904 (6)
	L_{32}	0.495 (4)	0.516 (4)	0.441 (4)	0.447 (4)	0.566 (4)	0.613 (4)
	L_{41}	1.035 (5)	1.267 (5)	0.635 (5)	0.678 (5)	1.321 (5)	1.875 (5)
	L_{42}	0.573 (4)	0.598 (4)	0.525 (4)	0.538 (4)	0.638 (4)	0.686 (4)

Table 8. Distribution of the nondimensional axial buckling load values and n_{cr} of laminated cylindrical shells with FG nanocomposite plies against the r/h with $T(\mathrm{K}) = T_0 + 400$ within ST and CT with and without elastic foundation.

r/h	Staking Sequences	$\overline{N}_0^{bucwp} \times 10,\ (n_{cr})$ for $(K_w,\ K_p) = (6\times10^8,\ 8\times10^4)$ and $T(\mathrm{K}) = T_0 + 400$					
		U		◇		X	
		ST	CT	ST	CT	ST	CT
20	SL_1	2.067 (3)	7.560 (3)	1.869 (3)	4.015 (3)	2.077 (3)	11.12 (3)
	L_{31}	2.171 (4)	7.427 (4)	1.929 (4)	3.772 (4)	2.166 (4)	11.10 (4)
	L_{32}	1.061 (3)	1.262 (3)	1.086 (3)	1.200 (3)	1.042 (3)	1.252 (2)
	L_{41}	2.234 (3)	6.871 (3)	1.857 (3)	3.126 (3)	2.250 (4)	10.64 (3)
	L_{42}	1.390 (3)	1.850 (3)	1.455 (3)	1.867 (3)	1.340 (3)	1.774 (2)
30	SL_1	1.743 (3)	3.632 (3)	1.428 (4)	2.061 (3)	1.857 (4)	5.220 (3)
	L_{31}	1.810 (4)	3.602 (4)	1.453 (4)	1.983 (4)	1.923 (4)	5.237 (4)
	L_{32}	0.868 (3)	0.916 (3)	0.870 (3)	0.895 (3)	0.884 (3)	0.972 (3)
	L_{41}	1.813 (4)	3.373 (4)	1.364 (4)	1.719 (4)	1.958 (4)	5.045 (4)
	L_{42}	1.064 (3)	1.176 (3)	1.090 (3)	1.189 (3)	1.059 (3)	1.196 (3)
40	SL_1	1.512 (4)	2.321 (3)	1.195 (4)	1.438 (4)	1.675 (4)	3.218 (3)
	L_{31}	1.567 (4)	2.327 (4)	1.221 (4)	1.421 (4)	1.733 (5)	3.248 (4)
	L_{32}	0.842 (3)	0.859 (3)	0.828 (4)	0.848 (4)	0.865 (3)	0.897 (3)
	L_{41}	1.548 (4)	2.199 (4)	1.143 (4)	1.273 (4)	1.746 (4)	3.142 (4)
	L_{42}	0.965 (3)	1.004 (3)	0.953 (4)	0.995 (4)	0.974 (3)	1.023 (3)
50	SL_1	1.386 (4)	1.782 (4)	1.108 (4)	1.219 (4)	1.561 (4)	2.358 (4)
	L_{31}	1.433 (5)	1.805 (5)	1.138 (5)	1.229 (5)	1.610 (5)	2.392 (5)
	L_{32}	0.895 (3)	0.902 (3)	0.856 (4)	0.864 (4)	0.918 (3)	0.932 (3)
	L_{41}	1.413 (4)	1.725 (4)	1.079 (4)	1.136 (4)	1.617 (4)	2.332 (4)
	L_{42}	0.978 (3)	0.995 (3)	0.939 (4)	0.957 (4)	0.992 (3)	1.013 (3)
r/h		$\overline{N}_0^{bucwp} \times 10,\ (n_{cr})$ for $(K_w,\ K_p) = (0,0)$ and $T(\mathrm{K}) = T_0 + 400$					
20	SL_1	1.802 (4)	7.312 (4)	1.603 (4)	3.761 (4)	1.813 (4)	10.87 (3)
	L_{31}	1.898 (4)	7.154 (4)	1.656 (4)	3.498 (4)	1.893 (4)	10.82 (4)
	L_{32}	0.816 (3)	1.017 (3)	0.841 (3)	0.955 (3)	0.797 (3)	1.027 (2)
	L_{41}	1.962 (4)	6.626 (3)	1.600 (4)	2.881 (3)	1.976 (4)	10.39 (4)
	L_{42}	1.145 (3)	1.604 (3)	1.210 (3)	1.622 (3)	1.095 (3)	1.550 (2)
30	SL_1	1.400 (5)	3.302 (5)	1.082 (5)	1.723 (5)	1.513 (5)	4.894 (4)
	L_{31}	1.459 (5)	3.261 (5)	1.111 (5)	1.649 (4)	1.562 (5)	4.888 (5)
	L_{32}	0.562 (3)	0.610 (3)	0.565 (3)	0.589 (3)	0.578 (3)	0.666 (3)
	L_{41}	1.479 (4)	3.038 (4)	1.029 (4)	1.385 (4)	1.623 (4)	4.711 (4)
	L_{42}	0.758 (3)	0.870 (3)	0.771 (4)	0.883 (3)	0.753 (3)	0.890 (3)
40	SL_1	1.073 (6)	1.889 (5)	0.753 (6)	1.000 (6)	1.237 (6)	2.787 (5)
	L_{31}	1.115 (5)	1.879 (5)	0.773 (5)	0.975 (5)	1.275 (6)	2.796 (5)
	L_{32}	0.451 (3)	0.468 (3)	0.409 (4)	0.429 (4)	0.474 (3)	0.506 (3)
	L_{41}	1.128 (5)	1.779 (4)	0.723 (4)	0.853 (4)	1.313 (5)	2.718 (5)
	L_{42}	0.574 (3)	0.613 (3)	0.534 (4)	0.575 (4)	0.583 (3)	0.632 (3)
50	SL_1	0.831 (6)	1.230 (6)	0.550 (6)	0.662 (6)	1.005 (6)	1.808 (6)
	L_{31}	0.863 (6)	1.238 (6)	0.572 (5)	0.663 (5)	1.033 (6)	1.819 (6)
	L_{32}	0.376 (4)	0.402 (3)	0.327 (4)	0.335 (4)	0.418 (3)	0.432 (3)
	L_{41}	0.864 (5)	1.180 (5)	0.535 (5)	0.595 (5)	1.060 (5)	1.778 (5)
	L_{42}	0.453 (4)	0.488 (4)	0.411 (4)	0.428 (4)	0.491 (3)	0.513 (3)

As the r/h ratio rises from 20 to 50 in the grounded and groundless cases and these are compared with each other at $T(\mathrm{K}) = 300$, 500, and 700, the significant pattern effects on the $\overline{N}_0^{buc}$ occur at different temperatures and alignments within the ST. For example, the most significant pattern effect on the nondimensional axial buckling within the ST occurs in the L_{41} alignment shell with the ◇-shaped plies (−38.65%) in the case without soil at $T(K)$ = 500 and r/h = 50, while in the case with soil, that influence occurs in the L_{31} alignment shell with the ◇-shaped plies (−35.57%) at $T_0(K)$ = 300 and r/h = 30 in the case with soil (see Figure 4a,b also).

With the increase in the r/h from 20 to 50, the influence of shear deformations on the $\overline{N}_0^{buc}$ of all lay-up shells reduces, while the presence of soil supports reduces that decrease, considering that the increase in temperature weakens that decrease. When the $\overline{N}_0^{buc}$ values of laminated shells in the r/h = 20, 30, 40, and 50 ratios are compared with each other in the grounded and groundless cases at $T(K)$ = 300, 500, and 700, the pronounced shear stress influences occur in the L_{31} array shell in U, ◇, and X shapes at all values of r/h in ground and groundless cases (except for U shape, where it occurs in the L_{41} array shell for r/h = 30 and 50). It is noted that most pronounced shear stress influences on the nondimensional axial buckling load occur in the L_{31} array shell with X-shaped plies at $T(K)$ = 700 for r/h = 20. That influence is (+%82.5) in the case without a foundation, while the shear stresses effect on the $\overline{N}_0^{buc}$ weakens by 2.02% in the presence of the elastic foundation (see Tables 6–8 and Figure 5 also).

As the r/h increases from 20 to 50, significant array effects occur at different $T(K)$ values but in the same arrangements when comparing the values of the $\overline{N}_0^{buc}$ for all layered shells with the $\overline{N}_0^{buc}$ values of the SL_1 shell with and without soil. For instance, the most significant array influence on the $\overline{N}_0^{buc}$ occurs at the X shape (−61.8%) for $T(K)$ = 700 and the L_{32} arrangement at r/h = 30 in the case without soil, while that influence occurs at the X shape (−55.9%) at $T(K) = T_0$ and L_{32} arrangement at r/h = 20 in the case with soil within the ST (see Figure 6 also).

In the grounded case and different r/h, as the nondimensional axial buckling load values for $T(K)$ = 500 and 700 are compared with the reference temperature (at $T_0(K) = 300$), the temperature influences on the nondimensional axial buckling load values for r/h = 20 and 30 are similar, while those influences for r/h = 40 and 50 differ according to the layer arrangement and shapes. For example, at $T(K)$ = 500 and 700, the most pronounced temperature effect at r/h = 20 occurs in the cylinder with the L_{31} stacking sequence with U and X shapes, while it occurs in the cylinder for the L_{32} stacking sequence with the ◇ shape. At the same temperatures, the most pronounced temperature influence for r/h = 30 is observed in the L_{32} array shell with U and ◇ shapes, while it occurs in the L_{31} array shell for X shapes. For $T(K)$ = 500 and r/h = 40, the most pronounced temperature influence occurs in the shell with the L_{31} arrangement at the U, ◇, and X shapes. For $T(K)$ = 500 and r/h = 50, the most significant temperature influence occurs in the L_{42} shell arrangement in U and X shapes (see Figure 7 also), while it occurs in the cylinder with the L_{32} arrangement in the ◇ shape. For $T(K)$ = 700 and at r/h = 40 and 50, the most pronounced pattern influence in the U, ◇, and X shapes in the grounded condition always occurs in the L_{32} arrangement cylinder (see Figure 7 also).

6. Conclusions

This paper demonstrates the stability characteristics of axially loaded laminated cylindrical shells consisting of FG nanocomposite orthotropic layers on the two-parameter elastic foundation and in the thermal environments in the framework of the FOST. The effective material properties of the laminated cylindrical shells consisting of FG nanocomposite layers are computed using the extended rule of mixture method and molecular dynamics techniques. An analytical approach is employed to obtain the nondimensional axial buckling load of laminated cylindrical shells consisting of FG nanocomposite orthotropic plies on the two-parameter elastic foundation and in thermal environments. After checking the accuracy of the solution method by comparing it with the results in the literature, the different influences on the nondimensional axial buckling load of laminated FG nanocomposite orthotropic cylindrical shells, which are sensitive to the elastic foundation and thermal environments, are generalized as follows:

1. The values of the nondimensional axial buckling load reduce as the ratio of the radius to the total thickness and $T(\mathrm{K})$ increase with and without an elastic foundation.
2. The presence of the elastic foundation significantly weakens the influence of the patterns on the nondimensional axial buckling load for all the ratios of the radius to the total thickness in thermal environments within the FOST and CT.
3. The influences of $\diamond$ and X shapes on the axial buckling load generally weaken with the increase in $T(\mathrm{K})$, as examined by the groundless and grounded cases within themselves for the r/h.
4. As the ratio of the radius to the total thickness rises in the grounded and groundless cases, the significant pattern influences on the axial buckling load occur at different temperatures and alignments within the FOST.
5. With the increase in the radius to the total thickness ratio, the influences of shear deformations on the axial buckling load of all laminated shells reduce, while the presence of soil supports reduces this decrease, considering that the increase in temperature weakens that decrease.
6. When the axial buckling loads of laminated shells in all r/h are compared with each other in the grounded and groundless cases, the most pronounced influence of the shear deformations on the axial buckling load occurs in the L_{31} array cylindrical shell with X-shaped plies at $T(\mathrm{K}) = 700$ for $r/h = 20$.
7. As the ratio of the radius to the total thickness ratio increases, significant array effects occur at different $T(\mathrm{K})$ but in the same L_{32} arrangement when comparing the values of the axial buckling load for laminated shells with those of the single-layer shell with and without an elastic foundation.
8. In the grounded case and for different r/h, as the nondimensional axial buckling loads for $T(\mathrm{K}) = 500$ and 700 are compared with the reference temperature, the temperature influences on the nondimensional axial buckling load for $r/h = 20$ and 30 are similar, while those effects for $r/h = 40$ and 50 differ according to the layer arrangement and patterns.

Author Contributions: Conceptualization, A.H.S. and M.A.; methodology, A.H.S.; software, M.A.; validation, M.A., A.H.S. and N.M.A.; formal analysis, M.A.; investigation, M.A.; resources, M.A. and N.M.A.; data curation, M.A. and N.M.A.; writing—original draft preparation, M.A.; writing—review and editing, A.H.S. and N.M.A.; visualization, M.A. and N.M.A. All authors have read and agreed to the published version of the manuscript.

Funding: This research received no external funding.

Data Availability Statement: All information supporting the calculation results is available in the article and in the references of the article used as a source.

Conflicts of Interest: The authors declare no conflict of interest.

Appendix A

$$
\begin{aligned}
&c_{11}=\Lambda_{11}^1 b_{11}+\Lambda_{12}^1 b_{21},\ c_{12}=\Lambda_{11}^1 b_{12}+\Lambda_{12}^1 b_{12},\ c_{13}=\Lambda_{11}^1 b_{13}+\Lambda_{12}^1 b_{23}+\Lambda_{11}^2, c_{14}=\Lambda_{11}^1 b_{14}+\Lambda_{12}^1 b_{24}+\Lambda_{12}^2,\\
&c_{15}=\Lambda_{11}^1 b_{15}+\Lambda_{12}^1 b_{25}+\Lambda_{15}^1,\ c_{18}=\Lambda_{11}^1 b_{18}+\Lambda_{12}^1 b_{28}+\Lambda_{18}^1, c_{21}=\Lambda_{21}^1 b_{11}+\Lambda_{22}^1 b_{21},\ c_{22}=\Lambda_{21}^1 b_{12}+\Lambda_{22}^1 b_{22},\\
&c_{23}=\Lambda_{21}^1 b_{13}+\Lambda_{22}^1 b_{23}+\Lambda_{21}^2, c_{24}=\Lambda_{21}^1 b_{14}+\Lambda_{22}^1 b_{24}+\Lambda_{22}^2,\ c_{25}=\Lambda_{21}^1 b_{15}+\Lambda_{22}^1 b_{25}+\Lambda_{25}^1,\ c_{28}=\Lambda_{21}^1 b_{18}+\Lambda_{22}^1 b_{28}+\Lambda_{28}^1,\\
&c_{31}=\Lambda_{66}^1 b_{31},\ \ c_{32}=\Lambda_{66}^1 b_{32}+2\Lambda_{66}^2,\ \ c_{35}=\Lambda_{35}^1-\Lambda_{66}^1 b_{35}, c_{38}=\Lambda_{38}^1-\Lambda_{66}^1 b_{38},\\
&\\
&\Lambda_{11}=a_{11}^1\Gamma_{11}+a_{12}^1\Gamma_{21},\ \Lambda_{12}=a_{11}^1\Gamma_{12}+a_{12}^1\Gamma_{22},\ \Lambda_{13}=a_{11}^1\Gamma_{13}+a_{12}^1\Gamma_{23}+a_{11}^2, \Lambda_{14}=a_{11}^1\Gamma_{14}+a_{12}^1\Gamma_{24}+a_{12}^2,\\
&\Lambda_{15}=a_{11}^1\Gamma_{15}+a_{12}^1\Gamma_{25}+a_{15}^1, \Lambda_{18}=a_{11}^1\Gamma_{18}+a_{12}^1\Gamma_{28}+a_{18}^1,\ \Lambda_{21}=a_{21}^1\Gamma_{11}+a_{22}^1\Gamma_{21}, \Lambda_{22}=a_{21}^1\Gamma_{12}+a_{22}^1\Gamma_{22},\\
&\Lambda_{23}=a_{21}^1\Gamma_{13}+A_{22}^1\Gamma_{23}+a_{21}^2,\ \Lambda_{24}=a_{21}^1\Gamma_{14}+a_{22}^1\Gamma_{24}+a_{22}^2,\ \Lambda_{25}=a_{21}^1\Gamma_{15}+a_{22}^1\Gamma_{25}+a_{25}^1,\\
&\Lambda_{28}=a_{21}^1\Gamma_{18}+a_{22}^1\Gamma_{28}+a_{28}^1, \Lambda_{31}=a_{66}^1\Gamma_{31},\ \Lambda_{32}=a_{66}^1\Gamma_{32}+2a_{66}^2,\ \Lambda_{35}=a_{35}^1-a_{66}^1\Gamma_{35},\ \Lambda_{38}=a_{38}^1-a_{66}^1\Gamma_{38},\\
&\\
&\Pi_3=\Pi_4=\sum_{i=1}^{N}\left[J^{(i)}(z_i)-J^{(i)}(z_{i-1})\right].
\end{aligned}
\tag{A1}
$$

where

$$
\begin{aligned}
&\Gamma_{11}=\tfrac{a_{22}^0}{\lambda},\ S_{12}=-\tfrac{a_{12}^0}{\lambda},\ \Gamma_{13}=\tfrac{a_{12}^0a_{21}^1-a_{11}^1a_{22}^0}{\lambda},\ \Gamma_{14}=\tfrac{a_{12}^0a_{22}^1-a_{12}^1a_{22}^0}{\lambda},\ \Gamma_{15}=\tfrac{a_{25}^0a_{12}^0-a_{15}^0a_{22}^0}{\lambda},\\
&\Gamma_{18}=\tfrac{a_{28}^0a_{12}^0-a_{18}^0a_{22}^0}{\lambda},\ \Gamma_{21}=-\tfrac{a_{21}^0}{\lambda},\ \Gamma_{22}=\tfrac{a_{11}^0}{\lambda},\ \Gamma_{23}=\tfrac{a_{11}^1a_{21}^0-a_{21}^1a_{11}^0}{\lambda},\ \Gamma_{24}=\tfrac{a_{12}^1a_{21}^0-a_{22}^1a_{11}^0}{\lambda},\\
&\Gamma_{25}=\tfrac{a_{15}^0a_{21}^0-a_{25}^0a_{11}^0}{\lambda},\ \Gamma_{31}=\tfrac{1}{a_{66}^0},\ \Gamma_{28}=\tfrac{a_{18}^0a_{21}^0-a_{28}^0a_{11}^0}{\lambda},\ \Gamma_{32}=-\tfrac{2a_{66}^1}{a_{66}^0},\ \Gamma_{35}=\tfrac{a_{35}^0}{a_{66}^0}, \Gamma_{38}=\tfrac{a_{38}^0}{a_{66}^0},\\
&\lambda=a_{11}^0a_{22}^0-a_{12}^0a_{21}^0,
\end{aligned}
$$

in which

$$
\begin{aligned}
&a_{11}^{i_1}=\sum_{i=1}^{N}\int_{z_{i-1}}^{z_i}U_{11(z,T)}^{(i)}z^{l_1}\mathrm{d}z,\ a_{12}^{i_1}=a_{21}^{i_1}=\sum_{i=1}^{N}\int_{z_{i-1}}^{z_i}U_{12(z,T)}^{(i)}z^{l_1}\mathrm{d}z=\sum_{i=1}^{N}\int_{z_{i-1}}^{z_i}U_{21(z,T)}^{(i)}z^{l_1}\mathrm{d}z, a_{22}^{i_1}=\sum_{i=1}^{N}\int_{z_{i-1}}^{z_i}U_{22(z,T)}^{(i)}z^{l_1}\mathrm{d}z,\\
&a_{66}^{i_1}=\sum_{i=1}^{N}\int_{z_{i-1}}^{z_i}U_{66(z,T)}^{(i)}z^{l_1}\mathrm{d}z,\ a_{15}^{i_2}=\sum_{i=1}^{N}\int_{z_{i-1}}^{z_i}U_{11(z,T)}^{(i)}\Pi_{1(z,T)}^{(i)}z^{l_2}\mathrm{d}z, a_{18}^{i_2}=\sum_{i=1}^{N}\int_{z_{i-1}}^{z_i}U_{12(z,T)}^{(i)}\Pi_{2(z,T)}^{(i)}z^{l_2}\mathrm{d}z,\\
&a_{25}^{i_2}=\sum_{i=1}^{N}\int_{z_{i-1}}^{z_i}U_{21(z,T)}^{(i)}\Pi_{1(z,T)}^{(i)}z^{l_2}\mathrm{d}z,\ a_{28}^{i_2}=\sum_{i=1}^{N}\int_{z_{i-1}}^{z_i}U_{22(z,T)}^{(i)}\Pi_{2(z,T)}^{(i)}z^{l_2}\mathrm{d}z,\ a_{35}^{i_2}=\sum_{i=1}^{N}\int_{z_{i-1}}^{z_i}U_{66(z,T)}^{(i)}\Pi_{1(z,T)}^{(i)}z^{l_2}\mathrm{d}z,\\
&a_{38}^{i_2}=\sum_{i=1}^{N}\int_{z_{i-1}}^{z_i}U_{66(z,T)}^{(i)}\Pi_{2(z,T)}^{(i)}z^{l_2}\mathrm{d}z,\ l_1=0,\,1,\,2;\ l_2=0,1.
\end{aligned}
\tag{A2}
$$

Appendix B

$$
\begin{aligned}
&Q_{11}=h\left[(\Lambda_{11}-\Lambda_{31})\overline{m}^2\overline{n}^2+\Lambda_{12}\overline{m}^4\right],\ Q_{12}=(\Lambda_{14}+\Lambda_{32})\overline{m}^2\overline{n}^2+\Lambda_{13}n_1{}^4,\ Q_{13}=\Lambda_{15}\overline{m}^3+\Lambda_{35}\overline{m}\overline{n}^2+\Pi_3\overline{m},\\
&Q_{14}=(\Lambda_{18}+\Lambda_{38})\overline{n}\overline{m}^2,\ Q_{21}=h\left[\Lambda_{21}\overline{n}^4+(\Lambda_{22}-\Lambda_{31})\overline{m}^2\overline{n}^2\right],\ Q_{22}=(\Lambda_{32}+\Lambda_{23})\overline{m}^2\overline{n}^2+\Lambda_{24}\overline{n}^4,\\
&Q_{23}=(\Lambda_{25}+\Lambda_{35})\overline{m}\overline{n}^2,\ Q_{24}=\Lambda_{28}n_2{}^3+\Lambda_{38}\overline{m}^2\overline{n}+\Pi_4\overline{n},\ Q_{31}=h\left[\Gamma_{22}\overline{m}^4+(\Gamma_{12}+\Gamma_{21}+\Gamma_{31})\overline{m}^2\overline{n}^2+\Gamma_{11}\overline{n}^4\right],\\
&Q_{32}=\Gamma_{23}\overline{m}^4+(\Gamma_{24}+\Gamma_{13}+\Gamma_{32})\overline{m}^2\overline{n}^2+\Gamma_{14}\overline{n}^4+\tfrac{\overline{m}^2}{r}, Q_{33}=\Gamma_{25}\overline{m}^3+(\Gamma_{15}+\Gamma_{35})\overline{m}\overline{n}^2,\\
&Q_{34}=(\Gamma_{28}+\Gamma_{38})\overline{m}^2\overline{n}+\Gamma_{18}\overline{n}^3,\ Q_{41}=\tfrac{\overline{m}^2h}{r},\ Q_{42}=N_0\overline{m}^2-K_w-K_p(\overline{m}^2+\overline{n}^2),\ Q_{43}=\Pi_3\overline{m},\ Q_{44}=\Pi_4\overline{n}.
\end{aligned}
\tag{A3}
$$

References

1. Winkler, E. *Die Lehre von der Elastizität und Festigkeit*; Dominicus: Prague, Czech Republic, 1867.
2. Hetenyi, M. Beams and plates on elastic foundations and related problems. *Appl. Mech. Rev.* **1966**, *19*, 95–102.
3. Kerr, A.D. Elastic and viscoelastic foundation models. *J. Appl. Mech.* **1964**, *31*, 491–498. [CrossRef]
4. Vlasov, V.Z.; Leont'ev, N. *Beams, Plates and Shells on Elastic Foundation*; Israel Program for Scientific Translation: Jerusalem, Israel, 1966.
5. Engel, R.S. Dynamic stability of an axially loaded beam on an elastic foundation with damping. *J. Sound Vib.* **1991**, *146*, 463–477. [CrossRef]
6. Pasternak, P.L. *On a New Method of Analysis of an Elastic Foundation by Means of Two Foundation Constants*; Gosudarstvennoe Izdatelstro Liberaturi po Stroitelstvui Arkhitekture: Moscow, Russia, 1954.
7. Praveen, A.P.; Rajamohan, V.; Mathew, A.T. Recent developments in investigation on buckling and post buckling responses of laminated composite shells. *Polym. Compos.* **2018**, *39*, 4231–4242. [CrossRef]
8. Ambartsumian, S.A. *Theory of Anisotropic Shells*; NASA: Washington, DC, USA, 1964.
9. Reddy, J.N. *Mechanics of Laminated Composite Plates and Shells: Theory and Analysis*, 2nd ed.; CRC Press: New York, NY, USA, 2004.

10. Simitses, G.J.; Han, B. Analysis of anisotropic laminated cylindrical shells subjected to destabilizing loads. Part I: Theory and solution procedure. *Compos. Struct.* **1991**, *17*, 167–181. [CrossRef]
11. Han, B.; Simitses, G.J. Analysis of anisotropic laminated cylindrical shells subjected to destabilizing loads. Part II: Numerical results. *Compos. Struct.* **1991**, *17*, 183–205. [CrossRef]
12. Li, J.; Xiang, Z.H.; Xue, M.D. Buckling analysis of rotationally periodic laminated composite shells by a new multilayered shell element. *Compos. Struct.* **2005**, *70*, 24–32. [CrossRef]
13. Shen, H.S. Boundary layer theory for the buckling and postbuckling of an anisotropic laminated cylindrical shell. Part I: Prediction under axial compression. *Compos. Struct.* **2008**, *82*, 346–361. [CrossRef]
14. Shen, H.S. Postbuckling of axially-loaded laminated cylindrical shells surrounded by an elastic medium. *Mech. Adv. Mater. Struc.* **2013**, *20*, 130–150. [CrossRef]
15. Sofiyev, A.H. Influences of elastic foundations and boundary conditions on the buckling of laminated shell structures subjected to combined loads. *Compos. Struct.* **2011**, *93*, 2126–2134. [CrossRef]
16. Odegard, G.M.; Gates, T.S.; Wise, K.E.; Park, C.; Siochi, E. Constitutive modeling of nanotube-reinforced polymer composites. *Compos. Sci. Techn.* **2003**, *63*, 1671–1687. [CrossRef]
17. Lordi, V.; Yao, N. Molecular mechanics of binding in carbon-nanotube–polymer composites. *J. Mater. Res.* **2000**, *15*, 2770–2779. [CrossRef]
18. Griebel, M.; Hamaekers, J. Molecular dynamics simulations of the elastic moduli of polymer–carbon nanotube composites. *Comput. Meth. Appl. Mech. Eng.* **2004**, *193*, 1773–1788. [CrossRef]
19. Valavala, P.K.; Clancy, T.C.; Odegard, G.M.; Gates, T.S. Nonlinear multiscale modeling of polymer materials. *Int. J. Solid. Struct.* **2007**, *44*, 1161–1179. [CrossRef]
20. Coleman, J.N.; Khan, U.; Blau, W.J.; Gun'ko, Y.K. Small but strong: A review of the mechanical properties of carbon nanotube-polymer composites. *Carbon* **2006**, *44*, 1624–1652. [CrossRef]
21. Njuguna, J.; Pielichowski, K.; Fan, J. Polymer nanocomposites for aerospace applications. In *Advances in Polymer Nanocomposites: Types and Applications*; Woodhead Publishing Ltd.: Sawston, UK, 2012; pp. 472–539.
22. Gatos, K.G.; Leong, Y.W. Classification of Nanomaterials and Nanocomposites. In *Nanocomposite Materials: Synthesis, Properties and Applications*; CRC: Boca Raton, FL, USA, 2017; pp. 5–36.
23. Okamoto, M. Polymer Nanocomposites. *ENG* **2023**, *4*, 457–479. [CrossRef]
24. Ali, Z.; Yaqoob, S.; Yu, J.; D'Amore, A. Critical review on the characterization, preparation, and enhanced mechanical, thermal, and electrical properties of carbon nanotubes and their hybrid filler polymer composites for various applications. *Compos. Part C Open Access* **2024**, *13*, 100434. [CrossRef]
25. Sahu, R.; Harursampath, D.; Ponnusami, S.A. Mechanical behaviour of carbon nanotube composites: A review of various modelling techniques. *J. Compos. Mater.* **2024**, *58*, 791–825. [CrossRef]
26. Shen, H.S. Postbuckling of nanotube-reinforced composite cylindrical shells in thermal environments, Part I: Axially-loaded shells. *Compos. Struct.* **2011**, *93*, 2096–2108. [CrossRef]
27. Shen, H.S.; Xiang, Y.; Fan, Y. Postbuckling of functionally graded graphene-reinforced composite laminated cylindrical panels under axial compression in thermal environments. *Int. J. Mech. Sci.* **2018**, *135*, 398–409. [CrossRef]
28. Hieu, P.T.; Tung, H.V. Buckling of shear deformable FG-CNTRC cylindrical shells and toroidal shell segments under mechanical loads in thermal environments. *ZAMM-J. Appl. Math. Mech.* **2020**, *100*, e201900243. [CrossRef]
29. Sofiyev, A.H. On the vibration and stability behaviors of heterogeneous-CNTRC-truncated conical shells under axial load in the context of FSDT. *Thin-Wall. Struct.* **2020**, *151*, 106747. [CrossRef]
30. Soni, S.K.; Thomas, B.; Swain, A.; Roy, T. Functionally graded carbon nanotubes reinforced composite structures: An extensive review. *Compos. Struct.* **2022**, *299*, 116075. [CrossRef]
31. Twinkle, C.M.; Pitchaimani, J. A semi-analytical nonlocal elasticity model for static stability and vibration behaviour of agglomerated CNTs reinforced nano cylindrical panel under non-uniform edge loads. *Appl. Math. Model.* **2022**, *103*, 68–90.
32. Rad, M.H.G.; Hosseini, S.M. Buckling analysis of multilayer FG-CNT reinforced nanocomposite cylinders assuming CNT waviness, agglomeration, and interphase effects using the CUF-EFG method. *Mech. Adv. Mater. Struct.* **2023**, *30*, 1309–1325.
33. Majumder, R.; Chakraborty, S.; Mishra, S.K. Reliability analysis and design of randomly imperfect thin cylindrical shells against post-critical drops. *Thin-Wall. Struct.* **2023**, *185*, 110594. [CrossRef]
34. Wu, S.; Li, Y.; Bao, Y.; Zhu, J.; Wu, H. Examination of beam theories for buckling and free vibration of functionally graded porous beams. *Materials* **2024**, *17*, 3080. [CrossRef] [PubMed]
35. Sofiyev, A.H. Modeling and solution of eigenvalue problems of laminated cylindrical shells consisting of nanocomposite plies in thermal environments. *Arch. Appl. Mech.* **2024**, *94*, 3071–3099. [CrossRef]
36. Shen, H.S.; Xiang, Y. Postbuckling of axially compressed nanotube-reinforced composite cylindrical panels resting on elastic foundations in thermal environments. *Compos. Part B Eng.* **2014**, *67*, 50–61. [CrossRef]

37. Lei, Z.X.; Zhang, L.W.; Liew, K.M. Buckling analysis of CNT reinforced functionally graded laminated composite plates. *Compos. Struct.* **2016**, *152*, 62–73. [CrossRef]
38. Chakraborty, S.; Dey, T.; Kumar, R. Stability and vibration analysis of CNT-Reinforced functionally graded laminated composite cylindrical shell panels using semi-analytical approach. *Compos. Part B Eng.* **2019**, *168*, 1–14. [CrossRef]
39. Mohammadi, M.; Arefi, M.; Dimitri, R.; Tornabene, F. Higher-order thermo-elastic analysis of FG-CNTRC cylindrical vessels surrounded by a Pasternak foundation. *Nanomaterials* **2019**, *9*, 79. [CrossRef]
40. Ipek, C.; Sofiyev, A.H.; Fantuzzi, N.; Efendiyeva, S.P. Buckling behavior of nanocomposite plates with functionally graded properties under compressive loads in elastic and thermal environments. *J. Appl. Comput. Mech.* **2023**, *9*, 974–986.
41. Monge, J.C.; Mantari, J.L.; Llosa, M.N.; Hinostroza, M.A. A size-dependent 3D solution of functionally graded shallow nanoshells. *Curved Layer. Struct.* **2023**, *10*, 20220215. [CrossRef]
42. Monge, J.C.; Mantari, J.L. 3D nonlocal solution with layerwise approach and DQM for multilayered functionally graded shallow nanoshells. *Mech. Adv. Mater. Struct.* **2024**. [CrossRef]
43. Mantari, J.L.; Monge, J.C. Semi-analytical layerwise solutions for FG MEE complex shell structures. *Eur. J. Mech.-A/Solids* **2025**, *109*, 105446.

Mathematical and Computational Applications

MDPI

Article

Polynomial Approximation over Arbitrary Shape Domains

Mohammad J. Mahtabi [1,*], Arash Ghasemi [1], Amirehsan Ghasemi [2] and James C. Newman III [1]

1 Department of Mechanical Engineering, University of Tennessee at Chattanooga, Chattanooga, TN 37403, USA; arash-ghasemi@utc.edu (A.G.); james-newman@utc.edu (J.C.N.III)
2 Bredesen Center for Interdisciplinary Research and Graduate Education, University of Tennessee, Knoxville, TN 37996, USA; aghasemi@vols.utk.edu
* Correspondence: mohammad-mahtabi@utc.edu

Abstract: In spectral/finite element methods, a robust and stable high-order polynomial approximation method for the solution can significantly reduce the required number of degrees of freedom (DOFs) to achieve a certain level of accuracy. In this work, a closed-form relation is proposed to approximate the Fekete points (AFPs) on arbitrary shape domains based on the singular value decomposition (SVD) of the Vandermonde matrix. In addition, a novel method is derived to compute the moments on highly complex domains, which may include discontinuities. Then, AFPs are used to generate compatible basis functions using SVD. Equations are derived and presented to determine orthogonal/orthonormal modal basis functions, as well as the Lagrange basis. Furthermore, theorems are proved to show the convergence and accuracy of the proposed method, together with an explicit form of the Weierstrass theorem for polynomial approximation. The method was implemented and some classical cases were analyzed. The results show the superior performance of the proposed method in terms of convergence and accuracy using many fewer DOFs and, thus, a much lower computational cost. It was shown that the orthogonal modal basis is the best choice to decrease the DOFs while maintaining a small Lebesgue constant when very high degree of polynomial is employed.

Keywords: higher-order methods; approximation theory; spectral elements; approximate Fekete points; Weierstrass theorem

1. Introduction

In multiscale simulation of physical phenomena, it is necessary to achieve maximum resolution per wavelength while preserving an acceptable efficiency. It is equally important, and necessary, for the numerical method to be robust enough to handle nonlinearity, discontinuities, geometrical complexities, and singularities. The conventional approach in spectral/finite element methods to achieve a higher accuracy is to tessellate a convex or concave domain to finer elements by triangulation/quadrilateralization. Clearly, in triangulation, many interior edges are generated, which, in turn, require additional (interpolation) points per edge for higher-order elements. This unavoidable fact significantly increases the number of degrees of freedom (DOFs). Ideally, if we could use the original domain without the need for triangulation/quadrilateralization, there would be semi-global basis functions, which would have the same order of accuracy as a conventional finite element but fewer DOFs due to no interior edges. Such an objective can be, in some cases, achieved by a high-order polynomial approximation of the solution (i.e., p-refinement). This, in turn, requires a suitable set of ingredients for robust polynomial approximation: a set of suitable interpolation points and representative basis functions.

A suitable choice of interpolation points is one that minimizes the Lebesgue constant [1] as a measure of the interpolation error. In the case of 1D space, Chebyshev points have proven [2] to be an ideal case of interpolation points. In higher dimensions, the Chebyshev points are determined by the tensor product of 1D distribution, and hence, the interpolation domain Ω is limited to quadrilaterals and hexahedrons in 2D and 3D, respectively, for which quad/hex tessellation is possible. However, a quad/hex tessellation of the domain may violate the optimal partitioning of a complex-shape domain, and hence, imposes extra DOFs, and thus, requires a higher computational cost [3]. Furthermore, polynomial approximation over arbitrary shape domains may have specific applications in various fields. For instance, in crystal plasticity, each grain—in general a non-quad/hex shape—can be modeled as a single element, thus greatly reducing the DOFs of the model and facilitating the post-processing of the result. Therefore, different approaches were proposed in the past for polynomial approximations [4–7] or discontinuous Galerkin finite element (FE) [8,9] formulations over complex geometries, including polygonal and polyhedral geometries. For non-quad/hex domains, Fekete points, representing the minimum potential points, were shown to be suitable interpolation points [10]. However, the determination of exact Fekete points on non-quad/hex domains is a Nondeterministic Polynomial (NP) problem and the computation may be undertaken using expensive optimization techniques [10]. There are approaches based on finding a local minimum using an equilibrium potential minimization, which has an $O(N^3)$ cost [11], but there is no guarantee that a global minimum (i.e., exact Fekete points) is found.

In this paper, a set of compatible ingredients for polynomial approximation/interpolation over arbitrary shape domains is presented. We propose an explicit formulation to determine the approximate Fekete points (AFPs) based on the singular value decomposition (SVD) of the Vandermonde matrix. The AFPs are determined from a pool of candidate points. Next, nodal and modal basis functions are introduced to be used with the AFPs. Furthermore, a formulation is presented to determine these functions with a small computational cost. Theories are proven to show the low Lebesgue constant of the proposed approach. Finally, based on the proposed approach, a new proof of the Weierstrass theorem is presented with an explicit formulation for the polynomial approximant over the arbitrary shape domain $\Omega \subset \mathbb{R}^d$.

2. Singular Value Decomposition (SVD) for AFPs

The Q-space of d-variate polynomials of degree $< n_i$ for each variable, obtained by the product of one-dimensional monomials, is represented by

$$f_Q = \{\prod_{i=1}^{d} {x_i}^{d_i} \ \mid \ 0 \le d_i < n_i\} \tag{1}$$

with $N_Q = \dim(f_Q) = \prod_{i=1}^{d} n_i$ terms, defined in $\Omega \subset \mathbb{R}^d$. The constrained subspace of Equation (1) for $\sum_i d_i < n$ is called the P-space of polynomials denoted by

$$f_P = \{\prod_{i=1}^{d} {x_i}^{d_i} \ \mid \ \sum_{k=1}^{d} d_k < n\} \tag{2}$$

where $N_P = \dim(f_P) = \binom{n+d-1}{d}$. For a sufficiently large number of *interpolation points* in Ω:

$$\hat{X} = \{\hat{x}_i\} \subset \Omega, \quad 1 \le i \le M, \quad M \gg N, \tag{3}$$

where $N = N_P \; or \; N_Q$, depending on the case. The transpose of the rectangular Vandermonde matrix can be constructed column-wise by using f defined in either Equation (1) or Equation (2) as

$$\hat{\mathcal{V}}^T = [f(\hat{x}_1) \mid f(\hat{x}_2) \mid \ \ldots \ | f(\hat{x}_M)] \in \mathbb{R}^{N \times M}. \tag{4}$$

The set of a large number of points $\hat{X} = \{\hat{x}_{i=1\ldots M}\}$ in Equation (3) is called *candidate points*. *Approximate Fekete points (AFPs)*, denoted by $\tilde{X}_F = \{\tilde{x}_{i=1\ldots N}\}$, are selected from the candidate points so that they mimic the Gauss–Lobatto quadrature points inside Ω. Since these are good *estimates* of Fekete points, they are called approximate Fekete points [12]. To start, consider the univariate case (we extend this to the multivariate formulation in Section 3.1 in Equation (14)). We are interested in finding $\tilde{X}$ so that the Lagrange polynomials constructed by

$$l_j(x) = \prod_{\substack{1 \leq i \leq N \\ i \neq j}} \frac{x - x_i}{x_j - x_i} \tag{5}$$

satisfying $l_j(\tilde{x}_i) = \delta_{ij}$ have small Lebesgue constants [1], defined by the operator norm of the d-dimensional interpolation

$$\Lambda_N = \max\left(\sum_{j=1}^{N} |l_j(x)| \right), \quad x \in \Omega, \tag{6}$$

which determines an upper-bound for the interpolation error

$$\|u - I_u\| \leq (1 + \Lambda_N)\|u - p^*\| \tag{7}$$

where p^* is the best polynomial approximant of u of degree $\leq N$, and $\|u - I_u\|$ is the norm of the difference between the exact value of u and an interpolated value I_u at any point $x \in \Omega$ given as

$$I_u(x) = \sum_{j=1}^{N} l_j(x)\tilde{f}_j, \tag{8}$$

where $\tilde{f}_j$s are the *sampled* values of the function at the interpolation points. The existence of a polynomial approximant for u is guaranteed by the Weierstrass approximation theorem and it can be shown that the best approximant exists and is unique (c.f. Theorem 10.1 of [2] for the proof). For equispaced points in 1D, which form the popular FE Lagrange basis, it is possible to show that the Lebesgue constant grows exponentially as $\Lambda_N \sim 2^{N+1}/(e\,N\log N)$ [1] due to the well-known Runge phenomenon. Therefore, according to Equation (7), for very high-order approximations, these points result in a significant deviation from the optimal result. It is possible—and desirable—to decrease the Lebesgue constant by choosing Chebyshev points (with $\Lambda_N < \frac{2}{\pi}\log(N+1) + 1$) [2]. However, as mentioned before, for such points, the domain Ω is limited to quadrilaterals and hexahedrons in 2D and 3D (i.e., tensor product spaces), respectively.

Another approach to decrease the Lebesgue constant is by selecting a set of quadrature points as the interpolation points in Equation (3) [12]. In this method, which is applicable to arbitrary shape domains, the best linear approximation for the jth moment $m_j = \int_\Omega f_j(x)d\mu$ can be obtained by solving the following underdetermined system:

$$\sum_{i=1}^{M} w_i f_j(\hat{x}_i) = \hat{\mathfrak{V}}^T w,\ 1 \leq j \leq N \qquad \Longleftrightarrow \qquad \hat{\mathfrak{V}}^T w = m \tag{9}$$

For simple geometries, the moments m_j can be obtained analytically. However, for complex geometries, methods such as sub-triangulation and composite integration and the polygonal Gauss-like method [13] are proposed to compute the moments.

In order to find the AFPs, first, the given arbitrary domain needs to be filled with a sufficiently *dense* set of candidate points. This can be achieved using the *fill pattern method* or the *iterative gravitational method*. The fill pattern method is a fast way to fill an arbitrary subset of $\mathbb{R}^d$ with a large number of uniformly distributed points inside its bounding box. Then, each point is explicitly checked using the polygonal point inclusion test [14] and is removed from the set if it is outside the bounding box. The result of this algorithm is very close to a uniform distribution, except near the boundaries of the polyhedra, where a gap is generated. In the iterative gravitational method, first, the bounding box of the domain is filled with a random set of points. Then, a gravitational equilibrium approach with an artificial time dependency algorithm similar to [15] is used to smooth the distribution of these points. This algorithm can generate a uniform distribution of points near the boundaries.

Once the candidate points are generated, we can perform SVD on their Vandermonde matrix to find the AFPs as follows. Using a compact SVD of the initially rectangular Vandermonde matrix, one can write

$$\hat{\mathcal{V}} = \hat{U}\hat{S}\hat{V}^T \tag{10}$$

where $\hat{U}$ and $\hat{V}$ are orthonormal matrices and $\hat{S}$ is a diagonal matrix, in which the diagonal elements are the singular values of $\hat{\mathcal{V}}$. It was proved that any matrix $\hat{\mathcal{V}}$ has $r = \text{rank}(\hat{\mathcal{V}})$ singular values, where $r \leq min(M, N)$. For the initial Vandermonde matrix $\hat{\mathcal{V}}$, since the points are distinct and $N \leq M$, the rank is equal to N. Thus, $\hat{S}$ will have N nonzero diagonal values $\sigma_{i=1,\dots,N}$, conventionally sorted in descending order. Since, according to SVD, the best N-degree approximation of $\hat{\mathcal{V}}$ can be written based on these rows, one can conclude that the points corresponding to these rows form the best set of size N representing $\hat{\mathcal{V}}$, which are, in fact, AFPs. An example of AFP determination using this approach is shown in Figure 1 for a complex domain including discontinuities. Once the AFPs $\tilde{x}_{i=1\dots N}$ are determined, we can construct the corresponding Vandermonde matrix $\tilde{\mathcal{V}}$. In the rest of this paper, we indicate all the AFP-related quantities as $\tilde{\square}$.

By replacing $\tilde{\mathcal{V}}$ with its full-rank SVD, Equation (9) can be written as

$$\tilde{\mathcal{V}}^T w = \tilde{V}\tilde{S}^T\tilde{U}^T w = m \tag{11}$$

where the diagonal elements of $\tilde{S}$ are $\sigma_{j=1,\dots N}$, the singular values of $\tilde{\mathcal{V}}$. Defining $\tilde{P} = \tilde{V}\tilde{S}^{-1}$, left-multiplying both sides of the last equality by $\tilde{P}^T$, and using the orthonormal property of $\tilde{V}$, one obtains

$$\tilde{P}^T\tilde{\mathcal{V}}^T w = \tilde{P}^T m = \mu \tag{12}$$

or

$$\tilde{U}^T w = \mu, \quad if \;\; w \neq 0, \tag{13}$$

where $\tilde{U}$ is the left unitary matrix in the SVD of $\tilde{\mathcal{V}}$, corresponding to AFPs. Solving Equation (13) yields a set of nonzero weights that are mostly positive.

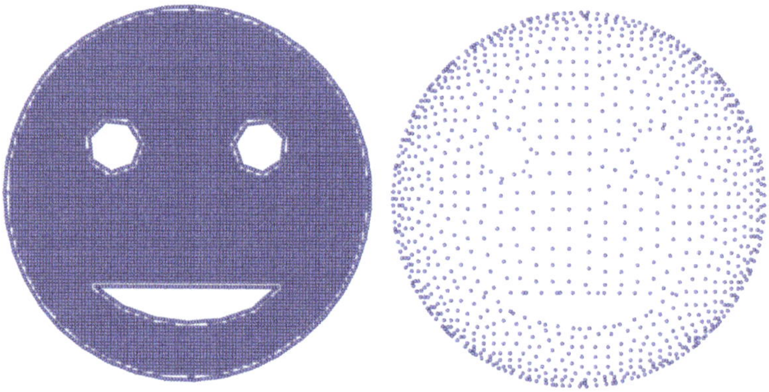

(a) Candidate Points *(b) Approximate Fekete Points*

Figure 1. Application of the SVD-based approach of Equation (10) to candidate points (**a**) and selecting AFPs (**b**) on a concave domain.

3. Basis Functions

3.1. Nodal Basis Functions

The value of the jth nodal basis function ψ_j of degree at most $N(= N_P \text{ or } N_Q)$ in the d-dimensional space at point $x = (x_1, x_2, \ldots, x_d)$ can be obtained by the product of row matrix $f(= f_P \text{ or } f_Q)$ and column matrix a_j, thus:

$$\psi_j(x) = \psi_j(x_1, x_2, \ldots, x_d) = \underbrace{\left[1, x_1, x_1^2, \ldots, x_2, x_2^2, \ldots, x_d, x_d^2, \ldots\right]_{1\times N}}_{\text{either } f_P \text{ or} f_Q} [a_j]_{N\times 1} = f a_j \quad (14)$$

where the terms involving multiple variables are not explicitly shown. The N possible cases of coefficient vectors a_j yields the $1 \times N$ point-wise basis matrix at the general point x:

$$\begin{aligned} \psi = [\psi_1, \ldots, \psi_N]_{1\times N} &= [f(x)a_1, f(x)a_2, \ldots, f(x)a_N] \\ &= [f(x)]_{1\times N}[a_1 \,|a_2 \,| \,\ldots \,|a_N]_{N\times N} \\ &= [f(x)]_{1\times N}[a]_{N\times N} \end{aligned} \quad (15)$$

Subsequently, the terms of all basis functions evaluated at a specific AFP $\tilde{x}_i$ are denoted by $\psi^{(i)}$. Evaluating Equation (15) at all $\tilde{X}_F = \{\tilde{x}_{i,\, i=1\ldots N}\}$ gives the nodal basis function matrix Ψ:

$$\Psi = \left[\psi_j^{(i)}\right] = \begin{bmatrix} \psi^{(1)} \\ \psi^{(2)} \\ \vdots \\ \psi^{(N)} \end{bmatrix}_{N\times N} = \begin{bmatrix} [f(\tilde{x}_1)]_{1\times N} \\ [f(\tilde{x}_2)]_{1\times N} \\ \vdots \\ [f(\tilde{x}_N)]_{1\times N} \end{bmatrix}_{N\times N} [a]_{N\times N} \quad (16)$$

By using the definition of the Vandermonde matrix, Equation (16) can be represented in the following compact form:

$$\Psi = \tilde{V}a, \quad (17)$$

In Equation (17), the numerical value of the jth basis function evaluated at point $\tilde{x}_i$ (i.e., $\psi_j^{(i)}$) is located at entry $\Psi(i,j)$. Applying Equation (5) to Equation (17) yields

$$\tilde{V}a = I, \quad (18)$$

Hence, the coefficients of the nodal basis functions can be determined by inverting the Vandermonde matrix of AFPs $\tilde{V}$ by replacing it in Equation (18) with its SVD from Equation (9):

$$\tilde{U}\tilde{S}\tilde{V}^T a = I, \quad (19)$$

which gives the unknown coefficients of the *nodal* approximate Fekete basis (AFB) as

$$a = \tilde{V}\, \tilde{S}^{-1}\, \tilde{U}^T. \quad (20)$$

The coefficient matrix a needs to be calculated *only once* and can be tabulated to an arbitrary order of approximation and for a variety of geometries. Then, at any general point $x \in \Omega$, the value of the jth basis function can be efficiently calculated with $\mathcal{O}(N)$ operations by evaluating f_P or f_Q at that point and performing the vector product in Equation (14). In order to obtain the explicit form of the nodal AFB at a general point $x \in \Omega$, let us substitute Equation (20) into Equation (15) to obtain

$$\psi = [\psi_1, \ldots, \psi_N]_{1\times N} = [f(x)]_{1\times N}\tilde{V}_{N\times N}\, \tilde{S}^{-1}_{N\times N}\, \tilde{U}^T_{N\times N} \quad (21)$$

where x is not necessarily an interpolation point.

3.2. Modal Basis Functions

Right-multiplying Equation (21) with the unitary matrix $\tilde{U}$ yields

$$\bar{\psi}_j = \psi_j \tilde{U} = [f(x)]_{1\times N} \tilde{V}_{N\times N}\, \tilde{S}^{-1}_{N\times N}, \tag{22}$$

which are the modal basis functions. In the following section, we prove characteristic properties of these basis functions, such as orthogonality, that are essential for successful polynomial approximation.

4. Approximation Theory over Arbitrary Shape Domains

This section summarizes some important theorems that are necessary to prove the convergence of the expansion of a function using the nodal and modal basis functions introduced [16]. We start by proving the orthogonality and Parseval theorems for the modal basis functions. Then, the Weierstrass theorem is proved for a particular form of this expansion, which utilizes an orthonormal basis.

Theorem 1. *The set of functions $\bar{\psi}_j$ forms an orthogonal set of basis functions for $i = 1 \ldots N$.*

Proof. According to Equation (22), $\bar{\psi}_k = 1/\sigma_k f \tilde{V}_{(k)}$, with σ_k being the kth singular value of $\tilde{V}$. Therefore, multiplying $\bar{\psi}_k = 1/\sigma_k f \tilde{V}_{(k)}$ and $\bar{\psi}_l = 1/\sigma_l f \tilde{V}_{(l)}$ $(1 \le k, l \le N)$ and integrating over Ω yields

$$\int_\Omega \bar{\psi}_k \bar{\psi}_l d\Omega = \frac{1}{\sigma_k \sigma_l} \int_\Omega \tilde{V}^T_{(k)} f^T f \tilde{V}_{(l)} \tag{23}$$

or

$$\int_\Omega \bar{\psi}_k \bar{\psi}_l d\Omega = \frac{\left(\tilde{V}^T_{(k)} \tilde{V}_{(l)} = \delta_{kl}\right)}{\sigma_k \sigma_l} \int_\Omega f^T f d\Omega = \frac{\|f\|_2^2 \delta_{kl}}{\sigma_k \sigma_l}, \tag{24}$$

where $\|f\|_2 = \sqrt{\int_\Omega f^T f d\Omega}$ is the L_2 norm of the moments. Equation (24) is finite (since $\sigma_{j=1\ldots N} \neq 0$) and is only nonzero when $k = l$, and hence, $\bar{\psi}_k$ and $\bar{\psi}_l$ are orthogonal, and thus, the proof is complete. □

Since in the standard SVD, the singular values are ordered from *larger* to *smaller values*, the modes corresponding to $\bar{\psi}_j$ also start from the lowest-frequency mode for $j = 1$ and range to the highest-frequency mode for $j = N$.

Remark 1. *As a result of Theorem 1, the set of bases*

$$\tilde{\psi}_k = \frac{f}{\|f\|_2} \tilde{V}_{(k)}, \tag{25}$$

is orthonormal. However, we should note that this will be only used for the proof of theorems and is not used in the spectral element formulation in this paper since it requires extra computations for the calculation of the norm of the moment vector over the domain, although the latter can be pre-computed and tabulated.

Any given function u can be *approximated* as the sum of $\bar{\psi}$s with the converging property, i.e., a higher accuracy is obtained when higher modes are included in the approximation. To show this, we call $\mathbb{I}_u^{(m)}$ the projection of u into a subset of the modal space with $m \le N$ modes:

$$u \approx \mathbb{I}_u^{(m)} = \sum_{k=1}^{m} c_k \bar{\psi}_k. \tag{26}$$

Substituting $\bar{\psi}_k$ from Equation (22) in Equation (26) yields

$$\mathbb{I}_u^{(m)} = [f(x)]_{1\times N} \tilde{V}_{N\times m}\, \tilde{S}^{-1}_{m\times m} c_{m\times 1} \tag{27}$$

Definition 1. *Inspired by the terminology "Fourier Coefficients" given in (Ref. [17], p. 27) for the polynomial approximation of one-dimensional functions, we consistently extend it to Generalized Fourier Coefficients/Amplitudes (GFCs) of the $\mathbb{R}^d$ approximation $u \approxeq \sum c_k \bar{\psi}_k$, where the c_ks are the GFCs.*

Theorem 2. *Parseval theorem for the orthogonal expansion given in Equation (26):*

$$\int_\Omega \left(\sum_{k=1}^m c_k \bar{\psi}_k \right)^2 d\Omega = \|f\|_2^2 \sum_{k=1}^m \left(\frac{c_k}{\sigma_k} \right)^2. \tag{28}$$

Proof.

$$\begin{aligned} \left(\sum_{k=1}^m c_k \bar{\psi}_k \right)^2 &= c_1^2(\bar{\psi}_1)^2 + c_2^2(\bar{\psi}_2)^2 + \ldots + c_m^2(\bar{\psi}_m)^2 \\ &+ c_1c_2\bar{\psi}_1\bar{\psi}_2 + c_1c_3\bar{\psi}_1\bar{\psi}_3 + \ldots + c_2c_1\bar{\psi}_2\bar{\psi}_1 + \ldots \\ &= \sum_{k=1}^m \sum_{l=1}^m c_k c_l \bar{\psi}_k \bar{\psi}_l. \end{aligned} \tag{29}$$

Integrating Equation (29) on Ω yields

$$\int_\Omega \left(\sum_{k=1}^m c_k \bar{\psi}_k \right)^2 d\Omega = \int_\Omega \sum_{k=1}^m \sum_{l=1}^m c_k c_l \bar{\psi}_k \bar{\psi}_l d\Omega = \sum_{k=1}^m \sum_{l=1}^m c_k c_l \int_\Omega \bar{\psi}_k \bar{\psi}_l d\Omega. \tag{30}$$

Using the result of Theorem 1 by substituting Equation (24) in Equation (30), one obtains

$$\begin{aligned} \int_\Omega \left(\sum_{k=1}^m c_k \bar{\psi}_k \right)^2 d\Omega &= \sum_{k=1}^m \sum_{l=1}^m c_k c_l \int_\Omega \bar{\psi}_k \bar{\psi}_l d\Omega \\ &= \sum_{k=1}^m \sum_{l=1}^m c_k c_l \frac{\delta_{kl}}{\sigma_k \sigma_l} \|f\|_2^2 = \|f\|_2^2 \sum_{k=1}^m \frac{c_k c_k}{\sigma_k \sigma_k} \\ &= \|f\|_2^2 \sum_{k=1}^m \left(\frac{c_k}{\sigma_k} \right)^2. \end{aligned} \tag{31}$$

□

Theorem 3. *Let $u(x)$ be defined for $x \in \Omega \subset \mathbb{R}^d$. Then, the GFCs c_k in the series expansion $u \approx \sum_{k=1}^m c_k \bar{\psi}_k, 1 \leq m \leq N$, decay.*

Proof. We need to show that for any $l = 1 \ldots (N-1)$, the ratio of the upper bounds of two consequent GFCs is less than unity. Consider N *distinct* points $\check{x}_{l=1\ldots N} \in \Omega$. Then, interpolating at $\check{x}$ using Equation (27) yields

$$u = \underbrace{\begin{bmatrix} f(\check{x}_1) \\ f(\check{x}_2) \\ \vdots \\ f(\check{x}_N) \end{bmatrix}_{N\times N}}_{\check{\mathcal{V}}} \tilde{V}_{N\times m}\, \tilde{S}^{-1}_{m\times m} c_{m\times 1}. \tag{32}$$

since $\check{x}_{l=1\ldots N}$ are distinct; then, $\check{\mathcal{V}}$ is invertible, and hence, Equation (32) can be written as

$$\check{u} = \check{\mathcal{V}}^{-1} u = \tilde{V}_{N\times m}\, \tilde{S}^{-1}_{m\times m} c_{m\times 1}. \tag{33}$$

Left-multiplying Equation (33) with the qth column of $\tilde{V}_{N\times m}$ yields

$$[\tilde{V}_{(q)}]^T_{1\times N}\, \check{u}_{N\times 1} = [\tilde{V}_{(q)}]^T_{1\times N}\, \tilde{V}_{N\times m}\, \tilde{S}^{-1}_{m\times m} c_{m\times 1} = \frac{c_q}{\sigma_q}. \tag{34}$$

Note that since $\tilde{V}_{N\times m}$ is unitary, the product of its qth column with itself generates a vector of zeros, except unity at the qth location, and hence, the final result of the vector product is the ratio of the qth GFC c_q to the qth singular value σ_q. Equation (34) can be further expanded as given below:

$$\left|\frac{c_q}{\sigma_q}\right| = \frac{|c_q|}{\sigma_q} = \left\|\tilde{V}^T_{(q)}\check{u}\right\| \leq \left\|\tilde{V}^T_{(q)}\right\| \|\check{u}\| = \|\check{u}\| \tag{35}$$

Since $\tilde{V}$ is unitary, $\left\|\tilde{V}^T_{(q)}\right\| = 1$ was used in the last equality of Equation (35). Furthermore, we can write

$$\frac{|c_{q+1}|}{\|\check{u}\|} \leq \sigma_{q+1}, \tag{36}$$

$$\frac{|c_q|}{\|\check{u}\|} \leq \sigma_q, \tag{37}$$

which determines the maximum possible magnitudes of the GFCs as

$$\max(|c_{q+1}|) = \sigma_{q+1}\|\check{u}\|, \tag{38}$$

$$\max(|c_q|) = \sigma_q\|\check{u}\|, \tag{39}$$

and according to the property of singular value decomposition, where $\sigma_N \leq \sigma_{N-1} \leq \ldots \leq \sigma_2 \leq \sigma_1$:

$$\frac{\max(|c_{q+1}|)}{\max(|c_q|)} = \frac{\sigma_{q+1}}{\sigma_q} \leq 1. \tag{40}$$

Therefore, the GFCs are decaying (not necessarily monotonically) in an envelope shaped by the decay of the singular values (see dashed bars in Figure 2). Therefore, the proof is complete. □

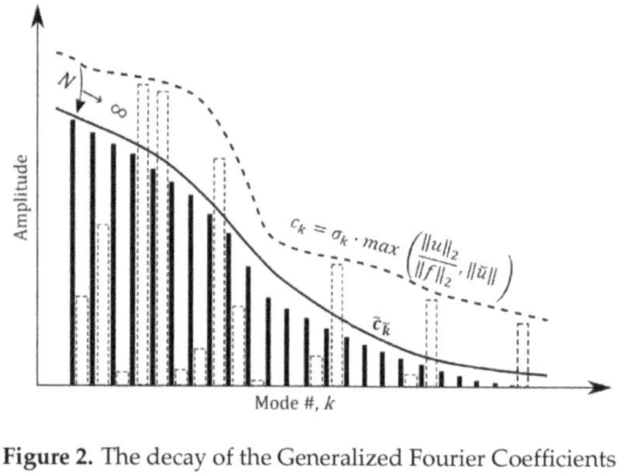

Figure 2. The decay of the Generalized Fourier Coefficients (GFCs): dashed bars correspond to the orthogonal basis $\bar{\psi}$ and the solid bars correspond to the orthonormal basis $\tilde{\psi}$, which, according to Theorem 7, monotonically decrease.

Theorem 4. *For any bounded u defined on $\Omega \subset \mathbb{R}^d$, the GFCs of the orthogonal modal basis functions in Equation (26) are given by*

$$c = \tilde{U}^T u \tag{41}$$

Proof. Similar to the proof of Theorem 3, this time, consider the N distinct points to be the AFPs $\tilde{x}_{l=1...N}$. Then, interpolation using Equation (27) yields

$$u = \begin{bmatrix} f(\tilde{x}_1) \\ f(\tilde{x}_2) \\ \vdots \\ f(\tilde{x}_N) \end{bmatrix}_{N\times N} \tilde{V}_{N\times m}\, \tilde{S}^{-1}_{m\times m} c_{m\times 1}. \tag{42}$$

Substituting the SVD of the Vandermonde matrix $\tilde{V} = \tilde{U}\tilde{S}\tilde{V}^T$ into Equation (42) yields

$$u = \tilde{U}_{N\times N}\tilde{S}_{N\times N}\tilde{V}^T_{N\times N}\tilde{V}_{N\times m}\tilde{S}^{-1}_{m\times m}c_{m\times 1}. \tag{43}$$

But

$$\tilde{V}^T_{N\times N}\tilde{V}_{N\times m} = I_{N\times m} = \begin{bmatrix} \begin{bmatrix} 1 & & \\ & \ddots & \\ & & 1 \end{bmatrix}_{m\times m} \\ \begin{bmatrix} 0 & & \\ & \ddots & \\ & & 0 \end{bmatrix}_{(N-m)\times m} \end{bmatrix}. \tag{44}$$

Substituting Equation (44) into Equation (43) yields

$$u = \tilde{U}_{N\times N}\tilde{S}_{N\times N}I_{N\times m}\tilde{S}^{-1}_{m\times m}c_{m\times 1}. \tag{45}$$

Similarly, the product of a singular value matrix $\tilde{S}_{N\times N}$ with the truncated identity matrix $I_{N\times m}$ is the truncated diagonal matrix given below:

$$\tilde{S}_{N\times N}I_{N\times m} = \tilde{S}_{N\times m} = \begin{bmatrix} \begin{bmatrix} \sigma_1 & & \\ & \ddots & \\ & & \sigma_m \end{bmatrix}_{m\times m} \\ \begin{bmatrix} 0 & & \\ & \ddots & \\ & & 0 \end{bmatrix}_{(N-m)\times m} \end{bmatrix}. \tag{46}$$

Substituting Equation (46) into Equation (45) and multiplying both sides by $\tilde{U}^T$ yields

$$\tilde{U}^T u = \tilde{S}_{N\times m}\tilde{S}^{-1}_{m\times m}c_{m\times 1}. \tag{47}$$

Since

$$\tilde{S}_{N\times m}\tilde{S}^{-1}_{m\times m} = \begin{bmatrix} \begin{bmatrix} \sigma_1 & & \\ & \ddots & \\ & & \sigma_m \end{bmatrix}_{m\times m} \\ \begin{bmatrix} 0 & & \\ & \ddots & \\ & & 0 \end{bmatrix}_{(N-m)\times m} \end{bmatrix} \begin{bmatrix} \frac{1}{\sigma_1} & & \\ & \ddots & \\ & & \frac{1}{\sigma_m} \end{bmatrix} = I_{N\times m}, \tag{48}$$

Equation (47) yields

$$\tilde{U}^T u = I_{N\times m} c_{m\times 1} = c_{m\times 1} \tag{49}$$

which shows that all GFCs are obtained with $\mathcal{O}(N^2)$ operations (i.e., matrix–vector product) when the full-rank unitary matrix $\tilde{U}_{N\times N}$ is invoked, i.e., $c_{1\ldots N} = \tilde{U}^T_{N\times N} u$. However, when only the first m columns of $\tilde{U}$ are used, the result is the first m GFCs, i.e., $c_{1\ldots m} = \tilde{U}^T_{N\times m} u$. □

In summary, we proved in Theorem 3 that the ratio of the upper bounds of two subsequent GFCs is less than unity. In addition, the GFCs of an orthogonal expansion of a function of Equation (26) are given by Equation (41) as $c = \tilde{U}^T u$ (Theorem 4) and that all GFCs are obtained with $\mathcal{O}(N^2)$ operations (matrix-vector product) when the full-rank unitary matrix $\tilde{U}_{N\times N}$ is invoked.

Remark 2. *The reader may notice that Equation (41) constitutes a Generalized Discrete Transform similar to a Discrete Fourier Transform by multiplying the given function u with the unitary matrix $\tilde{U}$. While the basic mechanism of $c = \tilde{U}^T u$ is similar to a DFT, Equation (41) generalizes the DFT to arbitrarily shaped and non-periodic domains. This important result reveals that the unitary matrix $\tilde{U}$ can, in fact, be regarded as a generalized convolution operator (matrix).*

Remark 3. *The truncated GFCs using $c_{1\ldots m} = \tilde{U}^T_{N\times(1\ldots m)} u$ offers a generalized* a posteriori *error estimator. In the classical Fourier analysis, the* tail *of the Fourier series (higher frequencies) can be eliminated to smooth the solution. This filtering strategy can be used here on an arbitrary shape domain by just using* the first m modes *in the series expansion $u \approxeq \sum c_k \bar{\psi}_k$ with the coefficients $c_{1\ldots m} = \tilde{U}^T_{N\times(1\ldots m)} u$. Strictly speaking, the norm of the eliminated tail, i.e., $\|\tilde{U}^T_{N\times(m+1)\ldots N)} u\|_2$, is an error estimator of the sum of the* eliminated energy *according to Parseval's theorem (Theorem 2).*

Next, we prove a theory regarding the convergence of the moments:

Theorem 5. *For an Ω selected as an arbitrary subset of $x_1 \times x_2 \times \ldots x_i \times \ldots \times x_d = \mathbb{R}^d$ inside a d-dimensional cube $|x_i| \le a = \tanh(\frac{1}{2}) = 0.4621\ldots$ (see Figure 3), $\int_\Omega \|f\|_2^2 d\Omega$ is monotonically increasing but convergent and*

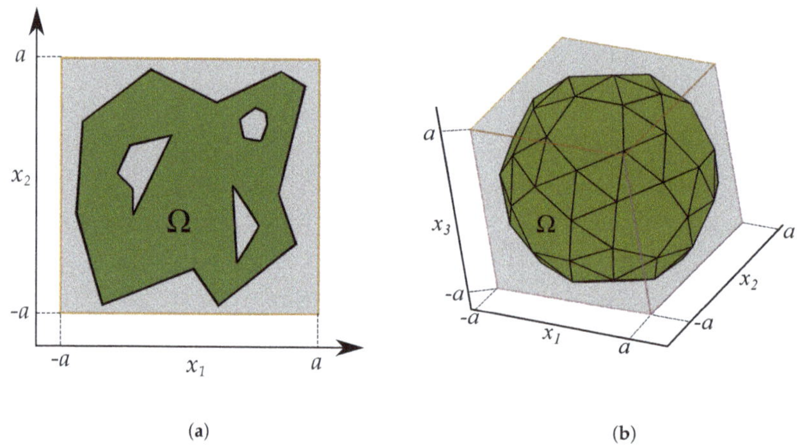

Figure 3. The transformation of Ω to a bounded area near the origin. Here, $a = \tanh(\frac{1}{2}) = 0.4621\ldots$. (**a**) Two-dimensional; (**b**) three-dimensional.

$$\int_\Omega \|f\|_2^2 d\Omega \le \int_\Omega \frac{1}{\prod_{k=1}^d (1-\xi_k^2)} d\xi_1 d\xi_2 \ldots d\xi_d \le 1, \quad \lim_{N\to\infty} \int_\Omega \|f_Q\|_2^2 d\Omega = 1. \tag{50}$$

Proof. To start, consider the one-dimensional space where, according to Equation (1), $f = x^{i=0\ldots N}$. Hence,

$$\begin{aligned}\int_\Omega \|f\|_2^2 d\Omega &= \int_\Omega \left[1, x, x^2, \ldots, x^N\right]\left[1, x, x^2, \ldots, x^N\right]^T d\Omega \\ &= \int_\Omega \left(1 + x^2 + x^4 + \ldots + x^{2N}\right) d\Omega.\end{aligned} \tag{51}$$

Obviously, the integral of the partial sum in Equation (51) always has a monotonically increasing rate since the area under the integrand is always increasing and positive. Now, in order to show that it converges as $N \to \infty$, let us rewrite Equation (51) as follows:

$$\int_\Omega \|f\|_2^2 d\Omega = \int_\Omega \frac{1 - x^{2(N+1)}}{1 - x^2} d\Omega. \tag{52}$$

Since Ω is now transformed to a box bounded by $|a| < 1$, $x^{2(N+1)} \to 0$ as $N \to \infty$, and thus, as $N \to \infty$, Equation (52) leads to

$$\int_\Omega \|f\|_2^2 d\Omega = \int_\Omega \frac{1}{1 - x^2} d\Omega = \int_\Omega \operatorname{arctanh}(\xi) d\Omega = \int_{-a}^{a} \operatorname{arctanh}(\xi) d\Omega = 2\operatorname{arctanh}(a) = 1. \tag{53}$$

Similarly, in the d-dimensional Q-space as $N \to \infty$, the transient terms depending on N vanish, and hence,

$$\begin{aligned}\int_\Omega \|f = f_Q\|_2^2 d\Omega &= \int_1 \frac{1}{1 - x_1^2} dx_1 \int_2 \frac{1}{1 - x_2^2} dx_2 \ldots \int_d \frac{1}{1 - x_d^2} dx_d = \prod_{i=1}^{d} \int_i \operatorname{arctanh}(\xi_i) d\xi_i \\ &= \int_{-a}^{a} \ldots \int_{-a}^{a} \operatorname{arctanh}(\xi_1)\operatorname{arctanh}(\xi_2) \ldots \operatorname{arctanh}(\xi_d) d\Omega \\ &= (2\operatorname{arctanh}(a))^d = 1.\end{aligned} \tag{54}$$

With a little investigation, we realize that $\int_\Omega \|f_P\|_2^2 d\Omega \leq \int_\Omega \|f_Q\|_2^2 d\Omega$ since the P-space is the lower triangular part of the Q-space. Thus, the above result is also valid for polynomial space P, and thus, the proof is complete. □

Note that the lth GFC in the expansion $u \approx \sum_{k=1}^{m} c_k \bar{\psi}_k$ can be obtained by multiplying both sides with $\bar{\psi}_l$ and integrating over Ω. The result is presented below:

$$\int_\Omega u \bar{\psi}_l d\Omega = \sum_{k=1}^{m} c_k \left(\int_\Omega \bar{\psi}_l \bar{\psi}_k\right). \tag{55}$$

Applying the orthogonality Theorem 1 (Equation (24)) to Equation (55) yields

$$\int_\Omega u \bar{\psi}_l d\Omega = \sum_{k=1}^{m} c_k \frac{\|f\|_2^2 \delta_{lk}}{\sigma_l \sigma_k} = \|f\|_2^2 \frac{c_l}{\sigma_l^2}. \tag{56}$$

Hence,

$$c_l = \frac{\sigma_l^2}{\|f\|_2^2} \int_\Omega u \bar{\psi}_l d\Omega, \tag{57}$$

which yields

$$\frac{c_k}{\sigma_k} = \frac{\sigma_k}{\|f\|_2^2} \int_\Omega u \bar{\psi}_k d\Omega. \tag{58}$$

By applying the Cauchy–Schwarz inequality, Equation (58) gives a new upper bound for c_k/σ_k as follows:

$$\frac{|c_k|}{\sigma_k} = \frac{\sigma_k}{\|f\|_2^2} \left\| \int_\Omega u \bar{\psi}_k d\Omega \right\| \leq \frac{\sigma_k}{\|f\|_2^2} \sqrt{\int_\Omega u^2 d\Omega} \sqrt{\int_\Omega (\bar{\psi}_k)^2 d\Omega}. \tag{59}$$

Since u is square-integrable, $\|u\|_2 = \sqrt{\int_\Omega u^2 d\Omega}$ is finite. Substituting the definition $\tilde{\psi}_k = f\tilde{V}_{(k)}/\sigma_k$ in Equation (59) yields

$$\frac{|c_k|}{\sigma_k} \leq \frac{\sigma_k}{\|f\|_2^2}\|u\|_2\sqrt{\left(\|f\frac{\tilde{V}_{(k)}}{\sigma_k}\|\right)^2} \leq \frac{\sigma_k}{\|f\|_2^2}\|u\|_2\|f\|_2\frac{1}{\sigma_k}, \tag{60}$$

or

$$\frac{|c_k|}{\sigma_k} \leq \frac{\|u\|_2}{\|f\|_2}. \tag{61}$$

Therefore, comparing Equation (37) and Equation (61), it can be concluded that the kth GFC is always bounded by

$$|c_k| \leq \sigma_k \max\left(\frac{\|u\|_2}{\|f\|_2}, \|\breve{u}\|\right) \tag{62}$$

This means that the magnitude of c_k is not necessarily monotonically decreasing, although its bound, i.e., $|c_k|_{max} = \sigma_k \times \max(\|u\|_2/\|f\|_2, \|\breve{u}\|)$, is always monotonically decreasing. This situation is graphically illustrated in Figure 2.

Theorem 6. *Parseval theorem for the orthonormal expansion given in Equation (25):*

$$\int_\Omega \left(\sum_{k=1}^{m} \tilde{c}_k\tilde{\psi}_k\right)^2 d\Omega = \sum_{k=1}^{m} \tilde{c}_k^2. \tag{63}$$

Proof.

$$\begin{aligned}
\int_\Omega \left(\sum_{k=1}^{m} \tilde{c}_k\tilde{\psi}_k\right)^2 d\Omega &= \int_\Omega \sum_{k=1}^{m}\sum_{l=1}^{m} \tilde{c}_k\tilde{c}_l\tilde{\psi}_k\tilde{\psi}_l d\Omega = \sum_{k=1}^{m}\sum_{l=1}^{m} \tilde{c}_k\tilde{c}_l \int_\Omega \tilde{\psi}_k\tilde{\psi}_l d\Omega \\
&= \sum_{k=1}^{m}\sum_{l=1}^{m} \tilde{c}_k\tilde{c}_l \int_\Omega \frac{f}{\|f\|_2}\tilde{V}_{(k)}\left(\frac{f}{\|f\|_2}\tilde{V}_{(l)}\right)^T d\Omega \\
&= \sum_{k=1}^{m}\sum_{l=1}^{m} \tilde{c}_k\tilde{c}_l \int_\Omega \frac{f}{\|f\|_2}\tilde{V}_{(k)}\tilde{V}_{(l)}^T\frac{f^T}{\|f\|_2} d\Omega = \sum_{k=1}^{m}\sum_{l=1}^{m} \frac{\tilde{c}_k\tilde{c}_l\delta_{kl}}{\|f\|_2^2}\int_\Omega ff^T d\Omega \\
&= \sum_{k=1}^{m}\sum_{l=1}^{m} \tilde{c}_k\tilde{c}_l\delta_{kl} = \sum_{k=1}^{m}\sum_{l=1}^{m} \tilde{c}_k\tilde{c}_k = \sum_{k=1}^{m} \tilde{c}_k^2.
\end{aligned} \tag{64}$$

□

Theorem 7 (Weierstrass approximation theorem for Ω, an arbitrary subset of $\mathbb{R}^d$)**.** *Assume that u is a bounded real-valued function on $\Omega \subset \mathbb{R}^d$. Then, for every $\epsilon > 0$, there exists a polynomial p such that for all $x \in \Omega$, $\|u - p\| < \epsilon$. Particularly, below we give an explicit relationship for the polynomial p:*

$$p = \left(\int_\Omega \tilde{\psi}_{\tilde{k}} u d\Omega\right)\tilde{\psi}_{\tilde{k}}, \tag{65}$$

where

$$\tilde{k} = \text{permutation}\left(\text{sort}_\downarrow\left[\int_\Omega f_1 u d\Omega, \int_\Omega f_2 u d\Omega, \ldots, \int_\Omega f_N u d\Omega\right]\left[\tilde{V}_{(1)}, \tilde{V}_{(2)}, \ldots, \tilde{V}_{(N)}\right]\right)$$

Proof. Using the orthonormality Theorem 6, multiplying $u \approx \sum_k \tilde{c}_k \tilde{\psi}_k$ with the lth orthonormal basis and integrating yields

$$\int_\Omega \tilde{\psi}_l u d\Omega = \int_\Omega \sum_k \tilde{c}_k \tilde{\psi}_k \tilde{\psi}_l d\Omega = \sum_k \tilde{c}_k \int_\Omega \tilde{\psi}_k \tilde{\psi}_l d\Omega = \sum_k \tilde{c}_k \delta_{lk} = \tilde{c}_l \tag{66}$$

Substituting $\tilde{c}_k$ from Equation (66) in $u \approx \sum_k \tilde{c}_k \tilde{\psi}_k$ yields

$$u \approx \sum_k \tilde{c}_k \tilde{\psi}_k = \sum_k \tilde{\psi}_k \left(\int_\Omega \tilde{\psi}_k u d\Omega \right), \tag{67}$$

which is the Gram–Schmidt process for the error vector $u_\perp$ that is normal to the span of all orthonormal modal basis functions, i.e.,

$$u_\perp = u - \frac{\langle u, \tilde{\psi}_1 \rangle}{\langle \tilde{\psi}_1, \tilde{\psi}_1 \rangle} \tilde{\psi}_1 - \frac{\langle u, \tilde{\psi}_2 \rangle}{\langle \tilde{\psi}_2, \tilde{\psi}_2 \rangle} \tilde{\psi}_2 - \ldots - \frac{\langle u, \tilde{\psi}_N \rangle}{\langle \tilde{\psi}_N, \tilde{\psi}_N \rangle} \tilde{\psi}_N \tag{68}$$

or

$$u = \langle u, \tilde{\psi}_1 \rangle \tilde{\psi}_1 + \langle u, \tilde{\psi}_2 \rangle \tilde{\psi}_2 + \ldots + \langle u, \tilde{\psi}_N \rangle \tilde{\psi}_N + u_\perp \tag{69}$$

observing that, according to Theorem 6, $\langle \tilde{\psi}_k, \tilde{\psi}_k \rangle = \int_\Omega (\tilde{\psi}_k)^2 d\Omega = 1$ since $\tilde{\psi}$s are orthonormal. Therefore, the Gram–Schmidt process results in monotonically decreasing residuals $u_\perp$ (and hence, the proof of the theorem) if we can show that in some way, the magnitude of the projections $\langle u, \tilde{\psi}_k \rangle$ can be made monotonically decreasing. In order to show this, let us focus on the integral $\int_\Omega \tilde{\psi}_k u d\Omega$ in Equation (67), which can be written as the summation of the Riemannian series on the quadrature points $\mathring{x}_i \in \Omega$ and the measure μ_i according to

$$\int_\Omega \tilde{\psi}_k u d\Omega = \sum_{i=1}^{\infty} \tilde{\psi}_k(\mathring{x}_i) u(\mathring{x}_i) \mu_i = [u(\mathring{x}_1)\mu_1, u(\mathring{x}_2)\mu_2, \ldots] \begin{bmatrix} \tilde{\psi}_k(\mathring{x}_1) \\ \tilde{\psi}_k(\mathring{x}_2) \\ \vdots \end{bmatrix}, \tag{70}$$

which can be further expanded using the definition $\tilde{\psi}_k = f/\|f\| \tilde{V}_{(k)}$ as follows:

$$\begin{aligned} \int_\Omega \tilde{\psi}_k u d\Omega &= [u(\mathring{x}_1)\mu_1, u(\mathring{x}_2)\mu_2, \ldots] \begin{bmatrix} \tilde{\psi}_k(\mathring{x}_1) \\ \tilde{\psi}_k(\mathring{x}_2) \\ \vdots \end{bmatrix} \\ &= [u(\mathring{x}_1)\mu_1, u(\mathring{x}_2)\mu_2, \ldots] \begin{bmatrix} \frac{f_1(\mathring{x}_1)}{\|f\|_2} & \frac{f_2(\mathring{x}_1)}{\|f\|_2} & \cdots & \frac{f_N(\mathring{x}_1)}{\|f\|_2} \\ \frac{f_1(\mathring{x}_2)}{\|f\|_2} & \frac{f_2(\mathring{x}_2)}{\|f\|_2} & \cdots & \frac{f_N(\mathring{x}_2)}{\|f\|_2} \\ \vdots & \vdots & \vdots & \vdots \end{bmatrix} \left[\tilde{V}_{(1)}, \tilde{V}_{(2)}, \ldots, \tilde{V}_{(N)} \right]. \end{aligned} \tag{71}$$

The first two terms on the *r.h.s.* of Equation (71) can be combined to give

$$\int_\Omega \tilde{\psi}_k u d\Omega = \frac{1}{\|f\|_2} \left[\sum_{i=1}^{\infty} u(\mathring{x}_i) f_1(\mathring{x}_i) \mu_i, \sum_{i=1}^{\infty} u(\mathring{x}_i) f_2(\mathring{x}_i) \mu_i, \ldots \right] \left[\tilde{V}_{(1)}, \tilde{V}_{(2)}, \ldots, \tilde{V}_{(N)} \right], \tag{72}$$

or

$$\int_\Omega \tilde{\psi}_k u d\Omega = \frac{1}{\|f\|_2} \left[\int_\Omega f_1 u d\Omega, \int_\Omega f_2 u d\Omega, \ldots, \int_\Omega f_N u d\Omega \right] \left[\tilde{V}_{(1)}, \tilde{V}_{(2)}, \ldots, \tilde{V}_{(N)} \right]. \tag{73}$$

According to Equation (73), the kth moment of inertia, i.e., $\int_\Omega f_k u d\Omega$, appears. Since u is bounded on Ω, all these integrals exist and are finite, and hence, the vector

$$W = \left[\int_\Omega f_1 u d\Omega, \int_\Omega f_2 u d\Omega, \ldots, \int_\Omega f_N u d\Omega \right], \tag{74}$$

exists and is finite. Therefore, using Equations (73) and (74), the coefficient of the Gram–Schmidt projection, i.e., $\int_\Omega \tilde{\psi}_k u d\Omega$, given as

$$\int_\Omega \tilde{\psi}_k u d\Omega = \frac{1}{\|f\|_2}[W_1, W_2, \ldots, W_N]\left[\tilde{V}_{(1)}, \tilde{V}_{(2)}, \ldots, \tilde{V}_{(N)}\right], \tag{75}$$

can be made monotonically decreasing by a matching pursuit procedure. First, we define the vector product of W with the kth column of the unitary matrix $\tilde{V}$ as:

$$\tilde{W}_k = W.\tilde{V}_{(k)} \quad , \quad k = 1 \ldots N. \tag{76}$$

This is the projection of W into the unitary space (matrix) $\tilde{V}$. Then, we find the permutation of integer indices k by sorting the result of vector product as follows:

$$\tilde{k} = \text{permutation}\big(\text{sort}_\downarrow(\tilde{W})\big). \tag{77}$$

$\tilde{k}$ is always monotonically decreasing, and hence, so is $\int_\Omega \tilde{\psi}_{\tilde{k}} u d\Omega$ (according to Equation (75)). Consequently, the Gram–Schmidt process always removes the component of u in span$(\tilde{\psi})$, starting from large values and moving to smaller values. Therefore, according to Equation (69), the error $u_\perp$ for the $\tilde{k}$ permutation is always decreasing, which means that by increasing the polynomial order, N, in the following expansion:

$$u = \sum_{\tilde{k}=1}^{N} \langle u, \tilde{\psi}_{\tilde{k}} \rangle \tilde{\psi}_{\tilde{k}} + u_\perp, \tag{78}$$

for some large enough N, we obtain $u_\perp = \epsilon$, and thus, the proof is complete. □

The monotonic decay of $\tilde{c}_{\tilde{k}}$ is compared with the decay of the coefficients of the orthogonal basis $\tilde{\psi}_k$, which decays in an envelope (bound), as can be seen in Figure 2.

5. Results and Discussion

5.1. Calculating the Lebesgue Constant

The general linear interpolation $\mathbb{I}_u^{(m)} = \mathcal{L}_N u$ can be written using the modal expansion Equation (26) as

$$\mathbb{I}_u^{(m)} = \mathcal{L}_N u = \sum_{k=1}^{m} c_k \tilde{\psi}_k. \tag{79}$$

It is our interest to study the error generated by such an interpolation. In particular, the conventional approach is to show that

$$E\left(\mathbb{I}_u^{(m)}\right) = \|u - \mathcal{L}_N u\|, \tag{80}$$

is small enough. Equation (80) can be written as

$$\|u - \mathcal{L}_N u\| = \|u - u^* + u^* - \mathcal{L}_N u\| \tag{81}$$

where u^* is the best approximant for which $\mathcal{L}_N u^* = u^*$ at point $x \in \Omega$. In fact, $\mathcal{L}_N$ is the Lagrange basis constructed at the approximate Fekete points $x = \tilde{x} \in \Omega$, and then used as a basis at any point $x \in \Omega$, in particular, $x = \tilde{x}$, where $\mathcal{L}_N = 1$, and hence, $u^* = \mathcal{L}_N u^*$. Next, by using the triangle inequality:

$$\begin{aligned} E\left(\mathbb{I}_u^{(m)}\right) &= \left\| u - u^* + \underbrace{u^*}_{\mathcal{L}_N u^*} - \mathcal{L}_N u \right\| \leq \|u - u^*\| + \|\mathcal{L}_N u^* - \mathcal{L}_N u\| \\ &\leq \|u - u^*\| + \|\mathcal{L}_N\| \|u - u^*\| \leq (1 + \|\mathcal{L}_N\|)\|u - u^*\| \end{aligned} \tag{82}$$

Therefore, the interpolation error is bounded by the norm of the interpolation operator, and hence, the Lebesgue constant can be defined as

$$\Lambda_N = \|\mathcal{L}_N\| \tag{83}$$

We are interested in the interpolation points that result in the minimal Lebesgue constant to maximize the accuracy of the interpolation according to Equation (82). The AFPs presented before have such a property. Exact calculation of the Lebesgue constant has always been difficult and mostly undertaken using empirical relations. The closed-form formulae are only available for the case of 1D and simple interpolants, like Chebyshev polynomials, as mentioned before. We derive an explicit relation for the Lebesgue constant of an arbitrary-shaped domain in $\mathbb{R}^d$. The key to achieving this is the minimum singular value of the orthogonal basis functions $\bar{\psi}_k$, as is shown below. Using Equation (22), Equation (83) leads to

$$\Lambda_N = \|\mathcal{L}_N\| = \left\|[f(x)]_{1\times N}\tilde{V}\,\tilde{S}^{-1}\right\| \tag{84}$$

or

$$\|\mathcal{L}_N\| = \sqrt{\int_\Omega \left([f(x)]_{1\times N}\tilde{V}\,\tilde{S}^{-1}\right)^T [f(x)]_{1\times N}\tilde{V}\,\tilde{S}^{-1} d\Omega} \tag{85}$$

or

$$\begin{aligned}\|\mathcal{L}_N\| &= \sqrt{\int_\Omega \tilde{S}^{-1}\tilde{V}^T\,(f^T f)\tilde{V}\,\tilde{S}^{-1} d\Omega} \\ &= \sqrt{\int_\Omega (f^T f) d\Omega\,\tilde{S}^{-1}\tilde{V}^T\tilde{V}\tilde{S}^{-1}} = \sqrt{\int_\Omega (f^T f) d\Omega}\,\tilde{S}^{-1}\end{aligned} \tag{86}$$

Therefore,

$$\|\mathcal{L}_N\|_{\max} = \frac{\sqrt{\int_\Omega (f^T f) d\Omega}}{\sigma_{\min}} \tag{87}$$

Remark 4. *It is crucially important to note that the norm of the moments, i.e.,* $\int_\Omega (f^T f) d\Omega$ *in the numerator of Equation (87), can be significantly large (especially for the higher-order polynomials) on a domain that is not centered around the origin. This leads to significantly inaccurate interpolation results because the Lebesgue constant increases rapidly according to Equation (82).*

Therefore, it is important to use domains centered around the origin (and additionally mapping them inside the unity box), where it can be shown that the result of $\int_\Omega (f^T f) d\Omega$ is always smaller than unity and monotonically converges to unity for an infinite-order polynomial (see Theorem 5). In this case, the upper bound in Equation (87) is very small, and for the basis functions evaluated on AFPs—since $\sigma_{\min}$ is close to unity—the interpolation remains very accurate for significantly higher-degree polynomials.

Comparison Between SVD and QR Approaches

As mentioned before, the QR algorithm of Sommariva et al. [12] needs at least two iterations to yield a well-conditioned AFP. This is mentioned as the rule of "twice is enough" by Ref. [18]. However, the proposed SVD-based approach, as explained before, results in a closed-form relation (Equation (10)) to approximate the Fekete points. In order to validate this, the two-dimensional function $u = \cos(3\pi x)\cos(3\pi y)$ was reconstructed on $\Omega = [-1,1] \times [-1,1]$ by evaluating the Vandermonde matrix on two different sets of points obtained by the SVD and QR methods using nodal basis functions. Since the SVD-based approach does not require iterations, for comparison, the number of iterations in the QR-based approach (which is an iterative method) was set to $s = 1$.

As shown in Figure 4, when increasing the degree of polynomial, the Lebesgue constant of the QR-based algorithm (based on one iteration) increased rapidly and the reconstructed function exhibited unacceptable errors. In contrast, the sum of the absolute values of the weights of the quadratures, i.e., w_i, obtained using the SVD-based formulation monotonically decreased. For both methods, $\sum_i w_i \approx 4$, which shows that the QR-based algorithm generated negative weights with an increased polynomial degree. Additionally, the Lebesgue constant of the SVD method remained smaller than that of the QR method. The same observation held for the L_2 norm of the SVD method compared with the QR approach.

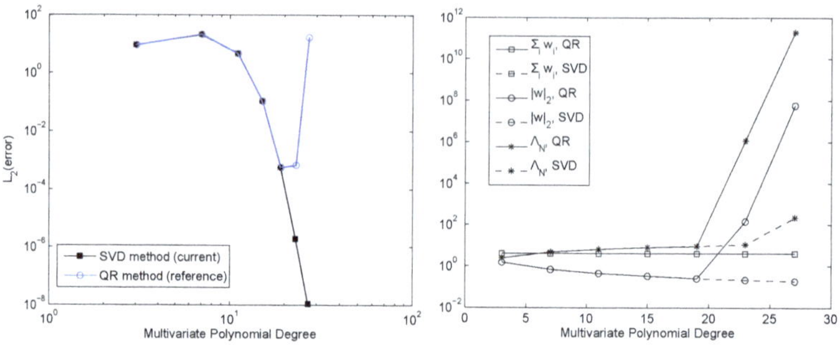

Figure 4. Comparison between SVD and QR (one iteration) approaches for finding AFPs: (**left**) the interpolation error versus polynomial degree and (**right**) various measures.

5.2. Numerical Results

5.2.1. Validating the Modal Basis Functions

Before assessing the accuracy of the interpolation via AFPs on general domains, we needed to *validate* the modal basis proposed in Equation (22) on a set of Chebyshev points. Therefore, in the first test case, a set of 20×20 Chebyshev points was generated by the tensor product of a one-dimensional distribution. Then, the Vandermonde matrix was evaluated on these points, and the modal basis Equation (22) was obtained. The results are plotted in Figure 5. As seen, the first and second modes had low-frequency contents, while the last mode had the highest frequency. Also, the symmetry was well preserved on the Chebyshev points.

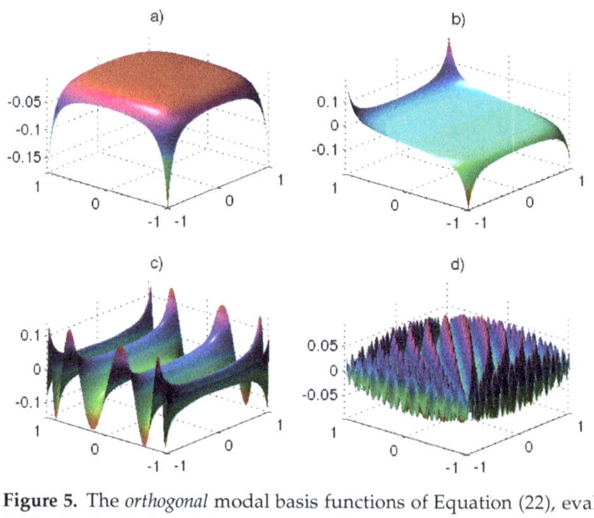

Figure 5. The *orthogonal* modal basis functions of Equation (22), evaluated on Chebyshev points. (**a**) $\bar{\psi}_1$; (**b**) $\bar{\psi}_2$; (**c**) $\bar{\psi}_{60}$; (**d**) last mode, i.e., $\bar{\psi}_{400}$.

To evaluate the effect of eliminating the higher modes, Figure 6 shows that the rank of the orthogonal basis was 400, corresponding to a full-rank SVD decomposition of the

Vandermonde matrix evaluated at Chebyshev points, as mentioned before. When all the bases were included, i.e., $m = 400$, the reconstructed function showed excellent agreement with the exact solution. Additionally, a ninety-percent reconstruction (i.e., $m = 360$) yielded an ideal reconstruction. It can be seen in Figure 6b with half of the required modes (i.e., $m = 200$), the reconstruction of the function without considering higher frequencies yielded an unacceptable result. These observations were in agreement with the preceding convergence theory.

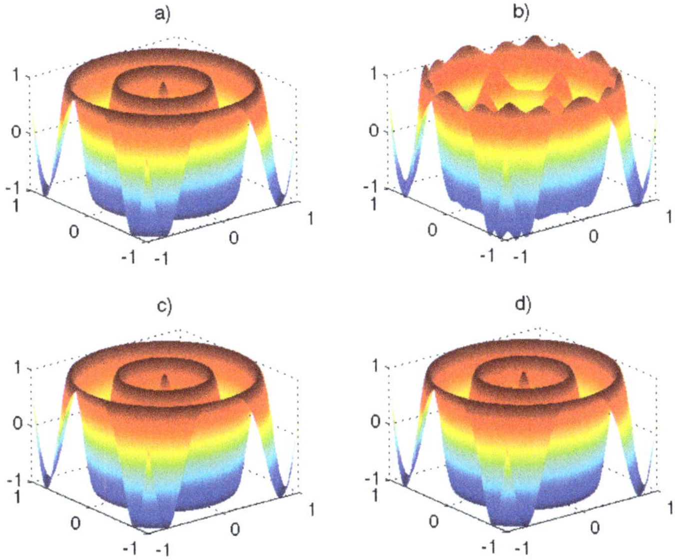

Figure 6. The spectral filtering of $u = \cos\left(4\pi\sqrt{x^2+y^2}\right)$ in Q-space by eliminating the higher-frequency orthogonal basis Equation (26). (**a**) $m = 400$, i.e., *full rank*; (**b**) $m = 200$, i.e., *half rank*; (**c**) $m = 360$, i.e., *ninety percent rank*; (**d**) exact.

5.2.2. Validating the Nodal Basis Functions

A plot of the *nodal* basis functions (Equation (21)) for a 16th-order P-space on a T-shaped domain is presented in the left column of Figure 7. In this figure, the top-left plot shows the first nodal basis ψ_1, and the bottom-left plot depicts the 200th nodal basis ψ_{200}. It should be noted that ψ_1 took a value of one at the top-right corner of the T-shaped domain and zero at the other AFPs. The right column of Figure 7 shows the modal basis functions (see Equation (22)) for a 16th-order P-space on a T-shaped domain, where the top plot corresponds to the first modal basis $\bar{\psi}_1$ and the bottom plot to the 200th modal basis $\bar{\psi}_{200}$.

The orthogonal modal basis functions, in addition to being well conditioned, were very accurate compared with the radial basis functions (RBFs) for the same number of DOFs. Figure 8 compares the reconstruction of two wavelengths of sinusoidal functions using an RBF basis (left column) and orthogonal modal basis functions $\bar{\Psi}$ (right column). As can be clearly seen, the RBF was either very inaccurate (top-left) or required many more DOFs to yield accurate results (bottom-left). However, $\bar{\Psi}$ yielded a spectral resolution with the minimum points per wavelength (see the middle of the right smiley-face domain). This resolution was comparable with the Fourier decomposition of the smooth functions on a simple rectangular geometry. These results, which demonstrate the superior accuracy/efficiency of the modal basis functions, can contribute to the field of meshfree methods, where RBF methods are extensively used.

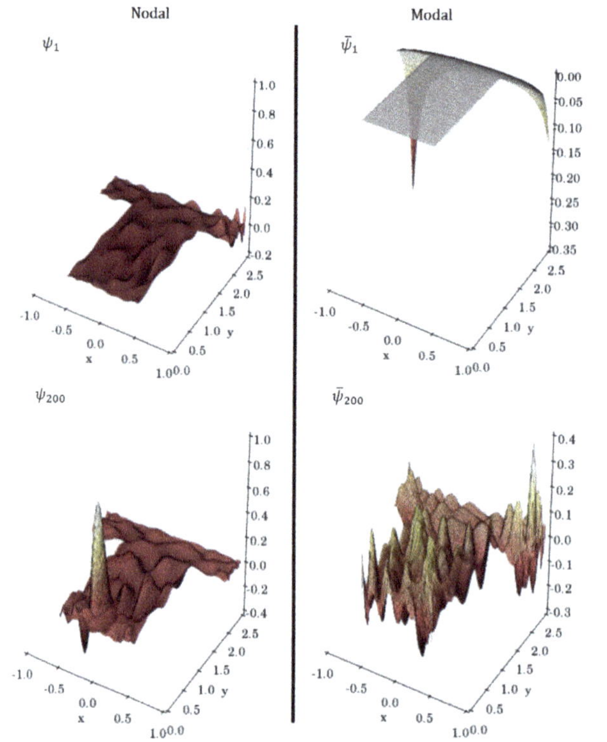

Figure 7. The first and the 200th basis functions of the *nodal* (**left column**) and *modal* (**right column**) approximate Fekete basis. **Top-left**: ψ_1, **bottom-left**: ψ_{200}, **top-right**: $\bar{\psi}_1$, and **bottom-right**: $\bar{\psi}_{200}$.

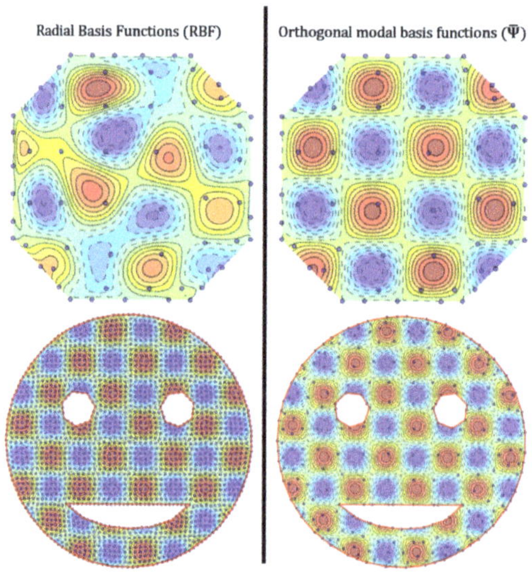

Figure 8. Comparison of the orthogonal modal basis functions ($\bar{\Psi}$) and RBFs in reconstructing the solution on two domains. (**Top** row) With the same DOF. (**Bottom** row) With same L_2 error. **Left** column shows the RBFs; **right** column corresponds to the orthogonal modal basis functions $\bar{\Psi}$.

To further assess the resolution of the orthogonal modal basis functions, the polynomial order on the smiley domain was increased. The result is presented in Figure 9 and demonstrates that six wavelengths could be reconstructed on this highly concave domain while the spectral accuracy was preserved.

Figure 9. Sub-elemental resolution of six wavelengths of $u = \sin(2\pi x)\sin(2\pi y)$ on a highly concave domain. As shown in the middle, the spectral accuracy corresponding to the optimal resolution is demonstrated.

5.2.3. Convergence Study

To demonstrate the superlinear convergence of the modal basis functions, a concave T-shaped domain was used to reconstruct the sinusoidal function. The result is presented in Figure 10, where the superlinear (spectral) convergence is shown.

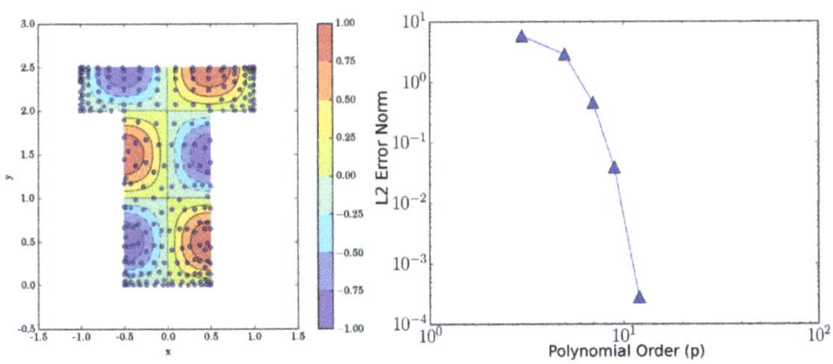

Figure 10. Superlinear convergence of the modal basis on the concave T-shape domain. (**Left**) Reconstructed function using the 16th-order modal basis constructed on the AFPs. (**Right**) L_2 error compared with the exact reconstruction.

Using the concept of GFCs (see Definition 1), it can be shown that the spectral content increases as the number of sides and/or the non-convexity of the domain increases. This can be a drawback of the generality of selecting *arbitrarily* shaped domains. This is shown in Figure 11, where the GFCs of the modal expansion is plotted against the corresponding modes for different domain shapes where, in all cases, the same function was reconstructed. As shown, more modes were required to closely reconstruct the function on a more complicated domain.

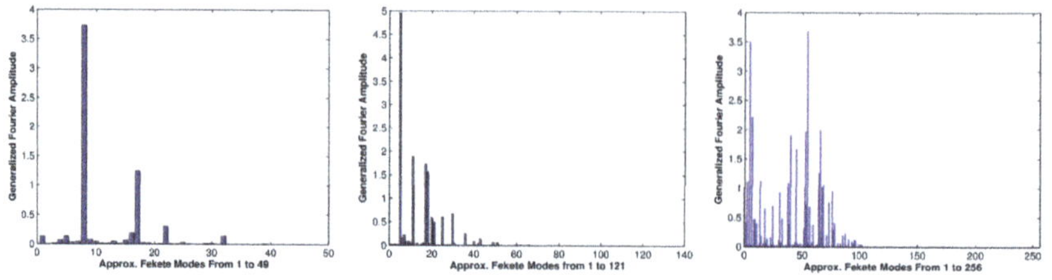

Figure 11. The spectra of $u = \sin(\pi x)\sin(\pi y)$ on different convex/concave elements. (**Left**) Using the 7th-order orthogonal modal basis Ψ on a quadrilateral element. (**Middle**) Using the 11th Ψ on a hexagonal element. (**Right**) Using the 16th Ψ on a T-shape element.

6. Summary and Conclusions

In this paper, a new approach based on the singular value decomposition (SVD) method is proposed to calculate the approximate Fekete points over an arbitrary shape domain. Explicit forms of equations are provided for the nodal and modal basis functions over such domains. Theorems are proved to show the convergence and accuracy of the proposed method. The method was implemented and some classical cases were analyzed. The results indicate superior performance of the proposed method in terms of the convergence and accuracy, while the computational cost was significantly reduced by reducing the degrees of freedom of the model. The proposed model has great potential to be implemented in computer programs and address multiphysics problems in various areas, with immediate application in spectral element methods [16]. As for the future extension of the model, the authors are working on the application of the proposed method for the fast and accurate simulations of various physical phenomena, such as conservation laws, problems in elasticity, and material science. In particular, in the area of materials science or mechanics of media with discontinuity (such as cracks or defects), where the modeling domain involves irregular geometries, this model is expected to provide a superior tool for fast and high-fidelity computations. The findings of this paper are summarized as follows:

- A closed-form relation is proposed to approximate the Fekete points on a general convex/concave polyhedral. The advantage of the current approach is that it also computes the weights of Gauss–Legendre/Lobatto, which can be used in a finite element formulation for the computation of quadrature points on arbitrary polygons.
- A new method to compute a set of modal basis functions using the SVD of the nodal Vandermonde matrix is developed, resulting in an orthogonal set basis Ψ and an orthonormal set $\tilde{\Psi}$.
- A generalization to a discrete Fourier transform for the case of the non-periodic polyhedral interval in $\mathbb{R}^d$ is presented. It is shown that the transpose of the left unitary matrix of the SVD of the Vandermonde matrix is the discrete Fourier matrix in this case.
- A closed-form formula is obtained to compute the Lebesgue constant of the interpolation on a general convex/concave polyhedral.
- The orthonormal modal basis provides a new way to look at the Weierstrass approximation theorem, where a new proof is provided for the general case in a subset of $\mathbb{R}^d$. This proof also implies the stability of modal basis expansion for arbitrary p-refinement.
- It is shown that the modal basis has superior accuracy/efficiency when compared with radial basis functions in a meshless approach.

Author Contributions: M.J.M.: development, writing, validation, visualization, and review and editing. A.G. (Arash Ghasemi): conceptualization, methodology, software, validation, visualization, formal analysis, writing—original draft, and review and editing. A.G. (Amirehsan Ghasemi): review and editing. J.C.N.III: review and editing. All authors have read and agreed to the published version of the manuscript.

Funding: This research did not receive any specific grant from funding agencies in the public, commercial, or not-for-profit sectors.

Data Availability Statement: No data were used for the research described in this article.

Conflicts of Interest: The authors declare no conflicts of interest.

References

1. Smith, S.J. Lebesgue constants in polynomial interpolation. In *Annales Mathematicae et Informaticae*; Eszterházy Károly College, Institute of Mathematics and Computer Science: Eger, Hungary, 2006; Volume 33, pp. 1787–5021.
2. Trefethen, L.N. *Approximation Theory and Approximation Practice, Extended Edition*; SIAM: Philadelphia, PA, USA, 2019.
3. Ghasemi, A.; Taylor, L.K.; Newman, J.C. Spectral/hp Hull: A Degree of Freedom Reducing Discontinuous Spectral Element Method for Conservation Laws with Application to Compressible Fluid Flow. *arXiv* **2016**, arXiv:1605.07443.
4. Perumal, L. A Brief Review on Polygonal/Polyhedral Finite Element Methods. *Math. Probl. Eng.* **2018**, *2018*, 5792372. [CrossRef]
5. Cesarano, C.; Cennamo, G.M.; Placidi, L. Humbert polynomials and functions in terms of Hermite polynomials towards applications to wave propagation. *WSEAS Trans. Math.* **2014**, *13*, 595–602.
6. Briani, M.; Sommariva, A.; Vianello, M. Computing Fekete and Lebesgue points: Simplex, square, disk. *J. Comput. Appl. Math.* **2012**, *236*, 2477–2486. [CrossRef]
7. Dattoli, G.; Ricci, P.E.; Cesarano, C. The Lagrange Polynomials, the Associated Generalizations, and the Umbral Calculus. *Integral Transform. Spec. Funct.* **2003**, *14*, 181–186. [CrossRef]
8. Jaśkowiec, J. Discontinuous Galerkin method on reference domain. *Comput. Assist. Methods Eng. Sci.* **2017**, *22*, 177–204.
9. Cangiani, A.; Georgoulis, E.H.; Houston, P. hp-version discontinuous Galerkin methods on polygonal and polyhedral meshes. *Math. Model. Methods Appl. Sci.* **2014**, *24*, 2009–2041. [CrossRef]
10. Taylor, M.A.; Wingate, B.A.; Vincent, R.E. An Algorithm for Computing Fekete Points in the Triangle. *SIAM J. Numer. Anal.* **2000**, *38*, 1707–1720. [CrossRef]
11. Bendito, E.; Carmona, A.; Encinas, A.; Gesto, J. Estimation of Fekete points. *J. Comput. Phys.* **2007**, *225*, 2354–2376. [CrossRef]
12. Sommariva, A.; Vianello, M. Computing approximate Fekete points by QR factorizations of Vandermonde matrices. *Comput. Math. Appl.* **2009**, *57*, 1324–1336. [CrossRef]
13. Sommariva, A.; Vianello, M. Product Gauss cubature over polygons based on Green's integration formula. *BIT Numer. Math.* **2007**, *47*, 441–453. [CrossRef]
14. Franklin, W. PNPOLY-Point Inclusion in Polygon Test-WR Franklin (WRF). 2006. Available online: https://wrfranklin.org/Research/Short_Notes/pnpoly.html (accessed on 28 September 2024).
15. Persson, P.O.; Strang, G. A simple mesh generator in MATLAB. *SIAM Rev.* **2004**, *46*, 329–345. [CrossRef]
16. Ghasemi, A. Spectral Hulls: A Degree of Freedom Reducing hp-Strategy in Space/Time. Ph.D. Thesis, University of Tennessee at Chattanooga, 2016. Available online: https://scholar.utc.edu/theses/476 (accessed on 28 September 2024).
17. Funaro, D. *Polynomial Approximation of Differential Equations*; Springer Science & Business Media: Berlin/Heidelberg, Germany, 2008; Volume 8.
18. Giraud, L.; Langou, J.; Rozložnik, M.; Eshof, J.v.d. Rounding error analysis of the classical Gram–Schmidt orthogonalization process. *Numer. Math.* **2005**, *101*, 87–100. [CrossRef]

Mathematical and Computational Applications

MDPI

Article

Variability on Functionally Graded Plates' Deflection Due to Uncertainty on Carbon Nanotubes' Properties

Alda Carvalho [1,2], Ana Martins [1,3], Ana F. Mota [1] and Maria A. R. Loja [1,4,*]

1 CIMOSM, Centro de Investigação em Modelação e Otimização de Sistemas Multifuncionais, ISEL/IPL, Instituto Superior de Engenharia de Lisboa, 1959-007 Lisboa, Portugal; alda.carvalho@uab.pt (A.C.); ana.martins@isel.pt (A.M.); anafilipa.s.mota@gmail.com (A.F.M.)
2 DCeT, Universidade Aberta & CEMAPRE/REM, ULisboa & CIMOSM, ISEL, 1269-001 Lisboa, Portugal
3 CIMA—Research Centre for Mathematics and Applications & CIMOSM, ISEL, 7000-671 Évora, Portugal
4 IDMEC, IST-Instituto Superior Técnico, Universidade de Lisboa, 1049-001 Lisboa, Portugal
* Correspondence: amelialoja@tecnico.ulisboa.pt

Abstract: Carbon nanotubes are widely used as material reinforcement in diverse fields of engineering. Being that their contribution is significant to improving the mean properties of the resulting materials, it is important to assess the influence of the variability on carbon nanotubes' material and geometrical properties to structures' responses. This work considers functionally graded plates constituted by an aluminum continuous phase reinforced with single-walled or multi-walled carbon. The nanotubes' weight fraction evolution through the thickness is responsible for the plates' functional gradient. The plates' samples are simulated considering that only the nanotubes' material and geometrical characteristics are affected by uncertainty. The results obtained from the multiple regression models developed allow us to conclude that the length of the nanotubes has no impact on the maximum transverse displacement of the plates in opposition to the carbon nanotubes' weight fraction evolution, their internal and external diameters, and the Young's modulus. The multiple regression models developed can be used as alternative prediction tools within the domain of the study.

Keywords: linear static finite element analysis; functionally graded plates; carbon nanotubes; Monte Carlo simulation; multiple regression modeling

1. Introduction

Functionally graded materials (FGM) are advanced composite materials with well-known advantages and applications [1] when compared to traditional composites. This is evident in the minimization of abrupt stress transitions which are characteristic of these latter. Simultaneously, the recognition of carbon nanotubes' (CNTs) attractive physicochemical structural abilities has motivated a large number of studies as well as applications in a wide range of sectors, as referred to in the review developed by Gupta et al. [2] 2019. More recent applications include CNTs composite fibers for electronic textiles, CNT-coated electrodes for probing neurons in the cerebrum, and bio-compatible materials for scaffolding in tissue engineering as mentioned by Rathinavel et al. [3].

A significant number of reviews focusing on a diversity of structural, mechanical, and physical characteristics of CNTs have been developed so far, those referenced here being only some of the most recent. Hence, among others, one may refer to the review paper by Liew et al. [4], which focused on the relevance of CNTs in functionally graded materials and the graded patterns of such reinforcements. The review also includes a survey of mechanical analysis of functionally graded carbon nanotube-reinforced composites and discusses recent advances and prospects in this field of research. Another review study was performed by Radhamani et al. [5] on carbon nanotubes' reinforced metal and steel nanocomposites. In this review, topics such as carbon nanotubes' dispersion uniformity, interfacial bonding, weight fraction, length, and alignment with the matrix are examined against the nanocomposites' properties enhancement. The authors also discuss possible paths to overcome technical challenges and potential applications of those nanocomposites. Vinyas et al. [6] performed a comprehensive review of the analysis of nanocomposites, covering the manufacturing processes to the properties' characterization, to identify the various methodologies, techniques, theories, and formulations that are used in nanocomposite technology. The use of graphene and its derivatives, particularly graphene platelets as relevant nanofillers for composites due to superior mechanical properties, was the object of a review work done by Zhao et al. [7]. The paper reviews graphene's mechanical properties, outlines functionally graded materials and functionally graded graphene platelets reinforced composites, discusses micromechanics models, and explores key problems and future research directions. Another review on CNTs, their properties, synthesis methods, and applications in micro and nanotechnology was developed by Shoukat and Khan [8]. In that work, various types of carbon nanotubes are explored, with details on their electrical conductance, resistivity, and thermal conductivity. Besides specific growth methods for the carbon nanotubes, the paper also describes formation methods, and applications of CNTs in electronics, biomedicine, and chemical sensors. Soni et al. [9] performed a comprehensive review of recent research on functionally graded carbon nanotubes reinforced composites, covering experimental and theoretical studies on the mechanical, vibration, thermal, thermo-mechanical, and low-velocity impact responses of those structures and/or structural components. The authors also discuss challenges and potential research paths.

From a more general perspective, functionally graded materials and the structures built from this type of advanced composites continue to draw the attention of several researchers. To name only a few, one can refer to the recent works of Valencia Murillo et al. [10], Kurpa et al. [11], and Alghanmi and Aljaghthami [12].

Considering the subject of the present work, it was relevant to compile references ranging from the CNTs properties' experimental and theoretical characterization to their modeling and integration as reinforcement into continuous material phases. A significant number of research works can be found in these domains. Among them, we can cite, for example, the investigation conducted by Ruoff and Lorents [13], which focused on the mechanical and thermal properties of CNTs. This study resulted in deriving the tensile and bending stiffness constants of ideal multi-walled and single-walled carbon nanotubes (MWCNTs, SWCNTs), and further extending the study to the characterization of their fundamental frequency. The authors suggested that the thermal expansion of CNTs would be essentially isotropic in contrast with the anisotropic character observed for carbon fibers and in graphite. The strength of the interface between the CNTs and the continuous matrix phase and the importance of achieving high-strength nanotube-reinforced composites was emphasized. Another research work involving the preparation of long carbon nanotubes, and the corresponding mechanical and physical property characterization, was carried out by Xie et al. [14], wherein they discussed the correlation among the obtained results with the CNTs microstructure.

A study on the thermo-mechanical properties of epoxy-based nanocomposites containing low-weight fractions of randomly oriented carbon nanotubes was developed by Fidelusa et al. [15]. The authors produced the nanocomposites with two epoxy resins and in both cases, a good dispersion of the nanotubes was exhibited. While moderate improvements in the tensile Young's modulus were observed, more significant enhancement in tensile impact toughness was evident for specific nanocomposites. The glass transition temperature showed no significant alterations and the elastic modulus of SWCNTs exceeded the Krenchel model predictions for short-fiber composites with random orientation.

Martone et al. [16] investigated the reinforcement efficiency arising from the use of CNTs with varying aspect ratios in an epoxy system. They concluded that this efficiency wasn't only influenced by the nanotubes' high modulus but also by their aspect ratio. Qiu and Yang [17] presented a study on the structure and properties of CNTs, where their geometric structure and their strong carbon–carbon chemical bonds were investigated, and found to contribute to relevant electronic, mechanical, and thermal properties. The authors also provided a summary and an outlook on foreseen potential developments in the field. The impact on the viscoelastic behavior of sandwich structures by integrating through-thickness graded core materials and nanocomposite skins with homogeneous or graded properties where the viscoelastic behavior of the sandwich core was modeled using the complex method was investigated by Loja [18]. It was concluded that effective design solutions for specific structural requirements can be achieved by considering such material design variables/profiles.

When the scale level of modeling requires a more refined approach because an average response is not sufficiently representative, the use of nonlocal approaches needs to be considered. This is well illustrated, for example, by the prediction needs arising from the increasing trend of electronic devices' miniaturization in different application fields and, from the use of functionally graded material systems in nano and microdevices. For such small-sized structures, the relevance of size dependency effects cannot be ignored, thus requiring the use of nonlocal approaches as noted by Eringen [19].

Many published works straightly related to the characterization of nanostructure and microstructure behavior can be found in the literature. Among others, one may refer to the literature review developed by Garg et al. [20] where the authors present a review of theories and methodologies used to investigate the behavior of nanostructures, where size-dependent and size-independent theories are discussed in detail.

To refer to some works in this context, Reddy and Pang [21] presented analytical solutions based on nonlocal approaches of the Euler–Bernoulli and Timoshenko beam theories to assess the size–dependency effect on the bending, buckling, and free natural vibrations of carbon nanotubes, modeled as straight beams. More recently, Kong et al. [22] investigated the influences of various parameters on the thermal buckling and post-buckling responses of functionally graded CNTs' reinforced nanobeams. To this purpose, the authors developed a formulation based on the Euler–Bernoulli theory, symmetry couple stress theory, and classical surface energy theory.

Reddy and Kim [23] studied the size effects on FGM nano and microplates by developing a general third-order theory of FGM plates accounting for a microstructure-dependent length scale parameter and the von Kármán nonlinearity. The theory considers temperature-dependent properties of the constituent materials, and the modified couple stress theory was used to incorporate a microstructural length scale parameter. Later, Liu et al. [24] presented a thin plate formulation based on isogeometric analysis, the modified couple stress theory, and the Kirchhoff theory to study the mechanical behavior of homogeneous and functionally graded microplates.

More recently, Thanh et al. [25] presented a study on the static bending behavior of functionally graded CNTs' reinforced composite nanoplates with different CNT distributions. The authors used isogeometric analysis in association with a refined plate theory and the modified couple stress theory to capture the size-dependent effects and to demonstrate the influence of the length scale on the bending behaviors of the nanoplates. A free vibration study of isotropic gradient elastic thick non-rectangular microplates was developed by Zhang et al. [26], where the microstructure-dependent effects of microplates were accounted for by considering a negative second-order gradient elastic theory with symmetry.

From another perspective, relevant to the present work, the non-deterministic character of real structures' behavior recommends its consideration in analyses. The uncertainty that affects the material and geometrical quantities involved in a problem definition and modeling has been the object of some studies. Different approaches and alternative descriptive and/or predictive models have been proposed for specific case studies. Although in a wider scope, one may refer in this context to the works by Sotiropoulos and Tserpes [27], Yin et al. [28], and Bouwer et al. [29].

Although theoretically, SWCNTs possess high ultimate strengths, experimental values demonstrate that these are considerably lower and exhibit variability, lacking clear information about this. Takakura et al. [30] presented the first experimental measurements of ultimate tensile strengths for individually defined SWCNTs. The authors found that the strength depends on the chiral structure with a small diameter. This led to the conclusion that near-armchair nanotubes display the highest strengths, thus pointing to the importance of, during the synthesis, targeting specific CNT structures.

In this context, recognizing the variability that affects structures and materials' properties, García-Macías et al. [31] explored the use of CNT in advanced cementitious composites with self-sensing capabilities, highlighting the limited understanding of uncertainties in functionally graded composite materials. They considered a stochastic representation of gradient profiles and studied the uncertainty propagation in the response of the plates. To characterize the response of these plates, the finite element method was used, and for representing stochastic uncertainties in overall composite material properties, they used probability theory. Pouresmaeeli and Fazelzadeh [32] studied the static instability of functionally graded carbon nanotube-reinforced composite beams considering material and geometrical uncertainties. A non-probabilistic approach was employed to model some variables' uncertainty propagation and sensitivity analysis was used to identify more significant ones. The influence of the nanotubes' volume fraction on the buckling load variability was also studied. Also recognizing that deterministic analyses are insufficient to more adequately characterize FGM plates' mechanical responses, Carvalho et al. [33] studied the effects of variability in material and geometrical parameters on the static and free vibration of those plates. Regression models were employed to describe these responses and to characterize the contribution of each model parameter to explaining response variability. A further study focused on exponentially graded plates with a functional gradient was developed by Rosa et al. [34]. In that study, the material and geometrical parameters for an exponentially graded plate were generated using a random multivariate normal distribution and Latin hypercube sampling. Subsequently, the linear static responses of these plates were obtained via the finite element method and correlated to the input parameters. Statistical models were established to serve as alternative description models.

Karsh et al. [35] proposed an approach to carry out a stochastic dynamic analysis of pre-twisted functionally graded plates. This approach was based on the combined use of an efficient neural network and the finite element method. From the results they achieved for the pre-twisted FGM cantilever plates, they assessed the influence of stochastic variations in geometric parameters, material properties, and temperature on the natural frequencies and mode shapes of those plates. The authors compared the efficiency and accuracy of artificial neural networks and polynomial neural networks to verify those results against direct Monte Carlo simulations. It was found that artificial neural networks can capture significant uncertainty effects on the dynamic responses of functionally graded plates without prejudice to the accuracy. Wang et al. [36] considered the use of extended support vector regression and Monte Carlo simulations to perform machine learning-aided stochastic free vibration analysis for FGM bar-type structures. The authors analyzed the influence of uncertainties on material properties, dimensions, and material gradient, and the approach was demonstrated to be computationally efficient and to provide accuracy. Gao et al. [37] presented a study on the probabilistic stability of functionally graded graphene platelets reinforced beams, using a non-inclusive Chebyshev metamodel with discrete singular convolution. Deterministic and probabilistic outcomes for critical buckling loads were obtained, including probability density functions, cumulative density functions (CDFs), means, and standard deviations. It was concluded that porosity distribution has a significant influence on the critical buckling load, followed by the porosity coefficient and graphene platelet weight fraction. A related investigation on the effects of the uncertainty in the free vibration responses of functionally graded porous nanocomposite shells with graphene platelet reinforcement was carried out by Baghlani et al. [38]. The authors considered the influence of material and geometry uncertainties, having used an interval analysis approach for the uncertainty analysis and Fourier differential quadrature for solving motion equations. It was found that the shells' type of curvature has a significant effect on uncertainty propagation and frequency sensitivity.

The present work aims to characterize the influence of introducing uncertainty regarding the geometrical and material properties of SWCNTs and MWCNTs on the maximum static deflection of functionally graded plates. Considering the scale level of modeling required for the present work, the use of a homogenized, local approach can be considered appropriate, thus being the one selected.

The remainder of this paper is organized as follows: Section 2 describes the materials and the methodology used in this study, Section 3 presents the results of a verification case, Section 4 describes the simulation process and the discussion of the obtained results, and Section 5 draws the main conclusions.

According to the authors' knowledge, and considering the literature search developed and illustrated in the present manuscript, no similar published works were found.

Overall, it is understood that a more complete understanding of the relative influence of CNTs' characterizing parameters will enable not only a more adequate selection of such nano inclusions for a specific application but may be also useful for customization purposes in manufacturing phases.

2. Materials and Methods

2.1. Functionally Graded Materials

This work aims to analyze the variability of the static deflection of functionally graded plates whose mixture composition results from the incorporation of SWCNTs and MWCNTs into an aluminum, continuous phase. Although other material and geometrical parameters associated with the plates' characterization can be considered as uncertainty sources, this work intends to analyze, solely, the variability induced by the uncertainty associated with CNTs characterizing parameters. Therefore, variables non-associated with CNT characterization are considered deterministic.

In this study, it is considered that the carbon nanotubes' weight fraction varies through the plate's thickness, as can be observed in Figure 1. On the lower surface of the plate, one has only aluminum, corresponding to material phase B, and at the upper surface, one has material phase A, which corresponds to a mixture of 2.5% in weight of carbon nanotubes with aluminum.

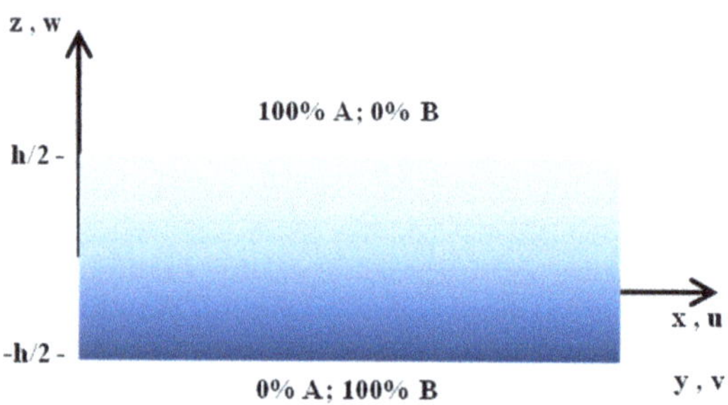

Figure 1. Schematic representation of the graded mixture of carbon nanotubes and aluminum through plates' thickness.

The mixture is governed by the known power law, presented in Equation (1), assuming that there is a perfect adhesion among phases and there are no porosities in the resulting material.

$$\begin{gathered} V_{f_{(A)}}(z) = \left(\frac{z}{h} + \frac{1}{2}\right)^{p}, \quad -\frac{h}{2} \leq z \leq \frac{h}{2} \\ V_{f_{(A)}}(z) + V_{f_{(B)}}(z) = 1 \end{gathered} \tag{1}$$

To predict the distribution through the thickness of the material properties, arising from the mixture of the nano-inclusions, one may consider Halpin–Tsai equations [39] to estimate Young's modulus, as presented in Equation (2).

$$
\begin{aligned}
E_{(C)} &= \frac{E_{(M)}}{8}\left[5\left(\frac{1+2\beta_{dd}V_{f\,(CNT)}}{1-\beta_{dd}V_{f\,(CNT)}}\right)+3\left(\frac{1+2\left(\frac{l_{(CNT)}}{d_{(CNT)}}\right)\beta_{dl}V_{f\,(CNT)}}{1-\beta_{dl}V_{f\,(CNT)}}\right)\right] \\
\beta_{dd} &= \frac{\frac{E_{(CNT)}}{E_{(M)}}-\frac{d_{(CNT)}}{4t_{(CNT)}}}{\frac{E_{(CNT)}}{E_{(M)}}+\frac{d_{(CNT)}}{2t_{(CNT)}}},\ \beta_{dl} = \frac{\frac{E_{(CNT)}}{E_{(M)}}-\frac{d_{(CNT)}}{4t_{(CNT)}}}{\frac{E_{(CNT)}}{E_{(M)}}+\frac{l_{(CNT)}}{2t_{(CNT)}}} \\
V_{f\,(CNT)} &= \frac{w_{(CNT)}}{w_{(CNT)}+\frac{\rho_{(CNT)}}{\rho_{(M)}}\left(1-w_{(CNT)}\right)}
\end{aligned}
\tag{2}
$$

where $E_{(C)}$, $E_{(M)}$, and $E_{(CNT)}$ represent respectively the Young's modulus of the mixture, of the aluminum matrix, and of the nanotubes. The nanotubes' outer diameter, thickness, and length are represented by $d_{(CNT)}$, $t_{(CNT)}$, and $l_{(CNT)}$, independently if one is considering single-walled or multi-walled nanotubes. The volume fraction of the nanotubes is determined by considering their weight fraction ($w_{(CNT)}$) in the mixture and the relation between the nanotubes and the aluminum densities. Besides being assumed that the resulting composite presents no porosities it is also assumed that there is a good dispersion of the nanotubes into the matrix, considering the low weight/volume fractions of the nanotubes used [40].

Voigt rule of mixtures was employed for determining the remaining material parameters, such as the Poisson's coefficient and shear modulus, according to Equation (3):

$$
P_{(FGM)} = P_{(A)}V_{f_{(A)}} + P_{(B)}V_{f_{(B)}} \tag{3}
$$

where $P_{(k)}$ stands for a generic property P of material k, and $V_{f_{(k)}}$ for its corresponding volume fraction. In this work, the material gradient is related to the evolution of the CNT weight fraction through the plates' thickness.

2.2. Displacement Field and Constitutive Relations

Considering the plates' geometrical characteristics that one intends to study, the first-order shear deformation theory, in which the displacement field is given in Equation (4), is used.

$$
\begin{aligned}
u(x,y,z) &= u_0(x,y) + z.\theta_x(x,y) \\
v(x,y,z) &= v_0(x,y) + z.\theta_y(x,y) \\
w(x,y) &= w_0(x,y)
\end{aligned}
\tag{4}
$$

In this equation, the parameters u, v, w stand for the displacements of a generic point in the directions oX, oY, and oZ, respectively. The displacements u^0, v^0, w^0 represent the position variation of a generic coordinate point $(x, y, 0)$ in the same directions. The rotations of the plate's transverse normals around the directions oY and oX are respectively denoted by θ_x^0 and θ_y^0. This displacement field is then characterized by presenting five degrees of freedom: $\{u^0, v^0, w^0, \theta_x^0, \theta_y^0\}$.

The corresponding deformations ε_{xx}, ε_{yy}, γ_{xy}, γ_{yz}, γ_{xz}, (Equation (5)) are subsequently obtained by applying to Equation (4), the kinematical relations from the elasticity theory for small deformations [41].

$$
\begin{aligned}
&\varepsilon_{xx} = \frac{\partial u^0}{\partial x} + z.\frac{\partial \theta_x^0}{\partial x}, \quad \varepsilon_{yy} = \frac{\partial v^0}{\partial y} + z.\frac{\partial \theta_y^0}{\partial y}, \\
&\gamma_{xy} = \left(\frac{\partial u^0}{\partial y} + \frac{\partial v^0}{\partial x}\right) + z\left(\frac{\partial \theta_x^0}{\partial y} + \frac{\partial \theta_y^0}{\partial x}\right), \\
&\gamma_{xz} = \frac{\partial w^0}{\partial x} + \theta_x^0, \gamma_{yz} = \frac{\partial w^0}{\partial y} + \theta_y^0
\end{aligned}
\tag{5}
$$

The stress and strain fields are described by the constitutive relations associated with the first-order shear deformation theory, as described in Equation (6).

$$\begin{Bmatrix} \sigma_{xx} \\ \sigma_{yy} \\ \tau_{xy} \end{Bmatrix} = \begin{bmatrix} Q_{11}(z) & Q_{12}(z) & 0 \\ Q_{12}(z) & Q_{22}(z) & 0 \\ 0 & 0 & Q_{66}(z) \end{bmatrix} \cdot \begin{Bmatrix} \varepsilon_{xx} \\ \varepsilon_{yy} \\ \gamma_{xy} \end{Bmatrix}$$
$$\begin{Bmatrix} \tau_{yz} \\ \tau_{xz} \end{Bmatrix} = \begin{bmatrix} k.Q_{44}(z) & 0 \\ 0 & k.Q_{55}(z) \end{bmatrix} \cdot \begin{Bmatrix} \gamma_{yz} \\ \gamma_{xz} \end{Bmatrix} \quad (6)$$

where the reduced elastic stiffness coefficients, Q_{ij}, are given in the literature, namely in [42], and the matrices are respectively associated with the membrane bending and transverse shear stiffness coefficients ($\boldsymbol{Q}_{mb}$ and $\boldsymbol{Q}_s$).

It is well known that the FSDT approach brings some limitations namely due to their through-thickness constant transverse shear deformations, γ_{yz}, γ_{xz}. To mitigate this, a shear correction factor, k, needs to be used. The use of $k = 5/6$, for homogeneous plates, is widely used, even when dealing with non-homogeneous plates. In this work, and to better adequate the shear correction factor to each specific plate, one can alternatively use the Singha et al. formulation [43], also implemented in [44].

$$k = \frac{\left(\int_{-\frac{h}{2}-d}^{\frac{h}{2}-d} \left(\int_{-\frac{h}{2}-d}^{z_{ns}} E(\xi).\xi d\xi \right) dz_{ns} \right)^2}{\int_{-\frac{h}{2}-d}^{z_{ns}} Q_{55} dz_{ns} . \int_{-\frac{h}{2}-d}^{\frac{h}{2}-d} \frac{\left(\int_{-\frac{h}{2}-d}^{z_{ns}} E(\xi).\xi d\xi \right)^2}{G(z_{ns})} dz_{ns}} \quad (7)$$

In Equation (7), the parameter z_{ns} represents the thickness coordinate corresponding to the neutral surface, h stands for the plate's thickness, and d represents the neutral surface' shift about the plate's mid-surface. This shifting of the neutral surface with respect to the plate middle surface and the adjustment in the power law to having it described in the neutral surface referential, are presented in Equation (8).

$$d = \frac{\int_{-h/2}^{h/2} E(z_{ms}).z_{ms} dz_{ms}}{\int_{-h/2}^{h/2} E(z_{ms}) dz_{ms}}$$
$$V_{f_{(A)}}(z_{ns}) = \left(\frac{z_{ns}+d}{h} + \frac{1}{2} \right)^p, \quad -\frac{h}{2} - d \leq z_{ns} \leq \frac{h}{2} - d \quad (8)$$

The parameters E, G, are the Young's and shear modulus of the functionally graded plates.

2.3. Finite Element Model

If one considers the minimization of the total potential energy of the system, it is achieved in the set of equilibrium Equation (9) for a generic plate element within a discretized domain [45]:

$$\boldsymbol{K}^e \boldsymbol{q}^e = \boldsymbol{F}^e \quad (9)$$

with $[K^e]$ being the element linear stiffness matrix, $\{q^e\}$ representing the vector of the element generalized displacements and $\{F^e\}$ the vector of the element generalized forces. The element stiffness matrix is given as described in Equation (10).

$$\boldsymbol{K}^e = \iiint_{V_e} \{ \boldsymbol{B}_{mb}^t . \boldsymbol{Q}_{mb} . \boldsymbol{B}_{mb} + \boldsymbol{B}_s^t . \boldsymbol{Q}_s . \boldsymbol{B}_s \} \, dV_e \quad (10)$$

The $\boldsymbol{Q}_{mb}$ and $\boldsymbol{Q}_s$ matrices have been defined in the previous section. Matrices $\boldsymbol{B}_{mb}$ and $\boldsymbol{B}_s$ express the relationships between the element nodal generalized displacements and the deformations and are closely related to the finite element implemented. In the present work, a bilinear Lagrange quadrilateral element is used (Q4). The constitution of these matrices is given for each element node as presented in Equation (11).

$$\boldsymbol{B}_{mb} = \begin{bmatrix} \frac{\partial N_i}{\partial x} & 0 & 0 & z.\frac{\partial N_i}{\partial x} & 0 \\ 0 & \frac{\partial N_i}{\partial y} & 0 & 0 & z.\frac{\partial N_i}{\partial y} \\ \frac{\partial N_i}{\partial y} & \frac{\partial N_i}{\partial x} & 0 & z.\frac{\partial N_i}{\partial y} & z.\frac{\partial N_i}{\partial x} \end{bmatrix}, \ \boldsymbol{B}_s = \begin{bmatrix} 0 & 0 & \frac{\partial N_i}{\partial y} & 0 & N_i \\ 0 & 0 & \frac{\partial N_i}{\partial x} & N_i & 0 \end{bmatrix} \tag{11}$$

where N_i is the interpolating function associated with the element i-th node. After the evaluation of all the element matrices and vectors and their assembly into the global stiffness matrix and global load vector, so the whole discretized domain is represented, the problem boundary conditions will be imposed to finally achieve the generalized nodal displacements.

2.4. Statistical Methods

Multiple linear regression is a statistical model used to predict the outcome of a dependent variable Y based on the values of two or more independent variables, $X_1, X_2, \ldots, X_p$, This model assumes a linear relationship between the dependent variable and the regressors is linear:

$$Y = \beta_0 + \beta_1 X_1 + \beta_2 X_2 + \ldots + \beta_p X_p + \varepsilon \tag{12}$$

As the individual data values, Y, for any given value of the independent variables vary randomly about the mean, an unobserved error or residual variable, ε, is introduced into the model to account for this random variation.

This model also assumes that the errors, ε, are uncorrelated with each other, follow a normal distribution with a mean of zero, and exhibit constant variance (homoscedasticity). For standard least squares estimation methods, the absence of perfect multicollinearity among the predictors is required, meaning that a linear relationship between two or more independent variables is not allowed.

To verify these assumptions, several tools can be employed. The Durbin–Watson two-sided test [46] is used to detect the presence of autocorrelation at lag 1 in the residuals. The Breusch–Pagan test [47] is applied to test for heteroskedasticity of the model's residuals. The Shapiro–Wilk test is used to examine the normality of the errors. The multicollinearity is examined with the VIF (Variance Inflation Factor) where a VIF value exceeding 5 indicates a problematic issue of correlation among the independent variables [48].

In multiple linear regression problems, specific hypothesis tests regarding the model parameters are useful for assessing the adequacy of the model. The ANOVA F test enables testing the joint significance of the regressors:

$$H_0: \beta_1 = \beta_2 = \ldots = \beta_p = 0 \quad vs \quad H_1: \exists \beta_j \neq 0 \quad (j = 1, \ldots, p) \tag{13}$$

Rejecting the null hypothesis of this test allows us to conclude that at least one of the independent variables significantly contributes to the model. However, this conclusion does not provide information about which regressions have a significant contribution to the model. Therefore, an individual independent variable test is needed—the t-test on the individual regression coefficient—to identify which regressors contribute significantly to the regression model:

$$H_0: \beta_j = 0 \quad vs \quad H_1: \beta_j \neq 0 \quad (j = 1, \ldots, p) \tag{14}$$

The Friedman Test

The Frieman test is a two-way analysis of variance by ranks, testing the null hypothesis that k-paired samples have been drawn from populations with the same median [49]. The R implementation is employed for this purpose [50]. If the null hypothesis of the Friedman test is rejected, it indicates that at least one of the populations' medians is different from the others. However, as the test result does not provide information about which medians differ from each other, pairwise comparisons between each pair of samples are performed using the Bonferroni correction.

3. Maximum Static Deflection: Verification Study

Before conducting the simulations required to obtain the results that will be post-processed to analyze the influence that the variability on the SWCNT and MWCNT material and geometrical properties will produce in the static maximum deflection of functionally graded plates, a verification case is performed.

To this purpose a sandwich simply supported square plate with unit edge and different edge-to-thickness ratios is analyzed. This plate is submitted to a 1 MPa uniformly distributed transverse load. The plate's core is constituted by alumina and the outer layers are composed of a functionally graded mixture of alumina and aluminum, that progresses to a fully metallic phase in the outer surfaces. This is done by considering different values for the power exponent law. The heights of the layers, progressing from the lower layer to the upper one, are respectively $2h/5$, $h/5$, and $2h/5$, being h the total thickness.

The plate is discretized in a 20 × 20 mesh of Q4 finite elements. The results are presented in a non-dimensional form using the multiplier $\overline{w} = \frac{10h^3 E_c}{a^4 q_0} \times w\left(\frac{a}{2}, \frac{b}{2}\right)$, where (a) and (b) represent the plate's dimensions with respect to the x and y directions respectively, (E_c) is the Young's modulus of alumina, and (q_0) the transverse load intensity.

The results obtained are presented in Table 1.

Table 1. Non-dimensional maximum static plate's deflection for different aspect ratios (a/h) and power law exponents (p).

	a/h					
	10			20		
p	$\overline{w}$ [51]	$\overline{w}$	$\delta_{\overline{w}}$ (%)	$\overline{w}$ [51]	$\overline{w}$	$\delta_{\overline{w}}$ (%)
0	0.4666	0.4655	−0.23	0.4494	0.4480	−0.31
0.5	0.6590	0.6574	−0.25	0.6401	0.6381	−0.31
2	1.0153	1.0129	−0.23	0.9945	0.9912	−0.33
10	1.4296	1.4194	−0.72	1.3997	1.3944	−0.38

The results obtained with the present model present very low relative deviations with respect to the reference [51], allowing us to conclude that the model has very good performance.

4. Case Study

4.1. Data Simulation for Carbon Nanotubes

In this subsection, a description of the simulation process employed in this case study is provided. To evaluate the impact of geometric and material properties of carbon nanotubes (CNTs) on the static response of functionally graded plates, a prior simulation of the CNTs was conducted using the values outlined in Figure 2. This figure presents in a tree schematic representation the reference values sourced from [https://www.cheaptubes.com (accessed on 15 February 2024)], where *d_ext* and *d_int* represent the outer and inner diameters of the carbon nanotube and *l* its length. The resulting cases represent the eight types of combinations obtained from the manufacturer's information.

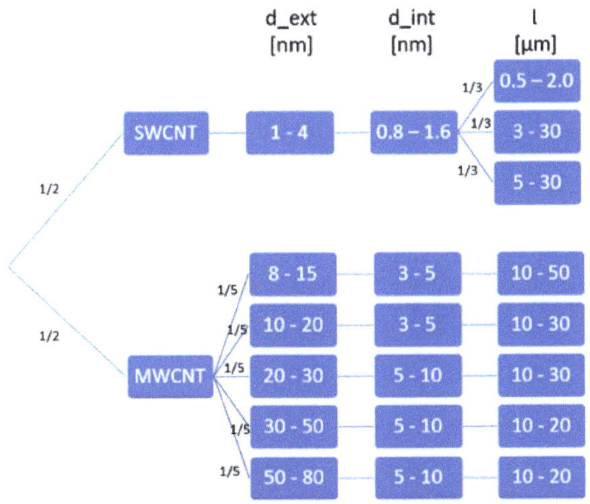

Figure 2. Illustrative flowchart of the simulation process.

Fifty nanotubes were simulated to create a reasonably sized sample that could effectively illustrate a real-world scenario. The uncertainty in input parameters arose from a dependency structure with a uniform assumption for each variable. This assumption of equiprobability aimed to translate the information provided by the manufacturer.

Initially, using equiprobability on the CNT type (SWCNT or MWCNT), the type was simulated. Subsequently, contingent on this outcome, the outer diameter of the nanotube was generated in accordance with the values provided in Figure 2. The other variables were simulated sequentially in the same fashion. For each nanotube combination obtained, a validation test was conducted. This allowed the elimination of impossible situations, such as the inner diameter being greater than the outer diameter.

The simulated carbon nanotubes are then integrated into an aluminum continuous phase (E = 70 GPa, ν = 0.3) in a graded manner through the thickness from which square plates are constituted. The FGM plates to be analyzed are considered in a simply supported condition and submitted to a unit uniform transverse pressure (1 Pa). The edge-to-thickness ratio (*a/h*) of the plates is equal to 20, with a unitary length edge (a = 1 m).

Considering the aim of the present study, the aluminum properties were considered not to be affected by uncertainty. The average elastic properties of the functionally graded mixture are estimated according to the Halpin–Tsai equation and Voigt rule of mixtures as referred to in Section 2. The plates are discretized in a 20×20 mesh of Q4 finite elements.

In Figure 3, one can see the results of the simulation as well as the maximum transverse displacement for $p = 0$. This case represents the maximum mixture in this study, the higher percentage of carbon in the nanotubes (Phase A: Aluminum + 2.5% CNTs). On the diagonal, the distribution of each of the variables is displayed. Also, below the diagonal, is the scatter plot, and above the diagonal are the values of the linear correlation coefficient for each pair of variables. The length presents a very low correlation with maximum transverse displacement. All the remainder input parameters present a positive and moderate correlation with the maximum transverse displacement. The low correlation between the diameters and Young's modulus is relevant when modeling the maximum transverse displacement using all input variables. This is discussed in the following section, where the variability of the maximum transverse displacement is described using a linear regression model with the input variables.

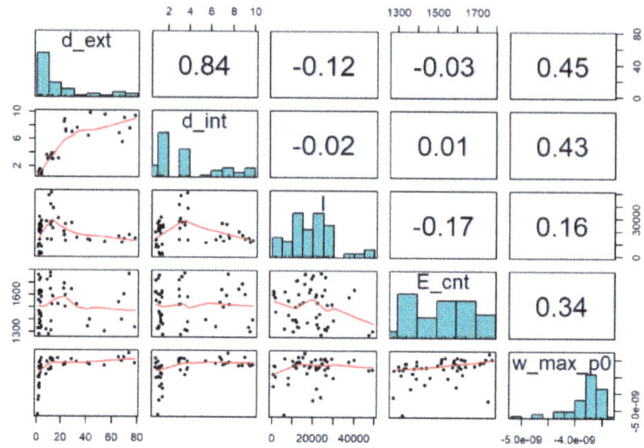

Figure 3. Matrix plot for the maximum transverse displacement, ($p = 0$), and all the input variables.

The input variables for this stage of analysis are the CNTs' length represented by l [μm], the CNT external and internal diameters respectively represented by *d_ext* and *d_int* [μm], the Young's modulus of the CNT, *E_cnt*, and the plate maximum transverse displacement *w_max* [m]. As expected, there is a high correlation between the diameters resulting from the simulation scheme (Figure 3). However, the correlation between the other inputs shows low values, which is important for a distinct contribution to explaining the variability of the maximum transverse displacement.

4.2. Plates' Maximum Transverse Displacement Distributions

In this work, both single-walled (SWCNT) and multi-walled (MWCNT) CNTs were used to integrate the plates, but separately. In Figure 4, we can see the maximum transverse displacement for the different values of the power-law exponent (p) in the two cases. It is possible to conclude that the maximum transverse displacement differs with the type of CNT.

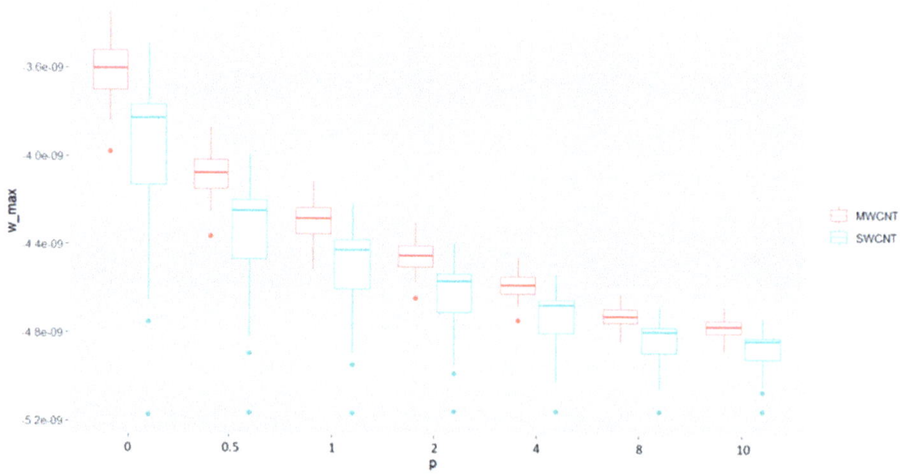

Figure 4. Plates' maximum transverse displacement [m] for the different values of the power law' exponent and CNT type.

Also, it is possible to observe that the plates' maximum transverse displacement has an inverse relationship with p. There is a clear difference in the value of the maximum transverse displacement among the exponents considered.

Since there is dependence between the exponent law samples, a Friedman test was applied to assess if these differences were significant. Considering the Friedman test result (p-value < 2.2×10^{-16}) and the pairwise comparison tests (results in Table 2), it is possible to conclude that the maximum transverse displacement values did not prove to be significantly different for $p = 8$ and $p = 10$ (p-value = 0.064) and are significant differences in this variable for all the remaining pairs. This result led to excluding the case $p = 10$ from the rest of the analysis because the conclusions would be similar.

Table 2. Comparison of maximum transverse displacement for the different values of the exponent of the power law: pairwise comparisons using the Bonferroni correction.

	p=0	p=0.5	p=1	p=2	p=4	p=8
$p = 0.5$	1.80×10^{-9}					
$p = 1$	1.20×10^{-11}	1.10×10^{-5}				
$p = 2$	4.30×10^{-13}	8.50×10^{-10}	1.70×10^{-5}			
$p = 4$	1.50×10^{-13}	1.10×10^{-11}	1.30×10^{-9}	3.00×10^{-5}		
$p = 8$	1.10×10^{-14}	2.90×10^{-13}	3.60×10^{-12}	1.90×10^{-10}	3.20×10^{-7}	
$p = 10$	4.90×10^{-15}	1.60×10^{-13}	6.20×10^{-13}	2.20×10^{-11}	3.40×10^{-9}	**0.064**

4.3. Model for Plates' Maximum Transverse Displacement—p = 0

The results obtained in the previous section led to the separation of the two cases (plates with SWCNT and plates with MWCNT). As we can see in Figures 5 and 6, the correlation between the variables differs with the CNT's type: SWCNT or MWCNT. Thus, the models were fitted for both cases, plates with SWCNT and plates with MWCNT, as well as for the various values of p (excluding $p = 10$, as in this case the maximum transverse displacement values did not prove to be significantly different from the case where $p = 8$).

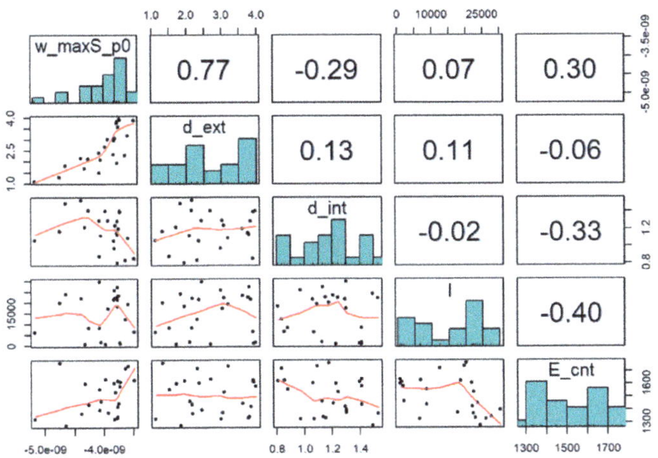

Figure 5. Matrix plot for the plates' maximum transverse displacement and all the input parameters: Plates with SWCNT.

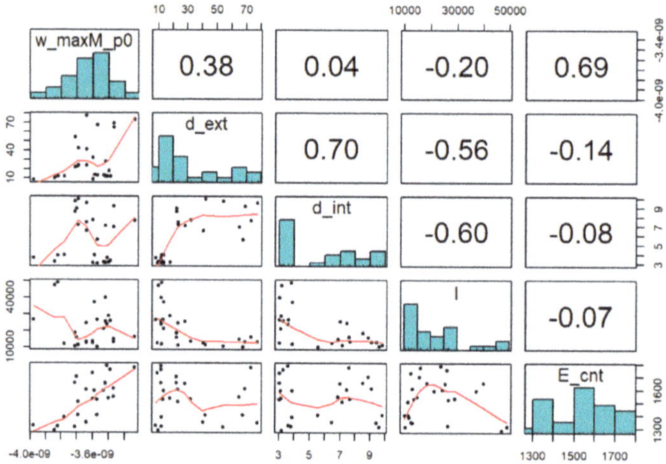

Figure 6. Matrix plot for the plates' maximum transverse displacement and all the input parameters: Plates with MWCNT.

As observed from the matrix plot in Figure 5, the external diameter of the SWCNTs presents a strong correlation to the maximum transverse deflection of the plates, followed by the Young's modulus with a weaker correlation coefficient. The internal diameter also shows a weaker correlation to the deflection although with an inverse trend when compared to the other parameters.

Figure 6 depicts a matrix plot considering the correlations among the parameters associated with the plates with MWCNTs. As one can conclude, in this case, the strongest correlation to the maximum transverse deflection of the plates is observed for the Young's modulus. A weaker, moderate correlation is observed for the external diameter.

It is thus possible to understand that for the two cases, the parameters Young's modulus and external diameter are the most relevant although differing from one case to another. The remaining input parameters present low correlation coefficients to the plates' maximum transverse displacement.

Considering the case of $p = 0$, the basis case, two linear regression models were fitted corresponding to plates with single and plates with multi-walled CNTs.

4.3.1. Model I—Plates with SWCNT

To choose the best model, all regression models based on the input variables were considered. This was done by using all possible combinations of inputs as input in the regression model. In the end, the model with the highest adjusted R^2 value $\left(R_a^2\right)$, was chosen:

$$W_{max} = \beta_0 + \beta_1 d_{int} + \beta_2 d_{ext} + \beta_3 \mathrm{E}_{\mathrm{cnt}} \quad (15)$$

This model is significant (F-test with p-value $= 3.974 \times 10^{-7}$) with $R_a^2 = 0.767$. The estimates of this model are presented in Table 3. Although, the residuals are not Gaussian (p-value $= 0.0019$ for Shapiro–Wilk test).

Table 3. Estimates of the model are defined in Equation (15). Plates with SWCNT: with $p = 0$ data.

	Estimate	**Std. Error**	t	p**-Value** [1]
Intercept	-5.252×10^{-9}	5.886×10^{-10}	-8.924	2.07×10^{-8} ***
d_{int}	-6.226×10^{-10}	2.081×10^{-10}	-2.992	0.00721 **
d_{ext}	3.686×10^{-10}	4.546×10^{-11}	8.109	9.44×10^{-8} ***
$\mathrm{E}_{\mathrm{cnt}}$	6.603×10^{-10}	2.989×10^{-13}	2.209	0.03901 *

[1] Significance codes: 0 '***' 0.001 '**' 0.01 '*' 0.05.

Also, all the other models are not suitable because they are not significant, have non-significant coefficients, or do not satisfy the residuals assumptions for a significance of 1%.

Thus, as the quality of this fit was not satisfactory, transformations were applied to linearize the data. Regarding all possible models combining input variables and the logarithm of input variables, the model with the highest $R_a^2 = 0.894$ was:

$$W_{max} = \beta_0 + \beta_1 \ln(d_{int}) + \beta_2 \ln(d_{ext}) + \beta_3 \ln(\mathrm{E_{cnt}}) \quad (16)$$

To assess the generalizability of this result, the F-test was conducted. The resulting p-value of 1.565×10^{-10} for this test indicates the significance of the model meaning that at least one of the input variables contributes significantly to explain the maximum transverse displacement. Furthermore, Table 4 displays the results of the t-tests showing all coefficients as significant at a significance level of α = 1%.

Table 4. Estimates of the model are defined in Equation (16). Plates with SWCNT: with p = 0 data.

	Estimate	**Std. Error**	t	p**-Value** [1]
Intercept	-11.732×10^{-9}	2.234×10^{-9}	-5.250	3.88×10^{-5} ***
$\ln(d_{int})$	-0.7828×10^{-9}	1.591×10^{-10}	-4.919	8.27×10^{-5} ***
$\ln(d_{ext})$	0.9688×10^{-9}	7.490×10^{-11}	12.935	3.57×10^{-11} ***
$\ln(\mathrm{E_{cnt}})$	0.9498×10^{-9}	3.043×10^{-10}	3.121	0.00538 **

[1] Significance codes: 0 '***' 0.001 '**' 0.01.

As mentioned in Section 2.4, the multiple regression model is constructed based on certain assumptions regarding the residuals. The highest VIF is 1.15, and the residuals exhibit homoscedasticity (Breusch-Pagan test), lack correlation (Durbin-Watson test), and follow a Gaussian distribution (Shapiro-Wilk test) considering α = 1%.

Note that the variable length of the nanotubes has never been included in the previous models. In fact, in all the possible models, this variable never achieved statistical significance.

4.3.2. Model II—Plates with MWCNT

In a similar way as for the plates with SWCNTs case, a model was selected with the highest R_a^2 from all possible linear models with input variables. The selected model is the one described in Equation (15).

This is significant (p-value $= 4.886 \times 10^{-8}$ for F-test) as well as all its parameters (Table 5) at α = 1%. The highest VIF is 2.003 and the residuals are fulfilling all the residuals assumptions for α = 1%.

Table 5. Estimates of the model are defined in Equation (15). Plates with MWCNT: with p = 0 data.

	Estimate	**Std. Error**	t	p**-Value** [1]
Intercept	-4.635×10^{-9}	1.331×10^{-10}	-34.815	$<2 \times 10^{-16}$ ***
d_{int}	-2.558×10^{-11}	7.277×10^{-12}	-3.515	0.00195 **
d_{ext}	4.849×10^{-12}	7.947×10^{-13}	6.101	3.85×10^{-6} ***
$\mathrm{E_{cnt}}$	6.647×10^{-13}	8.304×10^{-14}	8.004	5.85×10^{-8} ***

[1] Significance codes: 0 '***' 0.001 '**' 0.01.

Although this is a suitable model it does not have a very good fitting. $R_a^2 = 0.781$. Thus, for fitting improvement, transformations of input variables were considered.

An adjusted determination coefficient of 0.919 was achieved with the model in Equation (17). However, the coefficient of the length of the nanotube (l) is not significant (see Table 6).

$$W_{max} = \beta_0 + \beta_1 \ln(d_{int}) + \beta_2 \ln(d_{ext}) + \beta_3 \ln(\mathrm{E_{cnt}}) + \beta_4 \ln(\mathrm{l}) \quad (17)$$

Table 6. Estimates of the model are defined in Equation (17). Plates with MWCNT: with $p = 0$ data.

	Estimate	Std. Error	t	p-Value [1]
Intercept	-1.151×10^{-8}	6.169×10^{-10}	−18.656	1.50×10^{-14} ***
$\ln(d_{int})$	-2.489×10^{-10}	3.138×10^{-11}	−7.933	9.41×10^{-8} ***
$\ln(d_{ext})$	2.227×10^{-10}	1.948×10^{-11}	11.432	1.77×10^{-10} ***
$\ln(E_{cnt})$	1.001×10^{-11}	7.626×10^{-11}	13.129	1.36×10^{-11} ***
$\ln(l)$	2.708×10^{-11}	2.210×10^{-11}	1.226	0.234

[1] Significance codes: 0 '***' 0.001 0.1 ' ' 1.

The second model with the highest R_a^2 also was not suitable for similar reasons (instead of $ln(l)$ it was the variable l that has a non-significant coefficient). As occurred for the plates with SWCNTs case, again the length of the nanotube does not have a significant impact on the plate deformation.

The third best-fitting model was the one defined in Equation (16). This model has $R_a^2 = 0.917$ and it is significant the F-test (p-value $= 1.21 \times 10^{-12}$) with significant coefficients (Table 7) at $\alpha = 1\%$. The highest VIF is 3.05 and the residuals are homoscedastic (Breusch-Pagan test), uncorrelated (Durbin-Watson test) and Gaussian (Shapiro-Wilk test) considering $\alpha = 1\%$.

Table 7. Estimates of the model are defined in Equation (16). Plates with MWCNT: with $p = 0$ data.

	Estimate	Std. Error	t	p-Value [1]
Intercept	1.120×10^{-8}	5.697×10^{-10}	−19.659	1.91×10^{-15} ***
$\ln(d_{int})$	-2.576×10^{-10}	3.092×10^{-11}	−8.331	2.99×10^{-8} ***
$\ln(d_{ext})$	2.158×10^{-10}	1.886×10^{-11}	11.441	9.88×10^{-11} ***
$\ln(E_{cnt})$	1.001×10^{-9}	7.712×10^{-11}	12.974	8.76×10^{-12} ***

[1] Significance codes: 0 '***' 0.001.

In short, for $p = 0$ a similar best model was obtained for the maximum transverse deflection for plates with SWCNTs and MWCNTs. Both models present a very good fitting for the data, have statistical significance, and fulfill all the assumptions regarding the residuals. In both cases, the variable length of the nanotube has no impact on the deformation.

4.4. Model for Plates' Maximum Transverse Displacement—Other Values of p

The methodology for model selection described for the case of $p = 0$ was applied to the other cases regarding different values of p. Thus, the models were ranked by R_a^2, provided they met the following requirements:

- Significant overall model (F-test) and all model variables are significant (t-tests) at $\alpha = 1\%$;
- No multicollinearity issues (VIF less than 5 for all independent variables);
- Homoscedastic residuals (Breusch-Pagan test), uncorrelated residuals (Durbin–Watson test), and normal distribution of residuals (Shapiro-Wilk test) considering $\alpha = 1\%$.

The model fitted for $p = 0$ described in Equation (16) is also the best model for the other values of p regarding both the FGM plates with SWCNTs and with MWCNTs. For the SWCNTs case the partial slopes can be seen in Table 8, and for the MWCNTs case are presented in Table 9.

Table 8. Estimates of model defined in Equation (16) for plates with SWCNT with different values of p. The standard errors of the estimates are in parentheses.

	R_a^2	Intercept	$\ln(d_{int})$	$\ln(d_{ext})$	$\ln(E_{cnt})$
$p = 0$	0.894	-11.732×10^{-9} (2.234×10^{-9}) ***	-7.828×10^{-10} (1.591×10^{-10}) ***	9.688×10^{-10} (7.490×10^{-11}) ***	9.498×10^{-10} (3.043×10^{-10}) **
$p = 0.5$	0.909	-9.775×10^{-9} (1.453×10^{-9}) ***	-5.684×10^{-10} (1.035×10^{-10}) ***	6.834×10^{-10} (4.873×10^{-11}) ***	6.647×10^{-10} (1.980×10^{-10}) **
$p = 1$	0.912	-8.923×10^{-9} (1.161×10^{-9}) ***	-4.694×10^{-10} (8.273×10^{-11}) ***	5.552×10^{-10} (3.894×10^{-11}) ***	5.415×10^{-10} (1.582×10^{-10}) **
$p = 2$	0.913	-8.220×10^{-9} (9.283×10^{-10}) ***	-3.783×10^{-10} (6.613×10^{-11}) ***	4.465×10^{-10} (3.113×10^{-11}) ***	4.410×10^{-10} (1.265×10^{-10}) **
$p = 4$	0.917	-7.592×10^{-9} (7.434×10^{-10}) ***	-3.099×10^{-10} (5.295×10^{-11}) ***	3.675×10^{-10} (2.492×10^{-11}) ***	3.502×10^{-10} (1.013×10^{-10}) **
$p = 8$	0.925	-7.090×10^{-9} (5.367×10^{-10}) ***	-2.438×10^{-10} (3.823×10^{-11}) ***	2.778×10^{-10} (1.799×10^{-11}) ***	2.774×10^{-10} (7.311×10^{-11}) **

Significance codes: 0 '***' 0.001 '**' 0.01.

Table 9. Estimates of model defined in Equation (16) for plates with MWCNT with different values of p. The standard errors of the estimates are in parentheses.

	R_a^2	Intercept	$\ln(d_{int})$	$\ln(d_{ext})$	$\ln(E_{cnt})$
$p = 0$	0.917	-11.201×10^{-9} (5.697×10^{-10}) ***	-2.576×10^{-10} (3.092×10^{-11}) ***	2.158×10^{-10} (1.886×10^{-11}) ***	10.01×10^{-10} (7.712×10^{-11}) ***
$p = 0.5$	0.914	-9.799×10^{-9} (4.421×10^{-10}) ***	-1.977×10^{-10} (2.399×10^{-11}) ***	1.659×10^{-10} (1.464×10^{-11}) ***	7.532×10^{-10} (5.985×10^{-11}) ***
$p = 1$	0.919	-9.017×10^{-9} (3.554×10^{-10}) ***	-1.681×10^{-10} (1.928×10^{-11}) ***	1.383×10^{-10} (1.177×10^{-11}) ***	6.238×10^{-10} (4.811×10^{-11}) ***
$p = 2$	0.910	-8.329×10^{-9} (3.074×10^{-10}) ***	-1.311×10^{-10} (1.668×10^{-11}) ***	1.125×10^{-10} (1.018×10^{-11}) ***	5.103×10^{-10} (4.161×10^{-11}) ***
$p = 4$	0.910	-7.806×10^{-9} (2.563×10^{-10}) ***	-1.114×10^{-10} (1.391×10^{-11}) ***	0.942×10^{-10} (8.485×10^{-12}) ***	4.247×10^{-10} (3.469×10^{-11}) ***
$p = 8$	0.923	-7.306×10^{-9} (1.873×10^{-10}) ***	-0.869×10^{-10} (1.016×10^{-11}) ***	0.743×10^{-10} (6.200×10^{-12}) ***	3.403×10^{-10} (2.535×10^{-11}) ***

Significance codes: 0 '***' 0.001.

As a global result, the variable length, l, never achieved statistical significance. That implies the length of the nanotube has no impact on the plates' deformation. Concerning the plates with SWCNT case, it is concluded that the internal diameter parameter has a negative slope showing thus an inverse trend regarding the plates' deflection, while the external diameter as well as the Young's modulus have a direct proportional impact on those deflections. As p increases, the modulus of the intercept (β_0) and the coefficient of the internal diameter (β_1) also increases (decreases in modulus) and there is a decreasing trend in the other slopes (β_3 and β_4). Thus, the impact of the input variables—external and internal diameter and Young's modulus—on the maximum transverse displacement shows an opposite influence.

Concerning the MWCNTs' case similar conclusions can be taken about the same parameters' influence on the maximum transverse plates' deflection.

5. Conclusions

The objective of the present work is the characterization of the influence that geometrical and material properties' uncertainty of SWCNTs and MWCNTs has on the maximum static deflection of functionally graded plates. To this purpose, only these characteristics are subjected to variability.

According to the analyses conducted, different maximum transverse displacement results are obtained for SWCNT and MWCNT reinforced plates, which is expected considering the different contributions of these different carbon nanotubes to the plates' stiffening. It is also possible to verify that the exponent values considered, influence these displacements; however, it is concluded that the results obtained for $p = 10$, do not prove to be significantly different from the ones obtained when $p = 8$. This is also an expected result considering the evolution of the volume fraction distribution through the plates' thickness.

Multiple regression models are developed to describe the maximum transverse displacement of plates reinforced with SWCNT or MWCNT. For an exponent $p = 0$ a similar best regression model is obtained for the two cases. It is possible to conclude that the models present a very good fitting for the data, showing statistical significance and fulfilling all the assumptions regarding the residuals. In both cases, the variable length of the nanotube has no impact on the plates' deflection. The model fitted for the exponent $p = 0$ described in Equation (16) is also the best model for the other values of p regarding both plates reinforced with single-walled and multi-walled carbon nanotubes.

As a global result, the variable length never achieves statistical significance. This implies the length of the nanotube has no significant impact on the maximum transverse displacement of the plates.

Regarding the other input variables, considering the defined evolution of the materials mixture, it is demonstrated that the parameter associated with the nanotubes' internal diameter has a negative value (negative slope) thus an opposite trend influence on the plates' maximum deflection, and the external diameter as well as the Young's modulus have a direct trend influence on the plates' deflection.

As a complementary conclusion, it is possible to say that due to their quality characteristics, the multiple regression models developed can be used as alternative prediction tools within the domain of the study.

Author Contributions: Investigation. Conceptualization, M.A.R.L., A.C., A.M., and A.F.M.; Supervision, M.A.R.L. and A.C.; Methodology, M.A.R.L., A.C., A.M., and A.F.M.; software, validation, visualization, A.F.M., A.C., and A.M.; data curation, A.F.M., A.C., and A.M.; formal analysis, A.F.M., A.C., and A.M.; Writing—Original Draft, M.A.R.L., A.C. and A.M.; Writing—Review & Editing, M.A.R.L., A.C. and A.M. All authors have read and agreed to the published version of the manuscript.

Funding: This research received no external funding.

Data Availability Statement: Data is contained within the article.

Acknowledgments: M.A.R. Loja acknowledges the support of FCT/MEC through Project IDMEC. LAETA UIDB/50022/2020. Alda Carvalho is a CEMAPRE/REM member and has the support of Project CEMAPRE/REM—UIDB/05069/2020—financed by FCT/MCTES through national funds.

Conflicts of Interest: M.A.R. Loja, as co-guest editor of the present special issue, was not involved in the editorial review nor in the decision on the possible publication of this article. All the authors declare that there are no competing interests.

References

1. Birman, V.; Byrd, L.W. Modeling and analysis of functionally graded materials and structures. *Appl. Mech. Rev.* **2007**, *60*, 195–216. [CrossRef]
2. Gupta, N.; Gupta, S.M.; Sharma, S.K. Carbon nanotubes: Synthesis, properties and engineering applications. *Carbon Lett.* **2019**, *29*, 419–447. [CrossRef]

3. Rathinavel, S.; Priyadharshini, K.; Panda, D. A review on carbon nanotube: An overview of synthesis, properties, functionalization, characterization, and the application. *Mater. Sci. Eng.* **2021**, *268*, 11509. [CrossRef]
4. Liew, K.M.; Lei, Z.X.; Zhang, L.W. Mechanical analysis of functionally graded carbon nanotube reinforced composites: A review. *Compos. Struct.* **2015**, *120*, 90–97. [CrossRef]
5. Radhamani, A.V.; Chung Lau, H.; Ramakrishna, S. CNT-reinforced Metal and Steel Nanocomposites: A Comprehensive Assessment of Progress and Future Directions. *Compos. Part A Appl. Sci. Manuf.* **2018**, *114*, 170–187. [CrossRef]
6. Vinyas, M.; Atul, J.; Nguyen Thoi, T.; Loja, M.A.R. A Comprehensive Review on Analysis of Nanocomposites: From Manufacturing to Properties Characterization. *Mater. Res. Express* **2019**, *6*, 092002. [CrossRef]
7. Zhao, S.; Zhao, Z.; Yang, Z.; Ke, L.; Kitipornchai, S.; Yang, J. Functionally graded graphene reinforced composite structures: A review. *Eng. Struct.* **2020**, *210*, 110339. [CrossRef]
8. Shoukat, R.; Khan, M.I. Carbon nanotubes: A review on properties. synthesis methods and applications in micro and nanotechnology. *Microsyst. Technol.* **2021**, *27*, 4183–4192. [CrossRef]
9. Soni, S.K.; Thomas, B.; Swain, A.; Roy, T. Functionally graded carbon nanotubes reinforced composite structures: An extensive review. *Compos. Struct.* **2022**, *299*, 116075. [CrossRef]
10. Valencia Murillo, C.E.; Gutierrez Rivera, M.E.; Celaya Garcia, L.D. Thermal–Structural Linear Static Analysis of Functionally Graded Beams Using Reddy Beam Theory. *Math. Comput. Appl.* **2023**, *28*, 84. [CrossRef]
11. Kurpa, L.; Pellicano, F.; Shmatko, T.; Zippo, A. Free Vibration Analysis of Porous Functionally Graded Material Plates with Variable Thickness on an Elastic Foundation Using the R-Functions Method. *Math. Comput. Appl.* **2024**, *29*, 10. [CrossRef]
12. Alghanmi, R.A.; Aljaghthami, R.H. A Four-Variable Shear Deformation Theory for the Static Analysis of FG Sandwich Plates with Different Porosity Models. *Math. Comput. Appl.* **2024**, *29*, 20. [CrossRef]
13. Ruoff, R.S.; Lorents, D.C. Mechanical and Thermal Properties of Carbon Nanotubes. In *Carbon Nanotubes*; Elsevier: Amsterdam, The Netherlands, 1996; pp. 143–148.
14. Xie, S.; Li, W.; Pan, Z.; Chang, B.; Sun, L. Mechanical and physical properties on carbon nanotube. *J. Phys. Chem. Solids* **2000**, *61*, 1153–1158. [CrossRef]
15. Fidelusa, J.D.; Wiesela, E.; Gojnyb, F.H.; Schulteb, K.; Wagner, H.D. Thermo-mechanical properties of randomly oriented carbon/epoxy nanocomposites. *Compos. Part A* **2005**, *36*, 1555–1561. [CrossRef]
16. Martone, A.; Faiella, G.; Antonucci, V.; Giordano, M.; Zarrelli, M. The effect of the aspect ratio of carbon nanotubes on their effective reinforcement modulus in an epoxy matrix. *Compos. Sci. Technol.* **2011**, *71*, 1117–1123. [CrossRef]
17. Qiu, H.; Yang, J. Structure and Properties of Carbon Nanotubes. In *Industrial Applications of Carbon Nanotubes. Micro and Nano Technologies*; Peng, H., Li, Q., Chen, T., Eds.; Elsevier: Amsterdam, The Netherlands, 2017; pp. 47–69.
18. Loja, M.A.R. Dynamic Response of Soft Core Sandwich Beams with Metal-Graphene Nanocomposite Skins. *Shock Vib.* **2017**, *2017*, 7842413. [CrossRef]
19. Eringen, A.C. *Nonlocal Continuum Field Theories*; Springer: New York, NY, USA, 2002.
20. Garg, A.; Chalak, H.D.; Zenkour, A.M.; Belarbi, M.-O.; Houari, M.-S.-A. A Review of Available Theories and Methodologies for the Analysis of Nano Isotropic, Nano Functionally Graded, and CNT Reinforced Nanocomposite Structures. *Arch. Comput. Methods Eng.* **2022**, *29*, 2237–2270. [CrossRef]
21. Reddy, J.N.; Pang, S.D. Nonlocal continuum theories of beams for the analysis of carbon nanotubes. *J. Appl. Phys.* **2008**, *103*, 23511. [CrossRef]
22. Kong, L.; Zhang, B.; Li, C. Thermal Buckling and Postbuckling Behaviors of Couple Stress and Surface Energy-Enriched FG-CNTR Nanobeams. *Symmetry* **2022**, *14*, 2228. [CrossRef]
23. Reddy, J.N.; Kim, J. A nonlinear modified couple stress-based third-order theory of functionally graded plates. *Compos. Struct.* **2012**, *94*, 1128–1143. [CrossRef]
24. Liu, S.; Yu, T.; Bui, T.Q.; Xia, S. Size-dependent analysis of homogeneous and functionally graded microplates using IGA and a non-classical Kirchhoff plate theory. *Compos. Struct.* **2017**, *172*, 34–44. [CrossRef]
25. Thanh, C.-L.; Vu-Huu, T.; Phung-Van, P.; Nguyen-Xuan, H.; Abdel Wahab, M. Size-Dependent Analysis for FG-CNTRC Nanoplates Based on Refined Plate Theory and Modified Couple Stress. In Proceedings of the 1st International Conference on Numerical Modelling in Engineering, NME 2018, Ghent, Belgium, 28–29 August 2018; Lecture Notes in Civil Engineering, 20. Springer: Singapore, 2019; pp. 225–237.
26. Zhang, B.; Li, C.; Zhang, L.; Xie, F. Size-Dependent Free Vibration of Non-Rectangular Gradient Elastic Thick Microplates. *Symmetry* **2022**, *14*, 2592. [CrossRef]
27. Sotiropoulos, D.G.; Tserpes, K. Interval-Based Computation of the Uncertainty in the Mechanical Properties and the Failure Analysis of Unidirectional Composite Materials. *Math. Comput. Appl.* **2022**, *27*, 38. [CrossRef]
28. Yin, S.; Qin, H.; Gao, Q. An Efficient Orthogonal Polynomial Method for Auxetic Structure Analysis with Epistemic Uncertainties. *Math. Comput. Appl.* **2022**, *27*, 49. [CrossRef]
29. Bouwer, J.M.; Wilke, D.N.; Kok, S. Spatio-Temporal Gradient Enhanced Surrogate Modeling Strategies. *Math. Comput. Appl.* **2023**, *28*, 57. [CrossRef]
30. Takakura, A.; Beppu, K.; Nishihara, T.; Fukui, A.; Kozeki, T.; Namazu, T.; Miyauchi, Y.; Itami, K. Strength of carbon nanotubes depends on their chemical structures. *Nat. Commun.* **2019**, *10*, 3040. [CrossRef]

31. García-Macías, E.; Castro-Triguero, R.; Friswell, M.I.; Adhikari, S.; Sáez, A. Metamodel-based approach for stochastic free vibration analysis of functionally graded carbon nanotube reinforced plates. *Compos. Struct.* **2016**, *152*, 183–198. [CrossRef]
32. Pouresmaeeli, S.; Fazelzadeh, S.A. Uncertain Buckling and Sensitivity Analysis of Functionally Graded Carbon Nanotube-Reinforced Composite Beam. *Int. J. Appl. Mech.* **2017**, *9*, 1750071. [CrossRef]
33. Carvalho, A.; Silva, T.A.N.; Loja, M.A.R.; Damásio, F.R. Assessing the influence of material and geometrical uncertainty on the mechanical behavior of FGM plates. *Mech. Adv. Mater. Struct.* **2017**, *24*, 417–426. [CrossRef]
34. Rosa, R.S.B.; Loja, M.A.R.; Carvalho, A.C.J.V.N. Toward variability characterization and statistic models constitution for the prediction of exponentially graded plates' static response. *J. Compos. Sci.* **2018**, *2*, 59. [CrossRef]
35. Karsh, P.K.; Mukhopadhyay, T.; Dey, S. Stochastic dynamic analysis of twisted functionally graded plates. *Compos. Part B Eng.* **2018**, *147*, 259–278. [CrossRef]
36. Wang, Q.; Wu, D.; Tin-Loi, F.; Gao, W. Machine learning aided stochastic structural free vibration analysis for functionally graded bar-type structures. *Thin-Walled Struct.* **2019**, *144*, 106315. [CrossRef]
37. Gao, K.; Do, D.M.; Li, R.; Kitipornchai, S.; Yang, J. Probabilistic stability analysis of functionally graded graphene reinforced porous beams. *Aerosp. Sci. Technol.* **2020**, *98*, 105738. [CrossRef]
38. Baghlani, A.; Najafgholipour, M.A.; Khayat, M. The influence of mechanical uncertainties on the free vibration of functionally graded graphene-reinforced porous nanocomposite shells of revolution. *Eng. Struct.* **2021**, *228*, 111356. [CrossRef]
39. Halpin, J.C.; Kardos, J.L. The Halpin-Tsai Equations: A Review. *Polym. Eng. Sci.* **1976**, *16*, 344–352.
40. Costa, D.M.S.; Loja, M.A.R. Assessing the static behavior of hybrid CNT-metal-ceramic composite plates. *AIMS Mater. Sci.* **2016**, *3*, 808–831. [CrossRef]
41. Reddy, J.N. An evaluation of equivalent-single-layer and layerwise theories of composite laminates. *Compos. Struct.* **1993**, *25*, 21–35. [CrossRef]
42. Reddy, J.N. *Mechanics of Laminated Composite Plates and Shells*, 2nd ed.; CRC Press: Boca Raton, FL, USA, 2003.
43. Singha, M.K.; Prakash, T.; Ganapathi, M. Finite element analysis of functionally graded plates under transverse load. *Finite Elem. Anal. Des.* **2011**, *47*, 453–460. [CrossRef]
44. Mota, A.F.; Loja, M.A.R.; Barbosa, J.I.; Rodrigues, J.A. Porous Functionally Graded Plates: An Assessment of the Influence of Shear Correction Factor on Static Behavior. *Math. Comput. Appl.* **2020**, *25*, 25. [CrossRef]
45. Zienkiewicz, O.C.; Taylor, R.L. *The Finite Element Method*, 5th ed.; Butterworth-Heinemann: Oxford, UK, 2000; Volume 1.
46. Durbin, J.; Watson, G.S. Testing for Serial Correlation in Least Squares Regression. *Biometrika* **1951**, *38*, 159–179. [CrossRef] [PubMed]
47. Breusch, T.S.; Pagan, A.R. A Simple Test for Heteroskedasticity and Random Coefficient Variation. *Econometrica* **1979**, *47*, 1287–1294. [CrossRef]
48. James, G.; Witten, D.; Hastie, T.; Tibshirani, R. *An Introduction to Statistical Learning*; Springer: New York, NY, USA, 2013.
49. Siegel, S.; Castellan, N.J., Jr. *Nonparametric Statistics for the Behavioral Sciences*, 2nd ed.; Mcgraw-Hill Book Company: New York, NY, USA, 1988.
50. Hollander, M.; Wolfe, D.A. *Nonparametric Statistical Methods*; John Wiley & Sons: New York, NY, USA, 2013; pp. 139–146.
51. Demirhan, P.A.; Taskin, V. Levy solution for bending analysis of functionally graded sandwich plates based on four variable plate theory. *Compos. Struct.* **2017**, *177*, 80–95. [CrossRef]

Mathematical and Computational Applications

MDPI

Article

Free Vibration Analysis of Porous Functionally Graded Material Plates with Variable Thickness on an Elastic Foundation Using the R-Functions Method

Lidiya Kurpa [1], Francesco Pellicano [2], Tetyana Shmatko [3] and Antonio Zippo [2,*]

1 Department of Applied Mathematics, National Technical University "KhPI", Kyrpychova Str. 2, 61002 Kharkiv, Ukraine
2 Department of Engineering "Enzo Ferrari", Centre InterMech MoRe, University of Modena and Reggio Emilia, Via P. Vivarelli 10, 41124 Modena, Italy; francesco.pellicano@unimore.it
3 Department of Higher Mathematics, National Technical University "KhPI", Kyrpychova Str. 2, 61002 Kharkiv, Ukraine; ktv_ua@yahoo.com
* Correspondence: antonio.zippo@unimore.it

Abstract: Free vibrations of porous functionally graded material (FGM) plates with complex shapes are analyzed by using the R-functions method. The thickness of the plate is variable in the direction of one of the axes. Two types of porosity distributions through the thickness are considered: uniform (even) and non-uniform (uneven). The elastic foundation is defined by two parameters (Winkler and Pasternak). To obtain the mathematical model of the problem, the first-order shear deformation theory of the plate (FSDT) is used. The effective material properties in the thickness direction are modeled by means of a power law. Variational Ritz's method joined with the R-functions theory is used for obtaining a semi-analytical solution of the problem. The approach is applied to a number of case studies and validated by means of comparative analyses carried out on rectangular plates with a traditional finite element approach. The proof of the efficiency of the approach and its capability to handle actual engineering problems is fulfilled for FGM plates having complex shapes and various boundary conditions. The effect of different parameters, such as porosity distribution, volume fraction index, elastic foundation, FGM types, and boundary conditions, on the vibrations is studied.

Keywords: functionally graded material; R-function method; elastic foundation

1. Introduction

FGMs represent modern materials that are going to be widely used in many industries, with applications in aircraft and rockets, ships, nuclear reactors, and a number of components used in mechanical engineering. The intensive use of functionally graded materials has led to the need for a thorough study of their behavior during operation, considering such characteristics as porosity, elastic foundation, and varying plate or shell thickness. In this regard, many scientists focused their investigations on both theories related to the development of mathematical models [1–11] and experiments [12,13].

It can be noted that porosity can occur in functionally graded structures during the manufacturing process. So, many researchers took into account the influence of porosity while they were investigating mechanical, thermal, and other characteristics of FGM structures. Kim et al. [14] used the classical and first-order shear deformation theory to investigate buckling, bending, and free vibration characteristics of porous FG plates. Higher-order shear deformation theory (HSDT) was applied by Cong et al. [15] for analytical modeling of the buckling and post-buckling behavior of porous FGM plates subjected to thermal and mechanical loads. Zur and Jankowski [16] carried out a multiparametric investigation of the free vibration behavior of circular porous FGM plates using the classical plate theory. Li et al. [17] considered a semi-analytical approach to investigate the free vibration behavior of porous FG cylindrical shells. Wang and Wu [18] examined the free vibration characteristics of porous FG cylindrical shells with different boundary conditions by applying the sinusoidal shear deformation theory (SSDT). In the last few decades, functionally graded materials have been increasingly applied to nanocomposite structures in thermal and magnetic environments [19].

The literature on the vibration analysis of FGM plates resting on elastic foundations has been enriched by many scientific contributions in the last few years; the elastic foundation model based on the Winkler and Pasternak interaction has been widely applied: the Winkler model was developed for railroad tracks, and the Pasternak model introduced a new parameter to include the spring displacement in the longitudinal and lateral directions. Yang and Shen [20] conducted a vibration analysis of an initially stressed FGM plate resting on an elastic foundation; they used a simple power law for material gradation with clamped boundary conditions. Amini et al. [21] carried out a three-dimensional vibration analysis of the FGM plate resting on a Winkler foundation; Chebyshev polynomials and the Ritz method were applied to obtain the vibration modes. Results for free vibration and buckling analysis of an S-FGM (Sigmoid FGM) sandwich plate supported on an elastic foundation were reported by Singh and Harsh [22]. Malekzaden and Karami [23] studied the free vibration behavior of a homogeneous linearly varying thick plate resting on an elastic foundation using differential quadrature methods. Investigations on porous FGM structures with even and uneven distributions of porosity have been observed in the last few years. Rezaei and Saidi [24,25] analyzed the free vibration and flexural response of porous plates with different boundary conditions. Zenkour [6] investigated the static response of porous FGM single-layered and sandwich plates using a quasi-3D shear deformation theory. Trinh et al. [26] examined the effect of evenly distributed and unevenly distributed porosities on the dynamic behaviors of FG cylindrical, spherical, and hyperbolic paraboloid shells by means of the FSDT.

Nguen et al. [27] used the first-order shear deformation theory for deriving theoretical formulations and illustrating the nonlinear response of FG porous plates under thermal and mechanical loads supported by Pasternak's model of an elastic foundation. Evenly and unevenly distributed porosities were included in a distribution law for the calculation of the effective properties of FGM plates. Thrin et al. [28] developed a three-variable refined shear deformation theory to investigate the free vibration and bending behavior of porous FG doubly curved shallow shells exposed to uniform and sinusoidal pressure. Two porosity types influence parameters that influence the material properties and structure behaviors in different aspects. Kumar et al. [29] applied the first-order shear deformation theory for the presentation of a displacement model of the kinematic equations for tapered, porous FGM plates with variable thickness resting on a two-parameter elastic foundation. The solutions for constant and varying thick plates were investigated. Vinh and Huy [30] examined the static bending, free vibration, and buckling of FG sandwich plates with porosity using the finite element model based on a hyperbolic shear deformation theory. Most of the works cited above and the most of scientific literature dealt with rectangular plates. Balak et al. [31] studied the dynamic behavior of an elliptical multilayer plate with a saturated porous filler resting on an elastic foundation; these authors considered the case of the face sheet layers being piezoelectric. To solve the problem, the authors applied the first-order shear deformation theory and Galerkin's method.

Based on the above literature, it seems that many studies were conducted for the vibration analysis of FGM plates. But investigations in the field of porous FGM plates and shells with variable thickness resting on an elastic foundation are in demand now and are still limited. In particular, there is a need to investigate FGM plates and shells with complex planform and different boundary conditions.

In Ref. [32], nonlinear dynamics of spherical caps were numerically investigated, with an exploration of chaos-induced symmetry breaking. Nonlinear random vibrations of circular cylindrical shells were experimentally investigated in Ref. [33]. Modal localizations due to small imperfections in circular cylindrical shells were numerically investigated in Ref. [34]. A complex dynamic scenario of shells in contact with a non-Newtonian fluid was experimentally investigated in Ref [35].

In the present paper, the authors propose an approach combining the R-functions theory and variational Ritz method for studying the free vibration behavior of porous FGM plates of different forms with a hole of complex geometry. These plates are resting on an elastic foundation. The method allows the construction of admissible functions in an analytical form and the consideration of different boundary conditions for the hole and outside border. The thickness of the FGM plate can be varied using a linear or nonlinear law. Moreover, FEM analyses have been carried out with COMSOL Multiphysics in order to investigate the advantages and disadvantages of finite element modeling and boundary condition sensitivity and to carry out comparisons with the analytical method.

2. Formulation of the Problem

Consider a porous plate on an elastic foundation with variable thickness. Assume that a plate (Figure 1A) is made of functionally graded material (FGM), namely a mixture of ceramics (top of the plate) and metal (bottom). The distribution law of thickness for the general case is shown in Figure 1B. The plate may have an arbitrary shape.

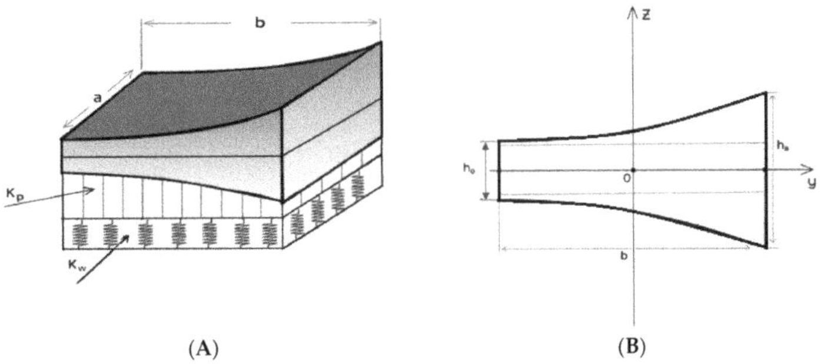

Figure 1. (**A**) FGM plate on elastic foundation with variable thickness; (**B**) distribution law of thickness for general case.

Two porosity distribution types are studied: even (Figure 2a) and uneven (Figure 2b). The effective material properties through the thickness such as Young's modulus E and mass density ρ can vary with a power law for an FGM with the porosity distribution factor α [24–26]:

Figure 2. (**a**) Even distribution of porosity; (**b**) uneven distribution of porosity.

Type I (even) is given as follows:

$$P_{ef}(z) = (P_m(T) - P_c(T))\left(\frac{z}{h} + \frac{1}{2}\right)^p + P_c(T) - \frac{\alpha}{2}(P_c(T) + P_m(T)) \quad (1)$$

Type II (uneven) is presented as follows:

$$P_{ef}(z) = (P_m(T) - P_c(T))\left(\frac{z}{h} + \frac{1}{2}\right)^p + P_c(T) - \frac{\alpha}{2}(P_c(T) + P_m(T))\left(1 - 2\frac{|z|}{h(x,y)}\right) \quad (2)$$

Here, p is the positive volume fraction index (gradient index). The mechanical characteristics of ceramics P_c and metal P_m depend on temperature T. This dependence is defined by known formulas presented in Refs. [6–8].

Equations (1) and (2) represent the general formulas for the determination of the elastic modulus E and the density ρ of the composite.

The stress and strain resultants in matrix form are as follows:

$$\{N\} = [A]\left\{\varepsilon^0\right\} + [B]\{\chi\},\ \{M\} = [B]\left\{\varepsilon^0\right\} + [D]\{\chi\},\ \{Q\} = K_s A_{33}\{\gamma_{13}, \gamma_{23}\}^T \quad (3)$$

where $\{N\} = \{N_{11}, N_{22}, N_{12}\}^T$ are forces per unit edge length in the middle surface of a plate, $\{M\} = \{M_{11}, M_{22}, M_{12}\}^T$ are bending and twisting moments per unit edge length, and $Q = (Q_x, Q_y)^T$ are transverse resultants; the coefficient K_s^2 denotes the shear correction factor. The components of the vectors $\{\varepsilon^0\} = \{\varepsilon_{11}^0, \varepsilon_{22}^0, \gamma_{12}^0\}^T$ and $\{\chi\} = \{\chi_{11}, \chi_{22}, \chi_{12}\}^T$ are defined in the following way:

$$\varepsilon_{11}^0 = u_{,x}\ \varepsilon_{22}^0 = v_{,y}\ \gamma_{12}^0 = u_{,y} + v_{,x}, \gamma_{13} = w_{,x} + \psi_x,\ \gamma_{23} = w_{,y} + \psi_y, \quad (4)$$

$$\chi_{11} = \psi_{x,x},\ \chi_{22} = \psi_{y,y},\ \chi_{12} = \psi_{x,y} + \psi_{y,x}$$

where u and v are middle surface displacements along the axes Ox and Oy, respectively; w is the transverse deflection of the plate along the axis Oz; and ψ_x, ψ_y are angles of rotations of the normal to the middle surface about the axes Oy and Ox. Matrices $[A]$, $[B]$, $[D]$ have the following form:

$$[A] = \begin{bmatrix} A_{11} & A_{12} & 0 \\ A_{12} & A_{22} & 0 \\ 0 & 0 & A_{66} \end{bmatrix}, [B] = \begin{bmatrix} B_{11} & B_{12} & 0 \\ B_{12} & B_{22} & 0 \\ 0 & 0 & B_{66} \end{bmatrix}, [D] = \begin{bmatrix} D_{11} & D_{12} & 0 \\ D_{12} & D_{22} & 0 \\ 0 & 0 & D_{66} \end{bmatrix}, \quad (5)$$

Elements of the matrixes $[A]$, $[B]$, $[D]$ are calculated as follows:

$$([A], [B], [D]) \int_{-\frac{h(x,y)}{2}}^{\frac{h(x,y)}{2}} E_{eff}(z)[C]\left(1, z, z^2\right)dz,\ [C] = \frac{1}{1-\nu^2}\begin{bmatrix} 1 & \nu & 0 \\ \nu & 1 & 0 \\ 0 & 0 & \frac{1-\nu}{2} \end{bmatrix} \quad (6)$$

Assuming that Poisson's ratio ν is constant and the same for metal and ceramics, we can calculate exactly the values of the elements A_{ij}, B_{ij}, $D_{ij}(i,j = 1,2,6)$ of matrices (5):

$$\begin{aligned} A_{11} &= A_{22} = \tfrac{1}{1-\nu^2}\left(\tfrac{E_m - E_c}{p+1} + E_c - \tfrac{\alpha}{2}(E_c + E_m) + \delta\left(\tfrac{\alpha(E_c+E_m)}{4}\right)\right)h(x,y), \\ A_{12} &= \nu A_{11},\ A_{66} = A_{44} = A_{55} = \tfrac{A_{11}(1-\nu)}{2} \end{aligned} \quad (7)$$

$$B_{11} = B_{22} = \frac{(E_m - E_c)p}{(1-\nu^2)(p+1)(p+2)}\frac{h^2(x,y)}{2},\ B_{12} = \nu B_{11},\ B_{66} = B_{44} = B_{55} = \frac{B_{11}(1-\nu)}{2} \quad (8)$$

$$D_{11} = D_{22} = \frac{h^3(x,y)}{1-\nu^2}\left(\frac{E_c}{12} - \frac{\alpha}{24}(E_c + E_m) + (E_m - E_c)\left(\frac{1}{p+3} - \frac{1}{p+2} + \frac{1}{4(p+1)}\right) + \delta\left(\frac{\alpha(E_c + E_m)}{32}\right)\right),$$

$$D_{12} = \nu D_{11},\ D_{66} = D_{44} = D_{55} = \frac{D_{11}(1-\nu)}{2} \quad (9)$$

where α is the porosity distribution factor; the indicator δ is the tracing, and this constant is equal to 0 for the even porosity and 1 for the uneven porosity.

The influence of the elastic foundation is taken into account as the reaction–deflection relation of Pasternak using the following formula [4,27]:

$$p_0 = K_w w - K_P \nabla^2 w \quad (10)$$

where $\nabla^2 w = \frac{\partial^2 w}{\partial x^2} + \frac{\partial^2 w}{\partial y^2}$, and K_w, K_P are the Winkler foundation stiffness and the shear stiffness of the Pasternak foundation, respectively.

The equations of motion for the FGM plates are the following:

$$\begin{aligned}
\frac{\partial N_{11}}{\partial x}+\frac{\partial N_{12}}{\partial y} &= I_0\frac{\partial^2 u}{\partial t^2}+I_1\frac{\partial^2 \psi_x}{\partial t^2};\\
\frac{\partial N_{22}}{\partial y}+\frac{\partial N_{12}}{\partial x} &= I_0\frac{\partial^2 v}{\partial t^2}+I_1\frac{\partial^2 \psi_y}{\partial t^2};\\
\frac{\partial Q_x}{\partial x}+\frac{\partial Q_y}{\partial y}-\left(K_w w-K_P\nabla^2 w\right) &= I_0\frac{\partial^2 w}{\partial t^2};\\
\frac{\partial M_{11}}{\partial x}+\frac{\partial M_{12}}{\partial y}-Q_x &= I_2\frac{\partial^2 \psi_x}{\partial t^2}+I_1\frac{\partial^2 u}{\partial t^2};\\
\frac{\partial M_{22}}{\partial y}+\frac{\partial M_{12}}{\partial x}-Q_y &= I_2\frac{\partial^2 \psi_y}{\partial t^2}+I_1\frac{\partial^2 v}{\partial t^2},
\end{aligned} \tag{11}$$

where

$$(I_0, I_1, I_2) = \int_{\frac{-h(x,y)}{2}}^{\frac{h(x,y)}{2}} \rho(z)\left(1,z,z^2\right)dz \tag{12}$$

By integrating relation (12), we obtain analytical expressions of these coefficients in the following form:

$$I_0 = \left(\frac{\rho_m-\rho_c}{p+1}+\rho_c-\frac{\alpha}{2}(\rho_c+\rho_m)+\delta\left(\frac{\alpha(\rho_c+\rho_m)}{4}\right)\right)h(x,y) \tag{13}$$

$$I_1 = \frac{(\rho_m-\rho_c)p}{(1-\nu^2)(p+1)(p+2)}\frac{h^2(x,y)}{2}, \tag{14}$$

$$I_2 = h^3(x,y)\left(\frac{\rho_c}{12}-\frac{\alpha}{24}(\rho_c+\rho_m)+(\rho_m-\rho_c)\left(\frac{1}{p+3}-\frac{1}{p+2}+\frac{1}{4(p+1)}\right)+\delta\left(\frac{\alpha(\rho_c+\rho_m)}{32}\right)\right) \tag{15}$$

The total potential energy of the system is expressed as

$$\Pi = U+V_e-T \tag{16}$$

where strain energy U, potential V_e and kinetic energy T in this case are defined by the following expressions:

$$U = \int_{\Omega}\left(N_{11}\varepsilon_{11}^{(0)}+N_{22}\varepsilon_{22}^{(0)}+N_{12}\gamma_{12}^{(0)}+M_{11}\chi_{11}+M_{22}\chi_{22}+M_{12}\chi_{12}+Q_1\gamma_{13}+Q_2\gamma_{23}\right)d\Omega \tag{17}$$

$$V_e = \frac{1}{2}\int_{\Omega}\left(K_w w^2+K_p\left(\vec{\nabla} w\right)^2\right)d\Omega \tag{18}$$

$$T = \frac{1}{2}\int_{\Omega}\left(\left(I_0\left(\left(\frac{\partial u_0}{\partial t}\right)^2+\left(\frac{\partial v_0}{\partial t}\right)^2+\left(\frac{\partial w_0}{\partial t}\right)^2\right)+2I_1\left(\frac{\partial \psi_x}{\partial t}\frac{\partial u_0}{\partial t}+\frac{\partial \psi_y}{\partial t}\frac{\partial v_0}{\partial t}\right)+I_2\left(\left(\frac{\partial \psi_x}{\partial t}\right)^2+\left(\frac{\partial \psi_y}{\partial t}\right)^2\right)\right)\right)d\Omega \tag{19}$$

3. Solution Method

To solve this problem, we use the Ritz method, which is an effective method with some drawbacks in application. For example, the main difficulty, arising in the case of complex geometry, is the construction of admissible functions; such a problem can be solved by using the R-functions theory. The application of the Ritz method in combination with the R-functions theory (RFM) allows one to represent the unknown solution in an analytical form. This is a great advantage of this method compared to other numerical methods. The R-functions theory offers approaches to the construction of so-called solution structures [36–39]. Those solution structures are the base for constructing the system of admissible functions. For example, let us construct the solution structures and set of admissible functions for the clamped plate shown in Figure 3a.

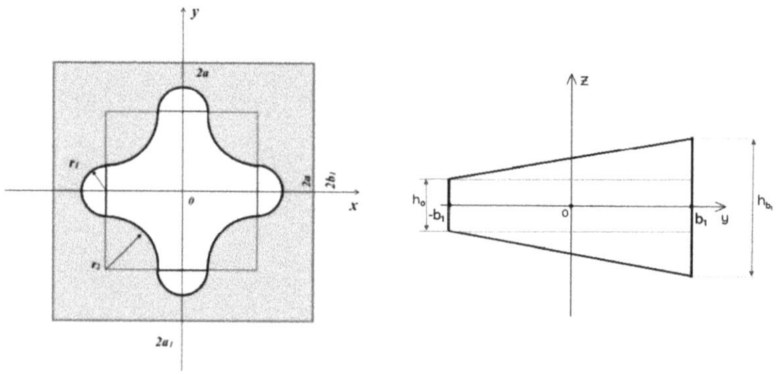

Figure 3. (**a**) Planform of plate with complex hole; (**b**) distribution law of thickness for plate with complex geometry.

The boundary conditions for a plate clamped on the whole border including the cut (CL-CL) are

$$w = 0,\ u = 0,\ v = 0,\ \psi_x = 0,\ \psi_y = 0,\ \forall(x,y) \in \partial\Omega \tag{20}$$

For these boundary conditions, the solution structure has the following form:

$$w = \omega\Phi_1,\ u = \omega\Phi_2,\ v = \omega\Phi_3,\ \psi_x = \omega\Phi_4,\ \psi_y = \omega\Phi_5\,. \tag{21}$$

The functions $\omega(x,y)$ are constructed using the R-functions theory and satisfy the following conditions:

$$\omega(x,y) = 0,\ \forall(x,y) \in \partial\Omega,$$
$$\omega(x,y) > 0,\ \forall(x,y) \in \Omega\,.$$

In the given case, the functions $\omega(x,y)$ have the following form:

$$\omega(x,y) = (f_1 \wedge_0 f_2) \wedge_0 \omega_{cut} \tag{22}$$

$$\omega_{cut}(x,y) = -(((f_3 \vee_0 f_4) \vee_0 f_{12}) \wedge_0 ((f_5 \vee_0 f_6) \vee_0 f_{11}) \wedge_0 ((f_7 \wedge_0 f_8) \wedge_0 (f_9 \wedge_0 f_{10}))) \tag{23}$$

where symbols $\wedge_0, \vee_0$ denote the R-operations of the R_0-system [36], which have the following form:

- $x_1 \wedge_0 x_2 \equiv x_1 + x_2 - \sqrt{x_1^2 + x_2^2}$ is the R-conjunction, which describes the intersection of the domains;
- $x_1 \vee_0 x_2 \equiv x_1 + x_2 + \sqrt{x_1^2 + x_2^2}$ is the R-disjunction, which describes the union of the domains.

Functions $f_i,\ i = \overline{1,12}$ in relations (22) and (23) are defined as follows:

$$\begin{gathered}
f_1 = (a_1^2 - x^2)/2a_1 \geq 0,\ f_{11} = (a^2 - x^2)/2a \geq 0, \\
f_2 = (b_1^2 - y^2)/2b_1 \geq 0,\ f_{12} = (a^2 - y^2)/2a \geq 0, \\
f_3 = \left(r_1^2 - x^2 - (y-a)^2\right)/2r_1 \geq 0,\ f_4 = \left(r_1^2 - x^2 - (y+a)^2\right)/2r_1 \geq 0, \\
f_5 = \left(r_1^2 - (x-a)^2 - y^2\right)/2r_1 \geq 0,\ f_6 = \left(r_1^2 - (x+a)^2 - y^2\right)/2r_1 \geq 0, \\
f_7 = \left((x-a)^2 + (y+a)^2 - r_2^2\right)/2r_2 \geq 0,\ f_8 = \left((x+a)^2 + (y-a)^2 - r_2^2\right)/2r_2 \geq 0, \\
f_9 = \left((x-a)^2 + (y-a)^2 - r_2^2\right)/2r_2 \geq 0,\ f_{10} = \left((x+a)^2 + (y+a)^2 - r_2^2\right)/2r_2 \geq 0,
\end{gathered} \tag{24}$$

In Formulas (21), the functions $\Phi_i(x,y)$, $(i = \overline{1,5})$ are indefinite components of the structure solutions. These components are expanded in series on some complete system of functions $\left\{\varphi_i^{(k)}\right\}$, $(k = 1,2,3,4,5)$:

$$\Phi_1 = \sum_{i=1}^{N_1} a_i\varphi_i^{(1)}, \Phi_2 = \sum_{i=N_1+1}^{N_2} a_i\varphi_i^{(2)}, \Phi_3 = \sum_{i=N_2+1}^{N_3} a_i\varphi_i^{(3)}, \Phi_4 = \sum_{i=N_3+1}^{N_4} a_i\varphi_i^{(4)}, \Phi_5 = \sum_{i=N_4+1}^{N_5} a_i\varphi_i^{(5)}, \quad (25)$$

where a_i, $i = 1,2,\cdots N_5$ are indefinite coefficients.

After the substitution of expressions (25) into (21), the following representation of the sought solution can be obtained:

$$\begin{aligned} w(x,y) &= \sum_{i=1}^{N_1} a_i w_i(x,y),\ u(x,y) = \sum_{i=N_1+1}^{N_2} a_i u_i(x,y),\ v(x,y) = \sum_{i=N_2+1}^{N_3} a_i v_i(x,y), \\ \psi_x(x,y) &= \sum_{i=N_3+1}^{N_2} a_i\psi_{xi}(x,y),\ \psi_y(x,y) = \sum_{i=N_4+1}^{N_3} a_i\psi_{yi}(x,y) \end{aligned} \quad (26)$$

The functions

$$\begin{aligned} w_i &= \omega(x,y)\varphi_i^{(1)}(x,y),\ u_i = \omega(x,y)\varphi_i^{(2)}(x,y),\ v_i = \omega(x,y)\varphi_i^{(3)}(x,y), \\ \psi_{xi} &= \omega(x,y)\varphi_i^{(4)}(x,y),\ \psi_{yi} = \omega(x,y)\varphi_i^{(5)}(x,y) \end{aligned} \quad (27)$$

are basic functions that satisfy boundary conditions (20) for any choice of the indefinite coefficients. These coefficients are sought by the Ritz method from the condition for the corresponding functional to have a stationary point. It is easy to show that in the given case, for harmonic vibrations, this functional has the following form:

$$J = U + V_e - \lambda^2 P \quad (28)$$

where U, V_e and P are the maximum potential and kinetic energies, respectively. Let us note that expressions for U and V_e coincide with (17) and (18).

The maximum kinetic energy T takes the following form:

$$P = \frac{1}{2}\iint_{\Omega}\left(I_0\left(u^2+v^2+w^2\right) + 2I_1\left(u\psi_x + v\psi_y\right) + I_2\left({\psi_x}^2 + {\psi_y}^2\right)\right)dxdy \quad (29)$$

Here, λ is a natural frequency of the harmonic vibrations in Equation (28).

4. Numerical Results and Discussion

4.1. Validation of the Approach

To prove the effectiveness of the proposed method and the accuracy of numerical results, a validation analysis was carried out for square FGM plates; different cases were considered by changing the parameters of porosity, volume exponent, elastic foundation, FGM type, and boundary conditions. The following five tests describe several comparative examples.

Test 1

Free vibrations of a simply supported FGM $Si_3N_4/SUS304$ square plate with porosity (Type 1) are considered. The mechanical characteristics of the mixture are as follows:

Si_3N_4:	$E = 322.27$ GPa,	$\nu = 0.3$,	$\rho = 2370\ \mathrm{kg/m^3}$;
$SUS304$:	$E = 207.78$ GPa,	$\nu = 0.3$,	$\rho = 8166\ \mathrm{kg/m^3}$.

This plate is porous with porosity distribution factor α = 0, 0.1, 0.2 and changing gradient index p = 0, 1, 2, 5, 10, 100. Values of non-dimensional fundamental frequency $\Lambda = \lambda\,(2a)^2 h_0\sqrt{\rho_c/E_c}$ for this study are presented in Table 1. A comparative analysis was carried out via comparisons with Ref. [28]. It is observed that there is an excellent agreement.

Table 1. Comparison of non-dimensional fundamental frequency $\Lambda = \lambda\,(2a)^2 h_0 \sqrt{\rho_c/E_c}$ for simply supported porous $Si_3N_4/SUS304$ FG plates ($\frac{a}{b} = 1, \frac{h}{2a} = 0.1$) with Ref. [28].

p	$\alpha = 0$		$\alpha = 0.1$		$\alpha = 0.2$	
	RFM	**[28]**	**RFM**	**[28]**	**RFM**	**[28]**
0	0.0249	0.0250	0.0241	0.0241	0.0231	0.0231
1	0.0348	0.0348	0.0347	0.0348	0.0347	0.0347
2	0.0394	0.0394	0.0399	0.0399	0.0406	0.0406
5	0.0460	0.0460	0.0477	0.0477	0.0502	0.0501
10	0.0503	0.0503	0.0531	0.0530	0.0572	0.0571
100	0.0567	0.0567	0.0613	0.0614	0.0688	0.0688

Test 2

An investigation of the free vibration of a square FGM plate on an elastic foundation made of aluminum and alumina (Al/Al_2O_3) without porosity ($\alpha = 0$) is conducted. The mechanical characteristics are as follows:

Al:	$E = 70$ GPa,	$\nu = 0.3$,	$\rho = 2707\ \text{kg/m}^3$
Al_2O_3:	$E = 380$ GPa,	$\nu = 0.3$,	$\rho = 3800\ \text{kg/m}^3$

Non-dimensional fundamental frequencies $\Lambda = \lambda\,(2a)^2 h_0 \sqrt{\rho_m/E_m}$ were obtained for $K_s = \frac{\pi^2}{12}$ using the FSDT. The elastic stiffnesses of Winkler and Pasternak foundations are defined as follows:

$$\overline{K}_W = \frac{K_W h_0^3}{(2b)^4 12(1-\nu_m\nu_c)},\ \overline{K}_P = \frac{K_P h_0^3}{(2b)^2 12(1-\nu_m\nu_c)}$$

Four different values of the volume exponent index $p = 0, 1, 2, 5$ are taken. Table 2 shows a comparison with results from Refs. [29,40]; an additional comparison with the finite element method (FEM) using COMSOL Multiphysics V6.2 is presented in Table 2.

Table 2. Comparison of non-dimensional fundamental frequency $\Lambda = \lambda\,(2a)^2 h_0 \sqrt{\rho_m/E_m}$ for simply supported (without porosity) FG (Al/Al_2O_3) plates ($\frac{a}{b} = 1, \frac{h_0}{2a} = 0.05, K_s = \frac{\pi^2}{12}$) on elastic foundation with Refs. [29,40] and FEM.

K_w	K_p	**Method**	$p = 0$	$p = 1$	$p = 2$	$p = 5$
0	0	RFM	0.0291	0.0222	0.0202	0.0191
		[29]	0.0291	0.0222	0.0202	0.0191
		[40]	0.0291	0.0222	0.0202	0.0191
		FEM	0.0286	0.0219	0.0199	0.0187
0	100	RFM	0.0406	0.0378	0.0374	0.0377
		[29]	0.0406	0.0378	0.0374	0.0377
		[40]	0.0406	0.0378	0.0374	0.0377
		FEM	0.0384	0.0352	0.0347	0.0347
100	0	RFM	0.0298	0.0233	0.0214	0.0205
		[29]	0.0298	0.0233	0.0214	0.0205
		[40]	0.0298	0.0233	0.0214	0.0205
100	100	RFM	0.0411	0.0384	0.0381	0.0384
		[29]	0.0411	0.0384	0.0381	0.0384
		[40]	0.0411	0.0384	0.0381	0.0384

A comparison of the results obtained shows that the deviation of the frequencies calculated using the FEM is over 7% for the case of Pasternak's elastic foundation, while the results obtained using the RFM are in good agreement with the values from Refs. [29,40].

Test 3

Verification of the proposed method for square isotropic plates with various thicknesses a/h_0 = 5, 10, 100 and different boundary conditions is performed. The following conditions are considered: The plate is simply supported on the whole boundary (SSSS); the plate is completely clamped on the whole boundary (CCCC); the plate has two opposite sides clamped and two other sides simply supported (CSCS); the plate has two adjacent sides clamped and two other adjacent sides simply supported (CCSS). The thickness of the plate varies linearly in the y-direction [29]. Taper ratio β is set equal to 0.25. A comparison of the present fundamental frequencies $\Lambda = \lambda\,(2a)^2\sqrt{\rho_m/E_m}/h_0$ with Refs. [27,31] is presented in Table 3.

Table 3. Comparison of the fundamental frequencies $\Lambda = \lambda\,(2a)^2\sqrt{\rho_m/E_m}/h_0$ for isotropic square tapered plates, β = 0.25, with different boundary conditions and thicknesses with Refs. [27,31].

a/h_0	Method	SSSS	CCCC	CSCS	CCSS
100	RFM	22.176	40.310	35.578	32.473
	[31]	22.164	40.309	-	32.441
	[27]	22.308	41.998	-	32.306
10	RFM	21.209	35.668	31.909	29.273
	[31]	21.224	35.65	-	29.339
	[27]	21.351	38.098	-	29.856
5	RFM	19.012	28.192	25.645	23.590
	[31]	19.057	28.154		23.887
	[27]	19.1493	30.976		25.043

Table 4 shows the fundamental frequencies $\Lambda = \lambda\,(2a)^2\sqrt{\rho_m/E_m}/h_0$ given by the present approach for isotropic square simply supported tapered plates with different thicknesses a/h = 5, 10, 100 and values of ratio tapers, β = 0.5 and β = 1, compared with the results of Refs. [29,41] and with finite element method (COMSOL Multiphysics) for the case $a/h_0 = 100$.

Table 4. Comparison of the fundamental frequencies $\Lambda = \lambda\,(2a)^2\sqrt{\rho_m/E_m}/h_0$ for isotropic square simply supported square tapered plates with different thicknesses and taper ratios with Refs. [29,41].

Taper Ratio β	Method	a/h_0 = 100	a/h_0 = 10	a/h_0 = 5
0.5	RFM	24.554	23.258	20.450
	[41]	24.543	23.282	20.518
	[29]	25.059	23.728	20.834
	FEM	21.570	-	-
1	RFM	29.193	27.062	22.882
	[41]	29.184	27.120	23.031
	[29]	30.897	28.511	23.928
	FEM	25.430	-	-

For plates having a variable thickness, the deviation of the results obtained using the RFM does not exceed 2% compared to the results presented in Ref. [29], and the results obtained have a good agreement with the results in Ref. [41]. The results obtained using the FEM differ significantly from the results presented in Refs. [29,41], and the error is about 13%. The authors can suppose that the FEM is not very useful for this specific problem of plates with variable thickness due to the ratio between length and thickness.

Test 4

This example presents vibration analysis of square FGM plates (Al/Al_2O_3) with different boundary conditions (SSSS, CCCC, CSCS), changing gradient index p = 3, 5, and porosity distribution factor $\alpha = 0, 0.1, 0.2$. Two porosity distribution types (even and uneven) are considered; the taper ratio is β = 0.4. The shear deformation factor is taken as $K_s = \frac{\pi^2}{12}$. The results are shown in Table 5. Good agreement was found with Ref. [29] and with the finite element method (COMSOL Multiphysics) for the even distribution of porosity.

Table 5. Comparison of non-dimensional frequency parameter $\Lambda = \lambda (2a)^2 \sqrt{\rho_m/E_m}/h_0$ for square FGM (Al/Al_2O_3) plates with different boundary conditions, gradient index values, and porosity parameters (Type I and Type II), $K_s = \frac{\pi^2}{12}$, a/h_0 = 20, β = 0.4, with Ref. [29] and FEM.

	p	Method	$\alpha = 0$	$\alpha = 0.1$		$\alpha = 0.2$	
				Even	Uneven	Even	Uneven
SSSS	3	RFM	9.4060	8.7741	9.3335	7.7039	9.2250
		[29]	9.4611	8.8289	9.3890	7.7603	9.2819
		FEM	9.2800	8.6400	-	7.5500	-
	5	RFM	9.1969	8.5106	9.1143	7.2713	8.9880
		[29]	9.2501	8.5637	9.1687	7.3255	9.0437
		FEM	9.2300	8.5300	-	7.2500	-
CCCC	3	RFM	16.7182	15.6250	16.5544	13.7710	16.3894
		[29]	17.5125	16.3599	17.3756	14.4083	17.1745
		FEM	16.9200	15.7600	-	13.8100	-
	5	RFM	16.2971	15.1072	16.4071	12.9621	15.9080
		[29]	17.0913	15.8377	16.9332	13.5777	16.6951
		FEM	16.8000	15.5000	-	13.2000	-
CSCS	3	RFM	13.5327	12.6407	13.4251	11.1286	13.2670
		[29]	13.5449	12.6487	13.4400	11.1319	13.1480
		FEM	13.6100	12.6700	-	11.1000	-
	5	RFM	13.2024	12.2324	13.0778	10.4829	12.8912
		[29]	13.2271	12.2532	13.1069	10.4967	12.9247
		FEM	13.5300	12.4800	-	12.1000	-

The comparison with the literature leads to the conclusion that the present approach is quite accurate, and the model can be considered validated for porous FGM plates of variable thickness resting on an elastic foundation. Note that in this case, the results obtained using the RFM and FEM methods are close and differ by no more than 2%. In the following section, further analyses will be presented, focused on plates having a complex geometry. In certain instances, such as when p = 5, alpha = 0.2, and CSCS, a discrepancy arises, which may be attributed to an edge (boundary) layer issue that eludes detection in the FEM, as indicated in Ref. [11]. In the following section further analyses will be presented, focused on plates having a complex geometry.

4.2. Free Vibration Analysis for Porous FGM Plates with a Complex Geometry

In actual engineering problems, professionals often face complex geometries, including, for example, holes having regular (circles or squares) or other shapes. These geometries are typically very difficult to handle with analytical or semi-analytical methods. Here, we prove that the use of the R-functions method allows the aforementioned difficulties to be overcome in an efficient way.

In this section, a porous plate with variable thickness resting on an elastic foundation with different elastic stiffnesses of Winkler and Pasternak types is investigated. The Planform of the plate with complex geometry and the distribution law of its thickness are shown in Figure 3a,b.

The geometric parameters are

$$a_1/a = 3;\ a_1/b_1 = 1;\ r_1/2a = 0.15;\ r_2/2a = 0.35;\ h_0/2a = 0.05.$$

The thickness of the plate varies linearly in the y-direction:

$$h(y) = h_0\left(1 + \beta\left(\frac{y+b}{2b}\right)\right),\ \beta = \frac{h_b - h_0}{h_o}. \tag{30}$$

The shear correction factor $K_s = \frac{5}{6}$ was chosen for the current analysis. The following boundary conditions were considered for the numerical experiment:

1. CL-CL—the outside boundary and hole are clamped.
2. CL-F—outside boundary is clamped, hole is free.
3. SS-CL—outside boundary is simply supported, hole is clamped.
4. F-CL—outside boundary is free, hole is clamped.

The non-dimensional natural frequency is defined as $\Lambda = \Omega\,(2a)^2\sqrt{\rho_m/E_m}/h_0$ for all cases.

Case 1

An investigation of the influence of the gradient index (p = 0, 0.5, 1, 2, 5, 10) on the natural frequency for an ideal FGM plate with constant thickness and complex geometry (Figure 3a) made of Al/Al_2O_3 for four types of boundary conditions is fulfilled; the results are shown in Table 6.

Table 6. Effect of gradient index on natural frequency of FGM (Al/Al_2O_3) plate (Figure 3a) with different boundary conditions.

p	CL-CL	CL-F	SS-CL	F-CL
0	12.3781	2.7204	8.2491	1.9158
0.5	10.6016	2.3044	7.0379	1.6449
1	9.6044	2.0768	6.3645	1.4923
2	8.7202	1.8881	5.7809	1.3546
5	8.1172	1.7889	5.4146	1.2559
10	7.7652	1.7316	5.2021	1.1991

From this analysis, it follows that for all boundary conditions, the natural frequencies decrease with an increase in the gradient index p. The results obtained for plates with the boundary condition CL-CL are essentially greater than frequencies for plates with other types of boundary conditions. The smallest values of frequency and minor changes are observed for boundary condition F-CL.

Case 2

An investigation of the free vibrations of a clamped (CL-CL) FGM (Al/Al_2O_3) plate resting on an elastic foundation with various combinations of Winkler and Pasternak types and different values of the gradient index p = 0, 0.5, 1, 2, 5, 10 is conducted. The non-dimensional fundamental frequencies are graphically illustrated in Figure 4.

It can be seen that the influence of the Pasternak foundation parameter exceeds that of the Winkler foundation parameter in all cases. A Pasternak foundation contains the effect of transverse shear deformation of elastic springs.

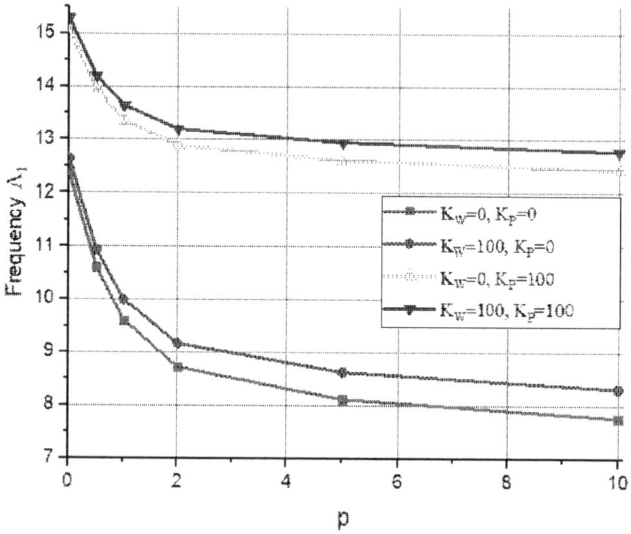

Figure 4. Effect of foundation stiffness K_w, K_p on natural frequency of FGM (Al/Al_2O_3) clamped plate on elastic foundation.

Case 3

An investigation of the vibrations of clamped (CL-CL) FGM plates having a complex geometry (Figure 3), resting on an elastic foundation (stiffness coefficients K_w = 100, K_p = 100), for different values of the porosity parameter α = 0, 0.1, 0.2, 0.3 is performed. The gradient index is varied as follows: p = 0, 0.5, 1, 2, 5, 10; three types of porosities are considered: ideal, even, and uneven. The non-dimensional fundamental frequencies are reported in Table 7. For this case, all of the natural frequencies do not increase significantly with an increase in the porosity parameter for both types—even and uneven distribution.

Table 7. Effect of the porosity parameter Type I and Type II on natural frequency of FGM (Al/Al_2O_3) clamped plate on elastic foundation (β = 0, K_w = 100, K_p = 100).

p	$\alpha = 0$	$\alpha = 0.1$		$\alpha = 0.2$		$\alpha = 0.3$	
	Ideal	**Even**	**Uneven**	**Even**	**Uneven**	**Even**	**Uneven**
0	15.2845	15.6671	15.5264	16.1161	15.7863	16.6514	16.0661
0.5	14.1874	14.5062	14.4108	14.8842	14.6519	15.3404	14.9133
1	13.6306	13.8831	13.8305	14.1729	14.0455	14.5053	14.2773
2	13.1943	13.3658	13.3646	13.5266	13.5434	13.6234	13.7305
5	12.9451	13.0728	13.0998	13.1276	13.2553	12.8635	13.4066
10	12.7809	12.9191	12.9407	12.9787	13.1009	12.5886	13.2544

Case 4

An investigation of free vibration behavior for a clamped (CL-CL) FGM plate (Al/Al_2O_3) with variable thickness on an elastic foundation is performed. For this experiment, the taper ratio is varied as follows: β = [0, 0.1, 0.2, 0.3]; the porosity parameter is α = 0.2, and the foundation stiffness coefficients are K_w = 50, K_p = 100. Two porosity distribution types are considered: even and uneven. The effect of the taper ratio β on the natural frequency of an FGM plate is tabulated in Table 8 and shown in Figure 5.

Table 8. Effect of taper ratio β and gradient index p on natural frequency of clamped FGM plate on elastic foundation (α = 0.2, Type I, II, K_w = 50, K_p = 100).

p	$\beta = 0$		$\beta = 0.1$		$\beta = 0.2$		$\beta = 0.3$	
	Even	**Uneven**	**Even**	**Uneven**	**Even**	**Uneven**	**Even**	**Uneven**
0	15.9938	15.6732	16.4946	16.1629	16.8211	16.4823	17.0981	16.2578
0.5	14.7343	14.5156	15.1997	14.9725	15.5032	15.2705	15.7629	15.5251
1	14.0044	13.8944	14.4487	14.3306	14.7388	14.6197	14.9889	14.8662
2	13.3365	13.3762	13.7609	13.7988	14.0396	14.0767	14.2821	14.3177
5	12.9157	13.0722	13.3287	13.4858	13.6052	13.7621	13.8484	14.0049
10	12.7579	12.9093	13.1689	13.3206	13.4500	13.5988	13.6981	13.8439

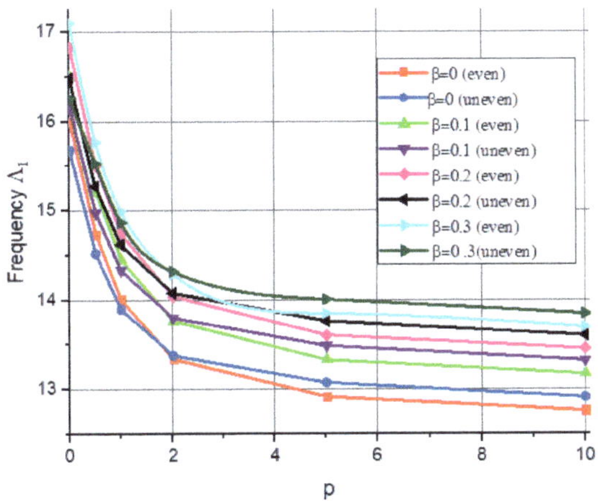

Figure 5. Effect of taper ratio β and volume fraction index p on natural frequency of clamped FGM plate on elastic foundation (α = 0.2, Type I, II, K_w = 50, K_p = 100).

The frequencies increase with the taper ratio, but they decrease with the increase in the gradient index, which is reasonable for this specific problem. The values of frequency for Type II (uneven distribution) are slightly lower than the frequencies for Type I for all values of the gradient index.

Case 5

An investigation of various types of FG materials is conducted. Two materials are considered in the FGM: ZrO_2 and Ti − 6Al − 4V; their mechanical properties are indicated as follows:

ZrO_2:	E = 200 GPa,	ν = 0.3,	ρ = 5700 kg/m^3;
Ti − 6Al − 4V:	E = 105.698 GPa,	ν = 0.3,	ρ = 4427 kg/m^3.

Further numerical experiments have been carried out for four FG materials:

- FGM-1: Al/Al_2O_3;
- FGM-2: Al/ZrO_2;
- FGM-3: Si_3N_4/SU S304;
- FGM-4: ZrO_2/Ti-6 Al-4V.

The FGM plate of Figure 3a is investigated. The variable thickness parameter is β = 0.3; the plate rests on an elastic foundation (K_w = 50, K_p = 100) and is clamped (CL-CL). The porosity parameter is α = 0.2 for two porosity distribution types—even and uneven; the power-law index is varied as follows p = 0, 0.5, 1, 2, 5, 10. The non-dimensional fundamental frequency is reported in Table 9 and Figure 6.

Table 9. Effect of the power index on natural frequency of clamped plates on elastic foundation $K_w = 50$, $K_p = 100$, with porosity $\alpha = 0.2$ and variable thickness $\beta = 0.3$, fabricated using different FGMs: FGM-1, FGM-2, FGM-3, FGM-4.

p	Al/Al_2O_3		Al/ZrO_2		Si_3N_4/SU S304		ZrO_2/Ti-6 Al-4V	
	Even	**Uneven**	**Even**	**Uneven**	**Even**	**Uneven**	**Even**	**Uneven**
0	17.0981	16.2578	11.3984	11.2181	33.1099	28.6338	13.4604	13.0954
0.5	15.7629	15.5251	11.7884	11.5483	20.4428	19.4449	13.4819	13.0915
1	14.9889	14.8662	12.1286	11.8418	17.7114	17.1402	13.5442	13.1377
2	14.2821	14.3177	12.6761	12.3071	15.7946	15.4595	13.6646	13.2342
5	13.8484	14.0049	13.5197	12.9885	14.3382	14.1478	13.8201	13.3554
10	13.6981	13.8439	13.9614	13.3197	13.7529	13.6123	13.8579	13.3784

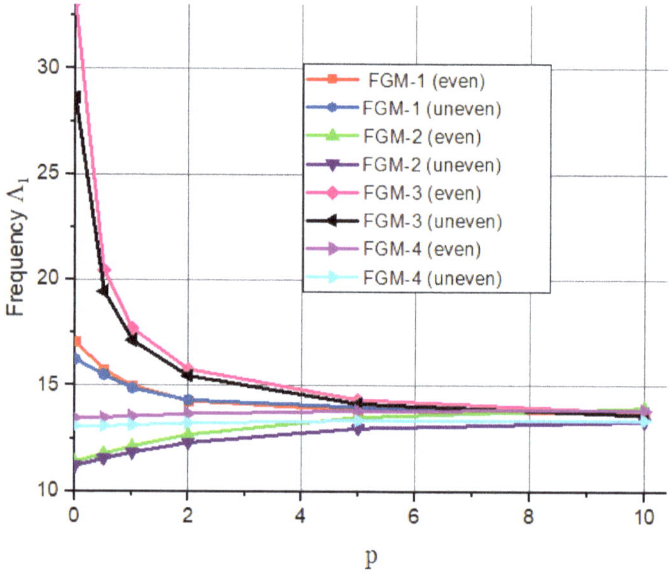

Figure 6. Effect of volume fraction index p on natural frequency of clamped FGM plate (different types of materials) on elastic foundation $K_w = 50$, $K_p = 100$ ($\alpha = 0.2$, $\beta = 0.3$).

For the case under consideration, there are several interesting points to discuss. First, as volume fraction index p increases, the frequencies decrease for the FGM-1 and FGM-3 materials, while for the other two, they increase insignificantly. Secondly, for all materials, the frequencies for FGM-2 are less than those for FGM-1. Thirdly, the frequencies for the FGM-3 material are significantly higher than those in other cases. Fourth, the frequencies for the FGM-4 material practically do not change.

Another free vibration analysis with four types of FG materials is fulfilled for clamped (CL-CL) FGM plates with different values of the porosity parameter: $\alpha = 0, 0.1, 0.2, 0.3, 0.4, 0.5, 0.6$. Now, the gradient index is $p = 1$, the taper ratio is $\beta = 0.3$, and the foundation stiffness parameters of Winkler and Pasternak are $K_w = 50$, $K_p = 100$. The non-dimensional fundamental frequencies for even and uneven porosity distribution types are presented in Table 10 and shown in Figure 7.

Table 10. Effect of the porosity parameter α of Types I and II on natural frequency of clamped plates, on elastic foundation $K_w = 50$, $K_p = 100$, made of different FGMs with taper ratio $\beta = 0.3$ and gradient index $p = 1$.

α	Al/Al_2O_3		Al/ZrO_2		Si_3N_4/SU S304		ZrO_2/Ti-6 Al-4V	
	Even	**Uneven**	**Even**	**Uneven**	**Even**	**Uneven**	**Even**	**Uneven**
0	14.4329	14.4329	11.4219	11.4219	16.4712	16.4712	12.6371	12.6371
0.1	14.6921	14.6417	11.7449	11.6236	17.0368	16.7923	13.0508	12.8773
0.2	14.9889	14.8662	12.1286	11.8418	17.7114	17.1402	13.5443	13.1377
0.3	15.3278	15.1082	12.5927	12.0789	18.5328	17.5187	14.1448	13.4209
0.4	15.7058	15.3699	13.1659	12.3376	19.5526	17.9325	14.8945	13.7305
0.5	16.0847	15.6541	13.8924	12.6213	20.8891	18.3873	15.8628	14.0707
0.6	16.1709	15.9633	14.8381	12.9341	22.6927	18.8903	17.1731	14.4467

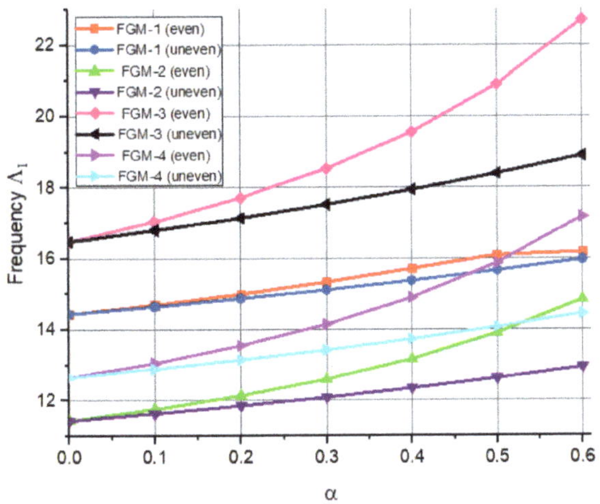

Figure 7. Effect of the porosity parameter α of Types I and II on natural frequency of clamped plates, on elastic foundation ($K_w = 50$, $K_p = 100$), made of different FGMs ($\beta = 0.3$, $p = 1$).

It can be noted that with an increase in the porosity parameter, the natural frequencies increase for all FG material types. A common trend is observed for all the materials in a small reduction in the frequency parameter for the uneven case of porosity. Material FGM-3 shows again the biggest values of non-dimensional frequency; frequencies of material FGM-1 are very close for cases of even and uneven porosity types.

5. Conclusions

This work considers for the first time the application of the R-functions theory to free vibration problems of porous FGM plates of a complex form, with variable thickness, resting on an elastic foundation. A mathematical formulation of the problem is developed in the framework of the first-order shear deformation theory for FGM plates. It is shown that the application of the R-functions theory together with the Ritz variational method makes it possible to solve a wide range of vibration problems for porous plates. The use of the Ritz variational method allows for taking into account the variability of the plate thickness analytically. A set of admissible functions, constructed using the R-functions theory, exactly satisfies the main boundary conditions, both on the outside region boundary and for holes. The approach was validated in a large number of case studies. New achievements of this work include the following:

(1) The highlight of this work is a demonstration of the effectiveness of the application of the R-functions theory for porous FGM plates of variable thickness resting on an elastic foundation with complex shapes.
(2) The method was used to investigate the free vibration of square plates with clamped holes having a complex form;
(3) A numerical experiment was conducted to study the effects of parameters such as the taper ratio, porosity distribution, foundation stiffness coefficients, volume fraction index, and type of FGM on the natural frequencies.
(4) The application of the R-functions theory is validated by means of a comparative analysis with a traditional finite element approach (COMSOL Multiphysics).

All these issues also allowed the identification of advantages and disadvantages of finite element modeling and boundary condition sensitivity for porous FGM plates with variable thickness.

Author Contributions: All authors contributed equally to conceptualization; methodology; validation; software; formal analysis; investigation; resources; writing—original draft preparation; writing—review and editing; visualization; funding acquisition. All authors have read and agreed to the published version of the manuscript.

Funding: This research was funded by NATO, project "Composite Metamaterials for Aerospace Structures—CoMetA", grant number G6176, under the framework of the Science for Peace and Security (SPS) Programme.

Data Availability Statement: Dataset available on request from the authors.

Conflicts of Interest: The authors declare no conflicts of interest.

References

1. Benachour, A.; Tahar, H.D.; Atmane, H.A.; Tounsi, A.; Ahmed, M.S. A four variable refined plate theory for free vibrations of functionally graded plates with arbitrary gradient. *Compos. B Eng.* **2011**, *42*, 1386–1394. [CrossRef]
2. Bert, C.W.; Malik, M. Free vibration analysis of tapered rectangular plates by differential quadrature method: A semi-analytical approach. *J. Sound Vib.* **1996**, *190*, 41–63. [CrossRef]
3. Demirhan, P.A.; Taskin, V. Bending and free vibration analysis of Levy-type porous functionally graded plate using state space approach. *Compos. B Eng.* **2019**, *160*, 661–676. [CrossRef]
4. Shahsavari, D.; Shahsavari, M.; Li, L.; Karami, B. A novel quasi-3D hyperbolic theory for free vibration of FG plates with porosities resting on Winkler/Pasternak/ Kerr foundation. *Aero. Sci. Technol.* **2018**, *72*, 134–149. [CrossRef]
5. Thai, H.T.; Choi, D.H. A simple first-order shear deformation theory for the bending and free vibration analysis of functionally graded plates. *Compos. Struct.* **2013**, *101*, 332–340. [CrossRef]
6. Zenkour, A.M. A quasi-3D refined theory for functionally graded single-layered and sandwich plates with porosities. *Compos. Struct.* **2018**, *201*, 38–48. [CrossRef]
7. Swaminathan, K.; Naveenkumar, D.T.; Zenkour, A.M.; Carrera, E. Stress, vibration and buckling analyses of FGM plates—A state-of-the-art-review. *Compos. Struct.* **2015**, *120*, 10–31. [CrossRef]
8. Shen, H.S. *Functionally Graded Materials*; Taylor & Francis: Abingdon, UK; CRC Press: Boca Raton, FL, USA, 2009.
9. Kiani, Y.; Akbarzadeh, A.H.; Chen, Z.T.; Eslami, M.R. Static and dynamic analysis of an FGM doubly curved panel resting on the Pasternak-type elastic foundation. *Compos. Struct.* **2012**, *94*, 2474–2484. [CrossRef]
10. Kiani, Y.; Sadighi, M.; Eslami, M.R. Dynamic analysis and active control of smart doubly curved FGM panels. *Compos. Struct.* **2013**, *102*, 205–216. [CrossRef]
11. Pellicano, F.; Zirilli, F. Boundary layers and non-linear vibrations in an axially moving beam. *Int. J. Non-Linear Mech.* **1998**, *33*, 691–711. [CrossRef]
12. Zippo, A.; Iarriccio, G.; Pellicano, F.; Shmatko, T. Vibrations of Plates with Complex Shape: Experimental Modal Analysis, Finite Element Method, and R-Functions Method. *Shock. Vib.* **2020**, *2020*, 8882867. [CrossRef]
13. Njim, E.K.; Al-Waily, M.; Sadeq, H.; Bakhy, A. Review of the Recent Research on the Experimental Tests of Functionally Graded Sandwich Panels. *J. Mech. Eng. Res. Dev.* **2021**, *44*, 420–441.
14. Kim, J.; Zur, K.K.; Reddy, J.N. Bending, free vibration, and buckling of modified couples stress-based functionally graded porous micro-plates. *Compos. Struct.* **2019**, *209*, 879–888. [CrossRef]
15. Cong, P.H.; Trinh, M.C.; Khoa, N.D.; Duc, N.D. Nonlinear thermomechanical buckling and post-buckling response of porous FGM plates using Reddy's HSDT. *Aerosp. Sci. Technol.* **2018**, *77*, 419–428. [CrossRef]
16. Zur, K.K.; Jankowski, P. Multiparametric analytical solution for the eigenvalue problem of FGM porous circular plates. *Symmetry* **2019**, *11*, 429. [CrossRef]

17. Li, H.; Pang, F.; Du, Y. Vibration analysis of functionally graded porous cylindrical shell with arbitrary boundary restraints by using a semi analytical method. *Compos. Part B Eng.* **2019**, *164*, 249–264. [CrossRef]
18. Wang, Y.; Wu, D. Free vibration of functionally graded porous cylindrical shell using a sinusoidal shear deformation theory. *Aerosp. Sci. Technol.* **2017**, *66*, 83–91. [CrossRef]
19. Dastjerdi, S.; Malikan, M.; Dimitri, R.; Tornabene, F. Nonlocal elasticity analysis of moderately thick porous functionally graded plates in a hygro-thermal environment. *Compos. Struct.* **2021**, *255*, 112925. [CrossRef]
20. Yang, J.; Shen, H.S. Dynamic response of initially stressed functionally graded rectangular thin plates. *Compos. Struct.* **2001**, *54*, 497–508. [CrossRef]
21. Amini, M.H.; Soleimani, M.; Rastgoo, A. Three-dimensional free vibration analysis of functionally graded material plates resting on an elastic foundation. *Smart Mater. Struct.* **2009**, *18*, 085015. [CrossRef]
22. Singh, S.J.; Harsha, S.P. Exact solution for free vibration and buckling of sandwich S-FGM plates on pasternak elastic foundation with various boundary conditions. *Int. J. Struct. Stabil. Dyn.* **2019**, *19*, 1950028. [CrossRef]
23. Malekzadeh, P.; Karami, G. Vibration of non-uniform thick plates on elastic foundation by differential quadrature method. *Eng. Struct.* **2004**, *26*, 1473–1482. [CrossRef]
24. Rezaei, A.S.; Saidi, A.R. Exact solution for free vibration of thick rectangular plates made of porous materials. *Compos. Struct.* **2015**, *134*, 1051–1060. [CrossRef]
25. Rezaei, A.S.; Saidi, A.R. Application of Carrera Unified Formulation to study the effect of porosity on natural frequencies of thick porous–cellular plates. *Compos. B Eng.* **2016**, *91*, 361–370. [CrossRef]
26. Trinh, M.C.; Duc, N.D.; Kim, S.E. Effects of porosity and thermomechanical loading on free vibration and nonlinear dynamic response of functionally graded sandwich shells with double curvature. *Aerosp. Sci. Technol.* **2019**, *87*, 119–132. [CrossRef]
27. Nguyen, D.D.; Vu, D.Q.; Pham, D.N.; Trinh, M.C. Nonlinear dynamic response of functionally graded porous plates on elastic foundation subjected to thermal and mechanical loads. *Appl. Comput. Mech.* **2018**, *4*, 245–259.
28. Trinh, M.C.; Kim, S.E. A three variable refined shear deformation theory for porous functionally graded doubly curved shell analysis. *Aerosp. Sci. Technol.* **2019**, *94*, 105356. [CrossRef]
29. Kumar, V.; Singh, S.J.; Saran, V.H.; Harsha, S.P. Vibration characteristics of porous FGM plate with variable thickness resting on Pasternak's foundation. *Eur. J. Mech. A Solids* **2021**, *85*, 104124. [CrossRef]
30. Vinh, P.V.; Huy, L.Q. Finite element analysis of functionally graded sandwich plates with porosity via a new hyperbolic shear deformation theory. *Def. Technol.* **2022**, *18*, 490–508. [CrossRef]
31. Balak, M.; Mehrabadi, S.J.; Monfared, H.M. Free vibration behavior of an elliptical sandwich microplate, consisting of a saturated porous core and two piezoelectric face layers, standing on an elastic foundation. *Acta Mech.* **2022**, *233*, 3253–3290. [CrossRef]
32. Iarriccio, G.; Zippo, A.; Pellicano, F. Asymmetric vibrations and chaos in spherical caps under uniform time-varying pressure fields. *Nonlinear Dyn.* **2022**, *107*, 313–329. [CrossRef]
33. Pellicano, F.; Zippo, A.; Iarriccio, G.; Barbieri, M. Experimental Study on Nonlinear Random Excitation. In *Design Tools and Methods in Industrial Engineering*; Lecture Notes in Mechanical Engineering; Springer: Cham, Switzerland, 2020; pp. 637–648. [CrossRef]
34. Hemmatnezhad, M.; Iarriccio, G.; Zippo, A.; Pellicano, F. Modal localization in vibrations of circular cylindrical shells with geometric imperfections. *Thin-Walled Struct.* **2022**, *181*, 110079. [CrossRef]
35. Zippo, A.; Iarriccio, G.; Bergamini, L.; Colombini, E.; Veronesi, P.; Pellicano, F. Fluid–Structure Interaction of a thin cylindrical shell filled with a non-Newtonian fluid. *J. Fluids Struct.* **2023**, *117*, 103829. [CrossRef]
36. Rvachev, V.L. *The R-Functions Theory and Its Some Application*; Naukova Dumka: Kiev, Ukraine, 1982; p. 552. (In Russian)
37. Awrejcewicz, J.; Kurpa, L.; Shmatko, T. Linear and nonlinear free vibration analysis of laminated functionally graded shallow shells with complex plan form and different boundary conditions. *J. Nonlinear Mech.* **2018**, *107*, 161–169. [CrossRef]
38. Kurpa, L.V.; Shmatko, T.V. Buckling and free vibration analysis of functionally graded sandwich plates and shallow shells by the Ritz method and the R-functions theory. *Proc. Inst. Mech. Eng. Part C* **2020**, *235*, 4582–4593. [CrossRef]
39. Awrejcewicz, J.; Kurpa, L.; Shmatko, T. Investigating geometrically nonlinear vibrations of laminated shallow shells with layers of variable thickness via the R-functions theory. *J. Compos. Struct.* **2015**, *125*, 575–585. [CrossRef]
40. Thai, H.T.; Choi, D.H. A refined shear deformation theory for free vibration of functionally graded plates on elastic foundation. *Compos. B Eng.* **2012**, *43*, 2335–2347. [CrossRef]
41. Manna, M.C. Free vibration of tapered isotropic rectangular plates. *JVC J. Vib. Control.* **2012**, *18*, 76–91. [CrossRef]

Mathematical and Computational Applications

MDPI

Article

Buckling of Cracked Euler–Bernoulli Columns Embedded in a Winkler Elastic Medium

José Antonio Loya *, Carlos Santiuste, Josué Aranda-Ruiz and Ramón Zaera

Department of Continuum Mechanics and Structural Analysis, University Carlos III of Madrid, Avda. de la Universidad, 30, 28911 Leganés, Madrid, Spain; csantius@ing.uc3m.es (C.S.); jaranda@ing.uc3m.es (J.A.-R.); rzaera@ing.uc3m.es (R.Z.)

* Correspondence: jloya@ing.uc3m.es

Abstract: This work analyses the buckling behaviour of cracked Euler–Bernoulli columns immersed in a Winkler elastic medium, obtaining their buckling loads. For this purpose, the beam is modelled as two segments connected in the cracked section by a mass-less rotational spring. Its rotation is proportional to the bending moment transmitted through the cracked section, considering the discontinuity of the rotation due to bending. The differential equations for the buckling behaviour are solved by applying the corresponding boundary conditions, as well as the compatibility and jump conditions of the cracked section. The proposed methodology allows calculating the buckling load as a function of the type of support, the parameter defining the elastic soil, the crack position and the initial length of the crack. The results obtained are compared with those published by other authors in works that deal with the problem in a partial way, showing the interaction and importance of the parameters considered in the buckling loads of the system.

Keywords: buckling loads; cracked Euler–Bernoulli columns; Winkler elastic medium

1. Introduction

The stability analysis of beam-type elements subjected to compressive loads is crucial for the design of structures in the civil, mechanical, aerospace, nuclear and offshore fields. Buckling is one of the most common modes of instability in columnar structures, as well as in elements supported by the ground, such as pipes, piles, footings, or railway tracks. Due to their geometric characteristics, these structures are often modelled as beams in civil engineering or railway engineering, with the Euler–Bernoulli or Timoshenko theory being the most commonly used. Additionally, when considering the effect exerted by the soil on the beam, the Winkler and the Pasternak model (or a combination of both) are frequently employed for elastic medium, where the soil is treated as a set of uniformly distributed linear springs without or with shear interaction between them. Thus, a beam-soil system can be analysed using the classical buckling theory, including in the governing equation one or two additional terms [1,2].

In the scientific literature of the last decade, one can find numerous papers dealing with the problem of beam buckling in elastic media. Some focus on the development of mathematical problem-solving techniques, while others focus on the treatment of beams with specific characteristics. In the first group are the works of Aristizabal-Ochoa [3], which deal with the treatment of generalised boundary conditions, that of Hassan and Hadima [4], which obtains the solution using the recursive differentiation method, the work of Anghel and Mares [5], which proposes an integral formulation for an elastic medium of the Winkler–Pasternak type, and that of Ike [6], which employs the Stodola–Vianello iterative method. In the second group, we find the work of Soltani for a tapered Timoshenko beam [7], that of Mohammed et al. [8], which considers FG Euler–Bernoulli beams supported on Winkler–Pasternak elastic foundation, the work of Nguyen et al. [9], that of Mellal et al. [10] for higher-order porous FG beams resting on variable elastic foundations, or the work by Xu et al. [11] for Timoshenko nanobeams resting on Winkler–Pasternak foundations submitted to thermal loads.

On the other hand, the presence of cracks in these types of structures can lead to a decrease in stiffness, the magnitude of which depends primarily on the element's geometry, support conditions, crack size and crack position. This decrease in stiffness has a significant effect on the beam's buckling load. The treatment of the crack involves representing the damaged section with a linear rotational spring, whose stiffness is related to the crack size and the geometry of the cross-section. Continuity in displacement, bending moment, and shear force are imposed on the cracked section, as well as a discontinuity in the rotation that is proportional to the transmitted bending moment. Using this methodology (as well as other equivalent alternatives that consider flexural stiffness singularities using the Dirac delta function), the problem of buckling in cracked beams has been studied in other works [12–16]. Recently, this methodology has also been applied to the analysis of buckling instabilities in FG beams [17] and in nanocantilevers [18].

In the works cited above, either the beam embedded in the elastic medium is not flawed, or the presence of a crack but not the effect of the surrounding elastic medium is taken into account. In the first case, the models do not allow consideration of the flexibilising effect of an eventual crack in the structural element, which leads to overestimates of the buckling load. In the second case, the models do not include the stabilising effect of the elastic medium, resulting in an oversizing of the cracked structural element. The joint consideration of the crack and the elastic medium has been taken into account for the vibratory analysis of beams [19], but not for the study of buckling instability. Therefore, the present study analyses the case of slender Euler–Bernoulli columns with cracks immersed in an elastic medium subjected to compression, considering the discontinuity of bending motion in that section. The effect of the crack length and position, stiffness of the surrounding medium, and type of supports on the determination of critical buckling loads are examined.

2. Euler–Benoulli Column Model in an Elastic Medium

2.1. Theoretical Formulation of an Intact Column

Consider a column without cracks, with length L, width B, height W, cross-sectional moment of inertia I, Young's modulus E, immersed in an elastic medium of Winkler type with stiffness k_w, and subjected to compression, as shown in Figure 1.

Following the classical Euler's theory, the equation governing the buckling behaviour of a column with a uniform cross-section embedded in an elastic medium can be presented as:

$$EI\frac{d^4v(x)}{dx^4} + P_c\frac{d^2v(x)}{dx^2} + k_w v(x) = 0 \tag{1}$$

where $v(x)$ is the transverse deflection of the column, x is the longitudinal Cartesian coordinate of the column with the origin at the bottom support, and P_c is the critical buckling load.

Considering the following dimensionless variables:

$$\xi = \frac{x}{L}, \quad V = \frac{v}{L}, \quad \lambda^2 = \frac{P_c L^2}{EI}, \quad K_w = \frac{k_w L^4}{EI} \tag{2}$$

Equation (1) can be rewritten as:

$$V(\xi)^{iv} + \lambda^2 V(\xi)'' + K_w V(\xi) = 0 \tag{3}$$

where $(\cdot)'$ represents the derivative with respect to ξ. The general solution for the equation with constant coefficients (3) can be expressed using hyperbolic functions. However, considering the definitions of rotation θ and stresses (bending moment, M, and shear force, Q), the corresponding nondimensional variables (rotation, bending moment, $\overline{M}$, and shear force $\overline{Q}$) can be written from their dimensional counterparts:

$$\theta = V', \quad \overline{M} = \frac{ML}{EI} = V'', \quad \overline{Q} = \frac{QL^2}{EI} = V''' + \lambda^2 V' \tag{4}$$

So, the solution of Equation (3) can be conveniently expressed in terms of the nondimensional displacement, slope, bending moment, and shear force at $\xi = 0$, $(V_0, \theta_0, \overline{M}_0, \overline{Q}_0)$, and Krylov–Duncan functions, $g_i(\xi)$ [20]:

$$V(\xi) = V_0 \cdot g_1(\xi) + \theta_0 \cdot g_2(\xi) + \overline{M}_0 \cdot g_3(\xi) + \overline{Q}_0 \cdot g_4(\xi) \tag{5}$$

where the following functions and parameters are defined:

$$g_1(\xi) = \cosh(\Lambda_1\xi) - \frac{\Lambda_1^2 \cosh(\Lambda_1\xi)}{(\Lambda_1^2 - \Lambda_2^2)} - \frac{\Lambda_1^2\Lambda_2^2 \cosh(\Lambda_2\xi)}{(\Lambda_1^2 - \Lambda_2^2)} \tag{6}$$

$$g_2(\xi) = \frac{\sinh(\Lambda_1\xi)}{\Lambda_1} - \frac{(\lambda^2 + \Lambda_1^2)\sinh(\Lambda_1\xi)}{\Lambda_1(\Lambda_1^2 - \Lambda_2^2)} + \frac{(\lambda^2 + \Lambda_1^2)\sinh(\Lambda_2\xi)}{\Lambda_2(\Lambda_1^2 - \Lambda_2^2)} \tag{7}$$

$$g_3(\xi) = \frac{\cosh(\Lambda_1\xi)}{(\Lambda_1^2 - \Lambda_2^2)} - \frac{\cosh(\Lambda_2\xi)}{(\Lambda_1^2 - \Lambda_2^2)} \tag{8}$$

$$g_4(\xi) = -\frac{\sinh(\Lambda_1\xi)}{\Lambda_1(\Lambda_1^2 - \Lambda_2^2)} + \frac{\sinh(\Lambda_2\xi)}{\Lambda_2(\Lambda_1^2 - \Lambda_2^2)} \tag{9}$$

with

$$\Lambda_{1,2} = \sqrt{\frac{-\lambda^2 \pm \sqrt{\lambda^4 - 4K_w}}{2}} \tag{10}$$

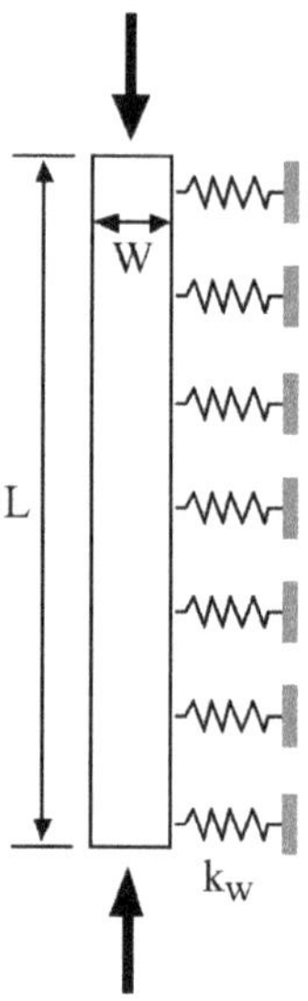

Figure 1. Euler–Bernoulli column in an elastic medium of Winkler type.

In order to solve it, the corresponding boundary conditions must be applied at each end (Table 1).

Table 1. Boundary Conditions.

Type of Support	Restrictions
Simple support	$V = \overline{M} = 0$
Fixed support	$V = \theta = 0$
Free end	$\overline{M} = \overline{Q} = 0$

2.2. Problem Formulation in Cracked Columns

Consider an open crack of length a located at a distance $\beta = (b/L)$ from the lower support, as sketched in Figure 2 (left). Following the method proposed by Freund and Herrmann in 1976 [21] and followed by many other authors [22–27], the cracked column is considered as two segments connected by elastic rotational springs, as shown in Figure 2 (right), whose stiffness depends on the crack depth and the geometry of the cracked section.

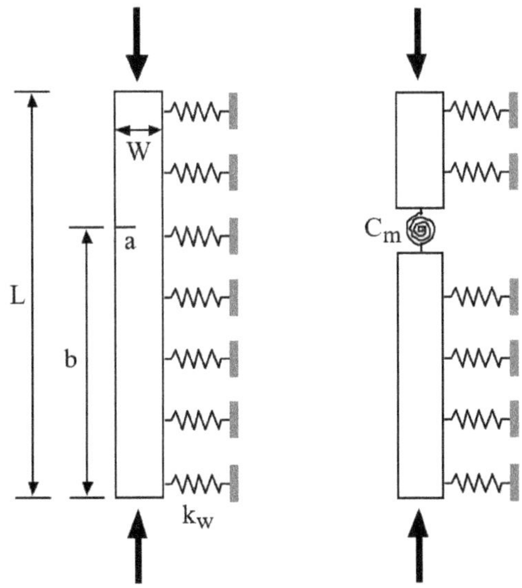

Figure 2. (**Left**): Cracked Euler–Bernoulli column in an elastic medium of Winkler type. (**Right**): Equivalent model with elastic spring for the cracked section.

The discontinuity in the deflection slope of the column at the cracked section, $\Delta\theta$, is proportional to the bending moment transmitted by that section, $M(b)$, as follows:

$$\Delta\theta = C_m M(x)|_{x=b} \tag{11}$$

$$C_m = \frac{W}{EI} m(\alpha, \text{cross-section geometry}) \tag{12}$$

with $\alpha = (a/W)$ being the dimensionless crack length and the function m evaluated by Tada et al. in 1985 [28] using the theory of Fracture Mechanics, which can be applied to linear elastic material behaviour. For the specific case of a rectangular cross-section beam, the function m takes the form expressed in Equation (13) [28]:

$$m(\alpha) = 2\left(\frac{\alpha}{1-\alpha}\right)^2 (5.93 - 19.69\alpha + 34.14\alpha^2 - 35.84\alpha^3 + 13.2\alpha^4) \tag{13}$$

Based on Equation (3), the governing equation for each of the two segments can be expressed as follows:

$$V_1(\xi)^{iv} + \lambda^2 V_1(\xi)'' + K_w V_1(\xi) = 0; \quad 0 < \xi < \beta \tag{14}$$

$$V_2(\xi)^{iv} + \lambda^2 V_2(\xi)'' + K_w V_2(\xi) = 0; \quad \beta < \xi < 1 \tag{15}$$

where λ is an eigenvalue of the cracked column in the elastic medium, related to the critical buckling load of the column with a crack-through expression (2).

The above equations must be solved by applying the corresponding boundary conditions, as well as the following continuity and jump conditions at the cracked section, $\xi = \beta$. These conditions are collected in the following Equations (16)–(19):

- Continuity in deflection:

$$\Delta V = V_2(\beta) - V_1(\beta) = 0 \tag{16}$$

- Continuity in bending moment:

$$V_2''(\beta) = V_1''(\beta) \tag{17}$$

- Continuity in shear force:

$$V_2'''(\beta) + \lambda^2 V_2'(\beta) = V_1'''(\beta) + \lambda^2 V_1'(\beta) \tag{18}$$

- Jump in the slope deflection:

$$\Delta\theta = V_2'(\beta) - V_1'(\beta) = \eta V_2''(\beta) \tag{19}$$

where $\eta = \frac{W}{L} m(\alpha) V_2$ is the parameter that controls the severity of the crack.

3. Direct Solution

The direct solution for the buckling forces can be obtained by separately analysing the column segments on each side of the crack. The solution which satisfies the compatibility conditions at the crack for each segment, $V_i(\xi)$, $i = 1, 2$, can be expressed in terms of displacements, rotations, and forces at the bottom support, $\xi = 0$, (V_0, θ_0, $\overline{M}_0$, $\overline{Q}_0$, respectively), as well as of the discontinuity in rotation, $\Delta\theta$, at the cracked section, $\xi = \beta$:

$$V_1(\xi) = V_0 \cdot g_1(\xi) + \theta_0 \cdot g_2(\xi) + \overline{M}_0 \cdot g_3(\xi) + \overline{Q}_0 \cdot g_4(\xi) \tag{20}$$

$$V_2(\xi) = V_1(\xi) + \Delta\theta \cdot g_2(\xi - \beta) \tag{21}$$

Applying the boundary conditions at the ends and the compatibility conditions at the cracked section (automatically satisfied by the expressions (20) and (21)), the displacement functions $V_{1,2}(\xi)$ lead to the corresponding eigenvalue problem, whose solution allows for obtaining the critical buckling loads of the system.

4. Numerical Results

4.1. Influence of the Crack on the Buckling Load

Firstly, the proposed model has been applied to Euler–Bernoulli columns without cracks and in the absence of an elastic medium ($k_w = 0$), with different boundary conditions (simply supported, clamped-clamped, clamped-free, clamped-supported). The obtained eigenvalues and the corresponding critical buckling loads, P_c, show perfect agreement with the cases described by other authors [16].

Subsequently, the influence of the severity of the crack and the position of the cracked section has been analysed in the absence of an elastic medium. The obtained critical loads for cracks with dimensionless length (a/W) ranging from 0 to 0.9, and located at a distance $\beta = 0.25$ and $\beta = 0.5$ from the bottom support, coincide with those calculated in other studies [16]. These results are normalised with respect to the value corresponding to the intact case and are represented in Figures 3 and 4, respectively.

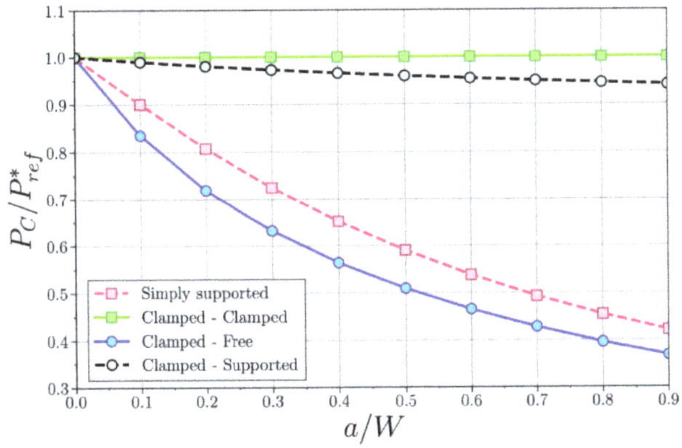

Figure 3. Variation of the first normalised critical buckling load with (a/W) for different boundary conditions and $\beta = 0.25$.

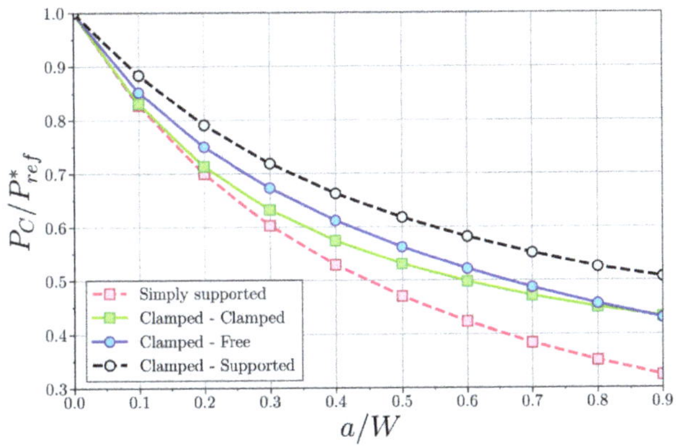

Figure 4. Variation of the first normalised critical buckling load with (a/W) for different boundary conditions and $\beta = 0.50$.

As expected, it is observed that the buckling load decreases with crack length. Regarding the position of the cracked section, it affects significantly. As a representative case, the clamped–clamped case can be observed: when the crack section is located at $\beta = 0.25$ (Figure 3), the crack has no effect on the first buckling load due to the null bending moment at the cracked section, in agreement with other works [16]. In the clamped–supported case, the bending moment in the cracked section at $\beta = 0.25$ (Figure 3) is small but not null, so the effect of the crack on the first buckling load is limited. These behaviours differ greatly in the case of $\beta = 0.50$ (Figure 4).

4.2. Influence of the Crack and Elastic Medium on the Buckling Load

To analyse the applicability of the model when the column is embedded in an elastic medium, the case of a simply supported intact steel column with a length $L = 1$ m, a moment of inertia $I = 833.333$ mm^4, and a Young's modulus $E = 200$ GPa [29] is considered. The values of the critical buckling load, P_c, obtained for different values of the dimensionless parameter representative of the Winkler medium, K_w [0, 5, 10, 50, 100], along with those calculated by Jančo in 2013 [29] using the analytical solution proposed for the simply supported column (Equation (22)), are presented in Table 2:

$$P_c = \frac{(K_w + \pi^4)EI}{\pi^2 L^2} \tag{22}$$

Table 2. Comparison of results for simply supported column without crack in an elastic medium.

P_c [N]	K_w				
	0	5	10	50	100
Theoretical [29]	1644.94	1729.36	1814.82	2489.28	3334.65
Proposed	1644.94	1729.44	1813.94	2489.95	3334.97
Error [%]	0	0	0.01	0.03	0.04

The comparison between the theoretical results [29] and the calculated ones for the simply supported case showed a good correlation between solutions. The maximum error was below 0.04%, validating the proposed solution for the elastic medium.

Additionally, Figure 5 shows the variation of the normalised critical load with the stiffness of the medium for other boundary conditions. In all cases, an increase in the critical load with K_w was observed, which was more pronounced as the boundary conditions become less rigid, as in the case of simply supported and cantilever beams.

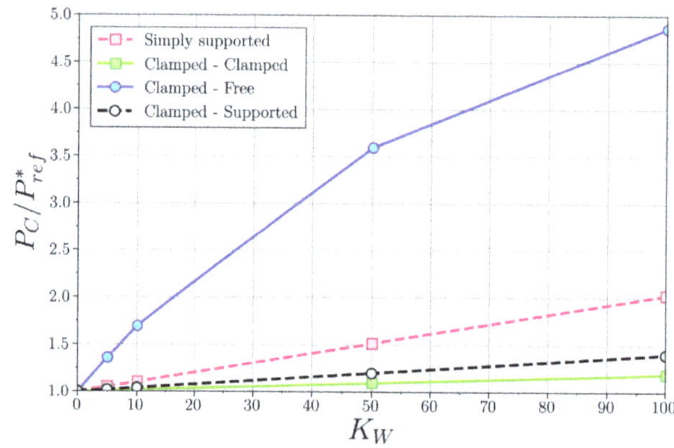

Figure 5. Variation of the first normalised critical buckling load with K_w and different boundary conditions for a non-cracked beam.

4.3. Combined Influence of the Crack and the Elastic Medium on the Buckling Load

In this section, the coupled effect of the cracked section, both at $\beta = 0.25$ and $\beta = 0.50$, and the elastic medium for different boundary conditions (simply supported, clamped–pinned, clamped–clamped, and cantilever) are analysed in Figures 6–13, respectively, representing the variation of the critical buckling load with the crack severity factor a/W and the Winkler stiffness K_w. In all cases, the load was normalised with that of an intact column in a surrounding elastic medium with zero stiffness, for the same boundary conditions.

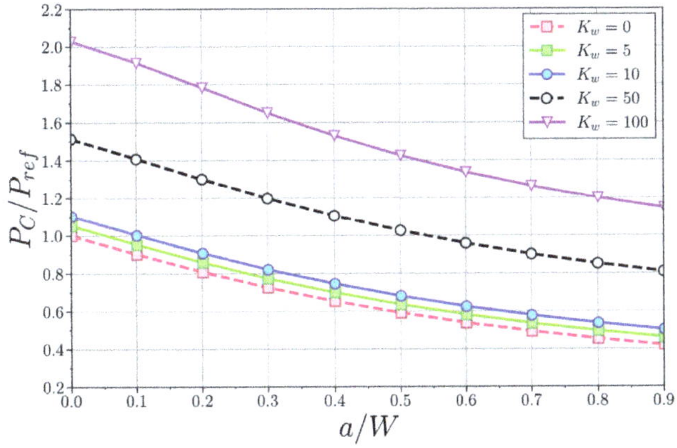

Figure 6. Simply supported column, $\beta = 0.25$. Variation of the first normalised critical buckling load with (a/W) and for different K_w.

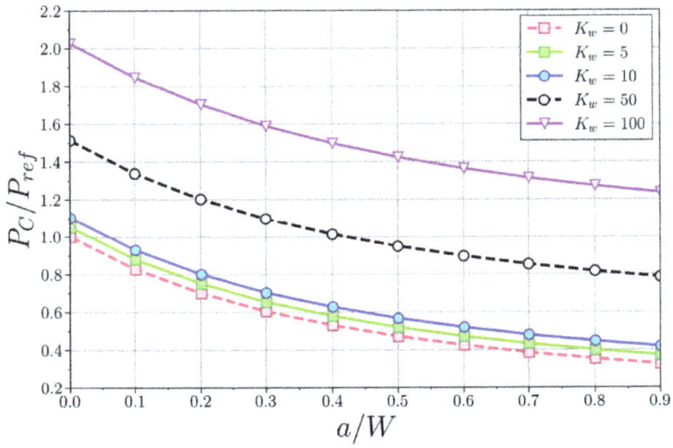

Figure 7. Simply supported column, $\beta = 0.5$. Variation of the first normalised critical buckling load with (a/W) and for different K_w.

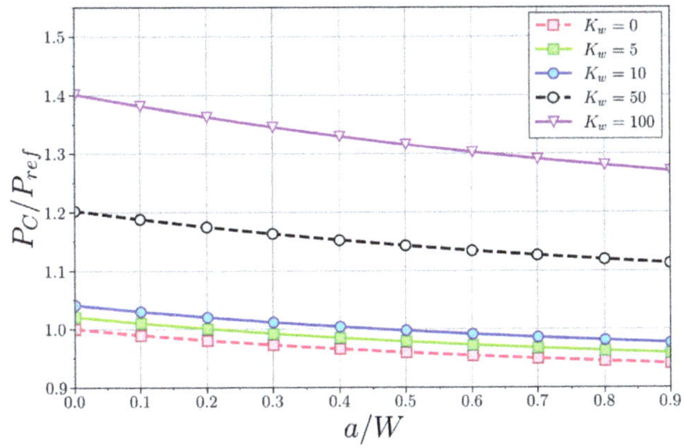

Figure 8. Clamped–supported column, $\beta = 0.25$. Variation of the first normalised critical buckling load with (a/W) and for different K_w.

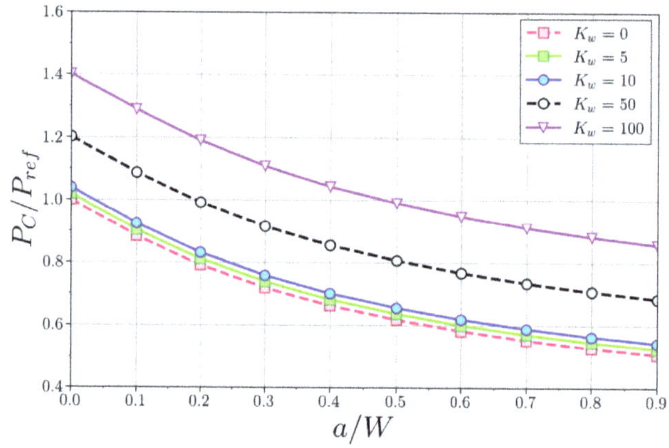

Figure 9. Clamped–supported column, $\beta = 0.5$. Variation of the first normalised critical buckling load with (a/W) and for different K_w.

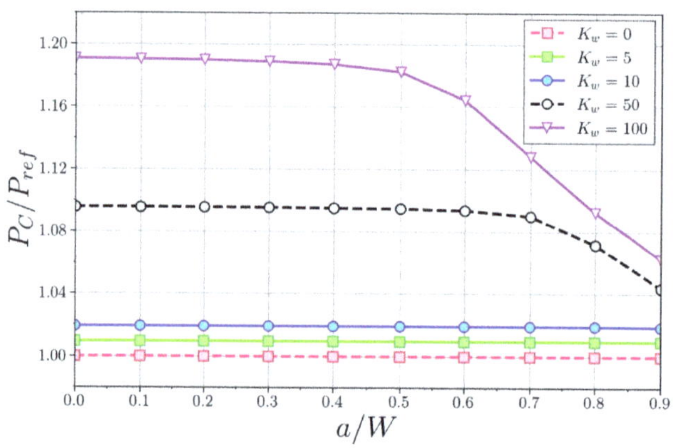

Figure 10. Clamped–clamped column, $\beta = 0.25$. Variation of the first normalised critical buckling load with (a/W) and for different K_w.

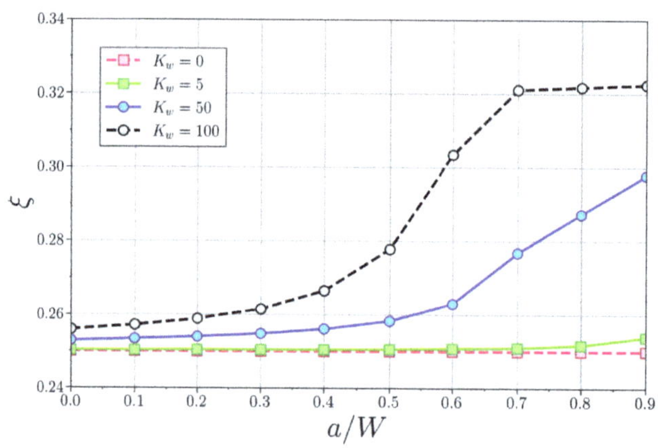

Figure 11. Position ξ at which the bending moment becomes null in a clamped–clamped column, for different crack lengths (a/W) and K_w.

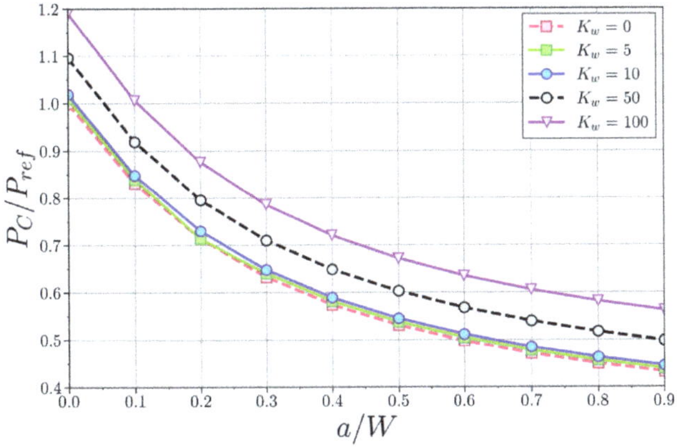

Figure 12. Clamped–clamped column, $\beta = 0.5$. Variation of the first normalised critical buckling load with (a/W) and for different K_w.

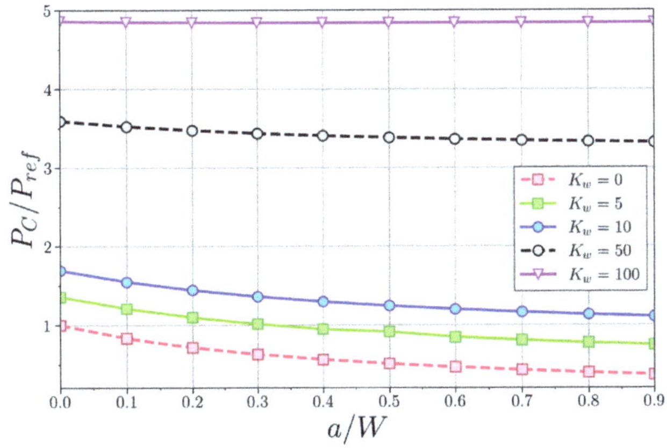

Figure 13. Cantilever column, $\beta = 0.25$. Variation of the first normalised critical buckling load with (a/W) and for different K_w.

4.3.1. Simply Supported Column

The first boundary conditions analysed were for simply supported columns, see Figures 6 and 7. In these cases, a decrease in the critical buckling load with the crack length was observed, while, on the other hand, the load increased with the stiffness of the medium due to the higher restriction to the column displacement. Although the trends were similar in all cases, the percentage decrease in the buckling load with crack severity was smaller as K_w increased due to the higher transverse stiffness of the system.

In general, these conclusions are also applicable to the other boundary conditions (clamped–clamped, clamped–pinned, and cantilever), with some particularities, as discussed below.

4.3.2. Clamped–Supported Column

The clamped–supported column behaviour is presented in Figures 8 and 9. Firstly, the influence of the elastic medium was weaker for these boundary conditions, as compared to the simply supported case, showing smaller increases in the buckling load as K_w rose (an average increase of 50% is observed compared to an increase of 170% in the case of simply supported column). Therefore, the potential benefit of the elastic confinement provided by the Winkler medium was reduced in the embedded–supported beam.

4.3.3. Clamped–Clamped Column

For the clamped–clamped column, and for the crack-position $\beta = 0.25$ (Figure 10), it is worth noting that the crack severity hardly affected the buckling load for low values of K_w. However, for large values, its influence begins to be noticeable for cracks larger than half the section height W.

Figure 11 represents the distance from the lower support, ξ, where the bending moment, M, was null in a clamped–clamped column with a cracked section at $\beta = 0.25$. Notice that for $Kw = 0$, $\overline{M} = 0$ at the cracked position for any crack severity, so no jump in slope deflection was achieved (Equation (19)). If the stiffness of the elastic medium increases, the position where $\overline{M} = 0$ does too, even in the case of an intact column. The contribution of the crack severity allows this position to increase from $\xi = 0.25$ up to $\xi = 0.32$ (close to $1/3$ length of the column). This implies that the bending moment at the cracked section is now non-nil, leading to a jump in the slope deflection in the cracked section.

For $\beta = 0.50$, see Figure 12, similar behaviour as in the simply supported case was appreciated, showing the importance of the crack position in the buckling behaviour for this boundary condition, which can strongly alter the trends.

4.3.4. Cantilever Column

The clamped-free (or cantilever) column leads to the lowest stiffness among all the boundary conditions considered. Here, the stabilising effect of the elastic medium was very relevant, as can be seen in Figures 13 and 14. Here, the buckling load increased by 500% in the whole range of Winkler stiffnesses, as compared to a scarce 20% in the clamped–clamped case (that with the higher structural stiffness and buckling load). This underlines the importance of the stiffness of the Winkler medium in the safety of cracked structures, especially for those with higher flexibility.

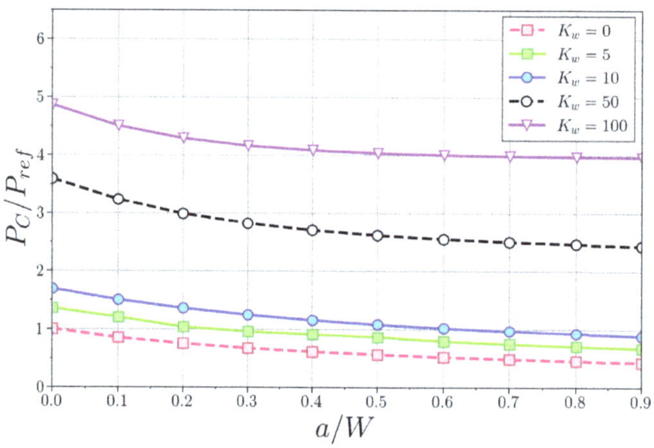

Figure 14. Cantilever column, $\beta = 0.5$. Variation of the first normalised critical buckling load with (a/W) and for different K_w.

5. Conclusions

It is known that the presence of cracks in a compression-loaded column reduces the buckling forces of the structure by making it more flexible. In this work, a theoretical model is proposed to determine these critical loads in cracked Euler–Bernoulli columns immersed in a Winkler-type elastic medium, under different boundary conditions. The described method divides the column into two segments connected by a rotational elastic massless spring, whose stiffness is related to the bending moment transmitted at the cracked section, and satisfies the corresponding continuity and jump conditions at the crack.

The proposed model has been independently validated against literature results for both the case of cracked columns in the absence of an elastic medium and intact columns immersed in a Winkler-type elastic medium.

Furthermore, the coupled effect of crack presence and the elastic medium was analysed, revealing the opposing effect on the critical buckling load produced by both considerations.

The present model has shown its capability to reproduce the buckling behaviour of a cracked beam in an elastic medium. However, some simplifying hypotheses were assumed and they can be modified in future works to obtain a better understanding of their limitations. For instance, the contribution of the shear forces can be added using a Timoshenko beam and/or modelling the elastic foundation with a Pasternak model.

Author Contributions: Conceptualisation, J.A.L. and R.Z.; methodology, J.A.L.; formal analysis, J.A.L. and R.Z.; investigation, J.A.L., C.S., J.A.-R. and R.Z.; writing—original draft preparation, J.A.L., C.S., J.A.-R. and R.Z.; writing—review and editing, J.A.L., C.S., J.A.-R. and R.Z.; supervision, J.A.L. and R.Z.; funding acquisition, C.S. and J.A.L. All authors have read and agreed to the published version of the manuscript.

Funding: This research was funded by the Spanish State Research Agency, grant number PID2020-118946RB-I00.

Conflicts of Interest: The authors declare no conflict of interest.

References

1. Eisenberger, M.; Clastornik, J. Vibrations and buckling of a beam on Winkler elastic foundation. *J. Sound Vib.* **1987**, *2*, 233–241. [CrossRef]
2. Stojanovic, V.; Kozic, P.; Janevski, G. Buckling instabilities of elastically connected Timoshenko beams on an elastic layer subjected to axial forces. *J. Mech. Mat. Struc.* **2012**, *7*, 363–374. [CrossRef]
3. Aristizabal-Ochoa, J.D. Stability of slender columns on an elastic foundation with generalised end conditions. *Ing. Investig.* **2013**, *33*, 34–40. [CrossRef]
4. Hassan, M.H.; Hadima, S.A. Analysis of nonuniform beams on elastic foundations using recursive differentiation method. *Eng. Mech.* **2015**, *22*, 83–94.
5. Anghel, V.; Mares, C. Integral formulation for stability and vibration analysis of beams on elastic foundation. *Proc. Rom. Acad. Ser. A* **2019**, *20*, 285–293.
6. Ike, C.C. Stodola-Vianello method for the buckling load analysis of Euler–Bernoulli beam on Winkler foundation. *UNIZIK J. Eng. Appl. Sci.* **2023**, *23*, 250–259.
7. Soltani, M. Finite element modeling for buckling analysis of tapered axially functionally graded Timoshenko beam on elastic foundation. *Mech. Adv. Compos. Struct.* **2020**, *7*, 203–218.
8. Mohammed, A.T.; Hareb, M.A.; Eqal, A.K. Investigation on the analysis of bending and buckling for FGM Euler–Bernoulli beam resting on Winkler-Pasternak elastic foundation. *J. Phys. Conf. Ser.* **2020**, *1773*, 012027. [CrossRef]
9. Nguyen, N.D.; Nguyen, T.N.; Nguyen, T.K.; Vo, T.P. A Legendre-Ritz solution for bending, buckling and free vibration behaviours of porous beams resting on the elastic foundation. *Structures* **2023**, *50*, 1934–1950. [CrossRef]
10. Mellal, F.; Bennai, R.; Avcar, M.; Nebab, M.; Atmane, H.A. On the vibration and buckling behaviors of porous FG beams resting on variable elastic foundation utilizing higher-order shear deformation theory. *Acta Mech.* **2023**, *234*, 3955–3977. [CrossRef]
11. Xu, C.; Li, Y.; Dai, Z. Investigation on buckling of Timoshenko nanobeams resting on Winkler–Pasternak foundations in a non-uniform thermal environment via stress-driven nonlocal elasticity and nonlocal heat conduction. *J. Therm. Stress* **2023**, *46*, 317–332. [CrossRef]
12. Wang, C.Y.; Wang, C.M.; Aung, T.M. Buckling of a weakened column. *J. Eng. Mech.* **2004**, *130*, 1373–1376. [CrossRef]
13. Biondi, B.; Cademi, S. Closed form solutions of Euler–Bernoulli beams with singularities. *Int. J. Solids Struct.* **2005**, *42*, 3027–3044. [CrossRef]
14. Biondi, B.; Cademi, S. Euler–Bernoulli beams with multiple singularities in the flexural stiffness. *Eur. J. Mech. A/Solids* **2007**, *26*, 789–809. [CrossRef]
15. Caddemi, S.; Caliò, I. Exact solution of the multi-cracked Euler–Bernoulli column. *Int. J. Solids Struct.* **2008**, *45*, 1332–1351. [CrossRef]
16. Loya, J.A.; Vadillo, G.; Fernández-Sáez, J. First-order solutions for the buckling loads of Euler–Bernoulli weakened columns. *J. Eng. Mech.* **2010**, *136*, 674–679. [CrossRef]

17. Saimi, A.; Bensaid, I.; Fellah, A. Effect of crack presence on the dynamic and buckling responses of bidirectional functionally graded beams based on quasi-3D beam model and differential quadrature finite element method. *Arch. Appl. Mech.* **2023**, *93*, 3131–3151. [CrossRef]
18. Darban, H.; Luciano, R.; Darban, R. Buckling of cracked micro- and nanocantilevers. *Acta Mech.* **2023**, *234*, 693–704. [CrossRef]
19. Loya, J.A.; Aranda-Ruiz, J.; Zaera, R. Natural frequencies of vibration in cracked Timoshenko beams within an elastic medium. *Theor. Appl. Frac. Mech.* **2022**, *118*, 103257. [CrossRef]
20. Karnovsky, I.A.; Lebed, O. *Advanced Methods of Structural Analysis*; Springer: Berlin/Heidelberg, Germany, 2010.
21. Freund, L.B.; Herrmann, G. Dynamic fracture of a beam or plate in plane bending. *Trans. ASME J. Appl. Mech.* **1976**, *43*, 112–116. [CrossRef]
22. Adams, R.; Cawley, P.; Pye, C.; Stone, B. A vibration technique for non-destructive assessing the integrity of structures. *Proc. Inst. Mech. Eng. Part C J. Mech. Eng. Sci.* **1978**, *20*, 93–100.
23. Morassi, A. Crack-induced changes in eigenfrequencies of beam structures. *J. Eng. Mech.* **1993**, *119*, 1798–1803. [CrossRef]
24. Narkis, Y. Identification of crack location in vibrating simply supported beams. *J. Sound Vib.* **1994**, *172*, 549–558. [CrossRef]
25. Fernández-Sáez, J.; Rubio, L.; Navarro, C. Approximate calculation of the fundamental frequency for bending vibrations of cracked beams. *J. Sound Vib.* **1999**, *225*, 345–352. [CrossRef]
26. Krawczuk, M.; Palacz, M.; Ostachowicz, W. The dynamic analysis of cracked Timoshenko beams by spectral element. *J. Sound Vib.* **2003**, *264*, 1139–1153. [CrossRef]
27. Loya, J.A.; Rubio, L.; Fernández-Sáez, J. Natural frequencies for bending vibrations of Timoshenko cracked beams. *J. Sound Vib.* **2006**, *290*, 640–653. [CrossRef]
28. Tada, H.; Paris, P.; Irwin, G. *The Stress Analysis of Cracks Handbook*; Paris Productions: St. Louis, MI, USA, 1985.
29. Jančo, R. Numerical and Exact Solution of Buckling Load For Beam on Elastic Foundation. *Trans. VŠB Tech. Univ. Ostrav. Mech. Ser.* **2013**, *59*, 21–26. [CrossRef] [PubMed]

Mathematical and Computational Applications

MDPI

Article

Thermal–Structural Linear Static Analysis of Functionally Graded Beams Using Reddy Beam Theory

Carlos Enrique Valencia Murillo, Miguel Ernesto Gutierrez Rivera * and Luis David Celaya Garcia

Department of Mechanical Engineering, University of Guanajuato, Salamanca 36885, Mexico; ce.valenciamurillo@ugto.mx (C.E.V.M.); ld.celayagarcia@ugto.mx (L.D.C.G.)
* Correspondence: miguel.gutierrez@ugto.mx

Abstract: In this work, a finite element model to perform the thermal–structural analysis of beams made of functionally graded material (FGM) is presented. The formulation is based on the third-order shear deformation theory. The constituents of the FGM are considered to vary only in the thickness direction, and the effective material properties are evaluated by means of the rule of mixtures. The volume distribution of the top constituent is modeled using the power law form. A comparison of the present finite element model with the numerical results available in the literature reveals that they are in good agreement. In addition, a routine to study functionally graded plane models in a commercial finite element code is used to verify the performance of the proposed model. In the present work, displacements for different values of the power law exponent and surface temperatures are presented. Furthermore, the normal stress variation along the thickness is shown for several power law exponents of functionally graded beams subjected to thermal and mechanical loads.

Keywords: beam; thermal analysis; third-order shear deformation theory; functionally graded material; finite element model

1. Introduction

Functionally graded materials (FGMs) are advanced materials made from a mixture of two or more constituents, and, therefore, they are not homogeneous. Typically, the mixture consists of a ceramic and a metallic material, and it is designed to have a continuous variation in material composition. The gradient of material properties allows the reduction of thermal and residual stresses, as well as the stress concentrations presented in laminated composite materials [1–5].

FGMs are often used in structures or applications that commonly operate under extreme temperature and/or environmental conditions, such as spacecrafts, aircrafts, and nuclear reactors [6–8]. The main reasons for their use are their outstanding thermo-mechanical properties, corrosion resistance, and high fracture toughness [9].

Many of the structural elements or components operating under these extreme environments are beams. For that reason, it is important to analyze the behavior of these types of elements [6]. Since the beam element is one of the most used in structural analysis, there are several theories available to describe its mechanical behavior. Among these are Euler–Bernoulli beam theory or classical beam theory (CBT), Timoshenko beam theory or first-order shear deformation theory (FSDT), Reddy–Bickford beam theory or third-order shear deformation theory (TSDT), and other higher-order shear deformation theories (HSDTs).

Static, dynamic, and modal analyses of functionally graded beams under mechanical loads have been made using these theories. Li [10] presented a unified approach to analyze the static and dynamic behavior of functionally graded beams (FGB), where the Euler–Bernoulli beam theory could be reduced from the Timoshenko beam theory as a special case. Alshorbagy et al. [11] investigated the free vibration response of FGB by means of the finite element method and the CBT. Moheimani and Ahmadian [12] studied the free vibration response of FGB using the Euler–Bernoulli beam theory and the non-local theory of elasticity. Chakraborty et al. [1] performed static and free vibration analyses of FGB using the FSDT. Nguyen et al. [13] studied the static and free vibration responses of axially loaded rectangular FGB using the FSDT. A higher-order finite element, based on the unified and integrated approach of Timoshenko beam theory, was developed by Katili et al. [14]. They performed static and free vibration analyses of FGB. Kadoli et al. [15] presented the static analysis of FGB using the TSDT. The free vibration of FGB was investigated by Aydogdu and Taskin [16] by means of a Navier-type solution method and different higher-order shear deformation theories. Mahi et al. [17] developed an exact model to study the free vibration response of FGB using a unified HSDT, where the material properties were taken as temperature-dependent. Thai and Vo [18] used different HSDTs to study the bending and free vibration of FGB. A similar analysis was made later by Vo et al. [19] using only a refined shear deformation theory. Şimşek and Reddy [20] studied the static bending and free vibration of functionally graded (FG) microbeams using a unified higher-order theory that contained various other theories by introducing a function into the displacement field that characterized the transverse shear and stress distribution along the thickness of the beam. Gao and Zhang [21] developed a non-classical third-order shear deformation beam theory for Reddy–Levinson beams using a modified couple stress theory and a surface elasticity theory that allowed them to consider the beam's microstructure, surface energy, and Poisson's effect.

The responses of functionally graded beams under thermal and mechanical loads have also been explored. Chakraborty and Gopalakrishnan [22] analyzed the wave propagation behavior of FGB subjected to high-frequency thermal or mechanical impulses using the spectral finite element method. Daneshmehr et al. [23] developed a micro-scale Reddy beam model based on the couple stress theory to analyze the thermal effect on the vibration, buckling, and static bending analyses. They obtained solutions using series expansions for the generalized displacements, which satisfied the boundary conditions. El-Megharbel [9] performed a theoretical analysis of FGB under thermal loads. De Pietro et al. [7] studied the thermo-elastic response of FGB using Carrera's unified formulation. Lim and Kim [24] used the FSDT to analyze the behavior of FGB with temperature-dependent material properties. Ebrahimi and Jafari [3] proposed a refined shear deformation beam theory for the thermo-mechanical analysis of FGB with porosities exposed to different thermal loads.

In this paper, a thermal-structural analysis of FGB is presented. The finite element model is developed using the TSDT. The material properties vary through the thickness according to the power law, and the temperature distribution along the same direction is obtained by means of a polynomial series. To verify the behavior of the present finite element model, plane models are developed using ANSYS APDL. Finally, to illustrate the performance of the model, some case studies are reported, where the power law exponent and the difference in the temperature between the top and bottom surfaces are varied.

2. Thermal–Structural Problem Description

To develop the present finite element model of FG beams under thermal and mechanical loads, the following conditions are considered:

- The FG beam has a rectangular cross-section of width b and thickness t, as shown in Figure 1, and the beam's length is L.
- The top and bottom surfaces, as seen in Figure 1, are exposed to the temperatures T_{top} and T_{bot}, respectively, where $T_{top} > T_{bot}$. The temperature only varies through the z coordinate, and it remains constant along the other directions.
- There is no internal heat generation, and convection heat transfer between the beam's surfaces and the surrounding media is not considered.
- In this case, a uniform distributed load q_0 is applied to the FG beam, as shown in Figure 1. However, the distributed load can also be function of the x coordinate.

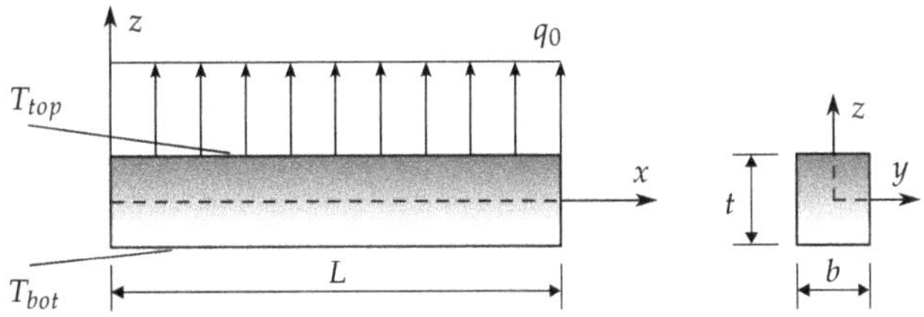

Figure 1. FG beam subjected to a distributed load with different temperatures of the top and bottom surfaces.

2.1. Mechanical Properties

In order to model the variation in the mechanical properties with the variation in the thickness of the beam, Voight's rule of mixtures is used [25], as follows:

$$P(z) = (P_{top} - P_{bot})V_{top}(z) + P_{bot}, \tag{1}$$

where P denotes the material property and the subscripts top and bot refer to the top and bottom constituent, respectively. $V_{top}(z)$ corresponds to the volume distribution of the top constituent through the thickness of the beam, which is defined by the power law as

$$V_{top}(z) = \left(\frac{2z+t}{2t}\right)^n, \tag{2}$$

where n is the power law exponent, which takes positive values.

2.2. Temperature Distribution

Following the assumptions stated in the problem description of Section 2, the governing equation of the heat transfer through the thickness of the beam is given by

$$\frac{\partial}{\partial z}\left[K(z)\frac{\partial T(z)}{\partial z}\right] = 0, \qquad -t/2 \le z \le t/2, \tag{3}$$

where $K(z)$ corresponds to the thermal conductivity, and it is calculated using Equation (1). In addition, the boundary conditions are

$$T(-t/2) = T_{bot}, \quad T(t/2) = T_{top}.$$

A solution to the above one-dimensional heat transfer equation was reported in the work of Javaheri and Eslami [26], and it is given as

$$T(z) = T_{bot} + \frac{T_{top} - T_{bot}}{H}\sum_{i=0}^{\eta}\left(\frac{1}{in+1}\right)\left(\frac{K_{bot} - K_{top}}{K_{bot}}\right)^i\left(\frac{2z+t}{2t}\right)^{(in+1)}, \tag{4}$$

with

$$H = \sum_{i=0}^{\eta}\left(\frac{1}{in+1}\right)\left(\frac{K_{bot} - K_{top}}{K_{bot}}\right)^i,$$

where i indicates the index of the sum and η denotes the number of terms used in the series for the approximation. One should also remember that n corresponds to the power law exponent presented previously in Equation (2).

3. Finite Element Model

This section briefly presents the development of the finite element model based on the TSDT. In order to obtain the equations for the present model (i.e., the stiffness matrix and generalized force vector), the definitions for the displacement field, strains, and constitutive equations are required. The displacement field of the TSDT is given by [27,28]

$$u_1(x) = u^0(x) + z\phi^0(x) - \kappa z^3\left[\phi^0(x) + \frac{\partial w^0(x)}{\partial x}\right], \tag{5}$$

$$u_3(x) = w^0(x), \tag{6}$$

where u^0 is the axial displacement, w^0 is the transverse displacement, ϕ^0 is the rotation of a point located at the centroidal axis x of the beam, and

$$\kappa = \frac{4}{3t^2}. \tag{7}$$

Considering the displacement field of Equations (5) and (6), the nonzero mechanical strains are defined as follows:

$$\varepsilon_{11}^{M} = \frac{\partial u^0}{\partial x} + z\frac{\partial \phi^0}{\partial x} - \kappa z^3\left(\frac{\partial \phi^0}{\partial x} + \frac{\partial^2 w^0}{\partial x^2}\right) \tag{8}$$

$$\gamma_{13}^{M} = \phi^0 - 3\kappa z^2\left(\phi^0 + \frac{\partial w^0}{\partial x}\right) + \frac{\partial w^0}{\partial x}. \tag{9}$$

where, for the sake of brevity, the x argument has been omitted and the superscript M stands for mechanical. On the other hand, the nonzero thermal strain is defined as

$$\varepsilon_{11}^{T} = \alpha(z)\left[T(z) - T_{ref}\right], \tag{10}$$

where $\alpha(z)$ denotes the thermal expansion coefficient, and its value is computed by means of the rule of mixtures defined in Equation (1). $T(z)$ is calculated using Equation (4), T_{ref} is the reference temperature at which the material is free of stress, and the superscript T stands for thermal.

Now, the constitutive equations are defined, i.e., the relation between stress and strain. In this case, the stresses, including thermal and mechanical effects, are considered to be defined by

$$\sigma_{11} = \sigma_{11}^{M} - \sigma_{11}^{T}, \quad \tau_{13} = \tau_{13}^{M}, \tag{11}$$

where

$$\sigma_{11}^{M} = E(z)\varepsilon_{11}^{M}, \quad \sigma_{11}^{T} = E(z)\varepsilon_{11}^{T}, \quad \tau_{13}^{M} = G(z)\gamma_{13}^{M}, \tag{12}$$

where $E(z)$ represents Young's modulus and $G(z)$ is the shear modulus, which is defined as $G(z) = \dfrac{E(z)}{2(1+\nu(z))}$, where $\nu(z)$ is Poisson's ratio.

3.1. Principle of Virtual Work

Here, to obtain the stiffness matrix and the force vector involved in the finite element model, the following definition of the principle of virtual work is used:

$$\delta W_I - \delta W_E = 0, \tag{13}$$

where δW_I is the virtual work carried out by internal forces and δW_E is the virtual work carried out by external forces, which are defined by the following expressions:

$$\delta W_I = \int_V \delta\boldsymbol{\varepsilon} \cdot \boldsymbol{\sigma}\, dV, \quad \delta W_E = \int_{h^e} \mathbf{f} \cdot \delta\mathbf{u}\, dx, \tag{14}$$

where $\mathbf{f}$ represents the vector associated with the external loads.

For the present model, introducing the strains and stresses defined in Equations (8)–(11) into Equation (14), the following expressions for the virtual works are found:

$$\delta W_I = \int_V \left[\delta\varepsilon_{11}^M E(z)\varepsilon_{11}^M + \delta\gamma_{13}^M G(z)\gamma_{13}^M - \delta\varepsilon_{11}^M E(z)\varepsilon_{11}^T\right] dV, \tag{15}$$

and

$$\delta W_E = \int_{h^e} q_0 \delta w^0(x) dx, \tag{16}$$

where h^e represents the one-dimensional domain of the element.

At this point, all the definitions required to obtain the equations involved in the finite element model have been introduced. In the following sections, the displacement vector, the stiffness matrix, and the generalized force vector are obtained.

3.2. Displacement Vector

In order to obtain the finite element model, the displacement field is approximated as follows:

$$u_j^0 = \sum_{j=0}^{p} \psi_j^u \Delta_j^{(1)}, \quad w_J^0 = \sum_{J=0}^{m} \psi_J^w \Delta_J^{(2)}, \quad \phi_k^0 = \sum_{k=0}^{p} \psi_k^\phi \Delta_k^{(3)}, \tag{17}$$

where the functions ψ_j^u and ψ_k^ϕ correspond to the linear Lagrange polynomials and the function ψ_J^w represents the Hermite cubic interpolation functions. Moreover, $\Delta_j^{(1)}$, $\Delta_J^{(2)}$, and $\Delta_k^{(3)}$ are nodal displacements associated with axial displacement, transverse displacement, and rotation, respectively. In this manner, the displacement vector of the finite element model has the form

$$\boldsymbol{\Delta} = \begin{bmatrix} \Delta^{(1)} & \Delta^{(2)} & \Delta^{(3)} \end{bmatrix}^{\mathrm{T}}. \tag{18}$$

3.3. Stiffness Matrix and Generalized Force Vector

Substituting the strains and stresses into Equation (15) and then replacing the displacements by their approximations defined by Equation (17), the stiffness matrix is found to have the form

$$\mathbf{K^e} = \begin{bmatrix} \mathbf{K}^{11} & \mathbf{K}^{12} & \mathbf{K}^{13} \\ \mathbf{K}^{21} & \mathbf{K}^{22} & \mathbf{K}^{23} \\ \mathbf{K}^{31} & \mathbf{K}^{32} & \mathbf{K}^{33} \end{bmatrix}, \tag{19}$$

where the components of the submatrices $\mathbf{K}^{ij}$ are given by

$$K_{ij}^{11} = \int_{h^e} A_{xx} \frac{d\,\psi_i^u}{dx}\frac{d\,\psi_j^u}{dx} dx, \quad K_{iJ}^{12} = \int_{h^e} -\kappa E_{xx} \frac{d\,\psi_i^u}{dx}\frac{d^2\,\psi_J^w}{dx^2} dx, \quad K_{il}^{13} = \int_{h^e} \hat{B}_{xx} \frac{d\,\psi_i^u}{dx}\frac{d\,\psi_l^\phi}{dx} dx,$$

$$K_{Ij}^{21} = K_{jI}^{12}, \quad K_{IJ}^{22} = \int_{h^e} \left[\kappa^2 H_{xx} \frac{d^2\,\psi_I^w}{dx^2}\frac{d^2\,\psi_J^w}{dx^2} + (\hat{A}_{xz} - \beta\hat{D}_{xz})\frac{d\,\psi_I^w}{dx}\frac{d\,\psi_J^w}{dx}\right] dx,$$

$$K_{Il}^{23} = \int_{h^e} \left[-\kappa \hat{F}_{xx} \frac{d^2\,\psi_I^w}{dx^2}\frac{d\,\psi_l^\phi}{dx} + (\hat{A}_{xz} - \beta\hat{D}_{xz})\frac{d\,\psi_I^w}{dx}\psi_l^\phi\right] dx, \quad K_{kj}^{31} = K_{li}^{13},$$

$$K_{kJ}^{32} = K_{lI}^{23}, \quad K_{kl}^{33} = \int_{h^e} \left[(\hat{D}_{xx} - \kappa\hat{F}_{xx})\frac{d\,\psi_k^\phi}{dx}\frac{d\,\psi_l^\phi}{dx} + (\hat{A}_{xz} - \beta\hat{D}_{xz})\psi_k^\phi\psi_l^\phi\right] dx,$$

and the resultants are defined as follows:

$$A_{xx} = \int_A E(z)dA, \quad B_{xx} = \int_A zE(z)dA, \quad D_{xx} = \int_A z^2E(z)dA,$$

$$E_{xx} = \int_A z^3E(z)dA, \quad F_{xx} = \int_A z^4E(z)dA, \quad H_{xx} = \int_A z^6E(z)dA,$$

$$\hat{B}_{xx} = B_{xx} - \kappa E_{xx}, \quad \hat{D}_{xx} = D_{xx} - \kappa F_{xx}, \quad \hat{F}_{xx} = F_{xx} - \kappa H_{xx},$$

$$A_{xz} = \int_A G(z)dA, \quad D_{xz} = \int_A z^2G(z)dA, \quad F_{xz} = \int_A z^4G(z)dA,$$

$$\hat{A}_{xz} = A_{xz} - \beta D_{xz}, \quad \hat{D}_{xz} = D_{xz} - \beta F_{xz},$$

where

$$\beta = 3\kappa.$$

Additionally, from the internal virtual work, the thermal force vector is defined as

$$\mathbf{F_T^e} = \begin{bmatrix} {}^T\mathbf{F}^1 & {}^T\mathbf{F}^2 & {}^T\mathbf{F}^3 \end{bmatrix}^{\mathrm{T}}, \tag{20}$$

where

$${}^TF_i^1 = \int_{h^e} L^T \frac{d\psi_i^u}{dx}dx, \quad {}^TF_I^2 = \int_{h^e} -N^T\frac{d^2\psi_I^w}{dx^2}dx, \quad {}^TF_k^3 = \int_{h^e} \left(M^T - N^T\right)\frac{d\psi_k^\phi}{dx}dx,$$

with

$$\left\{L^T, M^T, N^T\right\} = \int_A \left\{1, z, \kappa z^3\right\}\alpha(z)E(z)\left[T(z) - T_{ref}\right]dA.$$

Now, from the external virtual work, the force vector is given by

$$\mathbf{F_M^e} = \begin{bmatrix} 0 & {}^M\mathbf{F}^2 & 0 \end{bmatrix}^{\mathrm{T}}. \tag{21}$$

where

$${}^MF_I^2 = \int_{h^e} q_0\psi_I^w dx.$$

Finally, the thermo-mechanical finite element model has the following form:

$$\mathbf{K^e}\boldsymbol{\Delta} = \mathbf{F_M^e} + \mathbf{F_T^e}. \tag{22}$$

4. Numerical Results

This section is divided into four parts: a dependence study of η, the validation of the present model to perform static analysis, the validation of the thermal-structural analysis for isotropic beams, and a thermal-structural analysis of FG beams. Due to the lack of models using similar temperature distributions and the rule of mixtures in conjunction with the power law, the behavior of the present model is tested separately.

The results of the second part validate the behavior of the FGM model and allow us to perform a static analysis. The results of the third part validate the behavior of the thermo-mechanical model implemented for isotropic beams, and lastly, we perform a comparison with the numerical results obtained using a commercial software to verify the thermo-mechanical behavior of FG beams.

Unless otherwise specified, the mechanical properties of the constituents of the FG beams we used are presented in Table 1. The top constituent was ceramic.

Table 1. Mechanical properties of the FGM constituents.

Material	E (GPa)	ν	K (W/m°C)	α (1/°C)
Aluminum (Al)	70	0.3	204	23×10^{-6}
Alumina (Al_2O_3)	380	0.3	10.4	7.4×10^{-6}

In addition, the geometrical parameters of width and thickness are fixed values, where $b = 1$ m and $t = 1$ m. Thus, it is only needed to vary the length, L, to obtain different length-to-thickness ratios.

4.1. Dependence Study of Parameter η

Recalling that the temperature distribution (see Equation (4)) involves approximations depending on the numbers of terms used in the series (i.e., parameter η) and to achieve the accuracy and independence of η, it is proper to study the influence of this parameter on the results. Table 2 presents the displacements of a clamped-free FG beam under thermal load for several values of the parameter η. When $\eta > 100$, it is noted that the values of both displacements converge. Despite the slight difference in the results, in this work, 100 terms are used to evaluate the temperature distribution.

Table 2. Maximum displacements for a clamped-free FG beam subjected to only thermal load ($L/t = 5$, $T_{top} = 400$ °C, $T_{bot} = T_{ref} = 300$ °C).

	n = 0.5		n = 1		n = 5	
η	$u^0 \times 10^{-3}$	$w^0 \times 10^{-3}$	$u^0 \times 10^{-3}$	$w^0 \times 10^{-3}$	$u^0 \times 10^{-3}$	$w^0 \times 10^{-3}$
10	1.7247	−9.2646	1.9362	−8.9328	3.3252	−10.4942
25	1.4931	−8.7550	1.7070	−8.3815	3.1461	−10.0095
50	1.4283	−8.5021	1.6477	−8.1640	3.0990	−9.8696
100	1.4162	−8.4439	1.6369	−8.1186	3.0906	−9.8436
200	1.4156	−8.4410	1.6365	−8.1165	3.0902	−9.8425
400	1.4156	−8.4410	1.6365	−8.1165	3.0902	−9.8425

4.2. Static Analysis

A static analysis of various FG beams subjected to a distributed load was performed to verify the implementation of the FGM model in the present finite element model. The boundary conditions of the FG beam analyzed were clamped-free (C-F) and simply supported (S-R). Table 3 presents the mechanical properties of the two FGM constituents considered. In addition, it must be noted that the metal or ceramic may be the top or bottom constituent according to the boundary condition to be studied. The latter consideration is made to be consistent with the properties of FGM used in studies reported in the available literature.

Table 3. Mechanical properties of the FGM constituents for static analyses.

Material	E (GPa)	ν	C-F	S-R
Aluminum (Al)	70	0.3	Bottom	Top
Zirconia (ZnO_2)	200	0.3	Top	Bottom

To compare the results with those available in the literature, the following dimensionless parameter for the transverse deflection was used [14]:

$$\overline{w} = w \frac{E_{Al}}{q_0 L^4} \frac{bt^3}{12} \times 10^3. \quad (23)$$

Note that the values of the dimensionless parameter are only valid for the ceramic constituent considered in this static analysis.

In Tables 4–7, the numerical results of the present finite element model are compared with other formulations. The label Present denotes the results of the present model, the label Plane indicates the results obtained by means of a model made in the commercial software ANSYS using a mesh of PLANE182 elements, and references are used to label the literature results.

Tables 4 and 5 present the dimensionless transverse deflections for a C-F FG beam. The behavior is similar for both length-to-thickness ratios; that is, the nearest values to those of the present model are those reported in the work of Vo et al. [19], and those obtained with the plane model are within a relative error of 0.2% with respect to the present formulation. The similarity of the numerical results to the ones of Vo et al. [19] is expected since the latter were also obtained using a higher-order shear deformation theory.

Table 4. Maximum dimensionless transverse deflection of a C-F FG beam subjected to a uniform load distribution ($L/t = 4$).

Work	n = 0	n = 0.2	n = 1	n = 5	n = 10
Present	46.51490	54.00955	74.33885	94.71622	102.49537
Plane	46.57096	53.96973	74.24512	94.62760	102.51855
Vo et al. [19]	46.51500	54.01125	74.33875	94.71625	102.49625

Table 5. Maximum dimensionless transverse deflection of a C-F FG beam subjected to a uniform load distribution ($L/t = 16$).

Work	n = 0	n = 0.2	n = 1	n = 5	n = 10
Present	43.92621	51.13280	70.50375	88.53483	95.67928
Plane	43.86304	51.15649	70.39235	88.44528	95.62302
Vo et al. [19]	43.92625	51.13375	70.50250	88.53375	95.67875

Now, the dimensionless transverse deflections for S-R FG beams are shown in Tables 6 and 7. It can be noted that the results obtained by means of a higher-order shear deformation theory are very close to those of the present model, i.e., the results of Şimşek [29] and Vo et al. [19]. The numerical results reported by Şimşek [29] were obtained using a model based on the TSDT and the Ritz methods. In comparison with the plane model, the results are within a relative error of 0.83%, which is an acceptable value considering that the formulation of the plane element considers a two-dimensional model.

Table 6. Maximum dimensionless transverse deflection of an S-R FG beam subjected to a uniform load distribution ($L/t = 4$).

Work	n = 0	n = 0.5	n = 1	n = 5	n = 10
Present	15.04884	9.53850	8.36849	6.50747	6.00623
Plane	15.05273	9.54069	8.29951	6.49140	6.02041
Şimşek [29]	15.04922	9.53958	8.36862	6.50755	-
Vo et al. [19]	15.04948	9.53828	8.36823	6.50742	-

Table 7. Maximum dimensionless transverse deflection of an S-R FG beam subjected to a uniform load distribution ($L/t = 16$).

Work	n = 0	n = 0.5	n = 1	n = 5	n = 10
Present	13.14767	8.34089	7.38270	5.78671	5.31468
Plane	13.05415	8.28457	7.32718	5.74005	5.27186
Şimşek [29]	13.14779	8.34180	7.38268	5.78672	-
Vo et al. [19]	13.14714	8.34063	7.38255	5.78672	-

In general, the above comparisons show good agreement with the results reported in the literature, and thus, they validate the behavior of the FGM implemented in the present finite element model and the plane model.

4.3. Thermal–Structural Analysis of Isotropic Beams

In this section, isotropic beams subjected to thermal loads and different boundary conditions are analyzed as a first step to validate the thermal behavior of the present finite element model, as well as the plane model. Therefore, exact solutions of the transverse deflection for isotropic beams are used for comparison; the results of the exact solution are denoted with the label Exact. The exact solutions are reported in [30], and according to the boundary conditions, are as follows:

- For a C-F isotropic beam:

$$w(x) = -\frac{\alpha\left(T_{top} - T_{bot}\right)}{2t}x^2. \tag{24}$$

- For an S-R isotropic beam:

$$w(x) = -\frac{\alpha\left(T_{top} - T_{bot}\right)}{2t}\left(xL - x^2\right). \tag{25}$$

In this case, an isotropic beam made of aluminum is considered. The temperatures are assumed to be $T_{bot} = T_{ref} = 300$ °C and $T_{top} = 400$ °C. Tables 8 and 9 present the maximum transverse deflections of C-F and S-R isotropic beams, respectively, subjected to a thermal load for various length-to-thickness ratios. From these comparisons, it can be noted that the results of the present model are equal to those obtained with the exact solutions for both cases of boundary conditions. However, the PLANE model shows better behavior for long beams subjected to C-F conditions, having a maximum relative error value of 1.95% with respect to the exact solution for a ratio of $L/t = 3$. The PLANE model shows better behavior for short beams $(L/t = 3)$ in the case of the S-R condition, where the maximum relative error occurs for a ratio $L/t = 20$ and has a value of 1.50%.

In general, the thermo-mechanical responses for isotropic beams of the present model and the plane model are acceptable.

Table 8. Maximum transverse deflection for C-F isotropic beams subjected to a thermal load for various L/t ratios.

Model		**L/t**	
	3	**5**	**20**
Present	−0.010350	−0.028750	−0.46000
Plane	−0.010552	−0.029037	−0.46027
Exact	−0.010350	−0.028750	−0.46000

Table 9. Maximum transverse deflection for S-R isotropic beams subjected to a thermal load for various L/t ratios.

Model		**L/t**	
	3	**5**	**20**
Present	0.0025875	0.0071875	0.115
Plane	0.0025765	0.0071092	0.11327
Exact	0.0025875	0.0071875	0.115

4.4. Thermal–Structural Analysis of FG Beams

After verifying the performance for the static analysis of FG beams and the thermal–structural analysis of isotropic beams for the present model, the thermo-mechanical response of FG beams was examined. For this purpose, the temperatures of the top and bottom surfaces were: $T_{top} = 400$ °C, $T_{bot} = 300$ °C. Moreover, a uniform distributed load $q_0 = 100$ N/m was applied to the FG beam.

The maximum axial displacements and transverse deflections for C-F FG beams with different values of the power law exponent are shown in Table 10. The axial displacement increases as the power law exponent increases; this is a common behavior seen in the mechanical response of FG beams. Conversely, the ceramic volume distribution decreased; however, note that for a value of $n = 1$, the transverse deflection is smaller than the one obtained when $n = 0.5$ due to the presence of the thermal load.

Table 10. Maximum displacements of a C-F FG beam subjected to thermal load and distributed load $q_0 = 100$ N/m ($T_{top} = 400$ °C, $T_{bot} = 300$ °C, and $T_{ref} = 300$ °C).

	Model	n = 0.5 $u^0 \times 10^{-3}$	$w^0 \times 10^{-3}$	n = 1 $u^0 \times 10^{-3}$	$w^0 \times 10^{-3}$	n = 5 $u^0 \times 10^{-3}$	$w^0 \times 10^{-3}$	n = 10 $u^0 \times 10^{-3}$	$w^0 \times 10^{-3}$
$L/t = 3$	Present	0.8497	−3.0410	0.9822	−2.9236	1.8544	−3.5354	2.2992	−4.7209
	Plane	0.8514	−3.0958	0.9955	−2.9825	1.9406	−3.6603	2.4064	−4.9210
$L/t = 5$	Present	1.4162	−8.4435	1.6370	−8.1181	3.0906	−9.8428	3.8312	−13.1500
	Plane	1.4182	−8.5175	1.6506	−8.1941	3.1780	−10.0020	3.9411	−13.4360
$L/t = 10$	Present	2.8325	−33.7633	3.2740	−32.4618	6.1814	−39.4007	7.6611	−52.6523
	Plane	2.8356	−33.8830	3.2889	−32.5950	6.2720	−39.7390	7.7786	−53.3280
$L/t = 20$	Present	5.6653	−134.9740	6.5487	−129.7477	12.3642	−157.4974	15.3221	−210.5132
	Plane	5.6725	−134.9600	6.5690	−129.8300	12.4650	−158.3800	15.4580	−212.4600

From the comparisons presented in Table 10, the maximum relative errors are

- $L/t = 3$: 1.98% for $n = 0.5$ and 1, and 4.45% for $n = 5$ and 10, respectively.
- $L/t = 5$: 0.93% for $n = 0.5$ and 1, and 2.79% for $n = 5$ and 10, respectively.
- $L/t = 10$: 0.45% for $n = 0.5$ and 1, and 1.51% for $n = 5$ and 10, respectively.
- $L/t = 20$: 0.31% for $n = 0.5$ and 1, and 0.88% for $n = 5$ and 10, respectively.

It can be observed that most of the above relative errors are below 2.79%, while the maximum values are obtained for a short beam $(L/t = 3)$, and $n = 5$ and 10. According to the relative errors obtained, the behavior of the present model is acceptable.

Now, Table 11 presents the maximum axial displacement and transverse deflection for an S-R FG beam with different values of the power law exponent. It is worthwhile to mention that the maximum axial displacement is obtained at $x = L$ and the maximum transverse deflection occurs at $x = L/2$. In comparison with the absolute values of displacement and deflection that the C-F FG beam undergoes for the same mechanical and thermal loads, the transverse deflections are smaller in the S-R FG beam. Moreover, it can be noted that the axial displacements are very similar since the boundary conditions in the axial direction are equal; that is, for an S-R FG beam, the axial displacement at $x = 0$ is restricted, and at $x = L$, it is not, as occurs in the C-F FG beam. However, due to the axial bending coupling generated by the FGM, it is also expected to obtain axial displacements with a small difference between both cases of boundary conditions.

For the results presented in Table 11, the maximum relative errors are

- $L/t = 3$: 2.38% for $n = 0.5$ and 1, and 5.70% for $n = 5$ and 10, respectively.
- $L/t = 5$: 1.39% for $n = 0.5$ and 1, and 3.54% for $n = 5$ and 10, respectively.
- $L/t = 10$: 0.65% for $n = 0.5$ and 1, and 1.89% for $n = 5$ and 10, respectively.
- $L/t = 20$: 0.26% for $n = 0.5$ and 1, and 1.07% for $n = 5$ and 10, respectively.

Note that the maximum relative error is obtained for short beams with higher power law indices, and it is equal to 5.70%. With respect to the second-highest relative error, the values are below 3.54%. Thus, given the above results, the present model can be considered to have an acceptable behavior.

Table 11. Maximum displacements of an S-R FG beam subjected to thermal load and distributed load $q_0 = 100$ N/m ($T_{top} = 400$ °C, $T_{bot} = 300$ °C, and $T_{ref} = 300$ °C).

	Model	n = 0.5 $u^0 \times 10^{-3}$	$w^0 \times 10^{-3}$	n = 1 $u^0 \times 10^{-3}$	$w^0 \times 10^{-3}$	n = 5 $u^0 \times 10^{-3}$	$w^0 \times 10^{-3}$	n = 10 $u^0 \times 10^{-3}$	$w^0 \times 10^{-3}$
$L/t = 3$	Present	0.8496	0.7618	0.9822	0.7320	1.8544	0.8743	2.3005	1.1647
	Plane	0.8299	0.7606	0.9806	0.7324	1.9665	0.8841	2.4383	1.1980
$L/t = 5$	Present	1.4161	2.1125	1.6369	2.0308	3.0906	2.4514	3.8324	3.2722
	Plane	1.3967	2.1124	1.6356	2.0342	3.2037	2.4735	3.9729	3.3271
$L/t = 10$	Present	2.8323	8.4445	3.2738	8.1194	6.1811	9.8449	7.6621	13.1523
	Plane	2.8139	8.4458	3.2736	8.1329	6.2972	9.9199	7.8097	13.3030
$L/t = 20$	Present	5.6646	33.7796	6.5473	32.4830	12.3613	39.4332	15.3207	52.6880
	Plane	5.6500	33.7210	6.5522	32.4700	12.4870	39.6530	15.4860	53.1430

To complement the above numerical results, Figure 2 shows the transverse deflection for various power law exponents of FG beams subjected to thermal and mechanical loads. Figure 2a,b shows the transverse deflection of C-F and S-R FG beams, respectively. For both boundary conditions, the minimum transverse deflection is obtained when $n = 1$.

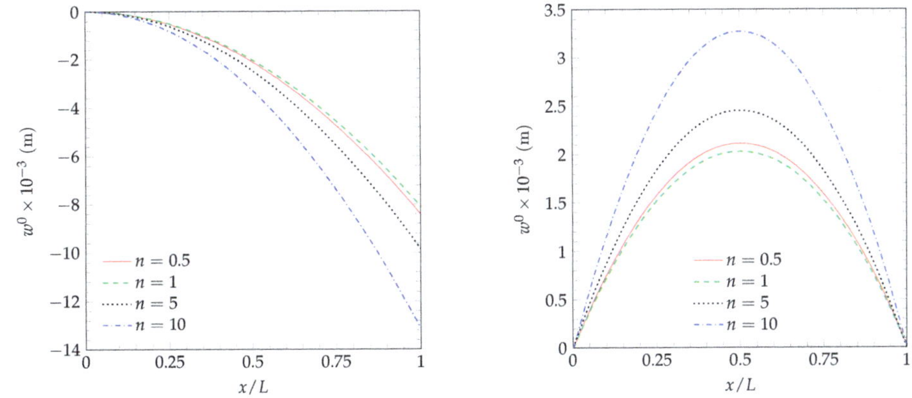

(**a**) (**b**)

Figure 2. Transverse deflection of various FG beams subjected to thermal and distributed loads where $q_0 = 100$ N/m ($T_{top} = 400$ °C, $T_{bot} = 300$ °C, and $T_{ref} = 300$ °C) under (**a**) C-F and (**b**) S-R boundary conditions.

4.5. Thermal–Structural Analysis of FG Beams, for $n = 1$

In this section, the thermo-mechanical response of the FG beam with a power law exponent $n = 1$ is studied for the C-F and an S-R boundary conditions. For this analysis, a distributed load $q_0 = -10^4$ N/m was applied to the FG beam, and the top surface temperature was considered to vary, while the other temperatures remained fixed; that is, the temperature of reference and bottom surface temperature were considered to be constant with the following values: $T_{ref} = 0$ °C and $T_{bot} = 20$ °C. The latter consideration allowed us to obtain the behavior of the FG beam as it is exposed to various temperature differences between its top and bottom surfaces, such that $\Delta T = T_{top} - T_{ref}$. Moreover, several length-to-thickness ratios were studied.

The maximum axial displacements and transverse deflections for the C-F FG beam are presented in Table 12; also, numerical results obtained using the plane model are included for comparison purposes. The influence of increasing the top surface temperature can be noted as an increment in both displacements, and the maximum displacements are obtained when $\Delta T = 400$ °C. In addition, a plot of the transverse deflection along the x axis of the FG beam is shown in Figure 3a, where greater deflections are observed as the temperature of the top surface increases.

Table 12. Maximum displacements of a C-F FG beam ($n = 1$) subjected to various ΔT and a distributed load $q_0 = -10^4$ N/m ($T_{bot} = 20$ ° C and $T_{ref} = 0$ °C).

		$\Delta T = 100$ °C		$\Delta T = 200$ °C		$\Delta T = 300$ °C		$\Delta T = 400$ °C	
L/h	Model	$u^0 \times 10^{-3}$	$w^0 \times 10^{-3}$	$u^0 \times 10^{-3}$	$w^0 \times 10^{-3}$	$u^0 \times 10^{-3}$	$w^0 \times 10^{-3}$	$u^0 \times 10^{-3}$	$w^0 \times 10^{-3}$
3	Present	1.8938	−1.5267	2.8760	−4.4503	3.8582	−7.3739	4.8403	−10.2976
	Plane	1.9195	−1.5620	2.9150	−4.5445	3.9105	−7.5270	4.9060	−10.5100
5	Present	3.1554	−4.2698	4.7924	−12.3883	6.4293	−20.5069	8.0662	−28.6255
	Plane	3.1814	−4.2973	4.8320	−12.4920	6.4826	−20.6870	8.1332	−28.8810
10	Present	6.3018	−17.6686	9.5756	−50.1384	12.8495	−82.6082	16.1234	−115.0780
	Plane	6.3288	−17.7010	9.6176	−50.3030	12.9060	−82.9060	16.1950	−115.5100
20	Present	12.5308	−80.1733	19.0785	−210.0480	25.6263	−339.9227	32.1740	−469.7974
	Plane	12.5620	−80.1610	19.1300	−210.1200	25.6980	−340.0800	32.2660	−470.0300

The comparisons of the results presented in Table 12 give the following ranges for the relative errors (ε_r):

- $L/t = 3$: $1.34 \leq \varepsilon_r \leq 2.26\%$.
- $L/t = 5$: $0.64 \leq \varepsilon_r \leq 0.88\%$.
- $L/t = 10$: $0.18 \leq \varepsilon_r \leq 0.44\%$.
- $L/t = 20$: $0.02 \leq \varepsilon_r \leq 0.29\%$.

As noted before, higher values of relative errors are obtained for the C-F FG beam of ratio $L/t = 3$. For moderately short to long beams, the values are below 0.9%. Therefore, the present model shows good behavior for the thermo-mechanical response of FG beams at different temperatures.

Now, regarding the S-R FG beam, the axial displacements and transverse deflections are presented in Table 13. In this case, the similarities with the axial displacements of C-F FG beam are only observed in short beams; notable differences are observed as the length-to-thickness ratio increases. The transverse deflection of the S-R FG beam is shown in Figure 3b, where again greater deflections are observed as the temperature of the top surface increases.

Table 13. Maximum displacements of an S-R FG beam ($n = 1$) subjected to various ΔT and a distributed load $q_0 = -10^4$ N/m ($T_{bot} = 20$ °C and $T_{ref} = 0$ °C).

		$\Delta T = 100$ °C		$\Delta T = 200$ °C		$\Delta T = 300$ °C		$\Delta T = 400$ °C	
L/h	Model	$u^0 \times 10^{-3}$	$w^0 \times 10^{-3}$	$u^0 \times 10^{-3}$	$w^0 \times 10^{-3}$	$u^0 \times 10^{-3}$	$w^0 \times 10^{-3}$	$u^0 \times 10^{-3}$	$w^0 \times 10^{-3}$
3	Present	1.8943	0.3802	2.8765	1.1122	3.8587	1.8443	4.8408	2.5763
	Plane	1.8927	0.3807	2.8732	1.1131	3.8538	1.8455	4.8343	2.5779
5	Present	3.1577	1.0502	4.7946	3.0809	6.4316	5.1117	8.0685	7.1425
	Plane	3.1563	1.0540	4.7919	3.0882	6.4276	5.1224	8.0632	7.1565
10	Present	6.3199	4.1343	9.5938	12.2529	12.8677	20.3715	16.1416	28.4900
	Plane	6.3194	4.1525	9.5931	12.2840	12.8670	20.4170	16.1400	28.5490
20	Present	12.6762	15.5429	19.2240	48.0127	25.7718	80.4825	32.3195	112.9523
	Plane	12.6790	15.5870	19.2310	48.0440	25.7840	80.5010	32.3370	112.9600

The ranges of relative errors for the results presented in Table 13 are

- $L/t = 3$: $0.06 \leq \varepsilon_r \leq 0.13\%$.
- $L/t = 5$: $0.04 \leq \varepsilon_r \leq 0.36\%$.
- $L/t = 10$: $0.01 \leq \varepsilon_r \leq 0.44\%$.
- $L/t = 20$: $0.01 \leq \varepsilon_r \leq 0.28\%$.

From Tables 12 anf 13, it can be observed that the displacements have similar behavior as presented in the static analyses of FG beams; that is, for a larger length-to-thickness ratio, higher displacements and deflections are presented. Furthermore, higher displacements and deflections are obtained as the temperature of the top surface increases, which is expected since the thermal effects also depend on ΔT.

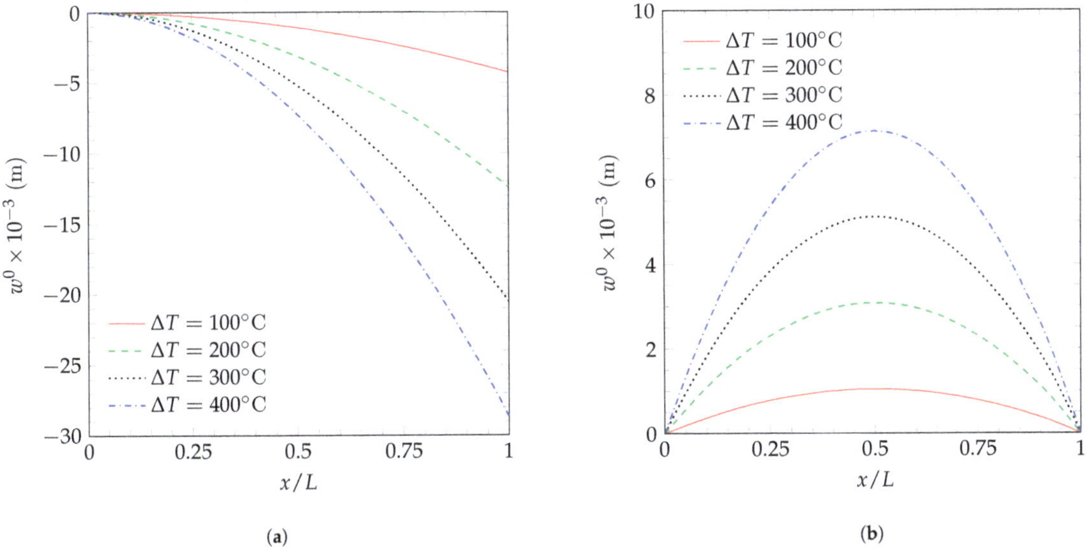

Figure 3. Transverse deflection of FG beams ($n = 1$) subjected to various ΔT and a distributed load $q_0 = -10^4$ N/m ($T_{bot} = 20$ °C and $T_{ref} = 0$ °C) under (**a**) C-F and (**b**) S-R boundary conditions.

In addition to the displacements presented in Table 12, the normal stresses through the thickness of a C-F FG beam with $n = 1$ at the clamped end are shown in Figure 4 for the ratios $L/t = 5$ and $L/t = 20$. Additionally, the normal stress obtained by means of the plane model is plotted to compare with the present model's results; from this comparison, a similar behavior of both models is observed. The normal stress is highly influenced by the length-to-thickness ratio since significant variations are observed in the FG beam with $L/t = 20$. It should be recalled that, in accordance with the temperature distribution and the temperatures considered, higher contributions due to thermal effects are observed at the top surface, where the difference $T(z) - T_{ref}$ reaches its maximum value.

In addition to the results presented in Table 13 for an S-R FG beam with $n = 1$, the variation of the normal stress through the thickness at the mid-span is shown in Figure 5 for the ratios $L/t = 5$ and $L/t = 20$. In the case of S-R conditions, contrary to the C-F condition, a significant influence of the length-to-thickness ratio is not observed on the normal stress.

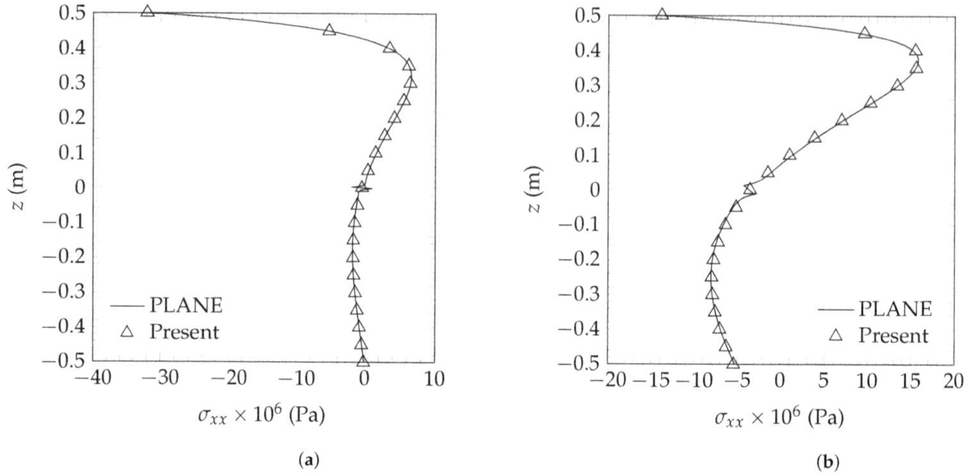

Figure 4. Variation of the normal stress σ_{xx} of a C-F FG beam subjected to a mechanical and thermal load for $n = 1$ and (**a**) $L/h = 5$; (**b**) $L/h = 20$ ($q_0 = -10^4$ N/m, $T_{bot} = 20$ ° C, and $T_{ref} = 0$ °C).

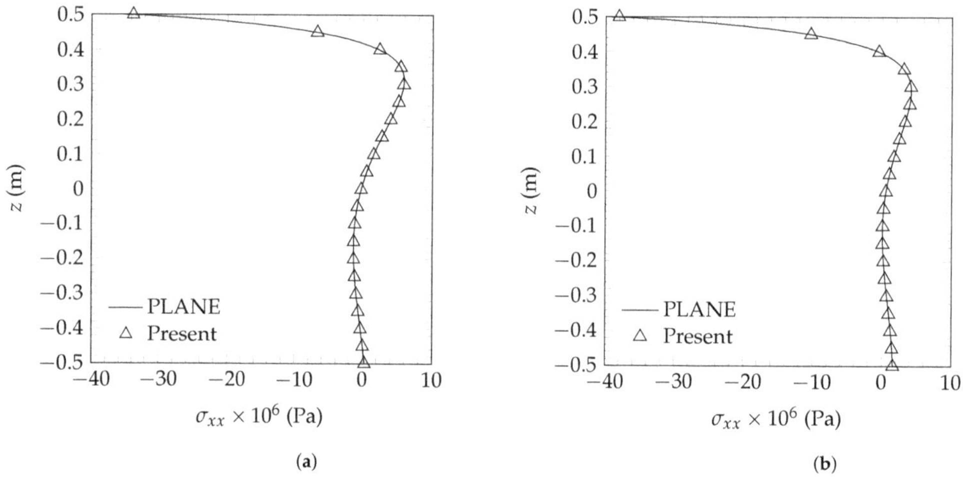

Figure 5. Variation of the normal stress σ_{xx} of an S-R FG beam subjected to a mechanical and thermal load for $n = 1$ and (**a**) $L/h = 5$; (**b**) $L/h = 20$ ($q_0 = -10^4$ N/m, $T_{bot} = 20$ ° C, and $T_{ref} = 0$ °C).

For completeness, the behavior of the normal stress when $\Delta T = 100$ °C for different values of the power law exponent n and a length to thickness ratio $L/t = 5$ is presented in Figure 6. It can be observed that, the behavior is similar for the C-F and S-R boundary conditions, with the maximum tensile stress being achieved for higher values of n (for the results presented here, it occurs when $n = 10$).

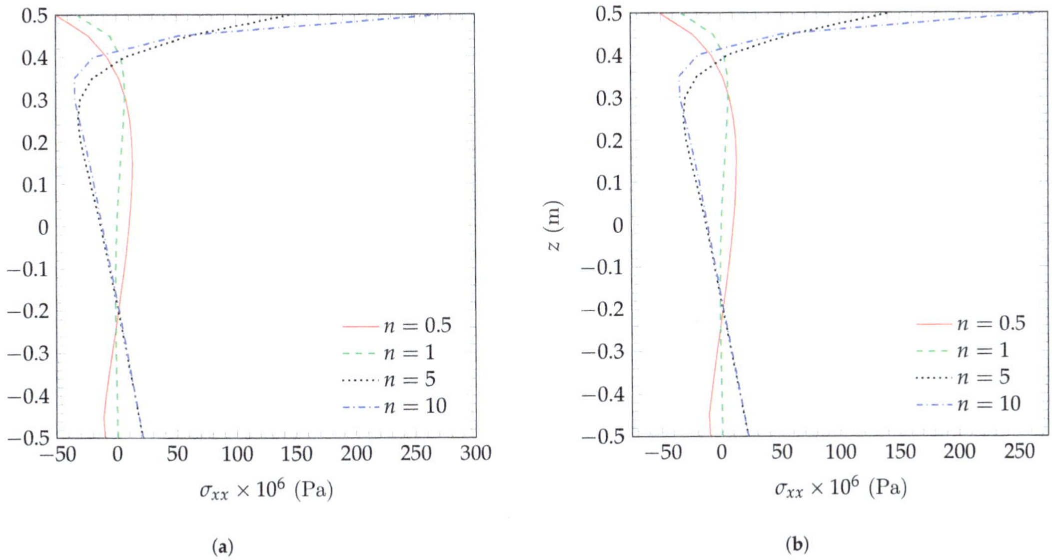

Figure 6. Normal stress (σ_{xx}) of various FG beams subjected to thermal and distributed loads where $q_0 = -10^4$ N/m ($T_{top} = 120$ °C, $T_{bot} = 20$ °C, and $T_{ref} = 0$ °C) under (**a**) C-F and (**b**) S-R boundary conditions.

5. Conclusions

In this paper, a finite element model based on TSDT to obtain the thermo-mechanical responses of FG beams subjected to distributed loads and thermal loads was presented. Moreover, the verification of the model's behavior was made in the following order: the mechanical response of FG beams, the thermo-mechanical response of isotropic beams, and, finally, the thermo-mechanical response of FG beams. The latter verification is made by a comparison with the results obtained using plane elements. Slight variations are expected in the comparisons since the formulation of the present model is distinct from the formulations used in the literature and simulations. In general, the following conclusions can be drawn:

- The present finite element model incorporated the rule of mixtures to evaluate the effective mechanical and thermal properties of the FG constituents, where the volume distribution of the ceramic was considered by means of the power law.
- The behavior of the present finite element model was checked by a comparison with the literature and simulations in a finite element commercial code, with the findings showing that the aforementioned results are close to the present ones and behave in a similar manner. Maximum axial displacements and transverse deflections are now available for a comparison with studies that have dealt with the thermal–structural problem presented here.
- In the thermal–structural analysis of FG beams subject to the boundary conditions considered in this article, the higher relative errors were obtained when short beams (e.g., $L/h = 3$) were modeled.
- In addition, we found that normal stresses predicted by the present finite element model were in good agreement with those obtained using plane elements.

Author Contributions: Conceptualization, C.E.V.M. and M.E.G.R.; software, C.E.V.M. and M.E.G.R.; validation, C.E.V.M. and L.D.C.G.; formal analysis, C.E.V.M. and M.E.G.R.; investigation, C.E.V.M. and L.D.C.G.; writing—original draft preparation, C.E.V.M., M.E.G.R. and L.D.C.G.; writing—review and editing, C.E.V.M. and M.E.G.R.; visualization, C.E.V.M. and M.E.G.R. All authors have read and agreed to the published version of the manuscript.

Funding: This research received no external funding.

Data Availability Statement: The data presented in this study are available on request from the corresponding author. The data are not publicly available.

Conflicts of Interest: The authors declare no conflict of interest.

Abbreviations

The following abbreviations are used in this manuscript:

FGM	Functionally graded material
CBT	Classical beam theory
FSDT	First-order shear deformation theory
TSDT	Third-order shear deformation theory
HSDT	Higher-order shear deformation theory
FGB	Functionally graded beams
FG	Functionally graded
L	Beam length
b	Beam width
t	Beam thickness
T_{top}, T_{bot}	Top and bottom surface temperatures
q_0	Uniform distributed load
x, y, z	Rectangular coordinate variables
P	Material property
P_{top}	Top constituent property
P_{bot}	Bottom constituent property
V_{top}	Volume distribution of the top constituent
n	Power law exponent
$K(z)$	Thermal conductivity
K_{top}, K_{bot}	Thermal conductivity of top and bottom constituents
i	Index of the sum
η	Number of terms used in the series for the approximation
u^0, w^0, ϕ^0	Axial displacement, transverse displacement, and rotation of a point located at the centroidal axis x
$(\cdot)^M$	Quantity related to mechanical effects
$(\cdot)^T$	Quantity related to thermal effects
$\varepsilon_{11}, \gamma_{13}$	Axial and transverse strains
$\alpha(z)$	Thermal expansion coefficient
T_{ref}	Temperature of reference
σ_{11}, γ_{13}	Normal and shear stresses
$E(z), G(z)$	Young's and shear moduli
$\nu(z)$	Poisson's ratio
$\delta W_I, \delta W_E$	Internal and external virtual works
$\mathbf{f}$	Vector of external forces
h_e	One-dimensional domain
ψ	Interpolation functions
$\mathbf{K^e}$	Element's stiffness matrix
$\mathbf{K}^{ij}$	Submatrices of element's stiffness matrix
$\mathbf{F_T^e}$	Element's thermal force vector
$\mathbf{F_M^e}$	Element's force vector
Al	Aluminum

Al_2O_3	Alumina
C-F	Clamped-free boundary conditions
ΔT	Temperature difference between top surface temperature and reference temperature
S-R	Simply supported boundary conditions
ZnO_2	Zirconia
Present	Numerical results of the present model
Plane	Numerical results of the plane model
Exact	Exact solution results
ε_r	Relative error

References

1. Chakraborty, A.; Gopalakrishnan, S.; Reddy, J. A new beam finite element for the analysis of functionally graded materials. *Int. J. Mech. Sci.* **2003**, *45*, 519–539. [CrossRef]
2. Elishakoff, I.E.; Pentaras, D.; Gentilini, C. *Mechanics of Functionally Graded Material Structures*; World Scientific: Singapore, 2015.
3. Ebrahimi, F.; Jafari, A. A four-variable refined shear-deformation beam theory for thermo-mechanical vibration analysis of temperature-dependent FGM beams with porosities. *Mech. Adv. Mater. Struct.* **2018**, *25*, 212–224. [CrossRef]
4. Xia, Y.M.; Li, S.R.; Wan, Z.Q. Bending solutions of FGM Reddy–Bickford beams in terms of those of the homogenous Euler–Bernoulli beams. *Acta Mech. Solida Sin.* **2019**, *32*, 499–516. [CrossRef]
5. Mahamood, R.; Jen, T.; Akinlabi, S.; Hassan, S.; Shatalov, M.; Murashkin, E.; Akinlabi, E.T. Functionally Graded Materials: An Introduction. In *Functionally Graded Materials (FGMs)*; CRC Press: Boca Raton, FL, USA, 2021; pp. 1–12.
6. Giunta, G.; Crisafulli, D.; Belouettar, S.; Carrera, E. A thermo-mechanical analysis of functionally graded beams via hierarchical modelling. *Compos. Struct.* **2013**, *95*, 676–690. [CrossRef]
7. De Pietro, G.; Hui, Y.; Giunta, G.; Belouettar, S.; Carrera, E.; Hu, H. Hierarchical one-dimensional finite elements for the thermal stress analysis of three-dimensional functionally graded beams. *Compos. Struct.* **2016**, *153*, 514–528. [CrossRef]
8. Malik, P.; Kadoli, R. Thermo-elastic response of SUS316-Al_2O_3 functionally graded beams under various heat loads. *Int. J. Mech. Sci.* **2017**, *128–129*, 206–223. [CrossRef]
9. El-Megharbel, A. A theoretical analysis of functionally graded beam under thermal loading. *World J. Eng. Technol.* **2016**, *4*, 437–449. [CrossRef]
10. Li, X.F. A unified approach for analyzing static and dynamic behaviors of functionally graded Timoshenko and Euler–Bernoulli beams. *J. Sound Vib.* **2008**, *318*, 1210–1229. [CrossRef]
11. Alshorbagy, A.E.; Eltaher, M.; Mahmoud, F. Free vibration characteristics of a functionally graded beam by finite element method. *Appl. Math. Model.* **2011**, *35*, 412–425. [CrossRef]
12. Moheimani, R.; Ahmadian, M.T. On free vibration of functionally graded Euler-Bernoulli beam models based on the non-local theory. In *Vibration, Acoustics and Wave Propagation, Proceedings of the ASME International Mechanical Engineering Congress and Exposition, Houston, TX, USA, 9–15 November 2012*; ASME: New York, NY, USA, 2012; Volume 12, pp. 169–173.
13. Nguyen, T.K.; Vo, T.P.; Thai, H.T. Static and free vibration of axially loaded functionally graded beams based on the first-order shear deformation theory. *Compos. Part B Eng.* **2013**, *55*, 147–157. [CrossRef]
14. Katili, I.; Syahril, T.; Katili, A.M. Static and free vibration analysis of FGM beam based on unified and integrated of Timoshenko's theory. *Compos. Struct.* **2020**, *242*, 112130.
15. Kadoli, R.; Akhtar, K.; Ganesan, N. Static analysis of functionally graded beams using higher order shear deformation theory. *Appl. Math. Model.* **2008**, *32*, 2509–2525. [CrossRef]
16. Aydogdu, M.; Taskin, V. Free vibration analysis of functionally graded beams with simply supported edges. *Mater. Des.* **2007**, *28*, 1651–1656. [CrossRef]
17. Mahi, A.; Adda Bedia, E.; Tounsi, A.; Mechab, I. An analytical method for temperature-dependent free vibration analysis of functionally graded beams with general boundary conditions. *Compos. Struct.* **2010**, *92*, 1877–1887. [CrossRef]
18. Thai, H.T.; Vo, T.P. Bending and free vibration of functionally graded beams using various higher-order shear deformation beam theories. *Int. J. Mech. Sci.* **2012**, *62*, 57–66. [CrossRef]
19. Vo, T.P.; Thai, H.T.; Nguyen, T.K.; Inam, F. Static and vibration analysis of functionally graded beams using refined shear deformation theory. *Meccanica* **2014**, *49*, 155–168.
20. Şimşek, M.; Reddy, J.N. Bending and vibration of functionally graded microbeams using a new higher order beam theory and the modified couple stress theory. *Int. J. Eng. Sci.* **2013**, *64*, 37–53.
21. Gao, X.L.; Zhang, G.Y. A microstructure- and surface energy-dependent third-order shear deformation beam model. *Z. Angew. Math. Phys.* **2015**, *66*, 1871–1894.
22. Chakraborty, A.; Gopalakrishnan, S. A spectrally formulated finite element for wave propagation analysis in functionally graded beams. *Int. J. Solids Struct.* **2003**, *40*, 2421–2448. [CrossRef]
23. Daneshmehr, A.R.; Mohammad Abadi, M.; Rajabpoor, A. Thermal effect on static bending, vibration and buckling of Reddy beam based on modified couple stress theory. *Appl. Mech. Mater.* **2013**, *332*, 331–338. [CrossRef]
24. Lim, T.K.; Kim, J.H. Thermo-elastic effects on shear correction factors for functionally graded beam. *Compos. Part B Eng.* **2017**, *123*, 262–270. [CrossRef]

25. Praveen, G.N.; Reddy, J.N. Nonlinear transient thermoelastic analysis of functionally graded ceramic-metal plates. *Int. J. Solids Struct.* **1998**, *35*, 4457–4476. [CrossRef]
26. Javaheri, R.; Eslami, M.R. Thermal buckling of functionally graded plates. *AIAA J.* **2002**, *40*, 162–169. [CrossRef]
27. Reddy, J.N. On locking-free shear deformable beam finite elements. *Comput. Methods Appl. Mech. Eng.* **1997**, *149*, 113–132. [CrossRef]
28. Reddy, J.N. *Energy Principles and Variational Methods in Applied Mechanics*; John Wiley & Sons: Hoboken, NJ, USA, 2002.
29. Şimşek, M. Static analysis of a functionally graded beam under a uniformly distributed load by Ritz method. *Int. J. Eng. Appl. Sci.* **2009**, *1*, 1–11.
30. Hetnarski, R.B.; Eslami, M.R. Solid Mechanics and Its Applications. In *Thermal Stresses—Advanced Theory and Applications*; Springer: Dordrecht, The Netherlands, 2009; Volume 158.

Mathematical and Computational Applications

MDPI

Article

Thermal Stress Formation in a Functionally Graded Al_2O_3-Adhesive Single Lap Joint Subjected to a Uniform Temperature Field

Mustafa Kemal Apalak [1,*] and Junuthula N. Reddy [2]

[1] Department of Mechanical Engineering, Erciyes University, 38280 Kayseri, Türkiye
[2] Department of Mechanical Engineering, Texas A&M University, College Station, TX 77843-3123, USA; jnreddy@tamu.edu
* Correspondence: apalakmk@erciyes.edu.tr

Abstract: This study investigates the strain and stress states in an aluminum single lap joint bonded with a functionally graded Al_2O_3 micro particle reinforced adhesive layer subjected to a uniform temperature field. Navier equations of elasticity theory were designated by considering the spatial derivatives of Lamé constants and the coefficient of thermal expansion for local material composition. The set of partial differential equations and mechanical boundary conditions for a two-dimensional model was reduced to a set of linear equations by means of the central finite difference approximation at each grid point of a discretized joint. The through-thickness Al_2O_3-adhesive composition was tailored by the functional grading concept, and the mechanical and thermal properties of local adhesive composition were predicted by Mori–Tanaka's homogenization approach. The adherend–adhesive interfaces exhibited sharp discontinuous thermal stresses, whereas the discontinuous nature of thermal strains along bi-material interfaces can be moderated by the gradient power index, which controls the through-thickness variation of particle amount in the local adhesive composition. The free edges of the adhesive layer were also critical due to the occurrence of high normal and shear strains and stresses. The gradient power index can influence the distribution and levels of strain and stress components only for a sufficiently high volume fraction of particles. The grading direction of particles in the adhesive layer was not influential because the temperature field is uniform; namely, it can only upturn the low and high strain and stress regions so that the neat adhesive–adherend interface and the particle-rich adhesive–adherend interface can be relocated.

Keywords: functionally graded material; Al_2O_3; adhesive; thermal stress; elasticity theory; finite difference method; micro particles

1. Introduction

The adhesive bonding technique has been used successfully to join similar and different materials. In general, adhesive joints are designed so that they can withstand static and dynamic loadings [1,2]. However, today's adhesives can serve at cryogenic, low, and high temperatures. The thermal loads result in non-uniform thermal stress distributions, which appear in a discontinuous manner in vicinities of adhesive–adherend interfaces due to incompatible thermal strains as a result of different mechanical and thermal properties of the materials on both sides of bi-material interfaces [3]. A uniform or non-uniform temperature distribution, a non-uniform material property distribution, chemical and physical changes induced in the adhesive material during the adhesive curing process, the expansion of adhesive with changes in moisture and temperature levels also result in thermal stresses in adhesive joints [4,5].

In various types of mechanical loadings, the adhesive joints undergo stress concentrations, called edge effects, around the free edges of adhesive–adherend interfaces while the normal and shear stresses remain uniform at low levels in a large overlap region and increase uniformly towards the free edges of the adhesive layer and then become peak near these free edges. A large overlap region can also experience high stresses except for the adhesive-free edges depending on the type of thermal loading. In order to reduce the stress concentrations and to improve the joint strength, some joint geometry-specific measures were considered by adjusting the stiffness of adherends around these critical regions. However, the proposed geometrical measures to relieve these peak stresses can cause losses in the overall stiffness and strength of adhesive joint [1,2,6].

A layered composite structure, which can be joined easily by adhesive bonding technique, can exhibit better thermal and mechanical properties to single-composite material. Nevertheless, a thermal load can result in critical stress concentrations occurring along bi-material interfaces due to the sharp discontinuities in the material properties [7,8]. The concept of functionally graded materials (FGMs) is already utilized by biological interfaces in nature in order to reduce stress concentrations along bi-material interfaces. FGMs aim to achieve an equivalent performance to that of single-phase materials by unifying the better properties of the constituent phases with one- or more-dimensional continuously varying material composition; consequently, this can remove sharp discontinuity along the bi-material interface and relieve sudden jumps in the thermal stresses along bi-material interfaces [9–11].

Although the concept of FGMs is new, a large number of research studies have been carried out, and this field continues to expand fast [12,13]. Today, this concept can also be implemented to reduce stress concentrations appearing along the adherend–adhesive interfaces of the adhesive joints serving under static, dynamic, and thermal loads, i.e., use of functionally graded adherends and adhesives [14]. The stress distribution and peak stress levels can be controlled by tailoring one- or two-dimensional composition variation of adherends as well as an adhesive with one or more other constituents [14–16]. This method is especially helpful for relieving thermal stresses due to thermal loads.

Mathematical models and solutions on the thermal residual stress analysis of adhesive joints with functionally graded adherends have been continuously improved, and the functionally graded adherends were reported to relieve both stress and strain distributions and levels in the adhesive layer as well as in the adherends even though the adhesive layer was still in a functionally ungraded state [17].

An adhesive layer with variable modulus, which requires at least the use of two adhesives with different mechanical and thermal properties, has been proposed to relieve high-stress concentrations at the free edges of the adhesive layer and to have more uniform stress distributions along the overlap region [18–23]. This can be considered as a stepped functionally graded adhesive layer; namely, a stiff adhesive in the middle portion of the overlap region and a flexible adhesive around the free edges of the overlap region are applied. The concept of using multi-modulus adhesives can improve the overall joint strength and can also be implemented to the thermal stress problems of the adhesive joints to operate at low and high temperatures [24]. Namely, a high-temperature adhesive in the middle of the overlap region keeps the strength by transferring the entire load, whereas a low-temperature adhesive withstands loads at low temperatures by causing the high-temperature adhesive to undergo moderate stress levels [18,25,26].

The dual or mixed adhesive technique also brings some drawbacks. The stiff adhesive may tend to displace the ductile adhesive under the applied pressure; therefore, the bonded joint may be worse off than using the ductile adhesive alone in the manufacturing stage [18]. Another common method is to add various reinforcements of different scales, which are harder, stiffer, and more strength than adhesive material, to the adhesive layer. Therefore, the mechanical properties, electrical and thermal conductivities of adhesive material can be improved suitably depending on its application area [27]. In general various fillers at a specific weight/volume fraction are distributed uniformly through adhesive material, and a homogeneous distribution of fillers is desired as possible. The stress analyses of this reinforced adhesive layer under mechanical and thermal loadings are performed using its mechanical and thermal properties, which are predicted by various experimental or continuum mechanics-based homogenization methods [28–31].

New theoretical analyses propose the use of a continuous adhesive grading, such as for modulus or coefficient of thermal expansion, along one or two coordinate directions of the adhesive material, and indicate that the improved strength of adhesive joints can be achieved by controlling stress concentrations with an existing optimum material grading rule [14,15]. Nevertheless, the material grading distribution rules are not practical right now for production purposes. The implementation of fused deposition modeling (3D printing) to the adhesive joints is now promising for the production of a functionally graded adhesive layer [32–35]. Consequently, the practice of functionally graded adhesive is still in the development stage and needs many theoretical and experimental studies that consider all aspects of adhesive material and adhesive joint.

In this study, the strain and stress states in an aluminum single lap joint bonded with a through-thickness functionally graded Al_2O_3 micro particle reinforced adhesive layer were investigated under a uniform temperature field (Figure 1). The spatial derivatives of Lamé constants and the coefficient of thermal expansion of local adhesive composition were considered in Navier equations of two-dimensional elasticity theory. The mechanical and thermal properties of the local adhesive composition were predicted by Mori–Tanaka's homogenization approach. The set of partial differential equations was solved with mechanical boundary conditions at each grid point of a discretized joint using the central finite difference approach. The effect of gradient power index controlling the through-thickness volume-fraction variation of particles in the local adhesive composition was also analyzed on the strain and stress states of the adhesive layer and adherends.

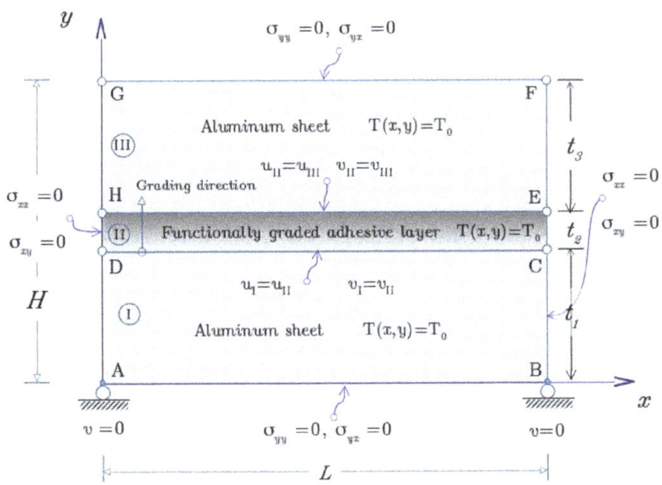

Figure 1. Boundary conditions of aluminum single-lap joint bonded with a through-thickness functionally graded adhesive layer.

2. Local Material Properties

The local composition of a functionally graded adhesive can be tailored along one or more spatial coordinate directions by means of a power function [9]. A continuous variation for any local mechanical property can be achieved; consequently, this can relieve discontinuities in thermal stresses which are encountered along the interfaces of layered material structures due to mismatches of mechanical and thermal properties.

The local mixture of both adhesive and micro-size (Al_2O_3) powders at any position through the adhesive thickness can be defined in terms of the volume fraction of (Al_2O_3) particles mixed through a two-component epoxy-based adhesive between a particle-rich adhesive interface and a neat adhesive interface. A well-known mixture rule can be implemented for the local composition of a particle-reinforced adhesive as

$$V_a(y) + V_p(y) = 1, \tag{1}$$

where a, p, $V_a(y)$ and $V_p(y)$ indicate adhesive and (Al_2O_3) particles and their volume fractions through the adhesive thickness. The maximum volume fraction of particles V_{max} in the vicinity of the particle-rich–adhesive interface is limited to a reasonable range of 0.01 and 0.1 because the adhesion between adhesive and aluminum adherend can not deteriorate. The volume fraction of (Al_2O_3) particles at any y—position through the adhesive thickness can be defined as

$$V_p(y) = \left(\frac{\bar{y}}{t_2}\right)^n V_{max} \quad \text{or} \quad V_p(y) = \left(1.0 - \left(\frac{\bar{y}}{t_2}\right)^n\right) V_{max}, \tag{2}$$

where t_2 is the adhesive thickness, $\bar{y} = y - t_2$ is the position relative to the lower adhesive interface. The power index n provides a desired variation form of the volume fraction of particles through the adhesive thickness in a range of 0.1 and 12.0. As shown in Figure 2, the first equation provides a composition variation from a neat lower adhesive interface to a particle-rich upper adhesive interface, and the second one acts in the reverse sense.

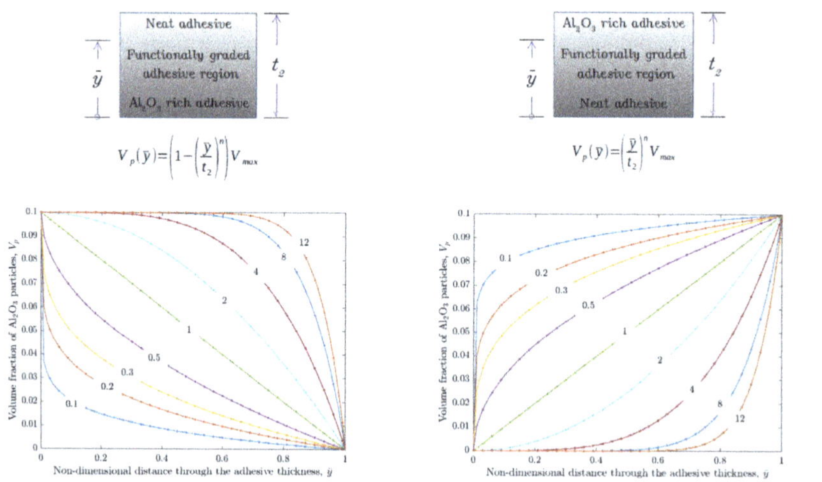

(**a**) Al_2O_3 rich adhesive (PRA) → neat adhesive (NA) (**b**) Neat adhesive (NA) → Al_2O_3 rich adhesive (PRA)

Figure 2. The volume fraction $V_p(\bar{y})$ variations of Al_2O_3 particles through the thickness of a functionally graded adhesive layer for different gradient power index (n) values ($V_{max} = 0.1$).

The mechanical and thermal properties of the local adhesive and particle mixture can be predicted using the Mori–Tanaka homogenization approach [28,29]. Thus, at any position $\bar{y}$ through the adhesive thickness, the overall bulk modulus

$$K(\bar{y}) = K_a + \frac{V_p(K_p - K_a)}{1 + (1 - V_p)\frac{3(K_p - K_a)}{3K_a + 4G_a}}, \tag{3}$$

the shear modulus

$$G(\bar{y}) = G_a + \frac{V_p(G_p - G_a)}{1 + (1 - V_p)\frac{G_p - G_a}{G_a + f_1}}, \tag{4}$$

where

$$f_1 = \frac{G_p(9K_p + 8G_p)}{6(K_p + 2G_p)}, \tag{5}$$

the modulus of elasticity

$$E(\bar{y}) = \frac{9KG}{3K + G}, \tag{6}$$

Poisson's ratio

$$v(\bar{y}) = \frac{3K - 2G}{2(3K + G)} \tag{7}$$

For isotropic particle-reinforced composite materials Wakashima-Tsukamoto [30] and Levin [31] propose the overall coefficient of thermal expansion in terms of the overall bulk modulus as

$$\alpha(\bar{y}) = \alpha_a + \left(\frac{1}{K} - \frac{1}{K_a}\right)\frac{\alpha_p - \alpha_a}{\frac{1}{K_p} - \frac{1}{K_a}} \tag{8}$$

3. Mathematical Model and Solution Method

Let x_1 and x_2 be spatial coordinate variables. In order to solve an elasticity problem, we need to consider the fundamental equations of elasticity theory [36] as follows:

Equilibrium

$$\frac{\partial \sigma_{ji}}{\partial x_i} + F_i = 0, \tag{9}$$

Strain-displacement relations

$$\varepsilon_{ij} = \frac{1}{2}\left(\frac{\partial u_i}{\partial x_j} + \frac{\partial u_j}{\partial x_i}\right), \tag{10}$$

Stress-strain relations

$$\sigma_{ij} = 2\mu\varepsilon_{ij} + \lambda\delta_{ij}\varepsilon_{nn} - \delta_{ij}(3\lambda + 2\mu)\alpha\bar{T}, \tag{11}$$

where δ_{ij} is kronecker delta and Lamé's constants

$$\lambda(x_2) = \frac{vE}{(1+v)(1-2v)}, \tag{12}$$

$$\mu(x_2) = \frac{E}{2(1+v)}, \tag{13}$$

the coefficient of thermal expansion $\alpha = \alpha(x_2)$, Poisson's ratio $v = v(x_2)$, the modulus of elasticity $E = E(x_2)$, the temperature difference $\bar{T} = T_o - T_{ref} =$ constant and the volumetric strain

$$\varepsilon_v = \varepsilon_{nn} = \frac{\partial u_k}{\partial x_k} = \varepsilon_{11} + \varepsilon_{22} + \varepsilon_{33} \tag{14}$$

Substituting Equations (10) and (14) into Equation (11) yields

$$\sigma_{ij} = \mu\left(\frac{\partial u_i}{\partial x_j} + \frac{\partial u_j}{\partial x_i}\right) + \lambda\delta_{ij}\frac{\partial u_k}{\partial x_k} - \delta_{ij}(3\lambda + 2\mu)\alpha\bar{T} \tag{15}$$

Finally, the substitution of Equation (15) into Equation (9) for $(F_i = 0)$ gives

$$\frac{\partial}{\partial x_j}\left(\mu\left(\frac{\partial u_i}{\partial x_j} + \frac{\partial u_j}{\partial x_i}\right) + \lambda\delta_{ij}\frac{\partial u_k}{\partial x_k} - \delta_{ij}(3\lambda + 2\mu)\alpha\bar{T}\right) = 0$$

After arranging the set of equations is obtained as follows

$$
\begin{aligned}
0 = {} & \frac{\partial \mu}{\partial x_j}\left(\frac{\partial u_i}{\partial x_j} + \frac{\partial u_j}{\partial x_i}\right) + \mu\frac{\partial^2 u_i}{\partial x_j^2} + \mu\frac{\partial^2 u_j}{\partial x_j x_i} + \frac{\partial \lambda}{\partial x_i}\frac{\partial u_k}{\partial x_k} + \lambda\frac{\partial}{\partial x_i}\left(\frac{\partial u_k}{\partial x_k}\right) \\
& - \left(3\frac{\partial \lambda}{\partial x_i} + 2\frac{\partial \mu}{\partial x_i}\right)\alpha\bar{T} - (3\lambda + 2\mu)\frac{\partial \alpha}{\partial x_i}\bar{T}
\end{aligned}
\tag{16}
$$

For a two-dimensional problem Equation (16) presents a set of two partial differential equations $(i = 1, 2)$ as

$$
\begin{aligned}
0 = {} & 2\frac{\partial \mu}{\partial x_1}\frac{\partial u_1}{\partial x_1} + \frac{\partial \mu}{\partial x_2}\left(\frac{\partial u_1}{\partial x_2} + \frac{\partial u_2}{\partial x_1}\right) + (\lambda + 2\mu)\frac{\partial^2 u_1}{\partial x_1^2} \\
& + (\lambda + \mu)\frac{\partial^2 u_2}{\partial x_1 \partial x_2} + \mu\frac{\partial^2 u_1}{\partial x_2^2} + \frac{\partial \lambda}{\partial x_1}\left(\frac{\partial u_1}{\partial x_1} + \frac{\partial u_2}{\partial x_2}\right) \\
& - \left(3\frac{\partial \lambda}{\partial x_1} + 2\frac{\partial \mu}{\partial x_1}\right)\alpha\bar{T} - (3\lambda + 2\mu)\frac{\partial \alpha}{\partial x_1}\bar{T},
\end{aligned}
\tag{17}
$$

$$
\begin{aligned}
0 = {} & \frac{\partial \mu}{\partial x_1}\left(\frac{\partial u_2}{\partial x_1} + \frac{\partial u_1}{\partial x_2}\right) + 2\frac{\partial \mu}{\partial x_2}\frac{\partial u_2}{\partial x_2} + (\lambda + 2\mu)\frac{\partial^2 u_2}{\partial x_2^2} \\
& + (\lambda + \mu)\frac{\partial^2 u_1}{\partial x_1 \partial x_2} + \mu\frac{\partial^2 u_2}{\partial x_1^2} + \frac{\partial \lambda}{\partial x_2}\left(\frac{\partial u_1}{\partial x_1} + \frac{\partial u_2}{\partial x_2}\right) \\
& - \left(3\frac{\partial \lambda}{\partial x_2} + 2\frac{\partial \mu}{\partial x_2}\right)\alpha\bar{T} - (3\lambda + 2\mu)\frac{\partial \alpha}{\partial x_2}\bar{T}
\end{aligned}
\tag{18}
$$

Let $x = x_1$, $y = x_2$, $u(x, y) = u_1(x_1, x_2)$ and $v(x, y) = u_2(x_1, x_2)$ for convenience. Equations (17) and (18) become

$$
\begin{aligned}
0 = {} & 2\frac{\partial \mu}{\partial x}\frac{\partial u}{\partial x} + \frac{\partial \mu}{\partial y}\left(\frac{\partial u}{\partial y} + \frac{\partial v}{\partial x}\right) + (\lambda + 2\mu)\frac{\partial^2 u}{\partial y} \\
& + (\lambda + \mu)\frac{\partial^2 v}{\partial x \partial y} + \mu\frac{\partial^2 u}{\partial y^2} + \frac{\partial \lambda}{\partial x}\left(\frac{\partial u}{\partial x} + \frac{\partial v}{\partial y}\right) \\
& - \left(3\frac{\partial \lambda}{\partial x} + 2\frac{\partial \mu}{\partial x}\right)\alpha\bar{T} - (3\lambda + 2\mu)\frac{\partial \alpha}{\partial x}\bar{T},
\end{aligned}
\tag{19}
$$

$$
\begin{aligned}
0 = {} & \frac{\partial \mu}{\partial x}\left(\frac{\partial v}{\partial x} + \frac{\partial u}{\partial y}\right) + 2\frac{\partial \mu}{\partial y}\frac{\partial v}{\partial y} + (\lambda + 2\mu)\frac{\partial^2 v}{\partial y^2} \\
& + (\lambda + \mu)\frac{\partial^2 u}{\partial x \partial y} + \mu\frac{\partial^2 v}{\partial x^2} + \frac{\partial \lambda}{\partial y}\left(\frac{\partial u}{\partial x} + \frac{\partial v}{\partial y}\right) \\
& - \left(3\frac{\partial \lambda}{\partial y} + 2\frac{\partial \mu}{\partial y}\right)\alpha\bar{T} - (3\lambda + 2\mu)\frac{\partial \alpha}{\partial y}\bar{T}
\end{aligned}
\tag{20}
$$

3.1. Boundary Conditions

Boundary conditions are described (Figure 1) as

$$\bar{T}(x, y) = T_0 \quad \text{constant,} \tag{21}$$

$$v = 0 \quad \text{at} \quad A(0, 0) \quad \text{and} \quad B(0, L), \tag{22}$$

$$\sigma_{xx} = 0, \;\; \sigma_{xy} = 0 \quad (x = 0, \;\; 0 < y < H), \tag{23}$$

$$\sigma_{xx} = 0, \;\; \sigma_{xy} = 0 \quad (x = L, \;\; 0 < y < H), \tag{24}$$

$$\sigma_{yy} = 0, \;\; \sigma_{yx} = 0 \quad (y = 0, \;\; 0 < x < L), \tag{25}$$

$$\sigma_{yy} = 0, \;\; \sigma_{yx} = 0 \quad (y = H, \;\; 0 < x < L), \tag{26}$$

$$\sigma_{xx} = 0, \ \ \sigma_{yy} = 0, \ \ \sigma_{xy} = 0 \quad [A(0,0), B(L,0), G(0,H), F(L,H)], \tag{27}$$

respectively.

3.2. Finite Difference Discretization

Let $\psi = \psi(x,y)$ be a continuous, differentiable two-variable function and be defined at each grid point (i,j) with spatial coordinates (x_i, y_i) of a two-dimensional region $\Re$ with a uniform grid distribution (Figure 3). i and j indicate positions along the coordinate axes x and y, respectively. The first and second-order partial derivatives of the function $\psi = \psi(x,y)$ with respect to spatial variables x and y can be discretized by means of forward, backward, and central difference equations.

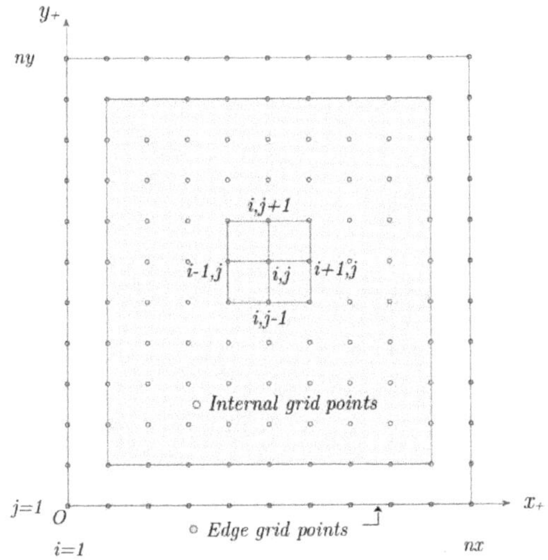

Figure 3. Representation of grid-point distributions in the solution region $\Re$ of adhesive single lap joint (not scaled).

The central-difference operators of the first-order partial derivatives of a function $\psi = \psi(x,y)$ at an internal grid point (i,j) with respect to spatial variables x and y are

$$\nabla_x \, \psi_{i,j} = \left.\frac{\partial \psi}{\partial x}\right|_{i,j} = \frac{\psi_{i+1,j} - \psi_{i-1,j}}{2\Delta x}, \tag{28}$$

$$\nabla_y \, \psi_{i,j} = \left.\frac{\partial \psi}{\partial y}\right|_{i,j} = \frac{\psi_{i,j+1} - \psi_{i,j-1}}{2\Delta y} \tag{29}$$

As the boundary conditions are applied, the central-difference operators can be modified in a forward sense as

$$\overrightarrow{\Gamma}_x \, \psi_{i,j} = \left.\frac{\partial \psi}{\partial x}\right|_{i,j} = \frac{-3\psi_{i,j} + 4\psi_{i+1,j} - \psi_{i+2,j}}{2\Delta x}, \tag{30}$$

$$\overrightarrow{\Gamma}_y \, \psi_{i,j} = \left.\frac{\partial \psi}{\partial y}\right|_{i,j} = \frac{-3\psi_{i,j} + 4\psi_{i,j+1} - \psi_{i,j+2}}{2\Delta y}, \tag{31}$$

or in a backward sense as

$$\overleftarrow{\Gamma}_x \, \psi_{i,j} = \left.\frac{\partial \psi}{\partial x}\right|_{i,j} = \frac{3\psi_{i,j} - 4\psi_{i-1,j} + \psi_{i-2,j}}{2\Delta x}, \tag{32}$$

$$\overleftarrow{\Gamma}_y \, \psi_{i,j} = \left.\frac{\partial \psi}{\partial y}\right|_{i,j} = \frac{3\psi_{i,j} - 4\psi_{i,j-1} + \psi_{i,j-2}}{2\Delta y} \tag{33}$$

The central-difference operators of the second-order partial derivatives of a function $\psi = \psi(x, y)$ at a internal grid point (i, j) with respect to spatial variables x and y are

$$\nabla_{xx} \, \psi_{i,j} = \left.\frac{\partial^2 \psi}{\partial x^2}\right|_{i,j} = \frac{\psi_{i+1,j} - 2\psi_{i,j} + \psi_{i-1,j}}{(\Delta x)^2}, \tag{34}$$

$$\nabla_{yy} \, \psi_{i,j} = \left.\frac{\partial^2 \psi}{\partial y^2}\right|_{i,j} = \frac{\psi_{i,j+1} - 2\psi_{i,j} + \psi_{i,j-1}}{(\Delta y)^2}, \tag{35}$$

$$\nabla_{xy} \, \psi_{i,j} = \left.\frac{\partial^2 \psi}{\partial x \partial y}\right|_{i,j} = \frac{\psi_{i+1,j+1} - \psi_{i+1,j-1} - \psi_{i-1,j+1} + \psi_{i-1,j-1}}{4\Delta x \Delta y} \tag{36}$$

As the boundary conditions are applied, the central-difference operators can be modified in a forward or backward sense as

$$\overrightarrow{\Gamma}_{xx} \, \psi_{i,j} = \left.\frac{\partial^2 \psi}{\partial x^2}\right|_{i,j} = \frac{-\psi_{i+3,j} + 4\psi_{i+2,j} - 5\psi_{i+1,j} + 2\psi_{i,j}}{(\Delta x)^2}, \tag{37}$$

$$\overleftarrow{\Gamma}_{xx} \, \psi_{i,j} = \left.\frac{\partial^2 \psi}{\partial x^2}\right|_{i,j} = \frac{2\psi_{i,j} - 5\psi_{i-1,j} + 4\psi_{i-2,j} - \psi_{i-3,j}}{(\Delta x)^2}, \tag{38}$$

$$\overrightarrow{\Gamma}_{yy} \, \psi_{i,j} = \left.\frac{\partial^2 \psi}{\partial y^2}\right|_{i,j} = \frac{-\psi_{i,j+3} + 4\psi_{i,j+2} - 5\psi_{i,j+1} + 2\psi_{i,j}}{(\Delta y)^2}, \tag{39}$$

$$\overleftarrow{\Gamma}_{yy} \, \psi_{i,j} = \left.\frac{\partial^2 \psi}{\partial y^2}\right|_{i,j} = \frac{2\psi_{i,j} - 5\psi_{i,j-1} + 4\psi_{i,j-2} - \psi_{i,j-3}}{(\Delta y)^2} \tag{40}$$

3.3. Internal Grid Points

Navier partial differential Equations (19) and (20) at each internal grid point, (i, j) of coordinates (x_i, y_i) inside the region $\Re$ (Figure 3) can be reduced to the linear difference equations by applying the relevant difference operators to the first and second order derivatives as follows

$$\begin{aligned} 0 = {} & 2(\nabla_x \mu_{i,j})(\nabla_x u_{i,j}) + (\nabla_y \mu_{i,j})(\nabla_y u_{i,j} + \nabla_x v_{i,j}) \\ & + (\lambda + 2\mu)_{i,j}(\nabla_{xx} u_{i,j}) + (\lambda + \mu)_{i,j}(\nabla_{xy} v_{i,j}) \\ & + \mu_{i,j}(\nabla_{yy} u_{i,j}) + (\nabla_x \lambda_{i,j})(\nabla_x u_{i,j} + \nabla_y v_{i,j}) \\ & - (3 \nabla_x \lambda_{i,j} + 2 \nabla_x \mu_{i,j})\alpha_{i,j}\bar{T}_{i,j} - (3\lambda + 2\mu)_{i,j}(\nabla_x \alpha_{i,j})\bar{T}_{i,j}, \end{aligned} \tag{41}$$

$$\begin{aligned} 0 = {} & (\nabla_x \mu_{i,j})(\nabla_x v_{i,j} + \nabla_y u_{i,j}) + 2(\nabla_y \mu_{i,j})(\nabla_y v_{i,j}) \\ & + (\lambda + 2\mu)_{i,j}(\nabla_{yy} v_{i,j}) + \mu_{i,j}(\nabla_{xx} v_{i,j}) \\ & + (\lambda + \mu)_{i,j}(\nabla_{xy} u_{i,j}) + (\nabla_y \lambda_{i,j})(\nabla_x u_{i,j} + \nabla_y v_{i,j}) \\ & - (3 \nabla_y \lambda_{i,j} + 2 \nabla_y \mu_{i,j})\alpha_{i,j}\bar{T}_{i,j} - (3\lambda + 2\mu)_{i,j}(\nabla_y \alpha_{i,j})\bar{T}_{i,j} \end{aligned} \tag{42}$$

3.4. Boundary Grid Points

Boundary conditions (22)–(27) at each grid point (i, j) of coordinates (x_i, y_i) along the outer boundaries of the region $\Re$ (Figures 1 and 3) can be implemented by means of the difference equations of the stress components

$$\sigma_{xx} = (\lambda + 2\mu)\frac{\partial u}{\partial x} + \lambda\frac{\partial v}{\partial y} - (3\lambda + 2\mu)\alpha\bar{T}, \tag{43}$$

$$\sigma_{yy} = (\lambda + 2\mu)\frac{\partial v}{\partial y} + \lambda\frac{\partial u}{\partial x} - (3\lambda + 2\mu)\alpha\bar{T}, \tag{44}$$

$$\sigma_{xy} = \sigma_{yx} = \mu\left(\frac{\partial u}{\partial y} + \frac{\partial v}{\partial x}\right), \tag{45}$$

as follows

1. Along the edge AG (Equation (23)):

$$0 = (\lambda + 2\mu)_{i,j}\left(\overrightarrow{\Gamma}_x\, u_{i,j}\right) + \lambda_{i,j}(\nabla_y v_{i,j}) - (3\lambda + 2\mu)_{i,j}\alpha_{i,j}\bar{T}_{i,j}, \tag{46}$$

$$0 = \mu_{i,j}\left(\nabla_y u_{i,j} + \overrightarrow{\Gamma}_x\, v_{i,j}\right), \tag{47}$$

2. Along the edge BF (Equation (24)):

$$0 = (\lambda + 2\mu)_{i,j}\left(\overleftarrow{\Gamma}_x\, u_{i,j}\right) + \lambda_{i,j}(\nabla_y v_{i,j}) - (3\lambda + 2\mu)_{i,j}\alpha_{i,j}\bar{T}_{i,j}, \tag{48}$$

$$0 = \mu_{i,j}\left(\nabla_y u_{i,j} + \overleftarrow{\Gamma}_x\, v_{i,j}\right), \tag{49}$$

3. Along the edge AB (Equation (25)):

$$0 = (\lambda + 2\mu)_{i,j}\left(\overrightarrow{\Gamma}_y\, v_{i,j}\right) + \lambda_{i,j}(\nabla_x u_{i,j}) - (3\lambda + 2\mu)_{i,j}\alpha_{i,j}\bar{T}_{i,j}, \tag{50}$$

$$0 = \mu_{i,j}\left(\overrightarrow{\Gamma}_y\, u_{i,j} + \nabla_x v_{i,j}\right), \tag{51}$$

4. Along the edge GF (Equation (26)):

$$0 = (\lambda + 2\mu)_{i,j}\left(\overleftarrow{\Gamma}_y\, v_{i,j}\right) + \lambda_{i,j}(\nabla_x u_{i,j}) - (3\lambda + 2\mu)_{i,j}\alpha_{i,j}\bar{T}_{i,j}, \tag{52}$$

$$0 = \mu_{i,j}\left(\overleftarrow{\Gamma}_y\, u_{i,j} + \nabla_x v_{i,j}\right), \tag{53}$$

5. At the corner A (Equation (27)):

$$0 = (\lambda + 2\mu)_{i,j}\left(\overrightarrow{\Gamma}_x\, u_{i,j}\right) + \lambda_{i,j}\left(\overrightarrow{\Gamma}_y\, v_{i,j}\right) - (3\lambda + 2\mu)_{i,j}\alpha_{i,j}\bar{T}_{i,j}, \tag{54}$$

$$0 = (\lambda + 2\mu)_{i,j}\left(\overrightarrow{\Gamma}_y\, v_{i,j}\right) + \lambda_{i,j}\left(\overrightarrow{\Gamma}_x\, u_{i,j}\right) - (3\lambda + 2\mu)_{i,j}\alpha_{i,j}\bar{T}_{i,j}, \tag{55}$$

$$0 = \mu_{i,j}\left(\overrightarrow{\Gamma}_y\, u_{i,j} + \overrightarrow{\Gamma}_x\, v_{i,j}\right), \tag{56}$$

6. At the corner G (Equation (27)):

$$0 = (\lambda + 2\mu)_{i,j}\left(\overrightarrow{\Gamma}_x\, u_{i,j}\right) + \lambda_{i,j}\left(\overleftarrow{\Gamma}_y\, v_{i,j}\right) - (3\lambda + 2\mu)_{i,j}\alpha_{i,j}\bar{T}_{i,j}, \tag{57}$$

$$0 = (\lambda + 2\mu)_{i,j}\left(\overleftarrow{\Gamma}_y\, v_{i,j}\right) + \lambda_{i,j}\left(\overrightarrow{\Gamma}_x\, u_{i,j}\right) - (3\lambda + 2\mu)_{i,j}\alpha_{i,j}\bar{T}_{i,j}, \tag{58}$$

$$0 = \mu_{i,j}\left(\overleftarrow{\Gamma}_y\, u_{i,j} + \overrightarrow{\Gamma}_x\, v_{i,j}\right), \tag{59}$$

7. At the corner B (Equation (27)):

$$0 = (\lambda + 2\mu)_{i,j}\left(\overleftarrow{\Gamma}_x\, u_{i,j}\right) + \lambda_{i,j}\left(\overrightarrow{\Gamma}_y\, v_{i,j}\right) - (3\lambda + 2\mu)_{i,j}\alpha_{i,j}\bar{T}_{i,j}, \tag{60}$$

$$0 = (\lambda + 2\mu)_{i,j}\left(\overrightarrow{\Gamma}_y\, v_{i,j}\right) + \lambda_{i,j}\left(\overleftarrow{\Gamma}_x\, u_{i,j}\right) - (3\lambda + 2\mu)_{i,j}\alpha_{i,j}\bar{T}_{i,j}, \tag{61}$$

$$0 = \mu_{i,j}\left(\overrightarrow{\Gamma}_y\, u_{i,j} + \overleftarrow{\Gamma}_x\, v_{i,j}\right), \tag{62}$$

8. At the corner F (Equation (27)):

$$0 = (\lambda + 2\mu)_{i,j}\left(\overleftarrow{\Gamma}_x\, u_{i,j}\right) + \lambda_{i,j}\left(\overleftarrow{\Gamma}_y\, v_{i,j}\right) - (3\lambda + 2\mu)_{i,j}\alpha_{i,j}\bar{T}_{i,j}, \tag{63}$$

$$0 = (\lambda + 2\mu)_{i,j}\left(\overleftarrow{\Gamma}_y\, v_{i,j}\right) + \lambda_{i,j}\left(\overleftarrow{\Gamma}_x\, u_{i,j}\right) - (3\lambda + 2\mu)_{i,j}\alpha_{i,j}\bar{T}_{i,j}, \tag{64}$$

$$0 = \mu_{i,j}\left(\overleftarrow{\Gamma}_y\, u_{i,j} + \overleftarrow{\Gamma}_x\, v_{i,j}\right) \tag{65}$$

3.5. Discretization of Continuity Conditions along Interfaces

The adherend and adhesive sides of interfaces are of different material properties. In single material regions, the finite difference discretization of Navier equations and boundary conditions can be made easily. The bi-material interfaces result in sudden changes in the through-thickness mechanical and thermal properties of local material. Consequently, the thermal strains and stresses become discontinuous while the total normal strains, as well as displacement components, are continuous.

In the infinitesimal neighborhood of bi-material interfaces, twin grid points can be defined (Figure 3), then Navier equations and boundary conditions can be discretized with material properties of the grid points on both sides $(-,+)$ of interfaces in sequence, and the predicted displacement components can be equated. Thus,

$$u^-_{i,j} = u^+_{i,j}, \tag{66}$$

$$v^-_{i,j} = v^+_{i,j} \tag{67}$$

3.5.1. Internal Grid Points of Interfaces

The Navier Equation (41) can be discretized with material properties of the internal grid points on both sides $(-,+)$ of interfaces as

$$\begin{aligned}0 = {} & 2(\nabla_x\mu_{i,j})^-(\nabla_x u_{i,j}) + (\nabla_y\mu_{i,j})^-(\nabla_y u_{i,j} + \nabla_x v_{i,j}) \\ & + (\lambda + 2\mu)^-_{i,j}(\nabla_{xx}u_{i,j}) + (\lambda + \mu)^-_{i,j}(\nabla_{xy}v_{i,j}) \\ & + \mu^-_{i,j}(\nabla_{yy}u_{i,j}) + (\nabla_x\lambda_{i,j})^-(\nabla_x u_{i,j} + \nabla_y v_{i,j}) \\ & - (3\nabla_x\lambda_{i,j} + 2\nabla_x\mu_{i,j})^-\alpha^-_{i,j}\bar{T}_{i,j} - (3\lambda + 2\mu)^-_{i,j}(\nabla_x\alpha_{i,j})^-\bar{T}_{i,j},\end{aligned} \tag{68}$$

$$\begin{aligned}0 = {} & 2(\nabla_x\mu_{i,j})^+(\nabla_x u_{i,j}) + (\nabla_y\mu_{i,j})^+(\nabla_y u_{i,j} + \nabla_x v_{i,j}) \\ & + (\lambda + 2\mu)^+_{i,j}(\nabla_{xx}u_{i,j}) + (\lambda + \mu)^+_{i,j}(\nabla_{xy}v_{i,j}) \\ & + \mu^+_{i,j}(\nabla_{yy}u_{i,j}) + (\nabla_x\lambda_{i,j})^+(\nabla_x u_{i,j} + \nabla_y v_{i,j}) \\ & - (3\nabla_x\lambda_{i,j} + 2\nabla_x\mu_{i,j})^+\alpha^+_{i,j}\bar{T}_{i,j} - (3\lambda + 2\mu)^+_{i,j}(\nabla_x\alpha_{i,j})^+\bar{T}_{i,j},\end{aligned} \tag{69}$$

respectively. In Equations (68) and (69), $j+1$ is replaced by $j+2$, and $j-1$ by $j-2$ in all finite difference operators for the grid points along the lower and upper twins of interfaces, respectively.

Similarly, the Navier Equation (42) can be discretized with material properties of the internal grid points on the both sides $(-,+)$ of interfaces as

$$\begin{aligned}0 = {} & (\nabla_x\mu_{i,j})^-(\nabla_x v_{i,j} + \nabla_y u_{i,j}) + 2(\nabla_y\mu_{i,j})^-(\nabla_y v_{i,j}) \\ & + (\lambda + 2\mu)^-_{i,j}(\nabla_{yy}v_{i,j}) + \mu^-_{i,j}(\nabla_{xx}v_{i,j}) \\ & + (\lambda + \mu)^-_{i,j}(\nabla_{xy}u_{i,j}) + (\nabla_y\lambda_{i,j})^-(\nabla_x u_{i,j} + \nabla_y v_{i,j}) \\ & - (3\nabla_y\lambda_{i,j} + 2\nabla_y\mu_{i,j})^-\alpha^-_{i,j}\bar{T}_{i,j} - (3\lambda + 2\mu)^-_{i,j}(\nabla_y\alpha_{i,j})^-\bar{T}_{i,j},\end{aligned} \tag{70}$$

$$
\begin{aligned}
0 = & \left(\nabla_x \mu_{i,j}\right)^+ \left(\nabla_x v_{i,j} + \nabla_y u_{i,j}\right) + 2\left(\nabla_y \mu_{i,j}\right)^+ \left(\nabla_y v_{i,j}\right) \\
& + (\lambda + 2\mu)^+_{i,j} \left(\nabla_{yy} v_{i,j}\right) + \mu^+_{i,j} \left(\nabla_{xx} v_{i,j}\right) \\
& + (\lambda + \mu)^+_{i,j} \left(\nabla_{xy} u_{i,j}\right) + \left(\nabla_y \lambda_{i,j}\right)^+ \left(\nabla_x u_{i,j} + \nabla_y v_{i,j}\right) \\
& - \left(3 \nabla_y \lambda_{i,j} + 2 \nabla_y \mu_{i,j}\right)^+ \alpha^+_{i,j} \bar{T}_{i,j} - (3\lambda + 2\mu)^+_{i,j} \left(\nabla_y \alpha_{i,j}\right)^+ \bar{T}_{i,j}
\end{aligned} \tag{71}
$$

The displacement components $u_{i,j}$ and $v_{i,j}$ can be calculated at each twin node in the infinitesimal neighborhood of both interfaces.

3.5.2. Grid Points at the Free Edges of Interfaces

The boundary conditions at the grid points along the free edges AG $(x = 0)$ and BF $(x = L)$ of both interfaces can be implemented with the previous approach as

1. At the free edge AG of both interfaces:

$$\sigma^-_{xx} = 0 = (\lambda + 2\mu)^-_{i,j} \left(\overrightarrow{\Gamma}_x\, u_{i,j}\right) + \lambda^-_{i,j} \left(\nabla_y v_{i,j}\right) - (3\lambda + 2\mu)^-_{i,j} \alpha^-_{i,j} \bar{T}_{i,j}, \tag{72}$$

$$\sigma^+_{xx} = 0 = (\lambda + 2\mu)^+_{i,j} \left(\overrightarrow{\Gamma}_x\, u_{i,j}\right) + \lambda^+_{i,j} \left(\nabla_y v_{i,j}\right) - (3\lambda + 2\mu)^+_{i,j} \alpha^+_{i,j} \bar{T}_{i,j}, \tag{73}$$

$$\sigma^-_{xy} = 0 = \mu^-_{i,j} \left(\nabla_y u_{i,j} + \overrightarrow{\Gamma}_x\, v_{i,j}\right), \tag{74}$$

$$\sigma^+_{xy} = 0 = \mu^+_{i,j} \left(\nabla_y u_{i,j} + \overrightarrow{\Gamma}_x\, v_{i,j}\right), \tag{75}$$

2. At the edge BF of both interfaces:

$$\sigma^-_{xx} = 0 = (\lambda + 2\mu)^-_{i,j} \left(\overleftarrow{\Gamma}_x\, u_{i,j}\right) + \lambda^-_{i,j} \left(\nabla_y v_{i,j}\right) - (3\lambda + 2\mu)^-_{i,j} \alpha^-_{i,j} \bar{T}_{i,j}, \tag{76}$$

$$\sigma^+_{xx} = 0 = (\lambda + 2\mu)^+_{i,j} \left(\overleftarrow{\Gamma}_x\, u_{i,j}\right) + \lambda^+_{i,j} \left(\nabla_y v_{i,j}\right) - (3\lambda + 2\mu)^+_{i,j} \alpha^+_{i,j} \bar{T}_{i,j}, \tag{77}$$

$$\sigma^-_{xy} = 0 = \mu^-_{i,j} \left(\nabla_y u_{i,j} + \overleftarrow{\Gamma}_x\, v_{i,j}\right), \tag{78}$$

$$\sigma^+_{xy} = 0 = \mu^+_{i,j} \left(\nabla_y u_{i,j} + \overleftarrow{\Gamma}_x\, v_{i,j}\right) \tag{79}$$

3.6. Solution Method

After Navier equations and the boundary conditions are discretized in the solution region $\Re$, unknown displacement components $u_{i,j}$ and $v_{i,j}$ at each grid point (i, j) can be calculated by implementing a recursive error reducing method.

Let $u^k_{i,j}$ and $v^k_{i,j}$ be displacement components at an iteration index k. The finite difference representations for Navier Equations (41)–(42) and (68)–(71) and boundary conditions (46)–(65) and (72)–(79) can be written as

$$
\begin{aligned}
c_{i,j} u^k_{i,j} &= F^k_{i,j}, \\
d_{i,j} v^k_{i,j} &= G^k_{i,j}
\end{aligned} \tag{80}
$$

The error levels for iteration k are calculated as

$$
\begin{aligned}
\mathrm{erru}^k_{i,j} &= F^k_{i,j} - \tfrac{1}{c_{i,j}} u^k_{i,j}, \\
\mathrm{errv}^k_{i,j} &= G^k_{i,j} - \tfrac{1}{d_{i,j}} v^k_{i,j}
\end{aligned} \tag{81}
$$

The displacement components for iteration $k + 1$ are predicted as

$$
\begin{aligned}
u^{k+1}_{i,j} &= u^k_{i,j} - \frac{\mathrm{erru}^k_{i,j}}{c_{i,j}}, \\
v^{k+1}_{i,j} &= v^k_{i,j} - \frac{\mathrm{errv}^k_{i,j}}{d_{i,j}}
\end{aligned} \tag{82}
$$

The summation of errors is calculated as

$$\text{SumError} = \sum_{i=1}^{m} \sum_{j=1}^{n} \left(\text{erru}_{i,j}^{k} + \text{errv}_{i,j}^{k} \right) \tag{83}$$

where m and n are division numbers of the uniform grid for the region $\Re$ along the coordinate axes x and y, respectively. The loop between (80) and (83) is repeated until SumError is reduced to a specific error level of eps $= 10^{-8}$ by equating $u_{i,j}^{k+1}$ and $v_{i,j}^{k+1}$ to $u_{i,j}^{k}$ and $v_{i,j}^{k}$.

4. Results and Discussion

The geometry, dimensions, and boundary conditions of an aluminum single lap joint bonded with a functionally graded adhesive are shown in Figure 1. The joint length $L = 15$ mm, aluminum adherend thickness $t_1 = t_3 = 1.5$ mm, and adhesive thickness $t_2 = 0.5$ mm. The displacements of the left and right lower corners are fixed only in the $y-$direction, and the normal and shear stresses are considered as zero along the free edges of the adhesive joint. A constant temperature change of $\Delta T = 30$ °C is assumed at all grid points. The thermal and mechanical properties of adherend, micro-sized powder, and adhesive materials are given in Table 1. The solution domain was discretized into a mesh grid of 631 × 150 with increments of $dx = dy = 0.02381$ mm along the x- and y-directions, respectively.

Table 1. Thermal and mechanical properties of the adherend, adhesive, and micro-sized particles.

		Units	Aluminium	Al_2O_3	Epoxy
Modulus of elasticity	E	MPa	68,900.0	379,211.0	4391.43
Poisson's ratio	υ		0.33	0.19	0.34
Coefficient of thermal expansion	α	1/m·K	23.58×10^{-6}	7.6×10^{-6}	40.47×10^{-6}
Shear modulus	G	MPa	26,000.0	150,000.0	1638.6
Bulk modulus	K	MPa	67,549.0	203,876.9	4574.4

The composition of functionally graded adhesive consists of (Al_2O_3) micro-particles and two-component epoxy-based adhesive mixed at specific volume fractions. The volume fraction of micro-particles V_p through the thickness of the adhesive layer is tailored by obeying a power rule including a gradient power index n (Equation (2)). Two grading directions are also considered, thus, the variations of volume fraction of particles through the adhesive thickness between a particle-rich adhesive around the lower interface and a neat adhesive around the upper interface (PRA→NA, Figure 2a), and between a neat adhesive around the lower interface and a particle-rich adhesive around the upper interface (NA→PRA, Figure 2b), respectively. The volume fraction of particles V_p around the particle-rich adhesive interface is limited by the maximum volume fraction of particles as $V_{max} = 0.01, 0.1, 0.3$ because the adhesion between adhesive and aluminum adherend has not deteriorated. The volume fraction of particles V_p can have a desired through-thickness form with the power index $n = 0.1, 0.2, 0.3, 0.5, 1.0, 2.0, 4.0, 8.0$ and 12.0 (Figure 2).

Consequently, this study aims to determine the effects of the gradient power index n, maximum volume fraction V_{max}, and grading direction through the adhesive thickness on the adhesive strain and stress distributions induced by a uniform temperature change through the adhesive joint and on reliving their critical levels. The thermal stress analyses were carried out for various maximum volume fractions of particles and power index values. The strain and stress components exhibited almost similar distributions except for their levels of low-volume fractions of particles. The left and right free edges of the adhesive layer appeared as symmetrical stress and strain concentration regions. Therefore, the distributions of strain and stress components will be discussed via their contour plots.

Figures 4–6 show the effects of the power index (n) and the maximum volume fraction of particles (V_{max}) on the distributions of strain $\varepsilon_{ij}(x,y)$ and stress $\sigma_{ij}(x,y)$ components around the left free ends of both lower and upper interfaces of a functionally graded adhesive layer. The normal strain ε_{xx} concentrates around the lower and upper adhesive interfaces, propagates towards the overlapping center, and decreases uniformly (Figure 4). A graded variation of normal strain appears, especially in the vicinity of both interfaces. The free edges of the adhesive layer undergo higher normal strain levels than two adherends because the overall coefficient of thermal expansion of adhesive composition is larger than those of aluminum adherends. Similar symmetrical distributions also appear around the right-hand sides of both interfaces. The general form of distributions is not affected by the power index n for a low maximum volume fraction ($V_{max} = 0.01$), while its effect becomes more apparent for a through-thickness quite particle-rich composition ($V_{max} = 0.3$). The normal strain levels decrease as the adhesive is enriched by particles through the adhesive thickness ($n = 1.0 \rightarrow 12$). Thus, the higher strain levels occur around the free end of the upper interface and in the vicinity of this interface. The normal strain decreases slightly through the adhesive thickness towards the vicinity of the lower interface. The normal strain distribution exhibits a dependency on the through-thickness variation of particles in the adhesive composition. The normal stress σ_{xx} concentrates in the vicinity of both interfaces and exhibits discontinuous distributions at different levels on the adherend and adhesive sides of interfaces (Figure 4). The normal stress levels in the adhesive layer are rather lower than in the adherends because aluminum adherends are of higher modulus than the adhesive composition. The normal stress distribution and levels remain similar for a low maximum volume fraction of particles (0.01), and the effect of the power index is negligible. The power index has a more apparent effect on the normal stress distributions and levels for a high volume fraction of particles (0.3). Namely, the higher stress levels occur on the adherend side in the vicinity of the neat adhesive–upper adherend interface in comparison with those around the particle-rich adhesive–lower adherend interface as the adhesive is enriched by particles through its thickness.

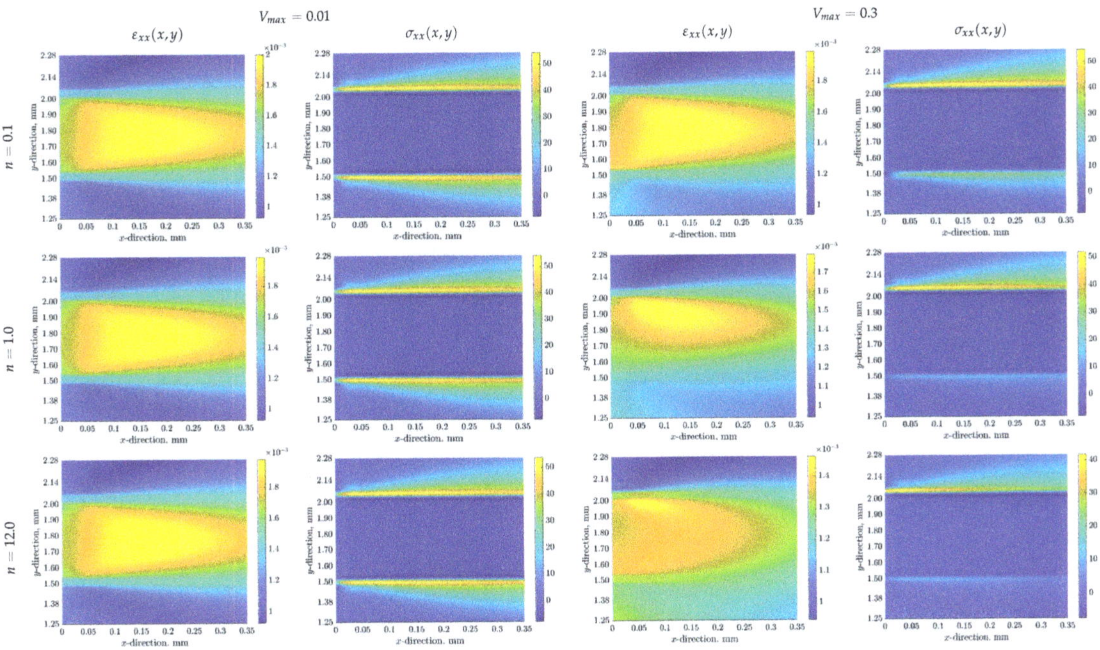

Figure 4. Effects of the gradient power index (n) and the maximum volume fraction of particles (V_{max}) on the normal strain $\varepsilon_{xx}(x,y)$ and stress $\sigma_{xx}(x,y)$ distributions around the left free-end of the PRA $\rightarrow$ NA functionally graded adhesive layer and interfaces.

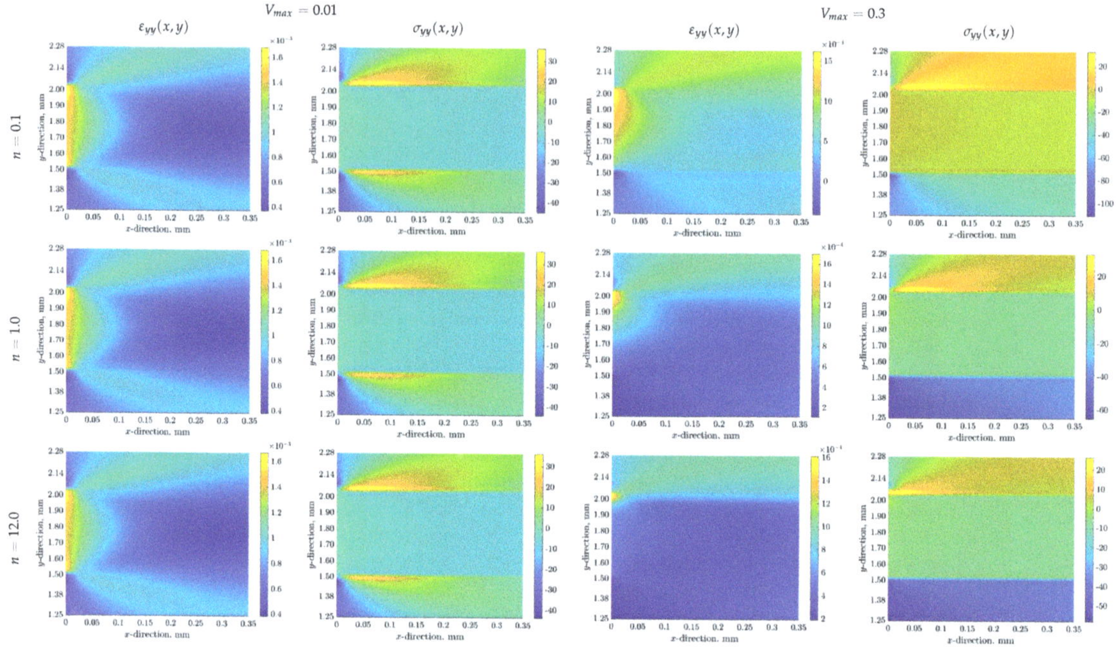

Figure 5. Effects of the gradient power index (n) and the maximum volume fraction of particles (V_{max}) on the normal strain $\varepsilon_{yy}(x, y)$ and stress $\sigma_{yy}(x, y)$ distributions around the left free-end of the PRA $\rightarrow$ NA functionally graded adhesive layer and interfaces.

The normal strain ε_{yy} exhibits similar distributions; thus, the concentration zones appear around the free edges of the adhesive layer and both adhesive interfaces, and then continuously relieve through the adherend and adhesive regions neighboring to the interfaces towards the center of overlap region (Figure 5). Especially, the concentration regions around the free ends of the adhesive layer expand through the adhesive thickness towards the center of the overlap region. The normal strain decreases along a symmetrical diffusing band-form region on the adherend sides of two interfaces. The normal strain levels are higher in the adhesive layer because the adhesive layer is of a larger overall coefficient of thermal expansion. The distribution manner and levels of the normal strain ε_{yy} around the free edges of the adhesive layer, and both interfaces are not affected notably by the power index for a low maximum volume fraction of particles (0.01). The power index becomes more effective on the normal strain distributions and levels for a high volume fraction of particles (0.3). Namely, the strain concentration zone at the adhesive-free edge gets narrower towards the free end of the upper neat adhesive–adherend interface, and occurs in the vicinity of this interface towards the center of the overlap region. In addition, the diffusing zone in the upper adherend becomes more apparent in comparison with those in the lower adherend as the adhesive is enriched by particles through its thickness. The normal stress σ_{yy} exhibits concentration zones with discontinuous distributions in the vicinity of both interfaces and different levels on the adherend and adhesive sides of interfaces (Figure 5). The normal stress levels in the adhesive layer are rather lower, whereas the adherend regions neighboring both interfaces undergo higher stress levels diffusing towards the center of the overlap region and through adherend thickness. The normal stress distribution and levels remain similar, and the effect of the power index is negligible for a low maximum volume fraction of particles (0.01). However, the power index affects evidently the normal stress distributions and levels only for a high volume fraction of particles (0.3). The higher tensile stress levels occur on the adherend side in the vicinity of the neat adhesive–upper adherend interface, whereas the higher compressive stress levels occur on the adherend side in the vicinity of the particle-rich adhesive–lower adherend interface. The high-stress levels relieve considerably in these concentration zones as the adhesive is enriched by particles through its thickness.

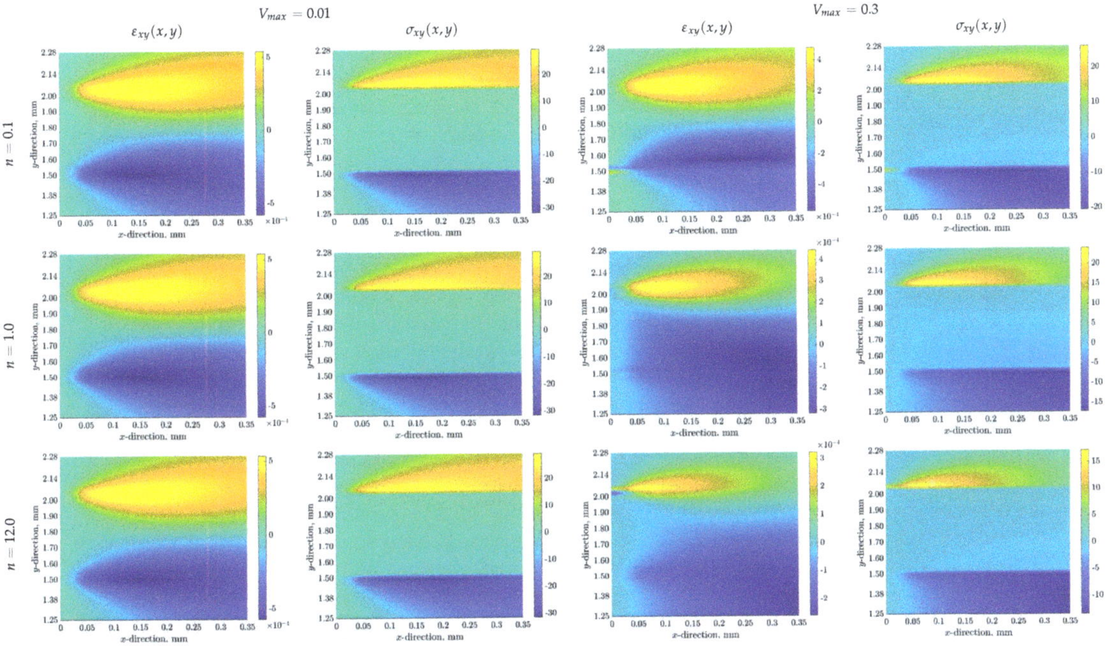

Figure 6. Effects of the gradient power index (n) and the maximum volume fraction of particles (V_{max}) on the shear strain $\varepsilon_{xy}(x, y)$ and stress $\sigma_{xy}(x, y)$ distributions around the left free-end of the PRA $\rightarrow$ NA functionally graded adhesive layer and interfaces.

The shear strain ε_{xy} concentrates in the neighborhood of both interfaces except their free edges (Figure 6). A narrow concentration zone initiates at a small distance from the free ends of both interfaces and expands through the adherend and adhesive thicknesses. The shear deformations occur symmetrically but in opposite directions along the lower and upper interfaces. The power index has a negligible effect on both distribution manner and levels of the shear strain ε_{xy} around the free edges of the adhesive layer and both interfaces for a low maximum volume fraction of particles (0.01), whereas this effect becomes apparent on the shear strain distributions and levels for a high volume fraction of particles (0.3). Thus, the symmetrical concentration zones near both interfaces degenerate, and the shear strain levels around the neat adhesive–upper adherend interface reach partly higher levels, and the shear strain levels decrease as the through-thickness adhesive composition is enriched by particles. The neat adhesive interface forces the neighboring zones of both adhesive and adherend to more deformation in shear due to its tendency to a larger thermal expansion. The shear stress σ_{xy} concentrations occur in the neighborhood of both interfaces except their free edges and exhibit a discontinuous distribution along both interfaces (Figure 6). The adherend side experiences higher shear stresses than those on the adhesive side. The shear strain and stress distributions are conformable. The effect of the power index becomes apparent on the shear stress σ_{xy} distributions and levels in the regions near both interfaces only for a high volume fraction of particles (0.3). The symmetrical concentration zones near both interfaces become smaller towards the free ends of both interfaces, and the shear stress levels decrease as the through-thickness adhesive composition is enriched by particles. The shear stress is also as critical as the normal stresses. In general, a ductile adhesive composition is expected to tend to damage in shear.

In case an adhesive single lap joint is subjected to a uniform temperature distribution, the strain and stress components concentrate in the neighborhood of adherend–adhesive interfaces and around their free edges. They also decrease uniformly along the interfaces towards the center of the overlap region. The normal and shear strain components exhibit grading distributions along both bi-material interfaces, whereas the normal and shear stresses are of a discontinuous nature. Since the adhesive material is generally assumed to be a material of lower strength than adherends; hereafter, the evaluation of normal/shear strain and stress distributions around the free edges of the adhesive layer is in evidence as a more convenient way.

Figures 7–9 show the effects of both gradient power index (n) and maximum volume fraction of particles (V_{max}) on the distributions of strain $\varepsilon_{ij}(x,y)$ and stress $\sigma_{ij}(x,y)$ components around the left free end of a functionally graded adhesive layer. The normal strain ε_{xx} distributions are symmetrical with respect to the adhesive mid-line (Figure 7) for a low maximum volume fraction of particles (0.01). The high normal strain levels occur in a large adhesive zone in the vicinity of adhesive mid-line from at a small distance from the free ends of both interfaces and decrease uniformly towards the center of the overlap region. The power index exhibits a negligible effect on the normal strain distribution and levels for a low maximum volume fraction of particles. Increasing the maximum volume fractions of particles makes the effect of the power index to become more apparent. As the power index is increased, namely, the through-thickness adhesive composition is enriched by particles, the symmetrical distribution of normal strain disappears, and the concentration region contracts towards the neat adhesive–upper adherend interface. This indicates a reduced overall thermal expansion of remaining adhesive regions enriched by particles. The normal stress σ_{xx} acts in compression and is negligible near the adhesive-free ends. It increases through a limited expanding adhesive region towards the center of the overlap region in a symmetrical manner with respect to the adhesive mid-line (Figure 7) for a low maximum volume fraction of particles. In addition, the adhesive regions near the interfaces experience higher compressive stress levels. As the local adhesive composition through the adhesive thickness is enriched by particles, the power index has a negligible effect on the normal stress distribution and levels. However, a high maximum volume fraction of particles reveals the effect of the power index. The normal stress distribution is not symmetrical anymore with respect to the adhesive mid-line, and a larger adhesive region undergoes lower stress levels. The adhesive regions near the neat adhesive–adherend interface experience still higher compressive stress levels while the stress levels decrease apparently in the adhesive regions near the lower particle-rich adhesive–adherend interface with increasing power index.

The normal strain ε_{yy} distributions are also symmetrical with respect to the adhesive mid-line and concentrate around the free ends of the adhesive layer, lower and upper interfaces. It decreases uniformly towards the center of the overlap region (Figure 8). The remaining adhesive regions undergo lower normal strain levels. For a low maximum volume fraction of particles, the power index is of a small effect on the normal strain distribution and levels. The symmetrical distribution with respect to the adhesive mid-line disappears, and the high strain concentration zones distribute from the adhesive mid-line towards the free end of neat adhesive–upper adherend interface for a high maximum volume fraction of particles (0.3). The power index affects also the through-thickness variation of normal strain; thus, the normal strain levels are formed depending on the variation of volume fraction of particles through the adhesive thickness, and the strain concentration zone contracts around the free end of the neat adhesive–upper adherend interface. The adhesive zones near the neat adhesive–upper adherend interface experience higher normal strain levels and decrease uniformly towards the particle-rich adhesive–lower adherend interface. The normal stress σ_{yy} distributions (Figure 8) also conform with those of the normal strain ε_{yy}. The adhesive layer undergoes compressive stresses except for the adhesive-free edge. Symmetrical distribution of normal stress appears with respect to the adhesive mid-line for a low maximum volume fraction of particles. The power index has a negligible effect on both normal stress distribution and levels. However, the lower normal stress zones around the adhesive free end contract around the free end of the neat adhesive–upper adherend interface as the local adhesive composition through the adhesive thickness is enriched by particles for a higher maximum volume fraction of particles (0.3). The power index is more effective on the normal stress distribution and levels. The remaining adhesive regions undergo compressive stresses, which increase uniformly towards the free end of the particle-rich adhesive–lower adherend interface, while the normal stress levels increase slightly because Al_2O_3 particles with high modulus improve the overall modulus of the local adhesive composition.

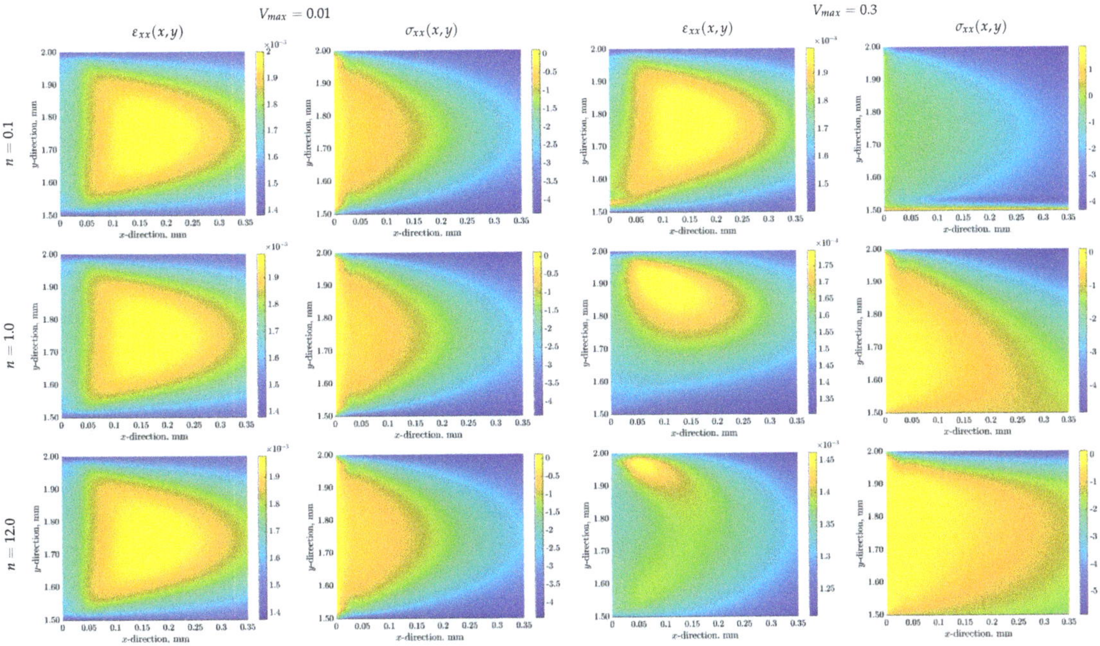

Figure 7. Effects of the gradient power index (n) and the maximum volume fraction of particles (V_{max}) on the normal strain $\varepsilon_{xx}(x,y)$ and stress $\sigma_{xx}(x,y)$ distributions around the left free-end of the PRA $\rightarrow$ NA functionally graded adhesive layer.

The shear strain ε_{xy} is of a symmetrical distribution with respect to the adhesive mid-line, which concentrates on the free ends of the lower and upper interfaces and expands uniformly through the adhesive regions near both interfaces towards the adhesive mid-line and the center of overlap region (Figure 9). The shear strain acts in opposite directions in the upper and lower adhesive portions. The remaining adhesive regions towards the center of the overlap region undergo negligible shear strain distributions. For a low maximum volume fraction of particles, the power index has a negligible effect on the shear strain distribution and levels, whereas a higher maximum volume fraction of particles (0.3) affects both shear strain distribution and levels. Namely, as the through-thickness adhesive composition is enriched by particles, the symmetrical distribution of shear strain degenerates fully, the high shear strain region in the adhesive upper portion contracts a narrower adhesive region near the upper neat adhesive–adherend interface and expands along the neighborhood of this interface towards the center of the overlap region. The shear strain levels also decrease uniformly, and its distribution is formed according to the variation of particle volume fraction through the adhesive thickness. The shear stress σ_{xy}

exhibits a symmetrical distribution with respect to the adhesive mid-line, concentrates around the free ends of the lower and upper interfaces, and high shear stress regions expand through the adhesive thickness uniformly towards the adhesive mid-line (Figure 9). The shear stress acts in opposite directions in the upper and lower adhesive portions. A large of the remaining overlap region experiences negligible shear stress levels. The shear stress distributions are less critical than those of two normal stress components. For a low maximum volume fraction of particles (0.01), the power index has a negligible effect on the shear stress distribution and levels. A higher maximum volume fraction of particles results in the effect of the power index becoming more apparent in the shear stress distribution and levels. Namely, the symmetrical shear stress distribution disappears, and the shear stresses in the particle-rich adhesive regions become more apparent. As the adhesive composition is enriched by particles, the shear stress levels decrease uniformly.

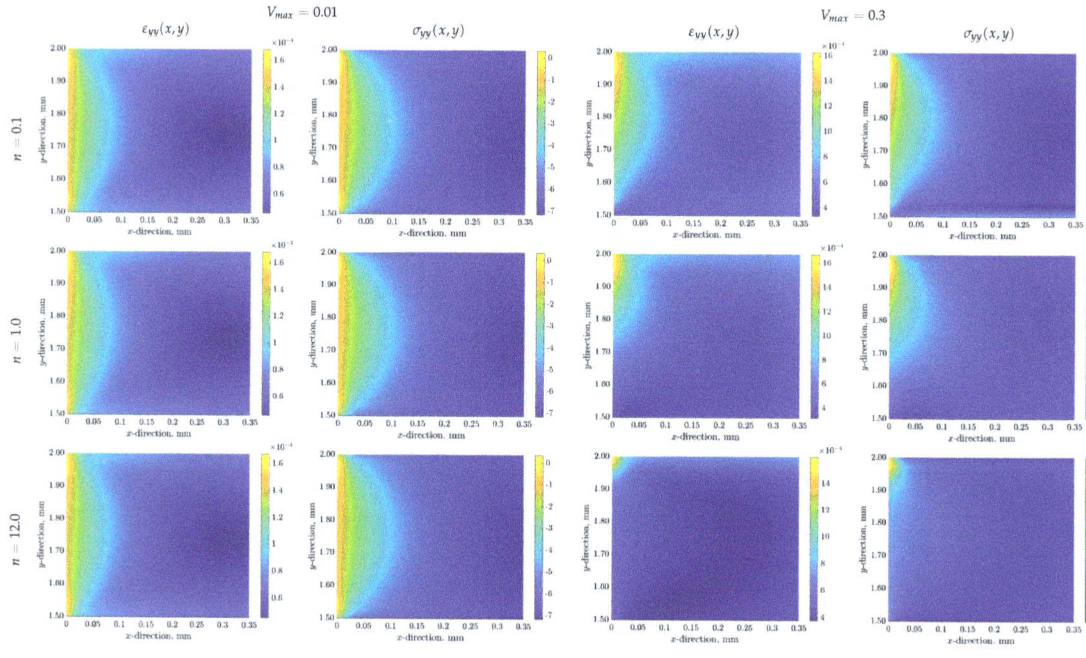

Figure 8. Effects of the gradient power index (n) and the maximum volume fraction of particles (V_{max}) on the normal strain $\varepsilon_{yy}(x, y)$ and stress $\sigma_{yy}(x, y)$ distributions around the left free-end of the PRA → NA functionally graded adhesive layer.

The free ends of the adhesive layer and the vicinities of the two interfaces appear as critical adhesive regions due to the high normal and shear strains. Therefore, the probable initiation of damage can be expected in these regions. The through-thickness distribution and levels of strain and stress components are also formed depending on the variation of particle volume fraction through the adhesive thickness. However, the effect of the power index becomes negligible, especially for a lower maximum volume fraction of particles. In order to determine the effects of the maximum volume fraction of particles V_{max} limiting the number of particles in the local adhesive composition and the power index n tailoring the variation of volume fraction of particles V_p through the adhesive thickness the variations of stress and strain components were evaluated along the upper aluminum adherend and lower aluminum adherend–adhesive interfaces (adhesive sides) and the adhesive mid-line. A grading direction was designated from the particle-rich adhesive–lower adherend interface to the neat adhesive–upper adherend interface.

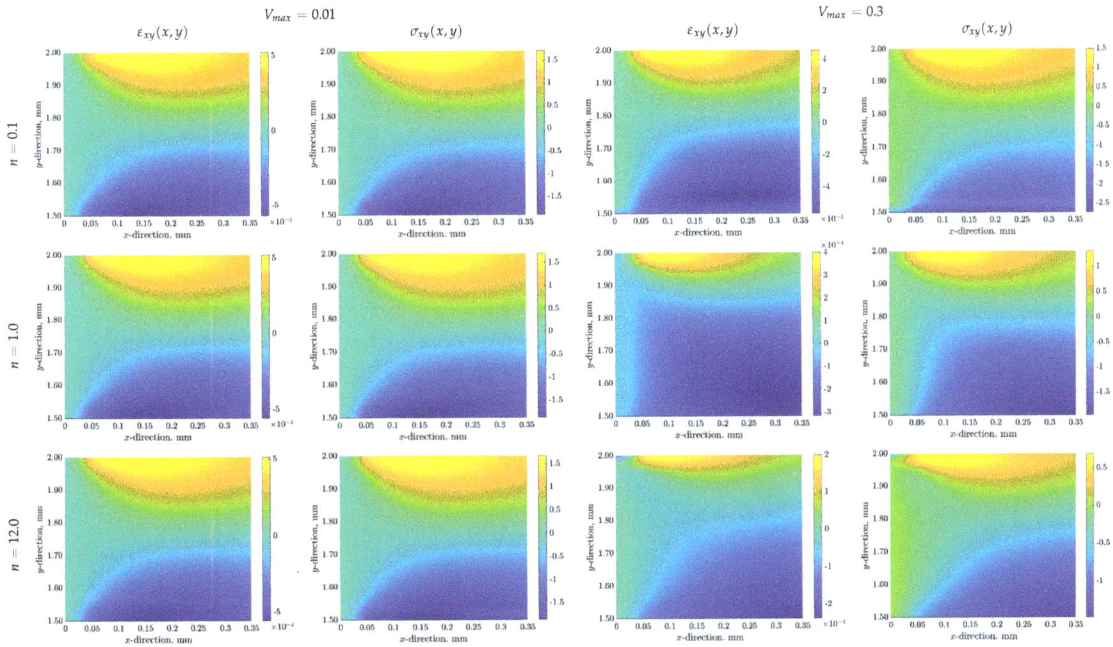

Figure 9. Effects of the gradient power index (n) and the maximum volume fraction of particles (V_{max}) on the shear strain $\varepsilon_{xy}(x, y)$ and stress $\sigma_{xy}(x, y)$ distributions around the left free-end of the PRA $\rightarrow$ NA functionally graded adhesive layer.

The normal strain ε_{xx} increases uniformly from low levels in the center of the overlap region towards the free edges of the adhesive layer and becomes peak near the free edges (Figure 10). Similar variations appear along the lower and upper interfaces and the adhesive mid-line for all power index values. The normal strain levels are lower along both interfaces than those along the adhesive mid-line. The normal stress σ_{xx} acts in compression and remains at high levels in a large overlap region and decreases towards the free edges of the adhesive layer, and then reaches zero levels (Figure 10). The effect of the power index becomes apparent on the normal strain and stress levels only for a high maximum volume fraction of particles, namely, the normal strain variations along the interfaces and adhesive mid-line are similar, but their levels decrease with increasing power index. The neat adhesive–upper adherend interface experiences higher normal stresses than the particle-rich adhesive–lower adherend interface. The power index affects normal stress levels rather than variation forms. The normal stress levels increase partly with increasing power index (enriched adhesive composition by particles) and decrease through the adhesive thickness from the neat adhesive–upper adherend interface to the particle-rich adhesive–lower adherend interface.

The normal strain ε_{yy} exhibits almost high levels in a large overlap region and decreases towards the free edges of the adhesive layer and then reaches peak levels suddenly at the free edges (Figure 11). Even though a similar behavior is observed along both interfaces and adhesive mid-line, the variation form remains similar, but the normal strain levels along the interfaces are partly higher. For a higher maximum volume fraction of particles (0.3), enriching the adhesive composition by particles results in apparent changes in normal strain levels rather than their variation forms, especially along the adhesive mid-line and the particle-rich adhesive–lower adherend interface. The normal strain ε_{yy} is more critical in a large overlap region in comparison to the adhesive-free edges. The normal stress σ_{yy} acts in compression and exhibits similar variations along the lower and upper interfaces and the adhesive mid-line, stays uniform at higher levels in a large overlap region and decreases uniformly towards the adhesive-free edges (Figure 11). The power index exhibits a negligible effect on the normal stress variations and levels for a low maximum volume fraction of particles. However, its influence becomes evident in the variation form and levels of normal stress, especially along the lower and upper interfaces, as the through-thickness adhesive composition is enriched by particles for a high maximum volume fraction of particles. A particle-rich adhesive composition variation results in lower normal strains but higher normal stresses.

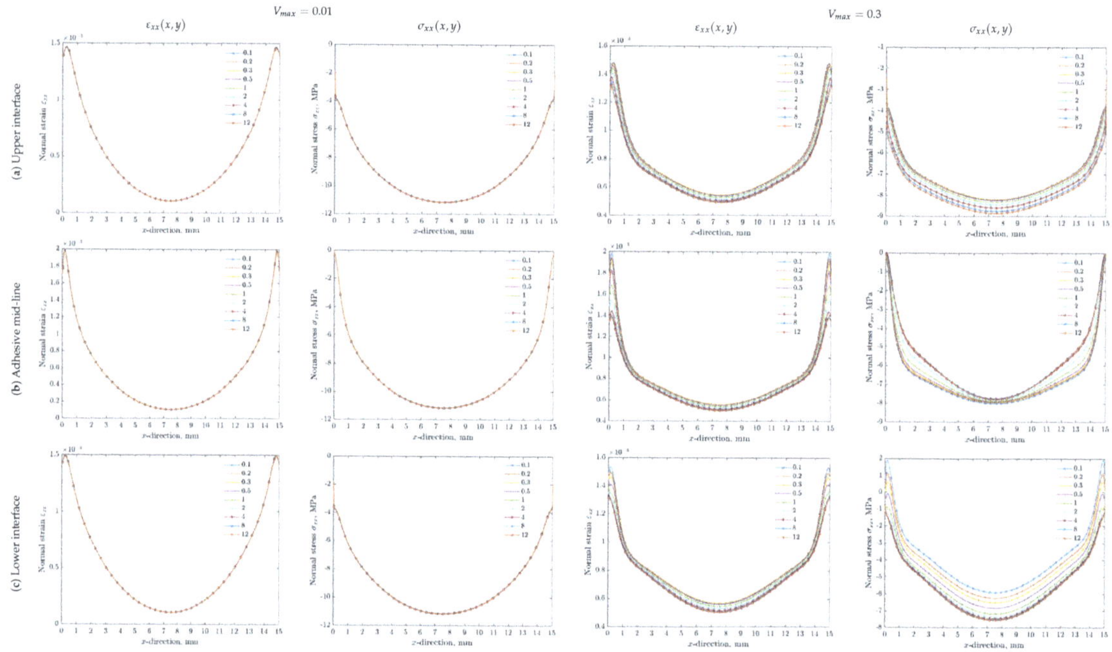

Figure 10. Effects of the gradient power index (n) and the maximum volume fraction of particles (V_{max}) on the normal strain $\varepsilon_{xx}(x, y)$ and stress $\sigma_{xx}(x, y)$ variations along (**a**) the upper interface, (**b**) the mid-line and (**c**) the lower interface of the PRA $\rightarrow$ NA functionally graded adhesive layer.

The shear strain ε_{xy} is uniform at negligible levels in a large overlap region and increases suddenly in the vicinity of the adhesive-free edges, and then decreases to zero levels at the adhesive-free edges (Figure 12). A symmetrical variation appears with respect to the center of the overlap region but in the opposite sense along both interfaces and adhesive mid-line. The lower and upper interfaces are of similar variations and levels but in the opposite sense. The shear strain exhibits a uniform increase along the adhesive mid-line in the center of the overlap region. In general, the power index and the maximum volume fraction of particles have a minor influence on the variations and levels of shear strain along both interfaces and adhesive mid-line. However, the peak values at the positions near the adhesive-free edges decrease with increasing power index. The shear stress σ_{xy} has a symmetrical variation but in the opposite sense along both interfaces and adhesive mid-line with respect to the center of overlap region (Figure 12). It remains uniform at negligible levels in a large of overlap region and increases suddenly in the vicinity of the adhesive-free edges, and then becomes negligible at the adhesive-free edges. Both lower and upper interfaces experience similar variations and levels but in the opposite sense. The power index and the maximum volume fraction of particles have a negligible effect on the various forms and levels of shear stress. However, for a higher maximum volume fraction of particles (0.3), the peak shear stress levels at the positions near adhesive-free edges decrease uniformly as the through-thickness adhesive composition is enriched by particles depending on the power index value.

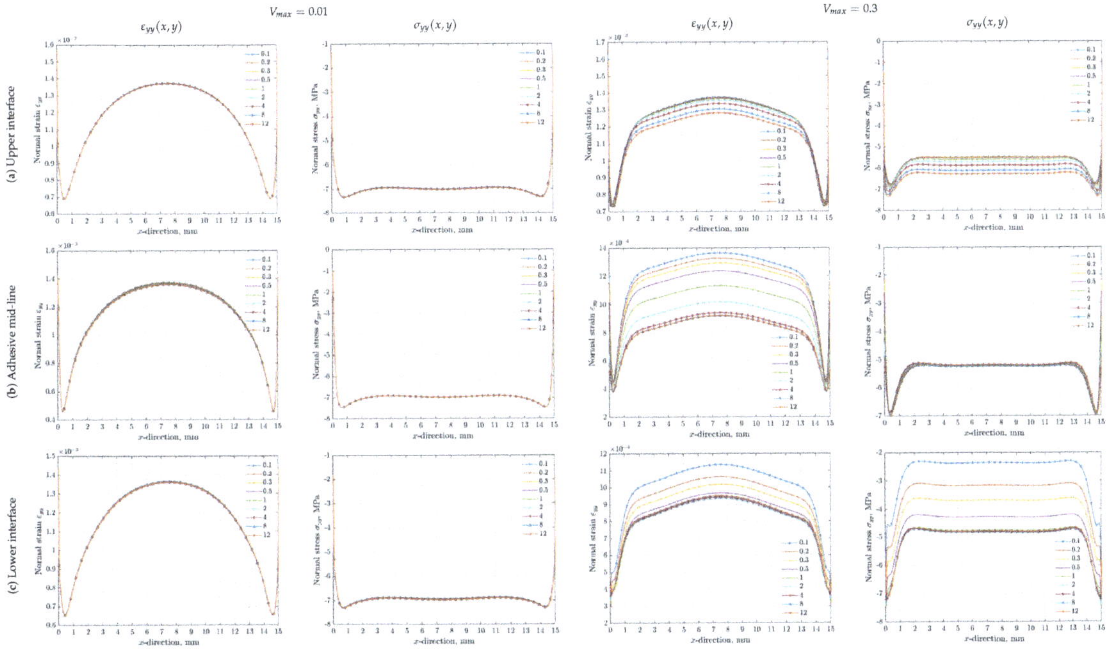

Figure 11. Effects of the gradient power index (n) and the maximum volume fraction of particles (V_{max}) on the normal strain $\varepsilon_{yy}(x, y)$ and stress $\sigma_{yy}(x, y)$ variations along (**a**) the upper interface, (**b**) the mid-line and (**c**) the lower interface of the PRA $\rightarrow$ NA functionally graded adhesive layer.

The thermal strain and stress states occurring in an adhesive composition with a low volume fraction of particles are influenced negligibly by the through-thickness grading manner under a uniform temperature field. However, the free edges of the adhesive layer experience high axial and shear strain and stress levels, whereas the transverse strain and stress become apparent in a large overlap region. As the adhesive composition is enriched by particles at high volume fraction, the power index becomes more influential on the strain and stress levels rather than their variation forms.

Figure 13 shows the effects of power index, the maximum volume fraction of particle, and grading direction on the through-thickness variations and levels of strain components ε_{ij} at the left free edge of adhesive layer $(x = 0)$. The normal strain ε_{xx} remains uniform at high levels in the vicinity of the adhesive mid-line, decreases uniformly towards both interfaces, and becomes minimum at both interfaces. An almost symmetrical through-thickness variation appears with respect to the adhesive mid-line. The power index influences only the normal strain levels rather than the variation manner, especially in a large region around the adhesive mid-line. As the through-thickness adhesive composition is enriched, the high normal strain levels reduce partly (increasing power index). In the case of an opposite grading direction, the general behavior of normal strain is the same as that in the previous grading direction. As the adhesive composition is enriched by particles at a higher volume fraction, the power index becomes more influential on both the strain variation and levels. Thus, the normal strain levels are uniform and maximum in a large region near the adhesive mid-line and become minimum at two interfaces. The through-thickness variation of normal strain is formed by the power index value. As the adhesive composition is enriched by particles, the normal strain levels decrease and become more uniform. The grading direction has a negligible effect on the variation form and levels of the normal strain, and only turns down the normal strain variations between two interfaces. The normal strain ε_{yy} is at uniform low levels in the adhesive region near the adhesive mid-line, increases uniformly from very near positions to both interfaces, becomes peak, and then decreases suddenly. However, its through-thickness variation is not symmetrical with respect to the adhesive mid-line on the contrary to that of the normal strain ε_{xx}, namely the adhesive zones near the neat adhesive–upper adherend interface experience higher normal strain levels. The power index has an effect on the normal strain levels rather than the through-thickness variation form for a lower maximum volume fraction of particles. An opposite grading direction does not influence the general behavior of normal strain, it turns down only the normal strain variations between two interfaces. However, both the levels and various forms of the normal strain change apparently depending on the power index value for a higher maximum volume fraction of particles (0.3). The shear strain ε_{xy} becomes peak at both interfaces by increasing suddenly from uniform negligible levels in a large middle region through the adhesive thickness. The shear strain acts in the opposite sense in the adhesive regions near both interfaces. This response at the free ends of both interfaces arises due to the incompatible mechanical and thermal properties of bi-material interfaces. The variation and level of shear strain are not influenced by the power index for a low maximum volume fraction of particles, whereas the shear strain levels in the adhesive zones near both interfaces increase slightly for particle-enriched adhesive compositions. In addition, the grading direction does not influence the through-thickness variation of shear strain at the adhesive-free edge.

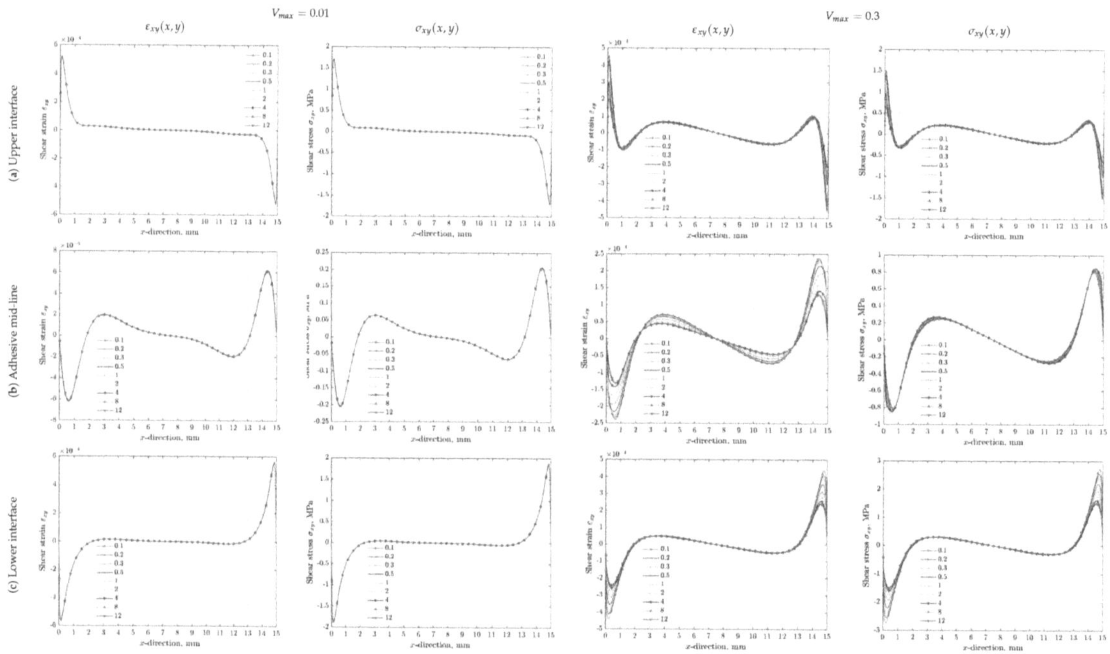

Figure 12. Effects of the gradient power index (n) and the maximum volume fraction of particles (V_{max}) on the shear strain $\varepsilon_{xy}(x,y)$ and stress $\sigma_{xy}(x,y)$ variations along (**a**) the upper interface, (**b**) the mid-line and (**c**) the lower interface of the PRA $\rightarrow$ NA functionally graded adhesive layer.

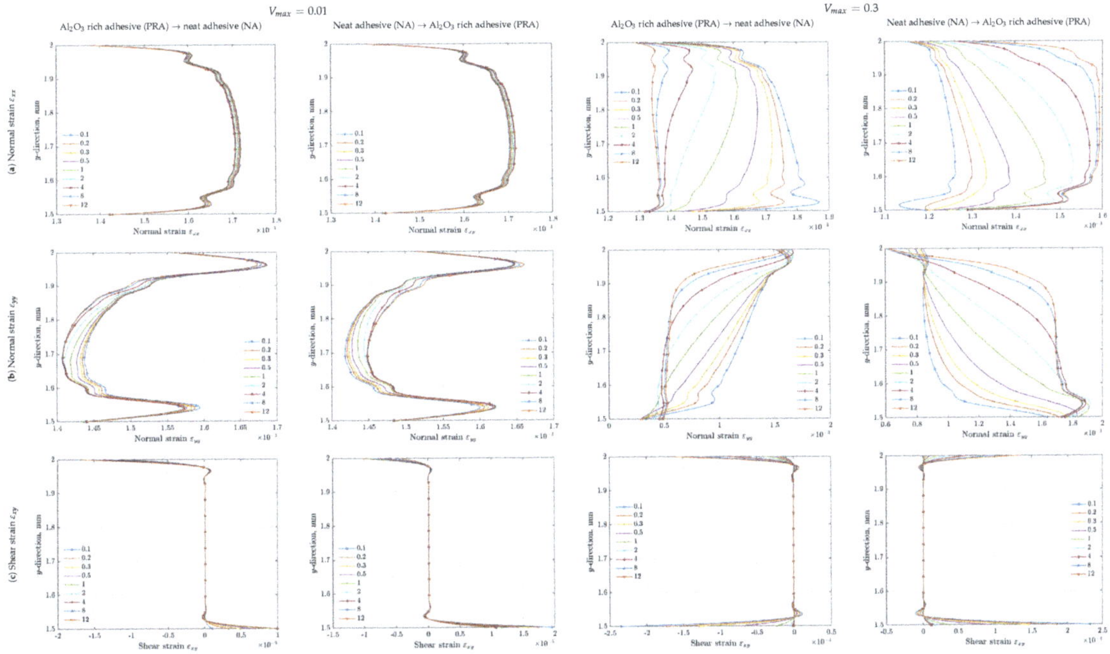

Figure 13. Effects of the gradient power index (n), the maximum volume fraction of particles (V_{max}) and the grading direction on (**a**) the normal strain ε_{xx}, (**b**) the normal strain ε_{yy} and (**c**) the shear strain ε_{xy} variations at the left free end $(x = 0)$ of the functionally graded adhesive layer.

Figure 14 shows the effects of power index, the maximum volume fraction of particle, and grading direction on the through-thickness variations and levels of normal and shear stress components σ_{ij} at the left free edge of adhesive layer $(x = 0)$. The normal stress σ_{xx} and shear stress σ_{xy} are negligible at the free edge due to the zero-stress condition at the free edge. However, a sudden change near both interfaces appears due to the continuity conditions along the interfaces. The normal stress σ_{yy} is uniform in the middle region of adhesive thickness and decreases towards a position near the interfaces, and then becomes maximum here by increasing towards both interfaces. The power index exhibits an evident influence on the through-thickness variation and levels of normal stress σ_{yy} for only a high maximum volume fraction of particles (0.3). As the local adhesive composition is enriched by particles, the stress levels decrease and become more uniform. The adhesive zones near the particle-rich adhesive–lower adherend interface experience higher stresses. The grading direction can only upturn the through-thickness variations of stress components, whereas the general trend of stress variations remains the same.

As a result, the different mechanical and thermal properties of adherend and adhesive materials in a single lap joint result in thermal stresses in both adherends and adhesive layer under a uniform temperature field. The thermal conductivity of the adhesive layer can be improved by mixing Al_2O_3 particles, and the larger coefficient of thermal expansion of the adhesive layer, which is the main reason for incompatible-thermal strain, can be reduced by tailoring the adhesive composition. The adherend–adhesive interfaces exhibit sharp discontinuous thermal stresses. The discontinuous nature of thermal strains along bi-material interfaces can be smoothed by the power index. The free edges of the adhesive layer are critical due to the occurrence of high normal/shear strains and stresses. The gradient power index, which controls through-thickness volume fraction variation of particles, can influence the distribution and levels of strain and stress components only for a sufficiently high volume fraction of particles. The grading direction of the volume fraction of particles in the adhesive layer is not influential because the temperature field is uniform, it can only reverse the low and high strain and stress regions because the neat adhesive–adherend interface and the particle-rich adhesive–adherend interface are relocated.

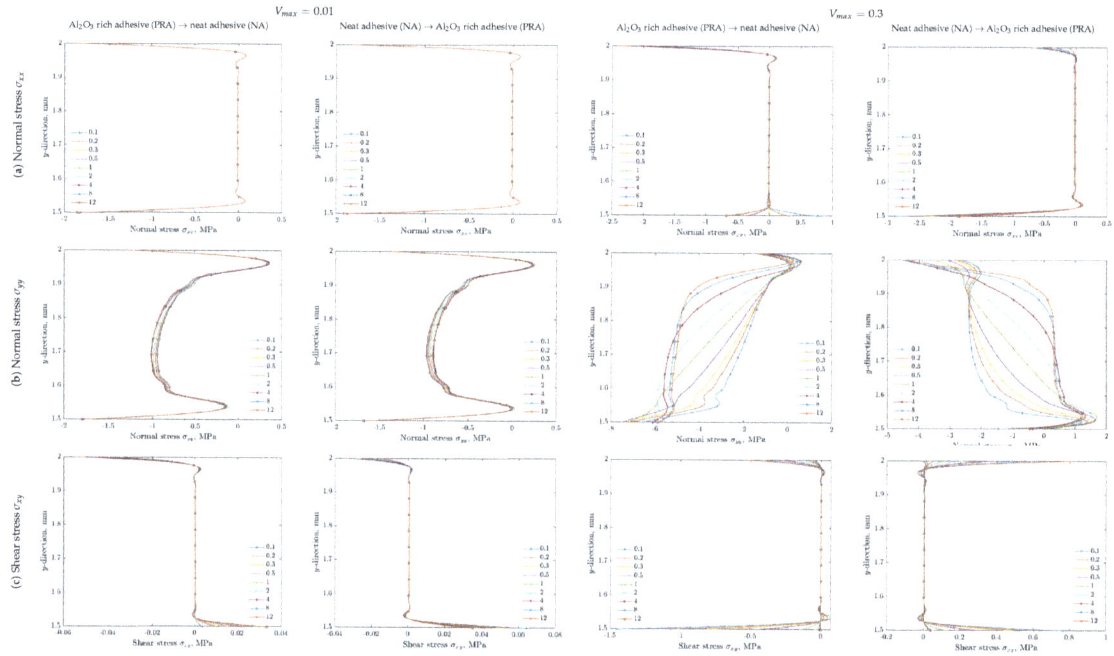

Figure 14. Effects of the gradient power index (n), the maximum volume fraction of particles (V_{max}) and the grading direction on (**a**) the normal stress σ_{xx}, (**b**) the normal stress σ_{yy} and (**c**) the shear stress σ_{xy} variations at the left free end $(x = 0)$ of the functionally graded adhesive layer.

5. Conclusions

The thermal stress analyses of an aluminum single lap joint bonded with a through-thickness functionally graded adhesive layer subjected to a uniform temperature field show that:

- A uniform temperature field causes both adherends and adhesive layers to experience apparent deformation and thermal stress states due to the mismatches of thermal and mechanical properties of aluminum and neat or particle-reinforced adhesives.
- The normal (xx) and shear (xy) components of strain and stress remain uniform at very low levels in a large overlap region and reach peak levels around/at the free edges of Al_2O_3 reinforced adhesive layer, whereas a large of overlap region undergoes still high normal strain and stress components (yy).
- In order to control the deformation and stress states induced by a uniform temperature field, a functionally graded material concept was implemented. However, the influence of the gradient power index, which tailors the through-thickness variation of the volume fraction of Al_2O_3 particles, becomes apparent only for a sufficiently high volume fraction of particles.
- An excessive volume fraction of particles is not desired because the adhesion quality between adherend and particle-reinforced adhesive, namely, interfacial bonding strength, is deteriorated. In this respect, the volume fraction of particles is recommended to limit a reliable range of 0.01 and 0.1.

- The grading direction through the adhesive thickness between the neat adhesive–adherend interface and the particle-rich adhesive–adherend interface has a small influence on the variations of total strain and thermal stress components, and can partly affect only their levels because the temperature field is uniform. In the case of a nonuniform temperature field induced by a constant/variable applied heat flux, the effect of grading direction needs to be investigated for a large range of volume fractions of particles.

Author Contributions: Conceptualization, M.K.A. and J.N.R.; methodology, M.K.A. and J.N.R.; software, M.K.A.; validation, M.K.A. and J.N.R.; formal analysis, M.K.A.; investigation, M.K.A.; resources, M.K.A. and J.N.R.; data curation, M.K.A.; writing—original draft preparation, M.K.A.; writing—review and editing, M.K.A. and J.N.R.; visualization, M.K.A.; supervision, J.N.R.; project administration, M.K.A.; funding acquisition, M.K.A. All authors have read and agreed to the published version of the manuscript.

Funding: This research was funded by the Scientific Research Project Division of Erciyes University under the grant number [FUI-2019-9219].

Data Availability Statement: The data presented in this study are available on request from the corresponding author subjected to the permission requested from the funder, the Scientific Research Project Division of Erciyes University, on behalf of the Presidency of Erciyes University. The data are not publicly available.

Conflicts of Interest: The authors declare no conflict of interest. The funder had no role in the design of the study; in the collection, analysis, or interpretation of data; in the writing of the manuscript; or in the decision to publish the results.

Abbreviations

The following abbreviations are used in this manuscript:

Al_2O_3	aluminum oxide
FGM	functionally graded material
NA	neat adhesive
PRA	Al_2O_3 particle-rich adhesive
a, p	adhesive, particle
dx, dy	increments between two neighbour grid points along the x- and y-directions
eps	specified error level
erru, errv	the differences of the calculated values of displacement components at iteration steps $k+1$ and k
i, j	indices of grid point along the x- and y-directions
k	iteration index
n	gradient power index
SumError	the total differences of the calculated values of displacement components at iteration step $k+1$ and k
t_1, t_3	lower and upper adherend thicknesses
t_2	adhesive thickness
u_i, u, v	displacement components along the x- and y-directions
x_i, x, y	spatial coordinate variables
$\bar{y}$	the position relative to the lower adhesive interface
E	modulus of elasticity
G, G_a, G_p	shear modulus (mixture, adhesive, particle)
H	joint height
K, K_a, K_p	bulk modulus (mixture, adhesive, particle)
L	adherend and adhesive (joint) length
T, T_0, T_{ref}	temperature
$\bar{T}$	temperature difference
V_a, V_p	volume fractions of adhesive and particles
V_{max}	maximum volume fractions of particles
α, α_a, α_p	coefficient of thermal expansion (mixture, adhesive, particle)

$\psi(x,y)$	a continuous, differentiable two-variable function
δ_{ij}	kronocker delta
λ, μ	Lamé's constants
∇_x, ∇_y	the central-difference operator of first-order partial derivative
∇_{xx}, ∇_{yy}, ∇_{xy}	the central-difference operator of second-order partial derivative
Γ_x, Γ_y	the central-difference operator of first-order partial derivative
Γ_{xx}, Γ_{yy}	the central-difference operator of second-order partial derivative
σ_{ij}	stress components
ε_{ij}	strain components
ε_v, ε_{nn}	volumetric strain
ν	Poisson's ratio
$\rightarrow$, $\leftarrow$	forward and backward sense
$-$, $+$	lower and upper sides of adhesive interfaces

References

1. Adams, R.D.; Wake, W.C. *Structural Adhesive Joints in Engineering*, 1st ed.; Elsevier Applied Science: London, UK, 1984.
2. Kinloch, A.J. *Adhesion and Adhesives: Science and Technology*, 1st ed.; Chapman and Hall: London, UK, 1987.
3. Apalak, M.K. Non-Linear thermal stresses in adhesive joints. In *Modeling of Adhesively Bonded Joints*; da Silva, L.F.M., Öchsner, A., Eds.; Springer: Berlin/Heidelberg, Germany, 2008; pp. 243–277.
4. Apalak, M.K. Thermal stresses in adhesively bonded joints/patches and their modeling. In *Progress in Adhesion and Adhesives*; Mittal, K.L., Ed.; Scrivener Publishing and John Wiley & Sons Inc.: New York, NY, USA, 2017; Volume 2, pp. 217–270.
5. Apalak, M.K. Ways to mitigate thermal stresses in adhesively bonded joints/patches. In *Progress in Adhesion and Adhesives*; Mittal, K.L., Ed.; Scrivener Publishing and John Wiley & Sons Inc.: New York, NY, USA, 2017; Volume 2, pp. 271–320.
6. Apalak, M.K. Effect of geometrical non-linearity on the stress and deformation states of adhesive joints. In *Adhesive Joints: Formation, Characteristics and Testing*; Mittal, K.L., Ed.; CRC Press: Boca Raton, FL, USA, 2002; Volume 2, pp. 221–256.
7. Ochoa, O.O.; Reddy, J.N. *Finite Element Analysis of Composite Laminates (Solid Mechanics and Its Applications)*; Springer: Dordrecht, The Netherlands, 1992.
8. Reddy, J.N. *Mechanics of Laminated Composite Plates and Shells: Theory and Analysis*, 2nd ed.; CRC Press: New York, NY, USA, 2003.
9. Koizumi, M. FGM Activities in Japan. *Compos. Part B* **1997**, *7*, 1–4. [CrossRef]
10. Kawasaki, A.; Watanabe, R. Finite element analysis of thermal stress of the metal/ceramic multi-layer composites with controlled compositional gradients. *Nippon Kinzoku Gakkaishi* **1987**, *51*, 525–529.
11. Yash, P.; Ponappa, K. Functionally graded materials: A review of computational materials science algorithms, production techniques, and their biomedical applications. *Proc. Inst. Mech. Eng. Part C* **2022**, *236*, 10969–10986.
12. El-Galy, I.M.; Saleh Bassiouny, I.; Ahmed Mahmoud, H. Functionally graded materials classifications and development trends from industrial point of view. *SN Appl. Sci.* **2019**, *1*, 1378. [CrossRef]
13. Jha, D.K.; Kant, T.; Singh, R.K. A critical review of recent research on functionally graded plates. *Compos. Struct.* **2013**, *96*, 833–849. [CrossRef]
14. Apalak, M.K. Functionally graded adhesively bonded joints. In *Progress in Adhesion and Adhesives*; Mittal, K.L., Ed.; Scrivener Publishing and John Wiley & Sons Inc.: Hoboken, NJ, USA, 2015; pp. 57–83.
15. Apalak, M.K. Functionally graded adhesively bonded joints. *Rev. Adhes. Adhes.* **2014**, *2*, 56–84. [CrossRef]
16. dos Reis, M.Q.; Marques, E.A.S.; Carbas, R.J.C.; da Silva, L.F.M. Functionally graded adherends in adhesive joints: An overview. *J. Adv. Join. Processes* **2020**, *2*, 100033. [CrossRef]
17. Apalak, M.K.; Demirbas, M.D. Improved mathematical models of thermal residual stresses in functionally graded adhesively bonded joints: A critical review. *Rev. Adhes. Adhes.* **2019**, *7*, 367–415. [CrossRef]
18. Hart-Smith, L.J. *Adhesive-Bonded Double-Lap Joints*; NASA CR 112235; NASA Langley Research Center: Hampton, VA, USA, 1973.
19. Srinivas, S. *Analysis of Bonded Joints*; NASA TN D-7855; NASA Langley Research Center: Hampton, VA, USA, 1975.
20. Pires, I.; Quintino, L.; Durodola, J.F.; Beevers, A. Performance of bi-adhesive bonded aluminium lap joints. *Int. J. Adhes. Adhes.* **2003**, *23*, 215–223. [CrossRef]
21. Fitton, M.D.; Broughton, J.G. Variable modulus adhesives: An approach to optimised joint performance. *Int. J. Adhes. Adhes.* **2005**, *25*, 329–336. [CrossRef]
22. Temiz, S. Application of bi-adhesive in double-strap joints subjected to bending moment. *J. Adhes. Sci. Technol.* **2006**, *20*, 1547–1560. [CrossRef]
23. Ferreira, C.L.; Campilho, R.D.S.G.; Moreira, R.D.F. Bonded structures improvement by the dual adhesive technique. *Procedia Struct. Integr.* **2020**, *28*, 1116–1124. [CrossRef]
24. Patrick, R.L. (Ed.) The National Materials Advisory Board of the National Research Council. In *Treatise on Adhesion and Adhesives: Structural Adhesives with Emphasis on Aerospace Applications*; Marcel Dekker: New York, NY, USA, 1976; Volume 4.
25. da Silva, L.F.M.; Adams, R.D. Adhesive joints at high and low temperatures using similar and dissimilar adherends and dual adhesives. *Int. J. Adhes. Adhes.* **2007**, *27*, 216–226. [CrossRef]

26. da Silva, L.F.M.; Adams, R.D. Joint strength predictions for adhesive joints to be used over a wide temperature range. *Int. J. Adhes. Adhes.* **2007**, *27*, 362–379. [CrossRef]
27. Nemati Giv, A.; Ayatollahi, M.R.; Ghaffari, S.H.; da Silva, L.F. Effect of reinforcements at different scales on mechanical properties of epoxy adhesives and adhesive joints: A review. *J. Adhes.* **2018**, *94*, 1082–1121. [CrossRef]
28. Mori, T.; Tanaka, K. Average stress in matrix and average elastic energy of materials with misfitting inclusions. *Acta Metall.* **1973**, *21*, 571–574. [CrossRef]
29. Benveniste, Y. A new approach to the application of Mori-Tanaka's theory in composite materials. *Mech. Mater.* **1987**, *6*, 147–157. [CrossRef]
30. Wakashima, K.; Tsukamoto, H. Mean-field micromechanics model and its application to the analysis of thermomechanical behaviour of composite materials. *Mater. Sci. Eng. A* **1991**, *146*, 291–316. [CrossRef]
31. Levin, V.M. On the coefficients of thermal expansion of heterogeneous materials. *Mech. Tverdogs Tela* **1967**, *2*, 88–94.
32. Kumar, S.; WarHart-Smithdle, B.L.; Arif, M.F. Strength and performance enhancement of bonded joints by spatial tailoring of adhesive compliance via 3D printing. *ACS Appl. Mater. Interfaces* **2017**, *9*, 884–891. [CrossRef]
33. Marques, J.B.; Barbosa, A.Q.; da Silva, C.I.; Carbas, R.J.C.; da Silva, L.F.M. An overview of manufacturing functionally graded adhesives – Challenges and prospects. *J. Adhes.* **2021**, *97*, 172–206. [CrossRef]
34. Naat, N.; Boutar, Y.S.; Naïmi, S.M.; da Silva, L.F.M. Effect of surface texture on the mechanical performance of bonded joints: A review. *J. Adhes.* **2023**, *99*, 166–258. [CrossRef]
35. Bergonzi, L.; Pirondi, A.; Moroni, F.; Frascio, M.; Avalle, M. A study on additive manufacturing build parameters as bonded joint design factors. *J. Adhes.* **2021**. [CrossRef]
36. Saada, A.S. *Elasticity: Theory and Applications*, 2nd ed.; J. Ross Publishing: Fort Laudedale, FL, USA, 2009.

MDPI AG
Grosspeteranlage 5
4052 Basel
Switzerland
Tel.: +41 61 683 77 34

Mathematical and Computational Applications Editorial Office
E-mail: mca@mdpi.com
www.mdpi.com/journal/mca

www.ingramcontent.com/pod-product-compliance
Lightning Source LLC
Chambersburg PA
CBHW061832210926
51850CB00006B/863
9783725858514